p. 43 Maxwell

Hydrodynamics

Horace Lamb, Cambridge at the University

BIBLIOLIFE

HYDRODYNAMICS

BY

HORACE LAMB, M.A., F.R.S.

PROFESSOR OF MATHEMATICS IN THE OWENS COLLEGE,
VICTORIA UNIVERSITY, MANCHESTER;
FORMERLY FELLOW OF TRINITY COLLEGE, CAMBRIDGE.

CAMBRIDGE:
AT THE UNIVERSITY PRESS.
1895

Cambridge:
PRINTED BY J. & C. F. CLAY,
AT THE UNIVERSITY PRESS.

PREFACE.

THIS book may be regarded as a second edition of a "Treatise on the Mathematical Theory of the Motion of Fluids," published in 1879, but the additions and alterations are so extensive that it has been thought proper to make a change in the title.

I have attempted to frame a connected account of the principal theorems and methods of the science, and of such of the more important applications as admit of being presented within a moderate compass. It is hoped that all investigations of fundamental importance will be found to have been given with sufficient detail, but in matters of secondary or illustrative interest I have often condensed the argument, or merely stated results, leaving the full working out to the reader.

In making a selection of the subjects to be treated I have been guided by considerations of physical interest. Long analytical investigations, leading to results which cannot be interpreted, have as far as possible been avoided. Considerable but, it is hoped, not excessive space has been devoted to the theory of waves of various kinds, and to the subject of viscosity. On the other hand, some readers may be disappointed to find that the theory of isolated vortices is still given much in the form in which it was left by the earlier researches of von Helmholtz and Lord Kelvin, and that little reference is made to the subsequent investigations of J. J. Thomson, W. M. Hicks, and others, in this field. The omission has been made with reluctance, and can be justified only on the ground that the investigations in question derive most of their interest from their bearing on kinetic theories of matter, which seem to lie outside the province of a treatise like the present.

I have ventured, in one important particular, to make a serious innovation in the established notation of the subject, by reversing the sign of the velocity-potential. This step has been taken not without hesitation, and was only finally decided upon when I found that it had the countenance of friends whose judgment I could trust; but the physical interpretation of the function, and the far-reaching analogy with the magnetic potential, are both so much improved by the change that its adoption appeared to be, sooner or later, inevitable.

I have endeavoured, throughout the book, to attribute to their proper authors the more important steps in the development of the subject. That this is not always an easy matter is shewn by the fact that it has occasionally been found necessary to modify references given in the former treatise, and generally accepted as correct. I trust, therefore, that any errors of ascription which remain will be viewed with indulgence. It may be well, moreover, to warn the reader, once for all, that I have allowed myself a free hand in dealing with the materials at my disposal, and that the reference in the footnote must not always be taken to imply that the method of the original author has been closely followed in the text. I will confess, indeed, that my ambition has been not merely to produce a text-book giving a faithful record of the present state of the science, with its achievements and its imperfections, but, if possible, to carry it a step further here and there, and at all events by the due coordination of results already obtained to lighten in some degree the labours of future investigators. I shall be glad if I have at least succeeded in conveying to my readers some of the fascination which the subject has exerted on so long a line of distinguished writers.

In the present subject, perhaps more than in any other department of mathematical physics, there is room for Poinsot's warning

"Gardons nous de croire qu'une science soit faite quand on l'a reduite à des formules analytiques." I have endeavoured to make the analytical results as intelligible as possible, by numerical illustrations, which it is hoped will be found correct, and by the insertion of a number of diagrams of stream-lines and other curves, drawn to scale, and reduced by photography. Some of these cases have, of course, been figured by previous writers, but many are new, and in every instance the curves have been calculated and drawn independently for the purposes of this work.

I am much indebted to various friends who have kindly taken an interest in the book, and have helped in various ways, but who would not care to be specially named. I cannot refrain, however, from expressing my obligations to those who have shared in the tedious labour of reading the proof sheets. Mr H. M. Taylor has increased the debt I was under in respect of the former treatise by giving me the benefit, so long as he was able, of his vigilant criticism. On his enforced retirement his place was kindly taken by Mr R. F. Gwyther, whose care has enabled me to correct many errors. Mr J. Larmor has read the book throughout, and has freely placed his great knowledge of the subject at my disposal; I owe to him many valuable suggestions. Finally, I have had the advantage, in the revision of the last chapter, of Mr A. E. H. Love's special acquaintance with the problems there treated.

Notwithstanding so much friendly help I cannot hope to have escaped numerous errors, in addition to the few which have been detected. I shall esteem myself fortunate if those which remain should prove to relate merely to points of detail and not of principle. In any case I shall be glad to have my attention called to them.

HORACE LAMB.

May, 1895.

CONTENTS.

CHAPTER I.

THE EQUATIONS OF MOTION.

CHAPTER II.

INTEGRATION OF THE EQUATIONS IN SPECIAL CASES.

CHAPTER III.

IRROTATIONAL MOTION.

CHAPTER IV.

MOTION OF A LIQUID IN TWO DIMENSIONS.

CHAPTER V.

IRROTATIONAL MOTION OF A LIQUID: PROBLEMS IN THREE DIMENSIONS.

CHAPTER VI.

ON THE MOTION OF SOLIDS THROUGH A LIQUID: DYNAMICAL THEORY.

CHAPTER VII.

VORTEX MOTION.

CHAPTER VIII.

TIDAL WAVES.

CHAPTER IX.

SURFACE WAVES.

CHAPTER X.

WAVES OF EXPANSION.

CHAPTER XI.

VISCOSITY.

CHAPTER XII.

EQUILIBRIUM OF ROTATING MASSES OF LIQUID.

ADDITIONS AND CORRECTIONS.

Page 109, equation (10). Lord Kelvin maintains that the type of motion here contemplated, with a surface of discontinuity, and a mass of 'dead water' in the rear of the lamina, has no resemblance to anything which occurs in actual fluids; and that the only legitimate application of the methods of von Helmholtz and Kirchhoff is to the case of free surfaces, as of a jet. *Nature*, t. l., pp. 524, 549, 573, 597 (1894).

Page 111, line 20, *for* $\alpha=0$ *read* $\alpha=90°$.

" 132, equation (4), *dele* $\mathbf{u}^2$.

" 156, equation (3), footnote. The author is informed that this solution was current in Cambridge at a somewhat earlier date, and is due to Dr Ferrers.

Page 305, footnote. To the list of works here cited must now be added: Gray and Mathews, *A Treatise on Bessel Functions and their Applications to Physics*, London, 1895.

Page 376, line 22, *for* $(g\lambda/2\pi)^{\frac{1}{2}}$ *read* $(2\pi g/\lambda)^{\frac{1}{2}}$.

" 381, line 10. Reference should be made to Scott Russell, *Brit. Ass. Rep.*, 1844, p. 369.

Page 386, equation (2). Attention has recently been called to some observations of Benjamin Franklin (in a letter dated 1762) on the behaviour of surfaces of separation of oil and water (*Complete Works*, 2nd ed., London, n. d., t. ii., p. 142). The phenomena depend for their explanation on the fact that the natural periods of oscillation of the surface of separation of two liquids of nearly equal density are very long compared with those of a free surface of similar extent.

Page 423, line 16, *for* the minimum condition......above given *read* the condition that $\delta(V-T_0)=0$, or $\delta(V+K)=0$.

Page 449, footnote, *for* Art. 302 *read* Art. 303.

" 482, line 16, *for* ϕ *read* $\bar{\phi}$.

" 487, footnote. The solution of the equation (1) of Art. 266 in spherical harmonics dates from Laplace, "Sur la diminution de la durée du jour, par le refroidissement de la Terre," *Conn. des Tems pour l'An* 1823, p. 245 (1820).

Page 491. *Dele* lines 9—18 and footnote.

HYDRODYNAMICS.

CHAPTER I.

THE EQUATIONS OF MOTION.

1. THE following investigations proceed on the assumption that the matter with which we deal may be treated as practically continuous and homogeneous in structure; *i.e.* we assume that the properties of the smallest portions into which we can conceive it to be divided are the same as those of the substance in bulk.

The fundamental property of a fluid is that it cannot be in equilibrium in a state of stress such that the mutual action between two adjacent parts is oblique to the common surface. This property is the basis of Hydrostatics, and is verified by the complete agreement of the deductions of that science with experiment. Very slight observation is enough, however, to convince us that oblique stresses may exist in fluids *in motion*. Let us suppose for instance that a vessel in the form of a circular cylinder, containing water (or other liquid), is made to rotate about its axis, which is vertical. If the motion of the vessel be uniform, the fluid is soon found to be rotating with the vessel as one solid body. If the vessel be now brought to rest, the motion of the fluid continues for some time, but gradually subsides, and at length ceases altogether; and it is found that during this process the portions of fluid which are further from the axis lag behind those which are nearer, and have their motion more rapidly checked. These phenomena point to the existence of mutual actions between contiguous elements which are partly tangential to the common surface. For if the mutual action were everywhere wholly normal, it is obvious that the moment of momentum, about the axis of the vessel, of any portion of fluid bounded by a surface of revolution about this axis, would be constant. We infer, moreover, that these tangential stresses are not called into play so long as the fluid moves as a solid body, but only whilst a change of shape of some portion of the mass is going on, and that their tendency is to oppose this change of shape.

2. It is usual, however, in the first instance to neglect the tangential stresses altogether. Their effect is in many practical cases small, and independently of this, it is convenient to divide the not inconsiderable difficulties of our subject by investigating first the effects of purely normal stress. The further consideration of the laws of tangential stress is accordingly deferred till Chapter XI.

If the stress exerted across any small plane area situate at a point P of the fluid be wholly normal, its intensity (per unit area) is the same for all aspects of the plane. The following proof of this theorem is given here for purposes of reference. Through P draw three straight lines PA, PB, PC mutually at right angles, and let a plane whose direction-cosines relatively to these lines

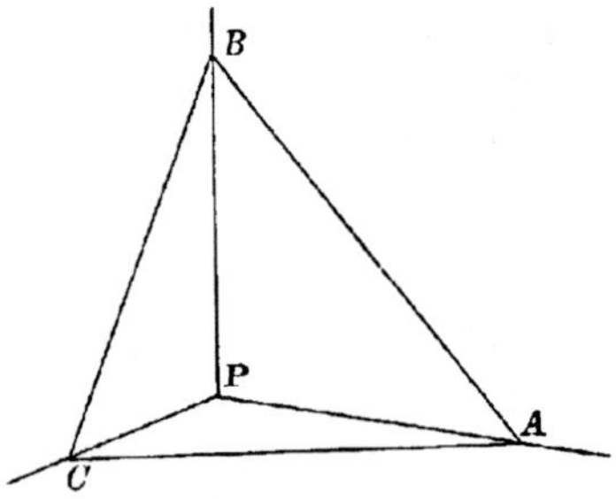

are l, m, n, passing infinitely close to P, meet them in A, B, C. Let p, p_1, p_2, p_3 denote the intensities of the stresses* across the faces ABC, PBC, PCA, PAB, respectively, of the tetrahedron $PABC$. If Δ be the area of the first-mentioned face, the areas of the others are in order $l\Delta$, $m\Delta$, $n\Delta$. Hence if we form the equation of motion of the tetrahedron parallel to PA we have $p_1 . l\Delta = pl . \Delta$, where we have omitted the terms which express the rate of change of momentum, and the component of the extraneous forces, because they are ultimately proportional to the mass of the tetrahedron, and therefore of the third order of small linear quantities, whilst the terms retained are of the second. We have then, ultimately, $p = p_1$, and similarly $p = p_2 = p_3$, which proves the theorem.

* Reckoned positive when pressures, negative when tensions. Most fluids are, however, incapable under ordinary conditions of supporting more than an exceedingly slight degree of tension, so that p is nearly always positive.

3. The equations of motion of a fluid have been obtained in two different forms, corresponding to the two ways in which the problem of determining the motion of a fluid mass, acted on by given forces and subject to given conditions, may be viewed. We may either regard as the object of our investigations a knowledge of the velocity, the pressure, and the density, at all points of space occupied by the fluid, for all instants; or we may seek to determine the history of any particle. The equations obtained on these two plans are conveniently designated, as by German mathematicians, the 'Eulerian' and the 'Lagrangian' forms of the hydrokinetic equations, although both forms are in reality due to Euler*.

The Eulerian Equations.

4. Let u, v, w be the components, parallel to the co-ordinate axes, of the velocity at the point (x, y, z) at the time t. These quantities are then functions of the independent variables x, y, z, t. For any particular value of t they express the motion at that instant at all points of space occupied by the fluid; whilst for particular values of x, y, z they give the history of what goes on at a particular place.

We shall suppose, for the most part, not only that u, v, w are finite and continuous functions of x, y, z, but that their space-derivatives of the first order (du/dx, dv/dx, dw/dx, &c.) are everywhere finite†; we shall understand by the term 'continuous motion,' a motion subject to these restrictions. Cases of exception, if they present themselves, will require separate examination. In continuous motion, as thus defined, the relative velocity of

* "Principes généraux du mouvement des fluides." *Hist. de l'Acad. de Berlin*, 1755.

"De principiis motus fluidorum." *Novi Comm. Acad. Petrop.* t. xiv. p. 1 (1759).

Lagrange gave three investigations of the equations of motion; first, incidentally, in connection with the principle of Least Action, in the *Miscellanea Taurinensia*, t. ii., (1760), *Oeuvres*, Paris, 1867–92, t. i.; secondly in his "Mémoire sur la Théorie du Mouvement des Fluides", *Nouv. mém. de l'Acad. de Berlin*, 1781, *Oeuvres*, t. iv.; and thirdly in the *Mécanique Analytique*. In this last exposition he starts with the second form of the equations (Art. 13, below), but translates them at once into the 'Eulerian' notation.

† It is important to bear in mind, with a view to some later developments under the head of Vortex Motion, that these derivatives need not be assumed to be continuous.

any two neighbouring particles P, P' will always be infinitely small, so that the line PP' will always remain of the same order of magnitude. It follows that if we imagine a small closed surface to be drawn, surrounding P, and suppose it to move with the fluid, it will always enclose the same matter. And *any* surface whatever, which moves with the fluid, completely and permanently separates the matter on the two sides of it.

5. The values of u, v, w for successive values of t give as it were a series of pictures of consecutive stages of the motion, in which however there is no immediate means of tracing the identity of any one particle.

To calculate the rate at which any function $F(x, y, z, t)$ varies for a moving particle, we remark that at the time $t + \delta t$ the particle which was originally in the position (x, y, z) is in the position $(x + u\delta t, y + v\delta t, z + w\delta t)$, so that the corresponding value of F is

$$F(x + u\delta t, y + v\delta t, z + w\delta t, t + \delta t)$$
$$= F + u\delta t \frac{dF}{dx} + v\delta t \frac{dF}{dy} + w\delta t \frac{dF}{dz} + \delta t \frac{dF}{dt}.$$

If, after Stokes, we introduce the symbol D/Dt to denote a differentiation following the motion of the fluid, the new value of F is also expressed by $F + DF/Dt \, . \, \delta t$, whence

$$\frac{DF}{Dt} = \frac{dF}{dt} + u\frac{dF}{dx} + v\frac{dF}{dy} + w\frac{dF}{dz} \quad \ldots\ldots\ldots\ldots\ldots(1).$$

6. To form the dynamical equations, let p be the pressure, ρ the density, X, Y, Z the components of the extraneous forces per unit mass, at the point (x, y, z) at the time t. Let us take an element having its centre at (x, y, z), and its edges δx, δy, δz parallel to the rectangular co-ordinate axes. The rate at which the x-component of the momentum of this element is increasing is $\rho\,\delta x\,\delta y\,\delta z\, Du/Dt$; and this must be equal to the x-component of the forces acting on the element. Of these the extraneous forces give $\rho\,\delta x\,\delta y\,\delta z\, X$. The pressure on the yz-face which is nearest the origin will be ultimately

$$(p - \tfrac{1}{2}dp/dx \, . \, \delta x)\,\delta y\,\delta z\,*,$$

* It is easily seen, by Taylor's theorem, that the mean pressure over any face of the element $\delta x\,\delta y\,\delta z$ may be taken to be equal to the pressure at the centre of that face.

that on the opposite face

$$(p + \tfrac{1}{2} dp/dx . \delta x)\, \delta y\, \delta z.$$

The difference of these gives a resultant $-dp/dx . \delta x \delta y \delta z$ in the direction of x-positive. The pressures on the remaining faces are perpendicular to x. We have then

$$\rho\, \delta x\, \delta y\, \delta z \frac{Du}{Dt} = \rho\, \delta x\, \delta y\, \delta z\, X - \frac{dp}{dx}\, \delta x\, \delta y\, \delta z.$$

Substituting the value of Du/Dt from (1), and writing down the symmetrical equations, we have

$$\left.\begin{aligned} \frac{du}{dt} + u\frac{du}{dx} + v\frac{du}{dy} + w\frac{du}{dz} &= X - \frac{1}{\rho}\frac{dp}{dx}, \\ \frac{dv}{dt} + u\frac{dv}{dx} + v\frac{dv}{dy} + w\frac{dv}{dz} &= Y - \frac{1}{\rho}\frac{dp}{dy}, \\ \frac{dw}{dt} + u\frac{dw}{dx} + v\frac{dw}{dy} + w\frac{dw}{dz} &= Z - \frac{1}{\rho}\frac{dp}{dz}. \end{aligned}\right\} \quad \text{.........(2).}$$

7. To these dynamical equations we must join, in the first place, a certain kinematical relation between u, v, w, ρ, obtained as follows.

If $\mathbf{v}$ be the volume of a moving element, we have, on account of the constancy of mass,

$$\frac{D . \rho \mathbf{v}}{Dt} = 0,$$

or

$$\frac{1}{\rho}\frac{D\rho}{Dt} + \frac{1}{\mathbf{v}}\frac{D\mathbf{v}}{Dt} = 0 \quad \text{........................(1).}$$

To calculate the value of $1/\mathbf{v} . D\mathbf{v}/Dt$, let the element in question be that which at time t fills the rectangular space $\delta x \delta y \delta z$ having one corner P at (x, y, z), and the edges PL, PM, PN (say) parallel to the co-ordinate axes. At time $t + \delta t$ the same element will form an oblique parallelepiped, and since the velocities of the particle L relative to the particle P are $du/dx . \delta x$, $dv/dx . \delta x$, $dw/dx . \delta x$, the projections of the edge PL become, after the time δt,

$$\left(1 + \frac{du}{dx}\delta t\right)\delta x, \quad \frac{dv}{dx}\delta t . \delta x, \quad \frac{dw}{dx}\delta t . \delta x,$$

respectively. To the first order in δt, the length of this edge is now

$$= \left(1 + \frac{du}{dx}\delta t\right)\delta x,$$

and similarly for the remaining edges. Since the angles of the parallelepiped differ infinitely little from right angles, the volume is still given, to the first order in δt, by the product of the three edges, *i.e.* we have

$$\mathbf{v} + \frac{D\mathbf{v}}{Dt}\delta t = \left\{1 + \left(\frac{du}{dx} + \frac{dv}{dy} + \frac{dw}{dz}\right)\delta t\right\}\delta x\,\delta y\,\delta z,$$

or

$$\frac{1}{\mathbf{v}}\frac{D\mathbf{v}}{Dt} = \frac{du}{dx} + \frac{dv}{dy} + \frac{dw}{dz} \quad\text{.....................(2).}$$

Hence (1) becomes

$$\frac{D\rho}{Dt} + \rho\left(\frac{du}{dx} + \frac{dv}{dy} + \frac{dw}{dz}\right) = 0 \quad\text{..................(3).}$$

This is called the 'equation of continuity.'

The expression $$\frac{du}{dx} + \frac{dv}{dy} + \frac{dw}{dz},$$

which, as we have seen, measures the rate of increase of volume of the fluid at the point (x, y, z), is conveniently called the 'expansion' at that point.

8. Another, and now more usual, method of obtaining the above equation is, instead of following the motion of a fluid element, to fix the attention on an element $\delta x\,\delta y\,\delta z$ of space, and to calculate the change produced in the included mass by the flow across the boundary. If the centre of the element be at (x, y, z), the amount of matter which per unit time enters it across the yz-face nearest the origin is

$$\left(\rho u - \tfrac{1}{2}\frac{d \, . \, \rho u}{dx}\delta x\right)\delta y\,\delta z,$$

and the amount which leaves it by the opposite face is

$$\left(\rho u + \tfrac{1}{2}\frac{d \, . \, \rho u}{dx}\delta x\right)\delta y\,\delta z.$$

The two faces together give a gain

$$-\frac{d \, . \, \rho u}{dx}\delta x\,\delta y\,\delta z,$$

per unit time. Calculating in the same way the effect of the flow across the remaining faces, we have for the total gain of mass, per unit time, in the space $\delta x \delta y \delta z$, the formula

$$-\left(\frac{d\,.\,\rho u}{dx}+\frac{d\,.\,\rho v}{dy}+\frac{d\,.\,\rho w}{dz}\right)\delta x \delta y \delta z.$$

Since the quantity of matter in any region can vary only in consequence of the flow across the boundary, this must be equal to

$$\frac{d}{dt}(\rho\,\delta x \delta y \delta z),$$

whence we get the equation of continuity in the form

$$\frac{d\rho}{dt}+\frac{d\,.\,\rho u}{dx}+\frac{d\,.\,\rho v}{dy}+\frac{d\,.\,\rho w}{dz}=0 \;\ldots\ldots\ldots\ldots\ldots(4).$$

9. It remains to put in evidence the physical properties of the fluid, so far as these affect the quantities which occur in our equations.

In an 'incompressible' fluid, or liquid, we have $D\rho/Dt = 0$, in which case the equation of continuity takes the simple form

$$\frac{du}{dx}+\frac{dv}{dy}+\frac{dw}{dz}=0 \;\ldots\ldots\ldots\ldots\ldots\ldots\ldots\ldots(1).$$

It is not assumed here that the fluid is of *uniform* density, though this is of course by far the most important case.

If we wished to take account of the slight compressibility of actual liquids, we should have a relation of the form

$$p = \kappa(\rho - \rho_0)/\rho_0 \;\ldots\ldots\ldots\ldots\ldots\ldots\ldots\ldots(2),$$

or

$$\rho/\rho_0 = 1 + p/\kappa \ldots\ldots\ldots\ldots\ldots\ldots\ldots\ldots\ldots(3),$$

where κ denotes what is called the 'elasticity of volume.'

In the case of a gas whose temperature is uniform and constant we have the 'isothermal' relation

$$p/p_0 = \rho/\rho_0 \ldots\ldots\ldots\ldots\ldots\ldots\ldots\ldots\ldots(4),$$

where p_0, ρ_0 are any pair of corresponding values for the temperature in question.

In most cases of motion of gases, however, the temperature is not constant, but rises and falls, for each element, as the gas is compressed or rarefied. When the changes are so rapid that we can ignore the gain or loss of heat by an element due to conduction and radiation, we have the 'adiabatic' relation

$$p/p_0 = (\rho/\rho_0)^{\gamma} \ldots\ldots\ldots\ldots\ldots\ldots\ldots\ldots(5),$$

where p_0 and ρ_0 are any pair of corresponding values for the element considered. The constant γ is the ratio of the two specific heats of the gas; for atmospheric air, and some other gases, its value is 1·408.

10. At the boundaries (if any) of the fluid, the equation of continuity is replaced by a special surface-condition. Thus at a *fixed* boundary, the velocity of the fluid perpendicular to the surface must be zero, *i.e.* if l, m, n be the direction-cosines of the normal,

$$lu + mv + nw = 0 \quad\text{.....................(1).}$$

Again at a surface of discontinuity, *i.e.* a surface at which the values of u, v, w change abruptly as we pass from one side to the other, we must have

$$l(u_1 - u_2) + m(v_1 - v_2) + n(w_1 - w_2) = 0 \quad\text{.........(2),}$$

where the suffixes are used to distinguish the values on the two sides. The same relation must hold at the common surface of a fluid and a moving solid.

The general surface-condition, of which these are particular cases, is that if $F(x, y, z, t) = 0$ be the equation of a bounding surface, we must have at every point of it

$$DF/Dt = 0 \quad\text{..........................(3).}$$

The velocity relative to the surface of a particle lying in it must be wholly tangential (or zero), for otherwise we should have a finite flow of fluid across it. It follows that the instantaneous rate of variation of F for a surface-particle must be zero.

A fuller proof, given by Lord Kelvin*, is as follows. To find the rate of motion (ν) of the surface $F(x, y, z, t) = 0$, normal to itself, we write

$$F(x + l\nu\delta t,\ y + m\nu\delta t,\ z + n\nu\delta t,\ t + \delta t) = 0,$$

where l, m, n are the direction-cosines of the normal at (x, y, z), whence

$$\nu\left(l\frac{dF}{dx} + m\frac{dF}{dy} + n\frac{dF}{dz}\right) + \frac{dF}{dt} = 0.$$

Since $$l, m, n = \frac{dF}{dx}, \frac{dF}{dy}, \frac{dF}{dz}, \div R,$$

* (W. Thomson) "Notes on Hydrodynamics," *Camb. and Dub. Math. Journ.* Feb. 1848. *Mathematical and Physical Papers*, Cambridge, 1882..., t. i., p. 83.

where $$R = \left\{\left(\frac{dF}{dx}\right)^2 + \left(\frac{dF}{dy}\right)^2 + \left(\frac{dF}{dz}\right)^2\right\}^{\frac{1}{2}},$$

this gives $$\dot{\nu} = -\frac{1}{R}\frac{dF}{dt} \quad \text{.........................(4).}$$

At every point of the surface we must have

$$\dot{\nu} = lu + mv + nw,$$

which leads, on substitution of the above values of l, m, n, to the equation (3).

The partial differential equation (3) is also satisfied by any surface moving with the fluid. This follows at once from the meaning of the operator D/Dt. A question arises as to whether the converse necessarily holds; *i.e.* whether a moving surface whose equation $F=0$ satisfies (3) will always consist of the same particles. Considering any such surface, let us fix our attention on a particle P situate on it at time t. The equation (3) expresses that the rate at which P is separating from the surface is at this instant zero; and it is easily seen that *if the motion be continuous* (according to the definition of Art. 4), the normal velocity, relative to the moving surface F, of a particle at an infinitesimal distance ζ from it is of the order ζ, viz. it is equal to $G\zeta$ where G is finite. Hence the equation of motion of the particle P relative to the surface may be written

$$D\zeta/Dt = G\zeta.$$

This shews that $\log\zeta$ increases at a finite rate, and since it is negative infinite to begin with (when $\zeta=0$), it remains so throughout, *i.e.* ζ remains zero for the particle P.

The same result follows from the nature of the solution of

$$\frac{dF}{dt} + u\frac{dF}{dx} + v\frac{dF}{dy} + w\frac{dF}{dz} = 0 \quad \text{.........................(i),}$$

considered as a partial differential equation in F*. The subsidiary system of ordinary differential equations is

$$dt = \frac{dx}{u} = \frac{dy}{v} = \frac{dz}{w} \quad \text{.............................. (ii),}$$

in which x, y, z are regarded as functions of the independent variable t. These are evidently the equations to find the paths of the particles, and their integrals may be supposed put in the forms

$$x = f_1(a, b, c, t), \quad y = f_2(a, b, c, t), \quad z = f_3(a, b, c, t) \quad \text{...........(iii),}$$

where the arbitrary constants a, b, c are any three quantities serving to identify a particle; for instance they may be the initial co-ordinates. The general solution of (i) is then found by elimination of a, b, c between (iii) and

$$F = \psi(a, b, c) \quad \text{...............................(iv),}$$

where ψ is an arbitrary function. This shews that a particle once in the surface $F=0$ remains in it throughout the motion.

* Lagrange, *Oeuvres*, t. iv., p. 706.

Equation of Energy.

11. In most cases which we shall have occasion to consider the extraneous forces have a potential; viz. we have

$$X = -\frac{d\Omega}{dx}, \quad Y = -\frac{d\Omega}{dy}, \quad Z = -\frac{d\Omega}{dz} \quad \text{............(1)}.$$

The physical meaning of Ω is that it denotes the potential energy, per unit mass, at the point (x, y, z), in respect of forces acting at a distance. It will be sufficient for the present to consider the case where the field of extraneous force is constant with respect to the time, *i.e.* $d\Omega/dt = 0$. If we now multiply the equations (2) of Art. 6 by u, v, w, in order, and add, we obtain a result which may be written

$$\tfrac{1}{2}\rho \frac{D}{Dt}(u^2 + v^2 + w^2) + \rho \frac{D\Omega}{Dt} = -\left(u\frac{dp}{dx} + v\frac{dp}{dy} + w\frac{dp}{dz}\right).$$

If we multiply this by $\delta x \delta y \delta z$, and integrate over any region, we find, since $D/Dt . (\rho\, \delta x \delta y \delta z) = 0$,

$$\frac{D}{Dt}(T + V) = -\iiint\left(u\frac{dp}{dx} + v\frac{dp}{dy} + w\frac{dp}{dz}\right) dx\,dy\,dz \quad \text{... (2)},$$

where

$$T = \tfrac{1}{2}\iiint \rho\,(u^2 + v^2 + w^2)\, dx\,dy\,dz, \quad V = \iiint \Omega \rho\, dx\,dy\,dx \quad \text{...(3)},$$

i.e. T and V denote the kinetic energy, and the potential energy in relation to the field of extraneous force, of the fluid which at the moment occupies the region in question. The triple integral on the right-hand side of (2) may be transformed by a process which will often recur in our subject. Thus, by a partial integration,

$$\iiint u\frac{dp}{dx}\, dx\,dy\,dz = \iint [pu]\, dy\,dz - \iiint p\frac{du}{dx}\, dx\,dy\,dz,$$

where $[pu]$ is used to indicate that the values of pu at the points where the boundary of the region is met by a line parallel to x are to be taken, with proper signs. If l, m, n be the direction-cosines of the *inwardly* directed normal to any element δS of this boundary, we have $\delta y \delta z = \pm\, l \delta S$, the signs alternating at the successive intersections referred to. We thus find that

$$\iint [pu]\, dy\,dz = -\iint pul\,dS,$$

where the integration extends over the whole bounding surface. Transforming the remaining terms in a similar manner, we obtain

$$\frac{D}{Dt}(T+V) = \iint p\,(lu + mv + nw)\,dS$$
$$+ \iiint p\left(\frac{du}{dx} + \frac{dv}{dy} + \frac{dw}{dz}\right) dx\,dy\,dz \;\ldots\ldots\ldots (4).$$

In the case of an incompressible fluid this reduces to the form

$$\frac{D}{Dt}(T+V) = \iint (lu + mv + nw)\,p\,dS \ldots\ldots\ldots\ldots\ldots (5).$$

Since $lu + mv + nw$ denotes the velocity of a fluid particle in the direction of the normal, the latter integral expresses the rate at which the pressures $p\delta S$ exerted from without on the various elements δS of the boundary are doing work. Hence the total increase of energy, kinetic and potential, of any portion of the liquid, is equal to the work done by the pressures on its surface.

In particular, if the fluid be bounded on all sides by fixed walls, we have

$$lu + mv + nw = 0$$

over the boundary, and therefore

$$T + V = \text{const.} \ldots\ldots\ldots\ldots\ldots\ldots\ldots\ldots (6).$$

A similar interpretation can be given to the more general equation (4), provided p be a function of ρ only. If we write

$$E = -\int p\,d\left(\frac{1}{\rho}\right) \ldots\ldots\ldots\ldots\ldots\ldots\ldots\ldots (7),$$

then E measures the work done by unit mass of the fluid against external pressure, as it passes, under the supposed relation between p and ρ, from its actual volume to some standard volume. For example*, if the unit mass were enclosed in a cylinder with a sliding piston of area A, then when the piston is pushed outwards through a space δx, the work done is $pA\,.\,\delta x$, of which the factor $A\delta x$ denotes the increment of volume, *i.e.* of ρ^{-1}. We may there-

* See any treatise on Thermodynamics. In the case of the adiabatic relation we find

$$E = \frac{1}{\gamma - 1}\left(\frac{p}{\rho} - \frac{p_0}{\rho_0}\right).$$

fore call E the intrinsic energy of the fluid, per unit mass. Now recalling the interpretation of the expression

$$\frac{du}{dx}+\frac{dv}{dy}+\frac{dw}{dz}$$

given in Art. 7 we see that the volume-integral in (4) measures the rate at which the various elements of the fluid are losing intrinsic energy by expansion*; it is therefore equal to $-DW/Dt$,

where $$W=\iiint E\rho\,dx\,dy\,dz, \qquad (8).$$

Hence $$\frac{D}{Dt}(T+V+W)=\iint p\,(lu+mv+nw)\,dS \qquad (9).$$

The total energy, which is now partly kinetic, partly potential in relation to a constant field of force, and partly intrinsic, is therefore increasing at a rate equal to that at which work is being done on the boundary by pressure from without.

Impulsive Generation of Motion.

12. If at any instant impulsive forces act bodily on the fluid, or if the boundary conditions suddenly change, a sudden alteration in the motion may take place. The latter case may arise, for instance, when a solid immersed in the fluid is suddenly set in motion.

Let ρ be the density, u, v, w the component velocities immediately before, u', v', w' those immediately after the impulse, X', Y', Z' the components of the extraneous impulsive forces per unit mass, ϖ the impulsive pressure, at the point (x, y, z). The change of momentum parallel to x of the element defined in Art. 6 is then $\rho\delta x\delta y\delta z\,(u'-u)$; the x-component of the extraneous impulsive forces is $\rho\delta x\delta y\delta z X'$, and the resultant impulsive pressure in the same direction is $-d\varpi/dx\,.\,\delta x\delta y\delta z$. Since an impulse is to be regarded as an infinitely great force acting for an infinitely short time (τ, say), the effects of all finite forces during this interval are neglected.

* Otherwise,

$$p\left(\frac{du}{dx}+\frac{dv}{dy}+\frac{dw}{dz}\right)\delta x\,\delta y\,\delta z$$

$$=-p\,.\,\frac{1}{\rho}\frac{D\rho}{Dt}\,.\,\delta x\,\delta y\,\delta z=p\,\frac{D}{Dt}\left(\frac{1}{\rho}\right).\,\rho\,\delta x\,\delta y\,\delta z=-\frac{DE}{Dt}\,.\,\rho\,\delta x\,\delta y\,\delta z.$$

Hence,

$$\rho\,\delta x\,\delta y\,\delta z\,(u'-u)=\rho\,\delta x\,\delta y\,\delta z\,X'-\frac{d\varpi}{dx}\,\delta x\,\delta y\,\delta z,$$

or

$$\left.\begin{aligned} u'-u &= X'-\frac{1}{\rho}\frac{d\varpi}{dx}.\\ v'-v &= Y'-\frac{1}{\rho}\frac{d\varpi}{dy},\\ w'-w &= Z'-\frac{1}{\rho}\frac{d\varpi}{dz}.\end{aligned}\right\}\quad\text{.................. (1).}$$

Similarly,

These equations might also have been deduced from (2) of Art. 6, by multiplying the latter by δt, integrating between the limits 0 and τ, putting

$$X'=\int_0^\tau X\,dt,\quad Y'=\int_0^\tau Y\,dt,\quad Z'=\int_0^\tau Z\,dt,\quad \varpi=\int_0^\tau p\,dt,$$

and then making τ vanish.

In a liquid an instantaneous change of motion can be produced by the action of impulsive pressures only, even when no impulsive forces act bodily on the mass. In this case we have $X', Y', Z'=0$, so that

$$\left.\begin{aligned} u'-u &= -\frac{1}{\rho}\frac{d\varpi}{dx},\\ v'-v &= -\frac{1}{\rho}\frac{d\varpi}{dy},\\ w'-w &= -\frac{1}{\rho}\frac{d\varpi}{dz}.\end{aligned}\right\}\quad\text{..................... (2).}$$

If we differentiate these equations with respect to x, y, z, respectively, and add, and if we further suppose the density to be uniform, we find by Art. 9 (1) that

$$\frac{d^2\varpi}{dx^2}+\frac{d^2\varpi}{dy^2}+\frac{d^2\varpi}{dz^2}=0.$$

The problem then, in any given case, is to determine a value of ϖ satisfying this equation and the proper boundary conditions*; the instantaneous change of motion is then given by (2).

* It will appear in Chapter III. that the value of ϖ is thus determinate, save as to an additive constant.

The Lagrangian Equations.

13. Let a, b, c be the initial co-ordinates of any particle of fluid, x, y, z its co-ordinates at time t. We here consider x, y, z as functions of the independent variables a, b, c, t; their values in terms of these quantities give the whole history of every particle of the fluid. The velocities parallel to the axes of co-ordinates of the particle (a, b, c) at time t are dx/dt, dy/dt, dz/dt, and the component accelerations in the same directions are d^2x/dt^2, d^2y/dt^2, d^2z/dt^2. Let p be the pressure and ρ the density in the neighbourhood of this particle at time t; X, Y, Z the components of the extraneous forces per unit mass acting there. Considering the motion of the mass of fluid which at time t occupies the differential element of volume $\delta x \delta y \delta z$, we find by the same reasoning as in Art. 6,

$$\frac{d^2x}{dt^2} = X - \frac{1}{\rho}\frac{dp}{dx},$$

$$\frac{d^2y}{dt^2} = Y - \frac{1}{\rho}\frac{dp}{dy},$$

$$\frac{d^2z}{dt^2} = Z - \frac{1}{\rho}\frac{dp}{dz}.$$

These equations contain differential coefficients with respect to x, y, z, whereas our independent variables are a, b, c, t. To eliminate these differential coefficients, we multiply the above equations by dx/da, dy/da, dz/da, respectively, and add; a second time by dx/db, dy/db, dz/db, and add; and again a third time by dx/dc, dy/dc, dz/dc, and add. We thus get the three equations

$$\left(\frac{d^2x}{dt^2} - X\right)\frac{dx}{da} + \left(\frac{d^2y}{dt^2} - Y\right)\frac{dy}{da} + \left(\frac{d^2z}{dt^2} - Z\right)\frac{dz}{da} + \frac{1}{\rho}\frac{dp}{da} = 0,$$

$$\left(\frac{d^2x}{dt^2} - X\right)\frac{dx}{db} + \left(\frac{d^2y}{dt^2} - Y\right)\frac{dy}{db} + \left(\frac{d^2z}{dt^2} - Z\right)\frac{dz}{db} + \frac{1}{\rho}\frac{dp}{db} = 0,$$

$$\left(\frac{d^2x}{dt^2} - X\right)\frac{dx}{dc} + \left(\frac{d^2y}{dt^2} - Y\right)\frac{dy}{dc} + \left(\frac{d^2z}{dt^2} - Z\right)\frac{dz}{dc} + \frac{1}{\rho}\frac{dp}{dc} = 0.$$

These are the 'Lagrangian' forms of the dynamical equations.

14. To find the form which the equation of continuity assumes in terms of our present variables, we consider the element of fluid which originally occupied a rectangular parallelepiped having its centre at the point (a, b, c), and its edges $\delta a, \delta b, \delta c$ parallel to the axes. At the time t the same element forms an oblique parallelepiped. The centre now has for its co-ordinates x, y, z; and the projections of the edges on the co-ordinate axes are respectively

$$\frac{dx}{da}\delta a,\quad \frac{dy}{da}\delta a,\quad \frac{dz}{da}\delta a;$$

$$\frac{dx}{db}\delta b,\quad \frac{dy}{db}\delta b,\quad \frac{dz}{db}\delta b;$$

$$\frac{dx}{dc}\delta c,\quad \frac{dy}{dc}\delta c,\quad \frac{dz}{dc}\delta c.$$

The volume of the parallelepiped is therefore

$$\begin{vmatrix} \dfrac{dx}{da}, & \dfrac{dy}{da}, & \dfrac{dz}{da} \\ \dfrac{dx}{db}, & \dfrac{dy}{db}, & \dfrac{dz}{db} \\ \dfrac{dx}{dc}, & \dfrac{dy}{dc}, & \dfrac{dz}{dc} \end{vmatrix} \delta a\,\delta b\,\delta c,$$

or, as it is often written,

$$\frac{d(x, y, z)}{d(a, b, c)}\delta a\,\delta b\,\delta c.$$

Hence, since the mass of the element is unchanged, we have

$$\rho\frac{d(x, y, z)}{d(a, b, c)} = \rho_0 \quad\text{.........................(1)},$$

where ρ_0 is the initial density at (a, b, c).

In the case of an incompressible fluid $\rho = \rho_0$, so that (1) becomes

$$\frac{d(x, y, z)}{d(a, b, c)} = 1 \quad\text{..........................(2)}.$$

Weber's Transformation.

15. If as in Art. 11 the forces X, Y, Z have a potential Ω, the dynamical equations of Art. 13 may be written

$$\frac{d^2x}{dt^2}\frac{dx}{da} + \frac{d^2y}{dt^2}\frac{dy}{da} + \frac{d^2z}{dt^2}\frac{dz}{da} = -\frac{d\Omega}{da} - \frac{1}{\rho}\frac{dp}{da}, \text{ \&c., \&c.}$$

Let us integrate these equations with respect to t between the limits 0 and t. We remark that

$$\int_0^t \frac{d^2x}{dt^2}\frac{dx}{da}dt = \left[\frac{dx}{dt}\frac{dx}{da}\right]_0^t - \int_0^t \frac{dx}{dt}\frac{d^2x}{da\,dt}dt$$
$$= \frac{dx}{dt}\frac{dx}{da} - u_0 - \tfrac{1}{2}\frac{d}{da}\int_0^t \left(\frac{dx}{dt}\right)^2 dt,$$

where u_0 is the initial value of the x-component of velocity of the particle (a, b, c). Hence if we write

$$\chi = \int_0^t \left[\int \frac{dp}{\rho} + \Omega - \tfrac{1}{2}\left\{\left(\frac{dx}{dt}\right)^2 + \left(\frac{dy}{dt}\right)^2 + \left(\frac{dz}{dt}\right)^2\right\}\right] dt \quad \text{...(1)},$$

we find

$$\left.\begin{aligned} \frac{dx}{dt}\frac{dx}{da} + \frac{dy}{dt}\frac{dy}{da} + \frac{dz}{dt}\frac{dz}{da} - u_0 &= -\frac{d\chi}{da}; \\ \frac{dx}{dt}\frac{dx}{db} + \frac{dy}{dt}\frac{dy}{db} + \frac{dz}{dt}\frac{dz}{db} - v_0 &= -\frac{d\chi}{db}; \\ \frac{dx}{dt}\frac{dx}{dc} + \frac{dy}{dt}\frac{dy}{dc} + \frac{dz}{dt}\frac{dz}{dc} - w_0 &= -\frac{d\chi}{dc}. \end{aligned}\right\} \quad \text{.........(2)*.}$$

These three equations, together with

$$\frac{d\chi}{dt} = \int \frac{dp}{\rho} + \Omega - \tfrac{1}{2}\left\{\left(\frac{dx}{dt}\right)^2 + \left(\frac{dy}{dt}\right)^2 + \left(\frac{dz}{dt}\right)^2\right\} \quad \text{.........(3)},$$

and the equation of continuity, are the partial differential equations to be satisfied by the five unknown quantities x, y, z, p, χ; ρ being supposed already eliminated by means of one of the relations of Art. 9.

The initial conditions to be satisfied are

$$x = a, \quad y = b, \quad z = c, \quad \chi = 0.$$

16. It is to be remarked that the quantities a, b, c need not be restricted to mean the initial co-ordinates of a particle; they may be any three quantities which serve to identify a particle, and which vary continuously from one particle to another. If we thus generalize the meanings of a, b, c, the form of the dynamical equations of Art. 13 is not altered; to find the form which the equation of continuity assumes, let x_0, y_0, z_0 now denote the initial co-ordinates of the particle to which a, b, c refer. The initial volume of the parallelepiped, whose centre is at

* H. Weber, "Ueber eine Transformation der hydrodynamischen Gleichungen", *Crelle*, t. lxviii. (1868).

(x_0, y_0, z_0) and whose edges correspond to variations δa, δb, δc of the parameters, a, b, c, is

$$\frac{d(x_0, y_0, z_0)}{d(a, b, c)} \delta a \delta b \delta c,$$

so that we have

$$\rho \frac{d(x, y, z)}{d(a, b, c)} = \rho_0 \frac{d(x_0, y_0, z_0)}{d(a, b, c)} \quad \text{..................(1)},$$

or, for an incompressible fluid,

$$\frac{d(x, y, z)}{d(a, b, c)} = \frac{d(x_0, y_0, z_0)}{d(a, b, c)} \quad \text{......................(2)}.$$

17. If we compare the two forms of the fundamental equations to which we have been led, we notice that the Eulerian equations of motion are linear and of the first order, whilst the Lagrangian equations are of the second order, and also contain products of differential coefficients. In Weber's transformation the latter are replaced by a system of equations of the first order, and of the second degree. The Eulerian equation of continuity is also much simpler than the Lagrangian, especially in the case of liquids. In these respects, therefore, the Eulerian forms of the equations possess great advantages. Again, the form in which the solution of the Eulerian equations appears corresponds, in many cases, more nearly to what we wish to know as to the motion of a fluid, our object being, in general, to gain a knowledge of the state of motion of the fluid mass at any instant, rather than to trace the career of individual particles.

On the other hand, whenever the fluid is bounded by a moving surface, the Lagrangian method possesses certain theoretical advantages. In the Eulerian method the functions u, v, w have no existence beyond this surface, and hence the range of values of x, y, z for which these functions exist varies in consequence of the motion which is itself the subject of investigation. In the other method, on the contrary, the range of the independent variables a, b, c is given once for all by the initial conditions*.

The difficulty, however, of integrating the Lagrangian equations has hitherto prevented their application except in certain very special cases. Accordingly in this treatise we deal almost exclusively with the Eulerian forms. The simplification and integration of these in certain cases form the subject of the following chapter.

* H. Weber, *l.c.*

CHAPTER II.

INTEGRATION OF THE EQUATIONS IN SPECIAL CASES.

18. In a large and important class of cases the component velocities u, v, w can be expressed in terms of a single function ϕ, as follows:

$$u = -\frac{d\phi}{dx}, \quad v = -\frac{d\phi}{dy}, \quad w = -\frac{d\phi}{dz} \text{..............(1).}$$

Such a function is called a 'velocity-potential,' from its analogy with the potential function which occurs in the theories of Attractions, Electrostatics, &c. The general theory of the velocity-potential is reserved for the next chapter; but we give at once a proof of the following important theorem:

If a velocity-potential exist, at any one instant, for any finite portion of a perfect fluid in motion under the action of forces which have a potential, then, provided the density of the fluid be either constant or a function of the pressure only, a velocity-potential exists for the same portion of the fluid at all instants before or after*.

In the equations of Art. 15, let the instant at which the

* Lagrange, "Mémoire sur la Théorie du Mouvement des Fluides," *Nouv. mém. de l'Acad. de Berlin*, 1781; *Oeuvres*, t. iv. p. 714. The argument is reproduced in the *Mécanique Analytique*.

Lagrange's statement and proof were alike imperfect; the first rigorous demonstration is due to Cauchy, "Mémoire sur la Théorie des Ondes," *Mém. de l'Acad. roy. des Sciences*, t. i. (1827); *Oeuvres Complètes*, Paris, 1882..., 1re Série, t. i. p. 38; the date of the memoir is 1815. Another proof is given by Stokes, *Camb. Trans.* t. viii. (1845) (see also *Math. and Phys. Papers*, Cambridge, 1880..., t. i. pp. 106, 158, and t. ii. p. 36), together with an excellent historical and critical account of the whole matter.

velocity-potential ϕ_0 exists be taken as the origin of time; we have then

$$u_0 da + v_0 db + w_0 dc = -d\phi_0,$$

throughout the portion of the mass in question. Multiplying the equations (2) of Art. 15 in order by da, db, dc, and adding, we get

$$\frac{dx}{dt}dx + \frac{dy}{dt}dy + \frac{dz}{dt}dz - (u_0 da + v_0 db + w_0 dc) = -d\chi,$$

or, in the 'Eulerian' notation,

$$udx + vdy + wdz = -d(\phi_0 + \chi) = -d\phi, \text{ say.}$$

Since the upper limit of t in Art. 15 (1) may be positive or negative, this proves the theorem.

It is to be particularly noticed that this continued existence of a velocity-potential is predicated, not of regions of space, but of portions of matter. A portion of matter for which a velocity-potential exists moves about and carries this property with it, but the part of space which it originally occupied may, in the course of time, come to be occupied by matter which did not originally possess the property, and which therefore cannot have acquired it.

The class of cases in which a velocity-potential exists includes all those where the motion has originated from rest under the action of forces of the kind here supposed; for then we have, initially,

$$u_0 da + v_0 db + w_0 dc = 0,$$

or

$$\phi_0 = \text{const.}$$

The restrictions under which the above theorem has been proved must be carefully remembered. It is assumed not only that the external forces X, Y, Z, estimated at per unit mass, have a potential, but that the density ρ is either uniform or a function of p only. The latter condition is violated for example, in the case of the convection currents generated by the unequal application of heat to a fluid; and again, in the wave-motion of a heterogeneous but incompressible fluid arranged originally in horizontal layers of equal density. Another important case of exception is that of 'electro-magnetic rotations.'

19. A comparison of the formulae (1) with the equations (2) of Art. 12 leads to a simple physical interpretation of ϕ.

Any actual state of motion of a liquid, for which a (single-valued) velocity-potential exists, could be produced instantaneously from rest

2—2

by the application of a properly chosen system of impulsive pressures. This is evident from the equations cited, which shew, moreover, that $\phi = \varpi/\rho + \text{const.}$; so that $\varpi = \rho\phi + C$ gives the requisite system. In the same way $\varpi = -\rho\phi + C$ gives the system of impulsive pressures which would completely stop the motion. The occurrence of an arbitrary constant in these expressions shews, what is otherwise evident, that a pressure uniform throughout a liquid mass produces no effect on its motion.

In the case of a gas, ϕ may be interpreted as the potential of the external impulsive forces by which the actual motion at any instant could be produced instantaneously from rest.

A state of motion for which a velocity-potential does not exist cannot be generated or destroyed by the action of impulsive pressures, or of extraneous impulsive forces having a potential.

20. The existence of a velocity-potential indicates, besides, certain *kinematical* properties of the motion.

A 'line of motion' or 'stream-line'* is defined to be a line drawn from point to point, so that its direction is everywhere that of the motion of the fluid. The differential equations of the system of such lines are

$$\frac{dx}{u} = \frac{dy}{v} = \frac{dz}{w} \quad \text{...............................} \quad (2).$$

The relations (1) shew that when a velocity-potential exists the lines of motion are everywhere perpendicular to a system of surfaces, viz. the 'equipotential' surfaces $\phi = \text{const.}$

Again, if from the point (x, y, z) we draw a linear element δs in the direction (l, m, n), the velocity resolved in this direction is $lu + mv + nw$, or

$$-\frac{d\phi}{dx}\frac{dx}{ds} - \frac{d\phi}{dy}\frac{dy}{ds} - \frac{d\phi}{dz}\frac{dz}{ds}, \text{ which} = -\frac{d\phi}{ds}.$$

The velocity in any direction is therefore equal to the rate of decrease of ϕ in that direction.

Taking δs in the direction of the normal to the surface $\phi = \text{const.}$ we see that if a series of such surfaces be drawn corresponding to

* Some writers prefer to restrict the use of the term 'stream-line' to the case of steady motion, as defined in Art. 22.

equidistant values of ϕ, the common difference being infinitely small, the velocity at any point will be inversely proportional to the distance between two consecutive surfaces in the neighbourhood of the point.

Hence, if any equipotential surface intersect itself, the velocity is zero at the intersection. The intersection of two *distinct* equipotential surfaces would imply an infinite velocity.

21. Under the circumstances stated in Art. 18, the equations of motion are at once integrable throughout that portion of the fluid mass for which a velocity-potential exists. For in virtue of the relations

$$\frac{dv}{dz}=\frac{dw}{dy},\quad \frac{dw}{dx}=\frac{du}{dz},\quad \frac{du}{dy}=\frac{dv}{dx},$$

which are implied in (1), the equations of Art. 6 may be written

$$-\frac{d^2\phi}{dxdt}+u\frac{du}{dx}+v\frac{dv}{dx}+w\frac{dw}{dx}=-\frac{d\Omega}{dx}-\frac{1}{\rho}\frac{dp}{dx},\quad \&c., \&c.$$

These have the integral

$$\int\frac{dp}{\rho}=\frac{d\phi}{dt}-\Omega-\tfrac{1}{2}q^2+F(t)\ \ldots\ldots\ldots\ldots\ldots (3),$$

where q denotes the resultant velocity $(u^2+v^2+w^2)^{\frac{1}{2}}$, and $F(t)$ is an arbitrary function of t. It is often convenient to suppose this arbitrary function to be incorporated in the value of $d\phi/dt$; this is permissible since, by (1), the values of u, v, w are not thereby affected.

Our equations take a specially simple form in the case of an incompressible fluid; viz. we then have

$$\frac{p}{\rho}=\frac{d\phi}{dt}-\Omega-\tfrac{1}{2}q^2+F(t)\ \ldots\ldots\ldots\ldots\ldots (4),$$

with the equation of continuity

$$\frac{d^2\phi}{dx^2}+\frac{d^2\phi}{dy^2}+\frac{d^2\phi}{dz^2}=0\ \ldots\ldots\ldots\ldots\ldots\ldots\ldots\ldots (5),$$

which is the equivalent of Art. 9 (1). When, as in many cases which we shall have to consider, the boundary conditions are purely kinematical, the process of solution consists in finding a function which shall satisfy (5) and the prescribed surface-conditions. The pressure p is then given by (4), and is thus far indeterminate to the extent of an additive function of t. It becomes determinate when the value of p at some point of the fluid is given for all values of t.

Suppose, for example, that we have a solid or solids moving through a liquid completely enclosed by fixed boundaries, and that it is possible (*e.g.* by means of a piston) to apply an arbitrary pressure at some point of the boundary. Whatever variations are made in the magnitude of the force applied to the piston, the motion of the fluid and of the solids will be absolutely unaffected, the pressure at all points instantaneously rising or falling by equal amounts. Physically, the origin of the paradox (such as it is) is that the fluid is treated as absolutely incompressible. In actual liquids changes of pressure are propagated with very great, but not infinite, velocity.

Steady Motion.

22. When at every point the velocity is constant in magnitude and direction, *i.e.* when

$$\frac{du}{dt}=0,\quad \frac{dv}{dt}=0,\quad \frac{dw}{dt}=0 \quad\ldots\ldots\ldots\ldots\ldots\ldots\ldots(1)$$

everywhere, the motion is said to be 'steady.'

In steady motion the lines of motion coincide with the paths of the particles. For if P, Q be two consecutive points on a line of motion, a particle which is at any instant at P is moving in the direction of the tangent at P, and will, therefore, after an infinitely short time arrive at Q. The motion being steady, the lines of motion remain the same. Hence the direction of motion at Q is along the tangent to the same line of motion, *i.e.* the particle continues to describe the line.

In steady motion the equation (3) of the last Art. becomes

$$\int\frac{dp}{\rho}=-\Omega-\tfrac{1}{2}q^2+\text{constant}\quad\ldots\ldots\ldots\ldots\ldots(2).$$

The equations may however in this case be integrated to a certain extent without assuming the existence of a velocity-potential. For if δs denote an element of a stream-line, we have $u=q\,dx/ds$, &c. Substituting in the equations of motion and remembering (1), we have

$$q\frac{du}{ds}=-\frac{d\Omega}{dx}-\frac{1}{\rho}\frac{dp}{dx},$$

with two similar equations. Multiplying these in order by dx/ds, dy/ds, dz/ds, and adding, we have

$$u\frac{du}{ds}+v\frac{dv}{ds}+w\frac{dw}{ds}=-\frac{d\Omega}{ds}-\frac{1}{\rho}\frac{dp}{ds},$$

or, integrating along the stream-line,

$$\int\frac{dp}{\rho}=-\Omega-\tfrac{1}{2}q^2+C \qquad\qquad (3).$$

This is similar in form to (2), but is more general in that it does not assume the existence of a velocity-potential. It must however be carefully noticed that the 'constant' of equation (2) and the 'C' of equation (3) have very different meanings, the former being an absolute constant, while the latter is constant along any particular stream-line, but may vary as we pass from one stream-line to another.

23. The theorem (3) stands in close relation to the principle of energy. If this be assumed independently, the formula may be deduced as follows*. Taking first the particular case of a liquid, let us consider the portion of an infinitely narrow tube, whose boundary follows the stream-lines, included between two cross sections A and B, the direction of motion being from A to B. Let p be the pressure, q the velocity, Ω the potential of the external forces, σ the area of the cross section, at A, and let the values of the same quantities at B be distinguished by accents. In each unit of time a mass $\rho q\sigma$ at A enters the portion of the tube considered, whilst an equal mass $\rho q'\sigma'$ leaves it at B. Hence $q\sigma=q'\sigma'$. Again, the work done on the mass entering at A is $pq\sigma$ per unit time, whilst the loss of work at B is $p'q'\sigma'$. The former mass brings with it the energy $\rho q\sigma(\tfrac{1}{2}q^2+\Omega)$, whilst the latter carries off energy to the amount $\rho q'\sigma'(\tfrac{1}{2}q'^2+\Omega')$. The motion being steady, the portion of the tube considered neither gains nor loses energy on the whole, so that

$$pq\sigma+\rho q\sigma(\tfrac{1}{2}q^2+\Omega)=p'q'\sigma'+\rho q'\sigma'(\tfrac{1}{2}q'^2+\Omega').$$

Dividing by $\rho q\sigma\,(=\rho q'\sigma')$, we have

$$\frac{p}{\rho}+\tfrac{1}{2}q^2+\Omega=\frac{p'}{\rho}+\tfrac{1}{2}q'^2+\Omega',$$

* This is really a reversion to the methods of Daniel Bernoulli, *Hydrodynamica*, Argentorati, 1738.

or, using C in the same sense as before,

$$\frac{p}{\rho} = -\Omega - \tfrac{1}{2}q^2 + C \qquad\qquad (4),$$

which is what the equation (3) becomes when ρ is constant.

To prove the corresponding formula for compressible fluids, we remark that the fluid entering at A now brings with it, in addition to its energies of motion and position, the intrinsic energy

$$-\int p\,d\left(\frac{1}{\rho}\right), \text{ or } -\frac{p}{\rho} + \int\frac{dp}{\rho},$$

per unit mass. The addition of these terms to (4) gives the equation (3).

The motion of a gas is as a rule subject to the adiabatic law

$$p/p_0 = (\rho/\rho_0)^\gamma \qquad\qquad (5),$$

and the equation (3) then takes the form

$$\frac{\gamma}{\gamma-1}\frac{p}{\rho} = -\Omega - \tfrac{1}{2}q^2 + C \qquad\qquad (6).$$

24. The preceding equations shew that, in steady motion, and for points along any one stream-line*, the pressure is, *cæteris paribus*, greatest where the velocity is least, and *vice versâ*. This statement, though opposed to popular notions, becomes evident when we reflect that a particle passing from a place of higher to one of lower pressure must have its motion accelerated, and *vice versâ*†.

It follows that in any case to which the equations of the last Art. apply there is a limit which the velocity cannot exceed‡. For instance, let us suppose that we have a liquid flowing from a reservoir where the motion may be neglected, and the pressure is p_0, and that we may neglect extraneous forces. We have then, in (4), $C = p_0/\rho$, and therefore

$$p = p_0 - \tfrac{1}{2}\rho q^2 \qquad\qquad (7).$$

Now although it is found that a liquid from which all traces

* This restriction is unnecessary when a velocity-potential exists.

† Some interesting practical illustrations of this principle are given by Froude, *Nature*, t. xiii., 1875.

‡ Cf. von Helmholtz, "Ueber discontinuirliche Flüssigkeitsbewegungen," *Berl. Monatsber.*, April, 1868; *Phil. Mag.*, Nov. 1868; *Gesammelte Abhandlungen*, Leipzig, 1882-3, t. i., p. 146.

of air or other dissolved gas have been eliminated can sustain a negative pressure, or tension, of considerable magnitude, this is not the case with fluids such as we find them under ordinary conditions. Practically, then, the equation (7) shews that q cannot exceed $(2p_0/\rho)^{\frac{1}{2}}$.

If in any case of fluid motion of which we have succeeded in obtaining the analytical expression, we suppose the motion to be gradually accelerated until the velocity at some point reaches the limit here indicated, a cavity will be formed there, and the conditions of the problem are more or less changed.

It will be shewn, in the next chapter, that in irrotational motion of a liquid, whether 'steady' or not, the place of least pressure is always at some point of the boundary, provided the extraneous forces have a potential Ω satisfying the equation

$$\frac{d^2\Omega}{dx^2} + \frac{d^2\Omega}{dy^2} + \frac{d^2\Omega}{dz^2} = 0.$$

This includes, of course, the case of gravity.

The limiting velocity, when no extraneous forces act, is of course that with which the fluid would escape from the reservoir into a vacuum. In the case of water at atmospheric pressure it is the velocity 'due to' the height of the water-barometer, or about 45 feet per second.

In the general case of a fluid in which p is a given function of ρ we have, putting $\Omega = 0$ in (3),

$$q^2 = 2\int_p^{p_0} \frac{dp}{\rho} \qquad \text{(8)}.$$

For a gas subject to the adiabatic law, this gives

$$q^2 = \frac{2\gamma}{\gamma - 1}\frac{p_0}{\rho_0}\left\{1 - \left(\frac{p}{p_0}\right)^{\frac{\gamma-1}{\gamma}}\right\} \qquad \text{(9)}$$

$$= \frac{2}{\gamma - 1}(c_0^2 - c^2) \qquad \text{(10)},$$

if $c, = (\gamma p/\rho)^{\frac{1}{2}}, = (dp/d\rho)^{\frac{1}{2}}$, denote the velocity of sound in the gas when at pressure p and density ρ, and c_0 the corresponding velocity for gas under the conditions which obtain in the reservoir. (See Chap. x.) Hence the limiting velocity is

$$\left(\frac{2}{\gamma - 1}\right)^{\frac{1}{2}} . c_0,$$

or, $2{\cdot}214\, c_0$, if $\gamma = 1{\cdot}408$.

25. We conclude this chapter with a few simple applications of the equations.

Efflux of Liquids.

Let us take in the first instance the problem of the efflux of a liquid from a small orifice in the walls of a vessel which is kept filled up to a constant level, so that the motion may be regarded as steady.

The origin being taken in the upper surface, let the axis of z be vertical, and its positive direction downwards, so that $\Omega = -gz$. If we suppose the area of the upper surface large compared with that of the orifice, the velocity at the former may be neglected. Hence, determining the value of C in Art. 23 (4) so that $p = P$ (the atmospheric pressure), when $z = 0$, we have

$$\frac{p}{\rho} = \frac{P}{\rho} + gz - \tfrac{1}{2}q^2 \qquad (1)^*.$$

At the surface of the issuing jet we have $p = P$, and therefore

$$q^2 = 2gz \qquad (2),$$

i.e. the velocity is that due to the depth below the upper surface. This is known as *Torricelli's Theorem.*

We cannot however at once apply this result to calculate the rate of efflux of the fluid, for two reasons. In the first place, the issuing fluid must be regarded as made up of a great number of elementary streams converging from all sides towards the orifice. Its motion is not, therefore, throughout the area of the orifice, everywhere perpendicular to this area, but becomes more and more oblique as we pass from the centre to the sides. Again, the converging motion of the elementary streams must make the pressure at the orifice somewhat greater in the interior of the jet than at the surface, where it is equal to the atmospheric pressure. The velocity, therefore, in the interior of the jet will be somewhat less than that given by (2).

Experiment shews however that the converging motion above spoken of ceases at a short distance beyond the orifice, and that (in the case of a circular orifice) the jet then becomes approximately cylindrical. The ratio of the area of the section S' of the jet at this point (called the 'vena contracta') to the area S of the orifice is called

* This result is due to D. Bernoulli, *l. c. ante* p. 23.

the 'coefficient of contraction.' If the orifice be simply a hole in a thin wall, this coefficient is found experimentally to be about ·62.

The paths of the particles at the vena contracta being nearly straight, there is little or no variation of pressure as we pass from the axis to the outer surface of the jet. We may therefore assume the velocity there to be uniform throughout the section, and to have the value given by (2), where z now denotes the depth of the vena contracta below the surface of the liquid in the vessel. The rate of efflux is therefore

$$(2gz)^{\frac{1}{2}} . \rho S' \qquad \text{.........................(3).}$$

The calculation of the form of the issuing jet presents difficulties which have only been overcome in a few ideal cases of motion in two dimensions. (See Chapter IV.) It may however be shewn that the coefficient of contraction must, in general, lie between $\frac{1}{2}$ and 1. To put the argument in its simplest form, let us first take the case of liquid issuing from a vessel the pressure in which, at a distance from the orifice, exceeds that of the external space by the amount P, gravity being neglected. When the orifice is closed by a plate, the resultant pressure of the fluid on the containing vessel is of course *nil*. If when the plate is removed, we assume (for the moment) that the pressure on the walls remains sensibly equal to P, there will be an unbalanced pressure PS acting on the vessel in the direction opposite to that of the jet, and tending to make it recoil. The equal and contrary reaction on the fluid produces in unit time the velocity q in the mass $\rho q S'$ flowing through the 'vena contracta,' whence

$$PS = \rho q^2 S' \qquad \text{....................................(i).}$$

The principle of energy gives, as in Art. 23,

$$P = \tfrac{1}{2}\rho q^2 \qquad \text{....................................(ii),}$$

so that, comparing, we have $S' = \frac{1}{2}S$. The formula (1) shews that the pressure on the walls, especially in the neighbourhood of the orifice, will in reality fall somewhat below the static pressure P, so that the left-hand side of (i) is too small. The ratio S'/S will therefore in general be $> \frac{1}{2}$.

In one particular case, viz. where a short cylindrical tube, projecting inwards, is attached to the orifice, the assumption above made is sufficiently exact, and the consequent value $\frac{1}{2}$ for the coefficient then agrees with experiment.

The reasoning is easily modified so as to take account of gravity (or other conservative forces). We have only to substitute for P the excess of the static pressure at the level of the orifice over the pressure outside. The difference of level between the orifice and the 'vena contracta' is here neglected*.

* The above theory is due to Borda (*Mém. de l'Acad. des Sciences*, 1766), who also made experiments with the special form of mouth-piece referred to, and found $S/S' = 1·942$. It was re-discovered by Hanlon, *Proc. Lond. Math. Soc.* t. iii. p. 4, (1869); the question is further elucidated in a note appended to this paper by Maxwell. See also Froude and J. Thomson, *Proc. Glasgow Phil. Soc.* t. x., (1876).

Efflux of Gases.

26. We consider next the efflux of a gas, supposed to flow through a small orifice from a vessel in which the pressure is p_0 and density ρ_0 into a space where the pressure is p_1. We assume that the motion has become steady, and that the expansion takes place according to the adiabatic law.

If the ratio p_0/p_1 of the pressures inside and outside the vessel do not exceed a certain limit, to be indicated presently, the flow will take place in much the same manner as in the case of a liquid, and the rate of discharge may be found by putting $p=p_1$ in Art. 24 (9), and multiplying the resulting value of q by the area S' of the vena contracta. This gives for the rate of discharge of mass

$$q_1\rho_1 S' = \left(\frac{2}{\gamma-1}\right)^{\frac{1}{2}} c_0\rho_0 \left\{\left(\frac{p_1}{p_0}\right)^{\frac{2}{\gamma}} - \left(\frac{p_1}{p_0}\right)^{\frac{\gamma+1}{\gamma}}\right\}^{\frac{1}{2}} . S' \quad \text{............ (i)*.}$$

It is plain, however, that there must be a limit to the applicability of this result; for otherwise we should be led to the paradoxical conclusion that when $p_1=0$, *i.e.* the discharge is into a vacuum, the flow of matter is *nil*. The elucidation of this point is due to Prof. Osborne Reynolds†. It is easily found by means of Art. 24 (8), that $q\rho$ is a maximum, *i.e.* the section of an elementary stream is a minimum, when $q^2=dp/d\rho$, that is, the velocity of the stream is equal to the velocity of sound in gas of the pressure and density which prevail there. On the adiabatic hypothesis this gives, by Art. 24 (10),

$$\frac{c}{c_0} = \left(\frac{2}{\gamma+1}\right)^{\frac{1}{2}} \quad \text{.................................. (ii),}$$

and therefore, since $c^2 \propto \rho^{\gamma-1}$,

$$\frac{\rho}{\rho_0} = \left(\frac{2}{\gamma+1}\right)^{\frac{1}{\gamma-1}}, \qquad \frac{p}{p_0} = \left(\frac{2}{\gamma+1}\right)^{\frac{\gamma}{\gamma-1}} \quad \text{.................. (iii),}$$

or, if $\gamma=1{\cdot}408$,

$$\rho = {\cdot}634\rho_0, \qquad p = {\cdot}527p_0 \quad \text{......................... (iv).}$$

If p_1 be less than this value, the stream after passing the point in question, widens out again, until it is lost at a distance in the eddies due to viscosity. The minimum sections of the elementary streams will be situate in the neighbourhood of the orifice, and their sum S may be called the virtual area of the latter. The velocity of efflux, as found from (ii), is

$$q = {\cdot}911c_0.$$

The rate of discharge is then $=q\rho S$, where q and ρ have the values just

* A result equivalent to this was given by de Saint Venant and Wantzel, *Journ. de l'École Polyt.*, t. xvi., p. 92 (1839).

† "On the Flow of Gases," *Proc. Manch. Lit. and Phil. Soc.*, Nov. 17, 1885; *Phil. Mag.*, March, 1876. A similar explanation was given by Hugoniot, *Comptes Rendus*, June 28, July 26, and Dec. 13, 1886. I have attempted, above, to condense the reasoning of these writers.

found, and is therefore approximately independent* of the external pressure p_1 so long as this falls below $\cdot 527 p_0$. The physical reason of this is (as pointed out by Reynolds) that, so long as the velocity at any point exceeds the velocity of sound under the conditions which obtain there, no change of pressure can be propagated backwards beyond this point so as to affect the motion further up the stream.

These conclusions appear to be in good agreement with experimental results.

Under similar circumstances as to pressure, the velocities of efflux of different gases are (so far as γ can be assumed to have the same value for each) proportional to the corresponding velocities of sound. Hence (as we shall see in Chap. X.) the velocity of efflux will vary inversely, and the rate of discharge of mass will vary directly, as the square root of the density†.

Rotating Liquid.

27. Let us next take the case of a mass of liquid rotating, under the action of gravity only, with constant and uniform angular velocity ω about the axis of z, supposed drawn vertically upwards.

By hypothesis,

$$u = -\omega y, \qquad v = \omega x, \qquad w = 0,$$
$$X = 0, \qquad Y = 0, \qquad Z = -g.$$

The equation of continuity is satisfied identically, and the dynamical equations of Art. 6 become

$$-\omega^2 x = -\frac{1}{\rho}\frac{dp}{dx}, \quad -\omega^2 y = -\frac{1}{\rho}\frac{dp}{dy}, \quad 0 = -\frac{1}{\rho}\frac{dp}{dz} - g \text{....(1).}$$

These have the common integral

$$\frac{p}{\rho} = \tfrac{1}{2}\omega^2 (x^2 + y^2) - gz + \text{const. .... (2).}$$

The free surface, $p = \text{const.}$, is therefore a paraboloid of revolution about the axis of z, having its concavity upwards, and its latus rectum $= 2g/\omega^2$.

Since $$\frac{dv}{dx} - \frac{du}{dy} = 2\omega,$$

a velocity-potential does not exist. A motion of this kind could not therefore be generated in a 'perfect' fluid, *i.e.* in one unable to sustain tangential stress.

28. Instead of supposing the angular velocity ω to be uniform, let us suppose it to be a function of the distance r from the

* The magnitude of the ratio p_0/p_1 will of course have *some* influence on the arrangement of the streams, and consequently on the value of S.

† Cf. Graham, *Phil. Trans.*, 1846.

axis, and let us inquire what form must be assigned to this function in order that a velocity-potential may exist for the motion. We find

$$\frac{dv}{dx} - \frac{du}{dy} = 2\omega + r\frac{d\omega}{dr},$$

and in order that this may vanish we must have $\omega r^2 = \mu$, a constant. The velocity at any point is then $= \mu/r$, so that the equation (2) of Art. 22 becomes

$$\frac{p}{\rho} = \text{const.} - \tfrac{1}{2}\frac{\mu^2}{r^2} \quad\ldots\ldots\ldots\ldots\ldots\ldots\ldots\quad (1),$$

if no extraneous forces act. To find the value of ϕ we have

$$\frac{d\phi}{dr} = 0, \qquad \frac{d\phi}{rd\theta} = -\frac{\mu}{r},$$

whence $$\phi = -\mu\theta + \text{const.} = -\mu\tan^{-1}\frac{y}{x} + \text{const.} \;\ldots\ldots\ldots\; (2).$$

We have here an instance of a 'cyclic' function. A function is said to be 'single-valued' throughout any region of space when we can assign to every point of that region a definite value of the function in such a way that these values shall form a continuous system. This is not possible with the function (2); for the value of ϕ, if it vary continuously, changes by $-2\pi\mu$ as the point to which it refers describes a complete circuit round the origin. The general theory of cyclic velocity-potentials will be given in the next chapter.

If gravity act, and if the axis of z be vertical, we must add to (1) the term $-gz$. The form of the free surface is therefore that generated by the revolution of the hyperbolic curve $x^2z = \text{const.}$ about the axis of z.

By properly fitting together the two preceding solutions we obtain the case of Rankine's 'combined vortex.' Thus the motion being everywhere in coaxial circles, let us suppose the velocity to be equal to ωr from $r = 0$ to $r = a$, and to $\omega a^2/r$ for $r > a$. The corresponding forms of the free surface are then given by

$$z = \frac{\omega^2}{2g}(r^2 - a^2) + C,$$

and $$z = \frac{\omega^2}{2g}\left(a^2 - \frac{a^4}{r^2}\right) + C,$$

these being continuous when $r=a$. The depth of the central depression below the general level of the surface is therefore ω^2a^2/g.

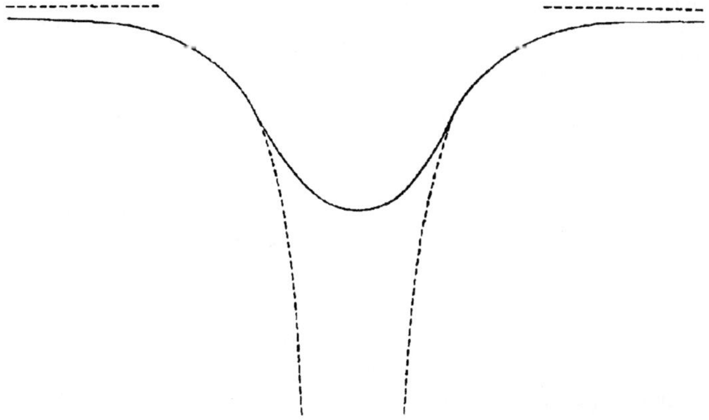

29. To illustrate, by way of contrast, the case of external forces not having a potential, let us suppose that a mass of liquid filling a right circular cylinder moves from rest under the action of the forces

$$X = Ax + By, \quad Y = B'x + Cy, \quad Z = 0,$$

the axis of z being that of the cylinder.

If we assume $u = -\omega y$, $v = \omega x$, $w = 0$, where ω is a function of t only, these values satisfy the equation of continuity and the boundary conditions. The dynamical equations become

$$\left.\begin{aligned} -y\frac{d\omega}{dt} - \omega^2 x &= Ax + By - \frac{1}{\rho}\frac{dp}{dx}, \\ x\frac{d\omega}{dt} - \omega^2 y &= B'x + Cy - \frac{1}{\rho}\frac{dp}{dy}, \end{aligned}\right\} \quad \ldots\ldots\ldots\ldots\ldots\ldots\ldots \text{(i)}.$$

Differentiating the first of these with respect to y, and the second with respect to x and subtracting, we eliminate p, and find

$$\frac{d\omega}{dt} = \tfrac{1}{2}(B' - B) \ldots\ldots\ldots\ldots\ldots\ldots\ldots\ldots\ldots\ldots \text{(ii)}.$$

The fluid therefore rotates as a whole about the axis of z with constantly accelerated angular velocity, except in the particular case when $B=B'$. To find p, we substitute the value of $d\omega/dt$ in (i) and integrate; we thus get

$$\frac{p}{\rho} = \tfrac{1}{2}\omega^2(x^2+y^2) + \tfrac{1}{2}(Ax^2 + 2\beta xy + Cy^2) + \text{const.},$$

where $2\beta = B + B'$.

30. As a final example, we will take one suggested by the theory of 'electro-magnetic rotations.'

If an electric current be made to pass radially from an axial wire, through a conducting liquid (*e.g.* a solution of $CuSO_4$), to the walls of a metallic containing cylinder, in a uniform magnetic field, the external forces will be of the type

$$X = -\mu y/r^2, \qquad Y = \mu x/r^2, \qquad Z = 0^*.$$

Assuming $u = -\omega y$, $v = \omega x$, $w = 0$, where ω is a function of r and t only, we find

$$\left.\begin{aligned} -y\frac{d\omega}{dt} - \omega^2 x &= -\frac{\mu y}{r^2} - \frac{1}{\rho}\frac{dp}{dx}, \\ x\frac{d\omega}{dt} - \omega^2 y &= \frac{\mu x}{r^2} - \frac{1}{\rho}\frac{dp}{dy}, \end{aligned}\right\} \quad \ldots\ldots\ldots\ldots\ldots\ldots\ldots\ldots (i).$$

Eliminating p, we obtain

$$2\frac{d\omega}{dt} + r\frac{d^2\omega}{dr\,dt} = 0.$$

The solution of this is

$$\omega = F(t)/r^2 + f(r),$$

where F and f denote arbitrary functions. Since $\omega = 0$ when $t = 0$, we have

$$F(0)/r^2 + f(r) = 0,$$

and therefore

$$\omega = \frac{F(t) - F(0)}{r^2} = \frac{\lambda}{r^2} \quad \ldots\ldots\ldots\ldots\ldots\ldots\ldots\ldots\ldots (ii),$$

where λ is a function of t which vanishes for $t = 0$. Substituting in (i), and integrating, we find

$$\frac{p}{\rho} = \left(\mu - \frac{d\lambda}{dt}\right)\tan^{-1}\frac{y}{x} - \tfrac{1}{2}\omega^2 r^2 + \chi(t).$$

Since p is essentially a single-valued function, we must have $d\lambda/dt = \mu$, or $\lambda = \mu t$. Hence the fluid rotates with an angular velocity which varies inversely as the square of the distance from the axis, and increases constantly with the time.

* If C denote the total flux of electricity outwards, per unit length of the axis, and γ the component of the magnetic force parallel to the axis, we have $\mu = \gamma C/2\pi\rho$. For the history of such experiments see Wiedemann, *Lehre v. d. Elektricität*, t. iii. p. 163. The above case is specially simple, in that the forces X, Y, Z, have a potential ($\Omega = -\mu\tan^{-1} y/x$), though a 'cyclic' one. As a rule, in electro-magnetic rotations, the mechanical forces X, Y, Z have not a potential at all.

CHAPTER III.

IRROTATIONAL MOTION.

31. THE present chapter is devoted mainly to an exposition of some general theorems relating to the kinds of motion already considered in Arts. 18—21; viz. those in which $udx + vdy + wdz$ is an exact differential throughout a finite mass of fluid. It is convenient to begin with the following analysis, due to Stokes*, of the motion of a fluid element in the most general case.

The component velocities at the point (x, y, z) being u, v, w, the relative velocities at an infinitely near point $(x + \mathbf{x}, y + \mathbf{y}, z + \mathbf{z})$ are

$$\left.\begin{aligned} \mathbf{u} &= \frac{du}{dx}\mathbf{x} + \frac{du}{dy}\mathbf{y} + \frac{du}{dz}\mathbf{z}, \\ \mathbf{v} &= \frac{dv}{dx}\mathbf{x} + \frac{dv}{dy}\mathbf{y} + \frac{dv}{dz}\mathbf{z}, \\ \mathbf{w} &= \frac{dw}{dx}\mathbf{x} + \frac{dw}{dy}\mathbf{y} + \frac{dw}{dz}\mathbf{z}. \end{aligned}\right\} \qquad (1).$$

If we write

$$a = \frac{du}{dx}, \quad b = \frac{dv}{dy}, \quad c = \frac{dw}{dz},$$

$$f = \tfrac{1}{2}\left(\frac{dw}{dy} + \frac{dv}{dz}\right), \quad g = \tfrac{1}{2}\left(\frac{du}{dz} + \frac{dw}{dx}\right), \quad h = \tfrac{1}{2}\left(\frac{dv}{dx} + \frac{du}{dy}\right),$$

$$\xi = \tfrac{1}{2}\left(\frac{dw}{dy} - \frac{dv}{dz}\right), \quad \eta = \tfrac{1}{2}\left(\frac{du}{dz} - \frac{dw}{dx}\right), \quad \zeta = \tfrac{1}{2}\left(\frac{dv}{dx} - \frac{du}{dy}\right),$$

equations (1) may be written

$$\left.\begin{aligned} \mathbf{u} &= a\mathbf{x} + h\mathbf{y} + g\mathbf{z} + \eta\mathbf{z} - \zeta\mathbf{y}, \\ \mathbf{v} &= h\mathbf{x} + b\mathbf{y} + f\mathbf{z} + \zeta\mathbf{x} - \xi\mathbf{z}, \\ \mathbf{w} &= g\mathbf{x} + f\mathbf{y} + c\mathbf{z} + \xi\mathbf{y} - \eta\mathbf{x}. \end{aligned}\right\} \qquad (2).$$

* "On the Theories of the Internal Friction of Fluids in Motion, &c." *Camb. Phil. Trans.*, t. viii. (1845); *Math. and Phys. Papers*, t. i., p. 80.

Hence the motion of a small element having the point (x, y, z) for its centre may be conceived as made up of three parts.

The first part, whose components are u, v, w, is a motion of *translation* of the element as a whole.

The second part, expressed by the first three terms on the right-hand sides of the equations (2), is a motion such that every point is moving in the direction of the normal to that quadric of the system

$$a\mathbf{x}^2 + b\mathbf{y}^2 + c\mathbf{z}^2 + 2f\mathbf{yz} + 2g\mathbf{zx} + 2h\mathbf{xy} = \text{const.} \quad \ldots\ldots\ldots (3),$$

on which it lies. If we refer these quadrics to their principal axes, the corresponding parts of the velocities parallel to these axes will be

$$\mathbf{u}' = a'\mathbf{x}', \quad \mathbf{v}' = b'\mathbf{y}', \quad \mathbf{w}' = c'\mathbf{z}' \ldots\ldots\ldots\ldots\ldots(4),$$

if

$$a'\mathbf{x}'^2 + b'\mathbf{y}'^2 + c'\mathbf{z}'^2 = \text{const.}$$

is what (3) becomes by the transformation. The formulæ (4) express that the length of every line in the element parallel to $\mathbf{x}'$ is being elongated at the (positive or negative) rate a', whilst lines parallel to $\mathbf{y}'$ and $\mathbf{z}'$ are being similarly elongated at the rates b' and c' respectively. Such a motion is called one of *pure strain* and the principal axes of the quadrics (3) are called the axes of the strain.

The last two terms on the right-hand sides of the equations (2) express a *rotation* of the element as a whole about an instantaneous axis; the component angular velocities of the rotation being ξ, η, ζ.

This analysis may be illustrated by the so-called 'laminar' motion of a liquid in which

$$u = 2\mu y, \quad v = 0, \quad w = 0,$$

so that

$$a, b, c, f, g, \xi, \eta = 0, \quad h = \mu, \quad \zeta = -\mu.$$

If A represent a rectangular fluid element bounded by planes parallel to the co-ordinate planes, then B represents the change produced in this in a short time by the strain, and C that due to the strain *plus* the rotation.

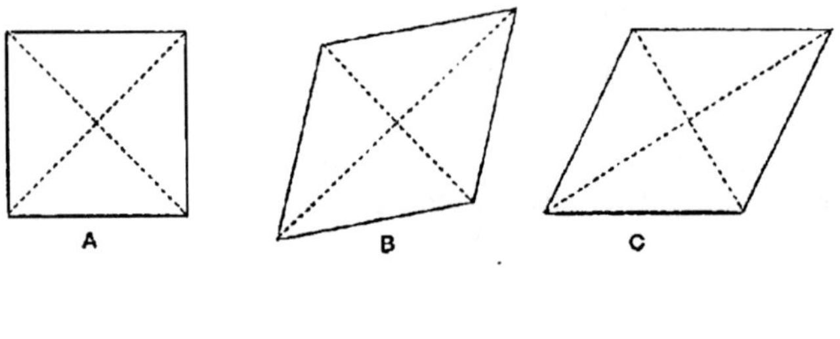

It is easily seen that the above resolution of the motion is unique. If we assume that the motion relative to the point (x, y, z) can be made up of a strain and a rotation in which the axes and coefficients of the strain and the axis and angular velocity of the rotation are arbitrary, then calculating the relative velocities $\mathbf{u}, \mathbf{v}, \mathbf{w}$, we get expressions similar to those on the right-hand sides of (2), but with arbitrary values of $a, b, c, f, g, h, \xi, \eta, \zeta$. Equating coefficients of $\mathbf{x}, \mathbf{y}, \mathbf{z}$, however, we find that a, b, c, &c. must have respectively the same values as before. Hence the directions of the axes of the strain, the rates of extension or contraction along them, and the axis and the angular velocity of rotation, at any point of the fluid, depend only on the state of relative motion at that point, and not on the position of the axes of reference.

When throughout a finite portion of a fluid mass we have ξ, η, ζ all zero, the relative motion of any element of that portion consists of a pure strain only, and is called 'irrotational.'

32. The value of the integral

$$\int (udx + vdy + wdz),$$

or

$$\int \left(u\frac{dx}{ds} + v\frac{dy}{ds} + w\frac{dz}{ds}\right) ds,$$

taken along any line $ABCD$, is called* the 'flow' of the fluid from A to D along that line. We shall denote it for shortness by $I(ABCD)$.

If A and D coincide, so that the line forms a closed curve, or circuit, the value of the integral is called the 'circulation' in that circuit. We denote it by $I(ABCA)$. If in either case the integration be taken in the opposite direction, the signs of dx/ds, dy/ds, dz/ds will be reversed, so that we have

$$I(AD) = -I(DA), \text{ and } I(ABCA) = -I(ACBA).$$

It is also plain that

$$I(ABCD) = I(AB) + I(BC) + I(CD).$$

Let us calculate the circulation in an infinitely small circuit surrounding the point (x, y, z). If $(x + \mathbf{x}, y + \mathbf{y}, z + \mathbf{z})$ be a point on the circuit, we have, by Art. 31 (2),

$$\mathbf{u}d\mathbf{x} + \mathbf{v}d\mathbf{y} + \mathbf{w}d\mathbf{z} = \tfrac{1}{2}d(a\mathbf{x}^2 + b\mathbf{y}^2 + c\mathbf{z}^2 + 2f\mathbf{yz} + 2g\mathbf{zx} + 2h\mathbf{xy})$$
$$+ \xi(\mathbf{y}d\mathbf{z} - \mathbf{z}d\mathbf{y}) + \eta(\mathbf{z}d\mathbf{x} - \mathbf{x}d\mathbf{z}) + \zeta(\mathbf{x}d\mathbf{y} - \mathbf{y}d\mathbf{x}) \ldots (1).$$

* Sir W. Thomson, "On Vortex Motion." *Edin. Trans.*, t. xxv. (1869).

Hence, integrating round a small closed circuit,

$$\int(\mathbf{u}d\mathbf{x}+\mathbf{v}d\mathbf{y}+\mathbf{w}d\mathbf{z})$$
$$=\xi\int(\mathbf{y}d\mathbf{z}-\mathbf{z}d\mathbf{y})+\eta\int(\mathbf{z}d\mathbf{x}-\mathbf{x}d\mathbf{z})+\zeta\int(\mathbf{x}d\mathbf{y}-\mathbf{y}d\mathbf{x})\ldots(2).$$

The coefficients of ξ, η, ζ in this expression are double the projections of the area of the circuit on the co-ordinate planes, these projections being reckoned positive or negative according to the direction of the integrations. In order to have a clear understanding on this point, we shall in this book suppose that the axes of co-ordinates form a *right-handed* system; thus if the axes of x and y point E. and N. respectively, that of z will point vertically upwards*. Now let δS be the area of the circuit, and let l, m, n be the direction-cosines of the normal to δS drawn in the direction which is related to that in which the circulation round the circuit is estimated, in the manner typified by a right-handed screw†. The formula (2) then shews that the circulation in the circuit is given by

$$2(l\xi+m\eta+n\zeta)\,\delta S\ldots\ldots\ldots\ldots\ldots\ldots(3),$$

or, twice the product of the area of the circuit into the component angular velocity of the fluid about the normal.

33. Any finite surface may be divided, by a double series of lines crossing it, into infinitely small elements. The sum of the circulations round the boundaries of these elements, taken all in the same sense, is equal to the circulation round the original boundary of the surface (supposed for the moment to consist of a single closed curve). For, in the sum in question, the flow

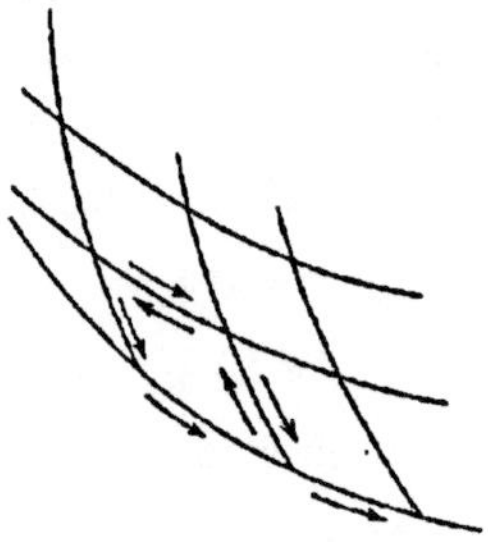

along each side common to two elements comes in twice, once for each element, but with opposite signs, and therefore disap-

* Maxwell, *Proc. Lond. Math. Soc.*, t. iii., pp. 279, 280.

† See Maxwell, *Electricity and Magnetism*, Oxford, 1873, Art. 23.

pears from the result. There remain then only the flows along those sides which are parts of the original boundary; whence the truth of the above statement.

Expressing this analytically we have, by (3),

$$\int(udx + vdy + wdz) = 2\iint(l\xi + m\eta + n\zeta)\,dS \quad\text{.........(4)},$$

or, substituting the values of ξ, η, ζ from Art. 31,

$$\int(udx + vdy + wdz) = \iint\left\{l\left(\frac{dw}{dy} - \frac{dv}{dz}\right) + m\left(\frac{du}{dz} - \frac{dw}{dx}\right) + n\left(\frac{dv}{dx} - \frac{du}{dy}\right)\right\}dS \quad\text{......(5)*};$$

where the single-integral is taken along the bounding curve, and the double-integral over the surface. In these formulæ the quantities l, m, n are the direction-cosines of the normal drawn always on one side of the surface, which we may term the positive side; the direction of integration in the ~~second member~~ is then that in which a man walking on the surface, on the positive side of it, and close to the edge, must proceed so as to have the surface always on his left hand.

The theorem (4) or (5) may evidently be extended to a surface whose boundary consists of two or more closed curves, provided the integration in the first member be taken round each of these in the proper direction, according to the rule just given.

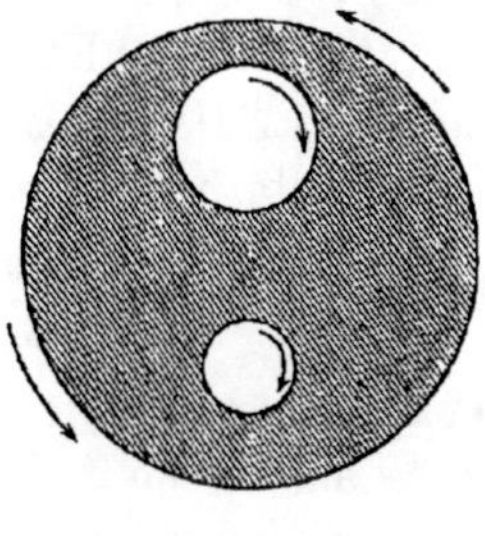

Thus, if the surface-integral in (5) extend over the shaded portion of the annexed figure, the directions in which the circulations in the several parts of the boundary are to be taken are shewn by

* This theorem is attributed by Maxwell to Stokes, *Smith's Prize Examination Papers for* 1854. The first published proof appears to have been given by Hankel, *Zur allgem. Theorie der Bewegung der Flüssigkeiten*, Göttingen, 1861, p. 35. That given above is due to Lord Kelvin, *l.c. ante* p. 35. See also Thomson and Tait, *Natural Philosophy*, Art. 190 (*j*), and Maxwell, *Electricity and Magnetism*, Art. 24.

the arrows, the positive side of the surface being that which faces the reader.

The value of the surface-integral taken over a *closed* surface is zero.

It should be noticed that (5) is a theorem of pure mathematics, and is true whatever functions u, v, w may be of x, y, z, provided only they be continuous over the surface*.

34. The rest of this chapter is devoted to a study of the kinematical properties of irrotational motion in general, as defined by the equations

$$\xi = 0, \quad \eta = 0, \quad \zeta = 0.$$

The existence and properties of the velocity-potential in the various cases that may arise will appear as consequences of this definition.

The physical importance of the subject rests on the fact that if the motion of any portion of a fluid mass be irrotational at any one instant it will under certain very general conditions continue to be irrotational. Practically, as will be seen, this has already been established by Lagrange's theorem, proved in Art. 18, but the importance of the matter warrants a repetition of the investigation, in the Eulerian notation, in the form originally given by Lord Kelvin†.

Consider first any terminated line AB drawn in the fluid, and suppose every point of this line to move always with the velocity of the fluid at that point. Let us calculate the rate at which the flow along this line, from A to B, is increasing. If $\delta x, \delta y, \delta z$ be the projections on the co-ordinate axes of an element of the line, we have

$$\frac{D}{Dt}(u\delta x) = \frac{Du}{Dt}\delta x + u\frac{D\delta x}{Dt}.$$

Now $D\delta x/Dt$, the rate at which δx is increasing in consequence of the motion of the fluid, is equal to the difference of the velocities parallel to x at its two ends, *i.e.* to δu; and the value of Du/Dt is given in Art. 6. Hence, and by similar considerations, we find, if ρ be a function of p only, and if the extraneous forces X, Y, Z have a potential Ω,

$$\frac{D}{Dt}(u\delta x + v\delta y + w\delta z) = -\frac{\delta p}{\rho} - \delta\Omega + u\delta u + v\delta v + w\delta w.$$

* It is not necessary that their differential coefficients should be continuous.

† *l.c. ante* p. 35.

Integrating along the line, from A to B, we get

$$\frac{D}{Dt}\int_A^B (udx + vdy + wdz) = \left[-\int\frac{dp}{\rho} - \Omega + \tfrac{1}{2}q^2\right]_A^B \text{.........(1)},$$

or, the rate at which the flow from A to B is increasing is equal to the excess of the value which $-\int dp/\rho - \Omega + \frac{1}{2}q^2$ has at B over that which it has at A. This theorem comprehends the whole of the dynamics of a perfect fluid. For instance, equations (2) of Art. 15 may be derived from it by taking as the line AB the infinitely short line whose projections were originally δa, δb, δc, and equating separately to zero the coefficients of these infinitesimals.

If Ω be single-valued, the expression within brackets on the right-hand side of (1) is a single-valued function of x, y, z. Hence if the integration on the left-hand be taken round a closed curve, so that B coincides with A, we have

$$\frac{D}{Dt}\int (udx + vdy + wdz) = 0 \text{..................(2)},$$

or, the circulation in any circuit moving with the fluid does not alter with the time.

It follows that if the motion of any portion of a fluid mass be initially irrotational it will always retain this property; for otherwise the circulation in every infinitely small circuit would not continue to be zero, as it is initially, by virtue of Art. 33 (4).

35. Considering now any region occupied by irrotationally-moving fluid, we see from Art. 33 (4) that the circulation is zero in every circuit which can be filled up by a continuous surface lying wholly in the region, or which is in other words capable of being contracted to a point without passing out of the region. Such a circuit is said to be 'reducible.'

Again, let us consider two paths ACB, ADB, connecting two points A, B of the region, and such that either may by continuous variation be made to coincide with the other, without ever passing out of the region. Such paths are called 'mutually reconcileable.' Since the circuit $ACBDA$ is reducible, we have $I(ACBDA) = 0$, or since $I(BDA) = -I(ADB)$,

$$I(ACB) = I(ADB);$$

i.e. the flow is the same along any two reconcileable paths.

A region such that *all* paths joining any two points of it are mutually reconcileable is said to be 'simply-connected.' Such a region is that enclosed within a sphere, or that included between two concentric spheres. In what follows, as far as Art. 46, we contemplate only simply-connected regions.

36. The irrotational motion of a fluid within a simply-connected region is characterized by the existence of a single-valued velocity-potential. Let us denote by $-\phi$ the flow to a variable point P from some fixed point A, viz.

$$\phi = -\int_A^P (udx + vdy + wdz) \qquad (1).$$

The value of ϕ has been shewn to be independent of the path along which the integration is effected, provided it lie wholly within the region. Hence ϕ is a single-valued function of the position of P; let us suppose it expressed in terms of the coordinates (x, y, z) of that point. By displacing P through an infinitely short space parallel to each of the axes of co-ordinates in succession, we find

$$u = -\frac{d\phi}{dx}, \quad v = -\frac{d\phi}{dy}, \quad w = -\frac{d\phi}{dz} \qquad (2),$$

i.e. ϕ is a velocity-potential, according to the definition of Art. 18.

The substitution of any other point B for A, as the lower limit in (1), simply adds an arbitrary constant to the value of ϕ, viz. the flow from A to B. The original definition of ϕ in Art. 18, and the physical interpretation in Art. 19, alike leave the function indeterminate to the extent of an additive constant.

As we follow the course of any line of motion the value of ϕ continually decreases; hence in a simply-connected region the lines of motion cannot form closed curves.

37. The function ϕ with which we have here to do is, together with its first differential coefficients, by the nature of the case, finite, continuous, and single-valued at all points of the region considered. In the case of incompressible fluids, which we now proceed to consider more particularly, ϕ must also satisfy the equation of continuity, (5) of Art. 21, or as we shall in future write it, for shortness,

$$\nabla^2\phi = 0 \qquad (1),$$

at every point of the region. Hence ϕ is now subject to mathematical conditions identical with those satisfied by the potential of masses attracting or repelling according to the law of the inverse square of the distance, at all points external to such masses; so that many of the results proved in the theories of Attractions, Electrostatics, Magnetism, and the Steady Flow of Heat, have also a hydrodynamical application. We proceed to develope those which are most important from this point of view.

In any case of motion of an incompressible fluid the surface-integral of the normal velocity taken over any surface, open or closed, is conveniently called the 'flux' across that surface. It is of course equal to the volume of fluid crossing the surface per unit time.

When the motion is irrotational, the flux is given by

$$-\iint \frac{d\phi}{dn} dS,$$

where δS is an element of the surface, and δn an element of the normal to it, drawn in the proper direction. In any region occupied wholly by liquid, the total flux across the boundary is zero, *i.e.*

$$\iint \frac{d\phi}{dn} dS = 0 \quad\text{..........................(2)},$$

the element δn of the normal being drawn always on one side (say inwards), and the integration extending over the whole boundary. This may be regarded as a generalized form of the equation of continuity (1).

The lines of motion drawn through the various points of an infinitesimal circuit define a tube, which may be called a tube of flow. The product of the velocity (q) into the cross-section (σ, say) is the same at all points of such a tube.

We may, if we choose, regard the whole space occupied by the fluid as made up of tubes of flow, and suppose the size of the tubes so adjusted that the product $q\sigma$ is the same for each. The flux across any surface is then proportional to the number of tubes which cross it. If the surface be closed, the equation (2) expresses the fact that as many tubes cross the surface inwards as outwards. Hence a line of motion cannot begin or end at a point of the fluid.

38. The function ϕ cannot be a maximum or minimum at a point in the interior of the fluid; for, if it were, we should have $d\phi/dn$ everywhere positive, or everywhere negative, over a small closed surface surrounding the point in question. Either of these suppositions is inconsistent with (2).

Further, the absolute value of the velocity cannot be a *maximum* at a point in the interior of the fluid. For let the axis of x be taken parallel to the direction of the velocity at any point P. The equation (1), and therefore also the equation (2), is satisfied if we write $d\phi/dx$ for ϕ. The above argument then shews that $d\phi/dx$ cannot be a maximum or a minimum at P. Hence there must be some point in the immediate neighbourhood of P for which $d\phi/dx$ has a numerically greater value, and therefore *a fortiori*, for which

$$\left\{\left(\frac{d\phi}{dx}\right)^2+\left(\frac{d\phi}{dy}\right)^2+\left(\frac{d\phi}{dz}\right)^2\right\}^{\frac{1}{2}}$$

is numerically greater than $d\phi/dx$, *i.e.* the velocity of the fluid at some neighbouring point is greater than at P*.

On the other hand, the velocity may be a *minimum* at some point of the fluid. The simplest case is that of a *zero* velocity; see, for example, the figure of Art. 69, below.

39. Let us apply (2) to the boundary of a finite spherical portion of the liquid. If r denote the distance of any point from the centre of the sphere, $\delta\varpi$ the elementary solid angle subtended at the centre by an element δS of the surface, we have

$$d\phi/dn=-d\phi/dr,$$

and $\delta S=r^2\delta\varpi$. Omitting the factor r^2, (2) becomes

$$\iint\frac{d\phi}{dr}\,d\varpi=0,$$

or

$$\frac{d}{dr}\iint\phi\,d\varpi=0 \qquad (3).$$

Since $1/4\pi\,.\iint\phi\,d\varpi$ or $1/4\pi r^2\,.\iint\phi\,dS$ measures the mean value of ϕ over the surface of the sphere, (3) shews that this mean value is independent of the radius. It is therefore the same for any sphere, concentric with the former one, which can be made to coincide

* This theorem was enunciated, in another connection, by Lord Kelvin, *Phil. Mag.*, Oct. 1850; *Reprint of Papers on Electrostatics, &c.*, London, 1872, Art. 665. The above demonstration is due to Kirchhoff, *Vorlesungen über mathematische Physik, Mechanik*, Leipzig, 1876, p. 186. For another proof see Art. 44 below.

with it by gradual variation of the radius, without ever passing out of the region occupied by the irrotationally moving liquid. We may therefore suppose the sphere contracted to a point, and so obtain a simple proof of the theorem, first given by Gauss in his memoir* on the theory of Attractions, that the mean value of ϕ over any spherical surface throughout the interior of which (1) is satisfied, is equal to its value at the centre.

The theorem, proved in Art. 38, that ϕ cannot be a maximum or a minimum at a point in the interior of the fluid, is an obvious consequence of the above.

The above proof appears to be due, in principle, to Frost†. Another demonstration, somewhat different in form, has been given by Lord Rayleigh‡. The equation (1), being linear, will be satisfied by the arithmetic mean of any number of separate solutions $\phi_1, \phi_2, \phi_3, \ldots$. Let us suppose an infinite number of systems of rectangular axes to be arranged uniformly about any point P as origin, and let $\phi_1, \phi_2, \phi_3, \ldots$ be the velocity-potentials of motions which are the same with respect to these systems as the original motion ϕ is with respect to the system x, y, z. In this case the arithmetic mean ($\bar{\phi}$, say) of the functions $\phi_1, \phi_2, \phi_3, \ldots$ will be a function of r, the distance from P, only. Expressing that in the motion (if any) represented by $\bar{\phi}$, the flux across any spherical surface which can be contracted to a point, without passing out of the region occupied by the fluid, would be zero, we have

$$4\pi r^2 \cdot \frac{d\bar{\phi}}{dr} = 0,$$

or $\bar{\phi} = \text{const.}$

Again, let us suppose that the region occupied by the irrotationally moving fluid is 'periphractic,'§ *i.e.* that it is limited internally by one or more closed surfaces, and let us apply (2) to the space included between one (or more) of these internal boundaries, and a spherical surface completely enclosing it and lying wholly in the fluid. If $4\pi M$ denote the total flux into this region, across the internal boundary, we find, with the same notation as before,

$$\iint \frac{d\phi}{dr} dS = -4\pi M,$$

* "Allgemeine Lehrsätze, u. s. w.," *Resultate aus den Beobachtungen des magnetischen Vereins*, 1839; *Werke*, Göttingen, 1870—80, t. v., p. 199.

† *Quarterly Journal of Mathematics*, t. xii. (1873).

‡ *Messenger of Mathematics*, t. vii., p. 69 (1878).

§ See Maxwell, *Electricity and Magnetism*, Arts. 18, 22. A region is said to be 'aperiphractic' when every closed surface drawn in it can be contracted to a point without passing out of the region.

the surface-integral extending over the sphere only. This may be written

$$\frac{1}{4\pi}\frac{d}{dr}\iint \phi\, d\varpi = -\frac{M}{r^2},$$

whence $$\frac{1}{4\pi r^2}\iint \phi\, dS = \frac{1}{4\pi}\iint \phi\, d\varpi = \frac{M}{r} + C \quad \text{..............} (4).$$

That is, the mean value of ϕ over any spherical surface drawn under the above-mentioned conditions is equal to $M/r + C$, where r is the radius, M an absolute constant, and C a quantity which is independent of the radius but may vary with the position of the centre*.

If however the original region throughout which the irrotational motion holds be unlimited externally, and if the first derivative (and therefore all the higher derivatives) of ϕ vanish at infinity, then C is the same for *all* spherical surfaces enclosing the whole of the internal boundaries. For if such a sphere be displaced parallel to x†, without alteration of size, the rate at which C varies in consequence of this displacement is, by (4), equal to the mean value of $d\phi/dx$ over the surface. Since $d\phi/dx$ vanishes at infinity, we can by taking the sphere large enough make the latter mean value as small as we please. Hence C is not altered by a displacement of the centre of the sphere parallel to x. In the same way we see that C is not altered by a displacement parallel to y or z; *i.e.* it is absolutely constant.

If the internal boundaries of the region considered be such that the total flux across them is zero, *e.g.* if they be the surfaces of solids, or of portions of incompressible fluid whose motion is rotational, we have $M = 0$, so that the mean value of ϕ over *any* spherical surface enclosing them all is the same.

40. (α) If ϕ be constant over the boundary of any simply-connected region occupied by liquid moving irrotationally, it has the same constant value throughout the interior of that region. For if not constant it would necessarily have a maximum or a minimum value at some point of the region.

* It is understood, of course, that the spherical surfaces to which this statement applies are reconcileable with one another, in a sense analogous to that of Art. 35.

† Kirchhoff, *Mechanik*, p. 191.

Otherwise: we have seen in Arts. 36, 37 that the lines of motion cannot begin or end at any point of the region, and that they cannot form closed curves lying wholly within it. They must therefore traverse the region, beginning and ending on its boundary. In our case however this is impossible, for such a line always proceeds from places where ϕ is greater to places where it is less. Hence there can be no motion, *i.e.*

$$\frac{d\phi}{dx} = 0, \quad \frac{d\phi}{dy} = 0, \quad \frac{d\phi}{dz} = 0,$$

and therefore ϕ is constant and equal to its value at the boundary.

(β) Again, if $d\phi/dn$ be zero at every point of the boundary of such a region as is above described, ϕ will be constant throughout the interior. For the condition $d\phi/dn = 0$ expresses that no lines of motion enter or leave the region, but that they are all contained within it. This is however, as we have seen, inconsistent with the other conditions which the lines must conform to. Hence, as before, there can be no motion, and ϕ is constant.

This theorem may be otherwise stated as follows: no continuous irrotational motion of a liquid can take place in a simply-connected region bounded entirely by fixed rigid walls.

(γ) Again, let the boundary of the region considered consist partly of surfaces S over which ϕ has a given constant value, and partly of other surfaces Σ over which $d\phi/dn = 0$. By the previous argument, no lines of motion can pass from one point to another of S, and none can cross Σ. Hence no such lines exist; ϕ is therefore constant as before, and equal to its value at S.

It follows from these theorems that the irrotational motion of a liquid in a simply-connected region is determinate when either the value of ϕ, or the value of the inward normal velocity $-d\phi/dn$, is prescribed at all points of the boundary, or (again) when the value of ϕ is given over part of the boundary, and the value of $-d\phi/dn$ over the remainder. For if ϕ_1, ϕ_2 be the velocity-potentials of two motions each of which satisfies the prescribed boundary-conditions, in any one of these cases, the function $\phi_1 - \phi_2$ satisfies the condition (α) or (β) or (γ) of the present Article, and must therefore be constant throughout the region.

41. A class of cases of great importance, but not strictly included in the scope of the foregoing theorems, occurs when the region occupied by the irrotationally moving liquid extends to infinity, but is bounded internally by one or more closed surfaces. We assume, for the present, that this region is simply-connected, and that ϕ is therefore single-valued.

If ϕ be constant over the internal boundary of the region, and tend everywhere to the same constant value at an infinite distance from the internal boundary, it is constant throughout the region. For otherwise ϕ would be a maximum or a minimum at some point.

We infer, exactly as in Art. 40, that if ϕ be given arbitrarily over the internal boundary, and have a given constant value at infinity, its value is everywhere determinate.

Of more importance in our present subject is the theorem that, if the normal velocity be zero at every point of the internal boundary, and if the fluid be at rest at infinity, then ϕ is everywhere constant. We cannot however infer this at once from the proof of the corresponding theorem in Art. 40. It is true that we may suppose the region limited externally by an infinitely large surface at every point of which $d\phi/dn$ is infinitely small; but it is conceivable that the integral $\iint d\phi/dn \,.\, dS$, taken over a portion of this surface, might still be finite, in which case the investigation referred to would fail. We proceed therefore as follows.

Since the velocity tends to the limit zero at an infinite distance from the internal boundary (S, say), it must be possible to draw a closed surface Σ, completely enclosing S, beyond which the velocity is everywhere less than a certain value ϵ, which value may, by making Σ large enough, be made as small as we please. Now in any direction from S let us take a point P at such a distance beyond Σ that the solid angle which Σ subtends at it is infinitely small; and with P as centre let us describe two spheres, one just excluding, the other just including S. We shall prove that the mean value of ϕ over each of these spheres is, within an infinitely small amount, the same. For if Q, Q' be points of these spheres on a common radius PQQ', then if Q, Q' fall within Σ the corresponding values of ϕ may differ by a finite amount; but since the portion of either spherical surface which falls within Σ is an infinitely small fraction of the whole, no finite difference in the mean values can arise from this cause. On the other hand, when Q, Q' fall without Σ, the corresponding values of ϕ cannot differ by so much as $\epsilon . QQ'$, for ϵ is by definition a superior limit to the rate of variation of ϕ. Hence, the mean values of ϕ over the two spherical surfaces must differ by less than $\epsilon . QQ'$. Since QQ' is finite, whilst ϵ may by taking Σ large enough be made as small as we please, the difference of the mean values may, by taking P sufficiently distant, be made infinitely small.

Now we have seen in Art. 39, that the mean value of ϕ over the inner sphere is equal to its value at P, and that the mean value over the outer sphere is (since $M = 0$) equal to a constant quantity C. Hence, ultimately, the value of ϕ at infinity tends everywhere to the constant value C.

The same result holds even if the normal velocity be not zero over the internal boundary; for in the theorem of Art. 39 M is divided by r, which is in our case infinite.

It follows that if $d\phi/dn = 0$ at all points of the internal boundary, and if the fluid be at rest at infinity, it must be everywhere at rest. For no lines of motion can begin or end on the internal boundary. Hence such lines, if they existed, must come from an infinite distance, traverse the region occupied by the fluid, and pass off again to infinity; *i.e.* they must form infinitely long courses between places where ϕ has, within an infinitely small amount, the same value C, which is impossible.

The theorem that, if the fluid be at rest at infinity, the motion is determinate when the value of $-d\phi/dn$ is given over the internal boundary, follows by the same argument as in Art. 40.

Green's Theorem.

42. In treatises on Electrostatics, &c., many important properties of the potential are usually proved by means of a certain theorem due to Green. Of these the most important from our present point of view have already been given; but as the theorem in question leads, amongst other things, to a useful expression for the kinetic energy in any case of irrotational motion, some account of it will properly find a place here.

Let U, V, W be any three functions which are finite, continuous, and single-valued at all points of a connected region completely bounded by one or more closed surfaces S; let δS be an element of any one of these surfaces, and l, m, n the direction-cosines of the normals to it drawn inwards. We shall prove in the first place that

$$\iint (lU + mV + nW)\, dS = -\iiint \left(\frac{dU}{dx} + \frac{dV}{dy} + \frac{dW}{dz}\right) dx\, dy\, dz \;\ldots\; (1),$$

where the triple-integral is taken throughout the region, and the double-integral over its boundary.

If we conceive a series of surfaces drawn so as to divide the region into any number of separate parts, the integral

$$\iint (lU + mV + nW)\, dS \;\ldots\ldots\ldots\ldots\ldots\ldots\; (2),$$

taken over the original boundary, is equal to the sum of the similar integrals each taken over the whole boundary of one of these parts. For, for every element $\delta\sigma$ of a dividing surface, we have, in the integrals corresponding to the parts lying on the two sides of this surface, elements $(lU + mV + nW)\,\delta\sigma$, and $(l'U + m'V + n'W)\,\delta\sigma$, respectively. But the normals to which l, m, n, and l', m', n' refer being drawn inwards in each case, we have $l' = -l$, $m' = -m$, $n' = -n$; so that, in forming the sum of the integrals spoken of, the elements due to the dividing surfaces disappear, and we have left only those due to the original boundary of the region.

Now let us suppose the dividing surfaces to consist of three systems of planes, drawn at infinitesimal intervals, parallel to yz, zx, xy, respectively. If x, y, z be the co-ordinates of the centre of one of the rectangular spaces thus formed, and $\delta x, \delta y, \delta z$ the lengths of its edges, the part of the integral (2) due to the yz-face nearest the origin is

$$\left(U - \tfrac{1}{2}\frac{dU}{dx}\,\delta x\right)\delta y\,\delta z,$$

and that due to the opposite face is

$$-\left(U + \tfrac{1}{2}\frac{dU}{dx}\,\delta x\right)\delta y\,\delta z.$$

The sum of these is $-dU/dx\,.\,\delta x\,\delta y\,\delta z$. Calculating in the same way the parts of the integral due to the remaining pairs of faces, we get for the final result

$$-\left(\frac{dU}{dx} + \frac{dV}{dy} + \frac{dW}{dz}\right)\delta x\,\delta y\,\delta z.$$

Hence (1) simply expresses the fact that the surface-integral (2), taken over the boundary of the region, is equal to the sum of the similar integrals taken over the boundaries of the elementary spaces of which we have supposed it built up.

The interpretation of this result when U, V, W denote the component velocities of a continuous substance is obvious. In the particular case of irrotational motion we obtain

$$\iint \frac{d\phi}{dn} dS = -\iiint \nabla^2\phi \, dx dy dz \text{..................} (3),$$

where δn denotes an element of the inwardly-directed normal to the surface S.

Again, if we put $U, V, W = \rho u, \rho v, \rho w$, respectively, we reproduce in substance the investigation of Art. 8.

Another useful result is obtained by putting $U, V, W = u\phi, v\phi, w\phi$, respectively, where u, v, w satisfy the relation

$$\frac{du}{dx} + \frac{dv}{dy} + \frac{dw}{dz} = 0$$

throughout the region, and make

$$lu + mv + nw = 0$$

over the boundary. We find

$$\iiint \left(u \frac{d\phi}{dx} + v \frac{d\phi}{dy} + w \frac{d\phi}{dz} \right) dx dy dz = 0 \text{ ....} (4).$$

The function ϕ is here merely restricted to be finite, single-valued, and continuous, and to have its first differential coefficients finite, throughout the region.

43. Now let ϕ, ϕ' be any two functions which, together with their first derivatives, are finite, continuous, and single-valued throughout the region considered; and let us put

$$U, V, W = \phi \frac{d\phi'}{dx}, \; \phi \frac{d\phi'}{dy}, \; \phi \frac{d\phi'}{dz},$$

respectively, so that

$$lU + mV + nW = \phi \frac{d\phi'}{dn}.$$

Substituting in (1) we find

$$\iint \phi \frac{d\phi'}{dn} dS = -\iiint \left(\frac{d\phi}{dx}\frac{d\phi'}{dx} + \frac{d\phi}{dy}\frac{d\phi'}{dy} + \frac{d\phi}{dz}\frac{d\phi'}{dz} \right) dx dy dz$$
$$- \iiint \phi \nabla^2 \phi' \, dx dy dz \text{.....................} (5)$$

By interchanging ϕ and ϕ' we obtain

$$\iint \phi' \frac{d\phi}{dn} dS = -\iiint \left(\frac{d\phi}{dx}\frac{d\phi'}{dx} + \frac{d\phi}{dy}\frac{d\phi'}{dy} + \frac{d\phi}{dz}\frac{d\phi'}{dz}\right) dxdydz$$
$$- \iiint \phi' \nabla^2 \phi \, dxdydz \ldots\ldots\ldots\ldots\ldots\ldots(6).$$

Equations (5) and (6) together constitute Green's theorem*.

44. If ϕ, ϕ' be the velocity-potentials of two distinct modes of irrotational motion of a liquid, so that

$$\nabla^2 \phi = 0, \quad \nabla^2 \phi' = 0 \ldots\ldots\ldots\ldots\ldots\ldots(1),$$

we obtain
$$\iint \phi \frac{d\phi'}{dn} dS = \iint \phi' \frac{d\phi}{dn} dS \ldots\ldots\ldots\ldots\ldots\ldots (2).$$

If we recall the physical interpretation of the velocity-potential, given in Art. 19, then, regarding the motion as generated in each case impulsively from rest, we recognize this equation as a particular case of the dynamical theorem that

$$\Sigma p_r \dot{q}_r' = \Sigma p_r' \dot{q}_r,$$

where p_r, $\dot{q}_r$ and p_r', $\dot{q}_r'$ are generalized components of impulse and velocity, in any two possible motions of a system†.

Again, in Art. 43 (6) let $\phi' = \phi$, and let ϕ be the velocity-potential of a liquid. We obtain

$$\iiint \left\{\left(\frac{d\phi}{dx}\right)^2 + \left(\frac{d\phi}{dy}\right)^2 + \left(\frac{d\phi}{dz}\right)^2\right\} dxdydz = -\iint \phi \frac{d\phi}{dn} dS \ldots\ldots (3).$$

To interpret this we multiply both sides by $\frac{1}{2}\rho$. Then on the right-hand side $-d\phi/dn$ denotes the normal velocity of the fluid inwards, whilst $\rho\phi$ is, by Art. 19, the impulsive pressure necessary to generate the motion. It is a proposition in Dynamics‡ that the work done by an impulse is measured by the product of the impulse into half the sum of the initial and final velocities, resolved in the direction of the impulse, of the point to which it is applied. Hence the right-hand side of (3), when modified as described, expresses the work done by the system of impulsive pressures which, applied to the surface S, would generate the actual motion; whilst the left-hand side gives the kinetic energy of this motion. The formula asserts that

* G. Green, *Essay on Electricity and Magnetism*, Nottingham, 1828, Art. 3. *Mathematical Papers* (ed. Ferrers), Cambridge, 1871, p. 23.

† Thomson and Tait, *Natural Philosophy*, Art. 313, equation (11).

‡ Thomson and Tait, *Natural Philosophy*, Art. 308.

these two quantities are equal. Hence if T denote the total kinetic energy of the liquid, we have the very important result

$$2T = -\rho \iint \phi \frac{d\phi}{dn} dS \quad \text{.....................} \quad (4).$$

If in (3), in place of ϕ, we write $d\phi/dx$, which will of course satisfy $\nabla^2 d\phi/dx = 0$, and apply the resulting theorem to the region included within a spherical surface of radius r having any point (x, y, z) as centre, then with the same notation as in Art. 39, we have

$$\tfrac{1}{2} r^2 \frac{d}{dr} \iint u^2 d\varpi = \iint u \frac{du}{dr} dS = -\iint \frac{d\phi}{dx} \frac{d}{dn}\left(\frac{d\phi}{dx}\right) dS$$

$$= \iiint \left\{ \left(\frac{d^2\phi}{dx^2}\right)^2 + \left(\frac{d^2\phi}{dx\,dy}\right)^2 + \left(\frac{d^2\phi}{dx\,dz}\right)^2 \right\} dx\,dy\,dz.$$

Hence, writing $q^2 = u^2 + v^2 + w^2$,

$$\tfrac{1}{2} r^2 \frac{d}{dr} \iint q^2 d\varpi = \iiint \left\{ \left(\frac{d^2\phi}{dx^2}\right)^2 + \left(\frac{d^2\phi}{dy^2}\right)^2 + \left(\frac{d^2\phi}{dz^2}\right)^2 + 2\left(\frac{d^2\phi}{dy\,dz}\right)^2 + 2\left(\frac{d^2\phi}{dz\,dx}\right)^2 + 2\left(\frac{d^2\phi}{dx\,dy}\right)^2 \right\} dx\,dy\,dz \quad \text{........} \quad \text{(i)}.$$

Since this latter expression is essentially positive, the mean value of q^2, taken over a sphere having any given point as centre, increases with the radius of the sphere. Hence q cannot be a maximum at any point of the fluid, as was proved otherwise in Art. 38.

Moreover, recalling the formula for the pressure in any case of irrotational motion of a liquid, viz.

$$\frac{p}{\rho} = \frac{d\phi}{dt} - \Omega - \tfrac{1}{2} q^2 + F(t) \quad \text{..........................} \quad \text{(ii)},$$

we infer that, provided the potential Ω of the external forces satisfy the condition

$$\nabla^2 \Omega = 0 \quad \text{.....................................} \quad \text{(iii)},$$

the mean value of p over a sphere described with any point in the interior of the fluid as centre will diminish as the radius increases. The place of least pressure will therefore be somewhere on the boundary of the fluid. This has a bearing on the point discussed in Art. 24.

45. In this connection we may note a remarkable theorem discovered by Lord Kelvin*, and afterwards generalized by him into an universal property of dynamical systems started impulsively from rest under prescribed velocity-conditions†.

The irrotational motion of a liquid occupying a simply-connected region has less kinetic energy than any other motion consistent with the same normal motion of the boundary.

* (W. Thomson) "On the Vis-Viva of a Liquid in Motion," *Camb. and Dub. Math. Journ.*, 1849; *Mathematical and Physical Papers*, t. i., p. 107.

† Thomson and Tait, *Natural Philosophy*, Art. 312.

Let T be the kinetic energy of the irrotational motion to which the velocity-potential ϕ refers, and T_1 that of another motion given by

$$u = -\frac{d\phi}{dx} + u_0, \quad v = -\frac{d\phi}{dy} + v_0, \quad w = -\frac{d\phi}{dz} + w_0 \text{......(5)},$$

where, in virtue of the equation of continuity, and the prescribed boundary-condition, we must have

$$\frac{du_0}{dx} + \frac{dv_0}{dy} + \frac{dw_0}{dz} = 0$$

throughout the region, and

$$lu_0 + mv_0 + nw_0 = 0$$

over the boundary. Further let us write

$$T_0 = \tfrac{1}{2}\rho \iiint (u_0^2 + v_0^2 + w_0^2)\, dx\,dy\,dz \text{ .... (6)}.$$

We find

$$T_1 = T + T_0 - \rho \iiint \left(u_0 \frac{d\phi}{dx} + v_0 \frac{d\phi}{dy} + w_0 \frac{d\phi}{dz}\right) dx\,dy\,dz.$$

Since the last integral vanishes, by Art. 42 (4), we have

$$T_1 = T + T_0 \text{.......................... (7)},$$

which proves the theorem.

46. We shall require to know, hereafter, the form assumed by the expression (4) for the kinetic energy when the fluid extends to infinity and is at rest there, being limited internally by one or more closed surfaces S. Let us suppose a large closed surface Σ described so as to enclose the whole of S. The energy of the fluid included between S and Σ is

$$-\tfrac{1}{2}\rho \iint \phi \frac{d\phi}{dn} dS - \tfrac{1}{2}\rho \iint \phi \frac{d\phi}{dn} d\Sigma \text{ .... (8)},$$

where the integration in the first term extends over S, that in the second over Σ. Since we have by the equation of continuity

$$\iint \frac{d\phi}{dn} dS + \iint \frac{d\phi}{dn} d\Sigma = 0,$$

(8) may be written

$$-\tfrac{1}{2}\rho \iint (\phi - C) \frac{d\phi}{dn} dS - \tfrac{1}{2}\rho \iint (\phi - C) \frac{d\phi}{dn} d\Sigma \text{ .... (9)},$$

where C may be any constant, but is here supposed to be the constant value to which ϕ was shewn in Art. 39 to tend at an infinite distance from S. Now the whole region occupied by the fluid may be supposed made up of tubes of flow, each of which must pass either from one point of the internal boundary to another, or from that boundary to infinity. Hence the value of the integral

$$\iint \frac{d\phi}{dn}\, d\Sigma,$$

taken over any surface, open or closed, finite or infinite, drawn within the region, must be finite. Hence ultimately, when Σ is taken infinitely large and infinitely distant all round from S, the second term of (9) vanishes, and we have

$$2T = -\rho \iint (\phi - C) \frac{d\phi}{dn}\, dS \qquad\qquad (10),$$

where the integration extends over the internal boundary only.

If the total flux across the internal boundary be zero, we have

$$\iint \frac{d\phi}{dn}\, dS = 0,$$

so that (10) becomes

$$2T = -\rho \iint \phi \frac{d\phi}{dn}\, dS \qquad\qquad (11),$$

simply.

On Multiply-connected Regions.

47. Before discussing the properties of irrotational motion in multiply-connected regions we must examine more in detail the nature and classification of such regions. In the following synopsis of this branch of the geometry of position we recapitulate for the sake of completeness one or two definitions already given.

We consider any connected region of space, enclosed by boundaries. A region is 'connected' when it is possible to pass from any one point of it to any other by an infinity of paths, each of which lies wholly in the region.

Any two such paths, or any two circuits, which can by continuous variation be made to coincide without ever passing out of the region, are said to be 'mutually reconcileable.' Any circuit which can be contracted to a point without passing out of the region is said to be 'reducible.' Two reconcileable paths, combined, form a reducible circuit. If two paths or two circuits be reconcileable, it must be possible to connect them by a continuous surface, which lies wholly within the region, and of which they form the complete boundary; and conversely.

It is further convenient to distinguish between 'simple' and 'multiple' irreducible circuits. A 'multiple' circuit is one which can by continuous variation be made to appear, in whole or in part, as the repetition of another circuit a certain number of times. A 'simple' circuit is one with which this is not possible.

A 'barrier,' or 'diaphragm,' is a surface drawn across the region, and limited by the line or lines in which it meets the boundary. Hence a barrier is necessarily a connected surface, and cannot consist of two or more detached portions.

A 'simply-connected' region is one such that all paths joining any two points of it are reconcileable, or such that all circuits drawn within it are reducible.

A 'doubly-connected' region is one such that two irreconcileable paths, and no more, can be drawn between any two points A, B of it; viz. any other path joining AB is reconcileable with one of these, or with a combination of the two taken each a certain number of times. In other words, the region is such that one (simple) irreducible circuit can be drawn in it, whilst all other circuits are either reconcileable with this (repeated, if necessary), or are reducible. As an example of a doubly-connected region we may take that enclosed by the surface of an anchor-ring, or that external to such a ring and extending to infinity.

Generally, a region such that n irreconcileable paths, and no more, can be drawn between any two points of it, or such that $n-1$ (simple) irreducible and irreconcileable circuits, and no more, can be drawn in it, is said to be 'n-ply-connected.'

The shaded portion of the figure on p. 37 is a triply-connected space of two dimensions.

It may be shewn that the above definition of an n-ply-connected space is self-consistent. In such simple cases as $n=2$, $n=3$, this is sufficiently evident without demonstration.

48. Let us suppose, now, that we have an n-ply-connected region, with $n-1$ simple independent irreducible circuits drawn in it. It is possible to draw a barrier meeting any one of these circuits in one point only, and not meeting any of the $n-2$ remaining circuits. A barrier drawn in this manner does not destroy the continuity of the region, for the interrupted circuit remains as a path leading round from one side to the other. The order of connection of the region is however diminished by unity; for every circuit drawn in the modified region must be reconcileable with one or more of the $n-2$ circuits not met by the barrier.

A second barrier, drawn in the same manner, will reduce the order of connection again by one, and so on; so that by drawing $n-1$ barriers we can reduce the region to a simply-connected one.

A simply-connected region is divided by a barrier into two separate parts; for otherwise it would be possible to pass from a point on one side the barrier to an adjacent point on the other side by a path lying wholly within the region, which path would in the original region form an irreducible circuit.

Hence in an n-ply-connected region it is possible to draw $n-1$ barriers, and no more, without destroying the continuity of the region. This property is sometimes adopted as the definition of an n-ply-connected space.

Irrotational Motion in Multiply-connected Spaces.

49. The circulation is the same in any two reconcileable circuits $ABCA$, $A'B'C'A'$ drawn in a region occupied by fluid moving irrotationally. For the two circuits may be connected by a continuous surface lying wholly within the region; and if we apply the theorem of Art. 33 to this surface, we have, remembering the rule as to the direction of integration round the boundary,

$$I(ABCA) + I(A'C'B'A') = 0,$$

or

$$I(ABCA) = I(A'B'C'A').$$

If a circuit $ABCA$ be reconcileable with two or more circuits $A'B'C'A'$, $A''B''C''A''$, &c., combined, we can connect all these circuits by a continuous surface which lies wholly within the region, and of which they form the complete boundary. Hence

$$I(ABCA) + I(A'C'B'A') + I(A''C''B''A'') + \&c. = 0,$$

or

$$I(ABCA) = I(A'B'C'A') + I(A''B''C''A'') + \&c.;$$

i.e. the circulation in any circuit is equal to the sum of the circulations in the several members of any set of circuits with which it is reconcileable.

Let the order of connection of the region be $n+1$, so that n independent simple irreducible circuits a_1, $a_2, \ldots a_n$ can be drawn in it; and let the circulations in these be κ_1, $\kappa_2, \ldots \kappa_n$, respectively. The sign of any κ will of course depend on the direction of integration round the corresponding circuit; let the direction in which κ is estimated be called the positive direction in the circuit. The value of the circulation in any other circuit can now be found at once. For the given circuit is necessarily reconcileable with some combination of the circuits a_1, $a_2, \ldots a_n$; say with a_1 taken p_1 times, a_2 taken p_2 times and so on, where of course any p is negative when the corresponding circuit is taken in the negative direction. The required circulation then is

$$p_1\kappa_1 + p_2\kappa_2 + \ldots + p_n\kappa_n \quad \ldots\ldots\ldots\ldots\ldots\ldots\ldots\ldots (1).$$

Since any two paths joining two points A, B of the region together form a circuit, it follows that the values of the flow in the two paths differ by a quantity of the form (1), where, of course, in particular cases some or all of the p's may be zero.

50. Let us denote by $-\phi$ the flow to a variable point P from a fixed point A, viz.

$$\phi = -\int_A^P (udx + vdy + wdz) \quad \ldots\ldots\ldots\ldots\ldots\ldots\ldots\ldots (2).$$

So long as the path of integration from A to P is not specified, ϕ is indeterminate to the extent of a quantity of the form (1).

If however n barriers be drawn in the manner explained in Art. 48, so as to reduce the region to a simply-connected one, and if the path of integration in (2) be restricted to lie within the region as thus modified (*i.e.* it is not to cross any of the barriers), then ϕ becomes a single-valued function, as in Art. 36. It is continuous throughout the modified region, but its values at two adjacent points on opposite sides of a barrier differ by $\pm\kappa$. To derive the value of ϕ when the integration is taken along any path in the unmodified region we must *subtract* the quantity (1), where any p denotes the number of times this path crosses the corresponding barrier. A crossing in the positive direction of the circuits interrupted by the barrier is here counted as positive, a crossing in the opposite direction as negative.

By displacing P through an infinitely short space parallel to each of the co-ordinate axes in succession, we find

$$u = -\frac{d\phi}{dx}, \quad v = -\frac{d\phi}{dy}, \quad w = -\frac{d\phi}{dz};$$

so that ϕ satisfies the definition of a velocity-potential (Art. 18). It is now however a many-valued or cyclic function; *i.e.* it is not possible to assign to every point of the original region a unique and definite value of ϕ, such values forming a continuous system. On the contrary, whenever P describes an irreducible circuit, ϕ will not, in general, return to its original value, but will differ from it by a quantity of the form (1). The quantities $\kappa_1, \kappa_2, \ldots \kappa_n$, which specify the amounts by which ϕ *decreases* as P describes the several independent circuits of the region, may be called the 'cyclic constants' of ϕ.

It is an immediate consequence of the 'circulation-theorem' of Art. 34 that under the conditions there presupposed the cyclic constants do not alter with the time. The necessity for these conditions is exemplified in the problem of Art. 30, where the potential of the extraneous forces is itself a cyclic function.

The foregoing theory may be illustrated by the case of Art. 28 (2), where the region (as limited by the exclusion of the origin, where the formula would give an infinite velocity) is doubly-connected; since we can connect any two points A, B of it by two irreconcileable paths passing on opposite sides of the axis of z, *e.g.* ACB, ADB in the figure. The portion of the plane zx for which x is positive may be taken as a barrier, and the region is thus made simply-connected. The circulation in any circuit meeting this barrier once only, *e.g.* in $ACBDA$, is $\int_0^{2\pi} \mu/r \,.\, r d\theta$, or $2\pi\mu$. That in any circuit not meeting the barrier is zero. In the modified region ϕ may be put equal to a single-valued function, viz. $-\mu\theta$, but its value on the positive side of the barrier is zero, that at an adjacent point on the negative side is $-2\pi\mu$.

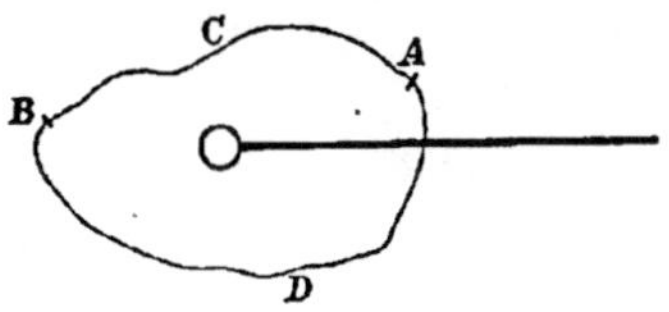

More complex illustrations of irrotational motion in multiply-connected spaces will present themselves in the next chapter.

51. Before proceeding further we may briefly indicate a somewhat different method of presenting the above theory.

Starting from the existence of a velocity-potential as the characteristic of the class of motions which we propose to study, and adopting the second definition of an $n+1$-ply-connected region, indicated in Art. 48, we remark that in a simply-connected region every equipotential surface must either be a closed surface, or else form a barrier dividing the region into two separate parts. Hence, supposing the whole system of such surfaces drawn, we see that if a closed curve cross any given equipotential surface once it must cross it again, and in the opposite direction. Hence, corresponding to any element of the curve, included between two consecutive equipotential surfaces, we have a second element such that the flow along it, being equal to the difference between the corresponding values of ϕ, is equal and opposite to that along the former; so that the circulation in the whole circuit is zero.

If however the region be multiply-connected, an equipotential surface may form a barrier without dividing it into two separate parts. Let as many such surfaces be drawn as it is possible to draw without destroying the continuity of the region. The number of these cannot, by definition, be greater than n. Every other equipotential surface which is not closed will be reconcileable (in an obvious sense) with one or more of these barriers. A curve drawn from one side of a barrier round to the other, without meeting any of the remaining barriers, will cross every equipotential surface reconcileable with the first barrier an odd number of times, and every other equipotential surface an even number of times. Hence the circulation in the circuit thus formed will not vanish, and ϕ will be a cyclic function.

In the method adopted above we have based the whole theory on the equations

$$\frac{dw}{dy}-\frac{dv}{dz}=0,\quad \frac{du}{dz}-\frac{dw}{dx}=0,\quad \frac{dv}{dx}-\frac{du}{dy}=0 \qquad \text{(i)},$$

and have deduced the existence and properties of the velocity-potential in the various cases as necessary consequences of these. In fact, Arts. 35, 36, and 49, 50 may be regarded as a treatise on the integration of this system of differential equations.

The integration of (i), when we have, on the right-hand side, instead of zero, known functions of x, y, z, will be treated in Chapter VII.

52. Proceeding now, as in Art. 37, to the particular case of an incompressible fluid, we remark that whether ϕ be cyclic or not, its first derivatives $d\phi/dx$, $d\phi/dy$, $d\phi/dz$, and therefore all the higher derivatives, are essentially single-valued functions, so that ϕ will still satisfy the equation of continuity

$$\nabla^2\phi = 0 \qquad \text{(1)},$$

or the equivalent form

$$\iint \frac{d\phi}{dn}\, dS = 0 \qquad \text{(2)},$$

where the surface-integration extends over the whole boundary of any portion of the fluid.

The theorem (α) of Art. 40, viz. that ϕ must be constant throughout the interior of any region at every point of which (1) is satisfied, if it be constant over the boundary, still holds when the region is multiply-connected. For ϕ, being constant over the boundary, is necessarily single-valued.

The remaining theorems of Art. 40, being based on the assumption that the stream-lines cannot form closed curves, will require modification. We must introduce the additional condition that the circulation is to be zero in each circuit of the region.

Removing this restriction, we have the theorem that the irrotational motion of a liquid occupying an n-ply-connected region is determinate when the normal velocity at every point of the boundary is prescribed, as well as the values of the circulations in each of the n independent and irreducible circuits which can be drawn in the region. For if ϕ_1, ϕ_2 be the (cyclic) velocity-potentials of two motions satisfying the above conditions, then $\phi = \phi_1 - \phi_2$ is a single-valued function which satisfies (1) at every point of the region, and makes $d\phi/dn = 0$ at every point of the boundary. Hence by Art. 40, ϕ is constant, and the motions determined by ϕ_1 and ϕ_2 are identical.

The theory of multiple connectivity seems to have been first developed by Riemann* for spaces of two dimensions, *à propos* of his researches on the theory of functions of a complex variable, in which connection also cyclic functions, satisfying the equation

$$\frac{d^2\phi}{dx^2} + \frac{d^2\phi}{dy^2} = 0$$

through multiply-connected regions, present themselves.

The bearing of the theory on Hydrodynamics, and the existence in certain cases of many-valued velocity-potentials were first pointed out by von Helmholtz†. The subject of cyclic irrotational motion in multiply-connected regions was afterwards taken up and fully investigated by Lord Kelvin in the paper on vortex-motion already referred to ‡.

* *Grundlagen für eine allgemeine Theorie der Functionen einer veränderlichen complexen Grösse*, Göttingen, 1851; *Mathematische Werke*, Leipzig, 1876, p. 3; "Lehrsätze aus der Analysis Situs," *Crelle*, t. liv. (1857); *Werke*, p. 84.

† *Crelle*, t. lv., 1858.

‡ See also Kirchhoff, "Ueber die Kräfte welche zwei unendlich dünne starre Ringe in einer Flüssigkeit scheinbar auf einander ausüben können," *Crelle*, t. lxxi. (1869); *Ges. Abh.*, p. 404.

Lord Kelvin's Extension of Green's Theorem.

53. It was assumed in the proof of Green's Theorem that ϕ and ϕ' were both single-valued functions. If either be a cyclic function, as may be the case when the region to which the integrations in Art. 43 refer is multiply-connected, the statement of the theorem must be modified. Let us suppose, for instance, that ϕ is cyclic; the surface-integral on the left-hand side of Art. 43 (5), and the second volume-integral on the right-hand side, are then indeterminate, on account of the indeterminateness in the value of ϕ itself. To remove this indeterminateness, let the barriers necessary to reduce the region to a simply-connected one be drawn, as explained in Art. 48. We may now suppose ϕ to be continuous and single-valued throughout the region thus modified; and the equation referred to will then hold, provided the two sides of each barrier be reckoned as part of the boundary of the region, and therefore included in the surface-integral on the left-hand side. Let $\delta\sigma_1$ be an element of one of the barriers, κ_1 the cyclic constant corresponding to that barrier, $d\phi'/dn$ the rate of variation of ϕ' in the positive direction of the normal to $\delta\sigma_1$. Since, in the parts of the surface-integral due to the two sides of $\delta\sigma_1$, $d\phi'/dn$ is to be taken with opposite signs, whilst the value of ϕ on the positive side exceeds that on the negative side by κ_1, we get finally for the element of the integral due to $\delta\sigma_1$, the value $\kappa_1 d\phi'/dn . \delta\sigma_1$. Hence Art. 43 (5) becomes, in the altered circumstances,

$$\iint \phi \frac{d\phi'}{dn} dS + \kappa_1 \iint \frac{d\phi'}{dn} d\sigma_1 + \kappa_2 \iint \frac{d\phi'}{dn} d\sigma_2 + \&c.$$

$$= -\iiint \left(\frac{d\phi}{dx}\frac{d\phi'}{dx} + \frac{d\phi}{dy}\frac{d\phi'}{dy} + \frac{d\phi}{dz}\frac{d\phi'}{dz}\right) dx dy dz$$

$$- \iiint \phi \nabla^2 \phi' \, dx dy dz \quad \ldots\ldots\ldots\ldots (1);$$

where the surface-integrations indicated on the left-hand side extend, the first over the original boundary of the region only, and the rest over the several barriers. The coefficient of any κ is evidently *minus* the total flux across the corresponding barrier, in a motion of which ϕ' is the velocity-potential. The values of ϕ in the first and last terms of the equation are to be assigned in the manner indicated in Art. 50.

If ϕ' also be a cyclic function, having the cyclic constants κ_1', κ_2', &c., then Art. 43 (6) becomes in the same way

$$\iint \phi' \frac{d\phi}{dn} dS + \kappa_1' \iint \frac{d\phi}{dn} d\sigma_1 + \kappa_2' \iint \frac{d\phi}{dn} d\sigma_2 + \ldots$$

$$= -\iiint \left(\frac{d\phi}{dx}\frac{d\phi'}{dx} + \frac{d\phi}{dy}\frac{d\phi'}{dy} + \frac{d\phi}{dz}\frac{d\phi'}{dz} \right) dx\,dy\,dz$$

$$- \iiint \phi' \nabla^2 \phi \, dx\,dy\,dz \quad \ldots\ldots (2).$$

Equations (1) and (2) together constitute Lord Kelvin's extension of Green's theorem.

54. If ϕ, ϕ' are both velocity-potentials of a liquid, we have

$$\nabla^2 \phi = 0, \quad \nabla^2 \phi' = 0 \quad \ldots\ldots (3),$$

and therefore

$$\iint \phi \frac{d\phi'}{dn} dS + \kappa_1 \iint \frac{d\phi'}{dn} d\sigma_1 + \kappa_2 \iint \frac{d\phi'}{dn} d\sigma_2 + \ldots$$

$$= \iint \phi' \frac{d\phi}{dn} dS + \kappa_1' \iint \frac{d\phi}{dn} d\sigma_1 + \kappa_2' \iint \frac{d\phi}{dn} d\sigma_2 + \ldots\ldots (4).$$

To obtain a physical interpretation of this theorem it is necessary to explain in the first place a method, imagined by Lord Kelvin, of generating any given cyclic irrotational motion of a liquid in a multiply-connected space.

Let us suppose the fluid to be enclosed in a perfectly smooth and flexible membrane occupying the position of the boundary. Further, let n barriers be drawn, as in Art. 48, so as to convert the region into a simply-connected one, and let their places be occupied by similar membranes, infinitely thin, and destitute of inertia. The fluid being initially at rest, let each element of the first-mentioned membrane be suddenly moved inwards with the given (positive or negative) normal velocity $-d\phi/dn$, whilst uniform impulsive pressures $\kappa_1\rho$, $\kappa_2\rho, \ldots \kappa_n\rho$ are simultaneously applied to the negative sides of the respective barrier-membranes. The motion generated will be characterized by the following properties. It will be irrotational, being generated from rest; the normal velocity at every point of the original boundary will have the prescribed value; the values of the impulsive pressure at two adjacent points on opposite sides of a membrane will differ by the corresponding value of $\kappa\rho$, and the values of the velocity-potential will therefore differ by the corresponding value of κ; finally, the motion on one side of a barrier will be continuous with that on the other. To prove the last statement we remark, first, that the velocities normal to the barrier at two adjacent points on opposite sides of it are the same, being each equal to the normal velocity of the adjacent portion of the membrane. Again, if P, Q be two consecutive points on a barrier, and if the corresponding values of ϕ be on the positive side ϕ_P, ϕ_Q, and on the negative side ϕ'_P, ϕ'_Q, we have

$$\phi_P - \phi'_P = \kappa = \phi_Q - \phi'_Q,$$

and therefore $$\phi_Q - \phi_P = \phi'_Q - \phi'_P,$$

i.e., if $PQ = \delta s$, $$d\phi/ds = d\phi'/ds.$$

Hence the tangential velocities at two adjacent points on opposite sides of the barrier also agree. If then we suppose the barrier-membranes to be liquefied immediately after the impulse, we obtain the irrotational motion in question.

The physical interpretation of (4), when multiplied by $-\rho$, now follows as in Art. 44. The values of $\rho\kappa$ are additional components of momentum, and those of $-\iint d\phi/dn\,.\,d\sigma$, the fluxes through the various apertures of the region, are the corresponding generalized velocities.

55. If in (2) we put $\phi' = \phi$, and suppose ϕ to be the velocity-potential of an incompressible fluid, we find

$$2T = \rho \iiint \left\{ \left(\frac{d\phi}{dx}\right)^2 + \left(\frac{d\phi}{dy}\right)^2 + \left(\frac{d\phi}{dz}\right)^2 \right\} dx\,dy\,dz$$

$$= -\rho \iint \phi \frac{d\phi}{dn} dS - \rho\kappa_1 \iint \frac{d\phi}{dn} d\sigma_1 - \rho\kappa_2 \iint \frac{d\phi}{dn} d\sigma_2 + \dots\dots\dots \quad (5).$$

The last member of this formula has a simple interpretation in terms of the artificial method of generating cyclic irrotational motion just explained. The first term has already been recognized as equal to twice the work done by the impulsive pressure $\rho\phi$ applied to every part of the original boundary of the fluid. Again, $\rho\kappa_1$ is the impulsive pressure applied, in the positive direction, to the infinitely thin massless membrane by which the place of the first barrier was supposed to be occupied; so that the expression

$$-\tfrac{1}{2} \iint \rho\kappa_1 \,.\, \frac{d\phi}{dn} d\sigma_1$$

denotes the work done by the impulsive forces applied to that membrane; and so on. Hence (5) expresses the fact that the energy of the motion is equal to the work done by the whole system of impulsive forces by which we may suppose it generated.

In applying (5) to the case where the fluid extends to infinity and is at rest there, we may replace the first term of the third member by

$$-\rho \iint (\phi - C) \frac{d\phi}{dn} dS \qquad (6),$$

where the integration extends over the internal boundary only. The proof is the same as in Art. 46. When the total flux across this boundary is zero, this reduces to

$$-\rho \iint \phi \frac{d\phi}{dn} dS \qquad (7).$$

The minimum theorem of Lord Kelvin, given in Art. 45, may now be extended as follows:

The irrotational motion of a liquid in a multiply-connected region has less kinetic energy than any other motion consistent with the same normal motion of the boundary and the same value of the total flux through each of the several independent channels of the region.

The proof is left to the reader.

Sources and Sinks.

56. The analogy with the theories of Electrostatics, the Steady Flow of Heat, &c., may be carried further by means of the conception of sources and sinks.

A 'simple source' is a point from which fluid is imagined to flow out uniformly in all directions. If the total flux outwards across a small closed surface surrounding the point be $4\pi m$*, then m is called the 'strength' of the source. A negative source is called a 'sink.' The continued existence of a source or a sink would postulate of course a continual creation or annihilation of fluid at the point in question.

* The factor 4π is introduced to keep up the analogy referred to.

The velocity-potential at any point P, due to a simple source, in a liquid at rest at infinity, is

$$\phi = m/r \qquad (1),$$

where r denotes the distance of P from the source. For this gives a radial flow from the point, and if δS, $= r^2\delta\varpi$, be an element of a spherical surface having its centre at the surface, we have

$$-\iint \frac{d\phi}{dr}\, dS = 4\pi m,$$

a constant, so that the equation of continuity is satisfied, and the flux outwards has the value appropriate to the strength of the source.

A combination of two equal and opposite sources $\pm m'$, at a distance δs apart, where, in the limit, δs is taken to be infinitely small, and m' infinitely great, but so that the product $m'\delta s$ is finite and equal to μ (say), is called a 'double source' of strength μ, and the line δs, considered as drawn in the direction from $-m'$ to $+m'$, is called its axis.

To find the velocity-potential at any point (x, y, z) due to a double source μ situate at (x', y', z'), and having its axis in the direction (l, m, n), we remark that, f being any continuous function,

$$f(x' + l\delta s,\ y' + m\delta s,\ z' + n\delta s) - f(x', y', z')$$

$$= \left(l\frac{d}{dx'} + m\frac{d}{dy'} + n\frac{d}{dz'}\right) f(x', y', z') \,.\, \delta s,$$

ultimately. Hence, putting $f(x', y', z') = m'/r$, where

$$r = \{(x - x')^2 + (y - y')^2 + (z - z')^2\}^{\frac{1}{2}},$$

we find

$$\phi = \mu\left(l\frac{d}{dx'} + m\frac{d}{dy'} + n\frac{d}{dz'}\right)\frac{1}{r} \qquad (2),$$

$$= -\mu\left(l\frac{d}{dx} + m\frac{d}{dy} + n\frac{d}{dz}\right)\frac{1}{r} \qquad (3),$$

$$= \mu\frac{\cos\vartheta}{r^2} \qquad (4),$$

where, in the latter form, ϑ denotes the angle which the line r, considered as drawn from (x', y', z') to (x, y, z), makes with the axis (l, m, n).

We might proceed, in a similar manner (see Art. 83), to build up sources of higher degrees of complexity, but the above is sufficient for our immediate purpose.

Finally, we may imagine simple or double sources, instead of existing at isolated points, to be distributed continuously over lines, surfaces, or volumes.

57. We can now prove that any continuous acyclic irrotational motion of a liquid mass may be regarded as due to a certain distribution of simple and double sources over the boundary.

This depends on the theorem, proved in Art. 44, that if ϕ, ϕ' be any two functions which satisfy $\nabla^2\phi=0$, $\nabla^2\phi'=0$, and are finite, continuous, and single-valued throughout any region, then

$$\iint \phi \frac{d\phi'}{dn} dS = \iint \phi' \frac{d\phi}{dn} dS \qquad (5),$$

where the integration extends over the whole boundary. In the present application, we take ϕ to be the velocity-potential of the motion in question, and put $\phi' = 1/r$, the reciprocal of the distance of any point of the fluid from a fixed point P.

We will first suppose that P is in the space occupied by the fluid. Since ϕ' then becomes infinite at P, it is necessary to exclude this point from the region to which the formula (5) applies; this may be done by describing a small spherical surface about P as centre. If we now suppose $\delta\Sigma$ to refer to this surface, and δS to the original boundary, the formula gives

$$\iint \phi \frac{d}{dn}\left(\frac{1}{r}\right) d\Sigma + \iint \phi \frac{d}{dn}\left(\frac{1}{r}\right) dS$$
$$= \iint \frac{1}{r}\frac{d\phi}{dn} d\Sigma + \iint \frac{1}{r}\frac{d\phi}{dn} dS \qquad (6).$$

At the surface Σ we have $d/dn\,(1/r) = -1/r^2$; hence if we put $\delta\Sigma = r^2 d\varpi$, and finally make $r=0$, the first integral on the left-hand becomes $= -4\pi\phi_P$, where ϕ_P denotes the value of ϕ at P, whilst the first integral on the right vanishes. Hence

$$\phi_P = -\frac{1}{4\pi}\iint \frac{1}{r}\frac{d\phi}{dn} dS + \frac{1}{4\pi}\iint \phi \frac{d}{dn}\left(\frac{1}{r}\right) dS \qquad (7).$$

This gives the value of ϕ at any point P of the fluid in terms of the values of ϕ and $d\phi/dn$ at the boundary. Comparing with the formulæ (1) and (2) we see that the first term is the velocity-potential due to a surface distribution of simple sources, with a density $-1/4\pi \cdot d\phi/dn$ per unit area, whilst the second term is the velocity-potential of a distribution of double sources, with axes normal to the surface, the density being $1/4\pi \cdot \phi$.

When the fluid extends to infinity and is at rest there, the surface-integrals in (7) may, on a certain understanding, be taken to refer to the internal boundary alone. To see this, we may take as external boundary an infinite sphere having the point P as centre. The corresponding part of the first integral in (7) vanishes, whilst that of the second is equal to C, the constant value to which, as we have seen in Art. 41, ϕ tends at infinity. It is convenient, for facility of statement, to suppose $C=0$; this is legitimate since we may always add an arbitrary constant to ϕ.

When the point P is external to the fluid, ϕ' is finite throughout the original region, and the formula (5) gives at once

$$0 = -\frac{1}{4\pi}\iint \frac{1}{r}\frac{d\phi}{dn}\,dS + \frac{1}{4\pi}\iint \phi \frac{d}{dn}\left(\frac{1}{r}\right) dS \quad \text{.........} \quad (8),$$

where, again, in the case of a liquid extending to infinity, and at rest there, the terms due to the infinite part of the boundary may be omitted.

58. The distribution expressed by (7) can, further, be replaced by one of simple sources only, or of double sources only, over the boundary.

Let ϕ be the velocity-potential of the fluid occupying a certain region, and let ϕ' now denote the velocity-potential of any possible acyclic irrotational motion through the rest of infinite space, with the condition that ϕ, or ϕ', as the case may be, vanishes at infinity. Then, if the point P be internal to the first region, and therefore external to the second, we have

$$\left.\begin{aligned} \phi_P &= -\frac{1}{4\pi}\iint \frac{1}{r}\frac{d\phi}{dn}\,dS + \frac{1}{4\pi}\iint \phi\,\frac{d}{dn}\left(\frac{1}{r}\right) dS, \\ 0 &= -\frac{1}{4\pi}\iint \frac{1}{r}\frac{d\phi'}{dn'}\,dS + \frac{1}{4\pi}\iint \phi'\,\frac{d}{dn'}\left(\frac{1}{r}\right) dS, \end{aligned}\right\} \quad \text{......}(9),$$

where δn, $\delta n'$ denote elements of the normal to dS, drawn inwards to the first and second regions respectively, so that $d/dn' = - d/dn$. By addition, we have

$$\phi_P = -\frac{1}{4\pi}\iint \frac{1}{r}\left(\frac{d\phi}{dn} + \frac{d\phi'}{dn'}\right) dS + \frac{1}{4\pi}\iint (\phi - \phi') \frac{d}{dn}\left(\frac{1}{r}\right) dS \ldots (10).$$

The function ϕ' will be determined by the surface-values of ϕ' or $d\phi'/dn'$, which are as yet at our disposal.

Let us in the first place make $\phi' = \phi$. The tangential velocities on the two sides of the boundary are then continuous, but the normal velocities are discontinuous. To assist the ideas, we may imagine a fluid to fill infinite space, and to be divided into two portions by an infinitely thin vacuous sheet within which an impulsive pressure $\rho\phi$ is applied, so as to generate the given motion from rest. The last term of (10) disappears, so that

$$\phi_P = -\frac{1}{4\pi}\iint \frac{1}{r}\left(\frac{d\phi}{dn} + \frac{d\phi'}{dn'}\right) dS \ldots\ldots\ldots\ldots\ldots (11),$$

that is, the motion (on either side) is that due to a surface-distribution of simple sources, of density

$$-\frac{1}{4\pi}\left(\frac{d\phi}{dn} + \frac{d\phi'}{dn'}\right)^*.$$

Secondly, we may suppose that $d\phi'/dn = d\phi/dn$. This gives continuous normal velocity, but discontinuous tangential velocity, over the original boundary. The motion may in this case be imagined to be generated by giving the prescribed normal velocity $- d\phi/dn$ to every point of an infinitely thin membrane coincident in position with the boundary. The first term of (10) now vanishes, and we have

$$\phi_P = \frac{1}{4\pi}\iint (\phi - \phi') \frac{d}{dn}\left(\frac{1}{r}\right) dS \ldots\ldots\ldots\ldots\ldots (12),$$

shewing that the motion on either side may be conceived as due to a surface-distribution of double sources, with density

$$\frac{1}{4\pi}(\phi - \phi').$$

It is obvious that *cyclic* irrotational motion of a liquid cannot be reproduced by any arrangement of simple sources. It is easily seen, however, that it may be represented by a certain distribution of double sources over

* This investigation was first given by Green, from the point of view of Electrostatics; *l.c. ante* p. 50.

the boundary, together with a uniform distribution of double sources over each of the barriers necessary to render the region occupied by the fluid simply-connected. In fact, with the same notation as in Art. 53, we find

$$\phi_P = \frac{1}{4\pi}\iint(\phi - \phi')\frac{d}{dn}\left(\frac{1}{r}\right)dS + \frac{\kappa_1}{4\pi}\iint\frac{d}{dn}\left(\frac{1}{r}\right)d\sigma_1 + \frac{\kappa_2}{4\pi}\iint\frac{d}{dn}\left(\frac{1}{r}\right)d\sigma_2 + \dots \qquad \text{(i)},$$

where ϕ is the single-valued velocity-potential which obtains in the modified region, and ϕ' is the velocity-potential of the acyclic motion which is generated in the external space when the proper normal velocity $-d\phi/dn$ is given to each element δS of a membrane coincident in position with the original boundary.

Another mode of representing the irrotational motion of a liquid, whether cyclic or not, will present itself in the chapter on Vortex Motion.

CHAPTER IV.

MOTION OF A LIQUID IN TWO DIMENSIONS.

59. If the velocities u, v be functions of x, y only, whilst w is zero, the motion takes place in a series of planes parallel to xy, and is the same in each of these planes. The investigation of the motion of a liquid under these circumstances is characterized by certain analytical peculiarities; and the solutions of several problems of great interest are readily obtained.

Since the whole motion is known when we know that in the plane $z=0$, we may confine our attention to that plane. When we speak of points and lines drawn in it, we shall understand them to represent respectively the straight lines parallel to the axis of z, and the cylindrical surfaces having their generating lines parallel to the axis of z, of which they are the traces.

By the flux across any curve we shall understand the volume of fluid which in unit time crosses that portion of the cylindrical surface, having the curve as base, which is included between the planes $z=0$, $z=1$.

Let A, P be any two points in the plane xy. The flux across any two lines joining AP is the same, provided they can be reconciled without passing out of the region occupied by the moving liquid; for otherwise the space included between these two lines would be gaining or losing matter. Hence if A be fixed, and P variable, the flux across any line AP is a function of the position of P. Let ψ be this function; more precisely, let ψ denote the flux across AP *from right to left*, as regards an observer placed on the curve, and looking along it from A in the direction of P. Analytically, if l, m be the direction-cosines of the normal (drawn to the left) to any element δs of the curve, we have

$$\psi = \int_A^P (lu + mv)\, ds \quad \text{.....................} \quad (1).$$

If the region occupied by the liquid be aperiphractic (see p. 43), ψ is necessarily a single-valued function, but in periphractic regions the value of ψ may depend on the nature of the path AP. For spaces of two dimensions, however, periphraxy and multiple-connectivity become the same thing, so that the properties of ψ, when it is a many-valued function, in relation to the nature of the region occupied by the moving liquid, may be inferred from Art. 50, where we have discussed the same question with regard to ϕ. The cyclic constants of ψ, when the region is periphractic, are the values of the flux across the closed curves forming the several parts of the internal boundary.

A change, say from A to B, of the point from which ψ is reckoned has merely the effect of adding a constant, viz. the flux across a line BA, to the value of ψ; so that we may, if we please, regard ψ as indeterminate to the extent of an additive constant.

If P move about in such a manner that the value of ψ does not alter, it will trace out a curve such that no fluid anywhere crosses it, *i.e.* a stream-line. Hence the curves ψ = const. are the stream-lines, and ψ is called the 'stream-function.'

If P receive an infinitesimal displacement $PQ\ (= \delta y)$ parallel to y, the increment of ψ is the flux across PQ from right to left, *i.e.* $\delta\psi = -u \,.\, PQ$, or

$$u = -\frac{d\psi}{dy} \quad \text{..........................} \quad (2).$$

Again, displacing P parallel to x, we find in the same way

$$v = \frac{d\psi}{dx} \quad \text{..........................} \quad (3).$$

The existence of a function ψ related to u and v in this manner might also have been inferred from the form which the equation of continuity takes in this case, viz.

$$\frac{du}{dx} + \frac{dv}{dy} = 0 \quad \text{.......................} \quad (4),$$

which is the analytical condition that $udy - vdx$ should be an exact differential*.

The foregoing considerations apply whether the motion be rotational or irrotational. The formulæ for the component angular velocities, given in Art. 31, become

$$\xi = 0, \quad \eta = 0, \quad \zeta = \tfrac{1}{2}\left(\frac{d^2\psi}{dx^2} + \frac{d^2\psi}{dy^2}\right) \text{ .... } (5);$$

so that in irrotational motion we have

$$\frac{d^2\psi}{dx^2} + \frac{d^2\psi}{dy^2} = 0 \text{ .... } (6).$$

60. In what follows we confine ourselves to the case of irrotational motion, which is, as we have already seen, characterized by the existence, in addition, of a velocity-potential ϕ, connected with u, v by the relations

$$u = -\frac{d\phi}{dx}, \quad v = -\frac{d\phi}{dy} \text{ .... } (1),$$

and, since we are considering the motion of incompressible fluids only, satisfying the equation of continuity

$$\frac{d^2\phi}{dx^2} + \frac{d^2\phi}{dy^2} = 0 \text{ .... } (2).$$

The theory of the function ϕ, and the relation between its properties and the nature of the two-dimensional space through which the irrotational motion holds, may be readily inferred from the corresponding theorems in three dimensions proved in the last chapter. The alterations, whether of enunciation or of proof, which are requisite to adapt these to the case of two dimensions are for the most part purely verbal.

An exception, which we will briefly examine, occurs however in the case of the theorem of Art. 39 and of those which depend on it.

If δs be an element of the boundary of any portion of the plane xy which is occupied wholly by moving liquid, and if δn be an element of the normal to δs drawn inwards, we have, by Art. 37,

$$\int \frac{d\phi}{dn} ds = 0 \text{ .... } (\text{i}),$$

* The function ψ was first introduced in this way by Lagrange, *Nouv. mém. de l'Acad. de Berlin*, 1781; *Oeuvres*, t. iv., p. 720. The kinematical interpretation is due to Rankine.

the integration extending round the whole boundary. If this boundary be a circle, and if r, θ be polar co-ordinates referred to the centre P of this circle as origin, the last equation may be written

$$\int_0^{2\pi} \frac{d\phi}{dr} \cdot r d\theta = 0, \text{ or } \frac{d}{dr}\int_0^{2\pi} \phi d\theta = 0.$$

Hence the integral
$$\frac{1}{2\pi}\int_0^{2\pi} \phi d\theta,$$

i.e. the mean-value of ϕ over a circle of centre P, and radius r, is independent of the value of r, and therefore remains unaltered when r is diminished without limit, in which case it becomes the value of ϕ at P.

If the region occupied by the fluid be periphractic, and if we apply (i) to the space enclosed between one of the internal boundaries and a circle with centre P and radius r surrounding this boundary, and lying wholly in the fluid, we have

$$\int_0^{2\pi} \frac{d\phi}{dr} \cdot r d\theta = -2\pi M \text{..............................(ii)};$$

where the integration in the first member extends over the circle only, and $2\pi M$ denotes the flux into the region across the internal boundary. Hence

$$\frac{d}{dr} \cdot \frac{1}{2\pi}\int_0^{2\pi} \phi d\theta = -\frac{M}{r},$$

which gives on integration

$$\frac{1}{2\pi}\int_0^{2\pi} \phi d\theta = -M \log r + C \text{ .... (iii)};$$

i.e. the mean value of ϕ over a circle with centre P and radius r is equal to $-M \log r + C$, where C is independent of r but may vary with the position of P. This formula holds of course only so far as the circle embraces the same internal boundary, and lies itself wholly in the fluid.

If the region be unlimited externally, and if the circle embrace the whole of the internal boundaries, and if further the velocity be everywhere zero at infinity, then C is an absolute constant; as is seen by reasoning similar to that of Art. 41. It may then be shewn that the value of ϕ at a very great distance r from the internal boundary tends to the value $-M \log r + C$. In the particular case of $M=0$ the limit to which ϕ tends at infinity is finite; in all other cases it is infinite, and of the opposite sign to M. We infer, as before, that there is only one single-valued function ϕ which 1° satisfies the equation (2) at every point of the plane xy external to a given system of closed curves, 2° makes the value of $d\phi/dn$ equal to an arbitrarily given quantity at every point of these curves, and 3° has its first differential coefficients all zero at infinity.

If we imagine point-sources, of the type explained in Art. 56, to be distributed uniformly along the axis of z, it is readily found that the velocity at a distance r from this axis will be in the direction of r, and equal to m/r, where m is a certain constant. This arrangement constitutes what may be called a 'line-source,' and its velocity-potential may be taken to be

$$\phi = -m \log r \text{................................(iv)}.$$

The reader who is interested in the matter will have no difficulty in working out a theory of two-dimensional sources and sinks, similar to that of Arts. 56—58 *.

61. The kinetic energy T of a portion of fluid bounded by a cylindrical surface whose generating lines are parallel to the axis of z, and by two planes perpendicular to the axis of z at unit distance apart, is given by the formula

$$2T = \rho \iint \left\{ \left(\frac{d\phi}{dx}\right)^2 + \left(\frac{d\phi}{dy}\right)^2 \right\} dx\, dy = -\rho \int \phi \frac{d\phi}{dn} ds \quad \text{......(1)},$$

where the surface-integral is taken over the portion of the plane xy cut off by the cylindrical surface, and the line-integral round the boundary of this portion. Since

$$d\phi/dn = -d\psi/ds,$$

the formula (1) may be written

$$2T = \rho \int \phi\, d\psi \quad \text{........................ (2)},$$

the integration being carried in the positive direction round the boundary.

If we attempt by a process similar to that of Art. 46 to calculate the energy in the case where the region extends to infinity, we find that its value is infinite, except when the total flux outwards ($2\pi M$) is zero. For if we introduce a circle of great radius r as the external boundary of the portion of the plane xy considered, we find that the corresponding part of the integral on the right-hand side of (1) tends, as r increases, to the value $\pi\rho M (M \log r - C)$, and is therefore ultimately infinite. The only exception is when $M = 0$, in which case we may suppose the line-integral in (1) to extend over the internal boundary only.

If the cylindrical part of the boundary consist of two or more separate portions one of which embraces all the rest, the enclosed region is multiply-connected, and the equation (1) needs a correction, which may be applied exactly as in Art. 55.

62. The functions ϕ and ψ are connected by the relations

$$\frac{d\phi}{dx} = \frac{d\psi}{dy}, \quad \frac{d\phi}{dy} = -\frac{d\psi}{dx} \quad \text{.................. (1)}.$$

These are the conditions that $\phi + i\psi$, where i stands for $\sqrt{-1}$, should be a function of the 'complex' variable $x + iy$. For if

* This subject has been treated very fully by C. Neumann, *Ueber das logarithmische und Newton'sche Potential*, Leipzig, 1877.

$$\phi + i\psi = f(x + iy) \text{ .... } (2),$$

we have
$$\frac{d}{dy}(\phi + i\psi) = if'(x + iy) = i\frac{d}{dx}(\phi + i\psi) \text{ ...... } (3),$$

whence, equating separately the real and the imaginary parts, we obtain (1).

Hence any assumption of the form (2) gives a possible case of irrotational motion. The curves ϕ = const. are the curves of equal velocity-potential, and the curves ψ = const. are the stream-lines. Since, by (1),

$$\frac{d\phi}{dx}\frac{d\psi}{dx} + \frac{d\phi}{dy}\frac{d\psi}{dy} = 0,$$

we see that these two systems of curves cut one another at right angles, as already proved. Since the relations (1) are unaltered when we write $-\psi$ for ϕ, and ϕ for ψ, we may, if we choose, look upon the curves ψ = const. as the equipotential curves, and the curves ϕ = const. as the stream-lines; so that every assumption of the kind indicated gives us *two* possible cases of irrotational motion.

For shortness, we shall through the rest of this Chapter follow the usual notation of the Theory of Functions, and write

$$z = x + iy \text{ .... } (4),$$
$$w = \phi + i\psi \text{ .... } (5).$$

At the present date the reader may be assumed to be in possession of at all events the elements of the theory referred to*. We may, however, briefly recall a few fundamental points which are of special importance in the hydrodynamical applications of the subject.

The complex variable $x+iy$ may be represented, after Argand and Gauss, by a vector drawn from the origin to the point (x, y). The result of adding two complex expressions is represented by the geometric sum of the corresponding vectors. Regarded as a multiplying *operator*, a complex expression $a+ib$ has the effect of increasing the length of a vector in the ratio $r : 1$, and of simultaneously turning it through an angle θ, where $r = (a^2+b^2)^{\frac{1}{2}}$, and $\theta = \tan^{-1} b/a$.

The fundamental property of a *function* of a complex variable is that it has a definite differential coefficient with respect to that variable. If ϕ, ψ denote any functions whatever of x and y, then corresponding to every value of $x+iy$ there must be one or more definite values of $\phi+i\psi$; but the ratio of the differential of this function to that of $x+iy$, viz.

$$\frac{\delta\phi + i\delta\psi}{\delta x + i\delta y}, \quad \text{or} \quad \frac{\left(\frac{d\phi}{dx} + i\frac{d\psi}{dx}\right)\delta x + \left(\frac{d\phi}{dy} + i\frac{d\psi}{dy}\right)\delta y}{\delta x + i\delta y},$$

* See, for example, Forsyth, *Theory of Functions*, Cambridge, 1893, cc. i., ii.

depends in general on the ratio $\delta x : \delta y$. The condition that it should be the same for all values of this ratio is

$$\frac{d\phi}{dy}+i\frac{d\psi}{dy}=i\left(\frac{d\phi}{dx}+i\frac{d\psi}{dx}\right) \qquad \text{(i)},$$

which is equivalent to (1) above. This property may therefore be taken, after Riemann, as the definition of a function of the complex variable $x+iy$; viz. such a function must have, for every assigned value of the variable, not only a definite value or system of values, but also for each of these values a definite differential coefficient. The advantage of this definition is that it is quite independent of the existence of an analytical expression for the function.

Now, w being any function of z, we have, corresponding to any point P of the plane xy (which we may call the plane of the variable z), one or more definite values of w. Let us choose any one of these, and denote it by a point P' of which ϕ, ψ are the rectangular co-ordinates in a second plane (the plane of the function w). If P trace out any curve in the plane of z, P' will trace out a corresponding curve in the plane of w. By mapping out the correspondence between the positions of P and P', we may exhibit graphically all the properties of the function w.

Let now Q be a point infinitely near to P, and let Q' be the corresponding point infinitely near to P'. We may denote PQ by δz, $P'Q'$ by δw. The vector $P'Q'$ may be obtained from the vector PQ by multiplying it by the differential coefficient dw/dz, whose value is by definition dependent only on the position of P, and not on the direction of the element δz or PQ. The effect of this operator dw/dz is to increase the length of PQ in some definite ratio, and to turn it through some definite angle. Hence, in the transition from the plane of z to that of w, all the infinitesimal vectors drawn from the point P have their lengths altered in the same ratio, and are turned through the same angle. Any angle in the plane of z is therefore equal to the corresponding angle in the plane of w, and any infinitely small figure in the one plane is similar to the corresponding figure in the other. In other words, corresponding figures in the planes of z and w are similar in their infinitely small parts.

For instance, in the plane of w the straight lines $\phi=\text{const.}$, $\psi=\text{const.}$, where the constants have assigned to them a series of values in arithmetical progression, the common difference being infinitesimal and the same in each case, form two systems of straight lines at right angles, dividing the plane into infinitely small squares. Hence in the plane xy the corresponding curves $\phi=\text{const.}$, $\psi=\text{const.}$, the values of the constants being assigned as before, cut one another at right angles (as has already been proved otherwise) and divide the plane into a series of infinitely small squares.

Conversely, if ϕ, ψ be any two functions of x, y such that the curves $\phi=m\epsilon$, $\psi=n\epsilon$, where ϵ is infinitesimal, and m, n are any integers, divide the plane xy into elementary squares, it is evident geometrically that

$$\frac{dx}{d\phi}=\pm\frac{dy}{d\psi}, \qquad \frac{dx}{d\psi}=\mp\frac{dy}{d\phi}.$$

If we take the upper signs, these are the conditions that $x+iy$ should be a function of $\phi + i\psi$. The case of the lower signs is reduced to this by reversing the sign of ψ. Hence the equation (2) contains the *complete* solution of the problem of orthomorphic projection from one plane to another*.

The similarity of corresponding infinitely small portions of the planes w and z breaks down at points where the differential coefficient dw/dz is zero or infinite. Since

$$\frac{dw}{dz} = \frac{d\phi}{dx} + i\frac{d\psi}{dx} \qquad \text{(ii)},$$

the corresponding value of the velocity, in the hydrodynamical application, is zero or infinite.

A 'uniform' or 'single-valued' function is one which returns to its original value whenever the representative point completes a closed circuit in the plane xy. All other functions are said to be 'multiform,' or 'many-valued.' A simple case of a multiform function is that of $z^{\frac{1}{2}}$. If we put

$$z = x + iy = r(\cos\theta + i\sin\theta),$$

we have

$$z^{\frac{1}{2}} = r^{\frac{1}{2}}(\cos\tfrac{1}{2}\theta + i\sin\tfrac{1}{2}\theta).$$

Hence when P describes a closed circuit surrounding the origin, θ increases by 2π, and the function $z^{\frac{1}{2}}$ does not return to its former value, the sign being reversed. A repetition of the circuit restores the original value.

A point (such as the origin in this example), at which two or more values of the function coincide, is called a 'branch-point.' In the hydrodynamical application 'branch-points' cannot occur in the interior of the space occupied by the fluid. They may however occur on the boundary, since the function will then be uniform throughout the region considered.

Many-valued functions of another kind, which may conveniently be distinguished as 'cyclic,' present themselves, in the Theory of Functions, as integrals with a variable upper limit. It is easily shewn that the value of the integral

$$\int f(z)\,dz \qquad \text{(iii)},$$

taken round the boundary of any portion of the plane xy throughout which $f(z)$, and its derivative $f'(z)$, are finite, is zero. This follows from the two-dimensional form of Stokes's Theorem, proved in Art. 33, viz.

$$\int (Pdx + Qdy) = \iint \left(\frac{dQ}{dx} - \frac{dP}{dy}\right) dx\,dy,$$

the restrictions as to the values of P, Q being as there stated. If we put $P = f(z)$, $Q = if(z)$, the result follows, since

$$\frac{d}{dy} f(z) = i\frac{d}{dx} f(z) \qquad \text{(iv)}.$$

Hence the value of the integral (iii), taken from a fixed point A to a variable point P, is the same for all paths which can be reconciled with one another without crossing points for which the above conditions are violated.

* Lagrange, "Sur la construction des cartes géographiques," *Nouv. mém. de l'Acad. de Berlin*, 1779; *Oeuvres*, t. iv., p. 636.

Points of the plane xy at which the conditions in question break down may be isolated by drawing a small closed curve round each. The rest of the plane is a multiply-connected region, and the value of the integral from A to P becomes a cyclic function of the position of P, as in Art. 50.

In the hydrodynamical applications, the integral (iii), considered as a function of the upper limit, is taken to be equal to $\phi+i\psi$. If we denote any cyclic constant of this function by $\kappa+i\mu$, then κ denotes the circulation in the corresponding circuit, and μ the flux across it outwards.

As a simple example we may take the *logarithmic* function, considered as defined by the equation

$$\log z=\int\frac{dz}{z} \quad\text{.................................. (v).}$$

Since z^{-1} is infinite at the origin, this point must be isolated, *e.g.* by drawing a small circle about it as centre. If we put

$$z=r(\cos\theta+i\sin\theta),$$

we have

$$\frac{dz}{z}=\frac{dr}{r}+id\theta,$$

so that the value of (v) taken round the circle is

$$\int id\theta=2\pi i.$$

Hence, in the simply-connected region external to the circle, the function (v) is many-valued, the cyclic constant being $-2\pi i$.

In the theory referred to, the *exponential* function is defined as the inverse function of (v), viz. if $w=\log z$, we have $e^w=z$. It follows that e^w is periodic, the period being $2\pi i$. The correspondence between the planes of z and w is illustrated by the annexed diagram. The circle of radius unity, described about the origin as centre, in the upper figure, corresponds over and over

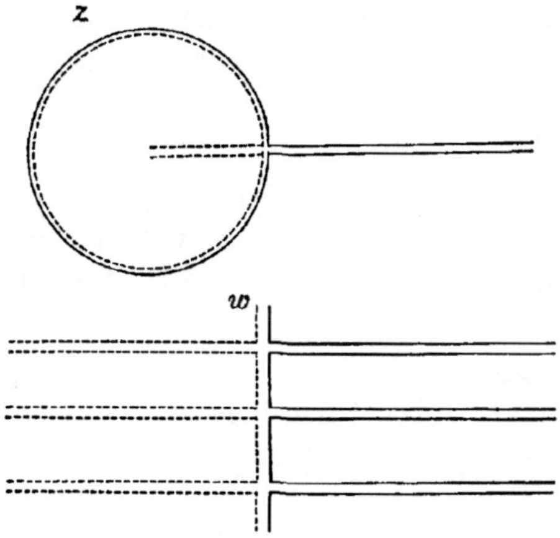

again to lengths 2π on the imaginary axis of w, whilst the inner and outer portions of the radial line $\theta=0$ correspond to a system of lines parallel to the real axis of w, drawn on the negative and positive sides, respectively*. The reader should examine these statements, as we shall have repeated occasion to use this transformation.

63. We can now proceed to some applications of the foregoing theory.

First let us assume $$w = Az^n,$$

A being real. Introducing polar co-ordinates r, θ, we have

$$\left.\begin{aligned}\phi &= Ar^n \cos n\theta,\\ \psi &= Ar^n \sin n\theta\end{aligned}\right\}\quad\text{.........................(1).}$$

The following cases may be noticed.

1°. If $n=1$, the stream-lines are a system of straight lines parallel to x, and the equipotential curves are a similar system parallel to y. In this case *any* corresponding figures in the planes of w and z are similar, whether they be finite or infinitesimal.

2°. If $n=2$, the curves $\phi=\text{const.}$ are a system of rectangular hyperbolas having the axes of co-ordinates as their principal axes, and the curves $\psi=\text{const.}$ are a similar system, having the co-ordinate axes as asymptotes. The lines $\theta=0$, $\theta=\frac{1}{2}\pi$ are parts of the same stream-line $\psi=0$, so that we may take the positive parts of the axes of x, y as fixed boundaries, and thus obtain the case of a fluid in motion in the angle between two perpendicular walls.

3°. If $n=-1$, we get two systems of circles touching the axes of co-ordinates at the origin. Since now $\phi = A/r \,.\, \cos\theta$, the velocity at the origin is infinite; we must therefore suppose the region to which our formulæ apply to be limited internally by a closed curve.

4°. If $n=-2$, each system of curves is composed of a double system of lemniscates. The axes of the system $\phi=\text{const.}$ coincide with x or y; those of the system $\psi=\text{const.}$ bisect the angles between these axes.

5°. By properly choosing the value of n we get a case of irrotational motion in which the boundary is composed of two rigid walls inclined at any angle α. The equation of the stream-lines being

$$r^n \sin n\theta = \text{const.}\quad\text{.........................(2),}$$

* It should be remarked that no attempt has been made to observe the same *scale* in corresponding figures, in this or in other examples, to be given later.

we see that the lines $\theta = 0$, $\theta = \pi/n$ are parts of the same stream-line. Hence if we put $n = \pi/\alpha$, we obtain the required solution in the form

$$\phi = A r^{\frac{\pi}{a}} \cos \frac{\pi\theta}{\alpha}, \quad \psi = A r^{\frac{\pi}{a}} \sin \frac{\pi\theta}{\alpha} \quad\dots\dots\dots\dots(3).$$

The component velocities along and perpendicular to r, are

$$-A \frac{\pi}{\alpha} r^{\frac{\pi}{a}-1} \cos \frac{\pi\theta}{\alpha}, \quad \text{and} \quad A \frac{\pi}{\alpha} r^{\frac{\pi}{a}-1} \sin \frac{\pi\theta}{\alpha};$$

and are therefore zero, finite, or infinite at the origin, according as α is less than, equal to, or greater than π.

64. We take next some cases of cyclic functions.

1°. The assumption

$$w = -\mu \log z \quad\dots\dots\dots\dots\dots\dots\dots(1)$$

gives $\phi = -\mu \log r, \quad \psi = -\mu\theta \quad\dots\dots\dots\dots\dots(2).$

The velocity at a distance r from the origin is μ/r; this point must therefore be isolated by drawing a small closed curve round it.

If we take the radii $\theta = \text{const.}$ as the stream-lines we get the case of a (two-dimensional) source at the origin. (See Art. 60.)

If the circles $r = \text{const.}$ be taken as stream-lines we get the case of Art. 28; the motion is now cyclic, the circulation in any circuit embracing the origin being $2\pi\mu$.

$$\int_0^{2\pi} \frac{\mu}{r} \cdot r\, d\theta = 2\mu$$

2°. Let us take

$$w = -\mu \log \frac{z-a}{z+a} \quad\dots\dots\dots\dots\dots\dots (3).$$

If we denote by r_1, r_2 the distances of any point in the plane xy from the points $(\pm a, 0)$, and by θ_1, θ_2, the angles which these distances make with positive direction of the axis of x, we have

$$z - a = r_1 e^{i\theta_1}, \quad z + a = r_2 e^{i\theta_2},$$

whence $\phi = -\mu \log r_1/r_2, \quad \psi = -\mu (\theta_1 - \theta_2) \dots\dots\dots (4).$

The curves $\phi = \text{const.}$, $\psi = \text{const.}$ form two orthogonal systems of 'coaxal' circles.

Either of these systems may be taken as the equipotential curves, and the other system will then form the stream-lines. In either case the velocity at the points ($\pm a$, 0) will be infinite.

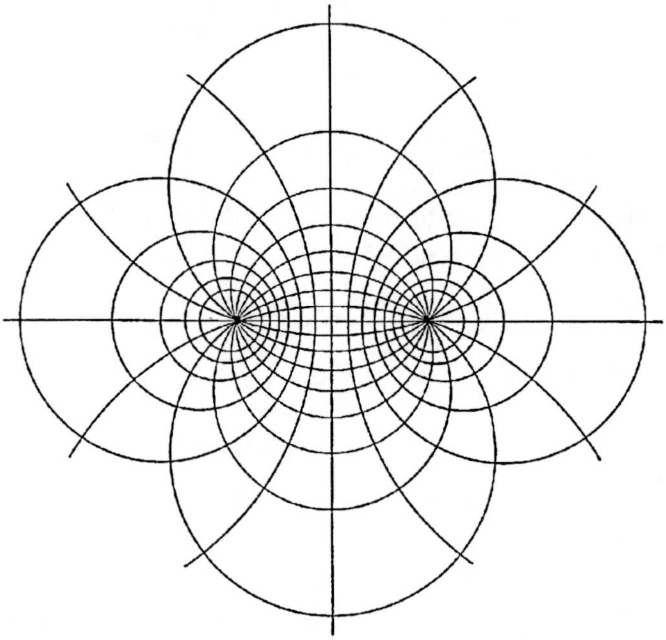

If these points be accordingly isolated by drawing closed curves round them, the rest of the plane xy becomes a triply-connected region.

If the circles $\theta_1 - \theta_2 = \text{const.}$ be taken as the stream-lines we have the case of a source and a sink, of equal intensities, situate at the points ($\pm a$, 0). If a is diminished indefinitely, whilst μa remains finite, we reproduce the assumption of Art. 63, 3°, which therefore corresponds to the case of a double line-source at the origin. (See the first diagram of Art. 68.)

If, on the other hand, we take the circles $r_1/r_2 = \text{const.}$ as the stream-lines we get a case of cyclic motion, viz. the circulation in any circuit embracing the first (only) of the above points is $2\pi\mu$, that in a circuit embracing the second is $-2\pi\mu$; whilst that in a circuit embracing both is zero. This example will have additional interest for us when we come to treat of 'Rectilinear Vortices.'

65. If w be a function of z, it follows at once from the definition of Art. 62 that z is a function of w. The latter form of assumption is sometimes more convenient analytically than the former.

The relations (1) of Art. 62 are then replaced by

$$\frac{dx}{d\phi}=\frac{dy}{d\psi},\quad \frac{dx}{d\psi}=-\frac{dy}{d\phi}\quad\text{.....................(1).}$$

Also since
$$\frac{dw}{dz}=\frac{d\phi}{dx}+i\frac{d\psi}{dx}=-u+iv,$$

we have
$$-\frac{dz}{dw}=\frac{1}{u-iv}=\frac{1}{q}\left(\frac{u}{q}+i\frac{v}{q}\right),$$

where q is the resultant velocity at (x, y). Hence if we write

$$\zeta=-\frac{dz}{dw}\quad\text{.......................... (2),}$$

and imagine the properties of the function ζ to be exhibited graphically in the manner already explained, the vector drawn from the origin to any point in the plane of ζ will agree in direction with, and be in magnitude the reciprocal of, the velocity at the corresponding point of the plane of z.

Again, since $1/q$ is the modulus of dz/dw, *i.e.* of $dx/d\phi+idy/d\phi$, we have

$$\frac{1}{q^2}=\left(\frac{dx}{d\phi}\right)^2+\left(\frac{dy}{d\phi}\right)^2\quad\text{..................... (3),}$$

which may, by (1), be put into the equivalent forms

$$\frac{1}{q^2}=\left(\frac{dx}{d\phi}\right)^2+\left(\frac{dx}{d\psi}\right)^2=\left(\frac{dy}{d\psi}\right)^2+\left(\frac{dy}{d\phi}\right)^2$$

$$=\left(\frac{dy}{d\psi}\right)^2+\left(\frac{dx}{d\psi}\right)^2=\frac{dx}{d\phi}\frac{dy}{d\psi}-\frac{dx}{d\psi}\frac{dy}{d\phi}\quad\text{.......... (4).}$$

The last formula, viz.

$$\frac{1}{q^2}=\frac{d(x, y)}{d(\phi, \psi)}\quad\text{...................... (5),}$$

simply expresses the fact that corresponding elementary areas in the planes of z and w are in the ratio of the square of the modulus of dz/dw to unity.

66. The following examples of this are important.

1°. Assume $$z = c\cosh w \qquad (1),$$

or $$\left.\begin{aligned} x &= c\cosh\phi\cos\psi \\ y &= c\sinh\phi\sin\psi \end{aligned}\right\} \qquad (2).$$

The curves $\phi = \text{const.}$ are the ellipses

$$\frac{x^2}{c^2\cosh^2\phi} + \frac{y^2}{c^2\sinh^2\phi} = 1 \qquad (3),$$

and the curves $\psi = \text{const.}$ are the hyperbolas

$$\frac{x^2}{c^2\cos^2\psi} - \frac{y^2}{c^2\sin^2\psi} = 1 \qquad (4),$$

these conics having the common foci $(\pm c, 0)$.

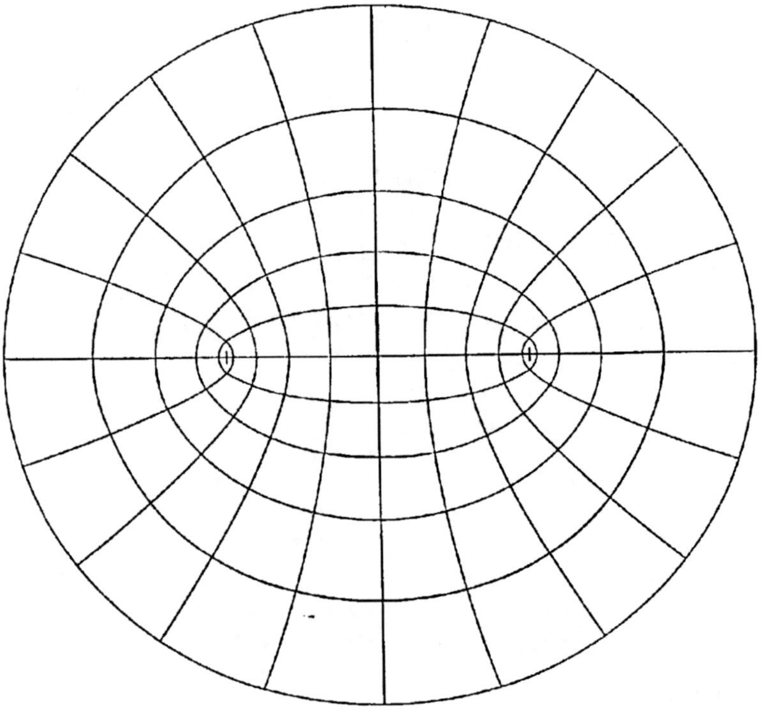

Since at the foci we have $\phi = 0$, $\psi = n\pi$, n being some integer, we see by (2) of the preceding Art. that the velocity there is infinite. If the hyperbolas be taken as the stream-lines, the portions of the axis of x which lie outside the points $(\pm c, 0)$ may be taken as rigid boundaries. We obtain in this manner the case of a liquid flowing from one side to the other of a thin plane partition, through an aperture of breadth $2c$; the velocity at the edges is however infinite.

If the ellipses be taken as the stream-lines we get the case of a liquid circulating round an elliptic cylinder, or, as an extreme case, round a rigid lamina whose section is the line joining the foci $(\pm c, 0)$.

At an infinite distance from the origin ϕ is infinite, of the order $\log r$, where r is the radius vector; and the velocity is infinitely small of the order $1/r$.

2°. Let $$z = w + e^{w} \qquad\qquad (5),$$

or $$x = \phi + e^{\phi} \cos\psi, \quad y = \psi + e^{\phi} \sin\psi \qquad\qquad (6).$$

The stream-line $\psi = 0$ coincides with the axis of x. Again the portion of the line $y = \pi$ between $x = -\infty$ and $x = -1$, considered

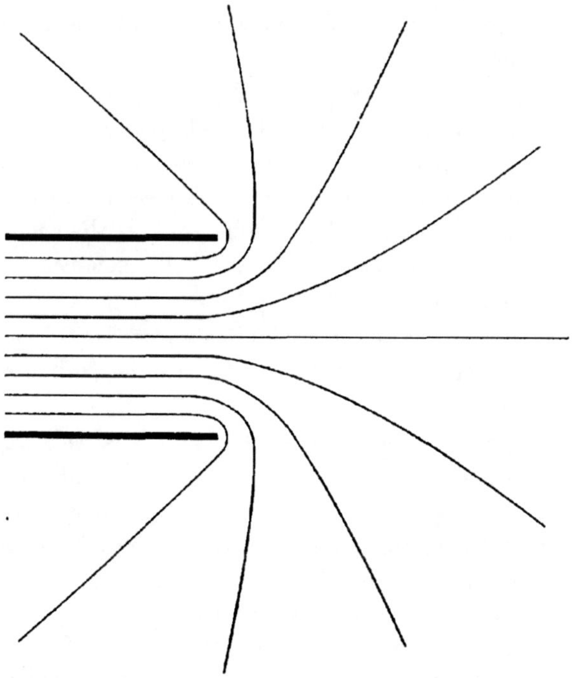

as a line bent back on itself, forms the stream-line $\psi = \pi$; viz. as ϕ decreases from $+\infty$ through 0 to $-\infty$, x increases from $-\infty$ to -1 and then decreases to $-\infty$ again. Similarly for the stream-line $\psi = -\pi$.

Since $\zeta = -dz/dw = -1 - e^{\phi}\cos\psi - ie^{\phi}\sin\psi$,
it appears that for large negative values of ϕ the velocity is in the direction of x-negative, and equal to unity, whilst for large positive values it is zero.

The above formulæ therefore express the motion of a liquid flowing into a canal bounded by two thin parallel walls from an open space. At the ends of the walls we have $\phi = 0$, $\psi = \pm\pi$, and therefore $\zeta = 0$, *i.e.* the velocity is infinite. The direction of the flow will be reversed if we change the sign of w in (5). The forms of the stream-lines, drawn, as in all similar cases in this chapter, for equidistant values of ψ, are shewn in the figure*.

67. A very general formula for the functions ϕ, ψ may be obtained as follows. It may be shewn that if a function $f(z)$ be finite, continuous, and single-valued, and have its first derivative finite, at all points of a space included between two concentric circles about the origin, its value at any point of this space can be expanded in the form

$$f(z) = A_0 + A_1 z + A_2 z^2 + \ldots + B_1 z^{-1} + B_2 z^{-2} + \ldots\ldots\ldots \quad (1).$$

If the above conditions be satisfied at all points within a circle having the origin as centre, we retain only the ascending series; if at all points without such a circle, the descending series, with the addition of the constant A_0, is sufficient. If the conditions be fulfilled for all points of the plane xy without exception, $f(z)$ can be no other than a constant A_0.

Putting $f(z) = \phi + i\psi$, introducing polar co-ordinates, and writing the complex constants A_n, B_n, in the forms $P_n + iQ_n$, $R_n + iS_n$, respectively, we obtain

$$\left.\begin{aligned} \phi &= P_0 + \Sigma_1^\infty r^n (P_n \cos n\theta - Q_n \sin n\theta) + \Sigma_1^\infty r^{-n}(R_n \cos n\theta + S_n \sin n\theta) \\ \psi &= Q_0 + \Sigma_1^\infty r^n (Q_n \cos n\theta + P_n \sin n\theta) + \Sigma_1^\infty r^{-n}(S_n \cos n\theta - R_n \sin n\theta) \end{aligned}\right\} \quad \ldots\ldots\ldots\ldots\ldots (2).$$

These formulæ are convenient in treating problems where we have the value of ϕ, or of $d\phi/dn$, given over the circular boundaries. This value may be expanded for each boundary in a series of sines and cosines of multiples of θ, by Fourier's theorem. The series thus found must be equivalent to those obtained from (2); whence, equating separately coefficients of $\sin n\theta$ and $\cos n\theta$, we obtain four systems of linear equations to determine P_n, Q_n, R_n, S_n.

* This example was given by von Helmholtz, *Berl. Monatsber.*, April 23, 1868; *Phil. Mag.*, Nov. 1868; *Ges. Abh.*, t. i., p. 154.

68. As an example let us take the case of an infinitely long circular cylinder of radius a moving with velocity $\mathbf{u}$ perpendicular to its length, in an infinite mass of liquid which is at rest at infinity.

Let the origin be taken in the axis of the cylinder, and the axes of x, y in a plane perpendicular to its length. Further let the axis of x be in the direction of the velocity $\mathbf{u}$. The motion, having originated from rest, will necessarily be irrotational, and ϕ will be single-valued. Also, since $\int d\phi/dn\,.\,ds$, taken round the section of the cylinder, is zero, ψ is also single-valued (Art. 59), so that the formulæ (2) apply. Moreover, since $d\phi/dn$ is given at every point of the internal boundary of the fluid, viz.

$$-\frac{d\phi}{dr} = \mathbf{u}\cos\theta, \text{ for } r = a \quad\text{.....................}\quad (3),$$

and since the fluid is at rest at infinity, the problem is determinate, by Art. 41. These conditions give $P_n = 0$, $Q_n = 0$, and

$$\mathbf{u}\cos\theta = \Sigma_1^\infty\, n a^{-n-1}(R_n\cos n\theta + S_n \sin n\theta),$$

which can be satisfied only by making $R_1 = \mathbf{u}a^2$, and all the other coefficients zero. The complete solution is therefore

$$\phi = \frac{\mathbf{u}a^2}{r}\cos\theta, \quad \psi = -\frac{\mathbf{u}a^2}{r}\sin\theta \quad\text{...............}\quad (4).$$

The stream-lines $\psi = \text{const.}$ are circles, as shewn on the next page.

The kinetic energy of the liquid is given by the formula (2) of Art. 61, viz.

$$2T = \rho\int\phi\,d\psi = \rho\mathbf{u}^2a^2\int_0^{2\pi}\cos^2\theta\,d\theta = \mathbf{m}'\mathbf{u}^2 \quad\text{.........}\quad (5),$$

if $\mathbf{m}', = \pi a^2\rho$, be the mass of fluid displaced by unit length of the cylinder. This result shews that the whole effect of the presence of the fluid may be represented by an addition $\mathbf{m}'$ to the inertia of the cylinder. Thus, in the case of rectilinear motion, if we have an extraneous force X acting on the cylinder, the equation of energy gives

$$\frac{d}{dt}(\tfrac{1}{2}\mathbf{m}\mathbf{u}^2 + \tfrac{1}{2}\mathbf{m}'\mathbf{u}^2) = X\mathbf{u},$$

or

$$(\mathbf{m} + \mathbf{m}')\frac{d\mathbf{u}}{dt} = X \quad\text{.....................}\quad (6),$$

where $\mathbf{m}$ represents the mass of the cylinder.

Writing this in the form

$$\mathbf{m}\frac{d\mathbf{u}}{dt} = X - \mathbf{m}'\frac{d\mathbf{u}}{dt},$$

we learn that the pressure of the fluid is equivalent to a force $-\mathbf{m}'\,d\mathbf{u}/dt$ in the direction of motion. This vanishes when $\mathbf{u}$ is constant.

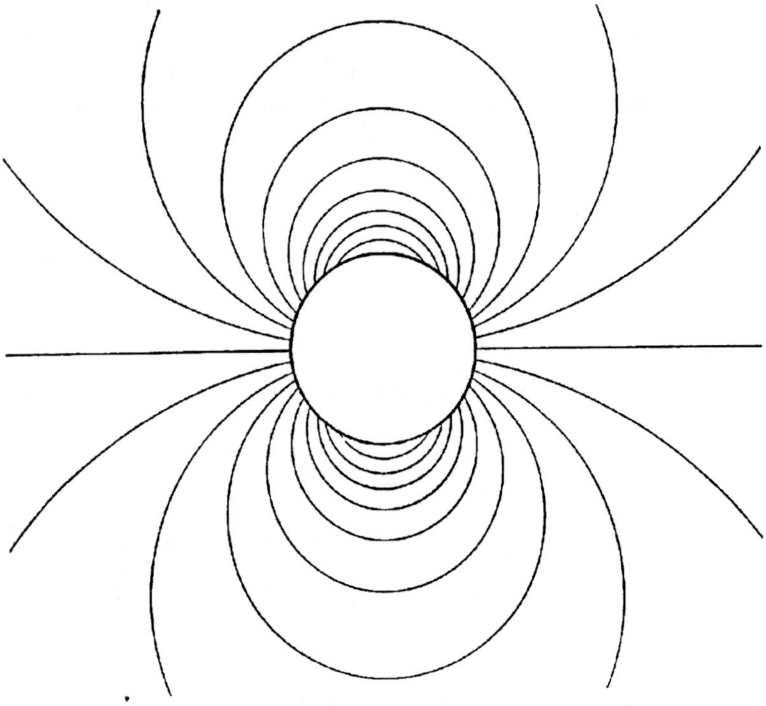

The above result may of course be verified by direct calculation. The pressure is given by the formula

$$\frac{p}{\rho} = \frac{d\phi}{dt} - \tfrac{1}{2}q^2 + F(t) \quad \text{.........................} \quad \text{(i)},$$

where we have omitted the term due to the extraneous forces (if any) acting on the fluid, the effect of which can be found by the rules of Hydrostatics. The term $d\phi/dt$ here expresses the rate at which ϕ is increasing at a fixed point of space, whereas the value of ϕ in (4) is referred to an origin which is in motion with the velocity $\mathbf{u}$. In consequence of this the value of r for any fixed point is increasing at the rate $-\mathbf{u}\cos\theta$, and that of θ at the rate $\mathbf{u}/r \,.\, \sin\theta$. Hence we must put

$$\frac{d\phi}{dt} = \frac{d\mathbf{u}}{dt}\frac{a^2}{r}\cos\theta - \mathbf{u}\cos\theta\frac{d\phi}{dr} + \frac{\mathbf{u}\sin\theta}{r}\frac{d\phi}{d\theta} = \frac{d\mathbf{u}}{dt}\frac{a^2}{r}\cos\theta + \frac{\mathbf{u}^2a^2}{r^2}\cos 2\theta.$$

Since, also, $q^2 = \mathbf{u}^2 a^4 / r^4$, the pressure at any point of the cylindrical surface $(r=a)$ is

$$p = \rho\left(a\frac{d\mathbf{u}}{dt}\cos\theta + \mathbf{u}^2\cos 2\theta - \tfrac{1}{2}\mathbf{u}^2 + F(t)\right) \text{..................(ii).}$$

The resultant force on unit length of the cylinder is evidently parallel to the initial line $\theta = 0$; to find its amount we multiply by $-a d\theta . \cos\theta$ and integrate with respect to θ between the limits 0 and π. The result is $-\mathbf{m}' d\mathbf{u}/dt$, as before.

If in the above example we impress on the fluid and the cylinder a velocity $-\mathbf{u}$ we have the case of a current flowing with the general velocity $\mathbf{u}$ past a fixed cylindrical obstacle. Adding to ϕ and ψ the terms $\mathbf{u}r\cos\theta$ and $\mathbf{u}r\sin\theta$, respectively, we get

$$\phi = \mathbf{u}\left(r + \frac{a^2}{r}\right)\cos\theta, \quad \psi = \mathbf{u}\left(r - \frac{a^2}{r}\right)\sin\theta \text{ .... (7).}$$

If no extraneous forces act, and if $\mathbf{u}$ be constant, the resultant force on the cylinder is zero.

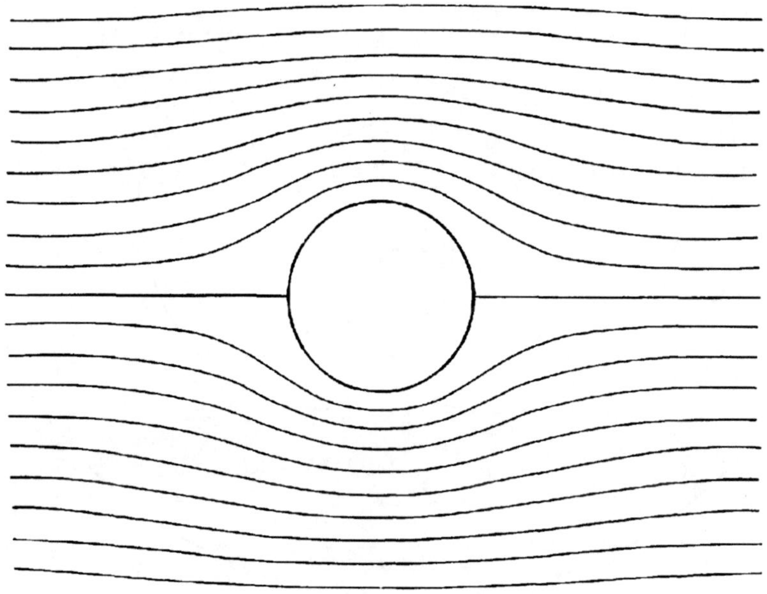

69. To render the formula (1) of Art. 67 capable of representing *any* case of irrotational motion in the space between two concentric circles, we must add to the right-hand side the term

$$A \log z \text{..............................(1).}$$

If $A = P + iQ$, the corresponding terms in ϕ, ψ are

$$P \log r - Q\theta, \quad P\theta + Q \log r \text{ ....} \quad (2),$$

respectively. The meaning of these terms is evident from Art. 64; viz. $2\pi P$, the cyclic constant of ψ, is the flux across the inner (or outer) circle; and $2\pi Q$, the cyclic constant of ϕ, is the circulation in any circuit embracing the origin.

For example, returning to the problem of the last Art., let us suppose that in addition to the motion produced by the cylinder we have an independent circulation round it, the cyclic constant being κ. The boundary-condition is then satisfied by

$$\phi = \mathbf{u}\frac{a^2}{r}\cos\theta - \frac{\kappa}{2\pi}\theta \text{ ....} \quad (3).$$

The effect of the cyclic motion, superposed on that due to the cylinder, will be to augment the velocity on one side, and to diminish (and, it may be, to reverse) it on the other. Hence

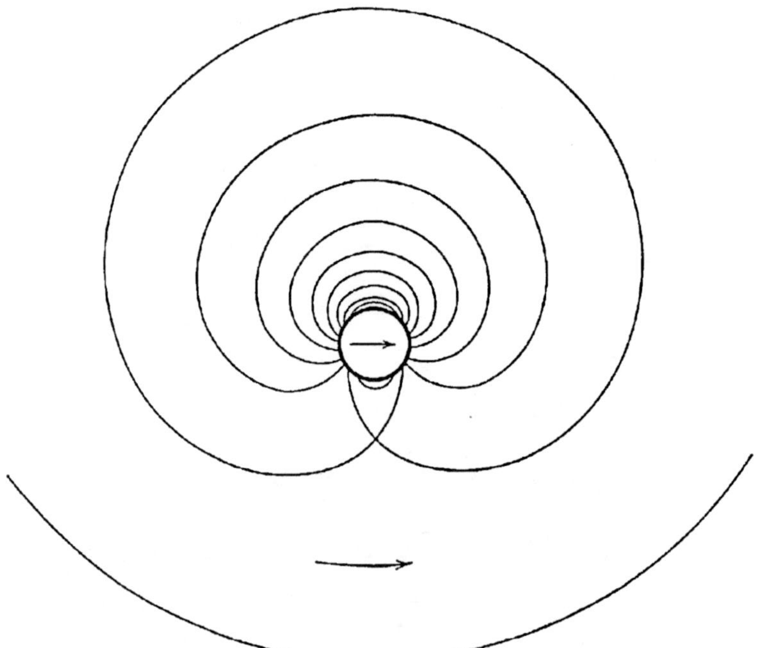

when the cylinder moves in a straight line with constant velocity, there will be a diminished pressure on one side, and an increased pressure on the other, so that a constraining force must be applied at right angles to the direction of motion.

The figure shews the lines of flow. At a distance from the origin they approximate to the form of concentric circles, the disturbance due to the cylinder becoming small in comparison with the cyclic motion. When, as in the case represented, $\mathrm{u} > \kappa/2\pi a$, there is a point of zero velocity in the fluid. The stream-line system has the same configuration in all cases, the only effect of a change in the value of u being to alter the scale, relative to the diameter of the cylinder.

To calculate the effect of the fluid pressures on the cylinder when moving in any manner we write

$$\phi = \frac{\mathrm{u}a^2}{r}\cos(\theta - \chi) - \frac{\kappa}{2\pi}\theta \text{..............................(i)},$$

where χ is the angle which the direction of motion makes with the axis of x. In the formula for the pressure [Art. 68 (i)] we must put, for $r = a$,

$$\frac{d\phi}{dt} = a\frac{d\mathrm{u}}{dt}\cos(\theta-\chi) + a\mathrm{u}\frac{d\chi}{dt}\sin(\theta-\chi) - \mathrm{u}\cos(\theta-\chi)\frac{d\phi}{dr} + \frac{\mathrm{u}}{a}\sin(\theta-\chi)\frac{d\phi}{d\theta}$$

$$= a\frac{d\mathrm{u}}{dt}\cos(\theta-\chi) + a\mathrm{u}\frac{d\chi}{dt}\sin(\theta-\chi) + \mathrm{u}^2\cos 2(\theta-\chi) - \frac{\kappa}{2\pi a}\mathrm{u}\sin(\theta-\chi) \text{...(ii)},$$

and

$$\tfrac{1}{2}q^2 = \tfrac{1}{2}\mathrm{u}^2 + \tfrac{1}{8}\frac{\kappa^2}{\pi^2 a^2} + \frac{\kappa}{2\pi a}\mathrm{u}\sin(\theta-\chi) \text{.................. (iii)}.$$

The resultant force on the cylinder is found to be made up of a component

$$-\mathrm{m}'\frac{d\mathrm{u}}{dt} \text{..(iv)},$$

in the direction of motion, and a component

$$\kappa\rho\mathrm{u} - \mathrm{m}'\mathrm{u}\frac{d\chi}{dt} \text{...................................(v)},$$

at right angles, where $\mathrm{m}' = \pi\rho a^2$ as before. Hence if P, Q denote the components of the extraneous forces, if any, in the directions of the tangent and the normal to the path, respectively, the equations of motion of the cylinder are

$$\left.\begin{aligned}(\mathrm{m}+\mathrm{m}')\frac{d\mathrm{u}}{dt} &= P,\\ (\mathrm{m}+\mathrm{m}')\mathrm{u}\frac{d\chi}{dt} &= \kappa\rho\mathrm{u} + Q\end{aligned}\right\} \text{........................(vi)}.$$

If there be no extraneous forces, u is constant, and writing $d\chi/dt = \mathrm{u}/R$, where R is the radius of curvature of the path, we find

$$R = (\mathrm{m}+\mathrm{m}')\,\mathrm{u}/\kappa\rho \text{................................(vii)}.$$

The path is therefore a circle, described in the direction of the cyclic motion*.

* Lord Rayleigh, "On the Irregular Flight of a Tennis Ball," *Mess. of Math.*, t. vii. (1878); Greenhill, *ibid.*, t. ix., p. 113 (1880).

If $\mathbf{x}$, $\mathbf{y}$ be the rectangular co-ordinates of the axis of the cylinder, the equations (vi) are equivalent to

$$\left.\begin{aligned}(\mathbf{m}+\mathbf{m}')\ddot{\mathbf{x}} &= -\kappa\rho\dot{\mathbf{y}}+X\\ (\mathbf{m}+\mathbf{m}')\ddot{\mathbf{y}} &= \kappa\rho\dot{\mathbf{x}}+Y\end{aligned}\right\}\text{..........................(viii)},$$

where X, Y are the components of the extraneous forces. To find the effect of a constant force, we may put

$$X=(\mathbf{m}+\mathbf{m}')g', \qquad Y=0\text{..........................(ix)}.$$

The solution then is

$$\left.\begin{aligned}\mathbf{x} &= \alpha+a\cos(nt+\epsilon),\\ \mathbf{y} &= \beta+\frac{g'}{n}t+a\sin(nt+\epsilon)\end{aligned}\right\}\text{..........................(x)},$$

provided

$$n=\kappa\rho/(\mathbf{m}+\mathbf{m}')\text{..................................(xi)}.$$

This shews that the path is a trochoid, described with a mean velocity g'/n perpendicular to x*. It is remarkable that the cylinder has on the whole no progressive motion in the direction of the extraneous force.

70. The formula (1) of Art. 67, as amended by the addition of the term $A\log z$, may readily be generalized so as to apply to any case of irrotational motion in a region with circular boundaries, one of which encloses all the rest. In fact, corresponding to each internal boundary we have a series of the form

$$A\log(z-c)+\frac{A_1}{z-c}+\frac{A_2}{(z-c)^2}+\ldots,$$

where c, $=a+ib$ say, refers to the centre, and the coefficients $A, A_1, A_2, \ldots$ are in general complex quantities. The difficulty however of determining these coefficients so as to satisfy given boundary conditions is now so great as to render this method of very limited application.

Indeed the determination of the irrotational motion of a liquid subject to given boundary conditions is a problem whose exact solution can be effected by direct processes in only a very few cases†. Most of the cases for which we know the solution have

* Greenhill, *l. c.*

† A very powerful method of transformation, applicable to cases where the boundaries of the fluid consist of fixed plane walls, has however been developed by Schwarz ("Ueber einige Abbildungsaufgaben," *Crelle*, t. lxx., *Gesammelte Abhandlungen*, Berlin, 1890, t. ii., p. 65), Christoffel ("Sul problema delle temperature stazionarie e la rappresentazione di una data superficie," *Annali di Matematica*, Serie II., t. i., p. 89), and Kirchhoff ("Zur Theorie des Condensators," *Berl. Monatsber.*, March 15, 1877; *Ges. Abh.*, p. 101). Many of the solutions which can be thus obtained are of great interest in the mathematically cognate subjects of Electrostatics, Heat-Conduction, &c. See for example, J. J. Thomson, *Recent Researches in Electricity and Magnetism*, Oxford, 1893, c. iii.

been obtained by an inverse process; viz. instead of trying to find a solution of the equation $\nabla^2\phi=0$ or $\nabla^2\psi=0$, satisfying given boundary conditions, we take some known solution of the differential equations and enquire what boundary conditions it can be made to satisfy. Examples of this method have already been given in Arts. 63, 64, and we may carry it further in the following two important cases of the general problem in two dimensions.

71. CASE I. The boundary of the fluid consists of a rigid cylindrical surface which is in motion with velocity **u** in a direction perpendicular to its length.

Let us take as axis of x the direction of this velocity **u**, and let δs be an element of the section of the surface by the plane xy.

Then at all points of this section the velocity of the fluid in the direction of the normal, which is denoted by $d\psi/ds$, must be equal to the velocity of the boundary normal to itself, or $-\mathbf{u}dy/ds$. Integrating along the section, we have

$$\psi=-\mathbf{u}y+\text{const.} \qquad\qquad (1).$$

If we take any admissible form of ψ, this equation defines a system of curves each of which would by its motion parallel to x give rise to the stream-lines $\psi=\text{const.}$* We give a few examples.

1°. If we choose for ψ the form $-\mathbf{u}y$, (1) is satisfied identically for all forms of the boundary. Hence the fluid contained within a cylinder of any shape which has a motion of translation only may move as a solid body. If, further, the cylindrical space occupied by the fluid be simply-connected, this is the only kind of motion possible. This is otherwise evident from Art. 40; for the motion of the fluid and the solid as one mass evidently satisfies all the conditions, and is therefore the only solution which the problem admits of.

2°. Let $\psi=A/r\,.\sin\theta$; then (1) becomes

$$\frac{A}{r}\sin\theta=-\mathbf{u}r\sin\theta+\text{const.} \qquad\qquad (2).$$

In this system of curves is included a circle of radius a, provided

* Cf. Rankine, "On Plane Water-Lines in Two Dimensions," *Phil. Trans.*, 1864, where the method is applied to obtain curves resembling the lines of ships.

$A/a = -\mathbf{u}a$. Hence the motion produced in an infinite mass of liquid by a circular cylinder moving through it with velocity $\mathbf{u}$ perpendicular to its length, is given by

$$\psi = -\frac{\mathbf{u}a^2}{r}\sin\theta \quad\text{.......................(3)},$$

which agrees with Art. 68.

3°. Let us introduce the elliptic co-ordinates ξ, η, connected with x, y by the relation

$$x + iy = c\cosh(\xi + i\eta) \quad\text{.....................(4)},$$

or

$$\left.\begin{aligned} x &= c\cosh\xi\cos\eta, \\ y &= c\sinh\xi\sin\eta \end{aligned}\right\} \quad\text{.....................(5)},$$

(cf. Art. 66), where ξ may be supposed to range from 0 to ∞, and η from 0 to 2π. If we now put

$$\phi + i\psi = Ce^{-(\xi+i\eta)} \quad\text{.......................(6)},$$

where C is some real constant, we have

$$\psi = -Ce^{-\xi}\sin\eta \quad\text{.......................(7)},$$

so that (1) becomes

$$Ce^{-\xi}\sin\eta = \mathbf{u}c\sinh\xi\sin\eta + \text{const.}$$

In this system of curves is included the ellipse whose parameter ξ_0 is determined by

$$Ce^{-\xi_0} = \mathbf{u}c\sinh\xi_0.$$

If a, b be the semi-axes of this ellipse we have

$$a = c\cosh\xi_0, \quad b = c\sinh\xi_0,$$

so that

$$C = \frac{\mathbf{u}bc}{a-b} = \mathbf{u}b\left(\frac{a+b}{a-b}\right)^{\frac{1}{2}}.$$

Hence the formula

$$\psi = -\mathbf{u}b\left(\frac{a+b}{a-b}\right)^{\frac{1}{2}} e^{-\xi}\sin\eta \quad\text{..................(8)}$$

gives the motion of an infinite mass of liquid produced by an elliptic cylinder of semi-axes a, b, moving parallel to the greater axis with velocity $\mathbf{u}$.

That the above formulæ make the velocity zero at infinity appears from the consideration that, when ξ is large, δx and δy are of the same order as $e^{\xi}\delta\xi$ or $e^{\xi}\delta\eta$, so that $d\psi/dx$, $d\psi/dy$ are of the order $e^{-2\xi}$ or $1/r^2$, ultimately, where r denotes the distance of any point from the axis of the cylinder.

If the motion of the cylinder were parallel to the minor axis the formula would be

$$\psi = \mathbf{v}a\left(\frac{a+b}{a-b}\right)^{\frac{1}{2}} e^{-\xi}\cos\eta \ldots\ldots\ldots\ldots\ldots\ldots(9).$$

The stream-lines are in each case the same for all confocal elliptic forms of the cylinder, so that the formulæ hold even when the section reduces to the straight line joining the foci. In this case (9) becomes

$$\psi = \mathbf{v}c\, e^{-\xi}\cos\eta \ldots\ldots\ldots\ldots\ldots\ldots\ldots(10),$$

which would give the motion produced by an infinitely long lamina of breadth $2c$ moving 'broadside on' in an infinite mass of

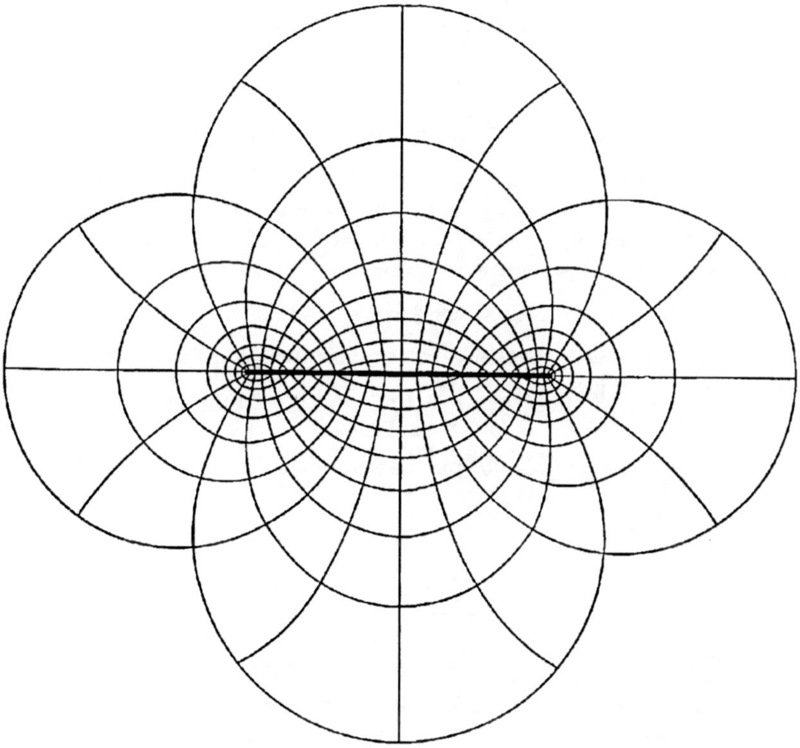

liquid. Since however this solution makes the velocity infinite at the edges, it is subject to the practical limitation already indicated in several instances*.

* This investigation was given in the *Quart. Journ. of Math.*, t. xiv. (1875). Results equivalent to (8), (9) had however been obtained, in a different manner, by Beltrami, "Sui principii fondamentali dell' idrodinamica razionale," *Mem. dell' Accad. delle Scienze di Bologna*, 1873, p. 394.

The kinetic energy of the fluid is given by

$$2T = \rho \int \phi \, d\psi = \rho C^2 e^{-2\xi_0} \int_0^{2\pi} \cos^2 \eta \, d\eta$$
$$= \pi \rho b^2 \mathbf{u}^2 \text{ .... } (11),$$

where b is the half-breadth of the cylinder perpendicular to the direction of motion.

If the units of length and time be properly chosen we may write

$$x + iy = \cosh(\xi + i\eta), \quad \phi + i\psi = e^{-(\xi + i\eta)},$$

whence $$x = \phi \left(1 + \frac{1}{\phi^2 + \psi^2}\right), \quad y = \psi \left(1 - \frac{1}{\phi^2 + \psi^2}\right).$$

These formulæ are convenient for tracing the curves $\phi = \text{const.}$, $\psi = \text{const.}$, which are figured on the preceding page.

By superposition of the results (8) and (9) we obtain, for the case of an elliptic cylinder having a motion of translation whose components are $\mathbf{u}$, $\mathbf{v}$,

$$\psi = -\left(\frac{a+b}{a-b}\right)^{\frac{1}{2}} e^{-\xi} (\mathbf{u} b \sin \eta - \mathbf{v} a \cos \eta) \text{ .... (i).}$$

To find the motion relative to the cylinder we must add to this the expression

$$\mathbf{u} y - \mathbf{v} x = c(\mathbf{u} \sinh \xi \sin \eta - \mathbf{v} \cosh \xi \cos \eta) \text{ .... (ii).}$$

For example, the stream-function for a current impinging at an angle of 45° on a plane lamina whose edges are at $x = \pm c$ is

$$\psi = -\frac{1}{\sqrt{2}} q_0 c \sinh \xi (\cos \eta - \sin \eta) \text{ .... (iii),}$$

where q_0 is the velocity at infinity. This immediately verifies, for it makes $\psi = 0$ for $\xi = 0$, and gives

$$\psi = -\frac{q_0}{\sqrt{2}} (x - y)$$

for $\xi = \infty$. The stream-lines for this case are shewn in the annexed figure

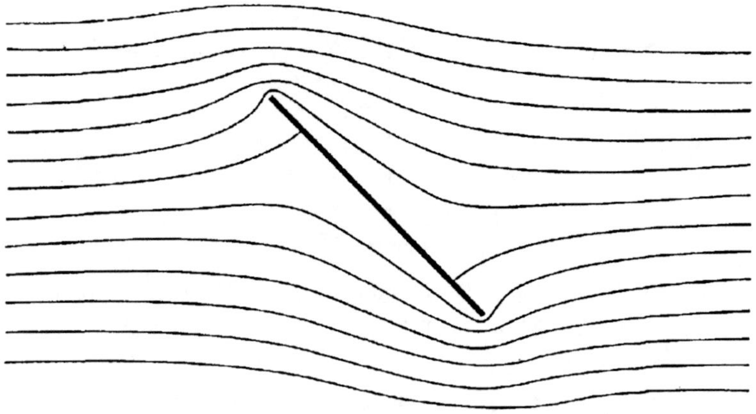

(turned through 45° for convenience). This will serve to illustrate some results to be obtained later in Chap. VI.

If we trace the course of the stream-line $\psi = 0$ from $\phi = +\infty$ to $\phi = -\infty$, we find that it consists in the first place of the hyperbolic arc $\eta = \frac{1}{4}\pi$, meeting the lamina at right angles; it then divides into two portions, following the faces of the lamina, which finally re-unite and are continued as the hyperbolic arc $\eta = \frac{5}{4}\pi$. The points where the hyperbolic arcs abut on the lamina are points of zero velocity, and therefore of maximum pressure. It is plain that the fluid pressures on the lamina are equivalent to a couple tending to set it broadside on to the stream; and it is easily found that the moment of this couple, per unit length, is $\frac{1}{2}\pi\rho q_0{}^2c^2$. Compare Art. 121.

72. Case II. The boundary of the fluid consists of a rigid cylindrical surface rotating with angular velocity ω about an axis parallel to its length.

Taking the origin in the axis of rotation, and the axes of x, y in a perpendicular plane, then, with the same notation as before, $d\psi/ds$ will be equal to the normal component of the velocity of the boundary, or

$$\frac{d\psi}{ds} = \omega r \frac{dr}{ds},$$

if r denote the radius vector from the origin. Integrating we have, at all points of the boundary,

$$\psi = \tfrac{1}{2}\omega r^2 + \text{const.} \quad \ldots\ldots\ldots\ldots\ldots\ldots\ldots(1).$$

If we assume any possible form of ψ, this will give us the equation of a series of curves, each of which would, by rotation round the origin, produce the system of stream-lines determined by ψ.

As examples we may take the following:

1°. If we assume

$$\psi = Ar^2 \cos 2\theta = A(x^2 - y^2) \quad \ldots\ldots\ldots\ldots\ldots\ldots(2),$$

the equation (1) becomes

$$(\tfrac{1}{2}\omega - A)x^2 + (\tfrac{1}{2}\omega + A)y^2 = C,$$

which, for any given value of A, represents a system of similar conics. That this system may include the ellipse

$$\frac{x^2}{a^2} + \frac{y^2}{b^2} = 1,$$

we must have $$(\tfrac{1}{2}\omega - A)a^2 = (\tfrac{1}{2}\omega + A)b^2,$$

or $$A = \tfrac{1}{2}\omega \cdot \frac{a^2 - b^2}{a^2 + b^2}.$$

Hence $$\psi = \tfrac{1}{2}\omega \cdot \frac{a^2 - b^2}{a^2 + b^2}(x^2 - y^2) \quad \ldots\ldots\ldots\ldots(3),$$

gives the motion of a liquid contained within a hollow elliptic cylinder whose semi-axes are a, b, produced by the rotation of the cylinder about its axis with angular velocity ω. The arrangement of the stream-lines $\psi =$ const. is given in the figure on p. 99.

The corresponding formula for ϕ is

$$\phi = -\omega \cdot \frac{a^2 - b^2}{a^2 + b^2} \cdot xy \quad \text{......................(4).}$$

The kinetic energy of the fluid, per unit length of the cylinder, is given by

$$2T = \rho \iint \left\{ \left(\frac{d\phi}{dx}\right)^2 + \left(\frac{d\phi}{dy}\right)^2 \right\} dx dy = \tfrac{1}{4} \frac{(a^2 - b^2)^2}{a^2 + b^2} \omega^2 \times \pi\rho ab \text{ ...(5).}$$

This is less than if the fluid were to rotate with the boundary, as one rigid mass, in the ratio of

$$\left(\frac{a^2 - b^2}{a^2 + b^2}\right)^2$$

to unity. We have here an illustration of Lord Kelvin's minimum theorem, proved in Art. 45.

2°. Let us assume

$$\psi = Ar^3 \cos 3\theta = A(x^3 - 3xy^2).$$

The equation (1) of the boundary then becomes

$$A(x^3 - 3xy^2) - \tfrac{1}{2}\omega(x^2 + y^2) = C \quad \text{..............(6).}$$

We may choose the constants so that the straight line $x = a$ shall form part of the boundary. The conditions for this are

$$Aa^3 - \tfrac{1}{2}\omega a^2 = C, \quad 3Aa + \tfrac{1}{2}\omega = 0.$$

Substituting the values of A, C hence derived in (6), we have

$$x^3 - a^3 - 3xy^2 + 3a(x^2 - a^2 + y^2) = 0.$$

Dividing out by $x - a$, we get

$$x^2 + 4ax + 4a^2 = 3y^2,$$

or

$$x + 2a = \pm\sqrt{3} \cdot y.$$

The rest of the boundary consists therefore of two straight lines passing through the point $(-2a, 0)$, and inclined at angles of 30° to the axis of x.

We have thus obtained the formulæ for the motion of the fluid contained within a vessel in the form of an equilateral prism, when the latter is rotating with angular velocity ω about an axis parallel to its length and passing through the centre of its section; viz. we have

$$\psi = -\tfrac{1}{6}\frac{\omega}{a}r^3\cos 3\theta, \quad \phi = \tfrac{1}{6}\frac{\omega}{a}r^3\sin 3\theta \qquad\qquad(7),$$

where $2\sqrt{3}a$ is the length of a side of the prism.

The problem of fluid motion in a rotating cylindrical case is to a certain extent mathematically identical with that of the torsion of a uniform rod or bar*. The above examples are mere adaptations of two of de Saint-Venant's solutions of the latter problem.

3°. In the case of a liquid contained in a rotating cylinder whose section is a circular sector of radius a and angle 2α, the axis of rotation passing through the centre, we may assume

$$\psi = \tfrac{1}{2}\omega r^2\frac{\cos 2\theta}{\cos 2\alpha} + \Sigma A_{2n+1}\left(\frac{r}{a}\right)^{(2n+1)\pi/2\alpha}\cos(2n+1)\frac{\pi\theta}{2\alpha} \qquad (8),$$

the middle radius being taken as initial line. For this makes $\psi = \tfrac{1}{2}\omega r^2$ for $\theta = \pm\alpha$, and the constants A_{2n+1} can be determined by Fourier's method so as to make $\psi = \tfrac{1}{2}\omega a^2$ for $r = a$. We find

$$A_{2n+1} = (-)^{n+1}\omega a^2\left\{\frac{1}{(2n+1)\pi - 4\alpha} - \frac{2}{(2n+1)\pi} + \frac{1}{(2n+1)\pi + 4\alpha}\right\} \qquad (9).$$

The conjugate expression for ϕ is

$$\phi = -\tfrac{1}{2}\omega r^2\frac{\sin 2\theta}{\cos 2\alpha} - \Sigma A_{2n+1}\left(\frac{r}{a}\right)^{(2n+1)\pi/2\alpha}\sin(2n+1)\frac{\pi\theta}{2\alpha} \qquad (10)\dagger,$$

where A_{2n+1} has the value (9).

The kinetic energy is given by

$$2T = -\rho\int\phi\frac{d\phi}{dn}ds = -2\rho\omega\int_0^a\phi_a r\,dr \qquad\qquad (11),$$

* See Thomson and Tait, *Natural Philosophy*, Art. 704, *et seq.*

† This problem was first solved by Stokes, "On the Critical Values of the Sums of Periodic Series," *Camb. Trans.*, t. viii. (1847), *Math. and Phys. Papers*, t. i., p. 305. See also papers by Hicks and Greenhill, *Mess. of Math.*, t. viii., pp. 42, 89, and t. x., p. 83.

where ϕ_α denotes the value of ϕ for $\theta = \alpha$, the value of $d\phi/dn$ being zero over the circular part of the boundary.

The case of the semicircle $\alpha = \frac{1}{2}\pi$ will be of use to us later. We then have

$$A_{2n+1} = (-)^{n+1} \frac{\omega a^2}{\pi} \left\{ \frac{1}{2n-1} - \frac{2}{2n+1} + \frac{1}{2n+3} \right\} \quad \text{......(12)},$$

and therefore

$$\int_0^a \phi_\alpha r dr = \frac{\omega a^4}{\pi} \Sigma \frac{1}{2n+3} \left\{ \frac{1}{2n-1} - \frac{2}{2n+1} + \frac{1}{2n+3} \right\}$$

$$= -\frac{\omega a^4}{\pi} \left(2 - \frac{\pi^2}{8} \right).$$

Hence*

$$2T = \tfrac{1}{2}\pi\rho\omega^2 a^4 \left(\frac{8}{\pi^2} - \tfrac{1}{2} \right) = \cdot 3106 a^2 \times \tfrac{1}{2}\pi\rho\omega^2 a^2 \quad \text{......(13)}.$$

This is less than if the fluid were solidified, in the ratio of ·6212 to 1. See Art. 45.

4°. With the same notation of elliptic coordinates as in Art. 71, 3°, let us assume

$$\phi + i\psi = Cie^{-2(\xi + i\eta)} \quad \text{......................(14)}.$$

Since $$x^2 + y^2 = \tfrac{1}{2}c^2 (\cosh 2\xi + \cos 2\eta),$$

the equation (1) becomes

$$Ce^{-2\xi} \cos 2\eta - \tfrac{1}{4}\omega c^2 (\cosh 2\xi + \cos 2\eta) = \text{const.}$$

This system of curves includes the ellipse whose parameter is ξ_0, provided

$$Ce^{-2\xi_0} - \tfrac{1}{4}\omega c^2 = 0,$$

or, using the values of a, b already given,

$$C = \tfrac{1}{4}\omega (a+b)^2,$$

so that

$$\left. \begin{aligned} \psi &= \tfrac{1}{4}\omega (a+b)^2 e^{-2\xi} \cos 2\eta, \\ \phi &= \tfrac{1}{4}\omega (a+b)^2 e^{-2\xi} \sin 2\eta. \end{aligned} \right\} \quad \text{...............(15)}.$$

At a great distance from the origin the velocity is of the order $1/r^3$.

* Greenhill, *l. c.*

The above formulæ therefore give the motion of an infinite mass of liquid, otherwise at rest, produced by the rotation of an elliptic cylinder about its axis with angular velocity ω*. The diagram shews the stream-lines both inside and outside a rigid elliptical cylindrical case rotating about its axis.

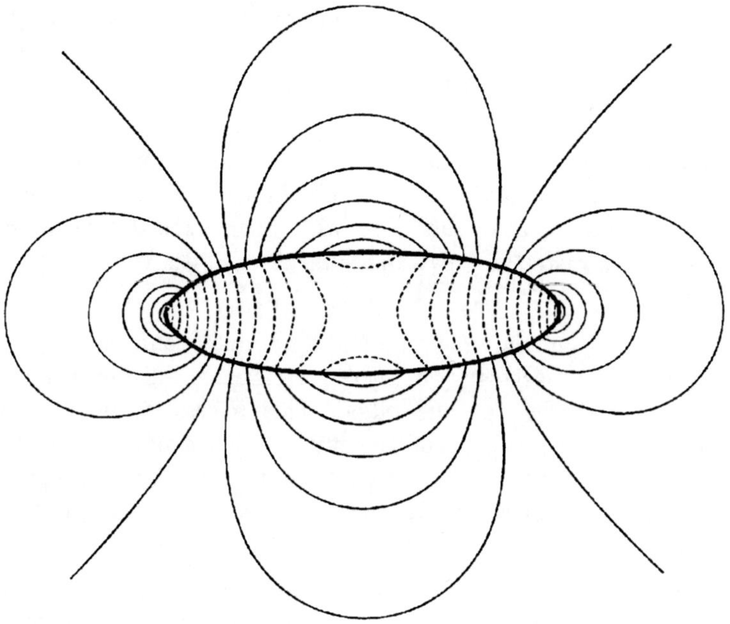

The kinetic energy of the external fluid is given by

$$2T = \tfrac{1}{8}\pi\rho c^4 . \omega^2 \qquad\qquad (16).$$

It is remarkable that this is the same for all confocal elliptic forms of the section of the cylinder.

Combining these results with those of Arts. 66, 71 we find that if an elliptic cylinder be moving with velocities **u**, **v** parallel to the principal axes of its cross-section, and rotating with angular velocity ω, and if (further) the fluid be circulating irrotationally round it, the cyclic constant being κ, then the stream-function relative to the aforesaid axes is

$$\psi = -\sqrt{\left(\frac{a+b}{a-b}\right)} e^{-\xi} (\mathbf{u} b \sin\eta - \mathbf{v} a \cos\eta) + \tfrac{1}{4}\omega (a+b)^2 e^{-2\xi} \cos 2\eta + \frac{\kappa}{2\pi}\xi.$$

* *Quart. Journ. Math.*, t. xiv. (1875); see also Beltrami, *l. c. ante* p. 93.

Discontinuous Motions.

73. We have, in the preceding pages, had several instances of the flow of a liquid round a sharp projecting edge, and it appeared in each case that the velocity there was infinite. This is indeed a necessary consequence of the assumed irrotational character of the motion, whether the fluid be incompressible or not, as may be seen by considering the configuration of the equipotential surfaces (which meet the boundary at right angles) in the immediate neighbourhood.

The occurrence of infinite values of the velocity may be avoided by supposing the edge to be slightly rounded, but even then the velocity near the edge will much exceed that which obtains at a distance great in comparison with the radius of curvature.

In order that the motion of a fluid may conform to such conditions, it is necessary that the pressure at a distance should greatly exceed that at the edge. This excess of pressure is demanded by the *inertia* of the fluid, which cannot be guided round a sharp curve, in opposition to centrifugal force, except by a distribution of pressure increasing with a very rapid gradient outwards.

Hence unless the pressure at a distance be very great, the maintenance of the motion in question would require a negative pressure at the corner, such as fluids under ordinary conditions are unable to sustain.

To put the matter in as definite a form as possible, let us imagine the following case. Let us suppose that a straight tube, whose length is large compared with the diameter, is fixed in the middle of a large closed vessel filled with frictionless liquid, and that this tube contains, at a distance from the ends, a sliding plug, or piston, P, which can be moved in any required manner by extraneous forces applied to it. The thickness of the walls of the tube is supposed to be small in comparison with the diameter; and the edges, at the two ends, to be rounded off, so that there are no sharp angles. Let us further suppose that at some point of the walls of the vessel there is a lateral tube, with a piston Q, by means of which the pressure in the interior can be adjusted at will.

Everything being at rest to begin with, let a slowly increasing velocity be communicated to the plug P, so that (for simplicity) the motion at any instant may be regarded as approximately

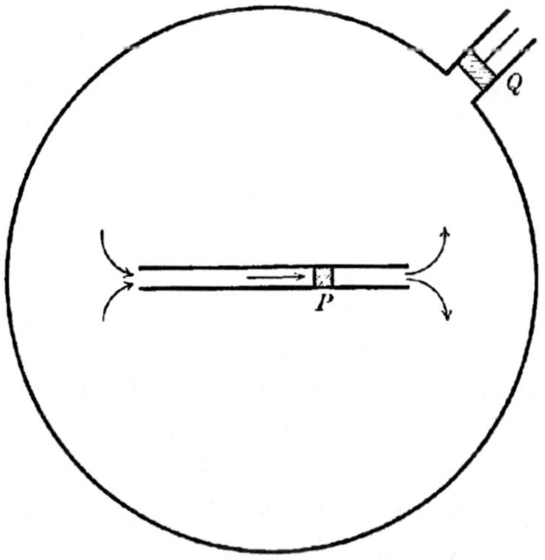

steady. At first, provided a sufficient force be applied to Q, a continuous motion of the kind indicated in the diagram on p. 83 will be produced in the fluid, there being in fact only one type of motion consistent with the conditions of the question. As the acceleration of the piston P proceeds, the pressure on Q may become enormous, even with very moderate velocities of P, and if Q be allowed to yield, an annular cavity will be formed at each end of the tube.

The further course of the motion in such a case has not yet been worked out from a theoretical stand-point. In actual liquids the problem is modified by viscosity, which prevents any slipping of the fluid immediately in contact with the tube, and must further exercise a considerable influence on such rapid differential motions of the fluid as are here in question.

As a matter of fact, the observed motions of fluids are often found to deviate very widely from the types shewn in our diagrams. In such a case as we have just described, the fluid issuing from the mouth of the tube does not immediately spread out in all directions, but forms, at all events for some distance, a more or less compact stream, bounded on all sides by fluid nearly at rest.

A familiar instance is the smoke-laden stream of gas issuing from a chimney.

74. Leaving aside the question of the manner in which the motion is established, von Helmholtz* and Kirchhoff† have endeavoured to construct types of steady motion of a frictionless liquid, in two dimensions, which shall resemble more closely what is observed in such cases as we have referred to. In the problems to be considered, there is either a free surface or (what comes to the same thing) a surface of discontinuity along which the moving liquid is in contact with other fluid at rest. In either case, the physical condition to be satisfied at this surface is that the pressure must be the same at all points of it; this implies, in virtue of the steady motion, and in the absence of extraneous forces, that the velocity must also be uniform along this surface.

The most general method we possess of treating problems of this class is based on the properties of the function ζ introduced in Art. 65. In the cases we shall discuss, the moving fluid is supposed bounded by stream-lines which consist partly of straight walls, and partly of lines along which the resultant velocity (q) is constant. For convenience, we may in the first instance suppose the units of length and time to be so adjusted that this constant velocity is equal to unity. Then in the plane of the function ζ the lines for which $q = 1$ are represented by arcs of a circle of unit radius, having the origin as centre, and the straight walls (since the direction of the flow along each is constant) by radial lines drawn outwards from the circumference. The points where these lines meet the circle correspond to the points where the bounding stream-lines change their character.

Consider, next, the function $\log \zeta$. In the plane of this function the circular arcs for which $q = 1$ become transformed into portions of the imaginary axis, and the radial lines into lines parallel to the real axis. It remains then to frame an assumption of the form

$$\log \zeta = f(w)$$

such that the now rectilinear boundaries shall correspond, in the

* *l. c. ante* p. 24.

† "Zur Theorie freier Flüssigkeitsstrahlen," *Crelle*, t. lxx. (1869), *Ges. Abh.*, p. 416; see also *Mechanik*, cc. xxi., xxii. Considerable additions to the subject have been recently made by Michell, "On the Theory of Free Stream Lines," *Phil. Trans.*, A., 1890.

plane of w, to straight lines $\psi = \text{constant}$. There are further conditions of correspondence between special points, one on the boundary, and one in the interior, of each area, which render the problem determinate. These will be specified, so far as is necessary, as occasion arises. The problem thus presented is a particular case of that solved by Schwarz, in the paper already cited. His method consists in the conformal representation of each area in turn on a half-plane*; we shall find that, in such simple cases as we shall have occasion to consider, this can be effected by the successive use of transformations already studied, and figured, in these pages.

When the correspondence between the planes of ζ and w has been established, the connection between z and w is to be found, by integration, from the relation $dz/dw = -\zeta$. The arbitrary constant which appears in the result is due to the arbitrary position of the origin in the plane of z.

75. We take first the case of fluid escaping from a large vessel by a straight canal projecting inwards†. This is the two-dimensional form of Borda's mouthpiece, referred to in Art. 25.

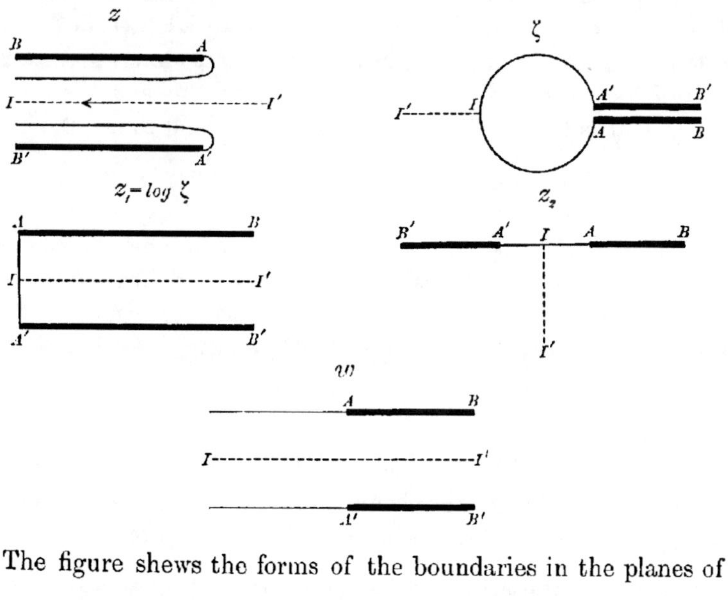

The figure shews the forms of the boundaries in the planes of

* See Forsyth, *Theory of Functions*, c. xx.

† This problem was first solved by von Helmholtz, *l. c. ante* p. 24.

z, ζ, w, and of two subsidiary variables z_1, z_2*. A reference to the diagram on p. 77 will shew that the relation

$$z_1 \equiv x_1 + iy_1 = \log \zeta \text{..........................(1)}$$

transforms the boundaries in the plane of ζ into the axis of x_1 from $(\infty, 0)$ to the origin, the axis of y_1 from the origin to $(0, -2\pi)$, and the line $y_1 = -2\pi$ from $(0, -2\pi)$ to $(\infty, -2\pi)$, respectively. If we now put

$$z_2 \equiv x_2 + iy_2 = \cosh \tfrac{1}{2}z_1 \text{......................(2),}$$

these boundaries become the portions of the axis of x_2 for which $x_2 > 1$, $1 > x_2 > -1$, and $x_2 < -1$, respectively; see Art. 66, 1°. It remains to transform the figure so that the positive and negative portions of the axis of x_2 shall correspond respectively to the two bounding stream-lines, and that the point $z_2 = 0$ (marked I in the figure) shall correspond to $w = -\infty$. All these conditions are satisfied by the assumption

$$w = \log z_2 \text{............................(3),}$$

(see Art. 62), provided the two bounding stream-lines be taken to be $\psi = 0$, $\psi = -\pi$ respectively. In other words the final breadth of the stream (where $q = 1$) is taken to be equal to π. This is equivalent to imposing a further relation between the units of length and time, in addition to that already adopted in Art. 74, so that these units are now, in any given case, determinate. An arbitrary constant might be added to (3); the equation, as it stands, makes the edge A of the canal correspond to $w = 0$.

Eliminating z_1, z_2, we get $\zeta^{\frac{1}{2}} + \zeta^{-\frac{1}{2}} = 2e^w$, whence, finally,

$$\zeta = -1 + 2e^{2w} + 2e^w(e^{2w} - 1)^{\frac{1}{2}} \text{...............(4).}$$

The free portion of the stream-line $\psi = 0$ is that for which ζ is complex and therefore $\phi < 0$. To trace its form we remark that along it we have $-d\phi/ds = q = 1$, and therefore $\phi = -s$, the arc being measured from the edge of the canal. Also $\zeta = dx/ds + idy/ds$. Hence

$$dx/ds = -1 + 2e^{-2s}, \quad dy/ds = -2e^{-s}(1 - e^{-2s})^{\frac{1}{2}} \text{...... (5),}$$

or, integrating,

$$x = 1 - s - e^{-2s}, \quad y = -\tfrac{1}{2}\pi + e^{-s}(1 - e^{-2s})^{\frac{1}{2}} + \sin^{-1} e^{-s} \text{... (6),}$$

the constants of integration being so chosen as to make the origin of (x, y) coincide with the point A of the first figure. For $s = \infty$,

* The heavy lines represent rigid boundaries, and the fine continuous lines the free surfaces. Corresponding points in the various figures are indicated by the same letters.

we have $y = -\frac{1}{2}\pi$, which shews that, on our scale, the total breadth of the canal is 2π. The coefficient of contraction is therefore $\frac{1}{2}$, in accordance with Borda's theory.

If we put $dx/ds = \cos\theta$, and therefore $s = \log\sec\frac{1}{2}\theta$, we get

$$x = \sin^2\tfrac{1}{2}\theta - \log\sec\tfrac{1}{2}\theta, \quad y = -\tfrac{1}{2}\theta + \tfrac{1}{2}\sin\theta \quad \text{.........(7)},$$

by means of which the curve in question is easily traced.

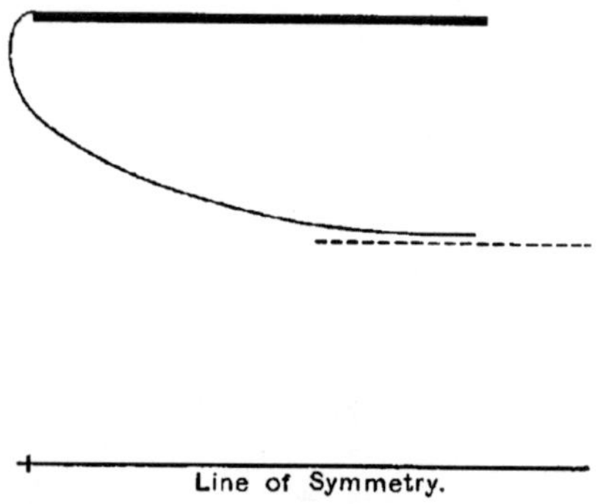

76. The solution for the case of fluid issuing from a large vessel by an aperture in a plane wall is analytically very similar. The successive steps of the transformation, viz.

$$z_1 = \log\zeta, \quad z_2 = \cosh z_1, \quad w = \log z_2 \quad \text{...........(1)},$$

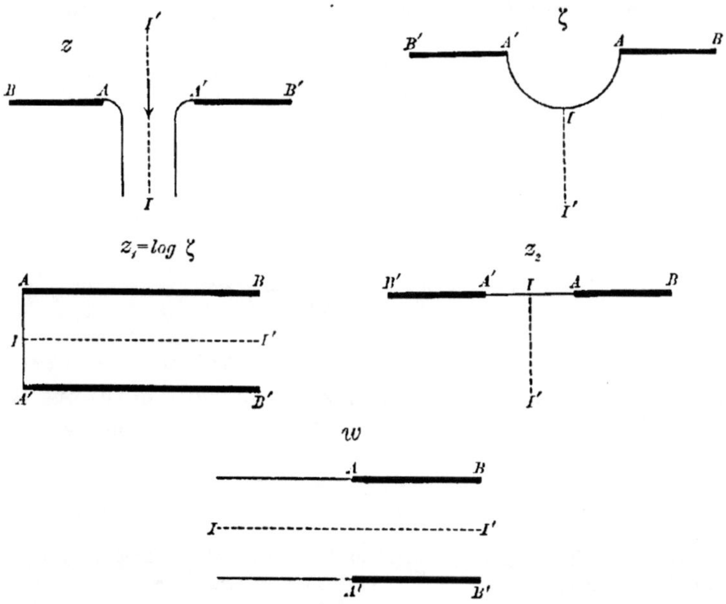

are sufficiently illustrated by the figures. We thus get

$$\zeta + \zeta^{-1} = 2e^{w},$$

or

$$\zeta = e^{w} + (e^{2w} - 1)^{\frac{1}{2}} \text{ .... (2).}$$

For the free stream-line starting from the edge A of the aperture we have $\psi = 0$, $\phi < 0$, whence

$$dx/ds = e^{-s}, \quad dy/ds = -(1 - e^{-2s})^{\frac{1}{2}} \text{ .... (3),}$$

or

$$x = 1 - e^{-s}, \quad y = (1 - e^{-2s})^{\frac{1}{2}} - \tfrac{1}{2}\log\frac{1 + (1 - e^{-2s})^{\frac{1}{2}}}{1 - (1 - e^{-2s})^{\frac{1}{2}}} \text{......(4)*,}$$

the origin being taken at the point A. If we put $dx/ds = \cos\theta$, these may be written

$$x = 2\sin^2\tfrac{1}{2}\theta, \quad y = \sin\theta - \log\tan(\tfrac{1}{4}\pi + \tfrac{1}{2}\theta) \text{......(5).}$$

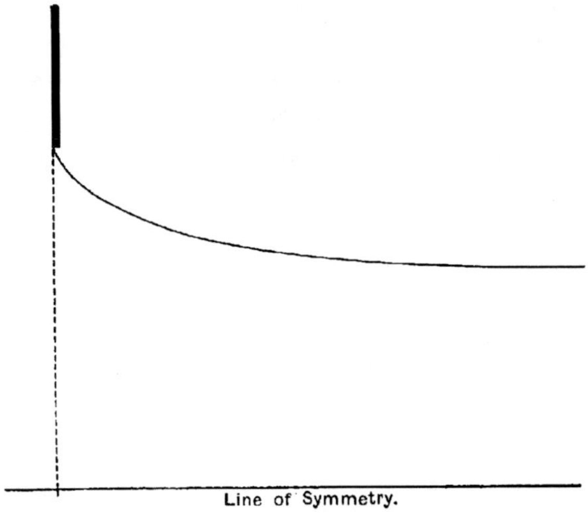

When $s = \infty$, we have $x = 1$; and therefore, since on our scale the final breadth of the stream is π, the total width of the aperture is represented by $\pi + 2$; *i.e.* the coefficient of contraction is

$$\pi/(\pi + 2), = \cdot 611.$$

* This example was given by Kirchhoff (*l. c.*), and discussed more fully by Lord Rayleigh, "Notes on Hydrodynamics," *Phil. Mag.*, December 1876.

77. The next example is of importance in the theory of the resistance of fluids. We suppose that a steady stream impinges directly on a fixed plane lamina, behind which is a region of dead water bounded on each side by a surface of discontinuity.

The middle stream-line, after meeting the lamina at right angles, branches off into two parts, which follow the lamina to the edges, and thence the surfaces of discontinuity. Let this be the line $\psi = 0$, and let us further suppose that at the point of divergence we have $\phi = 0$. The forms of the boundaries in the planes of z, ζ, w are shewn in the figures. The region occupied

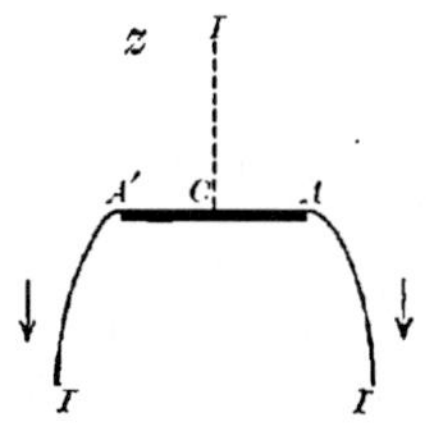

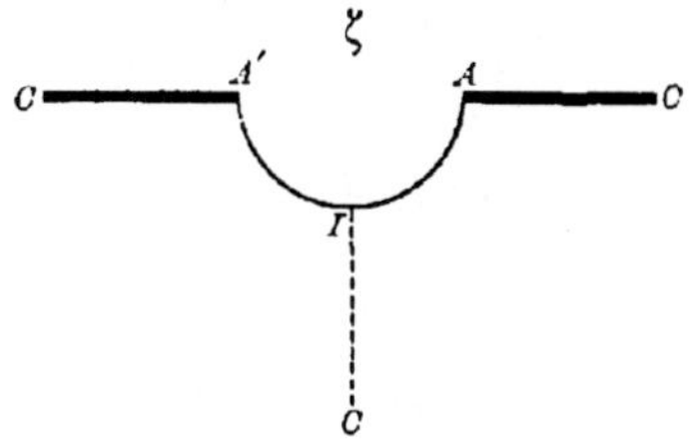

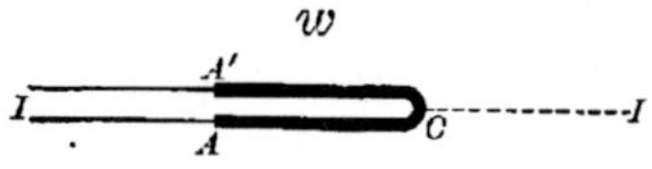

by the moving fluid corresponds to the whole of the plane of w, which must be regarded however as bounded internally by the two sides of the line $\psi = 0$, $\phi < 0$.

As in Art. 76, the transformations

$$\left.\begin{aligned} z_1 &= \log \zeta, \\ z_2 &= \cosh z_1 \end{aligned}\right\} \quad \text{.............................(1)},$$

give us as boundaries the segments of the axis $y_2 = 0$ made by the points $x_2 = \pm 1$. The further assumption

$$z_3 = -z_2^{\,2} \text{..............................(2)},$$

converts these into segments of the negative portion of the axis $y_3 = 0$, taken twice. The boundaries now correspond to those of the plane w, except that to $w = 0$ corresponds $z_3 = \infty$, and conversely. The transformation is therefore completed by putting

$$w = z_3^{-1} \quad \text{..............................(3)}.$$

Hence, finally,
$$\zeta = \left(-\frac{1}{w}\right)^{\frac{1}{2}} + \left(-\frac{1}{w} - 1\right)^{\frac{1}{2}} \quad \text{.............. (4)}.$$

For $\psi = 0$, and $0 > \phi > -1$, ζ is real; this corresponds to the portion *CA* of the stream-line. To find the breadth l of the lamina on the scale of our formulæ, we have, putting $\phi = -\phi'$,

$$l = 2\int_0^1 \frac{dx}{d\phi'} d\phi' = 2\int_0^1 \left\{\frac{1}{\phi'^{\frac{1}{2}}} + \left(\frac{1}{\phi'} - 1\right)^{\frac{1}{2}}\right\} d\phi' = 4 + \pi \quad \text{...(5).}$$

For the free portion *AI* of the stream-line, we have $\phi < -1$, and therefore, putting $\phi = -1 - s$,

$$\frac{dx}{ds} = \frac{1}{(1+s)^{\frac{1}{2}}}, \quad \frac{dy}{ds} = -\left(\frac{s}{1+s}\right)^{\frac{1}{2}} \quad \text{............(6).}$$

Hence, taking the origin at the centre of the lamina,

$$x = \tfrac{1}{2}\pi + 2(1+s)^{\frac{1}{2}}, \quad y = \{s(1+s)\}^{\frac{1}{2}} - \log\{s^{\frac{1}{2}} + (1+s)^{\frac{1}{2}}\},$$

or, putting $s = \tan^2\theta$,

$$x = \tfrac{1}{2}\pi + 2\sec\theta, \quad y = \tan\theta\sec\theta - \log\tan(\tfrac{1}{4}\pi + \tfrac{1}{2}\theta) \text{......(7).}$$

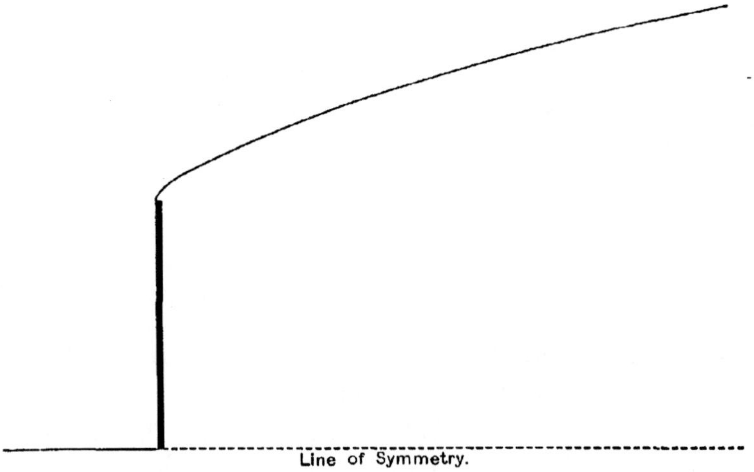

The excess of pressure at any point on the anterior face of the lamina is, by Art. 24 (7),

$$\tfrac{1}{2}\rho(1 - q^2) \quad \text{..........................(8),}$$

the constant being chosen so as to make this vanish at the surface of discontinuity. To find the resulting force on the lamina we must multiply by dx and integrate between the proper limits. Thus since, at the face of the lamina,

$$\frac{1}{q} = \frac{1}{\phi'^{\frac{1}{2}}} + \left(\frac{1}{\phi'} - 1\right)^{\frac{1}{2}}, \quad \frac{dx}{d\phi'} = \frac{1}{q},$$

we find

$$\rho\int_0^1 (1 - q^2)\frac{dx}{d\phi'}\,d\phi' = \rho\int_0^1\left(\frac{1}{q} - q\right)d\phi' = 2\rho\int_0^1\left(\frac{1}{\phi'} - 1\right)^{\frac{1}{2}}d\phi' = \pi\rho \quad \text{......(9)}.$$

This result has been obtained on the supposition of special units of length and time, or (if we choose so to regard the matter) of a special value (unity) of the general stream-velocity, and a special value $(4 + \pi)$ of the breadth of the lamina. It is evident from Art. 24 (7), and from the obvious geometrical similarity of the motion in all cases, that the resultant pressure (P_0, say) will vary directly as the square of the general velocity of the stream, and as the breadth of the lamina, so that for an arbitrary velocity q_0, and an arbitrary breadth l, the above result becomes

$$P_0 = \frac{\pi}{4 + \pi}\rho q_0^2 l \quad \text{......................(10)*},$$

or $\cdot 440\rho q_0^2 l$.

78. If the stream be *oblique* to the lamina, making an angle α, say, with its plane, the problem is altered in the manner indicated in the figures.

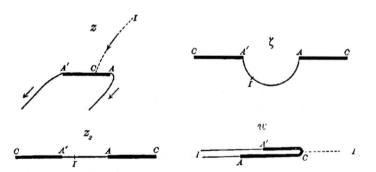

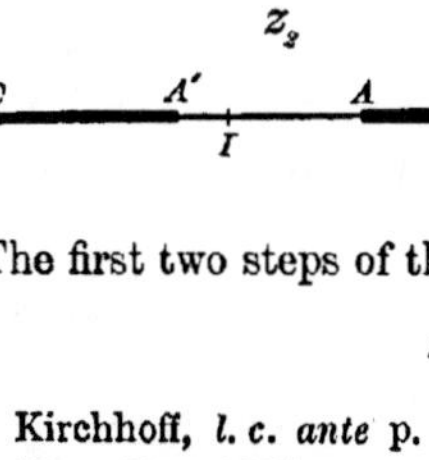

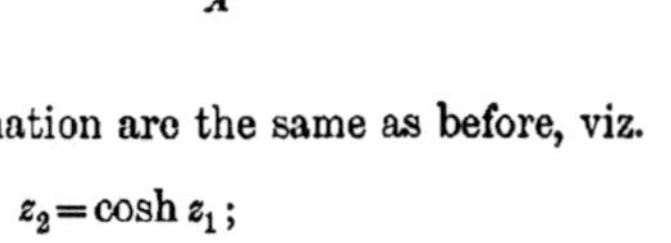

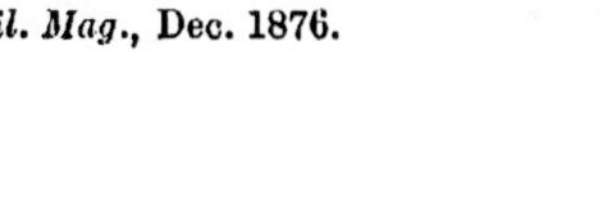

The first two steps of the transformation are the same as before, viz.

$$z_1 = \log \zeta, \qquad z_2 = \cosh z_1;$$

* Kirchhoff, *l. c. ante* p. 102; Lord Rayleigh, "On the Resistance of Fluids," *Phil. Mag.*, Dec. 1876.

and we note that for the point I which represents the parts of the stream-line $\psi=0$ for which $\phi=\pm\infty$, we now have

$$\zeta=e^{-i(\pi-\alpha)}, \qquad z_1=-(\pi-\alpha)i, \qquad z_2=-\cos\alpha.$$

The remaining step is then given by

$$(z_2+\cos\alpha)^2=-\frac{1}{w},$$

leading to

$$\zeta=-\cos\alpha+\left(-\frac{1}{w}\right)^{\frac{1}{2}}+\left\{\left(\frac{1}{(-w)^{\frac{1}{2}}}-\cos\alpha\right)^2-1\right\}^{\frac{1}{2}} \quad \text{.................(i)*.}$$

Along the surface of the lamina we have $\psi=0$ and ζ real, so that the corresponding values of ϕ range between the limits given by

$$\left(-\frac{1}{\phi}\right)^{\frac{1}{2}}-\cos\alpha=\pm 1.$$

The resultant pressure is to be found as in Art. 77 from the formula

$$\tfrac{1}{2}\rho\int(1-q^2)\,dx=\tfrac{1}{2}\rho\int\left(\frac{1}{q}-q\right)d\phi'=\rho\int\left\{\left(\frac{1}{\phi'^{\frac{1}{2}}}-\cos\alpha\right)^2-1\right\}^{\frac{1}{2}}d\phi'.$$

If we put

$$\frac{1}{\phi'^{\frac{1}{2}}}-\cos\alpha=\frac{1-\beta\cos\alpha}{\beta-\cos\alpha},$$

the limits of β are ±1, and the above expression becomes

$$\frac{2\rho}{\sin^3\alpha}\int_{-1}^{1}(1-\beta^2)^{\frac{1}{2}}\,d\beta=\frac{\pi}{\sin^3\alpha}\cdot\rho \quad \text{..........................(ii).}$$

The relation between x and β for any point of the lamina is given by

$$x=\int\frac{dx}{d\phi}\,d\phi=\int\left[-\cos\alpha+\frac{1}{\phi'^{\frac{1}{2}}}+\left\{\left(\frac{1}{\phi'^{\frac{1}{2}}}-\cos\alpha\right)^2-1\right\}^{\frac{1}{2}}\right]d\phi'$$

$$=\frac{2}{\sin^4\alpha}\int\{1-\beta\cos\alpha+\sin\alpha\,(1-\beta^2)^{\frac{1}{2}}\}\,d\beta$$

$$=\frac{1}{\sin^4\alpha}[2\beta+(1-\beta^2)\cos\alpha+\sin\alpha\,\{\beta\,(1-\beta^2)^{\frac{1}{2}}+\sin^{-1}\beta\}] \quad \text{.........(iii),}$$

the origin being chosen so that x shall have equal and opposite values when $\beta=\pm1$, *i.e.* it is taken at the centre of the lamina. The breadth is therefore, on the scale of our formulæ,

$$\frac{4+\pi\sin\alpha}{\sin^4\alpha} \quad \text{.................................... (iv).}$$

We infer from (ii) and (iv) that the resultant pressure (P_0) on a lamina of breadth l, inclined at an angle α to the general direction of a stream of velocity q_0, will be

$$P_0=\frac{\pi\sin\alpha}{4+\pi\sin\alpha}\,\rho q_0^2 l \quad \text{...................................(v).}$$

* The solution was carried thus far by Kirchhoff (*Crelle, l. c.*); the subsequent discussion is taken substantially from the paper by Lord Rayleigh.

To find the centre of pressure we take moments about the origin. Thus

$$\tfrac{1}{2}\rho\int(1-q^2)\,x\,dx=\tfrac{1}{2}\rho\int\left(\frac{1}{q}-q\right)x\,d\phi'$$

$$=\frac{2\rho}{\sin^3 a}\int_{-1}^{1}x(1-\beta^2)^{\frac{1}{2}}\,d\beta$$

$$=\frac{2\cos a}{\sin^7 a}\cdot\rho\int_{-1}^{1}(1-\beta^2)^{\frac{3}{2}}\,d\beta,$$

the remaining terms under the integral sign being odd functions of β and therefore contributing nothing to the final result. The value of the last integral is $\frac{3}{8}\pi$, so that the moment

$$=\frac{\pi}{\sin^3 a}\rho\times\frac{3\cos a}{4\sin^4 a}.$$

The first factor represents the total pressure; the abscissa $\bar{x}$ of the centre of pressure is therefore given by the second, or in terms of the breadth,

$$\bar{x}=\tfrac{3}{4}\cdot\frac{\cos a}{4+\pi\sin a}\cdot l \qquad\qquad \text{(vi)}.$$

This shews that the point in question is on the up-stream side of the centre. As a decreases from $\frac{1}{2}\pi$ to 0, $\bar{x}$ increases from 0 to $\frac{3}{16}l$. Hence if the lamina be free to turn about an axis in its plane coincident with the medial line, or parallel to this line at a distance of not more than $\frac{3}{16}$ of the breadth, the stable position will be that in which it is broadside on to the stream.

In the following table, derived from Lord Rayleigh's paper, the column I gives the excess of pressure on the anterior face, in terms of its value when $a=0$; whilst columns II and III give respectively the distances of the centre of pressure, and of the point where the stream divides, from the middle point of the lamina, expressed as fractions of the total breadth.

a	I	II	III
90°	1·000	·000	·000
70°	·965	·037	·232
50°	·854	·075	·402
30°	·641	·117	·483
20°	·481	·139	·496
10°	·273	·163	·500

The results contained in column I are in good agreement with some experiments by Vince (*Phil. Trans.* 1798).

79. An interesting variation of the problem of Art. 77 has been discussed by Bobyleff*. A stream is supposed to impinge symmetrically on a bent lamina whose section consists of two equal straight lines forming an angle.

If $2a$ be the angle, measured on the down-stream side, the boundaries of the plane of ζ can be transformed, so as to have the same shape as in the Art. cited, by the assumption

$$\zeta = C\zeta'^n,$$

provided C and n be determined so as to make $\zeta'=1$ when $\zeta=e^{-i(\frac{1}{2}\pi-a)}$, and $\zeta'=-1$ when $\zeta=e^{-i(\frac{1}{2}\pi+a)}$. This gives

$$C=e^{-i(\frac{1}{2}\pi-a)}, \qquad n=2a/\pi.$$

The problem is thus reduced to the former case, viz. we have

$$\zeta' = \left(-\frac{1}{w}\right)^{\frac{1}{2}} + \left(-\frac{1}{w}-1\right)^{\frac{1}{2}},$$

or

$$\zeta = e^{-i(\frac{1}{2}\pi-a)}\left\{\left(-\frac{1}{w}\right)^{\frac{1}{2}} + \left(-\frac{1}{w}-1\right)^{\frac{1}{2}}\right\}^n \text{ ....(i).}$$

Hence for $\psi=0$, and $0>\phi>-1$, we have, putting $\phi=-\phi'$ as before,

$$\frac{1}{q} = \text{mod. } \zeta = \left\{\frac{1}{\phi'^{\frac{1}{2}}} + \left(\frac{1}{\phi'}-1\right)^{\frac{1}{2}}\right\}^n \text{ ....(ii).}$$

The subsequent integrations are facilitated by putting $q=t^{\frac{1}{2}n}$, whence

$$\phi' = \frac{4t}{(1+t)^2}.$$

Thus

$$\int_0^1 \frac{1}{q}d\phi' = \left[\frac{\phi'}{q}\right]_0^1 + 2n\int_0^1 \frac{t^{-\frac{1}{2}n}}{(1+t)^2}dt = 1+n+n^2\int_0^1 \frac{t^{-\frac{1}{2}n}}{1+t}dt \text{.........(iii),}$$

$$\int_0^1 q\,d\phi' = \left[q\phi'\right]_0^1 - 2n\int_0^1 \frac{t^{\frac{1}{2}n}}{(1+t)^2}dt = 1+n-n^2\int_0^1 \frac{t^{\frac{1}{2}n-1}}{1+t}dt \text{...... (iv).}$$

We have here used the formulæ

$$\int_0^1 \frac{t^{-k}}{(1+t)^2}dt = \tfrac{1}{2}+k\int_0^1 \frac{t^{-k}}{1+t}dt,$$

$$\int_0^1 \frac{t^{k}}{(1+t)^2}dt = -\tfrac{1}{2}+k\int_0^1 \frac{t^{k-1}}{1+t}dt,$$

where $1>k>0$.

Since $q=d\phi'/ds$, where δs is an element of a stream-line, the breadth of either half of the lamina is given by (iii), viz. it is

$$1+\frac{2a}{\pi}+\frac{4a^2}{\pi^2}\int_0^1 \frac{t^{-a/\pi}}{1+t}dt \text{ .... (v).}$$

* *Journal of the Russian Physico-Chemical Society*, t. xiii. (1881); Wiedemann's *Beiblätter*, t. vi., p. 163.

The definite integral which occurs in this expression can be calculated from the formula

$$\int_0^1 \frac{t^{-k}}{1+t}\,dt = \frac{1}{(1-k)(2-k)} + \tfrac{1}{2}\Psi(1-\tfrac{1}{2}k) - \tfrac{1}{2}\Psi(\tfrac{1}{2}-\tfrac{1}{2}k) \quad \text{............(vi)},$$

where $\Psi(t)$, $=d/dt \,.\, \log \Pi(t)$, is the function introduced and tabulated by Gauss*.

The normal pressure on either half is, by the method of Art. 77,

$$= \tfrac{1}{2}\rho \int_0^1 \left(\frac{1}{q} - q\right) d\phi' = \tfrac{1}{2}\rho n^2 \int_0^\infty \frac{t^{-\frac{1}{2}n}}{1+t}\,dt$$

$$= \tfrac{1}{2}\rho n^2 \,.\, \frac{\pi}{\sin \frac{1}{2}n\pi}$$

$$= \rho \,.\, \frac{2a^2}{\pi \sin a}.$$

The resultant pressure in the direction of the stream is therefore

$$= \frac{4a^2}{\pi} \,.\, \rho \quad \text{.................................. (vii)}.$$

Hence, for any arbitrary velocity q_0 of the stream, and any breadth b of either half of the lamina, the resultant pressure is

$$P = \frac{4a^2}{\pi L} \,.\, \rho q_0^2 b \quad \text{................................(viii)},$$

where L stands for the numerical quantity (v).

For $a = \frac{1}{2}\pi$, we have $L = 2 + \frac{1}{2}\pi$, leading to the same result as in Art. 77 (10).

In the following table, taken (with a slight modification) from Bobyleff's paper, the second column gives the ratio P/P_0 of the resultant pressure to

a	P/P_0	$P/\rho q_0^2 b \sin a$	$P/P_0 \sin a$
10°	·039	·199	·227
20°	·140	·359	·409
30°	·278	·489	·555
40°	·433	·593	·674
45°	·512	·637	·724
50°	·589	·677	·769
60°	·733	·745	·846
70°	·854	·800	·909
80°	·945	·844	·959
90°	1·000	·879	1·000
100°	1·016	·907	1·031
110°	·995	·931	1·059
120°	·935	·950	1·079
130°	·840	·964	1·096
135°	·780	·970	1·103
140°	·713	·975	1·109
150°	·559	·984	1·119
160°	·385	·990	1·126
170°	·197	·996	1·132

* "Disquisitiones generales circa seriem infinitam," *Werke*, Göttingen, 1870—77, t. iii., p. 161.

that experienced by a plane strip of the same area. This ratio is a maximum when $a=100°$, about, the lamina being then concave on the up-stream side. In the third column the ratio of P to the distance ($2b \sin a$) between the edges of the lamina is compared with $\frac{1}{2}\rho q_0^2$. For values of a nearly equal to 180°, this ratio tends to the value unity, as we should expect, since the fluid within the acute angle is then nearly at rest, and the pressure-excess therefore practically equal to $\frac{1}{2}\rho q_0^2$. The last column gives the ratio of the resultant pressure to that experienced by a plane strip of breadth $2b \sin a$.

80. One remark, applicable to several of the foregoing investigations, ought not to be omitted here. It will appear at a later stage in our subject that surfaces of discontinuity are, as a rule, highly unstable. This instability may, however, be mitigated by viscosity; moreover it is possible, as urged by Lord Rayleigh, that in any case it may not seriously affect the character of the motion within some distance of the points on the rigid boundary at which the surfaces in question have their origin.

Flow in a Curved Stratum.

81. The theory developed in Arts. 59, 60, may be readily extended to the two-dimensional motion of a *curved* stratum of liquid, whose thickness is small compared with the radii of curvature. This question has been discussed, from the point of view of electric conduction, by Boltzmann*, Kirchhoff†, Töpler§, and others.

As in Art. 59, we take a fixed point A, and a variable point P, on the surface defining the form of the stratum, and denote by ψ the flux across any curve AP drawn on this surface. Then ψ is a function of the position of P, and by displacing P in any direction through a small distance δs, we find that the flux across the element δs is given by $d\psi/ds \,.\, \delta s$. The *velocity* perpendicular to this element will be $\delta\psi/h\delta s$, where h is the thickness of the stratum, not assumed as yet to be uniform.

If, further, the motion be irrotational, we shall have in addition a velocity-potential ϕ, and the equipotential curves $\phi=$ const. will cut the stream-lines $\psi=$ const. at right angles.

* *Wiener Sitzungsberichte*, t. lii., p. 214 (1865).

† *Berl. Monatsber.*, July 19, 1875; *Ges. Abh.*, p. 56.

§ *Pogg. Ann.*, t. clx., p. 375 (1877).

In the case of *uniform* thickness, to which we now proceed, it is convenient to write ψ for ψ/h, so that the velocity perpendicular to an element δs is now given indifferently by $d\psi/ds$ and $d\phi/dn$, δn being an element drawn at right angles to δs in the proper direction. The further relations are then exactly as in the plane problem; in particular the curves $\phi = \text{const.}$, $\psi = \text{const.}$, drawn for a series of values in arithmetic progression, the common difference being infinitely small and the same in each case, will divide the surface into elementary squares. For, by the orthogonal property, the elementary spaces in question are rectangles, and if δs_1, δs_2 be elements of a stream-line and an equipotential line, respectively, forming the sides of one of these rectangles, we have $d\psi/ds_2 = d\phi/ds_1$, whence $\delta s_1 = \delta s_2$, since by construction $\delta\psi = \delta\phi$.

Any problem of irrotational motion in a curved stratum (of uniform thickness) is therefore reduced by orthomorphic projection to the corresponding problem *in plano*. Thus for a spherical surface we may use, among an infinity of other methods, that of stereographic projection. As a simple example of this, we may take the case of a stratum of uniform depth covering the surface of a sphere with the exception of two circular islands (which may be of any size and in any relative position). It is evident that the only (two-dimensional) irrotational motion which can take place in the doubly-connected space occupied by the fluid is one in which the fluid circulates in opposite directions round the two islands, the cyclic constant being the same in each case. Since circles project into circles, the plane problem is that solved in Art. 64, 2°, viz. the stream-lines are a system of coaxal circles with real 'limiting points' (A, B, say), and the equipotential lines are the orthogonal system passing through A, B. Returning to the sphere, it follows from well-known theorems of stereographic projection that the stream-lines (including the contours of the two islands) are the circles in which the surface is cut by a system of planes passing through a fixed line, viz. the intersection of the tangent planes at the points corresponding to A and B, whilst the equipotential lines are the circles in which the sphere is cut by planes passing through these points*.

* This example is given by Kirchhoff, in the electrical interpretation, the problem considered being the distribution of current in a uniform spherical conducting sheet, the electrodes being situate at any two points A, B of the surface.

In any case of transformation by orthomorphic projection, whether the motion be irrotational or not, the velocity ($d\psi/dn$) is transformed in the inverse ratio of a linear element, and therefore the kinetic energies of the portions of the fluid occupying corresponding areas are equal (provided, of course, the density and the thickness be the same). In the same way the circulation ($\int d\psi/dn \,.\, ds$) in any circuit is unaltered by projection.

CHAPTER V.

IRROTATIONAL MOTION OF A LIQUID: PROBLEMS IN THREE DIMENSIONS.

82. Of the methods available for obtaining solutions of the equation

$$\nabla^2\phi = 0 \quad\quad\quad (1),$$

in three dimensions, the most important is that of Spherical Harmonics. This is especially suitable when the boundary conditions have relation to spherical or nearly spherical surfaces.

For a full account of this method we must refer to the special treatises*, but as the subject is very extensive, and has been treated from different points of view, it may be worth while to give a slight sketch, without formal proofs, or with mere indications of proofs, of such parts of it as are most important for our present purpose.

It is easily seen that since the operator ∇^2 is homogeneous with respect to x, y, z, the part of ϕ which is of any specified algebraic degree must satisfy (1) separately. Any such homogeneous solution of (1) is called a 'solid harmonic' of the algebraic degree in question. If ϕ_n be a solid harmonic of degree n, then if we write

$$\phi_n = r^n S_n \quad\quad\quad (2),$$

* Todhunter, *Functions of Laplace, &c.*, Cambridge, 1875. Ferrers, *Spherical Harmonics*, Cambridge, 1877. Heine, *Handbuch der Kugelfunctionen*, 2nd ed., Berlin, 1878. Thomson and Tait, *Natural Philosophy*, 2nd ed., Cambridge, 1879, t. i., pp. 171—218.

For the history of the subject see Todhunter, *History of the Theories of Attraction, &c.*, Cambridge, 1873, t. ii.

S_n will be a function of the direction (only) in which the point (x, y, z) lies with respect to the origin; in other words, a function of the position of the point in which the radius vector meets a unit sphere described with the origin as centre. It is therefore called a 'surface-harmonic' of order n.

To any solid harmonic ϕ_n of degree n corresponds another of degree $-n-1$, obtained by division by r^{2n+1}; *i.e.* $\phi = r^{-2n-1}\phi_n$ is also a solution of (1). Thus, corresponding to any surface harmonic S_n, we have the two solid harmonics $r^n S_n$ and $r^{-n-1} S_n$.

83. The most important case is when n is integral, and when the surface-harmonic S_n is further restricted to be finite over the unit sphere. In the form in which the theory (for this case) is presented by Thomson and Tait, and by Maxwell*, the primary solution of (1) is

$$\phi_{-1} = A/r \qquad (3).$$

This represents as we have seen (Art. 56) the velocity-potential due to a point-source at the origin. Since (1) is still satisfied when ϕ is differentiated with respect to x, y, or z, we derive a solution

$$\phi_{-2} = A\left(l\frac{d}{dx} + m\frac{d}{dy} + n\frac{d}{dz}\right)\frac{1}{r} \qquad (4).$$

This is the velocity-potential of a double-source at the origin, having its axis in the direction (l, m, n). The process can be continued, and the general type of solid harmonic obtainable in this way is

$$\phi_{-n-1} = A\frac{d^n}{dh_1 dh_2 \ldots dh_n}\frac{1}{r} \qquad (5),$$

where
$$\frac{d}{dh_s} = l_s\frac{d}{dx} + m_s\frac{d}{dy} + n_s\frac{d}{dz},$$

l_s, m_s, n_s being arbitrary direction-cosines.

This may be regarded as the velocity-potential of a certain configuration of simple sources about the origin, the dimensions of this system being small compared with r. To construct this system we premise that from any given system of sources we may

* *Electricity and Magnetism*, c. ix.

derive a system of higher order by first displacing it through a space $\frac{1}{2}h_s$ in the direction (l_s, m_s, n_s), and then superposing the *reversed* system, supposed displaced from its original position through a space $\frac{1}{2}h_s$ in the opposite direction. Thus, beginning with the case of a simple source O at the origin, a first application of the above process gives us two sources O_+, O_- equidistant from the origin, in opposite directions. The same process applied to the system O_+, O_- gives us four sources O_{++}, O_{-+}, O_{+-}, O_{--} at the corners of a parallelogram. The next step gives us eight sources at the corners of a parallelepiped, and so on. The velocity-potential, at a distance, due to an arrangement of 2^n sources obtained in this way, will be given by (5), where $A = m'h_1h_2...h_n$, m' being the strength of the original source at O. The formula becomes exact, for all distances r, when $h_1, h_2,...h_n$ are diminished, and m' increased, indefinitely, but so that A is finite.

The surface-harmonic corresponding to (5) is given by

$$S_n = Ar^{n+1}\frac{d^n}{dh_1 dh_2...dh_n}\frac{1}{r} \quad\text{..................}\quad (6),$$

and the complementary solid harmonic by

$$\phi_n = r^n S_n = r^{2n+1}\phi_{-n-1} \quad\text{..................}\quad (7).$$

By the method of 'inversion*,' applied to the above configuration of sources, it may be shewn that the solid harmonic (7) of positive degree n may be regarded as the velocity-potential due to a certain arrangement of 2^n simple sources at infinity.

The lines drawn from the origin in the various directions (l_s, m_s, n_s) are called the 'axes' of the solid harmonic (5) or (7), and the points in which these lines meet the unit sphere are called the 'poles' of the surface harmonic S_n. The formula (5) involves $2n+1$ arbitrary constants, viz. the angular co-ordinates (two for each) of the n poles, and the factor A. It can be shewn that this expression is equivalent to the most general form of surface-harmonic which is of integral order n and finite over the unit sphere†.

* Explained by Thomson and Tait, *Natural Philosophy*, Art. 515.

† Sylvester, *Phil. Mag.*, Oct. 1876.

84. In the original investigation of Laplace*, the equation $\nabla^2\phi = 0$ is first expressed in terms of spherical polar coordinates r, θ, ω, where

$$x = r\cos\theta, \quad y = r\sin\theta\cos\omega, \quad z = r\sin\theta\sin\omega.$$

The simplest way of effecting the transformation is to apply the theorem of Art. 37 (2) to the surface of a volume-element $r\delta\theta \,.\, r\sin\theta\delta\omega \,.\, \delta r$. Thus the difference of flux across the two faces perpendicular to r is

$$\frac{d}{dr}\left(\frac{d\phi}{dr} \,.\, r\delta\theta \,.\, r\sin\theta\delta\omega\right)\delta r.$$

Similarly for the two faces perpendicular to the meridian (ω=const.) we find

$$\frac{d}{d\theta}\left(\frac{d\phi}{rd\theta} \,.\, r\sin\theta\delta\omega \,.\, \delta r\right)\delta\theta,$$

and for the two faces perpendicular to a parallel of latitude (θ = const.)

$$\frac{d}{d\omega}\left(\frac{d\phi}{r\sin\theta d\omega} \,.\, r\delta\theta \,.\, \delta r\right)\delta\omega.$$

Hence, by addition,

$$\sin\theta\frac{d}{dr}\left(r^2\frac{d\phi}{dr}\right) + \frac{d}{d\theta}\left(\sin\theta\frac{d\phi}{d\theta}\right) + \frac{1}{\sin\theta}\frac{d^2\phi}{d\omega^2} = 0 \text{ ...(1).}$$

This might of course have been derived from Art. 82 (1) by the usual method of change of independent variables.

If we now assume that ϕ is homogeneous, of degree n, and put

$$\phi = r^n S_n,$$

we obtain

$$\frac{1}{\sin\theta}\frac{d}{d\theta}\left(\sin\theta\frac{dS_n}{d\theta}\right) + \frac{1}{\sin^2\theta}\frac{d^2 S_n}{d\omega^2} + n(n+1)S_n = 0 \text{ ...(2),}$$

which is the general differential equation of spherical surface-harmonics. Since the product $n(n+1)$ is unchanged in value when we write $-n-1$ for n, it appears that

$$\phi = r^{-n-1}S_n$$

will also be a solution of (1), as already stated.

* "Théorie de l'attraction des sphéroides et de la figure des planètes," *Mém. de l'Acad. roy. des Sciences*, 1782; *Oeuvres Complètes*, Paris, 1878..., t. x., p. 341; *Mécanique Céleste*, Livre 2me, c. ii.

85. In the case of symmetry about the axis of x, the term $d^2S_n/d\omega^2$ disappears, and putting $\cos\theta = \mu$ we get

$$\frac{d}{d\mu}\left\{(1-\mu^2)\frac{dS_n}{d\mu}\right\} + n(n+1)S_n = 0 \ldots\ldots\ldots\ldots(1),$$

the differential equation of 'zonal' harmonics*. This equation, containing only terms of two different dimensions in μ, is adapted for integration by series. We thus obtain

$$S_n = A\left\{1 - \frac{n(n+1)}{1.2}\mu^2 + \frac{(n-2)n(n+1)(n+3)}{1.2.3.4}\mu^4 - \ldots\right\}$$
$$+ B\left\{\mu - \frac{(n-1)(n+2)}{1.2.3}\mu^3 + \frac{(n-3)(n-1)(n+2)(n+4)}{1.2.3.4.5}\mu^5 - \ldots\right\}\ldots\ldots(2),$$

The series which here present themselves are of the kind called 'hypergeometric'; viz. if we write, after Gauss†,

$$F(\alpha,\beta,\gamma,x) = 1 + \frac{\alpha.\beta}{1.\gamma}x + \frac{\alpha.\alpha+1.\beta.\beta+1}{1.2.\gamma.\gamma+1}x^2 + \frac{\alpha.\alpha+1.\alpha+2.\beta.\beta+1.\beta+2}{1.2.3.\gamma.\gamma+1.\gamma+2}x^3 + \ldots(3),$$

we have

$$S_n = AF(-\tfrac{1}{2}n, \tfrac{1}{2}+\tfrac{1}{2}n, \tfrac{1}{2}, \mu^2) + B\mu F(\tfrac{1}{2}-\tfrac{1}{2}n, 1+\tfrac{1}{2}n, \tfrac{3}{2}, \mu^2)\ldots(4).$$

The series (3) is of course essentially convergent when x lies between 0 and 1; but when $x=1$ it is convergent if, and only if

$$\gamma - \alpha - \beta > 0.$$

In this case we have

$$F(\alpha,\beta,\gamma,1) = \frac{\Pi(\gamma-1).\Pi(\gamma-\alpha-\beta-1)}{\Pi(\gamma-\alpha-1).\Pi(\gamma-\beta-1)}\ldots\ldots\ldots\ldots\ldots\ldots(i),$$

where $\Pi(z)$ is in Gauss's notation the equivalent of Euler's $\Gamma(z+1)$.

The degree of divergence of the series (3) when

$$\gamma - \alpha - \beta < 0,$$

as x approaches the value 1, is given by the theorem

$$F(\alpha,\beta,\gamma,x) = (1-x)^{\gamma-\alpha-\beta}F(\gamma-\alpha,\gamma-\beta,\gamma,x)\ldots\ldots\ldots\ldots(ii)‡.$$

* So called by Thomson and Tait, because the nodal lines ($S_n=0$) divide the unit sphere into parallel belts.

† *l. c. ante* p. 113.

‡ Forsyth, *Differential Equations*, London, 1885, c. vi.

Since the latter series will now be convergent when $x=1$, we see that

$$F(\alpha, \beta, \gamma, x)$$

becomes divergent as $(1-x)^{\gamma-\alpha-\beta}$;

more precisely, for values of x infinitely nearly equal to unity, we have

$$F(\alpha, \beta, \gamma, x)=\frac{\Pi(\gamma-1).\Pi(\alpha+\beta-\gamma-1)}{\Pi(\alpha-1).\Pi(\beta-1)}(1-x)^{\gamma-\alpha-\beta} \qquad \text{(iii)},$$

ultimately.

For the critical case where $\gamma-\alpha-\beta=0$,

we may have recourse to the formula

$$\frac{d}{dx}F(\alpha, \beta, \gamma, x)=\frac{\alpha\beta}{\gamma}F(\alpha+1, \beta+1, \gamma+1, x) \qquad \text{(iv)},$$

which, with (ii), gives in the case supposed

$$\frac{d}{dx}F(\alpha, \beta, \gamma, x)=\frac{\alpha\beta}{\gamma}(1-x)^{-1}.F(\gamma-\alpha, \gamma-\beta, \gamma+1, x)$$

$$=\frac{\alpha\beta}{\gamma}(1-x)^{-1}.F(\alpha, \beta, \gamma+1, x) \qquad \text{(v)}.$$

The last factor is now convergent when $x=1$, so that $F(\alpha, \beta, \gamma, x)$ is ultimately divergent as $\log(1-x)$. More precisely we have, for values of x near this limit,

$$F(\alpha, \beta, \alpha+\beta, x)=\frac{\Pi(\alpha+\beta-1)}{\Pi(\alpha-1).\Pi(\beta-1)}\log\frac{1}{1-x} \qquad \text{(vi)}.$$

86. Of the two series which occur in the general expression Art. 85 (2) of a zonal harmonic, the former terminates when n is an even, and the latter when n is an odd integer. For other values of n both series are essentially convergent for values of μ between ± 1, but since in each case we have $\gamma-\alpha-\beta=0$, they diverge at the limits $\mu=\pm 1$, becoming infinite as $\log(1-\mu^2)$.

It follows that the terminating series corresponding to integral values of n are the only zonal surface-harmonics which are finite over the unit sphere. If we reverse the series we find that both these cases (n even, and n odd,) are included in the formula

$$P_n(\mu)=\frac{1.3.5...(2n-1)}{1.2.3...n}\left\{\mu^n-\frac{n(n-1)}{2(2n-1)}\mu^{n-2}\right.$$
$$\left.+\frac{n(n-1)(n-2)(n-3)}{2.4.(2n-1)(2n-3)}\mu^{n-4}-...\right\}...(1)^*,$$

* For n even this corresponds to $A=(-)^{\frac{1}{2}n}\dfrac{1.3.5...(n-1)}{2.4...n}$, $B=0$; whilst for n odd we have $A=0$, $B=(-)^{\frac{1}{2}(n-1)}\dfrac{3.5...n}{2.4...(n-1)}$. See Heine, t. i., pp. 12, 147.

where the constant factor has been adjusted so as to make $P_n(\mu) = 1$ for $\mu = 1$. The formula may also be written

$$P_n(\mu) = \frac{1}{2^n . n!} \frac{d^n}{d\mu^n} (\mu^2 - 1)^n \text{..............(2)*.}$$

The series (1) may otherwise be obtained by development of Art. 83 (6), which in the case of the zonal harmonic assumes the form

$$S_n = Ar^{n+1} \frac{d^n}{dx^n} \frac{1}{r} \text{ .... (3).}$$

As particular cases of (2) we have

$$P_0(\mu) = 1,$$
$$P_1(\mu) = \mu,$$
$$P_2(\mu) = \tfrac{1}{2}(3\mu^2 - 1),$$
$$P_3(\mu) = \tfrac{1}{2}(5\mu^3 - 3\mu).$$

The function $P_n(\mu)$ was first introduced into analysis by Legendre† as the coefficient of h^n in the expansion of

$$(1 - 2\mu h + h^2)^{-\frac{1}{2}}.$$

The connection of this with our present point of view is that if ϕ be the velocity-potential of a unit source on the axis of x at a distance c from the origin, we have, on Legendre's definition, for values of r less than c,

$$\phi = (c^2 - 2\mu cr + r^2)^{-\frac{1}{2}}$$
$$= \frac{1}{c} + P_1 \frac{r}{c^2} + P_2 \frac{r^2}{c^3} + \ldots \text{ .... (4).}$$

Each term in this expansion must separately satisfy $\nabla^2\phi = 0$, and therefore the coefficient P_n must be a solution of Art. 85 (1). Since P_n is obviously finite for all values of μ, and becomes equal to unity for $\mu = 1$, it must be identical with (1).

For values of r greater than c, the corresponding expansion is

$$\phi = \frac{1}{r} + P_1 \frac{c}{r^2} + P_2 \frac{c^2}{r^3} + \ldots \text{ ....(5).}$$

* The functions $P_1, P_2, \ldots P_7$ have been tabulated by Glaisher, for values of μ at intervals of ·01, *Brit. Ass. Reports*, 1879.

† "Sur l'attraction des sphéroides homogènes," *Mém. des Savans Étrangers*, t. x., 1785.

We can hence deduce expressions, which will be useful to us later, for the velocity-potential due to a *double-source* of unit strength, situate on the axis of x at a distance c from the origin, and having its axis pointing *from* the origin. This is evidently equal to $d\phi/dc$, where ϕ has either of the above forms; so that the required potential is, for $r < c$,

$$-\frac{1}{c^2} - 2P_1\frac{r}{c^3} - 3P_2\frac{r^2}{c^4} - \ldots\ldots\ldots\ldots\ldots\ldots (6),$$

and for $r > c$,

$$P_1\frac{1}{r^2} + 2P_2\frac{c}{r^3} + \ldots\ldots\ldots\ldots\ldots\ldots\ldots\ldots (7).$$

The remaining solution of Art. 85 (1), in the case of n integral, can be put into the more compact form*

$$Q_n(\mu) = \tfrac{1}{2}P_n(\mu)\log\frac{1+\mu}{1-\mu} - Z_n \ldots\ldots\ldots\ldots\ldots (8),$$

where

$$Z_n = \frac{2n-1}{1\,.\,n}P_{n-1} + \frac{2n-5}{3(n-1)}P_{n-3} + \ldots\ldots\ldots\ldots (9).$$

This function $Q_n(\mu)$ is sometimes called the zonal harmonic 'of the second kind.'

Thus

$$Q_0(\mu) = \tfrac{1}{2}\log\frac{1+\mu}{1-\mu},$$

$$Q_1(\mu) = \tfrac{1}{2}\mu\log\frac{1+\mu}{1-\mu} - 1,$$

$$Q_2(\mu) = \tfrac{1}{4}(3\mu^2-1)\log\frac{1+\mu}{1-\mu} - \tfrac{3}{2}\mu,$$

$$Q_3(\mu) = \tfrac{1}{4}(5\mu^3-3\mu)\log\frac{1+\mu}{1-\mu} - \tfrac{5}{2}\mu^2 + \tfrac{2}{3}.$$

* This is equivalent to Art. 84 (4) with, for n even, $A=0$, $B=(-)^{\frac{1}{2}n}\dfrac{2\,.\,4\ldots n}{1\,.\,3\ldots(n-1)}$; whilst for n odd we have $A=(-)^{\frac{1}{2}(n+1)}\dfrac{2\,.\,4\ldots(n-1)}{3\,.\,5\ldots n}$, $B=0$. See Heine, t. i., pp. 141, 147.

87. When we abandon the restriction as to symmetry about the axis of x, we may suppose S_n, if a finite and single-valued function of ω, to be expanded in a series of terms varying as $\cos s\omega$ and $\sin s\omega$ respectively. If this expansion is to apply to the whole sphere (*i.e.* from $\omega = 0$ to $\omega = 2\pi$), we may further (by Fourier's theorem) suppose the values of s to be integral. The differential equation satisfied by any such term is

$$\frac{d}{d\mu}\left\{(1-\mu^2)\frac{dS_n}{d\mu}\right\} + \left\{n(n+1) - \frac{s^2}{1-\mu^2}\right\} S_n = 0 \;\ldots\ldots(1).$$

If we put

$$S_n = (1-\mu^2)^{\frac{1}{2}s}\, v,$$

this takes the form

$$(1-\mu^2)\frac{d^2v}{d\mu^2} - 2(s+1)\mu\frac{dv}{d\mu} + (n-s)(n+s+1)\,v = 0,$$

which is suitable for integration by series. We thus obtain

$$\begin{aligned} S_n = A(1-\mu^2)^{\frac{1}{2}s}\Big\{1 &- \frac{(n-s)(n+s+1)}{1.2}\mu^2 \\ &+ \frac{(n-s-2)(n-s)(n+s+1)(n+s+3)}{1.2.3.4}\mu^4 - \ldots\Big\} \\ + B(1-\mu^2)^{\frac{1}{2}s}\Big\{\mu &- \frac{(n-s-1)(n+s+2)}{1.2.3}\mu^3 \\ &+ \frac{(n-s-3)(n-s-1)(n+s+2)(n+s+4)}{1.2.3.4.5}\mu^5 - \ldots\Big\} \;\ldots\ldots(2), \end{aligned}$$

the factor $\cos s\omega$ or $\sin s\omega$ being for the moment omitted. In the hypergeometric notation this may be written

$$\begin{aligned} S_n = (1-\mu^2)^{\frac{1}{2}s}\{&AF(\tfrac{1}{2}s - \tfrac{1}{2}n,\ \tfrac{1}{2} + \tfrac{1}{2}s + \tfrac{1}{2}n,\ \tfrac{1}{2},\ \mu^2) \\ &+ B\mu F(\tfrac{1}{2} + \tfrac{1}{2}s - \tfrac{1}{2}n,\ 1 + \tfrac{1}{2}s + \tfrac{1}{2}n,\ \tfrac{3}{2},\ \mu^2)\} \;\ldots\ldots(3). \end{aligned}$$

These expressions converge when $\mu^2 < 1$, but since in each case we have

$$\gamma - \alpha - \beta = -s,$$

the series become infinite as $(1-\mu^2)^{-s}$ at the limits $\mu = \pm 1$, unless they terminate*. The former series terminates when $n - s$ is an even, and the latter when it is an odd integer. By reversing the

* Lord Rayleigh, *Theory of Sound*, London, 1877, Art. 338.

series we can express both these finite solutions by the single formula

$$T_n^s(\mu)=\frac{(2n)!}{2^n(n-s)!\,n!}(1-\mu^2)^{\frac{1}{2}s}\left\{\mu^{n-s}-\frac{(n-s)(n-s-1)}{2.(2n-1)}\mu^{n-s-2}\right.$$

$$\left.+\frac{(n-s)(n-s-1)(n-s-2)(n-s-3)}{2.4.(2n-1)(2n-3)}\mu^{n-s-4}-\ldots\right\}\ldots\ldots(4).$$

On comparison with Art. 86 (1) we find that

$$T_n^s(\mu)=(1-\mu^2)^{\frac{1}{2}s}\frac{d^sP_n(\mu)}{d\mu^s}\ \ldots\ldots\ldots\ldots\ (5).$$

That this is a solution of (1) may of course be verified independently.

Collecting our results we learn that a surface-harmonic which is finite over the unit sphere is necessarily of integral order, and is further expressible, if n denote the order, in the form

$$S_n=A_0P_n(\mu)+\Sigma_{s=1}^{s=n}(A_s\cos s\omega+B_s\sin s\omega)\,T_n^s(\mu)\ldots(6),$$

containing $2n+1$ arbitrary constants. The terms of this involving ω are called 'tesseral' harmonics, with the exception of the last two, which are given by the formula

$$(1-\mu^2)^{\frac{1}{2}n}(A_n\cos n\omega+B_n\sin n\omega),$$

and are called 'sectorial' harmonics; the names being suggested by the forms of the compartments into which the unit sphere is divided by the nodal lines $S_n=0$.

The formula for the tesseral harmonic of rank s may be obtained otherwise from the general expression (6) of Art. 83 by making $n-s$ out of the n poles of the harmonic coincide at the point $\theta=0$ of the sphere, and distributing the remaining s poles evenly round the equatorial circle $\theta=\frac{1}{2}\pi$.

The remaining solution of (1), in the case of n integral may be put in the form

$$S_n=(A_s\cos s\omega+B_s\sin s\omega)\,U_n^s(\mu)\ \ldots\ldots\ldots\ldots\ (7),$$

where $$U_n^s(\mu)=(1-\mu^2)^{\frac{1}{2}s}\frac{d^sQ_n(\mu)}{d\mu^s}\ \ldots\ldots\ldots\ldots\ldots\ldots(8)^*.$$

This is sometimes called a tesseral harmonic 'of the second kind.'

* A table of the functions $Q_n(\mu)$, $U_n^s(\mu)$, for various values of n and s, has been given by Bryan, *Proc. Camb. Phil. Soc.*, t. vi., p. 297.

88. Two surface-harmonics S, S' are said to be 'conjugate' when

$$\iint SS'd\varpi = 0 \quad\text{......................(1)},$$

where $\delta\varpi$ is an element of surface of the unit sphere, and the integration extends over this sphere.

It may be shewn that any two surface-harmonics, of different orders, which are finite over the unit sphere, are conjugate, and also that the $2n+1$ harmonics of any given order n, of the zonal, tesseral, and sectorial types specified in Arts. 86, 87 are all mutually conjugate. It will appear, later, that the conjugate property is of great importance in the physical applications of the subject.

Since $\delta\varpi = \sin\theta\delta\theta\delta\omega = -\delta\mu\delta\omega$, we have, as particular cases of this theorem,

$$\int_{-1}^{1} P_m(\mu)\, d\mu = 0 \quad\text{..........................(2)},$$

$$\int_{-1}^{1} P_m(\mu) \,.\, P_n(\mu)\, d\mu = 0 \quad\text{.................. (3)},$$

and

$$\int_{-1}^{1} T_m^s(\mu) \,.\, T_n^s(\mu)\, d\mu = 0 \quad\text{.................. (4)},$$

provided m, n are unequal.

For $m = n$, it may be shewn that

$$\int_{-1}^{1} \{P_n(\mu)\}^2\, d\mu = \frac{2}{2n+1} \quad\text{..................(5)},$$

$$\int_{-1}^{1} \{T_n^s(\mu)\}^2\, d\mu = \frac{(n+s)!}{(n-s)!}\,\frac{2}{2n+1} \quad\text{......(6)*}.$$

Finally, we may quote the theorem that any arbitrary function of the position of a point on the unit sphere can be expanded in a series of surface-harmonics, obtained by giving n all integral values from 0 to ∞, in Art. 87 (6). The formulæ (5) and (6) are useful in determining the coefficients in this expansion. For the analytical proof of the theorem we must refer to the special treatises; the physical grounds for assuming the possibility of this and other similar expansions will appear, incidentally, in connection with various problems.

89. As a first application of the foregoing theory let us suppose that an arbitrary distribution of impulsive pressure is applied to the surface of a spherical mass of fluid initially at rest.

* Ferrers, p. 86.

This is equivalent to prescribing an arbitrary value of ϕ over the surface; the value of ϕ in the interior is thence determinate, by Art. 40. To find it, we may suppose the given surface value to be expanded, in accordance with the theorem quoted in Art. 88, in a series of surface-harmonics of integral order, thus

$$\phi = S_0 + S_1 + S_2 + \ldots + S_n + \ldots\ldots\ldots\ldots\ldots\ldots (1).$$

The required value is then

$$\phi = S_0 + \frac{r}{a} S_1 + \frac{r^2}{a^2} S_2 + \ldots + \frac{r^n}{a^n} S_n + \ldots\ldots\ldots\ldots (2),$$

for this satisfies $\nabla^2\phi = 0$, and assumes the prescribed form (1) when $r = a$, the radius of the sphere.

The corresponding solution for the case of a prescribed value of ϕ over the surface of a spherical cavity in an infinite mass of liquid initially at rest is evidently

$$\phi = \frac{a}{r} S_0 + \frac{a^2}{r^2} S_1 + \frac{a^3}{r^3} S_2 + \ldots + \frac{a^{n+1}}{r^{n+1}} S_n + \ldots\ldots\ldots\ldots (3).$$

Combining these two results we get the case of an infinite mass of fluid whose continuity is interrupted by an infinitely thin vacuous stratum, of spherical form, within which an arbitrary impulsive pressure is applied. The values (2) and (3) of ϕ are of course continuous at the stratum, but the values of the normal velocity are discontinuous, viz. we have, for the internal fluid,

$$\frac{d\phi}{dr} = \Sigma n S_n/a.$$

and for the external fluid

$$\frac{d\phi}{dr} = -\Sigma (n+1) S_n/a.$$

The motion, whether internal or external, is therefore that due to a distribution of simple sources with surface-density

$$\frac{1}{4\pi} \Sigma (2n+1) \frac{S_n}{a} \ldots\ldots\ldots\ldots\ldots\ldots\ldots\ldots (4)$$

over the sphere. See Art. 58.

90. Let us next suppose that, instead of the impulsive pressure, it is the normal velocity which is prescribed over the spherical surface; thus

$$\frac{d\phi}{dr} = S_1 + S_2 + \ldots + S_n + \ldots\ldots\ldots\ldots\ldots (1),$$

the term of zero order being necessarily absent, since we must have

$$\iint \frac{d\phi}{dr}\, d\varpi = 0 \quad\text{..........................(2)},$$

on account of the constancy of volume of the included mass.

The value of ϕ for the internal space is of the form

$$\phi = A_1 r S_1 + A_2 r^2 S_2 + \ldots + A_n r^n S_n + \ldots \quad\text{......(3)},$$

for this is finite and continuous, and satisfies $\nabla^2\phi = 0$, and the constants can be determined so as to make $d\phi/dr$ assume the given surface-value (1); viz. we have $nA_n a^{n-1} = 1$. The required solution is therefore

$$\phi = a\Sigma \frac{1}{n} \frac{r^n}{a^n} S_n \quad\text{........................(4)}.$$

The corresponding solution for the external space is found in like manner to be

$$\phi = -a\Sigma \frac{1}{n+1} \frac{a^{n+1}}{r^{n+1}} S_n \quad\text{..................(5)}.$$

The two solutions, taken together, give the motion produced in an infinite mass of liquid which is divided into two portions by a thin spherical membrane, when a prescribed normal velocity is given to every point of the membrane, subject to the condition (2).

The value of ϕ changes from $a\Sigma S_n/n$ to $-a\Sigma S_n/(n+1)$, as we cross the membrane, so that the *tangential* velocity is now discontinuous. The motion, whether inside or outside, is that due to a *double-sheet* of density

$$-\frac{1}{4\pi} a\Sigma \frac{2n+1}{n(n+1)} S_n.$$

See Art. 58.

The kinetic energy of the internal fluid is given by the formula (4) of Art. 44, viz.

$$2T = \rho \iint \phi \frac{d\phi}{dr}\, dS = \rho a^3 \Sigma \frac{1}{n} \iint S_n^2\, d\varpi \quad\text{...........(6)},$$

the parts of the integral which involve products of surface-harmonics of different orders disappearing in virtue of the conjugate property of Art. 88.

For the external fluid we have

$$2T = -\rho \iint \phi \frac{d\phi}{dr} dS = \rho a^3 \Sigma \frac{1}{n+1} \iint S_n^2 \, d\varpi \text{ ...... (7).}$$

91. A particular, but very important, case of the problem of the preceding Article is that of the motion of a solid sphere in an infinite mass of liquid which is at rest at infinity. If we take the origin at the centre of the sphere, and the axis of x in the direction of motion, the normal velocity at the surface is $\mathbf{u}x/r$, $= \mathbf{u}\cos\theta$, where $\mathbf{u}$ is the velocity of the centre. Hence the conditions to determine ϕ are (1°) that we must have $\nabla^2\phi = 0$ everywhere, (2°) that the space-derivatives of ϕ must vanish at infinity, and (3°) that at the surface of the sphere ($r = a$), we must have

$$-\frac{d\phi}{dr} = \mathbf{u}\cos\theta \text{ .... (1).}$$

The form of this suggests at once the zonal harmonic of the first order; we therefore assume

$$\phi = A \frac{d}{dx} \frac{1}{r} = -A \frac{\cos\theta}{r^2}.$$

The condition (1) gives $-2A/a^3 = \mathbf{u}$, so that the required solution is

$$\phi = \tfrac{1}{2}\mathbf{u} \frac{a^3}{r^2} \cos\theta \text{ .... (2)*.}$$

It appears on comparison with Art. 56 (4) that the motion of the fluid is the same as would be produced by a *double-source* of strength $\frac{1}{2}\mathbf{u}a^3$, situate at the centre of the sphere. For the forms of the stream-lines see p. 137.

To find the energy of the fluid motion we have

$$2T = -\rho \iint \phi \frac{d\phi}{dr} dS = \tfrac{1}{2}\rho a \mathbf{u}^2 \int_0^\pi \cos^2\theta \, . \, 2\pi a \sin\theta \, . \, a d\theta$$

$$= \tfrac{2}{3}\pi\rho a^3 \mathbf{u}^2 = \mathbf{m}'\mathbf{u}^2 \text{ .... (3),}$$

if $\mathbf{m}' = \frac{2}{3}\pi\rho a^3$. It appears, exactly as in Art. 68, that the effect of the fluid pressure is equivalent simply to an addition to the *inertia*

* Stokes, "On some cases of Fluid Motion," *Camb. Trans.* t. viii. (1843); *Math. and Phys. Papers*, t. i., p. 41.

Dirichlet, "Ueber einige Fälle in welchen sich die Bewegung eines festen Körpers in einem incompressibeln flüssigen Medium theoretisch bestimmen lässt," *Berl. Monatsber.*, 1852.

of the solid, the amount of the increase being now *half* the mass of the fluid displaced*.

Thus in the case of rectilinear motion of the sphere, if no external forces act on the fluid, the resultant pressure is equivalent to a force

$$-\mathbf{m}'\frac{d\mathbf{u}}{dt} \qquad\qquad (4),$$

in the direction of motion, vanishing when $\mathbf{u}$ is constant. Hence if the sphere be set in motion and left to itself, it will continue to move in a straight line with constant velocity.

The behaviour of a solid projected in an actual fluid is of course quite different; a continual application of force is necessary to maintain the motion, and if this be not supplied the solid is gradually brought to rest. It must be remembered however, in making this comparison, that in a 'perfect' fluid there is no dissipation of energy, and that if, further, the fluid be incompressible, the solid cannot lose its kinetic energy by transfer to the fluid, since, as we have seen in Chapter III., the motion of the fluid is entirely determined by that of the solid, and therefore ceases with it.

If we wish to verify the preceding results by direct calculation from the formula

$$\frac{p}{\rho}=\frac{d\phi}{dt}-\tfrac{1}{2}q^2+F(t) \qquad\qquad \text{(i)},$$

we must remember, as in Art. 68, that the origin is in motion, and that the values of r and θ for a fixed point of space are therefore increasing at the rates $-\mathbf{u}\cos\theta$, and $\mathbf{u}\sin\theta/r$, respectively. We thus find, for $r=a$,

$$\frac{p}{\rho}=\tfrac{1}{2}a\frac{d\mathbf{u}}{dt}\cos\theta+\tfrac{9}{16}\mathbf{u}^2\cos 2\theta-\tfrac{1}{16}\mathbf{u}^2+F(t) \qquad\qquad \text{(ii)}.$$

The last three terms are the same for surface-elements in the positions θ and $\pi-\theta$; so that, when $\mathbf{u}$ is constant, the pressures on the various elements of the anterior half of the sphere are balanced by equal pressures on the corresponding elements of the posterior half. But when the motion of the sphere is being accelerated there is an excess of pressure on the anterior, and a defect of pressure on the posterior half. The reverse holds when the motion is being retarded. The resultant effect in the direction of motion is

$$-\int_0^\pi 2\pi a\sin\theta \,.\, ad\theta \,.\, p\cos\theta,$$

which is readily found to be equal to $-\tfrac{2}{3}\pi\rho a^3\, d\mathbf{u}/dt$, as before.

* Green, "On the Vibration of Pendulums in Fluid Media," *Edin. Trans.*, 1833; *Math. Papers*, p. 322. Stokes, *l. c.*

92. The same method can be applied to find the motion produced in a liquid contained between a solid sphere and a fixed concentric spherical boundary, when the sphere is moving with given velocity **u**.

The centre of the sphere being taken as origin, it is evident, since the space occupied by the fluid is limited both externally and internally, that solid harmonics of both positive and negative degrees are admissible; they are in fact required, in order to satisfy the boundary conditions, which are

$$-d\phi/dr = \mathbf{u}\cos\theta,$$

for $r = a$, the radius of the sphere, and

$$d\phi/dr = 0,$$

for $r = b$, the radius of the external boundary, the axis of x being as before in the direction of motion.

We therefore assume

$$\phi = \left(Ar + \frac{B}{r^2}\right)\cos\theta \text{ .... (1)},$$

and the conditions in question give

$$A - \frac{2B}{a^3} = -\mathbf{u}, \quad A - \frac{2B}{b^3} = 0,$$

whence $$A = \frac{a^3}{b^3 - a^3}\mathbf{u}, \quad B = \tfrac{1}{2}\frac{a^3b^3}{b^3 - a^3}\mathbf{u} \text{ .... (2)}.$$

The kinetic energy of the fluid motion is given by

$$2T = -\rho\iint \phi\frac{d\phi}{dr}dS,$$

the integration extending over the inner spherical surface, since at the outer we have $d\phi/dr = 0$. We thus obtain

$$2T = \tfrac{2}{3}\pi\frac{b^3 + 2a^3}{b^3 - a^3}\rho a^3\mathbf{u}^2 \text{ ....(3)},$$

where $\mathbf{m}'$ stands for $\frac{4}{3}\pi\rho a^3$, as before. It appears that the effective addition to the inertia of the sphere is now

$$\tfrac{2}{3}\pi\frac{b^3 + 2a^3}{b^3 - a^3}\rho a^3\mathbf{u}^2 \text{ ....(4)*}.$$

* Stokes, *l. c. ante* p. 130.

As b diminishes from ∞ to a, this increases continually from $\frac{2}{3}\pi\rho a^3$ to ∞, in accordance with Lord Kelvin's minimum theorem (Art. 45). In other words, the introduction of a rigid spherical partition in an infinite mass of liquid acts as a constraint increasing the kinetic energy for a given velocity, and so virtually increasing the inertia of the system.

93. In all cases where the motion of a liquid takes place in a series of planes passing through a common line, and is the same in each such plane, there exists a stream-function analogous in some of its properties to the two-dimensional stream-function of the last Chapter. If in any plane through the axis of symmetry we take two points A and P, of which A is arbitrary, but fixed, while P is variable, then considering the annular surface generated by any line AP, it is plain that the flux across this surface is a function of the position of P. Denoting this function by $2\pi\psi$, and taking the axis of x to coincide with that of symmetry, we may say that ψ is a function of x and ϖ, where x is the abscissa of P, and ϖ, $= (y^2 + z^2)^{\frac{1}{2}}$, is its distance from the axis. The curves $\psi = \text{const.}$ are evidently stream-lines.

If P' be a point infinitely near to P in a meridian plane, it follows from the above definition that the velocity normal to PP' is equal to

$$\frac{2\pi d\psi}{2\pi\varpi \,.\, PP'},$$

whence, taking PP' parallel first to ϖ and then to x,

$$u = -\frac{1}{\varpi}\frac{d\psi}{d\varpi}, \quad v = \frac{1}{\varpi}\frac{d\psi}{dx} \quad\text{..................}\quad (1),$$

where u and v are the components of fluid velocity in the directions of x and ϖ respectively, the convention as to sign being similar to that of Art. 59.

These kinematical relations may also be inferred from the form which the equation of continuity takes under the present circumstances. If we express that the total flux into the annular space generated by the revolution of an elementary rectangle $\delta x \delta\varpi$ is zero, we find

$$\frac{d}{dx}(u \,.\, 2\pi\varpi\delta\varpi)\,\delta x + \frac{d}{d\varpi}(v \,.\, 2\pi\varpi\delta x)\,\delta\varpi = 0,$$

or $$\frac{d}{dx}(\varpi u) + \frac{d}{d\varpi}(\varpi v) = 0 \quad\ldots\ldots\ldots\ldots\ldots\ldots (2),$$

which shews that $$\varpi v \,.\, dx - \varpi u \,.\, d\varpi$$

is an exact differential. Denoting this by $d\psi$ we obtain the relations (1)*.

So far the motion has not been assumed to be irrotational; the condition that it should be so is

$$\frac{dv}{dx} - \frac{du}{d\varpi} = 0,$$

which leads to

$$\frac{d^2\psi}{dx^2} + \frac{d^2\psi}{d\varpi^2} - \frac{1}{\varpi}\frac{d\psi}{d\varpi} = 0 \quad\ldots\ldots\ldots\ldots\ldots\ldots (3).$$

The differential equation of ϕ is obtained by writing

$$u = -\frac{d\phi}{dx}, \quad v = -\frac{d\phi}{d\varpi}$$

in (2), viz. it is $$\frac{d^2\phi}{dx^2} + \frac{d^2\phi}{d\varpi^2} + \frac{1}{\varpi}\frac{d\phi}{d\varpi} = 0 \quad\ldots\ldots\ldots\ldots\ldots\ldots (4).$$

It appears that the functions ϕ and ψ are not now (as they were in Art. 62) interchangeable. They are, indeed, of different dimensions.

The kinetic energy of the liquid contained in any region bounded by surfaces of revolution about the axis is given by

$$\begin{aligned} 2T &= -\rho \iint \phi \frac{d\phi}{dn} dS \\ &= \rho \int \phi \frac{d\psi}{\varpi ds} \,.\, 2\pi\varpi ds \\ &= 2\pi\rho \int \phi d\psi \quad\ldots\ldots\ldots\ldots\ldots\ldots (5), \end{aligned}$$

δs denoting an element of the meridian section of the bounding surfaces, and the integration extending round the various parts of this section, in the proper directions. Compare Art. 61.

* The stream-function for the case of symmetry about an axis was introduced in this manner by Stokes, "On the Steady Motion of Incompressible Fluids," *Camb. Trans.*, t. vii. (1842); *Math. and Phys. Papers*, t. i., p. 14. Its analytical theory has been treated very fully by Sampson, "On Stokes' Current-Function," *Phil. Trans.* A., 1891.

94. The velocity-potential due to a unit source at the origin is

$$\phi = 1/r \quad\text{..............................(1).}$$

The flux through any closed curve is in this case numerically equal to the solid angle which the curve subtends at the origin. Hence for a circle with Ox as axis, whose radius subtends an angle θ at O, we have, attending to the sign,

$$2\pi\psi = -2\pi(1 - \cos\theta).$$

Omitting the constant term we have

$$\psi = \frac{x}{r} = \frac{dr}{dx} \quad\text{..............................(2).}$$

The solutions corresponding to any number of simple sources situate at various points of the axis of x may evidently be superposed; thus for the double-source

$$\phi = -\frac{d}{dx}\frac{1}{r} = \frac{\cos\theta}{r^2} \quad\text{.................. (3),}$$

we have

$$\psi = -\frac{d^2r}{dx^2} = -\frac{\varpi^2}{r^3} = -\frac{\sin^2\theta}{r} \quad\text{.............. (4).}$$

And, generally, to the zonal solid harmonic of degree $-n-1$, viz. to

$$\phi = A\frac{d^n}{dx^n}\frac{1}{r} \quad\text{........................(5),}$$

corresponds

$$\psi = A\frac{d^{n+1}r}{dx^{n+1}} \quad\text{..........................(6)*.}$$

A more general formula, applicable to harmonics of any degree, fractional or not, may be obtained as follows. Using spherical polar coordinates r, θ, the component velocities along r, and perpendicular to r in the plane of the meridian, are found by making the linear element PP' of Art. 93 coincide successively with $r\delta\theta$ and δr, respectively, viz. they are

$$-\frac{1}{r\sin\theta}\frac{d\psi}{rd\theta}, \qquad \frac{1}{r\sin\theta}\frac{d\psi}{dr} \quad\text{...............(7).}$$

* Stefan, "Ueber die Kraftlinien eines um eine Axe symmetrischen Feldes," *Wied. Ann.*, t. xvii. (1882).

Hence in the case of irrotational motion we have

$$\frac{d\psi}{\sin\theta d\theta} = r^2 \frac{d\phi}{dr}, \quad \frac{d\psi}{dr} = -\sin\theta \frac{d\phi}{d\theta} \text{ .... } (8).$$

Thus if

$$\phi = r^n S_n \text{..............................} (9),$$

where S_n is any surface-harmonic symmetrical about the axis, we have, putting $\mu = \cos\theta$,

$$\frac{d\psi}{d\mu} = -nr^{n+1} S_n, \quad \frac{d\psi}{dr} = r^n (1-\mu^2) \frac{dS_n}{d\mu}.$$

The latter equation gives

$$\psi = \frac{1}{n+1} r^{n+1} (1-\mu^2) \frac{dS_n}{d\mu} \text{ .... } (10),$$

which must necessarily also satisfy the former; this is readily verified by means of Art. 85 (1).

Thus in the case of the zonal harmonic P_n, we have as corresponding values

$$\phi = r^n P_n(\mu), \quad \psi = \frac{1}{n+1} r^{n+1} (1-\mu^2) \frac{dP_n}{d\mu} \text{ ...... } (11),$$

and

$$\phi = r^{-n-1} P_n(\mu), \quad \psi = -\frac{1}{n} r^{-n} (1-\mu^2) \frac{dP_n}{d\mu} \text{ ...... } (12),$$

of which the latter must be equivalent to (5) and (6). The same relations hold of course with regard to the zonal harmonic of the second kind, Q_n.

95. We saw in Art. 91 that the motion produced by a solid sphere in an infinite mass of liquid was that due to a double-source at the centre. Comparing the formulæ there given with Art. 94 (4), it appears that the stream-function due to the sphere is

$$\psi = -\tfrac{1}{2}\mathrm{u} \frac{a^3}{r} \sin^2\theta \text{........................} (1).$$

The forms of the stream-lines corresponding to a number of equidistant values of ψ are shewn on the opposite page. The stream-lines *relative to the sphere* are figured in the diagram near the end of Chapter VII.

Again, the stream-function due to two double-sources having their axes oppositely directed along the axis of x, will be of the form

$$\psi = \frac{A\varpi^2}{r_1^3} - \frac{B\varpi^2}{r_2^3} \quad\text{.........................(2)},$$

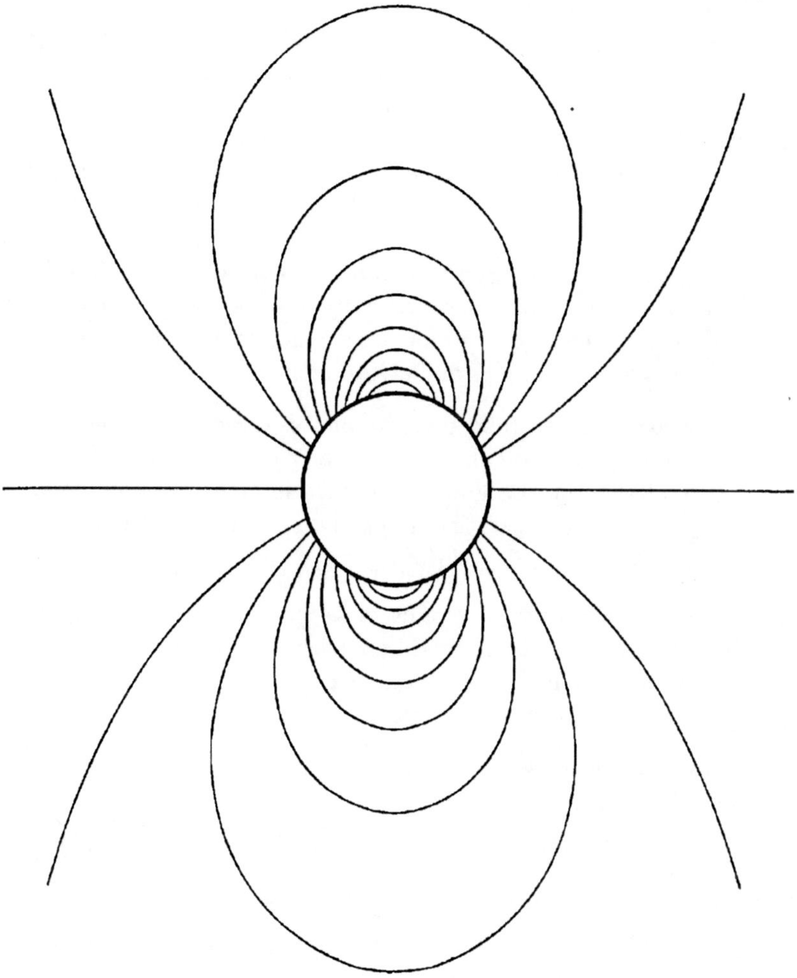

where r_1, r_2 denote the distances of any point from the positions, P_1 and P_2, say, of the two sources. At the stream-surface $\psi = 0$ we have

$$r_1/r_2 = (A/B)^{\frac{1}{3}},$$

i.e. the surface is a sphere in relation to which P_1 and P_2 are inverse points. If O be the centre of this sphere, and a its radius, we readily find

$$A/B = OP_1^3/a^3 = a^3/OP_2^3 \quad\quad (3).$$

This sphere may evidently be taken as a fixed boundary to the fluid on either side, and we thus obtain the motion due to a double-source (or say to an infinitely small sphere moving along Ox) in presence of a fixed spherical boundary. The disturbance of the stream-lines by the fixed sphere is that due to a double-source of the opposite sign placed at the 'inverse' point, the ratio of the strengths being given by (3)*. This fictitious double-source may be called the 'image' of the original one.

96. Rankine employed† a method similar to that of Art. 71 to discover forms of solids of revolution which will by motion parallel to their axes generate in a surrounding liquid any given type of irrotational motion symmetrical about an axis.

The velocity of the solid being $\mathbf{u}$, and δs denoting an element of the meridian, the normal velocity at any point of the surface is $\mathbf{u}d\varpi/ds$, and that of the fluid in contact is given by $-d\psi/\varpi ds$. Equating these and integrating along the meridian, we have

$$\psi = -\tfrac{1}{2}\mathbf{u}\varpi^2 + \text{const.} \quad\quad (1).$$

If in this we substitute any value of ψ satisfying Art. 93 (3), we obtain the equation of the meridian curves of a series of solids, each of which would by its motion parallel to x give rise to the given system of stream-lines.

In this way we may readily verify the solution already obtained for the sphere; thus, assuming

$$\psi = A\varpi^2/r^3 \quad\quad (2),$$

we find that (1) is satisfied for $r = a$, provided

$$A = -\tfrac{1}{2}\mathbf{u}a^3 \quad\quad (3),$$

which agrees with Art. 95 (1).

* This result was given by Stokes, "On the Resistance of a Fluid to Two Oscillating Spheres," *Brit. Ass. Report*, 1847; *Math. and Phys. Papers*, t. i., p. 230.

† "On the Mathematical Theory of Stream-Lines, especially those with Four Foci and upwards," *Phil. Trans.* 1871, p. 267.

97. The motion of a liquid bounded by *two* spherical surfaces can be found by successive approximations in certain cases. For two solid spheres moving in the line of centres the solution is greatly facilitated by the result given at the end of Art. 95, as to the 'image' of a double-source in a fixed sphere.

Let A, B be the centres, and let $\mathbf{u}$ be the velocity of A towards B, $\mathbf{u}'$ that of B towards A. Also, P being any point, let $AP=r$, $BP=r'$, $PAB=\theta$, $PBA=\theta'$. The velocity-potential will be of the form

$$\mathbf{u}\phi+\mathbf{u}'\phi' \quad \text{.......................................(i)},$$

where the functions ϕ and ϕ' are to be determined by the conditions that

$$\nabla^2\phi=0, \qquad \nabla^2\phi'=0 \quad \text{.............................(ii)},$$

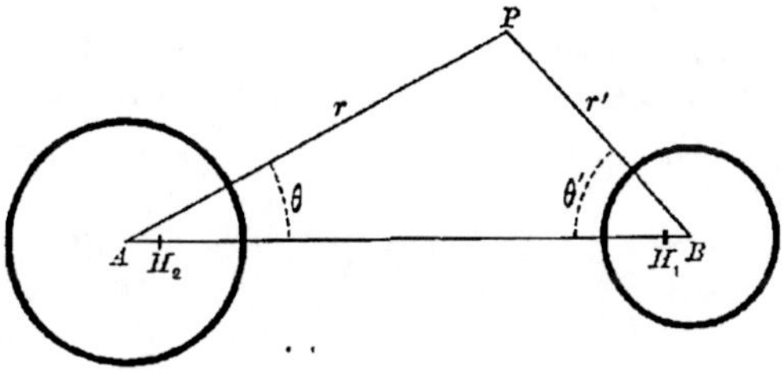

throughout the fluid; that their space-derivatives vanish at infinity; and that

$$\frac{d\phi}{dr}=-\cos\theta, \qquad \frac{d\phi'}{dr}=0 \quad \text{.......................(iii)},$$

over the surface of A, whilst

$$\frac{d\phi}{dr'}=0, \qquad \frac{d\phi'}{dr'}=-\cos\theta' \quad \text{.................(iv)},$$

over the surface of B. It is evident that ϕ is the value of the velocity-potential when A moves with unit velocity towards B, while B is at rest; and similarly for ϕ'.

To find ϕ, we remark that if B were absent the motion of the fluid would be that due to a certain double-source at A having its axis in the direction AB. The theorem of Art. 95 shews that we may satisfy the condition of zero normal velocity over the surface of B by introducing a double-source, viz. the 'image' of that at A in the sphere B. This image is at H_1, the inverse point of A with respect to the sphere B; its axis coincides with AB, and its strength μ_1 is given by

$$\mu_1=-\mu\, b^3/c^3,$$

where μ, $=\frac{1}{2}a^3$, is that of the original source at A. The resultant motion due to the two sources at A and H_1 will however violate the condition to be satisfied at the surface of the sphere A, and in order to neutralize the normal velocity at this surface, due to H_1, we must superpose a double-source at H_2, the image of H_1 in the sphere A. This will introduce a normal velocity at the surface of B, which may again be neutralized by adding the image of H_2 in B, and so on. If $\mu_1, \mu_2, \mu_3, \ldots$ be the strengths of the successive images, and $f_1, f_2, f_3, \ldots$ their distances from A, we have, if $AB=c$,

$$\left.\begin{array}{ll}\mu=\tfrac{1}{2}a^3, & \\ \mu_1/\mu=-b^3/c^3, & f_1=c-b^2/c, \\ \mu_2/\mu_1=-a^3/f_1^3, & f_2=a^2/f_1, \\ \mu_3/\mu_2=-b^3/(c-f_2)^3, & f_3=c-b^2/f_2, \\ \mu_4/\mu_3=-a^3/f_3^3, & f_4=a^2/f_3, \\ \mu_5/\mu_4=-b^3/(c-f_4)^3, & f_5=c-b^2/f_4,\end{array}\right\} \ldots\ldots\ldots\ldots\ldots \text{(v)},$$

and so on, the law of formation being now obvious. The images continually diminish in intensity, and this very rapidly if the radius of either sphere is small compared with the shortest distance between the two surfaces.

The formula for the kinetic energy is

$$2T=-\rho\iint(\mathrm{u}\phi+\mathrm{u}'\phi')\left(\mathrm{u}\frac{d\phi}{dn}+\mathrm{u}'\frac{d\phi'}{dn}\right)dS$$
$$=L\mathrm{u}^2+2M\mathrm{u}\mathrm{u}'+N\mathrm{u}'^2 \ldots\ldots\ldots\ldots\ldots\ldots\ldots\ldots \text{(vi)},$$

provided
$$\left.\begin{array}{l}L=-\rho\displaystyle\iint\phi\frac{d\phi}{dn}dS_A, \\ M=-\rho\displaystyle\iint\phi\frac{d\phi'}{dn}dS_B=-\rho\iint\phi'\frac{d\phi}{dn}dS_A, \\ N=-\rho\displaystyle\iint\phi'\frac{d\phi'}{dn}dS_B,\end{array}\right\} \ldots\ldots\ldots\ldots \text{(vii)},$$

where the suffixes indicate over which sphere the integration is to be effected. The equality of the two forms of M follows from Green's Theorem (Art. 44.)

The value of ϕ near the surface of A can be written down at once from the results (6) and (7) of Art. 86, viz. we have

$$\phi=(\mu+\mu_2+\mu_4+\ldots)\frac{\cos\theta}{r^2}-2\left(\frac{\mu_1}{f_1^3}+\frac{\mu_3}{f_3^3}+\ldots\right)r\cos\theta+\&c.\ldots\ldots \text{(viii)},$$

the remaining terms, involving zonal harmonics of higher orders, being omitted, as they will disappear in the subsequent surface-integration, in virtue of the conjugate property of Art. 88. Hence, putting $d\phi/dn=-\cos\theta$, we find with the help of (v)

$$L=\tfrac{4}{3}\pi\rho(\mu+3\mu_2+3\mu_4+\ldots)$$
$$=\tfrac{2}{3}\pi\rho a^3\left(1+3\frac{a^3b^3}{c^3f_1^3}+3\frac{a^6b^6}{c^3f_1^3(c-f_2)^3f_3^3}+\ldots\right)\ldots\ldots\ldots\ldots \text{(ix)}.$$

It appears that the inertia of the sphere A is in all cases increased by the presence of a fixed sphere B. Compare Art. 92.

The value of N may be written down from symmetry, viz. it is

$$N = \tfrac{2}{3}\pi\rho b^3 \left(1 + 3\frac{a^3b^3}{c^3 f_1'^3} + 3\frac{a^6b^6}{c^3 f_1'^3 (c-f_2')^3 f_3'^3} + \dots\right) \dots\dots\dots\dots (x),$$

where

$$\left.\begin{array}{ll} f_1' = c - a^2/c, & f_2' = b^2/f_1', \\ f_3' = c - a^2/f_2', & f_4' = b^2/f_3', \\ f_5' = c - a^2/f_4', & \end{array}\right\} \dots\dots\dots\dots (xi),$$

and so on.

To calculate M we require the value of ϕ' near the surface of the sphere A; this is due to double-sources μ', μ_1', μ_2', μ_3', ... at distances c, $c-f_1'$, $c-f_2'$, $c-f_3'$, ... from A, where

$$\left.\begin{array}{l} \mu' = -\tfrac{1}{2}b^3, \\ \mu_1'/\mu' = -a^3/c^3, \\ \mu_2'/\mu_1' = -b^3/f_1'^3, \\ \mu_3'/\mu_2' = -a^3/(c-f_2')^3, \\ \mu_4'/\mu_3' = -b^3/f_3'^3, \\ \mu_5'/\mu_4' = -a^3/(c-f_4')^3, \end{array}\right\} \dots\dots\dots\dots (xii),$$

and so on. This gives, for points near the surface of A,

$$\phi' = (\mu_1' + \mu_3' + \mu_5' + \dots)\frac{\cos\theta}{r^2}$$

$$- 2\left(\frac{\mu'}{c^3} + \frac{\mu_2'}{(c-f_2')^3} + \frac{\mu_4'}{(c-f_4')^3} + \dots\right) r\cos\theta + \&c. \dots\dots (xiii).$$

Hence

$$M = -\rho \iint \phi' \frac{d\phi}{dn} dS_A$$

$$= 4\pi\rho(\mu_1' + \mu_3' + \mu_5' + \dots)$$

$$= 2\pi\rho \frac{a^3b^3}{c^3}\left\{1 + \frac{a^3b^3}{f_1'^3(c-f_2')^3} + \frac{a^6b^6}{f_1'^3 f_3'^3 (c-f_2')^3 (c-f_4')^3} + \dots\right\} \dots (xiv).$$

When the ratios a/c and b/c are both small we have

$$\left.\begin{array}{l} L = \tfrac{2}{3}\pi\rho a^3\left(1 + 3\dfrac{a^3b^3}{c^6}\right), \\ M = 2\pi\rho\dfrac{a^3b^3}{c^3}, \\ N = \tfrac{2}{3}\pi\rho b^3\left(1 + 3\dfrac{a^3b^3}{c^6}\right), \end{array}\right\} \dots\dots\dots\dots (xv),*$$

approximately.

* To this degree of approximation these results may also be obtained by the method of the next Art.

If a, but not necessarily b, is small compared with the shortest distance between the spherical surfaces, we have

$$L=\tfrac{2}{3}\pi\rho a^3\left(1+3\frac{a^3b^3}{c^3f_1^{\,3}}+\dots\right)$$

$$=\tfrac{2}{3}\pi\rho a^3\left(1+3\frac{a^3b^3}{(c^2-b^2)^3}+\dots\right)\quad\text{(xvi)},$$

approximately. By putting $c=b+h$, and then making $b=\infty$, we get the formula for a sphere moving perpendicularly to a fixed plane wall at a distance h, viz.

$$2T=\tfrac{2}{3}\pi\rho a^3\left(1+\tfrac{3}{8}\frac{a^3}{h^3}+\dots\right)\mathbf{u}^2\quad\text{(xvii)},$$

a result due to Stokes.

This also follows from (vi) and (xv), by putting $b=a$, $\mathbf{u}'=\mathbf{u}$, $c=2h$, in which case the plane which bisects AB at right angles is evidently a plane of symmetry, and may therefore be taken as a fixed boundary to the fluid on either side.

98. When the spheres are moving at right angles to the line of centres the problem is more difficult; we shall therefore content ourselves with the first steps in the approximation, referring, for a more complete treatment, to the papers cited below.

Let the spheres be moving with velocities $\mathbf{v}$, $\mathbf{v}'$ in parallel directions at right angles to A, B, and let r, θ, ω and r', θ', ω' be two systems of spherical polar coordinates having their origins at A and B respectively, and their polar axes in the directions of the velocities $\mathbf{v}$, $\mathbf{v}'$. As before the velocity-potential will be of the form

$$\mathbf{v}\phi+\mathbf{v}'\phi',$$

with the surface conditions

$$\frac{d\phi}{dr}=-\cos\theta,\quad \frac{d\phi'}{dr}=0,\qquad \text{for } r=a,$$

and

$$\frac{d\phi}{dr'}=0,\quad \frac{d\phi'}{dr'}=-\cos\theta',\ \text{for } r'=b.$$

If the sphere B were absent the velocity-potential due to unit velocity of A would be

$$\tfrac{1}{2}\frac{a^3}{r^2}\cos\theta.$$

Since $r\cos\theta=r'\cos\theta'$, the value of this in the neighbourhood of B will be

$$\tfrac{1}{2}\frac{a^3}{c^3}r'\cos\theta',$$

approximately. The normal velocity due to this will be cancelled by the addition of the term

$$\tfrac{1}{4}\frac{a^3b^3}{c^3}\frac{\cos\theta'}{r'^2},$$

which, in the neighbourhood of A becomes equal to

$$\tfrac{1}{4}\frac{a^3b^3}{c^6}r\cos\theta,$$

nearly. To rectify the normal velocity at the surface of A, we add the term

$$\tfrac{1}{8}\frac{a^6b^3}{c^6}\frac{\cos\theta}{r^2}.$$

Stopping at this point, and collecting our results, we have, over the surface of A,

$$\phi=\tfrac{1}{2}a\left(1+\tfrac{3}{4}\frac{a^3b^3}{c^6}\right)\cos\theta,$$

and at the surface of B,

$$\phi=\tfrac{3}{4}b\,.\,\frac{a^3}{c^3}\cos\theta'.$$

Hence if we denote by P, Q, R the coefficients in the expression for the kinetic energy, viz.

$$2T=P\mathbf{v}^2+2Q\mathbf{v}\mathbf{v}'+R\mathbf{v}'^2 \ldots\ldots\ldots\ldots\ldots\ldots\ldots\ldots\text{(i)},$$

we have

$$\left.\begin{aligned}P&=-\rho\iint\phi\frac{d\phi}{dn}dS_A=\tfrac{2}{3}\pi\rho a^3\left(1+\tfrac{3}{4}\frac{a^3b^3}{c^6}\right),\\ Q&=-\rho\iint\phi\frac{d\phi'}{dn}dS_B=\pi\rho\frac{a^3b^3}{c^3},\\ R&=-\rho\iint\phi'\frac{d\phi'}{dn}dS_B=\tfrac{2}{3}\pi\rho b^3\left(1+\tfrac{3}{4}\frac{a^3b^3}{c^6}\right)\end{aligned}\right\}\ldots\ldots\text{(ii)}.$$

The case of a sphere moving parallel to a fixed plane boundary, at a distance h, is obtained by putting $b=a$, $\mathbf{v}=\mathbf{v}'$, $c=2h$, and halving the consequent value of T; thus

$$2T=\tfrac{2}{3}\pi\rho a^3\left(1+\tfrac{3}{16}\frac{a^3}{h^3}\right)\mathbf{v}^2 \ldots\ldots\ldots\ldots\ldots\ldots\text{(iii)}.$$

This result, which was also given by Stokes, may be compared with that of Art. 97 (xvii)*.

99. Another interesting problem is to calculate the kinetic energy of any given irrotational motion in a cyclic space bounded by fixed walls, as disturbed by a solid sphere moving in any manner, it being supposed that the radius of the sphere is small

* For a fuller analytical treatment of the problem of the motion of two spheres we refer to the following papers: W. M. Hicks, "On the Motion of Two Spheres in a Fluid," *Phil. Trans.*, 1880, p. 455; R. A. Herman, "On the Motion of Two Spheres in Fluid," *Quart. Journ. Math.*, t. xxii. (1887). See also C. Neumann, *Hydrodynamische Untersuchungen*, Leipzig, 1883.

in comparison with the distance from it of the nearest portion of the original boundary.

Let ϕ be the velocity-potential of the motion when the sphere is absent, and $\kappa_1, \kappa_2, \ldots$ the circulations in the various circuits. The kinetic energy of the original motion is therefore given by Art. 55 (5), viz.

$$2T_0 = -\Sigma\rho\kappa \iint \frac{d\phi}{dn}\, d\sigma \quad \text{.............................(i)},$$

where the integrations extend over the various barriers, drawn as in Art. 48. If we denote by $\phi+\phi'$ the velocity-potential in presence of the sphere, and by T the energy of the actual motion, we have

$$2T = -\rho \iint (\phi+\phi')\frac{d}{dn}(\phi+\phi')\, dS - \Sigma\rho\kappa \iint \frac{d}{dn}(\phi+\phi')\, d\sigma \quad \text{...... (ii)},$$

the cyclic constants of ϕ' being zero. The integration in the first term may be confined to the surface of the sphere, since we have $d\phi/dn = 0$ and $d\phi'/dn = 0$ over the original boundary. Now, by Art. 54 (4),

$$\iint \phi \frac{d\phi'}{dn}\, dS + \Sigma\kappa \iint \frac{d\phi'}{dn}\, d\sigma = \iint \phi' \frac{d\phi}{dn}\, dS,$$

so that (ii) reduces to

$$2T = 2T_0 - \rho \iint \phi' \frac{d}{dn}(2\phi+\phi')\, dS - \rho \iint \phi \frac{d\phi}{dn}\, dS \quad \text{......... (iii)}.$$

Let us now take the centre of the sphere as origin. Let a be the radius of the sphere, and $\mathbf{u}, \mathbf{v}, \mathbf{w}$ the components of its velocity in the directions of the coordinate axes; further, let u_0, v_0, w_0 be the component velocities of the fluid at the position of the centre, when the sphere is absent. Hence, in the neighbourhood of the sphere, we have, approximately

$$\left.\begin{aligned} \phi &= -u_0 x - v_0 y - w_0 z - \ldots \\ \phi' &= -(Ax+By+Cz)/r^3 - \ldots \end{aligned}\right\} \quad \text{.......................(iv)},$$

where the coefficients A, B, C are to be determined by the condition that

$$-\frac{d}{dr}(\phi+\phi') = \frac{x}{a}\mathbf{u} + \frac{y}{a}\mathbf{v} + \frac{z}{a}\mathbf{w},$$

for $r=a$. This gives

$$A = \tfrac{1}{2}a^3(u_0-\mathbf{u}), \quad B = \tfrac{1}{2}a^3(v_0-\mathbf{v}), \quad C = \tfrac{1}{2}a^3(w_0-\mathbf{w}) \quad \text{............ (v)}.$$

Again, $$-2\frac{d\phi}{dr} - \frac{d\phi'}{dr} = \frac{x}{a}(u_0+\mathbf{u}) + \frac{y}{a}(v_0+\mathbf{v}) + \frac{z}{a}(w_0+\mathbf{w}) \quad \text{............(vi)},$$

when $r=a$. Hence, substituting from (iv), (v), and (vi), in (iii), and remembering that $\iint x^2 dS = \tfrac{1}{3}a^2 . 4\pi a^2$, $\iint yz dS = 0$, &c., &c.,
we find

$$2T = 2T_0 + \tfrac{2}{3}\pi\rho a^3(\mathbf{u}^2+\mathbf{v}^2+\mathbf{w}^2) - 2\pi\rho a^3(u_0^2+v_0^2+w_0^2) \quad \text{...... (vii)}.$$

The dynamical consequences of the formula (vii) will be considered more fully in Art. 140; but in the meantime we may note that if the sphere be held at rest, so that **u**, **v**, **w** = 0, it experiences a force tending to diminish the energy of the system, and therefore urging it in the direction in which the square of the (undisturbed) fluid velocity, $u_0^2 + v_0^2 + w_0^2$, most rapidly increases*. Hence, by Art. 38, the sphere, if left to itself, cannot be in stable equilibrium at any point in the interior of the fluid mass.

Ellipsoidal Harmonics.

100. The method of Spherical Harmonics can also be adapted to the solution of the equation

$$\nabla^2\phi = 0 \quad\ldots\ldots\ldots\ldots(1),$$

under boundary-conditions having relation to ellipsoids of revolution†.

Beginning with the case where the ellipsoids are *prolate*, we write

$$\left.\begin{array}{l} x = k\cos\theta\cosh\eta = k\mu\zeta, \\ y = \varpi\cos\omega, \qquad z = \varpi\sin\omega, \\ \text{where} \quad \varpi = k\sin\theta\sinh\eta = k(1-\mu^2)^{\frac{1}{2}}(\zeta^2-1)^{\frac{1}{2}}. \end{array}\right\} \ldots\ldots\ldots(2).$$

The surfaces ζ = const., μ = const., are confocal ellipsoids, and hyperboloids of two sheets, respectively, the common foci being the points ($\pm k$, 0, 0). The value of ζ may range from 1 to ∞, whilst μ lies between ± 1. The coordinates μ, ζ, ω form an orthogonal system, and the values of the linear elements $\delta s_\mu, \delta s_\zeta, \delta s_\omega$ described by the point (x, y, z) when μ, ζ, ω separately vary, are respectively,

$$\delta s_\mu = k\left(\frac{\zeta^2-\mu^2}{1-\mu^2}\right)^{\frac{1}{2}}\delta\mu, \quad \delta s_\zeta = k\left(\frac{\zeta^2-\mu^2}{\zeta^2-1}\right)^{\frac{1}{2}}\delta\zeta,$$

$$\delta s_\omega = k(1-\mu^2)^{\frac{1}{2}}(\zeta^2-1)^{\frac{1}{2}}\delta\omega \quad\ldots\ldots\ldots(3).$$

To express (1) in terms of our new variables we equate to zero the total flux across the walls of a volume element $ds_\mu ds_\zeta ds_\omega$, and obtain

$$\frac{d}{d\mu}\left(\frac{d\phi}{ds_\mu}\delta s_\zeta\delta s_\omega\right)\delta\mu + \frac{d}{d\zeta}\left(\frac{d\phi}{ds_\zeta}\delta s_\mu\delta s_\omega\right)\delta\zeta + \frac{d}{d\omega}\left(\frac{d\phi}{ds_\omega}\delta s_\mu\delta s_\zeta\right)\delta\omega = 0,$$

* Sir W. Thomson, "On the Motion of Rigid Solids in a Liquid &c.," *Phil. Mag.*, May, 1873.

† Heine, "Ueber einige Aufgaben, welche auf partielle Differentialgleichungen führen," *Crelle*, t. xxvi., p. 185 (1843); *Kugelfunktionen*, t. ii., Art. 38. See also Ferrers, *Spherical Harmonics*, c. vi.

or, on substitution from (3),

$$\frac{d}{d\mu}\left\{(1-\mu^2)\frac{d\phi}{d\mu}\right\}+\frac{d}{d\zeta}\left\{(\zeta^2-1)\frac{d\phi}{d\zeta}\right\}+\frac{\zeta^2-\mu^2}{(1-\mu^2)(\zeta^2-1)}\frac{d^2\phi}{d\omega^2}=0.$$

This may also be written

$$\frac{d}{d\mu}\left\{(1-\mu^2)\frac{d\phi}{d\mu}\right\}+\frac{1}{1-\mu^2}\frac{d^2\phi}{d\omega^2}=\frac{d}{d\zeta}\left\{(1-\zeta^2)\frac{d\phi}{d\zeta}\right\}+\frac{1}{1-\zeta^2}\frac{d^2\phi}{d\omega^2}\quad\ldots(4).$$

101. If ϕ be a finite function of μ and ω from $\mu=-1$ to $\mu=+1$ and from $\omega=0$ to $\omega=2\pi$, it may be expanded in a series of surface harmonics of integral orders, of the types given by Art. 87 (6), where the coefficients are functions of ζ; and it appears on substitution in (4) that each term of the expansion must satisfy the equation separately. Taking first the case of the zonal harmonic, we write

$$\phi=P_n(\mu)\,.\,Z\quad\ldots\ldots(5),$$

and on substitution we find, in virtue of Art. 85 (1),

$$\frac{d}{d\zeta}\left\{(1-\zeta^2)\frac{dZ}{d\zeta}\right\}+n(n+1)Z=0\quad\ldots\ldots(6),$$

which is of the same form as the equation referred to. We thus obtain the solutions

$$\phi=P_n(\mu)\,.\,P_n(\zeta)\quad\ldots\ldots(7),$$

and

$$\phi=P_n(\mu)\,.\,Q_n(\zeta)\quad\ldots\ldots(8),$$

where

$$Q_n(\zeta)=P_n(\zeta)\int_\zeta^\infty\frac{d\zeta}{\{P_n(\zeta)\}^2(\zeta^2-1)},$$

$$=\tfrac{1}{2}P_n(\zeta)\log\frac{\zeta+1}{\zeta-1}-\frac{2n-1}{1\,.\,n}P_{n-1}(\zeta)-\frac{2n-5}{3\,(n-1)}P_{n-3}(\zeta)-\ldots,$$

$$=\frac{n!}{1\,.\,3\ldots(2n+1)}\left\{\zeta^{-n-1}+\frac{(n+1)(n+2)}{2\,(2n+3)}\zeta^{-n-3}+\frac{(n+1)(n+2)(n+3)(n+4)}{2\,.\,4\,(2n+3)(2n+5)}\zeta^{-n-5}+\ldots\right\}\quad\ldots(9)^*.$$

The solution (7) is finite when $\zeta=1$, and is therefore adapted to the space *within* an ellipsoid of revolution; whilst (8) is infinite for $\zeta=1$, but vanishes for $\zeta=\infty$, and is appropriate to the

* Ferrers, c. v.; Todhunter, c. vi.; Forsyth, *Differential Equations*, Arts. 96—99.

external region. As particular cases of the formula (9) we note

$$Q_0(\zeta) = \tfrac{1}{2}\log\frac{\zeta+1}{\zeta-1},$$

$$Q_1(\zeta) = \tfrac{1}{2}\zeta\log\frac{\zeta+1}{\zeta-1} - 1,$$

$$Q_2(\zeta) = \tfrac{1}{4}(3\zeta^2-1)\log\frac{\zeta+1}{\zeta-1} - \tfrac{3}{2}\zeta.$$

The definite-integral form of Q_n shews that

$$P_n Q_n' - P_n' Q_n = -\frac{1}{\zeta^2-1} \quad\text{..............} \quad (10),$$

where the accents indicate differentiations with respect to ζ.

The corresponding expressions for the stream-function are readily found; thus, from the definition of Art. 93,

$$\frac{d\phi}{ds_\zeta} = -\frac{1}{\varpi}\frac{d\psi}{ds_\mu}, \quad \frac{d\phi}{ds_\mu} = \frac{1}{\varpi}\frac{d\psi}{ds_\zeta} \quad\text{..............} \quad (11),$$

whence

$$\frac{d\psi}{d\mu} = -k(\zeta^2-1)\frac{d\phi}{d\zeta}, \quad \frac{d\psi}{d\zeta} = k(1-\mu^2)\frac{d\phi}{d\mu} \quad\text{......} \quad (12).$$

Thus, in the case of (7), we have

$$\frac{d\psi}{d\mu} = -k(\zeta^2-1)\frac{dP_n(\zeta)}{d\zeta}\,.\,P_n(\mu)$$

$$= \frac{k}{n(n+1)}(\zeta^2-1)\frac{dP_n(\zeta)}{d\zeta}\,.\,\frac{d}{d\mu}\left\{(1-\mu^2)\frac{dP_n(\mu)}{d\mu}\right\},$$

whence

$$\psi = \frac{k}{n(n+1)}(1-\mu^2)\frac{dP_n(\mu)}{d\mu}\,.\,(\zeta^2-1)\frac{dP_n(\zeta)}{d\mu} \quad\text{...} \quad (13).$$

The same result will follow of course from the second of equations (12).

In the same way, the stream-function corresponding to (8) is

$$\psi = \frac{k}{n(n+1)}(1-\mu^2)\frac{dP_n(\mu)}{d\mu}\,.\,(\zeta^2-1)\frac{dQ_n(\zeta)}{d\zeta} \quad\text{...} \quad (14).$$

102. We can apply this to the case of an ovary ellipsoid moving parallel to its axis in an infinite mass of liquid. The elliptic coordinates must be chosen so that the ellipsoid in question is a member of the confocal family, say that for which $\zeta = \zeta_0$. Comparing with Art. 100 (2) we see that if a, c be the polar and equatorial radii, and e the eccentricity of the meridian section we must have

$$k = ae, \qquad \zeta_0 = 1/e, \qquad k(\zeta_0^2 - 1)^{\frac{1}{2}} = c.$$

The surface condition is given by Art. 96 (1), viz. we must have

$$\psi = -\tfrac{1}{2}\mathbf{u}k^2(1-\mu^2)(\zeta^2-1) + \text{const.} \qquad \text{............(1)},$$

for $\zeta = \zeta_0$. Hence putting $n = 1$ in Art. 101 (14), and introducing an arbitrary multiplier A, we have

$$\psi = \tfrac{1}{2}Ak(1-\mu^2)(\zeta^2-1)\left\{\tfrac{1}{2}\log\frac{\zeta+1}{\zeta-1} - \frac{\zeta}{\zeta^2-1}\right\} \qquad \text{......(2)},$$

with the condition

$$A = \mathbf{u}k \div \left\{\frac{\zeta_0}{\zeta_0^2-1} - \tfrac{1}{2}\log\frac{\zeta_0+1}{\zeta_0-1}\right\}$$

$$= \mathbf{u}a \div \left\{\frac{1}{1-e^2} - \frac{1}{2e}\log\frac{1+e}{1-e}\right\} \qquad \text{.................. (3)}.$$

The corresponding formula for the velocity-potential is

$$\phi = A\mu\left\{\tfrac{1}{2}\zeta\log\frac{\zeta+1}{\zeta-1} - 1\right\} \qquad \text{..................(4)}.$$

The kinetic energy, and thence the inertia-coefficient due to the fluid, may be readily calculated, if required, by the formula (5) of Art. 93.

103. Leaving the case of symmetry, the solutions of $\nabla^2\phi = 0$ when ϕ is a tesseral or sectorial harmonic in μ and ω are found by a similar method to be of the types

$$\phi = T_n^s(\mu) \,.\, T_n^s(\zeta) \begin{matrix}\cos\\ \sin\end{matrix}\Big\} s\omega \qquad \text{.............. (1)},$$

$$\phi = T_n^s(\mu) \,.\, U_n^s(\zeta) \begin{matrix}\cos\\ \sin\end{matrix}\Big\} s\omega \qquad \text{.............. (2)},$$

where, as in Art. 87,

$$T_n^s(\mu) = (1-\mu^2)^{\frac{1}{2}s}\frac{d^sP_n(\mu)}{d\mu^s} \qquad \text{.............. (3)},$$

whilst (to avoid imaginaries) we write

$$T_n^s(\zeta) = (\zeta^2 - 1)^{\frac{1}{2}s} \frac{d^s P_n(\zeta)}{d\zeta^s} \quad \text{..................} \quad (4),$$

and

$$U_n^s(\zeta) = (\zeta^2 - 1)^{\frac{1}{2}s} \frac{d^s Q_n(\zeta)}{d\zeta^s} \quad \text{..................} \quad (5).$$

It may be shewn that

$$U_n^s(\zeta) = (-)^s \frac{(n+s)!}{(n-s)!} T_n^s(\zeta) \cdot \int_\zeta^\infty \frac{d\zeta}{\{T_n^s(\zeta)\}^2 \cdot (\zeta^2 - 1)} \quad \text{...} \quad (6).$$

As examples we may take the case of an ovary ellipsoid moving parallel to an *equatorial* axis, say that of y, or rotating about this axis.

In the former case, the surface-condition is

$$\frac{d\phi}{d\zeta} = -\mathbf{v}\frac{dy}{d\zeta},$$

for $\zeta = \zeta_0$, where $\mathbf{v}$ is the velocity of translation, or

$$\frac{d\phi}{d\zeta} = -\mathbf{v} \cdot \frac{k\zeta_0}{(\zeta_0^2 - 1)^{\frac{1}{2}}} \cdot (1 - \mu^2)^{\frac{1}{2}} \cos\omega \quad \text{...........} \quad (7).$$

This is satisfied by putting $n = 1$, $s = 1$, in (2), viz.

$$\phi = A(1 - \mu^2)^{\frac{1}{2}} (\zeta^2 - 1)^{\frac{1}{2}} \cdot \left\{\tfrac{1}{2}\log\frac{\zeta+1}{\zeta-1} - \frac{\zeta}{\zeta^2 - 1}\right\} \cos\omega \text{...} (8),$$

the constant A being given by

$$A\left\{\tfrac{1}{2}\log\frac{\zeta_0+1}{\zeta_0-1} - \frac{\zeta_0^2 - 2}{\zeta_0(\zeta_0^2 - 1)}\right\} = -k\mathbf{v} \quad \text{...........} \quad (9).$$

In the case of rotation about Oy, if $\mathbf{q}$ be the angular velocity, we must have

$$\frac{d\phi}{d\zeta} = -\mathbf{q}\left(z\frac{dx}{d\zeta} - x\frac{dz}{d\zeta}\right),$$

for $\zeta = \zeta_0$ or $\quad \dfrac{d\phi}{d\zeta} = k^2\mathbf{q} \cdot \dfrac{1}{(\zeta_0^2 - 1)^{\frac{1}{2}}} \cdot \mu(1 - \mu^2)^{\frac{1}{2}} \sin\omega \text{...........} (10).$

Putting $n = 2$, $s = 1$, in the formula (2) we find

$$\phi = A\mu(1 - \mu^2)^{\frac{1}{2}} (\zeta^2 - 1)^{\frac{1}{2}} \left\{\tfrac{3}{2}\zeta\log\frac{\zeta+1}{\zeta-1} - 3 - \frac{1}{\zeta^2 - 1}\right\} \sin\omega \text{...} (11),$$

A being determined by comparison with (10).

104. When the ellipsoid is of the *oblate* or "planetary" form, the appropriate coordinates are given by

$$\left.\begin{aligned} x &= k\cos\theta\sinh\eta = k\mu\zeta, \\ y &= \varpi\cos\omega, \qquad z = \varpi\sin\omega, \\ \text{where} \qquad \varpi &= k\sin\theta\cosh\eta = k(1-\mu^2)^{\frac{1}{2}}(\zeta^2+1)^{\frac{1}{2}}. \end{aligned}\right\} \quad \ldots\ldots (1).$$

Here ζ may range from 0 to ∞ (or, in some applications from $-\infty$ through 0 to $+\infty$), whilst μ lies between ± 1. The quadrics $\zeta = \text{const.}$, $\mu = \text{const.}$ are planetary ellipsoids, and hyperboloids of revolution of one sheet, all having the common focal circle $x = 0$, $\varpi = k$. As limiting forms we have the ellipsoid $\zeta = 0$, which coincides with the portion of the plane $x = 0$ for which $\varpi < k$, and the hyperboloid $\mu = 0$ coinciding with the remaining portion of this plane.

With the same notation as before we find

$$\delta s_\mu = k\left(\frac{\zeta^2+\mu^2}{1-\mu^2}\right)^{\frac{1}{2}}\delta\mu, \quad \delta s_\zeta = k\left(\frac{\zeta^2+\mu^2}{\zeta^2+1}\right)^{\frac{1}{2}}\delta\zeta,$$

$$\delta s_\omega = k(1-\mu^2)^{\frac{1}{2}}(\zeta^2+1)^{\frac{1}{2}}\,\delta\omega \ldots\ldots\ldots\ldots\ldots\ldots (2),$$

so that the equation of continuity becomes, by an investigation similar to that of Art. 100,

$$\frac{d}{d\mu}\left\{(1-\mu^2)\frac{d\phi}{d\mu}\right\} + \frac{d}{d\zeta}\left\{(\zeta^2+1)\frac{d\phi}{d\zeta}\right\} + \frac{\zeta^2+\mu^2}{(1-\mu^2)(\zeta^2+1)}\frac{d^2\phi}{d\omega^2} = 0,$$

or

$$\frac{d}{d\mu}\left\{(1-\mu^2)\frac{d\phi}{d\mu}\right\} + \frac{1}{1-\mu^2}\frac{d^2\phi}{d\omega^2} = -\frac{d}{d\zeta}\left\{(\zeta^2+1)\frac{d\phi}{d\zeta}\right\} + \frac{1}{\zeta^2+1}\frac{d^2\phi}{d\omega^2} \ldots (3).$$

This is of the same form as Art. 100 (4), with $i\zeta$ in place of ζ, and the same correspondence will of course run through the subsequent formulæ.

In the case of symmetry about the axis we have the solutions

$$\phi = P_n(\mu)\,.\,p_n(\zeta) \ldots\ldots\ldots\ldots\ldots\ldots\ldots (4),$$

and

$$\phi = P_n(\mu)\,.\,q_n(\zeta) \ldots\ldots\ldots\ldots\ldots\ldots\ldots (5),$$

where

$$p_n(\zeta) = \frac{1\,.\,3\,.\,5\ldots(2n-1)}{n\,!}\left\{\zeta^n + \frac{n(n-1)}{2(2n-1)}\zeta^{n-2} + \frac{n(n-1)(n-2)(n-3)}{2\,.\,4(2n-1)(2n-3)}\zeta^{n-4} + \ldots\right\} \ldots (6),$$

and $$q_n(\zeta) = p_n(\zeta)\int_\zeta^\infty \frac{d\zeta}{\{p_n(\zeta)\}^2(\zeta^2+1)}$$

$$= (-)^n\left\{p_n(\zeta)\cot^{-1}\zeta - \frac{2n-1}{1.n}p_{n-1}(\zeta) + \frac{2n-5}{3(n-1)}p_{n-3}(\zeta) - \ldots\right\}$$

$$= \frac{n!}{1.3.5\ldots(2n+1)}\left\{\zeta^{-n-1} - \frac{(n+1)(n+2)}{2(2n+3)}\zeta^{-n-3}\right.$$

$$\left. + \frac{(n+1)(n+2)(n+3)(n+4)}{2.4(2n+3)(2n+5)}\zeta^{-n-5} - \ldots\right\} \ldots\ldots\ldots (7)^*,$$

the latter expansion being however convergent only when $\zeta > 1$. As before, the solution (4) is appropriate to the region included within an ellipsoid of the family $\zeta =$ const., and (5) to the external space.

We note that

$$p_n q_n' - p_n' q_n = -\frac{1}{\zeta^2+1} \ldots\ldots\ldots\ldots\ldots\ldots (8).$$

As particular cases of the formula (7) we have

$$q_0(\zeta) = \cot^{-1}\zeta,$$

$$q_1(\zeta) = 1 - \zeta\cot^{-1}\zeta,$$

$$q_2(\zeta) = \tfrac{1}{2}(3\zeta^2+1)\cot^{-1}\zeta - \tfrac{3}{2}\zeta.$$

The formulæ for the stream-function corresponding to (4) and (5) are

$$\psi = \frac{k}{n(n+1)}(1-\mu^2)\frac{dP_n(\mu)}{d\mu}\,.\,(\zeta^2+1)\frac{dp_n(\zeta)}{d\zeta} \ldots\ldots (9),$$

and

$$\psi = \frac{k}{n(n+1)}(1-\mu^2)\frac{dP_n(\mu)}{d\mu}\,.\,(\zeta^2+1)\frac{dq_n(\zeta)}{d\zeta} \ldots (10).$$

105. The simplest case of Art. 104 (5) is when $n = 0$, viz.

$$\phi = A\cot^{-1}\zeta \ldots\ldots\ldots\ldots\ldots\ldots\ldots\ldots (1),$$

where ζ is supposed to range from $-\infty$ to $+\infty$. The formula (10) of the last Art. then assumes an indeterminate form, but we find by the method of Art. 101,

$$\psi = Ak\mu \ldots\ldots\ldots\ldots\ldots\ldots\ldots\ldots (2).$$

* The reader may easily adapt the demonstrations cited in Art. 101 to the present case.

This solution represents the flow of a liquid through a circular aperture in an infinite plane wall, viz. the aperture is the portion of the plane yz for which $\varpi < k$. The velocity at any point of the aperture ($\zeta=0$) is

$$u = -\frac{1}{\varpi}\frac{d\psi}{d\varpi} = \frac{A}{(k^2-\varpi^2)^{\frac{1}{2}}},$$

since, over the aperture, $k\mu = (k^2-\varpi^2)^{\frac{1}{2}}$. The velocity is therefore infinite at the edge. Compare Art. 66, 1°.

Again, the motion due to a planetary ellipsoid ($\zeta=\zeta_0$) moving with velocity $\mathbf{u}$ parallel to its axis in an infinite mass of liquid is given by

$$\phi = A\mu(1-\zeta\cot^{-1}\zeta) \quad\quad (3),$$

$$\psi = \tfrac{1}{2}Ak(1-\mu^2)(\zeta^2+1)\left\{\frac{\zeta}{\zeta^2+1} - \cot^{-1}\zeta\right\} \quad\quad (4),$$

where
$$A = -k\mathbf{u} \div \left\{\frac{\zeta_0}{\zeta_0^2+1} - \cot^{-1}\zeta_0\right\}.$$

Denoting the polar and equatorial radii by a and c, we have

$$a = k\zeta_0, \quad c = k(\zeta_0^2+1)^{\frac{1}{2}},$$

so that the eccentricity e of the meridian section is

$$e = (\zeta_0^2+1)^{-\frac{1}{2}}.$$

In terms of these quantities

$$A = -\mathbf{u}c \div \left\{(1-e^2)^{\frac{1}{2}} - \frac{1}{e}\sin^{-1}e\right\} \quad\quad (5).$$

The forms of the lines of motion, for equidistant values of ψ, are shewn on the opposite page.

The most interesting case is that of the circular disk, for which $e=1$, and $A = 2\mathbf{u}c/\pi$. The value (3) of ϕ for the two sides of the disk becomes equal to $\pm A\mu$, or $\pm A(1-\varpi^2/c^2)^{\frac{1}{2}}$, and the normal velocity $\pm\mathbf{u}$. Hence the formula (4) of Art. 44 gives

$$2T = -2\rho\int_0^c A(1-\varpi^2/c^2)^{\frac{1}{2}}.\mathbf{u}.2\pi\varpi\,d\varpi$$
$$= \frac{2}{\pi}.\tfrac{4}{3}\pi\rho c^3.\mathbf{u}^2 \quad\quad (6).$$

The effective addition to the inertia of the disk is therefore $2/\pi$ (=·6365) times the mass of a spherical portion of the fluid, of the same radius.

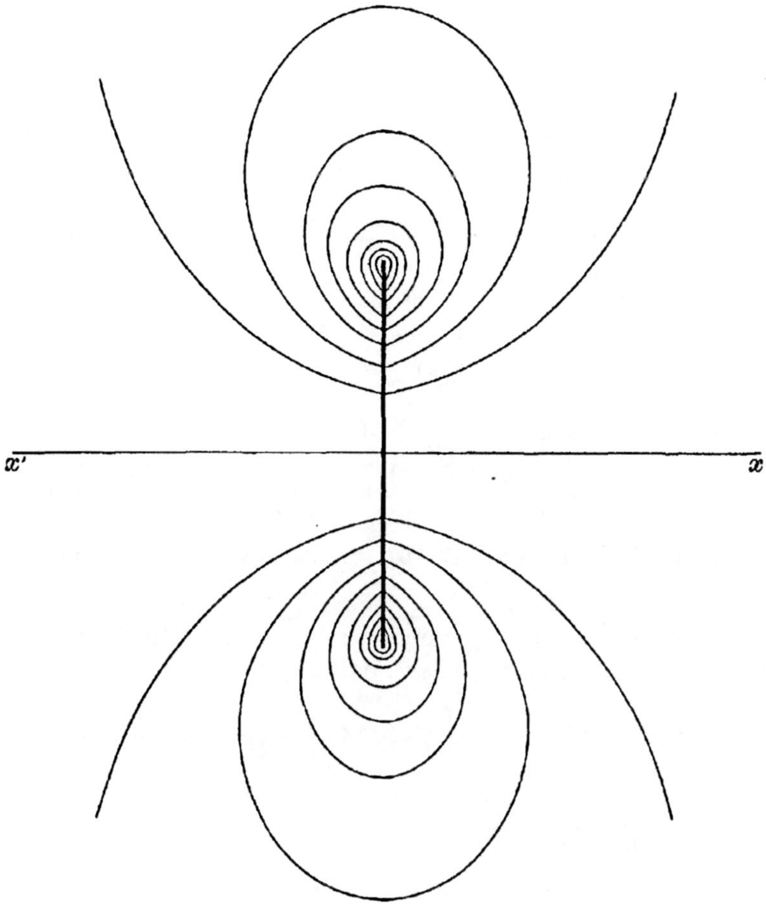

106. The solutions of the equation Art. **104** (3) in tesseral harmonics are

$$\phi = T_n^s(\mu) \, . \, t_n^s(\zeta) \, . \left.\begin{matrix}\cos\\ \sin\end{matrix}\right\} s\omega \qquad \text{.................. (1)},$$

and

$$\phi = T_n^s(\mu) \, . \, u_n^s(\zeta) \, . \left.\begin{matrix}\cos\\ \sin\end{matrix}\right\} s\omega \qquad \text{.................. (2)},$$

where

$$t_n^s(\zeta) = (\zeta^2+1)^{\frac{1}{2}s} \frac{d^s p_n(\zeta)}{d\zeta^s} \qquad \text{.................. (3)},$$

and

$$u_n^s(\zeta) = (\zeta^2+1)^{\frac{1}{2}s} \frac{d^s q_n(\zeta)}{d\zeta^s}$$

$$= (-)^s \frac{(n+s)!}{(n-s)!} \, . \, t_n^s(\zeta) \, . \int_\zeta^\infty \frac{d\zeta}{\{t_n^s(\zeta)\}^2 (\zeta^2+1)} \; \dots \text{(4)}.$$

These functions possess the property

$$u_n^{s'} t_n^s - u_n^s t_n^{s'} = (-)^{s+1} \frac{(n+s)!}{(n-s)!} \frac{1}{\zeta^2+1} \quad \text{......... (5).}$$

For the motion of a planetary ellipsoid ($\zeta = \zeta_0$) parallel to the axis of y we have $n = 1$, $s = 1$, as before, and thence

$$\phi = A(1-\mu^2)^{\frac{1}{2}} (\zeta^2+1)^{\frac{1}{2}} \left\{ \frac{\zeta}{\zeta^2+1} - \cot^{-1}\zeta \right\} \cos\omega \quad \text{...... (6),}$$

with A determined by the condition

$$\frac{d\phi}{d\zeta} = -\mathbf{v}\frac{dy}{d\zeta},$$

for $\zeta = \zeta_0$, $\mathbf{v}$ denoting the velocity of the solid. This gives

$$A\left\{\frac{\zeta_0^2+2}{\zeta_0(\zeta_0^2+1)} - \cot^{-1}\zeta_0\right\} = -k\mathbf{v} \quad \text{..............(7).}$$

In the case of the disk ($\zeta_0 = 0$), we have $A = 0$, as we should expect.

Again, for a planetary ellipsoid rotating about the axis of y with angular velocity $\mathbf{q}$, we have, putting $n = 2$, $s = 1$,

$$\phi = A\mu(1-\mu^2)^{\frac{1}{2}} (\zeta^2+1)^{\frac{1}{2}} \left\{ 3\zeta\cot^{-1}\zeta - 3 + \frac{1}{\zeta^2+1} \right\} \sin\omega \quad \text{......(8),}$$

with the surface condition

$$\frac{d\phi}{d\zeta} = -\mathbf{q}\left(z\frac{dx}{d\zeta} - x\frac{dz}{d\zeta}\right)$$

$$= -\frac{k^2\mathbf{q}}{(\zeta_0^2+1)^{\frac{1}{2}}} \cdot \mu(1-\mu^2)^{\frac{1}{2}} \sin\omega \quad \text{....................(9).}$$

For the circular disk ($\zeta_0 = 0$) this gives

$$\tfrac{3}{2}\pi A = -k^2\mathbf{q} \quad \text{.................... (10).}$$

At the two surfaces of the disk we have

$$\phi = \mp 2A\mu(1-\mu^2)^{\frac{1}{2}} \sin\omega, \quad \frac{d\phi}{dn} = \mp k\mathbf{q}(1-\mu^2)^{\frac{1}{2}} \sin\omega,$$

and substituting in the formula

$$2T = -\rho \iint \phi \frac{d\phi}{dn} \varpi d\varpi d\omega,$$

we obtain

$$2T = \tfrac{16}{45}\rho c^5 . \mathbf{q}^2 \quad \text{.................... (11).}$$

107. In questions relating to ellipsoids with three unequal axes we may use the method of Lamé's Functions*, or, as they are now often called, 'Ellipsoidal Harmonics.' Without attempting a complete account of this, we will investigate some solutions of the equation

$$\nabla^2\phi = 0 \qquad\qquad (1),$$

in ellipsoidal coordinates, which are analogous to spherical harmonics of the first and second orders, with a view to their hydrodynamical applications. It is convenient to begin with the motion of a liquid contained in an ellipsoidal envelope, which can be treated at once by Cartesian methods.

Thus when the envelope is in motion parallel to the axis of x with velocity $\mathbf{u}$, the enclosed fluid moves as a solid, and the velocity-potential is simply $\phi = -\mathbf{u}x$.

Next let us suppose that the envelope is rotating about a principal axis (say that of x) with angular velocity $\mathbf{p}$. The equation of the surface being

$$\frac{x^2}{a^2} + \frac{y^2}{b^2} + \frac{z^2}{c^2} = 1 \qquad\qquad (2),$$

the surface condition is

$$-\frac{x}{a^2}\frac{d\phi}{dx} - \frac{y}{b^2}\frac{d\phi}{dy} - \frac{z}{c^2}\frac{d\phi}{dz}$$

$$= -\frac{y}{b^2}\mathbf{p}z + \frac{z}{c^2}\mathbf{p}y.$$

We therefore assume $\phi = Ayz$, which is evidently a solution of (1), and obtain

$$A\left(\frac{1}{b^2} + \frac{1}{c^2}\right) = -\mathbf{p}\left(\frac{1}{c^2} - \frac{1}{b^2}\right),$$

or

$$\phi = -\frac{b^2 - c^2}{b^2 + c^2}\mathbf{p}\,.\,yz.$$

Hence, if the centre be moving with a velocity whose com-

* See, for example, Ferrers, *Spherical Harmonics*, c. vi.; W. D. Niven, "On Ellipsoidal Harmonics," *Phil. Trans.*, 1891, A.

ponents are **u**, **v**, **w** and if **p**, **q**, **r** be the angular velocities about the principal axes, we have by superposition

$$\phi = -\mathbf{u}x - \mathbf{v}y - \mathbf{w}z - \frac{b^2-c^2}{b^2+c^2}\mathbf{p}yz - \frac{c^2-a^2}{c^2+a^2}\mathbf{q}zx - \frac{a^2-b^2}{a^2+b^2}\mathbf{r}xy \quad \text{.......................(3)*}.$$

We may also include the case where the envelope is changing its form as well as position, but so as to remain ellipsoidal. If the axes are changing at the rates $\dot{a}$, $\dot{b}$, $\dot{c}$, respectively, the general boundary condition, Art. 10 (3), becomes

$$\frac{x^2}{a^3}\dot{a} + \frac{y^2}{b^3}\dot{b} + \frac{z^2}{c^3}\dot{c} + \frac{x}{a^2}\frac{d\phi}{dx} + \frac{y}{b^2}\frac{d\phi}{dy} + \frac{z}{c^2}\frac{d\phi}{dz} = 0 \quad \text{...... (4)},$$

which is satisfied by

$$\phi = -\tfrac{1}{2}\left(\frac{\dot{a}}{a}x^2 + \frac{\dot{b}}{b}y^2 + \frac{\dot{c}}{c}z^2\right) \quad \text{.................(5)†}.$$

The equation (1) requires that

$$\frac{\dot{a}}{a} + \frac{\dot{b}}{b} + \frac{\dot{c}}{c} = 0 \quad \text{..........................(6)},$$

which is in fact the condition which must be satisfied by the changing ellipsoidal surface in order that the enclosed volume $(\frac{4}{3}\pi abc)$ may be constant.

108. The solutions of the corresponding problems for an infinite mass of fluid bounded *internally* by an ellipsoid involve the use of a special system of orthogonal curvilinear coordinates.

If x, y, z be functions of three parameters λ, μ, ν, such that the surfaces

$$\lambda = \text{const.}, \quad \mu = \text{const.}, \quad \nu = \text{const.} \quad \text{...............(1)}$$

are mutually orthogonal at their intersections, and if we write

* This result appears to have been obtained independently by Beltrami, Bjerknes, and Maxwell, in 1873. See Hicks, "Report on Recent Progress in Hydrodynamics," *Brit. Ass. Rep.*, 1882.

† Bjerknes, "Verallgemeinerung des Problems von den Bewegungen, welche in einer ruhenden unelastischen Flüssigkeit die Bewegung eines Ellipsoids hervorbringt," *Göttinger Nachrichten*, 1873.

$$\left.\begin{aligned}\frac{1}{h_1^2}&=\left(\frac{dx}{d\lambda}\right)^2+\left(\frac{dy}{d\lambda}\right)^2+\left(\frac{dz}{d\lambda}\right)^2,\\ \frac{1}{h_2^2}&=\left(\frac{dx}{d\mu}\right)^2+\left(\frac{dy}{d\mu}\right)^2+\left(\frac{dz}{d\mu}\right)^2,\\ \frac{1}{h_3^2}&=\left(\frac{dx}{d\nu}\right)^2+\left(\frac{dy}{d\nu}\right)^2+\left(\frac{dz}{d\nu}\right)^2\end{aligned}\right\}\text{..............(2)},$$

the direction-cosines of the normals to the three surfaces which pass through (x, y, z) will be

$$\left.\begin{aligned}&h_1\frac{dx}{d\lambda},\quad h_1\frac{dy}{d\lambda},\quad h_1\frac{dz}{d\lambda},\\ &h_2\frac{dx}{d\mu},\quad h_2\frac{dy}{d\mu},\quad h_2\frac{dz}{d\mu},\\ &h_3\frac{dx}{d\nu},\quad h_3\frac{dy}{d\nu},\quad h_3\frac{dz}{d\nu}\end{aligned}\right\}\text{..................(3)},$$

respectively. It easily follows that the lengths of linear elements drawn in the directions of these normals will be

$$\delta\lambda/h_1,\quad \delta\mu/h_2,\quad \delta\nu/h_3,$$

respectively.

Hence if ϕ be the velocity-potential of any fluid motion, the total flux into the rectangular space included between the six surfaces $\lambda \pm \frac{1}{2}\delta\lambda$, $\mu \pm \frac{1}{2}\delta\mu$, $\nu \pm \frac{1}{2}\delta\nu$ will be

$$\frac{d}{d\lambda}\left(h_1\frac{d\phi}{d\lambda}\cdot\frac{\delta\mu}{h_2}\cdot\frac{\delta\nu}{h_3}\right)\delta\lambda+\frac{d}{d\mu}\left(h_2\frac{d\phi}{d\mu}\cdot\frac{\delta\nu}{h_3}\cdot\frac{\delta\lambda}{h_1}\right)\delta\mu+\frac{d}{d\nu}\left(h_3\frac{d\phi}{d\nu}\cdot\frac{\delta\lambda}{h_1}\cdot\frac{\delta\mu}{h_2}\right)\delta\nu.$$

It appears from Art. 42 (3) that the same flux is expressed by $\nabla^2\phi$ multiplied by the volume of the space, *i.e.* by $\delta\lambda\,\delta\mu\,\delta\nu/h_1h_2h_3$. Hence

$$\nabla^2\phi=h_1h_2h_3\left\{\frac{d}{d\lambda}\left(\frac{h_1}{h_2h_3}\frac{d\phi}{d\lambda}\right)+\frac{d}{d\mu}\left(\frac{h_2}{h_3h_1}\frac{d\phi}{d\mu}\right)+\frac{d}{d\nu}\left(\frac{h_3}{h_1h_2}\frac{d\phi}{d\nu}\right)\right\}\text{...(4)*}.$$

Equating this to zero, we obtain the general equation of continuity in orthogonal coordinates, of which particular cases have already been investigated in Arts. 84, 100, 104.

* The above method was given in a paper by W. Thomson, "On the Equations of Motion of Heat referred to Curvilinear Coordinates," *Camb. Math. Journ.*, t. iv. (1843); *Math. and Phys. Papers*, t. i., p. 25. Reference may also be made to Jacobi, "Ueber eine particuläre Lösung der partiellen Differentialgleichung......," *Crelle*, t. xxxvi, (1847), *Gesammelte Werke*, Berlin, 1881..., t. ii., p. 198.

The transformation of $\nabla^2\phi$ to general orthogonal coordinates was first effected by Lamé, "Sur les lois de l'équilibre du fluide éthéré," *Journ. de l'École Polyt.*, t. xiv., (1834). See also *Leçons sur les Coordonnées Curvilignes*, Paris, 1859, p. 22.

109. In the applications to which we now proceed the triple orthogonal system consists of the confocal quadrics

$$\frac{x^2}{a^2+\theta}+\frac{y^2}{b^2+\theta}+\frac{z^2}{c^2+\theta}-1=0 \quad\text{..............(1)},$$

whose properties are explained in books on Solid Geometry. Through any given point (x, y, z) there pass three surfaces of the system, corresponding to the three roots of (1), considered as a cubic in θ. If (as we shall for the most part suppose) $a > b > c$, one of these roots (λ, say) will lie between ∞ and $-c^2$, another (μ) between $-c^2$ and $-b^2$, and the third (ν) between $-b^2$ and $-a^2$. The surfaces λ, μ, ν are therefore ellipsoids, hyperboloids of one sheet, and hyperboloids of two sheets, respectively.

It follows immediately from this definition of λ, μ, ν, that

$$\frac{x^2}{a^2+\theta}+\frac{y^2}{b^2+\theta}+\frac{z^2}{c^2+\theta}-1=\frac{(\lambda-\theta)(\mu-\theta)(\nu-\theta)}{(a^2+\theta)(b^2+\theta)(c^2+\theta)} \quad\text{...(2)},$$

identically, for all values of θ. Hence multiplying by $a^2+\theta$, and afterwards putting $\theta=-a^2$, we obtain the first of the following equations:

$$\left.\begin{aligned} x^2&=\frac{(a^2+\lambda)(a^2+\mu)(a^2+\nu)}{(a^2-b^2)(a^2-c^2)}, \\ y^2&=\frac{(b^2+\lambda)(b^2+\mu)(b^2+\nu)}{(b^2-c^2)(b^2-a^2)}, \\ z^2&=\frac{(c^2+\lambda)(c^2+\mu)(c^2+\nu)}{(c^2-a^2)(c^2-b^2)} \end{aligned}\right\} \quad\text{...............(3)}.$$

These give

$$\frac{dx}{d\lambda}=\tfrac{1}{2}\frac{x}{a^2+\lambda},\quad \frac{dy}{d\lambda}=\tfrac{1}{2}\frac{y}{b^2+\lambda},\quad \frac{dz}{d\lambda}=\tfrac{1}{2}\frac{z}{c^2+\lambda} \quad\text{......(4)},$$

and thence, in the notation of Art. 108 (2),

$$\frac{1}{h_1^2}=\tfrac{1}{4}\left\{\frac{x^2}{(a^2+\lambda)^2}+\frac{y^2}{(b^2+\lambda)^2}+\frac{z^2}{(c^2+\lambda)^2}\right\} \quad\text{......... (5)}.$$

If we differentiate (2) with respect to θ and afterwards put $\theta=\lambda$, we deduce the first of the following three relations:

$$\left.\begin{aligned} h_1^2 &= 4\frac{(a^2+\lambda)(b^2+\lambda)(c^2+\lambda)}{(\lambda-\mu)(\lambda-\nu)},\\ h_2^2 &= 4\frac{(a^2+\mu)(b^2+\mu)(c^2+\mu)}{(\mu-\nu)(\mu-\lambda)},\\ h_3^2 &= 4\frac{(a^2+\nu)(b^2+\nu)(c^2+\nu)}{(\nu-\lambda)(\nu-\mu)} \end{aligned}\right\}\quad\ldots\ldots\ldots\ldots(6)^*.$$

The remaining relations of the sets (3) and (6) have been written down from symmetry.

Substituting in Art. 108 (4), we find

$$\nabla^2\phi = -\frac{4}{(\mu-\nu)(\nu-\lambda)(\lambda-\mu)}\left[(\mu-\nu)\left\{(a^2+\lambda)^{\frac{1}{2}}(b^2+\lambda)^{\frac{1}{2}}(c^2+\lambda)^{\frac{1}{2}}\frac{d}{d\lambda}\right\}^2\right.$$
$$+(\nu-\lambda)\left\{(a^2+\mu)^{\frac{1}{2}}(b^2+\mu)^{\frac{1}{2}}(c^2+\mu)^{\frac{1}{2}}\frac{d}{d\mu}\right\}^2$$
$$\left.+(\lambda-\mu)\left\{(a^2+\nu)^{\frac{1}{2}}(b^2+\nu)^{\frac{1}{2}}(c^2+\nu)^{\frac{1}{2}}\frac{d}{d\nu}\right\}^2\right]\phi$$
$$\ldots\ldots\ldots\ldots\ldots(7)\dagger.$$

110. The particular solutions of the transformed equation $\nabla^2\phi=0$ which first present themselves are those in which ϕ is a function of one (only) of the variables λ, μ, ν. Thus ϕ may be a function of λ alone, provided

$$(a^2+\lambda)^{\frac{1}{2}}(b^2+\lambda)^{\frac{1}{2}}(c^2+\lambda)^{\frac{1}{2}}\,d\phi/d\lambda = \text{const.},$$

whence
$$\phi = C\int_\lambda^\infty \frac{d\lambda}{\Delta}\quad\ldots\ldots\ldots\ldots\ldots\ldots\ldots\ldots(1),$$

if
$$\Delta = \{(a^2+\lambda)(b^2+\lambda)(c^2+\lambda)\}^{\frac{1}{2}}\quad\ldots\ldots\ldots\ldots\ldots\ldots(2),$$

the additive constant which attaches to ϕ being chosen so as to make ϕ vanish for $\lambda=\infty$.

In this solution, which corresponds to $\phi = A/r$ in spherical harmonics, the equipotential surfaces are the confocal ellipsoids, and the motion in the space external to any one of these (say that for which $\lambda=0$) is that due to a certain arrangement of simple sources over it. The velocity at any point is given by the formula

$$-\frac{d\phi}{dn} = -h_1\frac{d\phi}{d\lambda} = C\frac{h_1}{\Delta}\quad\ldots\ldots\ldots\ldots\ldots\ldots(3).$$

* It will be noticed that h_1, h_2, h_3 are double the perpendiculars from the origin on the tangent planes to the three quadrics λ, μ, ν.

† Cf. Lamé, "Sur les surfaces isothermes dans les corps solides homogènes en équilibre de température," *Liouville*, t. ii., (1837).

At a great distance from the origin the ellipsoids λ become spheres of radius $\lambda^{\frac{1}{2}}$, and the velocity is therefore ultimately equal to $2C/r^2$, where r denotes the distance from the origin. Over any particular equipotential surface λ, the velocity varies as the perpendicular from the centre on the tangent plane.

To find the distribution of sources over the surface $\lambda = 0$ which would produce the actual motion in the external space, we substitute for ϕ the value (1), in the formula (11) of Art. 58, and for ϕ' (which refers to the internal space) the constant value

$$\phi' = C\int_0^\infty \frac{d\lambda}{\Delta} \qquad\text{(4).}$$

The formula referred to then gives, for the surface-density of the required distribution,

$$\frac{C}{4\pi abc} \cdot h_1 \qquad\text{(5).}$$

The solution (1) may also be interpreted as representing the motion due to a change in dimensions of the ellipsoid, such that the ellipsoid remains similar to itself, and retains the directions of its axes unchanged in space. If we put

$$\dot{a}/a = \dot{b}/b = \dot{c}/c, \ = k, \text{ say},$$

the surface-condition Art. 107 (4) becomes

$$-\,d\phi/dn = \tfrac{1}{2}kh_1,$$

which is identical with (3), if we put $C = \frac{1}{2}kabc$.

A particular case of (5) is where the sources are distributed over the *elliptic disk* for which $\lambda = -c^2$, and therefore $z^2 = 0$. This is important in Electrostatics, but a more interesting application from the present point of view is to the flow through an *elliptic aperture*, viz. if the plane xy be occupied by a thin rigid partition with the exception of the part included by the ellipse

$$\frac{x^2}{a^2} + \frac{y^2}{b^2} = 1, \quad z = 0,$$

we have, putting $c = 0$ in the previous formulæ,

$$\phi = \mp A\int_0^\lambda \frac{d\lambda}{(a^2+\lambda)^{\frac{1}{2}}(b^2+\lambda)^{\frac{1}{2}}\lambda^{\frac{1}{2}}} \qquad\text{(6),}$$

where the upper limit is the positive root of

$$\frac{x^2}{a^2+\lambda}+\frac{y^2}{b^2+\lambda}+\frac{z^2}{\lambda}=1 \quad\text{.....................(7)},$$

and the negative or the positive sign is to be taken according as the point for which ϕ is required lies on the positive or the negative side of the plane xy. The two values of ϕ are continuous at the aperture, where $\lambda = 0$. As before, the velocity at a great distance is equal to $2A/r^2$, nearly. For points in the aperture the velocity may be found immediately from (6) and (7); thus we may put

$$\delta n = z = \lambda^{\frac{1}{2}}\left(1-\frac{x^2}{a^2}-\frac{y^2}{b^2}\right)^{\frac{1}{2}},$$

$$\delta\phi = -\,2A\lambda^{\frac{1}{2}}/ab,$$

approximately, since λ is small, whence

$$-\frac{d\phi}{dn}=\frac{2A}{ab}\cdot\left(1-\frac{x^2}{a^2}-\frac{y^2}{b^2}\right)^{-\frac{1}{2}} \quad\text{.................. (8)}.$$

This becomes infinite, as we should expect, at the edge. The particular case of a *circular* aperture has already been solved otherwise in Art. 105.

111. We proceed to investigate the solution of $\nabla^2\phi = 0$, finite at infinity, which corresponds, for the space external to the ellipsoid, to the solution $\phi = x$ for the internal space. Following the analogy of spherical harmonics we may assume for trial

$$\phi = x\chi \quad\text{..............................(1)},$$

which gives

$$\nabla^2\chi+\frac{2}{x}\frac{d\chi}{dx}=0 \quad\text{........................ (2)},$$

and inquire whether this can be satisfied by making χ equal to some function of λ only. On this supposition we shall have, by Art. 108 (3),

$$\frac{d\chi}{dx}=h_1\frac{d\chi}{d\lambda}\cdot h_1\frac{dx}{d\lambda},$$

and therefore, by Art. 109 (4), (6),

$$\frac{2}{x}\frac{d\chi}{dx}=4\frac{(b^2+\lambda)(c^2+\lambda)}{(\lambda-\mu)(\lambda-\nu)}\frac{d\chi}{d\lambda}.$$

On substitution from Art. 109 (7) the equation (2) becomes

$$\left\{(a^2+\lambda)^{\frac{1}{2}}(b^2+\lambda)^{\frac{1}{2}}(c^2+\lambda)^{\frac{1}{2}}\frac{d}{d\lambda}\right\}^2\chi = -(b^2+\lambda)(c^2+\lambda)\frac{d\chi}{d\lambda},$$

which may be written

$$\frac{d}{d\lambda}\log\left\{(a^2+\lambda)^{\frac{1}{2}}(b^2+\lambda)^{\frac{1}{2}}(c^2+\lambda)^{\frac{1}{2}}\frac{d\chi}{d\lambda}\right\} = -\frac{1}{a^2+\lambda},$$

whence
$$\chi = C\int_\lambda^\infty \frac{d\lambda}{(a^2+\lambda)^{\frac{3}{2}}(b^2+\lambda)^{\frac{1}{2}}(c^2+\lambda)^{\frac{1}{2}}} \quad\text{............(3)},$$

the arbitrary constant which presents itself in the second integration being chosen as before so as to make χ vanish at infinity.

The solution contained in (1) and (3) enables us to find the motion of a liquid, at rest at infinity, produced by the translation of a solid ellipsoid through it, parallel to a principal axis. The notation being as before, and the ellipsoid

$$\frac{x^2}{a^2}+\frac{y^2}{b^2}+\frac{z^2}{c^2}=1 \quad\text{........................ (4)}$$

being supposed in motion parallel to x with velocity $\mathbf{u}$, the surface-condition is

$$d\phi/d\lambda = -\mathbf{u}\,dx/d\lambda,\ \text{for}\ \lambda=0 \quad\text{.................(5)}.$$

Let us write, for shortness,

$$\alpha_0 = abc\int_0^\infty \frac{d\lambda}{(a^2+\lambda)\Delta},\quad \beta_0 = abc\int_0^\infty \frac{d\lambda}{(b^2+\lambda)\Delta},\quad \gamma_0 = abc\int_0^\infty \frac{d\lambda}{(c^2+\lambda)\Delta}$$
$$\text{.............. (6)},$$

where
$$\Delta = \{(a^2+\lambda)(b^2+\lambda)(c^2+\lambda)\}^{\frac{1}{2}} \quad\text{..............(7)}.$$

It will be noticed that these quantities α_0, β_0, γ_0 are pure numerics.

The conditions of our problem are now satisfied by

$$\phi = Cx\int_\lambda^\infty \frac{d\lambda}{(a^2+\lambda)\Delta} \quad\text{....................(8)},$$

provided
$$\frac{C}{2a^3bc}\alpha_0 - \frac{C}{a^3bc} = -\tfrac{1}{2}\frac{\mathbf{u}}{a^2},$$

that is
$$C = \frac{abc}{2-\alpha_0}\mathbf{u} \quad\text{.........................(9)}.$$

The corresponding solution when the ellipsoid moves parallel to y or z can be written down from symmetry, and by superposition we derive the case where the ellipsoid has any motion of translation whatever*.

At a great distance from the origin, the formula (8) becomes equivalent to

$$\phi = \tfrac{2}{3} C \frac{x}{r^3} \quad \text{.........................(10),}$$

which is the velocity-potential of a double source at the origin, of strength $\frac{2}{3}C$, or

$$\tfrac{2}{3} abc\mathbf{u}/(2 - \alpha_0).$$

Compare Art. 91.

The kinetic energy of the fluid is given by

$$2T = -\rho \iint \phi \frac{d\phi}{dn} dS = \rho \frac{\alpha_0}{2 - \alpha_0} \cdot \mathbf{u}^2 \cdot \iint xl dS,$$

where l is the cosine of the angle which the normal to the surface makes with the axis of x. The latter integral is equal to the volume of the ellipsoid, whence

$$2T = \frac{\alpha_0}{2 - \alpha_0} \cdot \tfrac{4}{3}\pi abc\rho \cdot \mathbf{u}^2 \quad \text{.................(11).}$$

The inertia-coefficient is therefore equal to the fraction $\alpha_0/(2 - \alpha_0)$ of the mass displaced by the solid. For the case of the sphere ($a=b=c$) we find $\alpha_0 = \frac{2}{3}$; this makes the fraction equal to $\frac{1}{2}$, in agreement with Art. 91. If we put $b = c$, we get the case of an ellipsoid of revolution, including (for $a = 0$) that of a circular disk. The identification with the results obtained by the methods of Arts. 102, 103, 105, 106 for these cases may be left to the reader.

112. We next inquire whether the equation $\nabla^2\phi = 0$ can be satisfied by

$$\phi = yz\chi \quad \text{............................(1),}$$

* This problem was first solved by Green, "Researches on the Vibration of Pendulums in Fluid Media," *Trans. R. S. Edin.*, 1833, *Math. Papers*, p. 315. The investigation is much shortened if we assume at once from the Theory of Attractions that (8) is a solution of $\nabla^2\phi = 0$, being in fact (save as to a constant factor) the x-component of the attraction of a homogeneous ellipsoid on an external point.

where χ is a function of λ only. This requires

$$\nabla^2\chi + \frac{2}{y}\frac{d\chi}{dy} + \frac{2}{z}\frac{d\chi}{dz} = 0 \text{ .... } (2).$$

Now, from Art. 109 (4), (6),

$$\frac{2}{y}\frac{d\chi}{dy} + \frac{2}{z}\frac{d\chi}{dz} = 2h_1^2\left(\frac{1}{y}\frac{dy}{d\lambda} + \frac{1}{z}\frac{dz}{d\lambda}\right)\frac{d\chi}{d\lambda}$$

$$= 4\frac{(a^2+\lambda)(b^2+\lambda)(c^2+\lambda)}{(\lambda-\mu)(\lambda-\nu)}\left(\frac{1}{b^2+\lambda} + \frac{1}{c^2+\lambda}\right)\frac{d\chi}{d\lambda}.$$

On substitution in (2) we find, by Art. 109 (7),

$$\frac{d}{d\lambda}\log\left\{(a^2+\lambda)^{\frac{1}{2}}(b^2+\lambda)^{\frac{1}{2}}(c^2+\lambda)^{\frac{1}{2}}\frac{d\chi}{d\lambda}\right\} = -\frac{1}{b^2+\lambda} - \frac{1}{c^2+\lambda},$$

whence

$$\chi = C\int_\lambda^\infty \frac{d\lambda}{(b^2+\lambda)(c^2+\lambda)\Delta} \text{ .... } (3),$$

the second constant of integration being chosen as before.

For a rigid ellipsoid rotating about the axis of x with angular velocity $\mathbf{p}$, the surface-condition is

$$d\phi/d\lambda = \mathbf{p}z\,dy/d\lambda - \mathbf{p}y\,dz/d\lambda \text{ .... } (4),$$

for $\lambda = 0$. Assuming

$$\phi = Cyz\int_\lambda^\infty \frac{d\lambda}{(b^2+\lambda)(c^2+\lambda)\Delta} \text{ .... } (5)^*,$$

we find that the surface-condition (4) is satisfied, provided

$$-\frac{C}{ab^3c^3} + \tfrac{1}{2}C\left(\frac{1}{b^2}+\frac{1}{c^2}\right)\frac{\gamma_0-\beta_0}{abc(b^2-c^2)} = \tfrac{1}{2}\mathbf{p}\left(\frac{1}{b^2}-\frac{1}{c^2}\right),$$

or

$$C = \frac{(b^2-c^2)^2}{2(b^2-c^2)+(b^2+c^2)(\beta_0-\gamma_0)}abc\mathbf{p} \text{ .... } (6).$$

* This expression differs only by a factor from

$$y\frac{d\Omega}{dz} - z\frac{d\Omega}{dy},$$

where Ω is the gravitation-potential of a uniform solid ellipsoid at an external point (x, y, z). Since $\nabla^2\Omega = 0$ it easily follows that the above is also a solution of the equation $\nabla^2\phi = 0$.

The formulæ for the cases of rotation about y or z can be written down from symmetry*.

The formula for the kinetic energy is

$$2T = -\rho \iint \phi \frac{d\phi}{dn} dS$$

$$= \rho C\mathbf{p} \,.\, \int_0^\infty \frac{d\lambda}{(a^2+\lambda)^{\frac{1}{2}} (b^2+\lambda)^{\frac{3}{2}} (c^2+\lambda)^{\frac{3}{2}}} \,.\, \iint (ny - mz)\, yz dS,$$

if (l, m, n) denote the direction-cosines of the normal to the ellipsoid. The latter integral

$$= \iiint (y^2 - z^2)\, dx dy dz = \tfrac{1}{5}(b^2 - c^2) \,.\, \tfrac{4}{3}\pi abc.$$

Hence we find

$$2T = \tfrac{1}{5} \,.\, \frac{(b^2 - c^2)^2 (\gamma_0 - \beta_0)}{2(b^2 - c^2) + (b^2 + c^2)(\beta_0 - \gamma_0)} \,.\, \tfrac{4}{3}\pi abc \rho \,.\, \mathbf{p}^2 \ldots (7).$$

The two remaining types of ellipsoidal harmonic of the second order, finite at the origin, are given by the expression

$$\frac{x^2}{a^2+\theta} + \frac{y^2}{b^2+\theta} + \frac{z^2}{c^2+\theta} - 1 \ldots\ldots\ldots\ldots\ldots\ldots\ldots\ldots\ldots\text{(i)},$$

where θ is either root of

$$\frac{1}{a^2+\theta} + \frac{1}{b^2+\theta} + \frac{1}{c^2+\theta} = 0 \ldots\ldots\ldots\ldots\ldots\ldots\ldots\ldots\ldots\text{(ii)},$$

this being the condition that (i) should satisfy $\nabla^2\phi = 0$.

The method of obtaining the corresponding solutions for the external space is explained in the treatise of Ferrers. These solutions would enable us to express the motion produced in a surrounding liquid by variations in the lengths of the axes of an ellipsoid, subject to the condition of no variation of volume

$$\dot{a}/a + \dot{b}/b + \dot{c}/c = 0 \ldots\ldots\ldots\ldots\ldots\ldots\ldots\ldots\ldots\text{(iii)}.$$

We have already found, in Art. 110, the solution for the case where the ellipsoid expands (or contracts) remaining similar to itself; so that by superposition we could obtain the case of an internal boundary changing its position and dimensions in any manner whatever, subject only to the condition of remaining ellipsoidal. This extension of the results arrived at by Green and Clebsch was first treated, though in a different manner from that here indicated, by Bjerknes†.

* The solution contained in (5) and (6) is due to Clebsch, "Ueber die Bewegung eines Ellipsoides in einer tropfbaren Flüssigkeit," *Crelle*, tt. lii., liii. (1856—7).

† *l. c. ante* p. 156.

113. The investigations of this chapter relate almost entirely to the case of spherical or ellipsoidal boundaries. It will be understood that solutions of the equation $\nabla^2\phi = 0$ can be carried out, on lines more or less similar, which are appropriate to other forms of boundary. The surface which comes next in interest, from the point of view of the present subject, is that of an anchor-ring, or 'torus'; this problem has been very ably treated, by distinct methods, by Hicks*, and Dyson†. We may also refer to the analytically remarkable problem of the spherical bowl, which has been investigated by Basset‡.

* "On Toroidal Functions," *Phil. Trans.*, 1881.

† "On the Potential of an Anchor-Ring," *Phil. Trans.*, 1893.

‡ "On the Potential of an Electrified Spherical Bowl, &c.," *Proc. Lond. Math. Soc.*, t. xvi. (1885).

CHAPTER VI.

ON THE MOTION OF SOLIDS THROUGH A LIQUID: DYNAMICAL THEORY.

114. IN this Chapter it is proposed to study the very interesting dynamical problem furnished by the motion of one or more solids in a liquid. The development of this subject is due mainly to Thomson and Tait* and to Kirchhoff†. The cardinal feature of the methods followed by these writers consists in this, that the solids and the fluid are treated as forming one dynamical system, and thus the troublesome calculation of the effect of the fluid pressures on the surfaces of the solids is avoided.

We begin with the case of a single solid moving through an infinite mass of liquid, and we shall suppose in the first instance that the motion of the fluid is entirely due to that of the solid, and is therefore irrotational and acyclic. Some special cases of this problem have been treated incidentally in the foregoing pages, and it appeared that the whole effect of the fluid might be represented by an increase in the *inertia* of the solid. The same result will be found to hold in general, provided we use the term 'inertia' in a somewhat extended sense.

Under the circumstances supposed, the motion of the fluid is characterized by the existence of a single-valued velocity-potential ϕ which, besides satisfying the equation of continuity

$$\nabla^2\phi = 0 \quad\quad\quad (1),$$

* *Natural Philosophy*, Art. 320.

† "Ueber die Bewegung eines Rotationskörpers in einer Flüssigkeit," *Crelle*, t. lxxi. (1869); *Ges. Abh.*, p. 376; *Mechanik*, c. xix.

fulfils the following conditions: (1°) the value of $-d\phi/dn$, where δn denotes as usual an element of the normal at any point of the surface of the solid, drawn on the side of the fluid, must be equal to the velocity of the surface at that point normal to itself, and (2°) the differential coefficients $d\phi/dx$, $d\phi/dy$, $d\phi/dz$ must vanish at an infinite distance, in every direction, from the solid. The latter condition is rendered necessary by the consideration that a finite velocity at infinity would imply an infinite kinetic energy, which could not be generated by finite forces acting for a finite time on the solid. It is also the condition to which we are led by supposing the fluid to be enclosed within a fixed vessel infinitely large and infinitely distant, all round, from the moving body. For on this supposition the space occupied by the fluid may be conceived as made up of tubes of flow which begin and end on the surface of the solid, so that the total flux across any area, finite or infinite, drawn in the fluid must be finite, and therefore the velocity at infinity zero.

It has been shewn in Arts. 40, 41, that under the above conditions the motion of the fluid is determinate.

115. In the further study of the problem it is convenient to follow the method introduced by Euler in the dynamics of rigid bodies, and to adopt a system of rectangular axes Ox, Oy, Oz fixed in the body, and moving with it. If the motion of the body at any instant be defined by the angular velocities p, q, r about, and the translational velocities u, v, w of the origin parallel to, the instantaneous positions of these axes, we may write, after Kirchhoff,

$$\phi = u\phi_1 + v\phi_2 + w\phi_3 + p\chi_1 + q\chi_2 + r\chi_3 \qquad \text{..........(2)},$$

where, as will appear immediately, ϕ_1, ϕ_2, ϕ_3, χ_1, χ_2, χ_3 are certain functions of x, y, z determined solely by the configuration of the surface of the solid, relative to the coordinate axes. In fact, if l, m, n denote the direction-cosines of the normal, drawn towards the fluid, at any point of this surface, the kinematical surface-condition is

$$-\frac{d\phi}{dn} = l(u + qz - ry) + m(v + rx - pz) + n(w + py - qx),$$

whence, substituting the value (2) of ϕ, we find

$$\left.\begin{array}{ll} -\dfrac{d\phi_1}{dn}=l, & -\dfrac{d\chi_1}{dn}=ny-mz \\ -\dfrac{d\phi_2}{dn}=m, & -\dfrac{d\chi_2}{dn}=lz-nx \\ -\dfrac{d\phi_3}{dn}=n, & -\dfrac{d\chi_3}{dn}=mx-ly \end{array}\right\}\ldots\ldots\ldots\ldots\ldots(3).$$

Since these functions must also satisfy (1), and have their derivatives zero at infinity, they are completely determinate, by Art. 41*.

116. Now whatever the motion of the solid and fluid at any instant, it might have been generated instantaneously from rest by a properly adjusted impulsive 'wrench' applied to the solid. This wrench is in fact that which would be required to counteract the impulsive pressures $\rho\phi$ on the surface, and, in addition, to generate the actual momentum of the solid. It is called by Lord Kelvin the 'impulse' of the system at the moment under consideration. It is to be noted that the impulse, as thus defined, cannot be asserted to be equivalent to the total momentum of the system, which is indeed in the present problem indeterminate. We proceed to shew however that the impulse varies, in consequence of extraneous forces acting on the solid, in exactly the same way as the momentum of a finite dynamical system.

Let us in the first instance consider any actual motion of a solid, from time t_0 to time t_1, under any given forces applied to it, in a *finite* mass of liquid enclosed by a fixed envelope of any form. Let us imagine the motion to have been generated from rest, previously to the time t_0, by forces (whether gradual or impulsive) applied to the solid, and to be arrested, in like manner, by forces applied to the solid after the time t_1. Since the momentum of the system is null both at the beginning and at the end of this process, the time-integrals of the forces applied to the solid, together with the time-integral of the pressures exerted on the fluid

* For the particular case of an ellipsoidal surface, their values may be written down from the results of Arts. 111, 112.

by the envelope, must form an equilibrating system. The effect of these latter pressures may be calculated from the formula

$$\frac{p}{\rho} = \frac{d\phi}{dt} - \tfrac{1}{2}q^2 + F(t) \text{.....................(1).}$$

A pressure uniform over the envelope has no resultant effect; hence, since ϕ is constant at the beginning and end, the only effective part of the integral pressure $\int p dt$ is given by the term

$$-\tfrac{1}{2}\rho \int q^2 dt \text{..........................(2).}$$

Let us now revert to the original form of our problem, and suppose the containing envelope to be infinitely large, and infinitely distant in every direction from the moving solid. It is easily seen by considering the arrangement of the tubes of flow (Art. 37) that the fluid velocity q at a great distance r from an origin in the neighbourhood of the solid will ultimately be, at most*, of the order $1/r^2$, and the integral pressure (2) therefore of the order $1/r^4$. Since the surface-elements of the envelope are of the order $r^2\delta\varpi$, where $\delta\varpi$ is an elementary solid angle, the force- and couple-resultants of the integral pressure (2) will now both be null. The same statement therefore holds with regard to the time-integral of the forces applied to the solid.

If we imagine the motion to have been started instantaneously at time t_0, and to be arrested instantaneously at time t_1, the result at which we have arrived may be stated as follows:

The 'impulse' of the motion (in Lord Kelvin's sense) at time t_1 differs from the 'impulse' at time t_0 by the time-integral of the extraneous forces acting on the solid during the interval $t_1 - t_0$†.

It will be noticed that the above reasoning is substantially unaltered when the single solid is replaced by a group of solids, which may moreover be flexible instead of rigid, and even when these solids are replaced by portions of fluid moving rotationally.

117. To express the above result analytically, let $\xi, \eta, \zeta, \lambda, \mu, \nu$ be the components of the force- and couple-constituents of the

* It is really of the order $1/r^3$ when, as in the case considered, the total flux outwards is zero.

† Sir W. Thomson, *l.c. ante* p. 35. The form of the argument given above was kindly suggested to the author by Mr Larmor.

impulse; and let X, Y, Z, L, M, N designate in the same manner the system of extraneous forces. The whole variation of $\xi, \eta, \zeta, \lambda, \mu, \nu$, due partly to the motion of the axes to which these quantities are referred, and partly to the action of the extraneous forces, is then given by the formulæ

$$\left.\begin{aligned} \frac{d\xi}{dt} &= r\eta - q\zeta + X, & \frac{d\lambda}{dt} &= w\eta - v\zeta + r\mu - q\nu + L, \\ \frac{d\eta}{dt} &= p\zeta - r\xi + Y, & \frac{d\mu}{dt} &= u\zeta - w\xi + p\nu - r\lambda + M, \\ \frac{d\zeta}{dt} &= q\xi - p\eta + Z, & \frac{d\nu}{dt} &= v\xi - u\eta + q\lambda - p\mu + N \end{aligned}\right\} \ldots(1)^*.$$

For at time $t + \delta t$ the moving axes make with their positions at time t angles whose cosines are

$$(1, r\delta t, -q\delta t), \; (-r\delta t, 1, p\delta t), \; (q\delta t, -p\delta t, 1),$$

respectively. Hence, resolving parallel to the new position of the axis of x,

$$\xi + \delta\xi = \xi + \eta \, . \, r\delta t - \zeta \, . \, q\delta t + X\delta t.$$

Again, taking moments about the new position of Ox, and remembering that O has been displaced through spaces $u\delta t$, $v\delta t$, $w\delta t$ parallel to the axes, we find

$$\lambda + \delta\lambda = \lambda + \eta \, . \, w\delta t - \zeta \, . \, v\delta t + \mu \, . \, r\delta t - \nu \, . \, q\delta t + L\delta t.$$

These, with the similar results which can be written down from symmetry, give the equations (1).

When no extraneous forces act, we verify at once that these equations have the integrals

$$\left.\begin{aligned} \xi^2 + \eta^2 + \zeta^2 &= \text{const.}, \\ \lambda\xi + \mu\eta + \nu\zeta &= \text{const.} \end{aligned}\right\} \ldots\ldots\ldots\ldots\ldots\ldots\ldots (2),$$

which express that the magnitudes of the force- and couple-resultants of the impulse are constant.

* Cf. Hayward, "On a Direct Method of Estimating Velocities, Accelerations, and all similar Quantities, with respect to Axes moveable in any manner in space." *Camb. Trans.*, t. x. (1856).

118. It remains to express ξ, η, ζ, λ, μ, ν in terms of u, v, w, p, q, r. In the first place let $\mathbf{T}$ denote the kinetic energy of the fluid, so that

$$2\mathbf{T} = -\rho \iint \phi \frac{d\phi}{dn} dS \qquad \text{(1)},$$

where the integration extends over the surface of the moving solid. Substituting the value of ϕ, from Art. 115 (2), we get

$$\begin{aligned} 2\mathbf{T} = {} & \mathbf{A}u^2 + \mathbf{B}v^2 + \mathbf{C}w^2 + 2\mathbf{A}'vw + 2\mathbf{B}'wu + 2\mathbf{C}'uv \\ & + \mathbf{P}p^2 + \mathbf{Q}q^2 + \mathbf{R}r^2 + 2\mathbf{P}'qr + 2\mathbf{Q}'rp + 2\mathbf{R}'pq \\ & + 2p\,(\mathbf{L}u + \mathbf{M}v + \mathbf{N}w) \\ & + 2q\,(\mathbf{L}'u + \mathbf{M}'v + \mathbf{N}'w) \\ & + 2r\,(\mathbf{L}''u + \mathbf{M}''v + \mathbf{N}''w) \qquad \text{(2)}, \end{aligned}$$

where the 21 coefficients **A**, **B**, **C**, &c. are certain constants determined by the form and position of the surface relative to the coordinate axes. Thus, for example,

$$\left.\begin{aligned} \mathbf{A} &= -\rho \iint \phi_1 \frac{d\phi_1}{dn} dS = \rho \iint \phi_1 l \, dS, \\ \mathbf{A}' &= -\tfrac{1}{2}\rho \iint \left(\phi_2 \frac{d\phi_3}{dn} + \phi_3 \frac{d\phi_2}{dn} \right) dS \\ &= -\rho \iint \phi_2 \frac{d\phi_3}{dn} dS = -\rho \iint \phi_3 \frac{d\phi_2}{dn} dS \\ &= \rho \iint \phi_2 n \, dS = \rho \iint \phi_3 m \, dS, \\ \mathbf{P} &= -\rho \iint \chi_1 \frac{d\chi_1}{dn} dS = \rho \iint \chi_1 (ny - mz) \, dS \end{aligned}\right\} \qquad \text{(3)},$$

the transformations depending on Art. 115 (3) and on a particular case of Green's Theorem (Art. 44 (2)). These expressions for the coefficients were given by Kirchhoff.

The actual values of the coefficients in the expression for 2T have been found in the preceding chapter for the case of the ellipsoid, viz. we have from Arts. 111, 112

$$\left.\begin{aligned} \mathbf{A} &= \frac{\alpha_0}{2-\alpha_0} \cdot \tfrac{4}{3}\pi\rho abc, \\ \mathbf{P} &= \tfrac{1}{5} \frac{(b^2-c^2)^2(\gamma_0-\beta_0)}{2(b^2-c^2)+(b^2+c^2)(\beta_0-\gamma_0)} \cdot \tfrac{4}{3}\pi\rho abc \end{aligned}\right\} \qquad \text{(i)},$$

with similar expressions for **B**, **C**, **Q**, **R**. The remaining coefficients, as will appear presently, in this case all vanish. We note that

$$\mathbf{A}-\mathbf{B}=\frac{2(\alpha_0-\beta_0)}{(2-\alpha_0)(2-\beta_0)}\cdot\tfrac{4}{3}\pi\rho abc \qquad \text{(ii)},$$

so that if $a>b>c$, then $\mathbf{A}<\mathbf{B}<\mathbf{C}$, as might have been anticipated.

The formulæ for an ellipsoid of revolution may be deduced by putting $b=c$; they may also be obtained independently by the method of Arts. 101–106. Thus for a circular disk ($a=0$, $b=c$) we have

$$\left.\begin{array}{ll}\mathbf{A}=\frac{8}{3}\rho c^3, & \mathbf{B}=\mathbf{C}=0,\\ \mathbf{P}=0, & \mathbf{Q}=\mathbf{R}=\frac{16}{45}\rho c^5\end{array}\right\} \qquad \text{(iii)}.$$

The kinetic energy, $\mathbf{T}_1$ say, of the solid alone is given by an expression of the form

$$\begin{aligned}2\mathbf{T}_1 &= \mathbf{m}(u^2+v^2+w^2)\\ &\quad+\mathbf{P}_1p^2+\mathbf{Q}_1q^2+\mathbf{R}_1r^2+2\mathbf{P}_1'qr+2\mathbf{Q}_1'rp+2\mathbf{R}_1'pq\\ &\quad+2\mathbf{m}\{p(\beta w-\gamma v)+q(\gamma u-\alpha w)+r(\alpha v-\beta u)\} \qquad \text{(4)}.\end{aligned}$$

Hence the total energy $\mathbf{T}+\mathbf{T}_1$, of the system, which we shall denote by T, is given by an expression of the same general form as (2), say

$$\begin{aligned}2T &= Au^2+Bv^2+Cw^2+2A'vw+2B'wu+2C'uv\\ &\quad+Pp^2+Qq^2+Rr^2+2P'qr+2Q'rp+2R'pq\\ &\quad+2p(Lu+Mv+Nw)\\ &\quad+2q(L'u+M'v+N'w)\\ &\quad+2r(L''u+M''v+N''w) \qquad \text{(5)},\end{aligned}$$

where the coefficients are printed in uniform type, although six of them have of course the same values as in (4).

119. The values of the several components of the impulse in terms of the velocities u, v, w, p, q, r can now be found by a well-known dynamical method*. Let a system of indefinitely great forces (X, Y, Z, L, M, N) act for an indefinitely short time τ on the solid, so as to change the impulse from $(\xi, \eta, \zeta, \lambda, \mu, \nu)$ to

$$(\xi+\Delta\xi,\ \eta+\Delta\eta,\ \zeta+\Delta\zeta,\ \lambda+\Delta\lambda,\ \mu+\Delta\mu,\ \nu+\Delta\nu).$$

* See Thomson and Tait, *Natural Philosophy*, Art. 313, or Maxwell, *Electricity and Magnetism*, Part IV., c. V.

The work done by the force X is

$$\int_0^\tau Xu\,dt,$$

which lies between

$$u_1\int_0^\tau X\,dt \text{ and } u_2\int_0^\tau X\,dt,$$

where u_1 and u_2 are the greatest and least values of u during the time τ, *i.e.* it lies between $u_1\Delta\xi$ and $u_2\Delta\xi$. If we now introduce the supposition that $\Delta\xi$, $\Delta\eta$, $\Delta\zeta$, $\Delta\lambda$, $\Delta\mu$, $\Delta\nu$ are infinitely small, u_1 and u_2 are each equal to u, and the work done is $u\Delta\xi$. In the same way we may calculate the work done by the remaining forces and couples. The total result must be equal to the increment of the kinetic energy, whence

$$u\Delta\xi+v\Delta\eta+w\Delta\zeta+p\Delta\lambda+q\Delta\mu+r\Delta\nu$$

$$=\Delta T=\frac{dT}{du}\Delta u+\frac{dT}{dv}\Delta v+\frac{dT}{dw}\Delta w+\frac{dT}{dp}\Delta p+\frac{dT}{dq}\Delta q+\frac{dT}{dr}\Delta r \ldots(1).$$

Now if the velocities be all altered in any given ratio, the impulses will be altered in the same ratio. If then we take

$$\frac{\Delta u}{u}=\frac{\Delta v}{v}=\frac{\Delta w}{w}=\frac{\Delta p}{p}=\frac{\Delta q}{q}=\frac{\Delta r}{r}=k,$$

it will follow that

$$\frac{\Delta\xi}{\xi}=\frac{\Delta\eta}{\eta}=\frac{\Delta\zeta}{\zeta}=\frac{\Delta\lambda}{\lambda}=\frac{\Delta\mu}{\mu}=\frac{\Delta\nu}{\nu}=k.$$

Substituting in (11), we find

$$u\xi+v\eta+w\zeta+p\lambda+q\mu+r\nu$$

$$=u\frac{dT}{du}+v\frac{dT}{dv}+w\frac{dT}{dw}+p\frac{dT}{dp}+q\frac{dT}{dq}+r\frac{dT}{dr}$$

$$=2T \ldots\ldots\ldots\ldots\ldots\ldots\ldots\ldots\ldots\ldots\ldots (2),$$

since T is a homogeneous quadratic function. Now performing the arbitrary variation Δ on the first and last members of (2), and omitting terms which cancel by (1), we find

$$\xi\Delta u+\eta\Delta v+\zeta\Delta w+\lambda\Delta p+\mu\Delta q+\nu\Delta r=\Delta T.$$

Since the variations Δu, Δv, Δw, Δp, Δq, Δr are all independent, this gives the required formulæ

$$\left.\begin{aligned} \xi = \frac{dT}{du}, \quad \eta = \frac{dT}{dv}, \quad \zeta = \frac{dT}{dw} \\ \lambda = \frac{dT}{dp}, \quad \mu = \frac{dT}{dq}, \quad \nu = \frac{dT}{dr} \end{aligned}\right\} \quad \ldots\ldots\ldots\ldots\ldots (3).$$

It may be noted that since $\xi, \eta, \zeta, \ldots$ are linear functions of $u, v, w, \ldots$, the latter quantities may also be expressed as linear functions of the former, and thence T may be regarded as a homogeneous quadratic function of $\xi, \eta, \zeta, \lambda, \mu, \nu$. When expressed in this manner we may denote it by T'. The equation (1) then gives at once

$$u\Delta\xi + v\Delta\eta + w\Delta\zeta + p\Delta\lambda + q\Delta\mu + r\Delta\nu$$
$$= \frac{dT'}{d\xi}\Delta\xi + \frac{dT'}{d\eta}\Delta\eta + \frac{dT'}{d\zeta}\Delta\zeta + \frac{dT'}{d\lambda}\Delta\lambda + \frac{dT'}{d\mu}\Delta\mu + \frac{dT'}{d\nu}\Delta\nu,$$

whence

$$\left.\begin{aligned} u = \frac{dT'}{d\xi}, \quad v = \frac{dT'}{d\eta}, \quad w = \frac{dT'}{d\zeta}, \\ p = \frac{dT'}{d\lambda}, \quad q = \frac{dT'}{d\mu}, \quad r = \frac{dT'}{d\nu} \end{aligned}\right\} \quad \ldots\ldots\ldots\ldots\ldots (4),$$

formulæ which are in a sense reciprocal to (3).

We can utilize this last result to obtain another integral of the equations of motion, in the case where no extraneous forces act, in addition to those obtained in Art. 117. Thus

$$\frac{dT'}{dt} = \frac{dT'}{d\xi}\frac{d\xi}{dt} + \ldots + \ldots + \frac{dT'}{d\lambda}\frac{d\lambda}{dt} + \ldots + \ldots$$
$$= u\frac{d\xi}{dt} + \ldots + \ldots + p\frac{d\lambda}{dt} + \ldots + \ldots,$$

which vanishes identically, by Art. 117 (1). Hence we have the equation of energy

$$T' = \text{const.} \ldots\ldots\ldots\ldots\ldots\ldots\ldots\ldots\ldots (5).$$

120. If in the formula (3) we put, in the notation of Art. 118,

$$T = \mathbf{T} + \mathbf{T}_1,$$

it is known from the dynamics of rigid bodies that the terms in $\mathbf{T}_1$ represent the linear and angular momentum of the solid by itself.

Hence the remaining terms, involving $\mathbf{T}$, must represent the system of impulsive pressures exerted by the surface of the solid on the fluid, in the supposed instantaneous generation of the motion from rest.

This is easily verified. For example, the x-component of the above system of impulsive pressures is

$$\iint \rho\phi l dS = -\rho \iint \phi \frac{d\phi_1}{dn} dS$$

$$= \mathbf{A}u + \mathbf{C}'v + \mathbf{B}'w + \mathbf{L}p + \mathbf{L}'q + \mathbf{L}''r$$

$$= \frac{d\mathbf{T}}{du} \quad \text{...(6)},$$

by the formulæ of Arts. 115, 118. In the same way, the moment of the impulsive pressures about Ox is

$$\iint \rho\phi\,(ny - mz)\,dS = -\rho \iint \phi \frac{d\chi_1}{dn} dS$$

$$= \mathbf{L}u + \mathbf{M}v + \mathbf{N}w + \mathbf{P}p + \mathbf{R}'q + \mathbf{Q}'r$$

$$= \frac{d\mathbf{T}}{dp} \quad \text{......................................(7)}.$$

121. The equations of motion may now be written

$$\left.\begin{aligned}
\frac{d}{dt}\frac{dT}{du} &= r\frac{dT}{dv} - q\frac{dT}{dw} + X, \\
\frac{d}{dt}\frac{dT}{dv} &= p\frac{dT}{dw} - r\frac{dT}{du} + Y, \\
\frac{d}{dt}\frac{dT}{dw} &= q\frac{dT}{du} - p\frac{dT}{dv} + Z, \\
\frac{d}{dt}\frac{dT}{dp} &= w\frac{dT}{dv} - v\frac{dT}{dw} + r\frac{dT}{dq} - q\frac{dT}{dr} + L, \\
\frac{d}{dt}\frac{dT}{dq} &= u\frac{dT}{dw} - w\frac{dT}{du} + p\frac{dT}{dr} - r\frac{dT}{dp} + M, \\
\frac{d}{dt}\frac{dT}{dr} &= v\frac{dT}{du} - u\frac{dT}{dv} + q\frac{dT}{dp} - p\frac{dT}{dq} + N
\end{aligned}\right\} \text{......(1)*}.$$

* See Kirchhoff, *l.c. ante* p. 167; also Sir W. Thomson, "Hydrokinetic Solutions and Observations," *Phil. Mag.*, Nov. 1871.

If in these we write $T = \mathbf{T} + \mathbf{T}_1$, and separate the terms due to $\mathbf{T}$ and $\mathbf{T}_1$ respectively, we obtain expressions for the forces exerted on the moving solid by the pressure of the surrounding fluid; thus the total component ($\mathbf{X}$, say) of the fluid pressure parallel to x is

$$\mathbf{X} = -\frac{d}{dt}\frac{d\mathbf{T}}{du} + r\frac{d\mathbf{T}}{dv} - q\frac{d\mathbf{T}}{dw} \quad \text{..............} (2),$$

and the moment ($\mathbf{L}$) of the same pressures about x is

$$\mathbf{L} = -\frac{d}{dt}\frac{d\mathbf{T}}{dp} + w\frac{d\mathbf{T}}{dv} - v\frac{d\mathbf{T}}{dw} + r\frac{d\mathbf{T}}{dq} - q\frac{d\mathbf{T}}{dr} \quad \text{.......} (3)^*.$$

For example, if the solid be constrained to move with a constant velocity (u, v, w), without rotation, we have

$$\left.\begin{array}{c} \mathbf{X} = 0, \quad \mathbf{Y} = 0, \quad \mathbf{Z} = 0, \\ \mathbf{L} = w\frac{d\mathbf{T}}{dv} - v\frac{d\mathbf{T}}{dw}, \quad \mathbf{M} = u\frac{d\mathbf{T}}{dw} - w\frac{d\mathbf{T}}{du}, \quad \mathbf{N} = v\frac{d\mathbf{T}}{du} - u\frac{d\mathbf{T}}{dv} \end{array}\right\} \quad \text{........................} (4),$$

where $\quad 2\mathbf{T} = \mathbf{A}u^2 + \mathbf{B}v^2 + \mathbf{C}w^2 + 2\mathbf{A}'vw + 2\mathbf{B}'wu + 2\mathbf{C}'uv.$

Hence the fluid pressures reduce to a couple, which moreover vanishes if

$$\frac{d\mathbf{T}}{du} : u = \frac{d\mathbf{T}}{dv} : v = \frac{d\mathbf{T}}{dw} : w,$$

i.e. provided the velocity (u, v, w) be in the direction of one of the principal axes of the ellipsoid

$$\mathbf{A}x^2 + \mathbf{B}y^2 + \mathbf{C}z^2 + 2\mathbf{A}'yz + 2\mathbf{B}'zx + 2\mathbf{C}'xy = \text{const.} \ldots (5).$$

Hence, as was first pointed out by Kirchhoff, there are, for any solid, three mutually perpendicular directions of permanent translation; that is to say, if the solid be set in motion parallel to one of these directions, without rotation, and left to itself, it will continue so to move. It is evident that these directions are determined solely by the configuration of the surface of the body. It must be observed however that the impulse necessary to produce one of

* The forms of these expressions being known, it is not difficult to verify them by direct calculation from the pressure-equation, Art. 21 (4). See a paper "On the Forces experienced by a Solid moving through a Liquid," *Quart. Journ. Math.*, t. xix. (1883).

these permanent translations does not in general reduce to a single force; thus if the axes of coordinates be chosen, for simplicity, parallel to the three directions in question, so that $A', B', C' = 0$, we have, corresponding to the motion u alone,

$$\xi = Au, \quad \eta = 0, \quad \zeta = 0,$$
$$\lambda = Lu, \quad \mu = L'u, \quad \nu = L''u,$$

so that the impulse consists of a wrench of pitch L/A.

With the same choice of axes, the components of the couple which is the equivalent of the fluid pressures on the solid, in the case of a uniform translation (u, v, w), are

$$\mathbf{L} = (\mathbf{B} - \mathbf{C})\, vw, \quad \mathbf{M} = (\mathbf{C} - \mathbf{A})\, wu, \quad \mathbf{N} = (\mathbf{A} - \mathbf{B})\, uv \ldots (6).$$

Hence if in the ellipsoid

$$\mathbf{A}x^2 + \mathbf{B}y^2 + \mathbf{C}z^2 = \text{const.} \ldots\ldots\ldots\ldots (7),$$

we draw a radius-vector r in the direction of the velocity (u, v, w) and erect the perpendicular h from the centre on the tangent plane at the extremity of r, the plane of the couple is that of h and r, its magnitude is proportional to $\sin(h, r)/h$, and its tendency is to turn the solid in the direction from h to r. Thus if the direction of (u, v, w) differs but slightly from that of the axis of x, the tendency of the couple is to diminish the deviation when $\mathbf{A}$ is the greatest, and to increase it when $\mathbf{A}$ is the least, of the three quantities $\mathbf{A}, \mathbf{B}, \mathbf{C}$, whilst if $\mathbf{A}$ is intermediate to $\mathbf{B}$ and $\mathbf{C}$ the tendency depends on the position of r relative to the circular sections of the above ellipsoid. It appears then that of the three permanent translations one only is thoroughly stable, viz. that corresponding to the greatest of the three coefficients $\mathbf{A}, \mathbf{B}, \mathbf{C}$. For example, the only stable direction of motion of an ellipsoid is that of its *least* axis; see Art. 118*.

122. The above, although the simplest, are not the only steady motions of which the body is capable, under the action of no external forces. The instantaneous motion of the body at any instant consists, by a well-known theorem of Kinematics, of a

* The physical cause of this tendency of a flat-shaped body to set itself broadside-on to the relative motion is clearly indicated in the diagram on p. 94. A number of interesting practical illustrations are given by Thomson and Tait, Art. 325.

twist about a certain screw; and the condition that this motion should be permanent is that it should not affect the configuration of the impulse (which is fixed in space) relatively to the body. This requires that the axes of the screw and of the corresponding impulsive wrench should coincide. Since the general equations of a straight line involve four independent constants, this gives four linear relations to be satisfied by the five ratios $u : v : w : p : q : r$. There exists then for every body, under the circumstances here considered, a singly-infinite system of possible steady motions.

Of these the next in importance to the three motions of permanent translation are those in which the impulse reduces to a *couple*. The equations (1) of Art. 117 are satisfied by $\xi, \eta, \zeta = 0$, and λ, μ, ν constant, provided

$$\lambda/p = \mu/q = \nu/r, \quad = k, \text{ say} \qquad \text{(i).}$$

If the axes of coordinates have the special directions referred to in the preceding Art., the conditions $\xi, \eta, \zeta = 0$ give us at once u, v, w in terms of p, q, r, viz.

$$\left.\begin{aligned} u &= -(Lp + L'q + L''r)/A,\\ v &= -(Mp + M'q + M''r)/B,\\ w &= -(Np + N'q + N''r)/C \end{aligned}\right\} \qquad \text{(ii).}$$

Substituting these values in the expressions for λ, μ, ν obtained from Art. 119 (3), we find

$$\lambda = \frac{d\Theta}{dp}, \quad \mu = \frac{d\Theta}{dq}, \quad \nu = \frac{d\Theta}{dr} \qquad \text{(iii),}$$

where $\quad 2\Theta(p, q, r) = \mathfrak{P}p^2 + \mathfrak{Q}q^2 + \mathfrak{R}r^2 + 2\mathfrak{P}'qr + 2\mathfrak{Q}'rp + 2\mathfrak{R}'pq \qquad \text{(iv)};$

the coefficients in this expression being determined by formulae of the types

$$\left.\begin{aligned} \mathfrak{P} &= P - \frac{L^2}{A} - \frac{M^2}{B} - \frac{N^2}{C},\\ \mathfrak{P}' &= P' - \frac{L'L''}{A} - \frac{M'M''}{B} - \frac{N'N''}{C} \end{aligned}\right\} \qquad \text{(v).}$$

These formulæ hold for any case in which the force-constituent of the impulse is zero. Introducing the conditions (i) of steady motion, the ratios $p : q : r$ are to be determined from the three equations

$$\left.\begin{aligned} \mathfrak{P}p + \mathfrak{R}'q + \mathfrak{Q}'r &= kp,\\ \mathfrak{R}'p + \mathfrak{Q}q + \mathfrak{P}'r &= kq,\\ \mathfrak{Q}'p + \mathfrak{P}'q + \mathfrak{R}r &= kr \end{aligned}\right\} \qquad \text{(vi).}$$

The form of these shews that the line whose direction-ratios are $p : q : r$ must be parallel to one of the principal axes of the ellipsoid

$$\Theta(x, y, z) = \text{const.} \qquad \text{(vii).}$$

There are therefore three permanent screw-motions such that the corresponding impulsive wrench in each case reduces to a couple only. The axes of these three screws are mutually at right angles, but do not in general intersect.

It may now be shewn that in all cases where the impulse reduces to a couple only, the motion can be completely determined. It is convenient, retaining the same directions of the axes as before, to change the origin. Now the origin may be transferred to any point (x, y, z) by writing

$$u+ry-qz, \qquad v+pz-rx, \qquad w+qx-py,$$

for u, v, w respectively. The coefficient of vr in the expression for the kinetic energy, Art. 118 (7), becomes $-Bx+M''$, that of wq becomes $Cx+N'$, and so on. Hence if we take

$$x=\tfrac{1}{2}\left(\frac{M''}{B}-\frac{N'}{C}\right), \quad y=\tfrac{1}{2}\left(\frac{N''}{C}-\frac{L''}{A}\right), \quad z=\tfrac{1}{2}\left(\frac{L'}{A}-\frac{M'}{B}\right) \quad \text{.........(viii)},$$

the coefficients in the transformed expression for $2T$ will satisfy the relations

$$M''/B=N'/C, \qquad N''/C=L''/A, \qquad L'/A=M'/B \quad \text{..............(ix)}.$$

If we denote the values of these pairs of equal quantities by α, β, γ respectively, the formulæ (ii) may now be written

$$u=-\frac{d\Psi}{dp}, \quad v=-\frac{d\Psi}{dq}, \quad w=-\frac{d\Psi}{dr} \quad \text{....................(x)},$$

where $$2\Psi(p, q, r)=\frac{L}{A}p^2+\frac{M'}{B}q^2+\frac{N''}{C}r^2+2\alpha qr+2\beta rp+2\gamma pq \quad \text{......(xi)}.$$

The motion of the body at any instant may be conceived as made up of two parts; viz. a motion of translation equal to that of the origin, and one of rotation about an instantaneous axis passing through the origin. Since $\xi, \eta, \zeta=0$ the latter part is to be determined by the equations

$$\frac{d\lambda}{dt}=r\mu-q\nu, \qquad \frac{d\mu}{dt}=p\nu-r\lambda, \qquad \frac{d\nu}{dt}=q\lambda-p\mu,$$

which express that the vector (λ, μ, ν) is constant in magnitude and has a fixed direction in space. Substituting from (iii),

$$\left.\begin{aligned} \frac{d}{dt}\frac{d\Theta}{dp}&=r\frac{d\Theta}{dq}-q\frac{d\Theta}{dr}, \\ \frac{d}{dt}\frac{d\Theta}{dq}&=p\frac{d\Theta}{dr}-r\frac{d\Theta}{dp}, \\ \frac{d}{dt}\frac{d\Theta}{dr}&=q\frac{d\Theta}{dp}-p\frac{d\Theta}{dq} \end{aligned}\right\} \quad \text{........................ (xii)}.$$

These are identical in form with the equations of motion of a rigid body about a fixed point, so that we may make use of Poinsot's well-known solution of the latter problem. The angular motion of the body is therefore obtained by making the ellipsoid (vii), which is fixed in the body, roll on the plane

$$\lambda x+\mu y+\nu z=\text{const.},$$

which is fixed in space, with an angular velocity proportional to the length OI of the radius vector drawn from the origin to the point of contact I. The representation of the actual motion is then completed by impressing on the whole system of rolling ellipsoid and plane a velocity of translation whose components are given by (x). This velocity is in the direction of the normal OM to the tangent plane of the quadric

$$\Psi(x, y, z) = -\epsilon^3 \qquad \text{(xiii)},$$

at the point P where OI meets it, and is equal to

$$\frac{\epsilon^3}{OP \cdot OM} \times \text{angular velocity of body} \qquad \text{(xiv)}.$$

When OI does not meet the quadric (xiii), but the conjugate quadric obtained by changing the sign of ϵ, the sense of the velocity (xiv) is reversed*.

123. The problem of the integration of the equations of motion of a solid in the general case has engaged the attention of several mathematicians, but, as might be anticipated from the complexity of the question, the meaning of the results is not easily grasped.

In what follows we shall in the first place inquire what simplifications occur in the formula for the kinetic energy, for special classes of solids, and then proceed to investigate one or two particular problems of considerable interest which can be treated without difficult mathematics.

1°. If the solid has a plane of symmetry, as regards both its form and the distribution of matter in its interior, then, taking this plane as that of xy, it is evident that the energy of the motion is unaltered if we reverse the signs of w, p, q, the motion being exactly similar in the two cases. This requires that A', B', P', Q', L, M, L', M', N'' should vanish. One of the directions of permanent translation is then parallel to z. The three screws of Art. 122 are now pure rotations; the axis of one of them is parallel to z; the axes of the other two are at right angles in the plane xy, but do not in general intersect the first.

2°. If the body have a second plane of symmetry, at right angles to the former one, let this be taken as the plane of zx. We find, in the same way, that in this case the coefficients

* The substance of this Art. is taken from a paper, "On the Free Motion of a Solid through an Infinite Mass of Liquid," *Proc. Lond. Math. Soc.*, t. viii. (1877). Similar results were obtained independently by Craig, "The Motion of a Solid in a Fluid," *Amer. Journ. of Math.*, t. ii. (1879).

C', R', N, L'' also must vanish, so that the expression for $2T$ assumes the form

$$2T = Au^2 + Bv^2 + Cw^2$$
$$+ Pp^2 + Qq^2 + Rr^2$$
$$+ 2N'wq + 2M''vr \text{ .... } (1).$$

The directions of permanent translation are now parallel to the three axes of coordinates. The axis of x is the axis of one of the permanent screws (now pure rotations) of Art. 122, and those of the other two intersect it at right angles (being parallel to y and z respectively), though not necessarily in the same point.

3°. If the body have a third plane of symmetry, viz. that of yz, at right angles to the two former ones, we have

$$2T = Au^2 + Bv^2 + Cw^2$$
$$+ Pp^2 + Qq^2 + Rr^2 \text{ .... } (2).$$

The axes of coordinates are in the directions of the three permanent translations; they are also the axes of the three permanent screw-motions (now pure rotations) of Art. 122.

4°. If, further, the solid be one of revolution, about x, say, the value (1) of $2T$ must be unaltered when we write v, q, $-w$, $-r$ for w, r, v, q, respectively; for this is merely equivalent to turning the axes of y, z through a right angle. Hence we must have $B = C$, $Q = R$, $M'' = -N'$. If we further transfer the origin to the point defined by Art. 122 (viii) we have $M'' = N'$. Hence we must have

$$M'' = 0, \quad N' = 0,$$

and
$$2T = Au^2 + B(v^2 + w^2)$$
$$+ Pp^2 + Q(q^2 + r^2) \text{ .... } (3).$$

The same reduction obtains in some other cases, for example when the solid is a right prism whose section is any regular polygon*. This is seen at once from the consideration that, the axis of x coinciding with the axis of the prism, it is impossible to assign any uniquely symmetrical directions to the axes of y and z.

* See Larmor, "On Hydrokinetic Symmetry," *Quart. Journ. Math.*, t. XX. (1885).

5°. If, in the last case, the form of the solid be similarly related to each of the coordinate planes (for example a sphere, or a cube), the expression (3) takes the form

$$2T = A\,(u^2 + v^2 + w^2) + P\,(p^2 + q^2 + r^2) \quad\text{..............(4).}$$

This again may be extended, for a like reason, to other cases, for example any regular polyhedron. Such a body is practically for the present purpose 'isotropic,' and its motion will be exactly that of a sphere under similar conditions.

6°. We may next consider another class of cases. Let us suppose that the body has a sort of skew symmetry about a certain axis (say that of x), viz. that it is identical with itself turned through two right angles about this axis, but has not necessarily a plane of symmetry*. The expression for $2T$ must be unaltered when we change the signs of v, w, q, r, so that the coefficients B', C', Q', R', M, N, L', L'' must all vanish. We have then

$$\begin{aligned} 2T = {} & Au^2 + Bv^2 + Cw^2 + 2A'vw \\ & + Pp^2 + Qq^2 + Rr^2 + 2P'qr \\ & + 2Lpu \\ & + 2q\,(M'v + N'w) \\ & + 2r\,(M''v + N''w) \quad\text{........................ (5).} \end{aligned}$$

The axis of x is one of the directions of permanent translation; and is also the axis of one of the three screws of Art. 122, the pitch being $-L/A$. The axes of the two remaining screws intersect it at right angles, but not in general in the same point.

7°. If, further, the body be identical with itself turned through *one* right angle about the above axis, the expression (5) must be unaltered when v, q, $-w$, $-r$ are written for w, r, v, q, respectively. This requires that $B = C$, $A' = 0$, $Q = R$, $P' = 0$, $M' = N''$, $N' = -M''$. If further we transfer the origin to the point chosen in Art. 122 we must have $N' = M''$, and therefore $N' = 0$, $M'' = 0$. Hence (5) reduces to

$$\begin{aligned} 2T = {} & Au^2 + B\,(v^2 + w^2) \\ & + Pp^2 + Q\,(q^2 + r^2) \\ & + 2Lpu \\ & + 2M'\,(vq + wr) \quad\text{.........................(6).†} \end{aligned}$$

* A two-bladed screw-propeller of a ship is an example of a body of this kind.

† This result admits of the same kind of generalization as (3), *e.g.* it applies to a body shaped like a screw-propeller with *three* symmetrically-disposed blades.

The form of this expression is unaltered when the axes of y, z are turned in their own plane through any angle. The body is therefore said to possess helicoidal symmetry about the axis of x.

8°. If the body possess the same properties of skew symmetry about an axis intersecting the former one at right angles, we must evidently have

$$\begin{aligned}2T = & A(u^2+v^2+w^2) \\ & + P(p^2+q^2+r^2) \\ & + 2L(pu+qv+rw) \quad \text{.....................} \quad (7).\end{aligned}$$

Any direction is now one of permanent translation, and any line drawn through the origin is the axis of a screw of the kind considered in Art. 122, of pitch $-L/A$. The form of (7) is unaltered by any change in the directions of the axes of coordinates. The solid is therefore in this case said to be 'helicoidally isotropic.'

124. For the case of a solid of revolution, or of any other form to which the formula

$$\begin{aligned}2T = & Au^2 + B(v^2+w^2) \\ & + Pp^2 + Q(q^2+r^2) \quad \text{.........................} (1)\end{aligned}$$

applies, the complete integration of the equations of motion was effected by Kirchhoff* in terms of elliptic functions.

The particular case where the solid moves without rotation about its axis, and with this axis always in one plane, admits of very simple treatment†, and the results are very interesting.

If the fixed plane in question be that of xy we have $p, q, w = 0$, so that the equations of motion, Art. 121 (1), reduce to

$$\left.\begin{aligned}A\frac{du}{dt} = rBv, \qquad & B\frac{dv}{dt} = -rAu, \\ Q\frac{dr}{dt} = (A-B)\,uv \quad & \end{aligned}\right\} \quad \text{............} (2).$$

Let $\mathbf{x}$, $\mathbf{y}$ be the coordinates of the moving origin relative to fixed axes in the plane (xy) in which the axis of the solid moves,

* *l.c. ante* p. 167.

† See Thomson and Tait, *Natural Philosophy*, Art. 322; and Greenhill, "On the Motion of a Cylinder through a Frictionless Liquid under no Forces," *Mess. of Math.*, t. ix. (1880).

the axis of **x** coinciding with the line of the resultant impulse (I, say) of the motion; and let θ be the angle which the line Ox (fixed in the solid) makes with **x**. We have then

$$Au = I\cos\theta, \quad Bv = -I\sin\theta, \quad r = \dot{\theta}.$$

The first two of equations (2) merely express the fixity of the direction of the impulse in space; the third gives

$$Q\ddot{\theta} + \frac{A-B}{AB} I^2 \sin\theta\cos\theta = 0 \quad\text{..................(3).}$$

We may suppose, without loss of generality, that $A > B$. If we write $2\theta = \vartheta$, (3) becomes

$$\ddot{\vartheta} + \frac{(A-B)I^2}{ABQ}\sin\vartheta = 0 \quad\text{..................(4),}$$

which is the equation of motion of the common pendulum. Hence the angular motion of the body is that of a 'quadrantal pendulum,' *i.e.* a body whose motion follows the same law in regard to a quadrant as the ordinary pendulum does in regard to a half-circumference. When θ has been determined from (3) and the initial conditions, **x**, **y** are to be found from the equations

$$\left.\begin{aligned} \dot{\mathbf{x}} &= u\cos\theta - v\sin\theta = \frac{I}{A}\cos^2\theta + \frac{I}{B}\sin^2\theta, \\ \dot{\mathbf{y}} &= u\sin\theta + v\cos\theta = \left(\frac{I}{A} - \frac{I}{B}\right)\sin\theta\cos\theta = \frac{Q}{I}\ddot{\theta} \end{aligned}\right\} \text{...(5),}$$

the latter of which gives

$$\mathbf{y} = \frac{Q}{I}\dot{\theta} \quad\text{............................(6),}$$

as is otherwise obvious, the additive constant being zero since the axis of **x** is taken to be coincident with, and not merely parallel to, the line of the impulse I.

Let us first suppose that the body makes complete revolutions, in which case the first integral of (3) is of the form

$$\dot{\theta}^2 = \omega^2(1 - k^2\sin^2\theta) \quad\text{.................... (7),}$$

where
$$k^2 = \frac{A-B}{ABQ}\cdot\frac{I^2}{\omega^2} \quad\text{........................ (8).}$$

Hence, reckoning t from the position $\theta = 0$, we have

$$\omega t = \int_0^\theta \frac{d\theta}{(1-k^2\sin^2\theta)^{\frac{1}{2}}} = F(k,\theta) \quad\text{..............(9),}$$

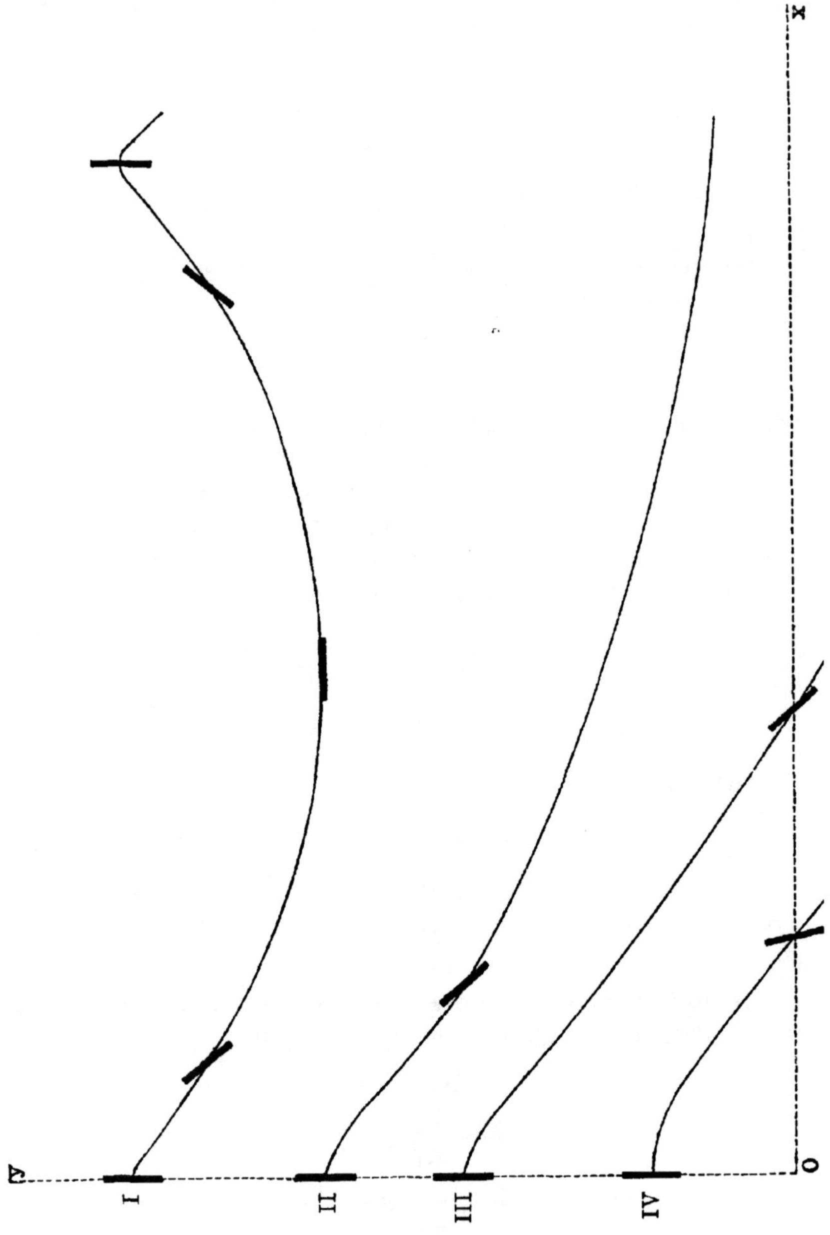
X
Y
O
I
II
III
IV

in the usual notation of elliptic integrals. If we eliminate t between (5) and (9), and then integrate with respect to θ, we find

$$\left.\begin{aligned}\mathbf{x} &= \left(\frac{I}{A\omega} + \frac{Q\omega}{I}\right) F(k, \theta) - \frac{Q\omega}{I} E(k, \theta), \\ \mathbf{y} &= \frac{Q}{I}\dot{\theta} = \frac{Q\omega}{I}(1 - k^2 \sin^2\theta)^{\frac{1}{2}}\end{aligned}\right\} \text{......} (10),$$

the origin of $\mathbf{x}$ being taken to correspond to the position $\theta = 0$. The path can then be traced, in any particular case, by means of Legendre's Tables. See the curve marked I in the figure.

If, on the other hand, the solid does not make a complete revolution, but oscillates through an angle α on each side of the position $\theta = 0$, the proper form of the first integral of (3) is

$$\dot{\theta}^2 = \omega^2 \left(1 - \frac{\sin^2\theta}{\sin^2\alpha}\right) \text{....................} (11),$$

where $$\sin^2\alpha = \frac{ABQ}{A - B} \cdot \frac{\omega^2}{I^2} \text{....................} (12).$$

If we put $$\sin\theta = \sin\alpha \sin\psi,$$

this gives $$\dot{\psi}^2 = \frac{\omega^2}{\sin^2\alpha}(1 - \sin^2\alpha \sin^2\psi),$$

whence $$\frac{\omega t}{\sin\alpha} = F(\sin\alpha, \psi) \text{....................} (13).$$

Transforming to ψ as independent variable, in (5), and integrating, we find

$$\left.\begin{aligned}\mathbf{x} &= \frac{I}{B\omega}\sin\alpha \,.\, F(\sin\alpha, \psi) - \frac{Q\omega}{I}\operatorname{cosec}\alpha \,.\, E(\sin\alpha, \psi), \\ \mathbf{y} &= \frac{Q\omega}{I}\cos\psi\end{aligned}\right\} \text{...} (14).$$

The path of the point O is here a sinuous curve crossing the line of the impulse at intervals of time equal to a half-period of the angular motion. This is illustrated by the curves III and IV of the figure.

There remains a critical case between the two preceding, where the solid just makes a half-revolution, θ having as asymptotic limits the two values $\pm\frac{1}{2}\pi$. This case may be obtained by putting $k=1$ in (7), or $\alpha=\frac{1}{2}\pi$ in (11); and we find

$$\dot{\theta}=\omega\cos\theta \quad\text{..............(15)},$$

$$\omega t=\log\tan\left(\tfrac{1}{4}\pi+\tfrac{1}{2}\theta\right) \quad\text{..............(16)},$$

$$\left.\begin{aligned}\mathbf{x}&=\frac{I}{B\omega}\log\tan\left(\tfrac{1}{4}\pi+\tfrac{1}{2}\theta\right)-\frac{Q\omega}{I}\sin\theta,\\ \mathbf{y}&=\frac{Q\omega}{I}\cos\theta\end{aligned}\right\}\quad\text{.........(17)}.$$

See the curve II of the figure*.

It is to be observed that the above investigation is not restricted to the case of a solid of revolution; it applies equally well to the case of a body with two perpendicular planes of symmetry, moving parallel to one of these planes, provided the origin be properly chosen. If the plane in question be that of xy, then on transferring the origin to the point $(M''/B, 0, 0)$ the last term in the formula (1) of Art. 123 disappears, and the equations of motion take the form (2) above. On the other hand, if the motion be parallel to zx we must transfer the origin to the point $(-N'/C, 0, 0)$.

The results of this Article, with the accompanying diagrams, serve to exemplify the statements made near the end of Art. 121. Thus the curve IV illustrates, with exaggerated amplitude, the case of a slightly disturbed *stable* steady motion parallel to an axis of permanent translation. The case of a slightly disturbed *unstable* steady motion would be represented by a curve contiguous to II, on one side or the other, according to the nature of the disturbance.

125. The mere question of the stability of the motion of a body parallel to an axis of symmetry may of course be more simply treated by approximate methods. Thus, in the case of a body

* In order to bring out the peculiar features of the motion, the curves have been drawn for the somewhat extreme case of $A=5B$. In the case of an infinitely thin disk, without inertia of its own, we should have $A/B=\infty$; the curves would then have *cusps* where they meet the axis of $\mathbf{y}$. It appears from (5) that $\dot{\mathbf{x}}$ has always the same sign, so that *loops* cannot occur in any case.

In the various cases figured the body is projected always with the same impulse, but with different degrees of rotation. In the curve I, the maximum angular velocity is $\sqrt{2}$ times what it is in the critical case II; whilst the curves III and IV represent oscillations of amplitude 45° and 18° respectively.

with three planes of symmetry, as in Art. 123, 3°, slightly disturbed from a state of steady motion parallel to x, we find, writing $u = u_0 + u'$, and assuming u', v, w, p, q, r to be all small,

$$\left.\begin{aligned} A\frac{du'}{dt} &= 0, \quad B\frac{dv}{dt} = -Au_0r, \qquad C\frac{dw}{dt} = Au_0q, \\ P\frac{dp}{dt} &= 0, \quad Q\frac{dq}{dt} = (C-A)\,u_0w, \quad R\frac{dr}{dt} = (A-B)\,u_0v \end{aligned}\right\} \ldots(1).$$

Hence $$B\frac{d^2v}{dt^2} + A\frac{(A-B)}{R}u_0^2v = 0,$$

with a similar equation for r, and

$$C\frac{d^2w}{dt^2} + A\frac{(A-C)}{Q}u_0^2w = 0 \quad \ldots\ldots\ldots\ldots\ldots (2),$$

with a similar equation for q. The motion is therefore stable only when A is the greatest of the three quantities A, B, C.

It is evident from ordinary Dynamics that the stability of a body moving parallel to an axis of symmetry will be increased, or its instability (as the case may be) will be diminished, by communicating to it a rotation about this axis. This question has been examined by Greenhill*.

Thus in the case of a solid of revolution slightly disturbed from a state of motion in which u and p are constant, while the remaining velocities are zero, if we neglect squares and products of small quantities, the first and fourth of equations (1) of Art. 121 give

$$du/dt = 0, \qquad dp/dt = 0,$$

whence $$u = u_0, \qquad p = p_0 \quad \ldots\ldots\ldots\ldots\ldots\ldots\ldots\ldots\ldots (i),$$

say, where u_0, p_0 are constants. The remaining equations then take, on substitution from Art. 123 (3), the forms

$$\left.\begin{aligned} B\left(\frac{dv}{dt} - p_0w\right) &= -Au_0r, \\ B\left(\frac{dw}{dt} + p_0v\right) &= \ \ Au_0q \end{aligned}\right\} \quad \ldots\ldots\ldots\ldots\ldots\ldots\ldots\ldots\ldots (ii),$$

$$\left.\begin{aligned} Q\frac{dq}{dt} + (P-Q)\,p_0r &= -(A-B)\,u_0w, \\ Q\frac{dr}{dt} - (P-Q)\,p_0q &= \ \ (A-B)\,u_0v \end{aligned}\right\} \quad \ldots\ldots\ldots\ldots\ldots\ldots (iii).$$

* "Fluid Motion between Confocal Elliptic Cylinders, &c.," *Quart. Journ. Math.*, t. xvi. (1879).

If we assume that v, w, q, r vary as $e^{i\lambda t}$, and eliminate their ratios, we find

$$Q\lambda^2 \pm (P-2Q)\, p_0\lambda - \left\{(P-Q)\, p_0^2 + \frac{A}{B}(A-B)\, u_0^2\right\} = 0 \text{.........(iv).}$$

The condition that the roots of this should be real is that

$$P^2 p_0^2 + 4\frac{A}{B}(A-B)\, Q u_0^2$$

should be positive. This is always satisfied when $A > B$, and can be satisfied in any case by giving a sufficiently great value to p_0.

This example illustrates the steadiness of flight which is given to an elongated projectile by rifling.

126. In the investigation of Art. 122 the term 'steady' was used to characterize modes of motion in which the 'instantaneous screw' preserved a constant relation to the moving solid. In the case of a solid of revolution, however, we may conveniently use the term in a somewhat wider sense, extending it to motions in which the velocities of translation and rotation are constant in magnitude, and make constant angles with the axis of symmetry and with each other, although their relation to particles of the solid not on the axis may continually vary.

The conditions to be satisfied in this case are most easily obtained from the equations of motion of Art. 121, which become, on substitution from Art. 123 (3),

$$\left.\begin{aligned} A\frac{du}{dt} &= B(rv - qw), & P\frac{dp}{dt} &= 0, \\ B\frac{dv}{dt} &= Bpw - Aru, & Q\frac{dq}{dt} &= -(A-B)\, uw - (P-Q)\, pr, \\ B\frac{dw}{dt} &= Aqu - Bpv, & Q\frac{dr}{dt} &= (A-B)\, uv + (P-Q)\, pq \end{aligned}\right\} \text{......(i).}$$

It appears that p is in any case constant, and that q^2+r^2 will also be constant provided

$$v/q = w/r, \quad = k, \text{ say} \text{..............................(ii).}$$

This makes $du/dt = 0$, and

$$v^2 + w^2 = \text{const.}$$

It follows that k will also be constant; and it only remains to satisfy the equations

$$kB\frac{dq}{dt} = (kBp - Au)\, r,$$

$$Q\frac{dq}{dt} = -\{(A-B)\, ku + (P-Q)\, p\}\, r,$$

which will be consistent provided

$$kB\{(A-B)ku+(P-Q)p\}+Q(kBp-Au)=0,$$

whence
$$u/p=kBP/\{AQ-k^2B(A-B)\} \quad\text{.........................(iii).}$$

Hence there are an infinite number of possible modes of steady motion, of the kind above defined. In each of these the instantaneous axis of rotation and the direction of translation of the origin are in one plane with the axis of the solid. It is easily seen that the origin describes a helix about the resultant axis of the impulse.

These results are due to Kirchhoff.

127. The only case of a body possessing helicoidal property, where simple results can be obtained, is that of the 'isotropic helicoid' defined by Art. 123 (7). Let O be the centre of the body, and let us take as axes of coordinates at any instant, a line Ox, parallel to the axis of the impulse, a line Oy drawn outwards from this axis, and a line Oz perpendicular to the plane of the two former. If I and G denote the force- and couple-constituents of the impulse, we have

$$\left.\begin{aligned} Au+Lp&=\xi=I, & Pp+Lu&=\lambda=G,\\ Av+Lq&=\eta=0, & Pq+Lv&=\mu=0,\\ Aw+Lr&=\zeta=0, & Pr+Lw&=\nu=I\varpi \end{aligned}\right\}\text{......(1),}$$

where ϖ denotes the distance of O from the axis of the impulse.

Since $AP-L^2 \neq 0$, the second and fifth of these equations shew that $v=0$, $q=0$. Hence ϖ is constant throughout the motion, and the remaining quantities are constant; in particular

$$\left.\begin{aligned} u&=(IP-GL)/(AP-L^2),\\ w&=-\varpi IL/(AP-L^2) \end{aligned}\right\}\text{............... (2).}$$

The origin O therefore describes a helix about the axis of the impulse, of pitch

$$G/I-P/L.$$

This example is due to Lord Kelvin*.

* *l.c. ante* p. 176. It is there pointed out that a solid of the kind here in question may be constructed by attaching vanes to a sphere, at the middle points of twelve quadrantal arcs drawn so as to divide the surface into octants. The vanes are to be perpendicular to the surface, and are to be inclined at angles of 45° to the respective arcs.

For some further investigations in this field see a paper by Miss Fawcett, "On the Motion of Solids in a Liquid," *Quart. Journ. Math.*, t. xxvi. (1893).

128. Before leaving this part of the subject we remark that the preceding theory applies, with obvious modifications, to the acyclic motion of a liquid occupying a cavity in a moving solid. If the origin be taken at the centre of inertia of the liquid, the formula for the kinetic energy of the fluid motion is of the type

$$2\mathbf{T} = \mathbf{m}(u^2 + v^2 + w^2)$$
$$+ \mathbf{P}p^2 + \mathbf{Q}q^2 + \mathbf{R}r^2 + 2\mathbf{P}'qr + 2\mathbf{Q}'rp + 2\mathbf{R}'pq \ldots\ldots(1).$$

For the kinetic energy is equal to that of the whole fluid mass ($\mathbf{m}$), supposed concentrated at the centre of mass and moving with this point, together with the kinetic energy of the motion relative to the centre of mass. The latter part of the energy is easily proved by the method of Arts. 115, 118 to be a homogeneous quadratic function of p, q, r.

Hence the fluid may be replaced by a solid of the same mass, having the same centre of inertia, provided the principal axes and moments of inertia be properly assigned.

The values of the coefficients in (1), for the case of an ellipsoidal cavity, may be calculated from Art. 107. Thus, if the axes of x, y, z coincide with the principal axes of the ellipsoid, we find

$$\mathbf{P} = \tfrac{1}{5}\mathbf{m}\frac{(b^2-c^2)^2}{b^2+c^2}, \quad \mathbf{Q} = \tfrac{1}{5}\mathbf{m}\frac{(c^2-a^2)^2}{c^2+a^2}, \quad \mathbf{R} = \tfrac{1}{5}\mathbf{m}\frac{(a^2-b^2)^2}{a^2+b^2},$$
$$\mathbf{P}'=0, \quad \mathbf{Q}'=0, \quad \mathbf{R}'=0.$$

Case of a Perforated Solid.

129. If the moving solid have one or more apertures or perforations, so that the space external to it is multiply-connected, the fluid may have a motion independent of that of the solid, viz. a cyclic motion in which the circulations in the several irreducible circuits which can be drawn through the apertures may have any given constant values. We will briefly indicate how the foregoing methods may be adapted to this case.

Let κ, κ', κ'',... be the circulations in the various circuits, and let $\delta\sigma$, $\delta\sigma'$, $\delta\sigma''$,... be elements of the corresponding barriers, drawn as in Art. 48. Further, let l, m, n denote direction-cosines of the normal, drawn towards the fluid, at any point of the surface of the solid, or drawn on the positive side at any point of a barrier. The velocity-potential is then of the form

$$\phi + \phi_0,$$

where

$$\left.\begin{aligned}\phi &= u\phi_1 + v\phi_2 + w\phi_3 + p\chi_1 + q\chi_2 + r\chi_3,\\ \phi_0 &= \kappa\omega + \kappa'\omega' + \kappa''\omega'' + \dots\end{aligned}\right\} \quad \dots\dots\dots(1).$$

The functions $\phi_1, \phi_2, \phi_3, \chi_1, \chi_2, \chi_3$ are determined by the same conditions as in Art. 115. To determine ω, we have the conditions: (1°) that it must satisfy $\nabla^2\omega = 0$ at all points of the fluid; (2°) that its derivatives must vanish at infinity; (3°) that $d\omega/dn = 0$ at the surface of the solid; and (4°) that ω must be a cyclic function, diminishing by unity whenever the point to which it refers completes a circuit cutting the first barrier once only in the positive direction, and recovering its original value whenever the point completes a circuit not cutting this barrier. It appears from Art. 52 that these conditions determine ω save as to an additive constant. In like manner the remaining functions $\omega', \omega'', \dots$ are determined.

By the formula (5) of Art. 55, twice the kinetic energy of the fluid is equal to

$$-\rho\iint(\phi + \phi_0)\frac{d}{dn}(\phi + \phi_0)\,dS$$

$$-\rho\kappa\iint\frac{d}{dn}(\phi + \phi_0)\,d\sigma - \rho\kappa'\int\frac{d}{dn}(\phi + \phi_0)\,d\sigma' - \dots \quad \dots(2).$$

Since the cyclic constants of ϕ are zero, we have, by Art. 54 (4),

$$\iint\phi_0\frac{d\phi}{dn}\,dS + \rho\kappa\iint\frac{d\phi}{dn}\,d\sigma + \rho\kappa'\iint\frac{d\phi}{dn}\,d\sigma' + \dots = \iint\phi\frac{d\phi_0}{dn}\,dS,$$

which vanishes, since $d\phi_0/dn = 0$ at the surface of the solid. Hence (2) reduces to

$$-\rho\iint\phi\frac{d\phi}{dn}\,dS - \rho\kappa\iint\frac{d\phi_0}{dn}\,d\sigma - \rho\kappa'\iint\frac{d\phi_0}{dn}\,d\sigma' - \dots \quad \dots(3).$$

Substituting the values of ϕ, ϕ_0 from (1), we find that the kinetic energy of the fluid is equal to

$$\mathbf{T} + K \quad \dots\dots\dots\dots\dots\dots\dots\dots(4),$$

where $\mathbf{T}$ is a homogeneous quadratic function of u, v, w, p, q, r of the form defined by Art. 118 (2), (3), and

$$2K = (\kappa, \kappa)\,\kappa^2 + (\kappa', \kappa')\,\kappa'^2 + \dots + 2\,(\kappa, \kappa')\,\kappa\kappa' + \dots \quad \dots\dots(5),$$

where, for example,

$$\left.\begin{aligned}(\kappa, \kappa) &= -\rho \iint \frac{d\omega}{dn} d\sigma \\ (\kappa, \kappa') &= -\tfrac{1}{2}\rho \iint \frac{d\omega'}{dn} d\sigma - \tfrac{1}{2}\rho \iint \frac{d\omega}{dn} d\sigma' \\ &= -\rho \iint \frac{d\omega'}{dn} d\sigma = -\rho \iint \frac{d\omega}{dn} d\sigma'\end{aligned}\right\} \text{.........} (6).$$

The identity of the two forms of (κ, κ') follows from Art. 54 (4).

Hence the total energy of fluid and solid is given by

$$T = \mathfrak{T} + K, \text{ .... } (7),$$

where $\mathfrak{T}$ is a homogeneous quadratic function of u, v, w, p, q, r of the same form as Art. 118 (5), and K is defined by (5) and (6) above.

130. The 'impulse' of the motion now consists partly of impulsive forces applied to the solid, and partly of impulsive pressures $\rho\kappa, \rho\kappa', \rho\kappa''$... applied uniformly (as explained in Art. 54) over the several membranes which are supposed for a moment to occupy the positions of the barriers. Let us denote by $\xi_1, \eta_1, \zeta_1, \lambda_1, \mu_1, \nu_1$ the components of the extraneous impulse applied to the solid. Expressing that the x-component of the momentum of the solid is equal to the similar component of the total impulse acting on it, we have

$$\begin{aligned}\frac{d\mathbf{T}_1}{du} &= \xi_1 - \rho \iint (\phi + \phi_0)\, l dS \\ &= \xi_1 + \rho \iint (u\phi_1 + \ldots + p\chi_1 + \ldots + \kappa\omega + \ldots) \frac{d\phi_1}{dn} dS \\ &= \xi_1 - \frac{d\mathbf{T}}{du} + \rho\kappa \iint \omega \frac{d\phi_1}{dn} dS + \rho\kappa' \iint \omega' \frac{d\phi_1}{dn} dS + \ldots \text{ ...} (1),\end{aligned}$$

where, as before, $\mathbf{T}_1$ denotes the kinetic energy of the solid, and $\mathbf{T}$ that part of the energy of the fluid which is independent of the cyclic motion. Again, considering the angular momentum of the solid about the axis of x,

$$\begin{aligned}\frac{d\mathbf{T}_1}{dp} &= \lambda_1 - \rho \iint (\phi + \phi_0)(ny - mz)\, dS \\ &= \lambda_1 + \rho \iint (u\phi_1 + \ldots + p\chi_1 + \ldots + \kappa\omega + \ldots) \frac{d\chi_1}{dn} dS \\ &= \lambda_1 - \frac{d\mathbf{T}}{dp} + \rho\kappa \iint \omega \frac{d\chi_1}{dn} dS + \rho\kappa' \iint \omega' \frac{d\chi_1}{dn} dS + \text{ ....} (2).\end{aligned}$$

Hence, since $\mathfrak{T} = \mathbf{T} + \mathbf{T}_1$, we have

$$\left.\begin{aligned}\xi_1 &= \frac{d\mathfrak{T}}{du} - \rho\kappa \iint \omega \frac{d\phi_1}{dn} dS - \rho\kappa' \iint \omega' \frac{d\phi_1}{dn} dS - \dots, \\ \lambda_1 &= \frac{d\mathfrak{T}}{dp} - \rho\kappa \iint \omega \frac{d\chi_1}{dn} dS - \rho\kappa' \iint \omega' \frac{d\chi_1}{dn} dS - \dots\end{aligned}\right\} \dots\dots (3).$$

By virtue of Lord Kelvin's extension of Green's theorem, already referred to, these may be written in the alternative forms

$$\left.\begin{aligned}\xi_1 &= \frac{d\mathfrak{T}}{du} + \rho\kappa \iint \frac{d\phi_1}{dn} d\sigma + \rho\kappa' \iint \frac{d\phi_1}{dn} d\sigma' + \dots, \\ \lambda_1 &= \frac{d\mathfrak{T}}{dp} + \rho\kappa \iint \frac{d\chi_1}{dn} d\sigma + \rho\kappa' \iint \frac{d\chi_1}{dn} d\sigma' + \dots\end{aligned}\right\} \dots\dots (4).$$

Adding to these the terms due to the impulsive pressures applied to the barriers, we have, finally, for the components of the total impulse of the motion,

$$\left.\begin{aligned}\xi &= \frac{d\mathfrak{T}}{du} + \xi_0, \quad \eta = \frac{d\mathfrak{T}}{dv} + \eta_0, \quad \zeta = \frac{d\mathfrak{T}}{dw} + \zeta_0, \\ \lambda &= \frac{d\mathfrak{T}}{dp} + \lambda_0, \quad \mu = \frac{d\mathfrak{T}}{dq} + \mu_0, \quad \nu = \frac{d\mathfrak{T}}{dr} + \nu_0\end{aligned}\right\} \dots\dots (5),$$

where, for example,

$$\left.\begin{aligned}\xi_0 &= \rho\kappa \iint \left(l + \frac{d\phi_1}{dn}\right) d\sigma + \rho\kappa' \iint \left(l + \frac{d\phi_1}{dn}\right) d\sigma' + \dots \\ \lambda_0 &= \rho\kappa \iint \left(ny - mz + \frac{d\chi_1}{dn}\right) d\sigma + \rho\kappa' \iint \left(ny - mz + \frac{d\chi_1}{dn}\right) d\sigma' + \dots\end{aligned}\right\} (6).$$

It is evident that the constants ξ_0, η_0, ζ_0, λ_0, μ_0, ν_0 are the components of the impulse of the cyclic fluid motion which remains when the solid is, by forces applied to it alone, brought to rest.

By the argument of Art. 116, the total impulse is subject to the same laws as the momentum of a finite dynamical system. Hence the equations of motion of the solid are obtained by substituting from (5) in the equations (1) of Art. 117*.

* This conclusion may be verified by direct calculation from the pressure-formula of Art. 21; see Bryan, "Hydrodynamical Proof of the Equations of Motion of a Perforated Solid,......," *Phil. Mag.*, May, 1893.

131. As a simple example we may take the case of an annular solid of revolution. If the axis of x coincide with that of the ring, we see by reasoning of the same kind as in Art. 123, 4° that if the situation of the origin on this axis be properly chosen we may write

$$\begin{aligned}2T = & Au^2 + B(v^2 + w^2) \\ & + Pp^2 + Q(q^2 + r^2) \\ & + (\kappa, \kappa)\kappa^2 \quad \text{.............................(1).}\end{aligned}$$

Hence
$$\left.\begin{aligned}\xi &= Au + \xi_0, & \eta &= Bv, & \zeta &= Bw, \\ \lambda &= Pp, & \mu &= Qq, & \nu &= Qr\end{aligned}\right\} \quad \text{...........(2).}$$

Substituting in the equations of Art. 117, we find $dp/dt = 0$, or $p = \text{const.}$, as is obviously the case. Let us suppose that the ring is slightly disturbed from a state of motion in which v, w, p, q, r are zero, *i.e.* a state of steady motion parallel to the axis. In the beginning of the disturbed motion v, w, p, q, r will be small quantities whose products we may neglect. The first of the equations referred to then gives $du/dt = 0$, or $u = \text{const.}$, and the remaining equations become

$$\left.\begin{aligned}B\frac{dv}{dt} &= -(Au + \xi_0)r, & Q\frac{dq}{dt} &= -\{(A - B)u + \xi_0\}w, \\ B\frac{dw}{dt} &= (Au + \xi_0)q, & Q\frac{dr}{dt} &= \{(A - B)u + \xi_0\}v\end{aligned}\right\} \quad \text{...(3).}$$

Eliminating r, we find

$$BQ\frac{d^2v}{dt^2} = -(Au + \xi_0)\{(A - B)u + \xi_0\}v \quad \text{.........(4).}$$

Exactly the same equation is satisfied by w. It is therefore necessary and sufficient for stability that the coefficient of v on the right-hand side of (4) should be negative; and the time of a small oscillation, in the case of disturbed stable motion, is

$$2\pi\left[\frac{BQ}{(Au + \xi_0)\{(A - B)u + \xi_0\}}\right]^{\frac{1}{2}} \quad \text{...........(5)*.}$$

We may also notice another case of steady motion of the ring, viz. where the impulse reduces to a couple about a diameter. It is easily seen that the equations of motion are satisfied by $\xi, \eta, \zeta, \lambda, \mu = 0$, and ν constant; in which case

$$u = -\xi_0/A, \quad r = \text{const.}$$

* Sir W. Thomson, *l. c. ante* p. 176.

The ring then rotates about an axis in the plane yz parallel to that of z, at a distance u/r from it.

For further investigations on the motion of a ring we refer to papers by Basset*, who has discussed in detail various cases where the axis moves in one plane, and Miss Fawcett†.

Equations of Motion in Generalized Coordinates.

132. When we have more than one moving solid, or when the fluid is bounded, wholly or in part, by fixed walls, we may have recourse to Lagrange's method of 'generalized coordinates.' This was first applied to hydrodynamical problems by Thomson and Tait§.

In any dynamical system whatever, if ξ, η, ζ be the Cartesian coordinates at time t of any particle m, and X, Y, Z be the components of the total force acting on it, we have of course

$$m\ddot{\xi} = X, \quad m\ddot{\eta} = Y, \quad m\ddot{\zeta} = Z \text{.................}(1).$$

Now let $\xi + \Delta\xi$, $\eta + \Delta\eta$, $\zeta + \Delta\zeta$ be the coordinates of the same particle in any arbitrary motion of the system differing infinitely little from the actual motion, and let us form the equation

$$\Sigma m (\ddot{\xi}\Delta\xi + \ddot{\eta}\Delta\eta + \ddot{\zeta}\Delta\zeta) = \Sigma (X\Delta\xi + Y\Delta\eta + Z\Delta\zeta) \text{......}(2),$$

where the summation Σ embraces all the particles of the system. This follows at once from the equations (1), and includes these, on account of the arbitrary character of the variations $\Delta\xi$, $\Delta\eta$, $\Delta\zeta$. Its chief advantages, however, consist in the extensive elimination of internal forces which, by imposing suitable restrictions on the values of $\Delta\xi$, $\Delta\eta$, $\Delta\zeta$ we are able to effect, and in the facilities which it affords for transformation of coordinates.

If we multiply (2) by δt and integrate between the limits t_0 and t_1, then since

$$\frac{d}{dt}\Delta\xi = \frac{d}{dt}(\xi + \Delta\xi) - \frac{d\xi}{dt} = \Delta\dot{\xi}, \ \ldots, \ \ldots,$$

* "On the Motion of a Ring in an Infinite Liquid," *Proc. Camb. Phil. Soc.*, t. vi. (1887).

† *l. c. ante* p. 191.

§ *Natural Philosophy* (1st ed.), Oxford, 1867, Art. 331.

we find

$$\left[\Sigma m(\dot{\xi}\Delta\xi+\dot{\eta}\Delta\eta+\dot{\zeta}\Delta\zeta)\right]_{t_0}^{t_1}-\int_{t_0}^{t_1}\Sigma m(\dot{\xi}\Delta\dot{\xi}+\dot{\eta}\Delta\dot{\eta}+\dot{\zeta}\Delta\dot{\zeta})\,dt$$

$$=\int_{t_0}^{t_1}\Sigma(X\Delta\xi+Y\Delta\eta+Z\Delta\zeta)\,dt.$$

If we put, as usual,

$$2T=\Sigma m(\dot{\xi}^2+\dot{\eta}^2+\dot{\zeta}^2) \quad\text{..................(3)},$$

this may be written

$$\int_{t_0}^{t_1}\{\Delta T+\Sigma(X\Delta\xi+Y\Delta\eta+Z\Delta\zeta)\}\,dt$$

$$=\left[\Sigma m(\dot{\xi}\Delta\xi+\dot{\eta}\Delta\eta+\dot{\zeta}\Delta\zeta)\right]_{t_0}^{t_1} \quad\text{..............(4)}.$$

If we now introduce the condition that in the varied motion the initial and final positions (at times t_0 and t_1) shall be respectively the same for each particle as in the actual motion, the quantities $\Delta\xi$, $\Delta\eta$, $\Delta\zeta$ vanish at both limits, and the above equation reduces to

$$\int_{t_0}^{t_1}\{\Delta T+\Sigma(X\Delta\xi+Y\Delta\eta+Z\Delta\zeta)\}\,dt=0 \quad\text{...... (5)}.$$

This formula is especially valuable in the case of a system whose freedom is limited more or less by constraints. If the variations $\Delta\xi$, $\Delta\eta$, $\Delta\zeta$ be such as are consistent with these constraints, some of the internal forces of the system disappear as a rule from the sum

$$\Sigma(X\Delta\xi+Y\Delta\eta+Z\Delta\zeta);$$

for example, all the internal reactions between the particles of a rigid body, and (as we shall prove presently) the *mutual* pressures between the elements of an incompressible perfect fluid.

In the case of a 'conservative system,' we have

$$\Sigma(X\Delta\xi+Y\Delta\eta+Z\Delta\zeta)=-\Delta V \quad\text{........... (6)},$$

where V is the potential energy, and the equation (5) takes the form

$$\Delta\int_{t_0}^{t_1}(T-V)\,dt=0 \quad\text{..................(7)*}.$$

* Sir W. R. Hamilton, "On a General Method in Dynamics," *Phil. Trans.* 1834, 1835.

133. In the systems ordinarily considered in books on Dynamics, the position of every particle at any instant is completely determined by the values of certain independent variables or 'generalized coordinates' $q_1, q_2, \ldots$, so that

$$\left.\begin{aligned}\dot{\xi} &= \frac{d\xi}{dq_1}\dot{q}_1 + \frac{d\xi}{dq_2}\dot{q}_2 + \ldots, \ldots, \ldots, \\ \Delta\xi &= \frac{d\xi}{dq_1}\Delta q_1 + \frac{d\xi}{dq_2}\Delta q_2 + \ldots, \ldots, \ldots,\end{aligned}\right\} \ldots\ldots\ldots\ldots(8).$$

The kinetic energy can then be expressed as a homogeneous quadratic function of the 'generalized velocity-components' $\dot{q}_1, \dot{q}_2, \ldots$, thus

$$2T = A_{11}\dot{q}_1^2 + A_{22}\dot{q}_2^2 + \ldots + 2A_{12}\dot{q}_1\dot{q}_2 + \ldots\ldots\ldots\ldots(9),$$

where, for example,

$$\left.\begin{aligned}A_{11} &= \Sigma m\left\{\left(\frac{d\xi}{dq_1}\right)^2 + \left(\frac{d\eta}{dq_1}\right)^2 + \left(\frac{d\zeta}{dq_1}\right)^2\right\}, \\ A_{12} &= \Sigma m\left\{\frac{d\xi}{dq_1}\frac{d\xi}{dq_2} + \frac{d\eta}{dq_1}\frac{d\eta}{dq_2} + \frac{d\zeta}{dq_1}\frac{d\zeta}{dq_2}\right\},\end{aligned}\right\} \ldots\ldots\ldots(10).$$

The quantities $A_{11}, A_{22}, \ldots, A_{12}, \ldots$ are called the 'inertia-coefficients' of the system; they are, of course, in general functions of the coordinates $q_1, q_2, \ldots$.

Again, we have

$$\Sigma(X\Delta\xi + Y\Delta\eta + Z\Delta\zeta) = Q_1\Delta q_1 + Q_2\Delta q_2 + \ldots\ldots (11),$$

where, for example,

$$Q_1 = \Sigma\left(X\frac{d\xi}{dq_1} + Y\frac{d\eta}{dq_1} + Z\frac{d\zeta}{dq_1}\right) \ldots\ldots\ldots (12).$$

The quantities $Q_1, Q_2, \ldots$ are called the 'generalised components of force.' In the case of a conservative system we have

$$Q_1 = -\frac{dV}{dq_1} \ldots\ldots\ldots\ldots\ldots\ldots\ldots\ldots (13).$$

If X', Y', Z' be the components of impulsive force by which the actual motion of the particle m could be produced instantaneously from rest, we have of course

$$m\dot{\xi} = X', \quad m\dot{\eta} = Y', \quad m\dot{\zeta} = Z' \ldots\ldots\ldots\ldots\ldots\ldots\ldots (i),$$

and therefore

$$\Sigma m(\dot{\xi}\Delta\xi + \dot{\eta}\Delta\eta + \dot{\zeta}\Delta\zeta) = \Sigma(X'\Delta\xi + Y'\Delta\eta + Z'\Delta\zeta) \ldots\ldots\ldots\ldots (ii).$$

Now, from (8) and (10),

$$\Sigma m(\dot{\xi}\Delta\xi+\dot{\eta}\Delta\eta+\dot{\zeta}\Delta\zeta)$$

$$=(A_{11}\dot{q}_1+A_{12}\dot{q}_2+\ldots)\,\Delta q_1+(A_{21}\dot{q}_1+A_{22}\dot{q}_2+\ldots)\,\Delta q_2+\ldots$$

$$=\frac{dT}{d\dot{q}_1}\Delta q_1+\frac{dT}{d\dot{q}_2}\Delta q_2+\ldots\ldots\ldots\ldots\ldots\text{(iii)},$$

by (9). Again

$$\Sigma(X'\Delta\xi+Y'\Delta\eta+Z'\Delta\zeta)=Q_1'\Delta q_1+Q_2'\Delta q_2+\ldots\ldots\ldots\ldots\text{(iv)},$$

where, for example,

$$Q_1'=\Sigma\left(X'\frac{d\xi}{dq_1}+Y'\frac{d\eta}{dq_1}+Z'\frac{d\zeta}{dq_1}\right)\ldots\ldots\ldots\ldots\text{(v)}.$$

It is evident, on comparison with (12), that Q_1', Q_2',... are the time-integrals of Q_1, Q_2,... taken over the infinitely short duration of the impulse, in other words they are the generalized components of the impulse. Equating the right-hand sides of (iii) and (v) we have, on account of the independence of the variations Δq_1, Δq_2,...,

$$\frac{dT}{d\dot{q}_1}=Q_1',\quad \frac{dT}{d\dot{q}_2}=Q_2',\ \ldots,\ \ldots\ldots\ldots\ldots\ldots\text{(vi)}.$$

The quantities

$$\frac{dT}{d\dot{q}_1},\quad \frac{dT}{d\dot{q}_2},\ \ldots,$$

are therefore called the 'generalized components of momentum' of the system, they are usually denoted by the symbols p_1, p_2,.... Since T is, by (9), a homogeneous quadratic function of $\dot{q}_1$, $\dot{q}_2$,..., it follows that

$$2T=p_1\dot{q}_1+p_2\dot{q}_2+\ldots\ldots\ldots\ldots\ldots\text{(vii)}.$$

In terms of the generalized coordinates q_1, q_2,... the equation (5) becomes

$$\int_{t_0}^{t_1}\{\Delta T+Q_1\Delta q_1+Q_2\Delta q_2+\ldots\}\,dt=0\ \ldots\ldots\ldots\ (14),$$

where

$$\Delta T=\frac{dT}{d\dot{q}_1}\Delta\dot{q}_1+\frac{dT}{d\dot{q}_2}\Delta\dot{q}_2+\ldots+\frac{dT}{dq_1}\Delta q_1+\frac{dT}{dq_2}\Delta q_2+\ldots\ (15).$$

Hence, by a partial integration, and remembering that, by hypothesis, Δq_1, Δq_2,... all vanish at the limits t_0, t_1, we find

$$\int_{t_0}^{t_1}\left\{\left(\frac{d}{dt}\frac{dT}{d\dot{q}_1}-\frac{dT}{dq_1}-Q_1\right)\Delta q_1+\left(\frac{d}{dt}\frac{dT}{d\dot{q}_2}-\frac{dT}{dq_2}-Q_2\right)\Delta q_2+\ldots\right\}dt=0$$
$$\ldots\ldots\ldots(16).$$

Since the values of Δq_1, Δq_2,... within the limits of integration are still arbitrary, their coefficients must separately vanish. We thus obtain Lagrange's equations

$$\left.\begin{aligned}\frac{d}{dt}\frac{dT}{d\dot{q}_1}-\frac{dT}{dq_1}&=Q_1,\\ \frac{d}{dt}\frac{dT}{d\dot{q}_2}-\frac{dT}{dq_2}&=Q_2,\\ \cdots\cdots\cdots\ &\cdots\cdots\cdots\end{aligned}\right\}\quad\ldots\ldots\ldots\ldots\ldots\ldots(17)^*.$$

134. Proceeding now to the hydrodynamical problem, let $q_1, q_2,\ldots$ be a system of generalised coordinates which serve to specify the configuration of the solids. We will suppose, for the present, that the motion of the fluid is entirely due to that of the solids, and is therefore irrotational and acyclic.

In this case the velocity-potential at any instant will be of the form

$$\phi=\dot{q}_1\phi_1+\dot{q}_2\phi_2+\ldots\ldots\ldots\ldots\ldots\ldots\ldots\ldots(1),$$

where $\phi_1, \phi_2,\ldots$ are determined in a manner analogous to that of Art. 115. The formula for the kinetic energy of the fluid is then

$$\begin{aligned}2\mathbf{T}&=-\rho\iint\phi\frac{d\phi}{dn}dS\\ &=\mathbf{A}_{11}\dot{q}_1^2+\mathbf{A}_{22}\dot{q}_2^2+\ldots+2\mathbf{A}_{12}\dot{q}_1\dot{q}_2+\ldots\ \ldots\ldots(2),\end{aligned}$$

where, for example,

$$\left.\begin{aligned}\mathbf{A}_{11}&=-\rho\iint\phi_1\frac{d\phi_1}{dn}dS,\\ \mathbf{A}_{12}&=-\rho\iint\phi_1\frac{d\phi_2}{dn}dS=-\rho\iint\phi_2\frac{d\phi_1}{dn}dS\end{aligned}\right\}\ldots\ldots\ldots(3),$$

the integrations extending over the instantaneous positions of the bounding surfaces of the fluid. The identity of the two forms of $\mathbf{A}_{12}$ follows from Green's Theorem. The coefficients $\mathbf{A}_{11}, \mathbf{A}_{12},\ldots$ will, of course, be in general functions of the coordinates $q_1, q_2,\ldots$.

* The above sketch is introduced with the view of rendering more intelligible the hydrodynamical investigations which follow. Lagrange's proof, directly from the variational equation of Art. 132 (2), is reproduced in most treatises on Dynamics. Another proof, by direct transformation of coordinates, not involving the method of 'variations,' was given in the first instance by Hamilton, *Phil. Trans.* 1835, p. 96; the same method was employed by Jacobi, *Vorlesungen über Dynamik* (ed. Clebsch), Berlin, 1864, p. 64, *Werke*, Supplementband, p. 64; by Bertrand in the notes to his edition of the *Mécanique Analytique*, Paris, 1853; and more recently by Thomson and Tait, *Natural Philosophy*, (2nd ed.) Art. 318.

If we add to (2) twice the kinetic energy, $\mathbf{T}_1$, of the solids themselves, we get an expression of the same form, with altered coefficients, say

$$2T = A_{11}\dot{q}_1^2 + A_{22}\dot{q}_2^2 + \ldots + 2A_{12}\dot{q}_1\dot{q}_2 + \ldots \qquad (4).$$

It remains to shew that the equations of motion of the solids can be obtained by substituting this value of T in the Lagrangian equations, Art. 133 (17). We cannot assume this without further consideration, for the positions of the various particles of the fluid are evidently *not* determined by the instantaneous values $q_1, q_2, \ldots$ of the coordinates of the solids.

Going back to the general formula

$$\int_{t_0}^{t_1} \{\Delta T + \Sigma (X\Delta\xi + Y\Delta\eta + Z\Delta\zeta)\} \, dt = \Big[\Sigma m (\dot{\xi}\Delta\xi + \dot{\eta}\Delta\eta + \dot{\zeta}\Delta\zeta)\Big]_{t_0}^{t_1} \qquad (5),$$

let us suppose that in the varied motion, to which the symbol Δ refers, the solids undergo no change of size or shape, and that the fluid remains incompressible, and has, at the boundaries, the same displacement in the direction of the normal as the solids with which it is in contact. It is known that under these conditions the terms due to the internal forces of the solids will disappear from the sum

$$\Sigma (X\Delta\xi + Y\Delta\eta + Z\Delta\zeta).$$

The terms due to the mutual pressures of the fluid elements are equivalent to

$$-\iiint \left(\frac{dp}{dx}\Delta\xi + \frac{dp}{dy}\Delta\eta + \frac{dp}{dz}\Delta\zeta\right) dx\,dy\,dz,$$

$$\text{or} \quad \iint p (l\Delta\xi + m\Delta\eta + n\Delta\zeta) \, dS + \iiint p \left(\frac{d\Delta\xi}{dx} + \frac{d\Delta\eta}{dy} + \frac{d\Delta\zeta}{dz}\right) dx\,dy\,dz,$$

where the former integral extends over the bounding surfaces, l, m, n denoting the direction-cosines of the normal, drawn towards the fluid. The volume-integral vanishes by the condition of incompressibility,

$$\frac{d\Delta\xi}{dx} + \frac{d\Delta\eta}{dy} + \frac{d\Delta\zeta}{dz} = 0.$$

The surface-integral vanishes at a fixed boundary, where

$$l\Delta\xi + m\Delta\eta + n\Delta\zeta = 0,$$

and in the case of a moving solid it is cancelled by the terms due to the pressure exerted by the fluid on the solid. Hence the symbols X, Y, Z may be taken to refer only to the *extraneous* forces acting on the system, and we may write

$$\Sigma(X\Delta\xi + Y\Delta\eta + Z\Delta\zeta) = Q_1\Delta q_1 + Q_2\Delta q_2 + \dots \dots\dots (6),$$

where Q_1, Q_2,... now denote the generalized components of extraneous force.

We have still to consider the right-hand side of (5). Let us suppose that in the arbitrarily varied motion the initial and final positions of the solids are respectively the same as in the actual motion. For every particle of the solids we shall then have

$$\Delta\xi = 0,\ \Delta\eta = 0,\ \Delta\zeta = 0,$$

at both limits, but the same will not hold as a rule with regard to the particles of the fluid. The corresponding part of the sum

$$\Sigma m(\dot{\xi}\Delta\xi + \dot{\eta}\Delta\eta + \dot{\zeta}\Delta\zeta)$$

will however vanish; viz. we have

$$-\rho\iiint\left(\frac{d\phi}{dx}\Delta\xi + \frac{d\phi}{dy}\Delta\eta + \frac{d\phi}{dz}\Delta\xi\right)dx\,dy\,dz$$

$$= \rho\iint\phi\,(l\Delta\xi + m\Delta\eta + n\Delta\zeta)\,dS$$

$$+\rho\iiint\phi\left(\frac{d\Delta\xi}{dx} + \frac{d\Delta\eta}{dy} + \frac{d\Delta\zeta}{dz}\right)dx\,dy\,dz,$$

of which the second term vanishes by the condition of incompressibility, and the first term vanishes at the limits t_0 and t_1, since we then have, by hypothesis,

$$l\Delta\xi + m\Delta\eta + n\Delta\zeta = 0$$

at the surfaces of the solids. Hence, under the above conditions, the right-hand side of (5) vanishes, and therefore

$$\int_{t_0}^{t_1}\{\Delta T + Q_1\Delta q_1 + Q_2\Delta q_2 + \dots\}\,dt = 0 \dots\dots\dots\dots(7).$$

The varied motion of the fluid has still a high degree of generality. We will now further limit it by supposing that whilst the solids are, by suitable forces applied to them, made to execute an arbitrary motion, subject to the conditions that Δq_1,

$\Delta q_2, \ldots = 0$ for $t = t_0$ and $t = t_1$, the fluid is left to take its own course in consequence of this. The varied motion of the fluid will now be irrotational, and therefore $T + \Delta T$ will be the same function of the varied coordinates $q + \Delta q$, and the varied velocities $\dot{q} + \Delta\dot{q}$, that T is of q and $\dot{q}$. Hence we may write, in (7),

$$\Delta T = \frac{dT}{d\dot{q}_1}\Delta\dot{q}_1 + \frac{dT}{d\dot{q}_2}\Delta\dot{q}_2 + \ldots + \frac{dT}{dq_1}\Delta q_1 + \frac{dT}{dq_2}\Delta q_2 + \ldots\ldots(8)^*.$$

The derivation of the Lagrangian equations then follows exactly as before.

It is a simple consequence of Lagrange's equations, thus established for the present case, that the generalized components of the impulse by which the actual motion at any instant could be generated instantaneously from rest are

$$\frac{dT}{d\dot{q}_1},\quad \frac{dT}{d\dot{q}_2}, \ldots,$$

If we put $T = \mathbf{T} + \mathbf{T}_1$, we infer that the terms

$$\frac{d\mathbf{T}}{d\dot{q}_1},\quad \frac{d\mathbf{T}}{d\dot{q}_2}, \ldots,$$

must represent the impulsive pressures which would be exerted by the solids on the fluid in contact with them.

This may be verified as follows. If $\Delta\xi$, $\Delta\eta$, $\Delta\zeta$ denote arbitrary variations subject only to the condition of incompressibility, and to the condition that the fluid is to remain in contact with the solids, it is found as above that, considering the fluid only,

$$\Sigma m(\dot{\xi}\Delta\xi + \dot{\eta}\Delta\eta + \dot{\zeta}\Delta\zeta)$$
$$= \rho\iint\phi(l\Delta\xi + m\Delta\eta + n\Delta\zeta)\,dS \ldots\ldots\ldots\ldots\ldots\ldots \text{(i)}.$$

Now by the kinematical condition to be satisfied at the surface, we have

$$l\Delta\xi + m\Delta\eta + n\Delta\zeta = -\frac{d\phi_1}{dn}\Delta q_1 - \frac{d\phi_2}{dn}\Delta q_2 - \ldots\ldots\ldots\ldots \text{(ii)},$$

and therefore

$$\Sigma m(\dot{\xi}\Delta\xi + \dot{\eta}\Delta\eta + \dot{\zeta}\Delta\zeta)$$
$$= -\rho\iint\phi\left(\frac{d\phi_1}{dn}\Delta q_1 + \frac{d\phi_2}{dn}\Delta q_2 + \ldots\right)dS$$
$$= (\mathbf{A}_{11}\dot{q}_1 + \mathbf{A}_{12}\dot{q}_2 + \ldots)\Delta q_1 + (\mathbf{A}_{21}\dot{q}_1 + \mathbf{A}_{22}\dot{q}_2 + \ldots)\Delta q_2 + \ldots$$
$$= \frac{d\mathbf{T}}{d\dot{q}_1}\Delta q_1 + \frac{d\mathbf{T}}{d\dot{q}_2}\Delta q_2 + \ldots\ldots\ldots\ldots\ldots\ldots \text{(iii)},$$

by (1), (2), (3) above. This proves the statement.

With the help of equation (iii) the reader may easily construct a proof of Lagrange's equations, for the present case, analogous to that usually given in text-books of Dynamics.

* This investigation is amplified from Kirchhoff, *l.c. ante* p. 167.

135. As a first application of the foregoing theory we may take an example given by Thomson and Tait, where a sphere is supposed to move in a liquid which is limited only by an infinite plane wall.

Taking, for brevity, the case where the centre moves in a plane perpendicular to that of the wall, let us specify its position at time t by rectangular coordinates x, y in this plane, of which y denotes the distance from the wall. We have

$$2T = A\dot{x}^2 + B\dot{y}^2 \quad\text{.......................(1)},$$

where A and B are functions of y only, it being plain that the term $\dot{x}\dot{y}$ cannot occur, since the energy must remain unaltered when the sign of $\dot{x}$ is reversed. The values of A, B can be written down from the results of Arts. 97, 98, viz. if $\mathbf{m}$ denote the mass of the sphere, and a its radius, we have

$$\left.\begin{aligned} A &= \mathbf{m} + \tfrac{2}{3}\pi\rho a^3\left(1 + \tfrac{3}{16}\frac{a^3}{y^3}\right), \\ B &= \mathbf{m} + \tfrac{2}{3}\pi\rho a^3\left(1 + \tfrac{3}{8}\frac{a^3}{y^3}\right) \end{aligned}\right\} \quad\text{..............(2)},$$

approximately, if y be great in comparison with a.

The equations of motion give

$$\left.\begin{aligned} &\frac{d}{dt}(A\dot{x}) = X, \\ &\frac{d}{dt}(B\dot{y}) - \tfrac{1}{2}\left(\frac{dA}{dy}\dot{x}^2 + \frac{dB}{dy}\dot{y}^2\right) = Y \end{aligned}\right\} \quad\text{............ (3)},$$

where X, Y are the components of extraneous force, supposed to act on the sphere in a line through the centre.

If there be no extraneous force, and if the sphere be projected in a direction normal to the wall, we have $\dot{x} = 0$, and

$$B\dot{y}^2 = \text{const.} \quad\text{..........................(4)}.$$

Since B diminishes as y increases, the sphere experiences an acceleration *from* the wall.

Again, if the sphere be constrained to move in a line parallel to the wall, we have $\dot{y} = 0$, and the necessary constraining force is

$$Y = -\tfrac{1}{2}\frac{dA}{dy}\dot{x}^2 \quad\text{....................... (5)}.$$

Since dA/dy is negative, the sphere appears to be *attracted* by the wall. The reason of this is easily seen by reducing the problem to one of steady motion. The fluid velocity will evidently be greater, and the pressure, therefore, will be less, on the side of the sphere next the wall than on the further side; see Art. 24.

The above investigation will also apply to the case of two spheres projected in an unlimited mass of fluid, in such a way that the plane $y = 0$ is a plane of symmetry as regards the motion.

136. Let us next take the case of two spheres moving in the line of centres.

The kinematical part of this problem has been treated in Art. 97. If we now denote by x, y the distances of the centres A, B from some fixed origin O in the line joining them, we have

$$2T = L\dot{x}^2 - 2M\dot{x}\dot{y} + N\dot{y}^2 \text{ ....(i)},$$

where the coefficients L, M, N are functions of c, $= y - x$. Hence the equations of motion are

$$\left.\begin{aligned} \frac{d}{dt}(L\dot{x} - M\dot{y}) + \tfrac{1}{2}\left(\frac{dL}{dc}\dot{x}^2 - 2\frac{dM}{dc}\dot{x}\dot{y} + \frac{dN}{dc}\dot{y}^2\right) &= X, \\ \frac{d}{dt}(-M\dot{x} + N\dot{y}) - \tfrac{1}{2}\left(\frac{dL}{dc}\dot{x}^2 - 2\frac{dM}{dc}\dot{x}\dot{y} + \frac{dN}{dc}\dot{y}^2\right) &= Y \end{aligned}\right\} \text{ ....(ii)},$$

where X, Y are the forces acting on the spheres along the line of centres. If the radii a, b are both small compared with c, we have, by Art. 97 (xv), keeping only the most important terms,

$$L = \mathbf{m} + \tfrac{2}{3}\pi\rho a^3, \qquad M = 2\pi\rho\frac{a^3 b^3}{c^3}, \qquad N = \mathbf{m}' + \tfrac{2}{3}\pi\rho b^3 \text{ ....(iii)}$$

approximately, where $\mathbf{m}$, $\mathbf{m}'$ are the masses of the two spheres. Hence to this order of approximation

$$\frac{dL}{dc} = 0, \quad \frac{dM}{dc} = -6\pi\rho\frac{a^3 b^3}{c^4}, \quad \frac{dN}{dc} = 0.$$

If each sphere be constrained to move with constant velocity, the force which must be applied to A to maintain its motion is

$$X = -\frac{dM}{dc}\dot{y}(\dot{y} - \dot{x}) - \frac{dM}{dc}\dot{x}\dot{y} = 6\pi\rho\frac{a^3 b^3}{c^4}\dot{y}^2 \text{ ....(iv)}.$$

This tends towards B, and depends only on the velocity of B. The spheres therefore appear to repel one another; and it is to be noticed that the apparent forces are not equal and opposite unless $\dot{x} = \pm\dot{y}$.

Again, if each sphere make small periodic oscillations about a mean position, the period being the same for each, the mean values of the first terms in (ii) will be zero, and the spheres therefore will appear to act on one another with forces equal to

$$6\pi\rho\frac{a^3 b^3}{c^4}[\dot{x}\dot{y}] \text{ .... (v)},$$

where $[\dot{x}\dot{y}]$ denotes the mean value of $\dot{x}\dot{y}$. If $\dot{x}, \dot{y}$ differ in phase by less than a quarter-period, this force is one of repulsion, if by more than a quarter-period it is one of attraction.

Next, let B perform small periodic oscillations, while A is held at rest. The mean force which must be applied to A to prevent it from moving is

$$X = \tfrac{1}{2}\frac{dN}{dc}[\dot{y}^2] \qquad \text{(vi)},$$

where $[\dot{y}^2]$ denotes the mean square of the velocity of B. To the above order of approximation dN/dc is zero, but on reference to Art. 97 (xv) we find that the most important term in it is $-12\pi\rho a^3 b^6/c^7$, so that the force exerted on A is attractive, and equal to

$$6\pi\rho\frac{a^3 b^6}{c^7}[\dot{y}^2] \qquad \text{(vii)}.$$

This result comes under a general principle enunciated by Lord Kelvin. If we have two bodies immersed in a fluid, one of which (A) performs small vibrations while the other (B) is held at rest, the fluid velocity at the surface of B will on the whole be greater on the side nearer A than on that which is more remote. Hence the average pressure on the former side will be less than that on the latter, so that B will experience on the whole an attraction towards A. As practical illustrations of this principle we may cite the apparent attraction of a delicately-suspended card by a vibrating tuning-fork, and other similar phenomena studied experimentally by Guthrie* and explained in the above manner by Lord Kelvin†.

Modification of Lagrange's Equations in the case of Cyclic Motion.

137. We return to the investigation of Art. 134, with the view of adapting it to the case where the fluid has cyclic irrotational motion through channels in the moving solids, or (it may be) in an enclosing vessel, independently of the motion of the solids themselves.

If $\kappa, \kappa', \kappa'', \ldots$, be the circulations in the various independent circuits which can be drawn in the space occupied by the fluid, the velocity-potential will now be of the form

$$\phi + \phi_0,$$

where
$$\phi = \dot{q}_1\phi_1 + \dot{q}_2\phi_2 + \ldots \qquad \text{(1)},$$

* "On Approach caused by Vibration," *Proc. Roy. Soc.*, t. xix., (1869); *Phil. Mag.*, Nov. 1870.

† *Reprint of Papers on Electrostatics, &c.*, Art. 741. For references to further investigations, both experimental and theoretical, by Bjerknes and others on the mutual influence of oscillating spheres in a fluid, see Hicks, "Report on Recent Researches in Hydrodynamics," *Brit. Ass. Rep.*, 1882, pp. 52...; Winkelmann, *Handbuch der Physik*, Breslau, 1891..., t. i., p. 435.

the functions $\phi_1, \phi_2, \ldots$, being determined by the same conditions as in Art. 134, and

$$\phi_0 = \kappa\omega + \kappa'\omega' + \ldots \qquad (2),$$

$\omega, \omega', \ldots$, being cyclic velocity-potentials determined as in Art. 129.

Let us imagine barrier-surfaces to be drawn across the several channels. In the case of channels in a containing vessel we shall suppose these ideal surfaces to be fixed in space, and in the case of channels in a moving solid we shall suppose them to be fixed relatively to the solid. Let us denote by $\dot\chi_0, \dot\chi_0', \ldots$, the portions of the fluxes across these barriers which are due to the cyclic motion alone, and which would therefore remain if the solids were held at rest in their instantaneous positions, so that, for example,

$$\dot\chi_0 = -\iint \frac{d\phi_0}{dn}\, d\sigma = -\kappa \iint \frac{d\omega}{dn}\, d\sigma - \kappa' \iint \frac{d\omega'}{dn}\, d\sigma' - \ldots \ldots (3),$$

where $\delta\sigma, \delta\sigma', \ldots$ are elements of the several barriers. The *total* fluxes across the respective barriers will be denoted by $\dot\chi + \dot\chi_0$, $\dot\chi' + \dot\chi_0', \ldots$, so that $\dot\chi, \dot\chi', \ldots$ would be the surface-integrals of the normal velocity of the fluid *relative to the barriers*, if the motion of the fluid were entirely due to that of the solids, and therefore acyclic.

The expression of Art. 55 for twice the kinetic energy of the fluid becomes, in our present notation,

$$-\rho \iint (\phi + \phi_0) \frac{d}{dn} (\phi + \phi_0)\, dS$$
$$- \rho\kappa \iint \frac{d}{dn} (\phi + \phi_0)\, d\sigma - \rho\kappa' \iint \frac{d}{dn} (\phi + \phi_0)\, d\sigma' - \ldots \ldots (4).$$

This reduces, exactly as in Art. 129, to the sum of two homogeneous quadratic functions of $\dot q_1, \dot q_2, \ldots$, and of $\kappa, \kappa', \ldots$, respectively*. Thus the kinetic energy of the fluid is equal to

$$\mathbf{T} + K \qquad (5),$$

with $$2\mathbf{T} = \mathbf{A}_{11}\dot q_1^2 + \mathbf{A}_{22}\dot q_2^2 + \ldots + 2\mathbf{A}_{12}\dot q_1 \dot q_2 + \ldots \ldots \qquad (6),$$

and $$2K = (\kappa, \kappa)\,\kappa^2 + (\kappa', \kappa')\,\kappa'^2 + \ldots + 2(\kappa, \kappa')\,\kappa\kappa' + \ldots \ldots (7),$$

where, for example,

$$\left.\begin{aligned} \mathbf{A}_{11} &= -\rho \iint \phi_1 \frac{d\phi_1}{dn}\, dS, \\ \mathbf{A}_{12} &= -\rho \iint \phi_1 \frac{d\phi_2}{dn}\, dS = -\rho \iint \phi_2 \frac{d\phi_1}{dn}\, dS \end{aligned}\right\} \ldots\ldots\ldots (8),$$

* An example of this reduction is furnished by the calculation of Art. 99.

and
$$\left.\begin{aligned}(\kappa, \kappa) &= -\rho \iint \frac{d\omega}{dn}\, d\sigma,\\ (\kappa, \kappa') &= -\rho \iint \frac{d\omega'}{dn}\, d\sigma = -\rho \iint \frac{d\omega}{dn}\, d\sigma'\end{aligned}\right\} \quad\ldots\ldots\ldots\ldots\ldots (9).$$

It is evident that K is the energy of the cyclic motion which remains when the solids are maintained at rest in the configuration $(q_1, q_2, \ldots)$. We note that, by (3), (7), and (9),

$$\rho\dot{\chi}_0 = \frac{dK}{d\kappa}, \quad \rho\dot{\chi}_0' = \frac{dK}{d\kappa'}, \ldots, \quad\ldots\ldots\ldots\ldots (10),$$

and
$$2K = \rho\kappa\dot{\chi}_0 + \rho\kappa'\dot{\chi}_0' + \ldots \quad\ldots\ldots\ldots\ldots\ldots (11).$$

If we add to (5) the kinetic energy of the solids themselves, we obtain for the total kinetic energy of the system an expression of the form

$$T = \mathfrak{T} + K \ldots\ldots\ldots\ldots\ldots\ldots\ldots\ldots\ldots (12),$$

where
$$2\mathfrak{T} = A_{11}\dot{q}_1^2 + A_{22}\dot{q}_2^2 + \ldots + 2A_{12}\dot{q}_1\dot{q}_2 + \ldots \ldots\ldots (13),$$

the coefficients being in general functions of $q_1, q_2, \ldots\ldots$

To obtain the equations of motion we have recourse as before to the formula

$$\int_{t_0}^{t_1} \{\Delta T + \Sigma (X\Delta\xi + Y\Delta\eta + Z\Delta\zeta)\}\, dt$$
$$= \left[\Sigma m (\dot{\xi}\Delta\xi + \dot{\eta}\Delta\eta + \dot{\zeta}\Delta\zeta)\right]_{t_0}^{t_1} \ldots\ldots\ldots (14).$$

The only new feature is in the treatment of the expression on the right-hand side. By the usual method of partial integration we find

$$-\rho \iiint \left\{\frac{d}{dx}(\phi + \phi_0)\,\Delta\xi + \frac{d}{dy}(\phi + \phi_0)\,\Delta\eta + \frac{d}{dz}(\phi + \phi_0)\,\Delta\zeta\right\} dx\,dy\,dz$$
$$= \rho \iint (\phi + \phi_0)(l\Delta\xi + m\Delta\eta + n\Delta\zeta)\, dS$$
$$+ \rho\kappa \iint (l\Delta\xi + m\Delta\eta + n\Delta\zeta)\, d\sigma + \rho\kappa' \iint (l\Delta\xi + m\Delta\eta + n\Delta\zeta)\, d\sigma' + \ldots$$
$$\ldots\ldots\ldots\ldots\ldots (15),$$

where l, m, n are the direction-cosines of the normal to any element δS of a bounding surface, drawn towards the fluid, or (as the case may be) of the normal to a barrier, drawn in the direction in which the circulation is estimated.

Let us now suppose that the slightly varied motion, to which Δ refers, is arbitrary as regards the solids, except only that the initial and final configurations are to be the same as in the actual motion, whilst the fluid is free to take its own course in accordance with the motion of the solids. On this supposition we shall have, both at time t_0 and at time t_1,

$$l\Delta\xi + m\Delta\eta + n\Delta\zeta = 0$$

for the fluid in contact with an element δS of the surface of a solid, and, at the barriers,

$$\iint (l\Delta\xi + m\Delta\eta + n\Delta\zeta)\, d\sigma = \Delta(\chi + \chi_0),\ \ldots,\ \ldots.$$

The right-hand side of (14) therefore reduces, under the present suppositions, to

$$\Big[\rho\kappa\Delta(\chi + \chi_0) + \rho\kappa'\Delta(\chi' + \chi_0') + \ldots\Big]_{t_0}^{t_1},$$

and the equation may be put into the form

$$\int_{t_0}^{t_1} \{\Delta T - \rho\kappa\Delta(\dot\chi + \dot\chi_0) - \rho\kappa'\Delta(\dot\chi' + \dot\chi_0') - \ldots$$
$$+ Q_1\Delta q_1 + Q_2\Delta q_2 + \ldots\}\, dt = 0 \quad\ldots\ldots(16)^*,$$

which now takes the place of Art. 134 (7).

Since the variation Δ does not affect the cyclic constants $\kappa, \kappa', \ldots$, we have by (11),

$$\rho\kappa\Delta\dot\chi_0 + \rho\kappa'\Delta\dot\chi_0' + \ldots = 2\Delta K,$$

and therefore, by (12),

$$\int_{t_0}^{t_1} \{\Delta\mathfrak{T} - \rho\kappa\Delta\dot\chi - \rho\kappa'\Delta\dot\chi' - \ldots - \Delta K$$
$$+ Q_1\Delta q_1 + Q_2\Delta q_2 + \ldots\}\, dt = 0 \quad\ldots\ldots(17).$$

It is easily seen that $\dot\chi, \dot\chi', \ldots$ are linear functions of $\dot q_1, \dot q_2, \ldots$, say

$$\left.\begin{aligned} \dot\chi &= \alpha_1\dot q_1 + \alpha_2\dot q_2 + \ldots \\ \dot\chi' &= \alpha_1'\dot q_1 + \alpha_2'\dot q_2 + \ldots \\ &\ldots\ldots\ldots\ldots\ldots\ldots \end{aligned}\right\} \quad\ldots\ldots\ldots\ldots\ldots\ldots(18),$$

where the coefficients are in general functions of $q_1, q_2, \ldots$. If we write

* Cf. Larmor, "On the Direct Application of the Principle of Least Action to the Dynamics of Solid and Fluid Systems," *Proc. Lond. Math. Soc.*, t. xv. (1884).

for shortness,

$$\left.\begin{aligned} \beta_1 &= \rho\kappa\alpha_1 + \rho\kappa'\alpha_1' + \ldots \\ \beta_2 &= \rho\kappa\alpha_2 + \rho\kappa'\alpha_2' + \ldots \\ &\ldots\ldots\ldots\ldots\ldots \end{aligned}\right\} \quad\ldots\ldots\ldots\ldots\ldots\ldots(19),$$

the formula (17) becomes

$$\int_{t_0}^{t_1} \{\Delta\mathfrak{T} - \Delta(\beta_1\dot{q}_1 + \beta_2\dot{q}_2 + \ldots) - \Delta K + Q_1\Delta q_1 + Q_2\Delta q_2 + \ldots\}\, dt = 0 \quad \ldots\ldots(20).$$

Selecting the terms in Δq_1, $\Delta\dot{q}_1$ from the expression to be integrated, we have

$$\left(\frac{d\mathfrak{T}}{d\dot{q}_1} - \beta_1\right)\Delta\dot{q}_1 + \left(\frac{d\mathfrak{T}}{dq_1} - \dot{q}_1\frac{d\beta_1}{dq_1} - \dot{q}_2\frac{d\beta_2}{dq_1} - \ldots - \frac{dK}{dq_1} + Q_1\right)\Delta q_1.$$

Hence by a partial integration, remembering that $\Delta q_1, \Delta q_2, \ldots$ vanish at both limits, and equating to zero the coefficients of $\Delta q_1, \Delta q_2, \ldots$ which remain under the integral sign, we obtain the first of the following symmetrical system of equations:

$$\left.\begin{aligned} &\frac{d}{dt}\frac{d\mathfrak{T}}{d\dot{q}_1} - \frac{d\mathfrak{T}}{dq_1} \qquad\qquad\qquad + (1, 2)\,\dot{q}_2 + (1, 3)\,\dot{q}_3 + \ldots + \frac{dK}{dq_1} = Q_1, \\ &\frac{d}{dt}\frac{d\mathfrak{T}}{d\dot{q}_2} - \frac{d\mathfrak{T}}{dq_2} + (2, 1)\,\dot{q}_1 \qquad\qquad\quad + (2, 3)\,\dot{q}_3 + \ldots + \frac{dK}{dq_2} = Q_2, \\ &\frac{d}{dt}\frac{d\mathfrak{T}}{d\dot{q}_3} - \frac{d\mathfrak{T}}{dq_3} + (3, 1)\,\dot{q}_1 + (3, 2)\,\dot{q}_2 \qquad\qquad + \ldots + \frac{dK}{dq_3} = Q_3, \\ &\ldots\ldots\ldots\ldots\ldots\ldots\ldots\ldots\ldots\ldots\ldots\ldots \end{aligned}\right\} (21)^*.$$

We have here introduced the notation

$$(r, s) = \frac{d\beta_s}{dq_r} - \frac{d\beta_r}{dq_s} \quad\ldots\ldots\ldots\ldots\ldots\ldots\ldots (22),$$

and it is important to notice that $(r, s) = -(s, r)$.

138. The foregoing investigation has been adopted as leading directly, and in conformity with our previous work, to the desired result; but it may be worth while to give another treatment of the question, which will bring out more fully the connection with the theory of 'gyrostatic' systems, and the method of 'ignoration of coordinates.'

* These equations were first given in a paper by Sir W. Thomson, "On the Motion of Rigid Solids in a Liquid circulating irrotationally through perforations in them or in a Fixed Solid," *Phil. Mag.*, May 1873. See also C. Neumann, *Hydrodynamische Untersuchungen* (1883).

It will be necessary to modify, to some extent, our previous notation. Let us now denote by $\dot{\chi}, \dot{\chi}', \dot{\chi}'', \ldots$ the total fluxes relative to the several barriers of the region, which we shall as before regard as ideal surfaces fixed relatively to the solid surfaces on which they abut; and let $\chi, \chi', \chi'', \ldots$ be the time-integrals of these fluxes, reckoned each from an arbitrary epoch. We shall shew, in the first place, that the Lagrangian equations (Art. 133 (17)) will still hold in the case of cyclic motion, provided these quantities $\chi, \chi', \chi'', \ldots$ are treated as additional generalized coordinates of the system.

Let $q_1, q_2, \ldots$ be, as before, the system of generalized coordinates which specify the positions of the moving solids. The motion of the fluid at any instant is completely determined by the values of the velocities $\dot{q}_1, \dot{q}_2, \ldots$, and of the fluxes $\dot{\chi}, \dot{\chi}', \ldots$, as above defined. For if there were two types of irrotational motion consistent with these values, then, in the motion which is the *difference* of these, the bounding surfaces, and therefore also the barriers, would be at rest, and the flux across each barrier would be zero. The formula (5) of Art. 55 shews that the kinetic energy of such a motion would be zero, and the velocity therefore everywhere null.

It follows that the velocity-potential (Φ, say) of the fluid motion can be expressed in the form

$$\Phi = \dot{q}_1\phi_1 + \dot{q}_2\phi_2 + \ldots + \dot{\chi}\omega + \dot{\chi}'\omega' + \ldots \quad \ldots\ldots\ldots(1),$$

where ϕ_1, for example, is the velocity-potential of the motion corresponding to

$$\dot{q}_1 = 1, \quad \dot{q}_2 = 0, \quad \dot{q}_3 = 0, \ldots,$$
$$\dot{\chi} = 0, \quad \dot{\chi}' = 0, \quad \dot{\chi}'' = 0, \ldots,$$

which we have just seen to be determinate.

The kinetic energy of the fluid is given by the expression

$$\tfrac{1}{2}\rho \iiint \left\{\left(\frac{d\Phi}{dx}\right)^2 + \left(\frac{d\Phi}{dy}\right)^2 + \left(\frac{d\Phi}{dz}\right)^2\right\} dx\,dy\,dz \quad \ldots\ldots\ldots(2).$$

Substituting the value of Φ from (1), and adding the energy of motion of the solids, we see that the total kinetic energy of the system (T, say) is a homogeneous quadratic function of the quantities $\dot{q}_1, \dot{q}_2, \ldots, \dot{\chi}, \dot{\chi}', \ldots$, with coefficients which are functions of $q_1, q_2, \ldots$, only.

We now recur to the formula (4) of Art. 132. The variations $\Delta\xi$, $\Delta\eta$, $\Delta\zeta$ being subject to the condition of incompressibility, the part of the sum

$$\Sigma m\,(\dot\xi\Delta\xi + \dot\eta\Delta\eta + \dot\zeta\Delta\zeta) \qquad (3)$$

which is due to the fluid is, in the present notation,

$$-\rho\iiint\left(\frac{d\Phi}{dx}\Delta\xi + \frac{d\Phi}{dy}\Delta\eta + \frac{d\Phi}{dz}\Delta\zeta\right)$$
$$= \rho\iint\Phi\,(l\Delta\xi + m\Delta\eta + n\Delta\zeta)\,dS$$
$$+\rho\kappa\Delta\chi + \rho\kappa'\Delta\chi' + \ldots \qquad (4),$$

where the surface-integral extends over the bounding surfaces of the fluid, and the symbols κ, κ',... denote as usual the cyclic constants of the actual motion. We will now suppose that the varied motion of the solids is subject to the condition that $\Delta q_1, \Delta q_2, \ldots = 0$, at both limits ($t_0$ and t_1), that the varied motion of the fluid is irrotational and consistent with the motion of the solids, and that the (varied) circulations are adjusted so as to make $\Delta\chi$, $\Delta\chi'$,... also vanish at the limits. Under these circumstances the right-hand side of the formula cited is zero, and we have

$$\int_{t_0}^{t_1}\{\Delta T + \Sigma\,(X\Delta\xi + Y\Delta\eta + Z\Delta\zeta)\} = 0 \qquad (5).$$

If we assume that the extraneous forces do on the whole no work when the boundary of the fluid is at rest, whatever relative displacements be given to the parts of the fluid, the generalized components of force corresponding to the coordinates χ, χ',... will be zero, and the formula may be written

$$\int_{t_0}^{t_1}\{\Delta T + Q_1\Delta q_1 + Q_2\Delta q_2 + \ldots\}\,dt = 0 \qquad (6),$$

where

$$\Delta T = \frac{dT}{d\dot q_1}\Delta\dot q_1 + \frac{dT}{d\dot q_2}\Delta\dot q_2 + \ldots + \frac{dT}{dq_1}\Delta q_1 + \frac{dT}{dq_2}\Delta q_2 + \ldots + \frac{dT}{d\dot\chi}\Delta\dot\chi + \frac{dT}{d\dot\chi'}\Delta\dot\chi'$$
$$+ \ldots \qquad (7).$$

139. If we now follow out the process indicated at the end of Art. 133, we arrive at the equations of motion for the present case, in the forms

$$\left.\begin{aligned}\frac{d}{dt}\frac{dT}{d\dot q_1} - \frac{dT}{dq_1} = Q_1, \quad \frac{d}{dt}\frac{dT}{d\dot q_2} - \frac{dT}{dq_2} = Q_2, \ldots,\\ \frac{d}{dt}\frac{dT}{d\dot\chi} = 0, \quad \frac{d}{dt}\frac{dT}{d\dot\chi'} = 0, \ldots,\end{aligned}\right\} \qquad (1).$$

Equations of this type present themselves in various problems of ordinary Dynamics, *e.g.* in questions relating to gyrostats, where the coordinates $\chi, \chi', \ldots$, whose absolute values do not affect the kinetic and potential energies of the system, are the angular coordinates of the gyrostats relative to their frames. The general theory of systems of this kind has been treated independently by Routh* and by Thomson and Tait†. It may be put, briefly, as follows.

We obtain from (1), by integration,

$$\frac{dT}{d\dot{\chi}} = C, \quad \frac{dT}{d\dot{\chi}'} = C', \ldots, \quad \ldots\ldots\ldots\ldots\ldots\ldots(2),$$

where, in the language of the general theory, $C, C', \ldots$ are the constant momenta corresponding to the coordinates $\chi, \chi', \ldots$. In the hydrodynamical problem, they are equal to $\rho\kappa, \rho\kappa', \ldots$, as will be shewn later, but we retain for the present the more general notation.

Let us write

$$\Theta = T - C\dot{\chi} - C'\dot{\chi}' - \ldots \quad \ldots\ldots\ldots\ldots\ldots\ldots(3).$$

The equations (2) when written in full, determine $\dot{\chi}, \dot{\chi}', \ldots$ as linear functions of $C, C', \ldots$ and $\dot{q}_1, \dot{q}_2, \ldots$; and by substitution in (3) we can express Θ as a quadratic function of $\dot{q}_1, \dot{q}_2, \ldots, C, C', \ldots$. On this supposition we have, performing the arbitrary variation Δ on both sides of (3), and omitting terms which cancel, by (2),

$$\frac{d\Theta}{d\dot{q}_1}\Delta\dot{q}_1 + \ldots + \frac{d\Theta}{dq_1}\Delta q_1 + \ldots + \frac{d\Theta}{dC}\Delta C + \ldots$$
$$= \frac{dT}{d\dot{q}_1}\Delta\dot{q}_1 + \ldots + \frac{dT}{dq_1}\Delta q_1 + \ldots - \dot{\chi}\Delta C - \ldots \ \ldots\ldots(4),$$

where, for brevity, only one term of each kind is exhibited.

Hence

$$\left.\begin{aligned} &\frac{d\Theta}{d\dot{q}_1} = \frac{dT}{d\dot{q}_1}, \quad \frac{d\Theta}{d\dot{q}_2} = \frac{dT}{d\dot{q}_2}, \ldots, \\ &\frac{d\Theta}{dq_1} = \frac{dT}{dq_1}, \quad \frac{d\Theta}{dq_2} = \frac{dT}{dq_2}, \ldots, \\ &\frac{d\Theta}{dC} = -\dot{\chi}, \quad \frac{d\Theta}{dC'} = -\dot{\chi}', \ldots \end{aligned}\right\} \ldots\ldots\ldots\ldots\ldots(5).$$

* *On the Stability of a given State of Motion* (Adams Prize Essay), London, 1877.

† *Natural Philosophy*, 2nd edition, Art. 319 (1879).

See also von Helmholtz, "Principien der Statik monocyclischer Systeme," *Crelle*, t. xcvii. (1884).

Hence the equations (1) now take the form

$$\left.\begin{array}{l}\dfrac{d}{dt}\dfrac{d\Theta}{d\dot{q}_1}-\dfrac{d\Theta}{dq_1}=Q_1,\\ \dfrac{d}{dt}\dfrac{d\Theta}{d\dot{q}_2}-\dfrac{d\Theta}{dq_2}=Q_2,\\ \dots\dots\dots\dots\end{array}\right\}\dots\dots\dots\dots(6)^*,$$

from which the velocities $\dot{\chi}, \dot{\chi}', \dots$ corresponding to the 'ignored' coordinates $\chi, \chi', \dots$ have been eliminated.

In the particular case where

$$C=0,\quad C'=0, \dots,$$

these equations are of the ordinary Lagrangian form, Θ being now equal to T, with the velocities $\dot{\chi}, \dot{\chi}', \dots$ eliminated by means of the relations

$$\frac{dT}{d\dot{\chi}}=0,\quad \frac{dT}{d\dot{\chi}'}=0, \dots,$$

so that Θ is now a homogeneous quadratic function of $\dot{q}_1, \dot{q}_2, \dots$. Cf. Art. 134 (4).

In the general case we proceed as follows. If we substitute in (3) from the last line of (5) we obtain

$$T=\Theta-\left(C\frac{d\Theta}{dC}+C'\frac{d\Theta}{dC'}+\dots\right)\dots\dots\dots\dots(7).$$

Now, remembering the composition of Θ, we may write, for a moment

$$\Theta=\Theta_{2,0}+\Theta_{1,1}+\Theta_{0,2}\dots\dots\dots\dots(8),$$

where $\Theta_{2,0}$ is a homogeneous quadratic function of $\dot{q}_1, \dot{q}_2, \dots$, without $C, C', \dots$; $\Theta_{1,1}$ is a bilinear function of these two sets of quantities; and $\Theta_{0,2}$ is a homogeneous quadratic function of $C, C', \dots$, without $\dot{q}_1, \dot{q}_2, \dots$. Substituting in (7), we find

$$T=\Theta_{2,0}-\Theta_{0,2}\dots\dots\dots\dots(9),$$

or, to return to our previous notation,

$$T=\mathfrak{T}+K\dots\dots\dots\dots(10),$$

where $\mathfrak{T}$ and K are homogeneous quadratic functions of $\dot{q}_1, \dot{q}_2, \dots$

* Routh, *l. c.*

and of C, C',..., respectively. Hence (8) may be written in the form

$$\Theta = \mathfrak{T} - K - \beta_1\dot{q}_1 - \beta_2\dot{q}_2 - \dots \quad\text{.............(11)},$$

where β_1, β_2,... are linear functions of C, C', ..., say

$$\left.\begin{aligned}\beta_1 &= \alpha_1 C + \alpha_1' C' + \dots,\\ \beta_2 &= \alpha_2 C + \alpha_2' C' + \dots,\\ &\dots\dots\dots\dots\end{aligned}\right\}\text{.................(12).}$$

The meaning of the coefficients α_1, α_2,..., α_1', α_2',..., ... appears from the last line of (5), viz. we have

$$\left.\begin{aligned}\dot{\chi} &= \frac{dK}{dC} + \alpha_1\dot{q}_1 + \alpha_2\dot{q}_2 + \dots,\\ \dot{\chi}' &= \frac{dK}{dC'} + \alpha_1'\dot{q}_1 + \alpha_2'\dot{q}_2 + \dots\\ &\dots\dots\dots\dots\end{aligned}\right\}\text{..............(13).}$$

Compare Art. 137 (18).

If we now substitute from (11) in the equations (6) we obtain the general equations of motion of a 'gyrostatic system,' in the form

$$\left.\begin{aligned}&\frac{d}{dt}\frac{d\mathfrak{T}}{d\dot{q}_1} - \frac{d\mathfrak{T}}{dq_1} \qquad\qquad + (1, 2)\,\dot{q}_2 + (1, 3)\,\dot{q}_3 + \dots + \frac{dK}{dq_1} = Q_1,\\ &\frac{d}{dt}\frac{d\mathfrak{T}}{d\dot{q}_2} - \frac{d\mathfrak{T}}{dq_2} + (2, 1)\,\dot{q}_1 \qquad\qquad + (2, 3)\,\dot{q}_3 + \dots + \frac{dK}{dq_2} = Q_2,\\ &\frac{d}{dt}\frac{d\mathfrak{T}}{d\dot{q}_3} - \frac{d\mathfrak{T}}{dq_3} + (3, 1)\,\dot{q}_1 + (3, 2)\,\dot{q}_2 \qquad\qquad + \dots + \frac{dK}{dq_3} = Q_3\\ &\dots\dots\dots\dots\dots\dots\dots\dots\end{aligned}\right\}\text{(14)*,}$$

where

$$(r, s) = \frac{d\beta_s}{dq_r} - \frac{d\beta_r}{dq_s} \quad\text{.....................(15).}$$

The equations (21) of Art. 137 are a particular case of these. To complete the identification it remains to shew that, in the hydrodynamical application,

$$C = \rho\kappa, \quad C' = \rho\kappa', \dots, \quad\text{..............................(i).}$$

For this purpose we may imagine that in the instantaneous generation of the actual motion from rest, the positions of the various barriers are occupied for a moment by membranes to which uniform impulsive pressures $\rho\kappa$, $\rho\kappa'$, ... are applied as in Art. 54, whilst impulsive forces are simultaneously applied to the respective solids, whose force and couple resultants are equal and opposite to those of the pressures†. In this way we obtain a system of generalized components of impulsive force, corresponding to the

* These equations were obtained, in a different manner, by Thomson and Tait, *l. c. ante* p. 214.

† Sir W. Thomson, *l. c. ante* p. 211.

coordinates χ, χ', ..., viz. the virtual moment of this system is zero for any infinitely small displacements of the solids, so long as χ, χ',... do not vary. We may imagine, for example, that the impulses are communicated to the membranes by some mechanism attached to the solids and reacting on these*. Denoting these components by X, X′, ..., and considering an arbitrary variation of χ, χ', ... only, we easily find, by an adaptation of the method employed near the end of Art. 134, that

$$\frac{dT}{d\dot{\chi}}\Delta\chi + \frac{dT}{d\dot{\chi}'}\Delta\chi' + \ldots = \mathrm{X}\Delta\chi + \mathrm{X}'\Delta\chi' + \ldots$$
$$= \rho\kappa\Delta\chi + \rho\kappa'\Delta\chi' + \ldots \qquad \text{(ii)},$$

whence the results (i) follow.

The same thing may be proved otherwise as follows. From the equations (2) and (1) of Art. 138, we find

$$\frac{dT}{d\dot{\chi}} = \rho\iiint\left(\frac{d\Phi}{dx}\frac{d\omega}{dx} + \frac{d\Phi}{dy}\frac{d\omega}{dy} + \frac{d\Phi}{dz}\frac{d\omega}{dz}\right)dx\,dy\,dz$$
$$= -\rho\iint\Phi\frac{d\omega}{dn}dS - \rho\kappa\iint\frac{d\omega}{dn}d\sigma - \rho\kappa'\iint\frac{d\omega}{dn}d\sigma' - \ldots \qquad \text{(iii)},$$

since $\nabla^2\omega = 0$. The conditions by which ω is determined are that it is the value of Φ when

$$\dot{q}_1 = 0, \quad \dot{q}_2 = 0, \quad \ldots, \quad \dot{\chi} = 1, \quad \dot{\chi}' = 0, \quad \ldots, \qquad \text{(iv)},$$

i.e. ω is the velocity-potential of a motion in which the boundaries, and therefore also the barriers, are fixed, whilst

$$-\iint\frac{d\omega}{dn}d\sigma = 1, \quad -\iint\frac{d\omega}{dn}d\sigma' = 0, \quad \ldots, \qquad \text{(v)}.$$

Hence the right-hand side of (iii) reduces to $\rho\kappa$, as was to be proved.

140. A simple application of the equations (21) of Art. 137 is to the case of a sphere moving through a liquid which circulates irrotationally through apertures in a fixed solid.

If the radius (a, say) of the sphere be small compared with its least distance from the fixed boundary, then $\mathfrak{T}$, the kinetic energy of the system when the motion of the fluid is acyclic, is given by Art. 91, viz.

$$2\mathfrak{T} = \mathbf{m}(\dot{x}^2 + \dot{y}^2 + \dot{z}^2) \qquad \text{(i)},$$

where $\mathbf{m}$ now denotes the mass of the sphere together with half that of the fluid displaced by it, and x, y, z are the Cartesian coordinates of the centre. And by the investigation of Art. 99, or more simply by a direct calculation, we have, for the energy of the cyclic motion by itself,

$$2K = \text{const.} - 2\pi\rho a^3(u^2 + v^2 + w^2) \qquad \text{(ii)}.$$

Again the coefficients α_1, α_2, α_3 of Art. 137 (18) denote the fluxes across the first barrier, when the sphere moves with unit velocity parallel to x, y, z, respectively. If we denote by Ω the flux across this barrier due to a unit simple-source at (x, y, z), then remembering the equivalence of a moving sphere to a double-source (Art. 91), we have

$$\alpha_1 = \tfrac{1}{2}a^3 d\Omega/dx, \quad \alpha_2 = \tfrac{1}{2}a^3 d\Omega/dy, \quad \alpha_3 = \tfrac{1}{2}a^3 d\Omega/dz \qquad \text{(iii)},$$

* Burton, *Phil. Mag.*, May, 1893.

so that the quantities denoted by (2, 3), (3, 1), (1, 2) in Art. 137 (21) vanish identically. The equations therefore reduce in the present case to

$$\mathrm{m}\ddot{x}=X+\frac{dW}{dx},\quad \mathrm{m}\ddot{y}=Y+\frac{dW}{dy},\quad \mathrm{m}\ddot{z}=Z+\frac{dW}{dz}\ \ldots\ldots\ldots\ldots\ \text{(iv)},$$

where

$$W=\pi\rho a^3(u^2+v^2+w^2)\ldots\ldots\ldots\ldots\ldots\ldots\text{(v)},$$

and X, Y, Z are the components of extraneous force applied to the sphere.

By an easy generalization it is seen that the equations (iv) must apply to any case where the liquid is in steady (irrotational) motion except in so far as it is disturbed by the motion of the small sphere. It is not difficult, moreover, to establish the equations by direct calculation of the pressures exerted on the sphere by the fluid.

When X, Y, $Z=0$, the sphere tends to move towards places where the undisturbed velocity of the fluid is greatest.

For example, in the case of cyclic motion round a fixed circular cylinder (Arts. 28, 64), the fluid velocity varies inversely as the distance from the axis. The sphere will therefore move as if under the action of a force towards this axis varying inversely as the cube of the distance. The projection of its path on a plane perpendicular to the axis will therefore be a Cotes' spiral*.

141. If in the equations (21) of Art. 137 we put $\dot{q}_1=0$, $\dot{q}_2=0,\ldots$, we obtain the generalized components of force which are required in order to maintain the solids at rest, viz.

$$Q_1=\frac{dK}{dq_1},\quad Q_2=\frac{dK}{dq_2},\ldots,\ \ldots\ldots\ldots\ldots\ldots\ \text{(1)}.$$

We are not dependent, of course, for this result, on the somewhat intricate investigation which precedes. If the solids be guided from rest in the configuration $(q_1, q_2,\ldots)$ to rest in the configuration $(q_1+\Delta q_1,\ q_2+\Delta q_2,\ldots)$, the work done on them is ultimately equal to

$$Q_1\Delta q_1+Q_2\Delta q_2+\ldots,$$

which must therefore be equal to the increment ΔK of the kinetic energy. This gives at once the equations (1).

The forces representing the pressures of the fluid on the solids (at rest) are obtained by reversing the sign in (1), viz. they are

$$-\frac{dK}{dq_1},\quad -\frac{dK}{dq_2},\ldots,\ \ldots\ldots\ldots\ldots\ldots\ \text{(2)}.$$

The solids tend therefore to move so that the kinetic energy of the cyclic motion diminishes.

* Sir W. Thomson, *l. c. ante* p. 211.

It appears from Art. 137 (10), that under the present circumstances the fluxes through the respective apertures are given by

$$\rho\dot{\chi}_0 = \frac{dK}{d\kappa}, \quad \rho\dot{\chi}_0' = \frac{dK}{d\kappa'}, \ldots, \quad \ldots\ldots\ldots\ldots\ldots\ldots(3).$$

By solving these equations, the circulations $\kappa, \kappa', \ldots$ can be expressed as linear functions of $\dot{\chi}_0, \dot{\chi}_0', \ldots$.

If these values of $\kappa, \kappa', \ldots$ be substituted in K we obtain a homogeneous quadratic function of $\dot{\chi}_0, \dot{\chi}_0', \ldots$. When so expressed, the kinetic energy of the cyclic motion may be denoted by T_0. We have then, exactly as in Art. 119,

$$T_0 + K = 2K = \rho\kappa\dot{\chi}_0 + \rho\kappa'\dot{\chi}_0' + \ldots \quad \ldots\ldots\ldots\ldots\ldots\ldots(4),$$

so that if, for the moment, the symbol Δ be used to indicate a perfectly general variation of these functions, we have

$$\frac{dT_0}{d\dot{\chi}_0}\Delta\dot{\chi}_0 + \frac{dT_0}{d\dot{\chi}_0'}\Delta\dot{\chi}_0' + \ldots + \frac{dT_0}{dq_1}\Delta q_1 + \frac{dT_0}{dq_2}\Delta q_2 + \ldots$$

$$+ \frac{dK}{d\kappa}\Delta\kappa + \frac{dK}{d\kappa'}\Delta\kappa' + \ldots + \frac{dK}{dq_1}\Delta q_1 + \frac{dK}{dq_2}\Delta q_2 + \ldots$$

$$= \rho\kappa\Delta\dot{\chi}_0 + \rho\kappa'\Delta\dot{\chi}_0' + \ldots + \rho\dot{\chi}_0\Delta\kappa + \rho\dot{\chi}_0'\Delta\kappa' + \ldots \quad \ldots\ldots\ldots(5).$$

Omitting terms which cancel by (3), and equating coefficients of the variations $\Delta\dot{\chi}_0, \Delta\dot{\chi}_0', \ldots, \Delta q_1, \Delta q_2, \ldots$, which form an independent system, we find

$$\rho\kappa = \frac{dT_0}{d\dot{\chi}_0}, \quad \rho\kappa' = \frac{dT_0}{d\dot{\chi}_0'}, \ldots, \quad \ldots\ldots\ldots\ldots\ldots\ldots(6),$$

and

$$\frac{dT_0}{dq_1} = -\frac{dK}{dq_1}, \quad \frac{dT_0}{dq_2} = -\frac{dK}{dq_2}, \ldots, \quad \ldots\ldots\ldots\ldots(7).$$

Hence the generalized components (2) of the pressures exerted by the fluid on the solids when held at rest may also be expressed in the forms

$$\frac{dT_0}{dq_1}, \quad \frac{dT_0}{dq_2}, \ldots, \quad \ldots\ldots\ldots\ldots\ldots\ldots\ldots\ldots(8).$$

It will be shown in Art. 152 that the energy K of the cyclic fluid motion is proportional to the energy of a system of electric current-sheets coincident with the surfaces of the fixed solids, the current-lines being orthogonal to the stream-lines of the fluid.

The electromagnetic forces between conductors carrying these currents are proportional* to the expressions (2) with the signs reversed. Hence in the hydrodynamical problem the forces on the solids are opposite to those which obtain in the electrical analogue. In the particular case where the fixed solids reduce to infinitely thin cores, round which the fluid circulates, the current-sheets in question are practically equivalent to a system of electric currents flowing in the cores, regarded as wires, with strengths κ, κ', ... respectively. For example, two thin circular rings, having a common axis, will repel or attract one another according as the fluid circulates in the same or in opposite directions through them†. This might have been foreseen of course from the principle of Art. 24.

Another interesting case is that of a number of open tubes, so narrow as not sensibly to impede the motion of the fluid outside them. If flow be established through the tubes, then as regards the external space the extremities will act as sources and sinks. The energy due to any distribution of positive or negative sources m_1, m_2, ... is given, so far as it depends on the relative configuration of these, by the integral

$$-\tfrac{1}{2}\rho\iint\phi\frac{d\phi}{dn}\,dS \quad\text{.............................(i)},$$

taken over a number of small closed surfaces surrounding m_1, m_2, ... respectively. If ϕ_1, ϕ_2, ... be the velocity-potentials due to the several sources, the part of this expression which is due to the simultaneous presence of m_1, m_2 is

$$-\tfrac{1}{2}\rho\iint\left(\phi_1\frac{d\phi_2}{dn}+\phi_2\frac{d\phi_1}{dn}\right)dS \quad\text{........................(ii)},$$

which is by Green's Theorem equal to

$$-\rho\iint\phi_1\frac{d\phi_2}{dn}\,dS \quad\text{.............................(iii)}.$$

Since the surface-integral of $d\phi_2/dn$ is zero over each of the closed surfaces except that surrounding m_2, we may ultimately confine the integration to the latter, and so obtain

$$-\rho\phi_1\iint\frac{d\phi_2}{dn}\,dS_2=4\pi\rho m_2\phi_1 \quad\text{........................(iv)}.$$

Since the value of ϕ_1 at m_2 is m_1/r_{12}, where r_{12} denotes the distance between m_1 and m_2, we obtain, for the part of the kinetic energy which varies with the relative positions of the sources, the expression

$$4\pi\rho\Sigma\frac{m_1m_2}{r_{12}} \quad\text{..................................(v)}.$$

* Maxwell, *Electricity and Magnetism*, Art. 573.

† The theorem of this paragraph was given by Kirchhoff, *l.c. ante* p. 59. See also Sir W. Thomson, "On the Forces experienced by Solids immersed in a Moving Liquid," *Proc. R. S. Edin.*, 1870; *Reprint*, Art. xli.; and Boltzmann, "Ueber die Druckkräfte welche auf Ringe wirksam sind die in bewegte Flüssigkeit tauchen," *Crelle*, t. lxxiii. (1871).

The quantities m_1, m_2, ... are in the present problem equal to $1/4\pi$ times the fluxes $\dot{\chi}_0$, $\dot{\chi}_0'$, ... across the sections of the respective tubes, so that (v) corresponds to the form T_0 of the kinetic energy. The force apparently exerted by m_1 on m_2, tending to increase r_{12}, is therefore, by (8),

$$4\pi\rho\,\frac{d}{dr_{12}}\cdot\frac{m_1 m_2}{r_{12}} = -4\pi\rho\,.\,\frac{m_1 m_2}{r_{12}^2}\,.$$

Hence two sources of like sign attract, and two of unlike sign repel, with forces varying inversely as the square of the distance*. This result, again, is easily seen to be in accordance with general principles. It also follows, independently, from the electric analogy, the tubes corresponding to Ampère's 'solenoids.'

We here take leave of this somewhat difficult part of our subject. To avoid the suspicion of vagueness which sometimes attaches to the use of 'generalized coordinates,' an attempt has been made in this Chapter to make the treatment as definite as possible, even at some sacrifice of generality in the results. There can be no doubt, for example, that with proper interpretations the equations of Art. 137 will apply to the case of *flexible* bodies surrounded by an irrotationally moving fluid, and even to cases of isolated vortices (see Chap. VII.), but the justification of such applications belongs rather to general Dynamics†.

* Sir W. Thomson, *Reprint*, Art. xli.

† For further investigations bearing on the subject of this Chapter see J. Purser, "On the Applicability of Lagrange's Equations in certain Cases of Fluid Motion," *Phil. Mag.*, Nov. 1878; Larmor, *l.c. ante* p. 210; Basset, *Hydrodynamics*, Cambridge, 1888, c. viii.

CHAPTER VII.

VORTEX MOTION.

142. OUR investigations have thus far been confined for the most part to the case of irrotational motion. We now proceed to the study of rotational or 'vortex' motion. This subject was first investigated by von Helmholtz*; other and simpler proofs of some of his theorems were afterwards given by Lord Kelvin in the paper on vortex motion already cited in Chapter III.

We shall, throughout this Chapter, use the symbols ξ, η, ζ to denote, as in Chap. III., the components of the instantaneous angular velocity of a fluid element, viz.

$$\xi = \tfrac{1}{2}\left(\frac{dw}{dy} - \frac{dv}{dz}\right), \quad \eta = \tfrac{1}{2}\left(\frac{du}{dz} - \frac{dw}{dx}\right), \quad \zeta = \tfrac{1}{2}\left(\frac{dv}{dx} - \frac{du}{dy}\right) \ldots (1).$$

A line drawn from point to point so that its direction is everywhere that of the instantaneous axis of rotation of the fluid is called a 'vortex-line.' The differential equations of the system of vortex-lines are

$$\frac{dx}{\xi} = \frac{dy}{\eta} = \frac{dz}{\zeta} \quad \ldots\ldots\ldots\ldots\ldots\ldots\ldots\ldots (2).$$

If through every point of a small closed curve we draw the corresponding vortex-line, we obtain a tube, which we call a

* "Ueber Integrale der hydrodynamischen Gleichungen welche den Wirbelbewegungen entsprechen," *Crelle*, t. lv. (1858); *Ges. Abh.*, t. i., p. 101.

'vortex-tube.' The fluid contained within such a tube constitutes what is called a 'vortex-filament,' or simply a 'vortex.'

Let ABC, $A'B'C'$ be any two circuits drawn on the surface of a vortex-tube and embracing it, and let AA' be a connecting line also drawn on the surface. Let us apply the theorem of Art. 33 to the circuit $ABCAA'C'B'A'A$ and the part of the surface of the

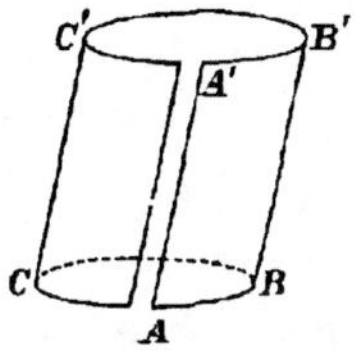

tube bounded by it. Since $l\xi + m\eta + n\zeta$ is zero at every point of this surface, the line-integral

$$\int (udx + vdy + wdz),$$

taken round the circuit, must vanish; *i.e.* in the notation of Art. 32

$$I(ABCA) + I(AA') + I(A'C'B'A') + I(A'A) = 0,$$

which reduces to

$$I(ABCA) = I(A'B'C'A').$$

Hence the circulation is the same in all circuits embracing the same vortex-tube.

Again, it appears from Art. 32 that the circulation round the boundary of any cross-section of the tube, made normal to its length, is $2\omega\sigma$, where $\omega, = (\xi^2 + \eta^2 + \zeta^2)^{\frac{1}{2}}$, is the angular velocity of the fluid, and σ the infinitely small area of the section.

Combining these results we see that the product of the angular velocity into the cross-section is the same at all points of a vortex. This product is conveniently termed the 'strength' of the vortex.

The foregoing proof is due to Lord Kelvin; the theorem itself was first given by von Helmholtz, as a deduction from the relation

$$\frac{d\xi}{dx} + \frac{d\eta}{dy} + \frac{d\zeta}{dz} = 0 \quad \text{.................................} \quad \text{(i)},$$

which follows at once from the values of ξ, η, ζ given by (1). In fact, writing in Art. 42 (1), ξ, η, ζ for U, V, W, respectively, we find

$$\iint (l\xi + m\eta + n\zeta)\, dS = 0 \text{..........................(ii)},$$

where the integration extends over any closed surface lying wholly in the fluid. Applying this to the closed surface formed by two cross-sections of a vortex-tube and the portion of the tube intercepted between them, we find $\omega_1\sigma_1 = \omega_2\sigma_2$, where ω_1, ω_2 denote the angular velocities at the sections σ_1, σ_2, respectively.

Lord Kelvin's proof shews that the theorem is true even when ξ, η, ζ are discontinuous (in which case there may be an abrupt bend at some point of a vortex), provided only that u, v, w are continuous.

An important consequence of the above theorem is that a vortex-line cannot begin or end at any point in the interior of the fluid. Any vortex-lines which exist must either form closed curves, or else traverse the fluid, beginning and ending on its boundaries. Compare Art. 37.

The theorem of Art. 33 (4) may now be enunciated as follows: The circulation in any circuit is equal to twice the sum of the strengths of all the vortices which it embraces.

143. It was proved in Art. 34 that, in a perfect fluid whose density is either uniform or a function of the pressure only, and which is subject to extraneous forces having a single-valued potential, the circulation in any circuit moving with the fluid is constant.

Applying this theorem to a circuit embracing a vortex-tube we find that the strength of any vortex is constant.

If we take at any instant a surface composed wholly of vortex-lines, the circulation in any circuit drawn on it is zero, by Art. 33, for we have $l\xi + m\eta + n\zeta = 0$ at every point of the surface. The preceding article shews that if the surface be now supposed to move with the fluid, the circulation will always be zero in any circuit drawn on it, and therefore the surface will always consist of vortex-lines. Again, considering two such surfaces, it is plain that their intersection must always be a vortex-line, whence we derive the theorem that the vortex-lines move with the fluid.

This remarkable theorem was first given by von Helmholtz for the case of liquids; the preceding proof, by Lord Kelvin, shews that it holds for all fluids subject to the conditions above stated.

One or two independent proofs of the theorem may be briefly indicated.

Of these perhaps the most conclusive is based upon a slight generalization of some equations given originally by Cauchy in his great memoir on Waves*, and employed by him to demonstrate Lagrange's velocity-potential theorem.

The equations (2) of Art. 15, yield, on elimination of the function χ by cross-differentiation,

$$\frac{du}{db}\frac{dx}{dc}-\frac{du}{dc}\frac{dx}{db}+\frac{dv}{db}\frac{dy}{dc}-\frac{dv}{dc}\frac{dy}{db}+\frac{dw}{db}\frac{dz}{dc}-\frac{dw}{dc}\frac{dz}{db}=\frac{dw_0}{db}-\frac{dv_0}{dc},$$

(where u, v, w have been written in place of dx/dt, dy/dt, dz/dt, respectively), with two symmetrical equations. If in these equations we replace the differential coefficients of u, v, w with respect to a, b, c, by their values in terms of differential coefficients of the same quantities with respect to x, y, z, we obtain

$$\left.\begin{aligned}\xi\frac{d(y,z)}{d(b,c)}+\eta\frac{d(z,x)}{d(b,c)}+\zeta\frac{d(x,y)}{d(b,c)}&=\xi_0,\\ \xi\frac{d(y,z)}{d(c,a)}+\eta\frac{d(z,x)}{d(c,a)}+\zeta\frac{d(x,y)}{d(c,a)}&=\eta_0,\\ \xi\frac{d(y,z)}{d(a,b)}+\eta\frac{d(z,x)}{d(a,b)}+\zeta\frac{d(x,y)}{d(a,b)}&=\zeta_0\end{aligned}\right\}\quad\text{.................(i).}$$

If we multiply these by dx/da, dx/db, dx/dc, in order, and add, then, taking account of the Lagrangian equation of continuity (Art. 14 (1)) we deduce the first of the following three symmetrical equations:

$$\left.\begin{aligned}\frac{\xi}{\rho}&=\frac{\xi_0}{\rho_0}\frac{dx}{da}+\frac{\eta_0}{\rho_0}\frac{dx}{db}+\frac{\zeta_0}{\rho_0}\frac{dx}{dc},\\ \frac{\eta}{\rho}&=\frac{\xi_0}{\rho_0}\frac{dy}{da}+\frac{\eta_0}{\rho_0}\frac{dy}{db}+\frac{\zeta_0}{\rho_0}\frac{dy}{dc},\\ \frac{\zeta}{\rho}&=\frac{\xi_0}{\rho_0}\frac{dz}{da}+\frac{\eta_0}{\rho_0}\frac{dz}{db}+\frac{\zeta_0}{\rho_0}\frac{dz}{dc}\end{aligned}\right\}\quad\text{........................ (ii).}$$

In the particular case of an incompressible fluid ($\rho=\rho_0$) these differ only in the use of the notation ξ, η, ζ from the equations given by Cauchy. They shew at once that if the initial values ξ_0, η_0, ζ_0 of the component rotations vanish for any particle of the fluid, then ξ, η, ζ are always zero for that particle. This constitutes in fact Cauchy's proof of Lagrange's theorem.

To interpret (ii) in the general case, let us take at time $t=0$ a linear element coincident with a vortex-line, say

$$\delta a=\epsilon\xi_0/\rho_0,\qquad \delta b=\epsilon\eta_0/\rho_0,\qquad \delta c=\epsilon\zeta_0/\rho_0,$$

where ϵ is infinitesimal. If we suppose this element to move with the fluid, the equations (ii) shew that its projections on the coordinate axes at any other time will be given by

$$\delta x=\epsilon\xi/\rho,\qquad \delta y=\epsilon\eta/\rho,\qquad \delta z=\epsilon\zeta/\rho,$$

* *l. c. ante* p. 18.

i.e. the element will still form part of a vortex-line, and its length (δs, say) will vary as ω/ρ, where ω is the resultant angular velocity. But if σ be the cross-section of a vortex-filament having δs as axis, the product $\rho\sigma\delta s$ is constant with regard to the time. Hence the strength $\omega\sigma$ of the vortex is constant*.

The proof given originally by von Helmholtz depends on a system of three equations which, when generalized so as to apply to any fluid in which ρ is a function of p only, become

$$\left.\begin{aligned} \frac{D}{Dt}\left(\frac{\xi}{\rho}\right) &= \frac{\xi}{\rho}\frac{du}{dx} + \frac{\eta}{\rho}\frac{du}{dy} + \frac{\zeta}{\rho}\frac{du}{dz}, \\ \frac{D}{Dt}\left(\frac{\eta}{\rho}\right) &= \frac{\xi}{\rho}\frac{dv}{dx} + \frac{\eta}{\rho}\frac{dv}{dy} + \frac{\zeta}{\rho}\frac{dv}{dz}, \\ \frac{D}{Dt}\left(\frac{\zeta}{\rho}\right) &= \frac{\xi}{\rho}\frac{dw}{dx} + \frac{\eta}{\rho}\frac{dw}{dy} + \frac{\zeta}{\rho}\frac{dw}{dz} \end{aligned}\right\} \quad \text{(iii)}\dagger.$$

These may be obtained as follows. The dynamical equations of Art. 6 may be written, when a force-potential Ω exists, in the forms

$$\left.\begin{aligned} \frac{du}{dt} - 2v\zeta + 2w\eta &= -\frac{d\chi'}{dx}, \\ \frac{dv}{dt} - 2w\xi + 2u\zeta &= -\frac{d\chi'}{dy}, \\ \frac{dw}{dt} - 2u\eta + 2v\xi &= -\frac{d\chi'}{dz} \end{aligned}\right\} \quad \text{(iv)},$$

provided

$$\chi' = \int \frac{dp}{\rho} + \tfrac{1}{2}q^2 + \Omega \quad \text{(v)},$$

where $q^2 = u^2 + v^2 + w^2$. From the second and third of these we obtain, eliminating χ' by cross-differentiation,

$$\frac{d\xi}{dt} + v\frac{d\xi}{dy} + w\frac{d\xi}{dz} - u\left(\frac{d\eta}{dy} + \frac{d\zeta}{dz}\right) = \eta\frac{du}{dy} + \zeta\frac{du}{dz} - \xi\left(\frac{dv}{dy} + \frac{dw}{dz}\right).$$

Remembering the relation

$$\frac{d\xi}{dx} + \frac{d\eta}{dy} + \frac{d\zeta}{dz} = 0 \quad \text{(vi)},$$

and the equation of continuity

$$\frac{D\rho}{Dt} + \rho\left(\frac{du}{dx} + \frac{dv}{dy} + \frac{dw}{dz}\right) = 0 \quad \text{(vii)},$$

we easily deduce the first of equations (iii).

To interpret these equations we take, at time t, a linear element whose projections on the coordinate axes are

$$\delta x = \epsilon\xi/\rho, \qquad \delta y = \epsilon\eta/\rho, \qquad \delta z = \epsilon\zeta/\rho \quad \text{(viii)},$$

where ϵ is infinitesimal. If this element be supposed to move with the fluid,

* See Nanson, *Mess. of Math.* t. iii., p. 120 (1874); Kirchhoff, *Mechanik*, Leipzig. 1876..., c. xv.; Stokes, *Math. and Phys. Papers*, t. ii., p. 47 (1883).

† Nanson, *l. c.*

the rate at which δx is increasing is equal to the difference of the values of u at the two ends, whence

$$\frac{D\delta x}{Dt} = \epsilon\frac{\xi}{\rho}\frac{du}{dx} + \epsilon\frac{\eta}{\rho}\frac{du}{dy} + \epsilon\frac{\zeta}{\rho}\frac{du}{dz}.$$

It follows, by (iii), that

$$\frac{D}{Dt}\left(\delta x - \epsilon\frac{\xi}{\rho}\right) = 0, \quad \frac{D}{Dt}\left(\delta y - \epsilon\frac{\eta}{\rho}\right) = 0, \quad \frac{D}{Dt}\left(\delta z - \epsilon\frac{\zeta}{\rho}\right) = 0 \;\ldots\ldots \text{(ix)}.$$

Von Helmholtz concludes that if the relations (viii) hold at time t, they will hold at time $t + \delta t$, and so on, continually. The inference is, however, not quite rigorous; it is in fact open to the criticisms which Sir G. Stokes* has directed against various defective proofs of Lagrange's velocity-potential theorem†.

By way of establishing a connection with Lord Kelvin's investigation we may notice that the equations (i) express that the circulation is constant in each of three infinitely small circuits initially perpendicular, respectively, to the three coordinate axes. Taking, for example, the circuit which initially bounded the rectangle $\delta b\,\delta c$, and denoting by A, B, C the areas of its projections at time t on the coordinate planes, we have

$$A = \frac{d(y, z)}{d(b, c)}\delta b\,\delta c, \quad B = \frac{d(z, x)}{d(b, c)}\delta b\,\delta c, \quad C = \frac{d(x, y)}{d(b, c)}\delta b\,\delta c,$$

so that the first of the equations referred to is equivalent to

$$\xi A + \eta B + \zeta C = \xi_0 \delta b\,\delta c \;\ldots\ldots\ldots\ldots \text{(x)}‡.$$

144. It is easily seen by the same kind of argument as in Art. 41 that no irrotational motion is possible in an incompressible fluid filling infinite space, and subject to the condition that the velocity vanishes at infinity. This leads at once to the following theorem:

The motion of a fluid which fills infinite space, and is at rest at infinity, is determinate when we know the values of the

* *l. c. ante* p. 18.

† It may be mentioned that, in the case of an incompressible fluid, equations somewhat similar to (iii) had been established by Lagrange, *Miscell. Taur.*, t. ii. (1760), *Oeuvres*, t. i., p. 442. The author is indebted for this reference, and for the above criticism of von Helmholtz' investigation, to Mr Larmor. Equations equivalent to those given by Lagrange were obtained independently by Stokes, *l. c.*, and made the basis of a rigorous proof of the velocity-potential theorem.

‡ Nanson, *Mess. of Math.*, t. vii., p. 182 (1878). A similar interpretation of von Helmholtz' equations was given by the author of this work in the *Mess. of Math.*, t. vii., p. 41 (1877).

Finally we may note that another proof of Lagrange's theorem, based on elementary dynamical principles, without special reference to the hydrokinetic equations, was indicated by Stokes (*Camb. Trans.*, t. viii.; *Math. and Phys. Papers*, t. i., p. 113), and carried out by Lord Kelvin, in his paper on Vortex Motion.

expansion (θ, say) and of the component angular velocities ξ, η, ζ, at all points of the region.

For, if possible, let there be two sets of values, u_1, v_1, w_1, and u_2, v_2, w_2, of the component velocities, each satisfying the equations

$$\frac{du}{dx}+\frac{dv}{dy}+\frac{dw}{dz}=\theta \text{ ....(1),}$$

$$\frac{dw}{dy}-\frac{dv}{dz}=2\xi,\quad \frac{du}{dz}-\frac{dw}{dx}=2\eta,\quad \frac{dv}{dx}-\frac{du}{dy}=2\zeta \text{.........(2),}$$

throughout infinite space, and vanishing at infinity. The quantities

$$u'=u_1-u_2,\quad v'=v_1-v_2,\quad w'=w_1-w_2,$$

will satisfy (1) and (2) with θ, ξ, η, ζ each put $=0$, and will vanish at infinity. Hence, in virtue of the result above stated, they will everywhere vanish, and there is only one possible motion satisfying the given conditions.

In the same way we can shew that the motion of a fluid occupying any *limited* simply-connected region is determinate when we know the values of the expansion, and of the component rotations, at every point of the region, and the value of the normal velocity at every point of the boundary. In the case of a multiply-connected region we must add to the above data the values of the circulations in the several independent circuits of the region.

145. If, in the case of infinite space, the quantities θ, ξ, η, ζ all vanish beyond some finite distance of the origin, the complete determination of u, v, w in terms of them can be effected as follows*.

The component velocities (u_1, v_1, w_1, say) due to the *expansion* can be written down at once from Art. 56 (1), it being evident that the expansion θ' in an element $\delta x'\delta y'\delta z'$ is equivalent to a simple source of strength $1/4\pi\,.\,\theta'\delta x'\delta y'\delta z'$. We thus obtain

$$u_1=-\frac{d\Phi}{dx},\quad v_1=-\frac{d\Phi}{dy},\quad w_1=-\frac{d\Phi}{dz} \text{ ....(1),}$$

where

$$\Phi=\frac{1}{4\pi}\iiint\frac{\theta'}{r}\,dx'dy'dz' \text{ ....(2),}$$

* The investigation which follows is substantially that given by von Helmholtz. The kinematical problem in question was first solved, in a slightly different manner, by Stokes, "On the Dynamical Theory of Diffraction," *Camb. Trans.*, t. ix. (1849), *Math. and Phys. Papers*, t. ii., pp. 254....

r denoting the distance between the point (x', y', z') at which the volume-element of the integral is situate and the point (x, y, z) at which the values of u_1, v_1, w_1 are required, viz.

$$r = \{(x-x')^2 + (y-y')^2 + (z-z')^2\}^{\frac{1}{2}},$$

and the integration including all parts of space at which θ' differs from zero.

To verify this result, we notice that the above values of u_1, v_1, w_1 make

$$\frac{du_1}{dx} + \frac{dv_1}{dy} + \frac{dw_1}{dz} = -\nabla^2\Phi = \theta,$$

by the theory of Attractions, and also vanish at infinity.

To find the velocities (u_2, v_2, w_2, say) due to the *vortices*, we assume

$$u_2 = \frac{dH}{dy} - \frac{dG}{dz}, \quad v_2 = \frac{dF}{dz} - \frac{dH}{dx}, \quad w_2 = \frac{dG}{dx} - \frac{dF}{dy}, \quad \text{......(3)},$$

and seek to determine F, G, H so as to satisfy the required conditions. In the first place, these formulæ make

$$\frac{du_2}{dx} + \frac{dv_2}{dy} + \frac{dw_2}{dz} = 0,$$

and so do not interfere with the result contained in (1). Also, they give

$$2\xi = \frac{dw_2}{dy} - \frac{dv_2}{dz} = \frac{d}{dx}\left(\frac{dF}{dx} + \frac{dG}{dy} + \frac{dH}{dz}\right) - \nabla^2 F.$$

Hence our problem will be solved if we can find three functions F, G, H satisfying

$$\frac{dF}{dx} + \frac{dG}{dy} + \frac{dH}{dz} = 0, \quad \text{......................(4)},$$

and $$\nabla^2 F = -2\xi, \quad \nabla^2 G = -2\eta, \quad \nabla^2 H = -2\zeta \quad \text{.........(5)}.$$

These latter equations are satisfied by making F, G, H equal to the potentials of distributions of matter whose volume-densities at the point (x, y, z) are $\xi/2\pi$, $\eta/2\pi$, $\zeta/2\pi$, respectively; thus

$$\left.\begin{aligned} F &= \frac{1}{2\pi}\iiint\frac{\xi'}{r}\,dx'dy'dz', \\ G &= \frac{1}{2\pi}\iiint\frac{\eta'}{r}\,dx'dy'dz', \\ H &= \frac{1}{2\pi}\iiint\frac{\zeta'}{r}\,dx'dy'dz' \end{aligned}\right\} \quad \text{..................(6)},$$

where the accents attached to ξ, η, ζ are used to distinguish the values of these quantities at the point (x', y', z'), and

$$r = \{(x-x')^2 + (y-y')^2 + (z-z')^2\}^{\frac{1}{2}},$$

as before. The integrations are to include, of course, all places at which ξ, η, ζ differ from zero.

It remains to shew that the above values of F, G, H really satisfy (4). Since $d/dx \,.\, r^{-1} = -d/dx' \,.\, r^{-1}$, we have

$$\frac{dF}{dx} + \frac{dG}{dy} + \frac{dH}{dz} = -\frac{1}{2\pi}\iiint\left(\xi'\frac{d}{dx'} + \eta'\frac{d}{dy'} + \zeta'\frac{d}{dz'}\right)\frac{1}{r}\,dx'dy'dz'$$

$$= \frac{1}{2\pi}\iint(l\xi' + m\eta' + n\zeta')\frac{dS'}{r} + \frac{1}{2\pi}\iiint\left(\frac{d\xi'}{dx'} + \frac{d\eta'}{dy'} + \frac{d\zeta'}{dz'}\right)\frac{dx'dy'dz'}{r} \quad \text{........(7)},$$

by the usual method of partial integration. The volume-integral vanishes, by Art. 142 (i), and the surface-integral also vanishes, since $l\xi + m\eta + n\zeta = 0$ at the bounding surfaces of the vortices. Hence the formulae (3) and (6) lead to the prescribed values of ξ, η, ζ, and give a zero velocity at infinity.

The complete solution of our problem is now obtained by superposition of the results contained in the formulæ (1) and (3), viz. we have

$$\left.\begin{aligned} u &= -\frac{d\Phi}{dx} + \frac{dH}{dy} - \frac{dG}{dz}, \\ v &= -\frac{d\Phi}{dy} + \frac{dF}{dz} - \frac{dH}{dx}, \\ w &= -\frac{d\Phi}{dz} + \frac{dG}{dx} - \frac{dF}{dy} \end{aligned}\right\} \quad \text{..................(8)},$$

where Φ, F, G, H have the values given in (2) and (6).

When the region occupied by the fluid is not unlimited, but is bounded (in whole or in part) by surfaces at which the normal velocity is given, and when further (in the case of a cyclic region) the value of the circulation in each of the independent circuits of the region is prescribed, the problem may by a similar analysis be reduced to one of irrotational motion, of the kind considered in Chap. III., and there proved to be determinate. This may be left to the reader, with the remark that if the vortices traverse the region, beginning and ending on the boundary, it is convenient to imagine them continued beyond it, or along its surface, in such a manner that they form re-entrant filaments, and to make the integrals (6) refer to the complete system of vortices thus obtained. On this understanding the condition (4) will still be satisfied.

146. There is a remarkable analogy between the analytical relations above developed and those which obtain in the theory of Electro-magnetism. If, in the equations (1) and (2) of Art. 144, we write

$$\begin{array}{lccccccc} & \alpha, & \beta, & \gamma, & \rho, & p, & q, & r \\ \text{for} & u, & v, & w, & \theta/4\pi, & \xi/2\pi, & \eta/2\pi, & \zeta/2\pi, \end{array}$$

respectively, we obtain

$$\left.\begin{array}{c} \dfrac{d\alpha}{dx}+\dfrac{d\beta}{dy}+\dfrac{d\gamma}{dz}=4\pi\rho, \\ \dfrac{d\gamma}{dy}-\dfrac{d\beta}{dz}=4\pi p, \quad \dfrac{d\alpha}{dz}-\dfrac{d\gamma}{dx}=4\pi q, \quad \dfrac{d\beta}{dx}-\dfrac{d\alpha}{dy}=4\pi r \end{array}\right\} \ldots(1)^*,$$

which are the fundamental relations of the subject referred to; viz. α, β, γ are the components of magnetic force, p, q, r those of electric current, and ρ is the volume-density of the imaginary magnetic matter by which any magnetization present in the field may be represented. Hence, if we disregard constant factors, the vortex-filaments correspond to electric circuits, the strengths of the vortices to the strengths of the currents in these circuits, sources and sinks to positive and negative magnetic poles, and, finally, fluid velocity to magnetic force†.

The analogy will of course extend to all results deduced from the fundamental relations; thus, in equations (8) of the preceding Art., Φ corresponds to the magnetic potential and F, G, H to the components of 'electro-magnetic momentum.'

147. To interpret the result contained in Art. 145 (8), we may calculate the values of u, v, w due to an isolated re-entrant vortex-filament situate in an infinite mass of incompressible fluid which is at rest at infinity.

Since $\theta=0$, we shall have $\Phi=0$. Again, to calculate the values of F, G, H, we may replace the volume-element $\delta x'\delta y'\delta z'$ by $\sigma'\delta s'$, where $\delta s'$ is an element of the length of the filament, and σ' its cross-section. Also, we have

$$\xi'=\omega'\frac{dx'}{ds'}, \quad \eta'=\omega'\frac{dy'}{ds'}, \quad \zeta'=\omega'\frac{dz'}{ds'},$$

* Cf. Maxwell, *Electricity and Magnetism*, Art. 607.

† This analogy was first pointed out by von Helmholtz; it has been extensively utilized by Lord Kelvin in his papers on *Electrostatics and Magnetism*.

where ω' is the angular velocity of the fluid. Hence the formulæ (6) of Art. 145 become

$$F = \frac{m'}{2\pi}\int \frac{dx'}{r}, \quad G = \frac{m'}{2\pi}\int \frac{dy'}{r}, \quad H = \frac{m'}{2\pi}\int \frac{dz'}{r} \quad \ldots\ldots (1),$$

where $m', = \omega'\sigma'$, measures the strength of the vortex, and the integrals are to be taken along the whole length of the filament.

Hence, by Art. 145 (8), we have

$$u = \frac{m'}{2\pi}\int \left(\frac{d}{dy}\frac{1}{r}\,.\,dz' - \frac{d}{dz}\frac{1}{r}\,.\,dy'\right),$$

with similar results for v, w. We thus find

$$\left.\begin{aligned} u &= \frac{m'}{2\pi}\int \left(\frac{dy'}{ds'}\frac{z-z'}{r} - \frac{dz'}{ds'}\frac{x-x'}{r}\right)\frac{ds'}{r^2}, \\ v &= \frac{m'}{2\pi}\int \left(\frac{dz'}{ds'}\frac{x-x'}{r} - \frac{dx'}{ds'}\frac{y-y'}{r}\right)\frac{ds'}{r^2}, \\ w &= \frac{m'}{2\pi}\int \left(\frac{dx'}{ds'}\frac{y-y'}{r} - \frac{dy'}{ds'}\frac{z-z'}{r}\right)\frac{ds'}{r^2}, \end{aligned}\right\} \ldots\ldots\ldots\ldots (2)^*.$$

If Δu, Δv, Δw denote the parts of these expressions which correspond to the element $\delta s'$ of the filament, it appears that the resultant of Δu, Δv, Δw is a velocity perpendicular to the plane containing the direction of the vortex-line at (x', y', z') and the line r, and that its sense is that in which the point (x, y, z) would be carried if it were attached to a rigid body rotating with the fluid element at (x', y', z'). For the magnitude of the resultant we have

$$\{(\Delta u)^2 + (\Delta v)^2 + (\Delta w)^2\}^{\frac{1}{2}} = \frac{m'}{2\pi}\frac{\sin\chi\,\delta s'}{r^2} \quad \ldots\ldots\ldots (3),$$

where χ is the angle which r makes with the vortex-line at (x', y', z').

With the change of symbols indicated in the preceding Art. this result becomes identical with the law of action of an electric current on a magnetic pole†.

* These are equivalent to the forms obtained by Stokes, *l. c. ante* p. 228.

† Ampère, *Théorie mathématique des phenomènes électro-dynamiques*, Paris, 1826.

Velocity-Potential due to a Vortex.

148. At points external to the vortices there exists of course a velocity-potential, whose value may be obtained as follows. Taking for shortness the case of a single re-entrant vortex, it was found in the preceding Art. that, in the case of an incompressible fluid,

$$u = \frac{m'}{2\pi}\int\left(\frac{d}{dz'}\frac{1}{r}.dy' - \frac{d}{dy'}\frac{1}{r}.dz'\right) \ldots \ldots\ldots (1).$$

By Stokes' Theorem (Art. 33 (5)) we can replace a line-integral extending round a closed curve by a surface-integral taken over any surface bounded by that curve; viz. we have, with a slight change of notation,

$$\int(Pdx' + Qdy' + Rdz')$$
$$= \iint\left\{l\left(\frac{dR}{dy'} - \frac{dQ}{dz'}\right) + m\left(\frac{dP}{dz'} - \frac{dR}{dx'}\right) + n\left(\frac{dQ}{dx'} - \frac{dP}{dy'}\right)\right\} dS'.$$

If we put

$$P = 0, \quad Q = \frac{d}{dz'}\frac{1}{r}, \quad R = -\frac{d}{dy'}\frac{1}{r},$$

we find

$$\frac{dR}{dy'} - \frac{dQ}{dz'} = -\left(\frac{d^2}{dy'^2} + \frac{d^2}{dz'^2}\right)\frac{1}{r} = \frac{d^2}{dx'^2}\frac{1}{r'},$$

$$\frac{dP}{dz'} - \frac{dR}{dx'} = \qquad \frac{d^2}{dx'dy'}\frac{1}{r'},$$

$$\frac{dQ}{dx'} - \frac{dP}{dy'} = \qquad \frac{d^2}{dx'dz'}\frac{1}{r'},$$

so that (1) may be written

$$u = \frac{m'}{2\pi}\iint\left(l\frac{d}{dx'} + m\frac{d}{dy'} + n\frac{d}{dz'}\right)\frac{d}{dx'}\frac{1}{r}dS'.$$

Hence, and by similar reasoning, we have, since

$$d/dx'.r^{-1} = -d/dx.r^{-1},$$

$$u = -\frac{d\phi}{dx}, \quad v = -\frac{d\phi}{dy}, \quad w = -\frac{d\phi}{dz}, \ldots\ldots\ldots\ldots\ldots (2),$$

where

$$\phi = \frac{m'}{2\pi}\iint\left(l\frac{d}{dx'} + m\frac{d}{dy'} + n\frac{d}{dz'}\right)\frac{1}{r}dS' \ldots \ldots\ldots (3).$$

Here l, m, n denote the direction-cosines of the normal to the element $\delta S'$ of any surface bounded by the vortex-filament.

The formula (3) may be otherwise written

$$\phi = \frac{m'}{2\pi}\iint \frac{\cos \vartheta}{r^2}\, dS' \quad\ldots\ldots\ldots\ldots\ldots\ldots (4),$$

where ϑ denotes the angle between r and the normal (l, m, n). Since $\cos\theta\,\delta S'/r^2$ measures the elementary solid angle subtended by $\delta S'$ at (x, y, z), we see that the velocity-potential at any point, due to a single re-entrant vortex, is equal to the product of $m'/2\pi$ into the solid angle which any surface bounded by the vortex subtends at that point.

Since this solid angle changes by 4π when the point in question describes a circuit embracing the vortex, we verify that the value of ϕ given by (4) is cyclic, the cyclic constant being twice the strength of the vortex. Cf. Art. 142.

Comparing (4) with Art. 56 (4) we see that a vortex is, in a sense, equivalent to a uniform distribution of double sources over any surface bounded by it. The axes of the double sources must be supposed to be everywhere normal to the surface, and the density of the distribution to be equal to the strength of the vortex divided by 2π. It is here assumed that the relation between the positive direction of the normal and the positive direction of the axis of the vortex-filament is of the 'right-handed' type. See Art. 32.

Conversely, it may be shewn that any distribution of double sources over a *closed* surface, the axes being directed along the normals, may be replaced by a system of closed vortex-filaments lying in the surface*. The same thing will appear independently from the investigation of the next Art.

Vortex-Sheets.

149. We have so far assumed u, v, w to be continuous. We will now shew how cases where surfaces present themselves at which these quantities are discontinuous may be brought within the scope of our theorems.

The case of a surface where the *normal* velocity is discontinuous has already been treated in Art. 58. If u, v, w denote the component velocities on one side, and u', v', w' those on the other,

* Cf. Maxwell, *Electricity and Magnetism*, Arts. 485, 652.

it was found that the circumstances could be represented by imagining a distribution of simple-sources, with surface density

$$\frac{1}{4\pi}\{l(u'-u)+m(v'-v)+n(w'-w)\},$$

where l, m, n denote the direction cosines of the normal drawn towards the side to which the accents refer.

Let us next consider the case where the *tangential* velocity (only) is discontinuous, so that

$$l(u'-u)+m(v'-v)+w(w'-w)=0 \qquad\text{..........(1).}$$

We will suppose that the lines of *relative* motion, which are defined by the differential equations

$$\frac{dx}{u'-u}=\frac{dy}{v'-v}=\frac{dz}{w'-w}, \qquad\text{..................(2),}$$

are traced on the surface, and that the system of orthogonal trajectories to these lines is also drawn. Let PQ, $P'Q'$ be linear elements drawn close to the surface, on the two sides, parallel to a line of the system (2), and let PP' and QQ' be normal to the surface and infinitely small in comparison with PQ or $P'Q'$. The circulation in the circuit $P'Q'QP$ will then be equal to $(q'-q)\,PQ$, where q, q' denote the absolute velocities on the two sides. This is the same as if the position of the surface were occupied by an infinitely thin stratum of vortices, the orthogonal trajectories above-mentioned being the vortex-lines, and the angular velocity ω and the (variable) thickness δn of the stratum being connected by the relation $2\omega\,.\,PQ\,.\,\delta n=(q'-q)\,PQ$, or

$$\omega\delta n=\tfrac{1}{2}(q'-q) \qquad\text{.......................(3).}$$

The same result follows from a consideration of the discontinuities which occur in the values of u, v, w as determined by the formulæ (3) and (6) of Art. 145, when we apply these to the case of a stratum of thickness δn within which ξ, η, ζ are infinite, but so that $\xi\delta n$, $\eta\delta n$, $\zeta\delta n$ are finite*.

It was shewn in Arts. 144, 145 that any continuous motion of a fluid filling infinite space, and at rest at infinity, may be regarded as due to a proper arrangement of sources and vortices distributed with finite density. We have now seen how by considerations of continuity we can pass to the case where the sources and vortices are distributed with infinite volume-density,

* Helmholtz, *l. c. ante* p. 222.

but finite surface-density, over surfaces. In particular, we may take the case where the infinite fluid in question is incompressible, and is divided into two portions by a closed surface over which the normal velocity is continuous, but the tangential velocity discontinuous, as in Art. 58 (12). This is equivalent to a vortex-sheet; and we infer that every continuous irrotational motion, whether cyclic or not, of an incompressible substance occupying any region whatever, may be regarded as due to a certain distribution of vortices over the boundaries which separate it from the rest of infinite space. In the case of a region extending to infinity, the distribution is confined to the *finite* portion of the boundary, provided the fluid be at rest at infinity.

This theorem is complementary to the results obtained in Art. 58.

The foregoing conclusions may be illustrated by means of the results of Art. 90. Thus when a normal velocity S_n was prescribed over the sphere $r=a$, the values of the velocity-potential for the internal and external space were found to be

$$\phi=\frac{a}{n}\left(\frac{r}{a}\right)^n S_n, \text{ and } \phi=-\frac{a}{n+1}\left(\frac{a}{r}\right)^{n+1} S_n,$$

respectively. Hence if $\delta\epsilon$ be the angle which any linear element drawn on the surface subtends at the centre, the relative velocity estimated in the direction of this element will be

$$\frac{2n+1}{n(n+1)}\frac{dS_n}{d\epsilon}.$$

The resultant relative velocity is therefore tangential to the surface, and perpendicular to the contour lines ($S_n=$ const.) of the surface-harmonic S_n, which are therefore the vortex-lines.

For example, if we have a thin spherical shell filled with and surrounded by liquid, moving as in Art. 91 parallel to the axis of x, the motion of the fluid, whether internal or external, will be that due to a system of vortices arranged in parallel circles on the sphere; the strength of an elementary vortex being proportional to the projection, on the axis of x, of the breadth of the corresponding strip of the surface*.

Impulse and Energy of a Vortex-System.

150. The following investigations relate to the case of a vortex-system of finite dimensions in an incompressible fluid which fills infinite space and is at rest at infinity.

* The same statements hold also for an ellipsoidal shell moving parallel to one of its principal axes. See Art. 111.

If X', Y', Z' be components of a distribution of impulsive force which would generate the actual motion (u, v, w) instantaneously from rest, we have by Art. 12 (1)

$$X' - \frac{1}{\rho}\frac{d\varpi}{dx} = u, \quad Y' - \frac{1}{\rho}\frac{d\varpi}{dy} = v, \quad Z' - \frac{1}{\rho}\frac{d\varpi}{dz} = w \quad \text{......(1)},$$

where ϖ is the impulsive pressure. The problem of finding X', Y', Z', ϖ in terms of u, v, w, so as to satisfy these three equations, is clearly indeterminate; but a sufficient solution for our purpose may be obtained as follows.

Let us imagine a simply-connected surface S to be drawn enclosing all the vortices. Over this surface, and through the external space, let us put

$$\varpi = \rho\phi \quad \text{..............................(2)},$$

where ϕ is the velocity-potential of the vortex-system, determined as in Art. 148. Inside S let us take as the value of ϖ any single-valued function which is finite and continuous, is equal to (2) at S, and also satisfies the equation

$$\frac{d\varpi}{dn} = \rho\frac{d\phi}{dn} \quad \text{..............................(3)},$$

at S, where δn denotes as usual an element of the normal. It follows from these conditions, which can evidently be satisfied in an infinite number of ways, that the space-derivatives $d\varpi/dx$, $d\varpi/dy$, $d\varpi/dz$ will be continuous at the surface S. The values of X', Y', Z' are now given by the formulæ (1); they vanish at the surface S, and at all external points.

The force- and couple-equivalents of the distribution X', Y', Z' constitute the 'impulse' of the vortex-system. We are at present concerned only with the instantaneous state of the system, but it is of interest to recall that, when no extraneous forces act, this impulse is, by the argument of Art. 116, constant in every respect.

Now, considering the matter inclosed within the surface S, we find, resolving parallel to x,

$$\iiint \rho X' dxdydz = \rho\iiint u\, dxdydz - \rho\iint l\phi\, dS \quad \text{..............(4)},$$

if l, m, n be the direction-cosines of the inwardly-directed normal to any element δS of the surface. Let us first take the case of a single vortex-filament of infinitely small section. The fluid velocity being everywhere finite and continuous, the parts of the volume-integral on the right-hand side of (4) which are due to the substance of the vortex itself may be neglected in comparison with those due to the remainder of the space included within S. Hence we may write

$$\iiint u\,dxdydz = -\iiint \frac{d\phi}{dx}\,dxdydz = \iint l\phi dS + 2m' \iint l dS' \;\ldots (5),$$

where ϕ has the value given by Art. 147 (4), m' denoting the strength of the vortex (so that $2m'$ is the cyclic constant of ϕ), and $\delta S'$ an element of any surface bounded by it. Substituting in (4), we infer that the components of the impulse parallel to the coordinate axes are

$$2m'\rho\iint l dS',\quad 2m'\rho\iint m dS',\quad 2m'\rho\iint n dS' \ldots\ldots\ldots\ldots\ldots (6).$$

Again, taking moments about Ox,

$$\iiint\rho\,(yZ' - zY')\,dxdydz$$
$$= \rho\iiint(yw - zv)\,dxdydz - \rho\iint(ny - mz)\,\phi dS \ldots\ldots\ldots (7).$$

For the same reason as before, we may substitute, for the volume-integral on the right-hand side,

$$-\iiint\left(y\frac{d\phi}{dz} - z\frac{d\phi}{dy}\right)dxdydz$$
$$= \iint(ny - mz)\,\phi dS + 2m'\iint(ny - mz)\,dS' \ldots\ldots\ldots (8).$$

Hence, and by symmetry, we find, for the moments of the impulse about the coordinate axes,

$$2m'\rho\iint(ny - mz)\,dS',\quad 2m'\rho\iint(lz - nx)\,dS',\quad 2m'\rho\iint(mx - ly)\,dS' \ldots (9).$$

The surface-integrals contained in (6) and (9) may be replaced by line-integrals taken along the vortex. In the case of (6) it is obvious that the coefficients of $m'\rho$ are double the projections on the coordinate axes of any area bounded by the vortex, so that the components in question take the forms

$$m'\int\left(y'\frac{dz'}{ds'} - z'\frac{dy'}{ds'}\right)ds',\quad m'\int\left(z'\frac{dx'}{ds'} - x'\frac{dz'}{ds'}\right)ds',$$
$$m'\int\left(x'\frac{dy'}{ds'} - y'\frac{dx'}{ds'}\right)ds', \ldots\ldots\ldots\ldots\ldots\ldots\ldots (10).$$

For the similar transformation of (9) we must have recourse to Stokes' Theorem; we obtain without difficulty the forms

$$m'\rho\int(y'^2+z'^2)\frac{dx'}{ds'}ds',\quad m'\rho\int(z'^2+x'^2)\frac{dy'}{ds'}ds',\quad m'\rho\int(x'^2+y'^2)\frac{dz'}{ds'}ds' \quad\ldots\ldots\ldots\ldots(11).$$

From (10) and (11) we can derive by superposition the components of the force- and couple- resultants of any finite system of vortices. Denoting these by P, Q, R, and L, M, N, respectively, we find, putting

$$m' = \omega'\sigma',$$

$$\omega'\frac{dx'}{ds'} = \xi',\quad \omega'\frac{dy'}{ds'} = \eta',\quad \omega'\frac{dz'}{ds'} = \zeta',$$

and replacing the volume-element $\sigma'\delta s'$ by $\delta x'\delta y'\delta z'$,

$$\left.\begin{aligned} P &= \rho\iiint(y\zeta - z\eta)\,dxdydz, & L &= \rho\iiint(y^2+z^2)\,\xi\,dxdydz,\\ Q &= \rho\iiint(z\xi - x\zeta)\,dxdydz, & M &= \rho\iiint(z^2+x^2)\,\eta\,dxdydz,\\ R &= \rho\iiint(x\eta - y\xi)\,dxdydz, & N &= \rho\iiint(x^2+y^2)\,\zeta\,dxdydz \end{aligned}\right\}\ldots(12)^*,$$

where the accents have been dropped, as no longer necessary.

151. Let us next consider the *energy* of the vortex-system. It is easily proved that under the circumstances presupposed, and in the absence of extraneous forces, this energy will be constant. For if T be the energy of the fluid bounded by any closed surface S, we have, putting $V=0$ in Art. 11 (5),

$$\frac{DT}{Dt} = \iint(lu + mv + nw)\,pdS \quad\ldots\ldots\ldots\ldots\ldots\ldots(1).$$

If the surface S enclose all the vortices, we may put

$$\frac{p}{\rho} = \frac{d\phi}{dt} - \tfrac{1}{2}q^2 + F(t) \quad\ldots\ldots\ldots\ldots\ldots\ldots\ldots\ldots(2),$$

and it easily follows from Art. 148 (4) that at a great distance R from the vortices p will be finite, and $lu+mv+nw$ of the order R^{-3}, whilst when the surface S is taken wholly at infinity,

* These expressions were given by J. J. Thomson, *On the Motion of Vortex Rings* (Adams Prize Essay), London, 1883, pp. 5, 6.

the elements δS ultimately vary as R^2. Hence, ultimately, the right-hand side of (1) vanishes, and we have

$$T = \text{const.} \qquad \text{(3).}$$

152. We proceed to investigate one or two important kinematical expressions for T, still confining ourselves, for simplicity, to the case where the fluid (supposed incompressible) extends to infinity, and is at rest there, all the vortices being within a finite distance of the origin.

The first of these is indicated by the electro-magnetic analogy pointed out in Art. 146. Since $\theta = 0$, and therefore $\Phi = 0$, we have

$$2T = \rho\iiint(u^2 + v^2 + w^2)\,dxdydz$$

$$= \rho\iiint\left\{u\left(\frac{dH}{dy} - \frac{dG}{dz}\right) + v\left(\frac{dF}{dz} - \frac{dH}{dx}\right) + w\left(\frac{dG}{dx} - \frac{dF}{dy}\right)\right\} dxdydz,$$

by Art. 145 (3). The last member may be replaced by the sum of a surface integral

$$\rho\iint\{F(mw - nv) + G(nu - lw) + H(lv - mu)\}\,dS,$$

and a volume integral

$$\rho\iiint\left\{F\left(\frac{dw}{dy} - \frac{dv}{dz}\right) + G\left(\frac{du}{dz} - \frac{dw}{dx}\right) + H\left(\frac{dv}{dx} - \frac{du}{dy}\right)\right\} dxdydz.$$

At points of the infinitely distant boundary, F, G, H are ultimately of the order R^{-2}, and u, v, w of the order R^{-3}, so that the surface-integral vanishes, and we have

$$T = \rho\iiint(F\xi + G\eta + H\zeta)\,dxdydz \qquad \text{(1),}$$

or, substituting the values of F, G, H from Art. 145 (6),

$$T = \frac{\rho}{2\pi}\iiiiiint\frac{\xi\xi' + \eta\eta' + \zeta\zeta'}{r}\,dxdydz\,dx'dy'dz' \quad \text{...(2),}$$

where each volume-integration extends over the whole space occupied by the vortices.

A slightly different form may be given to this expression as follows. Regarding the vortex-system as made up of filaments, let δs, $\delta s'$ be elements of length of any two filaments, σ, σ' the corresponding cross-sections, and ω, ω' the corresponding angular velocities. The elements of volume may be taken to be

$\sigma\delta s$ and $\sigma'\delta s'$, respectively, so that the expression following the integral signs in (2) is equivalent to

$$\frac{\cos \epsilon}{r} . \omega\sigma\delta s . \omega'\sigma'\delta s',$$

where ϵ is the angle between δs and $\delta s'$. If we put $\omega\sigma = m$, $\omega'\sigma' = m'$, so that m and m' denote the strengths of the two elementary vortices, we have

$$T = \frac{\rho}{\pi} \Sigma mm' \iint \frac{\cos \epsilon}{r} ds ds' \text{ .... (3)},$$

where the double integral is to be taken along the axes of the filaments, and the summation embraces every pair of such filaments which are present.

The factor of ρ/π in (3) is identical with the expression for the energy of a system of electric currents flowing along conductors coincident in position with the vortex-filaments, with strengths $m, m', \ldots$ respectively*. The above investigation is in fact merely an inversion of the argument given in treatises on Electro-magnetism, whereby it is proved that

$$\Sigma ii' \iint \frac{\cos \epsilon}{r} ds ds' = \frac{1}{8\pi} \iiint (\alpha^2 + \beta^2 + \gamma^2)\, dx dy dz,$$

i, i' denoting the strengths of the currents in the linear conductors whose elements are denoted by δs, $\delta s'$, and α, β, γ the components of magnetic force at any point of the field.

The theorem of this Art. is purely kinematical, and rests solely on the assumption that the functions u, v, w satisfy the equation of continuity,

$$\frac{du}{dx} + \frac{dv}{dy} + \frac{dw}{dz} = 0,$$

throughout infinite space, and vanish at infinity. It can therefore by an easy generalization be extended to the case considered in Art. 141, where a liquid is supposed to circulate irrotationally through apertures in fixed solids, the values of u, v, w being now taken to be zero at all points of space not occupied by the fluid. The investigation of Art. 149 shews that the distribution of velocity thus obtained may be regarded as due to a system of vortex-sheets coincident with the surfaces of the solids. The energy of this system will be given by an obvious adaptation of the formula (3) above, and will therefore be proportional to that of the correspond-

* See Maxwell, *Electricity and Magnetism*, Arts. 524, 637.

ing system of electric current-sheets. This proves a statement made by anticipation in Art. 141.

153. Under the circumstances stated at the beginning of Art. 152, we have another useful expression for T; viz.

$$T = 2\rho \iiint \{u(y\zeta - z\eta) + v(z\xi - x\zeta) + w(x\eta - y\xi)\}\, dx\,dy\,dz \ldots (4).$$

To verify this, we take the right-hand member, and transform it by the process already so often employed, omitting the surface-integrals for the same reason as in the preceding Art. The first of the three terms gives

$$\rho \iiint u \left\{ y\left(\frac{dv}{dx} - \frac{du}{dy}\right) - z\left(\frac{du}{dz} - \frac{dw}{dx}\right)\right\} dx\,dy\,dz$$

$$= -\rho \iiint \left\{(vy + wz)\frac{du}{dx} - u^2\right\} dx\,dy\,dz.$$

Transforming the remaining terms in the same way, adding, and making use of the equation of continuity, we obtain

$$\rho \iiint \left(u^2 + v^2 + w^2 + xu\frac{du}{dx} + yv\frac{dv}{dy} + zw\frac{dw}{dz}\right) dx\,dy\,dz,$$

or, finally, on again transforming the last three terms,

$$\tfrac{1}{2}\rho \iiint (u^2 + v^2 + w^2)\, dx\,dy\,dz.$$

In the case of a finite region the surface-integrals must be retained. This involves the addition to the right-hand side of (4) of the term

$$\rho \iint \{(lu + mv + nw)(xu + yv + zw) - \tfrac{1}{2}(lx + my + nz) q^2\}\, dS,$$

where $q^2 = u^2 + v^2 + w^2$. This simplifies in the case of a *fixed* boundary*.

The value of the expression (4) must be unaltered by any displacement of the origin of coordinates. Hence we must have

$$\left.\begin{aligned} &\iiint (v\zeta - w\eta)\, dx\,dy\,dz = 0, \\ &\iiint (w\xi - u\zeta)\, dx\,dy\,dz = 0, \\ &\iiint (u\eta - v\xi)\, dx\,dy\,dz = 0 \end{aligned}\right\} \ldots\ldots\ldots\ldots (i).$$

These equations, which may easily be verified by partial integration, follow also from the consideration that the components of the impulse parallel to the coordinate axes must be constant. Thus, taking first the case of a fluid enclosed in a fixed envelope of finite size, we have, in the notation of Art. 150,

$$P = \rho \iiint u\, dx\,dy\,dz - \rho \iint l\phi\, dS \ldots\ldots\ldots\ldots (ii),$$

whence

$$\frac{dP}{dt} = \rho \iiint \frac{du}{dt} dx\,dy\,dz - \rho \iint l \frac{d\phi}{dt} dS$$

$$= -\rho \iiint \frac{d\chi'}{dx} dx\,dy\,dz + 2\rho \iiint (v\zeta - w\eta)\, dx\,dy\,dz - \rho \iint l\frac{d\phi}{dt} dS \ldots\ldots (iii),$$

* Cf. J. J. Thomson, *l.c.*

by Art. 143 (iv). The first and third terms of this cancel, since at the envelope we have $\chi' = d\phi/dt$. Hence for any re-entrant system of vortices enclosed in a fixed vessel, we have

$$\frac{dP}{dt} = 2\rho \iiint (v\zeta - w\eta)\, dx\,dy\,dz \quad \text{.......................(iv)},$$

with two similar equations. If now the containing vessel be supposed infinitely large, and infinitely distant from the vortices, it follows from the argument of Art. 116 that P is constant. This gives the first of equations (i).

Conversely from (i), established otherwise, we could infer the constancy of the components P, Q, R of the impulse*.

Rectilinear Vortices.

154. When the motion is in two dimensions xy we have $w = 0$, whilst u, v are functions of x, y, only. Hence $\xi = 0$, $\eta = 0$, so that the vortex-lines are straight lines parallel to z. The theory then takes a very simple form.

The formulæ (8) of Art. 145 are now replaced by

$$u = -\frac{d\phi}{dx} - \frac{d\psi}{dy}, \quad v = -\frac{d\phi}{dy} + \frac{d\psi}{dx} \quad \text{..............(1)},$$

the functions ϕ, ψ being subject to the equations

$$\nabla_1^2\phi = -\theta, \quad \nabla_1^2\psi = 2\zeta \quad \text{....................(2)},$$

where $\nabla_1^2 = d^2/dx^2 + d^2/dy^2$,

and to the proper boundary-conditions.

In the case of an incompressible fluid, to which we will now confine ourselves, we have

$$u = -\frac{d\psi}{dy}, \quad v = \frac{d\psi}{dx} \quad \text{.......................(3)},$$

where ψ is the stream-function of Art. 59. It is known from the theory of Attractions that the solution of

$$\nabla_1^2\psi = 2\zeta \quad \text{............................(4)},$$

where ζ is a given function of x, y, is

$$\psi = \frac{1}{\pi}\iint \zeta' \log r\, dx'\,dy' + \psi_0 \quad \text{.............. (5)},$$

* Cf. J. J. Thomson, *Motion of Vortex Rings*, p. 5.

where ζ' denotes the value of ζ at the point (x', y'), and r now stands for

$$\{(x-x')^2+(y-y')^2\}^{\frac{1}{2}}.$$

The 'complementary function' ψ_0 may be any solution of

$$\nabla_1^2\psi_0 = 0 \quad \text{.........................} \quad (6);$$

it enables us to satisfy the boundary-conditions.

In the case of an unlimited mass of liquid, at rest at infinity, we have $\psi_0 = \text{const.}$ The formulæ (3) and (5) then give

$$\left.\begin{aligned} u &= -\frac{1}{\pi}\iint \zeta' \frac{y-y'}{r^2}\, dx'\, dy', \\ v &= \frac{1}{\pi}\iint \zeta' \frac{x-x'}{r^2}\, dx'\, dy' \end{aligned}\right\} \quad \text{...............} \quad (7).$$

Hence a vortex-filament whose coordinates are x', y' and whose strength is m' contributes to the motion at (x, y) a velocity whose components are

$$-\frac{m'}{\pi}\cdot\frac{y-y'}{r^2}, \text{ and } \frac{m'}{\pi}\cdot\frac{x-x'}{r^2}.$$

This velocity is perpendicular to the line joining the points (x, y), (x', y'), and its amount is $m'/\pi r$.

Let us calculate the integrals $\iint u\zeta dxdy$, and $\iint v\zeta dxdy$, where the integrations include all portions of the plane xy for which ζ does not vanish. We have

$$\iint u\zeta dxdy = -\frac{1}{\pi}\iiiint \zeta\zeta' \frac{y-y'}{r^2}\, dxdy\, dx'\, dy',$$

where each double integration includes the sections of all the vortices. Now, corresponding to any term

$$\zeta\zeta' \frac{y-y'}{r^2}\, dxdy\, dx'\, dy'$$

of this result, we have another term

$$\zeta\zeta' \frac{y'-y}{r^2}\, dxdy\, dx'\, dy',$$

and these two terms neutralize one another. Hence

$$\iint u\zeta dxdy = 0 \quad \text{.........................} \quad (8),$$

and, by the same reasoning,

$$\iint v\zeta\, dx\, dy = 0 \text{ ....(9).}$$

If as before we denote the strength of a vortex by m, these results may be written

$$\Sigma mu = 0, \quad \Sigma mv = 0 \text{ ....(10).}$$

We have seen above that the strength of each vortex is constant with regard to the time. Hence (10) express that the point whose coordinates are

$$\bar{x} = \frac{\Sigma mx}{\Sigma m}, \qquad \bar{y} = \frac{\Sigma my}{\Sigma m},$$

is fixed throughout the motion. This point, which coincides with the centre of inertia of a film of matter distributed over the plane xy with the surface-density ζ, may be called the 'centre' of the system of vortices, and the straight line parallel to z of which it is the projection may be called the 'axis' of the system.

155. Some interesting examples are furnished by the case of one or more isolated vortices of infinitely small section. Thus:

1°. Let us suppose that we have only one vortex-filament present, and that the rotation ζ has the same sign throughout its infinitely small section. Its centre, as just defined, will lie either within the substance of the filament, or at all events infinitely close to it. Since this centre remains at rest, the filament as a whole will be stationary, though its parts may experience relative motions, and its centre will not necessarily lie always in the same element of fluid. Any particle at a finite distance r from the centre of the filament will describe a circle about the latter as axis, with constant velocity $m/\pi r$. The region external to the filament is doubly-connected; and the circulation in any (simple) circuit embracing the filament is $2m$. The irrotational motion of the fluid external to the filament is the same as in Art. 28 (2).

2°. Next suppose that we have two vortices, of strengths m_1, m_2, respectively. Let A, B be their centres, O the centre of the system. The motion of each filament as a whole is entirely due to the other, and is therefore always perpendicular to AB. Hence the two filaments remain always at the same distance from one another, and rotate with constant angular velocity about O, which is fixed. This angular velocity is easily found; we have only to divide the velocity of A (say), viz. $m_2/(\pi . AB)$, by the distance AO, where

$$AO = \frac{m_2}{m_1 + m_2} AB,$$

and so obtain

$$\frac{m_1 + m_2}{\pi . AB^2}$$

for the angular velocity required.

If m_1, m_2 be of the same sign, *i.e.* if the directions of rotation in the two filaments be the same, O lies between A and B; but if the rotations be of opposite signs, O lies in AB, or BA, produced.

If $m_1 = - m_2$, O is at infinity; in this case it is easily seen that A, B move with constant velocity $m_1/(\pi . AB)$ perpendicular to AB, which remains fixed in direction. The motion at a distance from the filaments is given at any instant by the formulæ of Art. 64, 2°.

Such a combination of two equal and opposite rectilinear vortices may be called a 'vortex-pair.' It is the two-dimensional analogue of a circular vortex-ring (Art. 162), and exhibits many of the characteristic properties of the latter.

The motion at all points of the plane bisecting AB at right angles is in this latter case tangential to that plane. We may therefore suppose the plane to form a fixed rigid boundary of the fluid in either side of it, and so obtain the solution of the case where we have a single rectilinear vortex in the neighbourhood of a fixed plane wall to which it is parallel. The filament moves parallel to the plane with the velocity $m/2\pi d$, where d is the distance of the vortex from the wall.

The stream-lines due to a vortex-pair, at distances from the vortices great in comparison with the linear dimensions of the cross-sections, form a system of coaxal circles, as shewn in the diagram on p. 80.

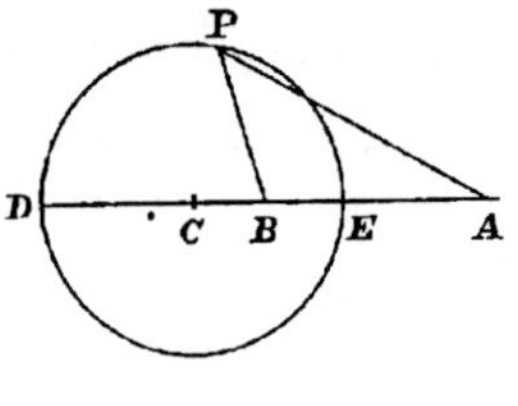

We can hence derive the solution of the case where we have a single vortex-filament in a mass of fluid which is bounded, either internally or externally, by a fixed circular cylinder. Thus, in the figure, let EPD be the section of the cylinder, A the position of the vortex (supposed in this case external), and let B be the 'image' of A with respect to the circle EPD, viz. C being the centre, let

$$CB . CA = c^2,$$

where c is the radius of the circle. If P be any point on the circle, we have

$$\frac{AP}{BP}=\frac{AE}{BE}=\frac{AD}{BD}=\text{const.};$$

so that the circle occupies the position of a stream-line due to a pair of vortices, whose strengths are equal and opposite in sign, situated at A, B in an unlimited mass of fluid. Since the motion of the vortex A would then be perpendicular to AB, it is plain that all the conditions of the problem will be satisfied if we suppose A to describe a circle about the axis of the cylinder with the constant velocity

$$-\frac{m}{\pi \,.\, AB}=-\frac{m \,.\, CA}{\pi\,(CA^2-c^2)},$$

where m denotes the strength of A.

In the same way a single vortex of strength m, situated inside a fixed circular cylinder, say at B, would describe a circle with constant velocity

$$\frac{m \,.\, CB}{\pi\,(c^2-CB^2)}.$$

It is to be noticed, however*, that in the case of the external vortex the motion is not completely determinate unless, in addition to the strength m of the vortex, the value of the circulation in a circuit embracing the cylinder (but not the vortex) is prescribed. In the above solution, this circulation is that due to the vortex-image at B and is $-2m$. This may be annulled by the superposition of an additional vortex $+m$ at C, in which case we have, for the velocity of A,

$$-\frac{m \,.\, CA}{\pi\,(CA^2-c^2)}+\frac{m}{\pi \,.\, CA}=-\frac{mc^2}{\pi \,.\, CA\,(CA^2-c^2)}.$$

For a prescribed circulation κ we must add to this the term $\kappa/2\pi \,.\, CA$.

3°. If we have four parallel rectilinear vortices whose centres form a rectangle $ABB'A'$, the strengths being m for the vortices A', B, and $-m$ for the vortices A, B', it is evident that the centres will always form a rectangle. Further, the various rotations having the directions indicated in the figure, we see that

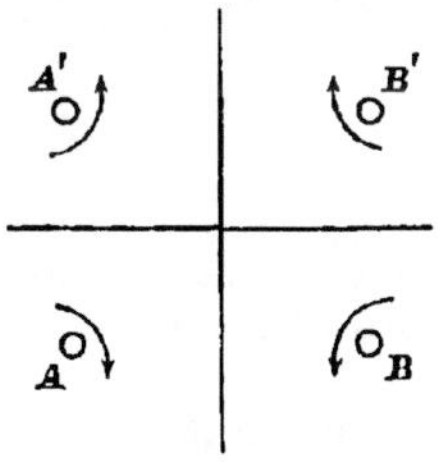

* See F. A. Tarleton, "On a Problem in Vortex Motion," *Proc. R. I. A.*, December 12, 1892.

the effect of the presence of the pair A, A' on B, B' is to separate them, and at the same time to diminish their velocity perpendicular to the line joining them. The planes which bisect AB, AA' at right angles may (either or both) be taken as fixed rigid boundaries. We thus get the case where a pair of vortices, of equal and opposite strengths, move towards (or from) a plane wall, or where a single vortex moves in the angle between two perpendicular walls.

If x, y be the coordinates of the vortex B' relative to the planes of symmetry, we readily find

$$\dot{x} = -\frac{m}{2\pi} \cdot \frac{x^2}{yr^2}, \quad \dot{y} = \frac{m}{2\pi} \cdot \frac{y^2}{xr^2} \quad \text{.........................(i)},$$

where $r^2 = x^2 + y^2$. By division we obtain the differential equation of the path, viz.

$$\frac{dx}{x^3} + \frac{dy}{y^3} = 0,$$

whence $$a^2 (x^2 + y^2) = 4x^2y^2,$$

a being an arbitrary constant, or, transforming to polar coordinates,

$$r = a/\sin 2\theta \quad \text{...................................(ii)}.$$

Also since $$x\dot{y} - y\dot{x} = m/2\pi,$$

the vortex moves as if under a centre of force at the origin. This force is repulsive, and its law is that of the inverse cube*.

156. When, as in the case of a vortex-pair, or a system of vortex-pairs, the algebraic sum of the strengths of all the vortices is zero, we may work out a theory of the 'impulse,' in two dimensions, analogous to that given in Arts. 116, 149 for the case of a finite vortex-system. The detailed examination of this must be left to the reader. If P, Q denote the components of the impulse parallel to x and y, and N its moment about Oz, all reckoned per unit depth of the fluid parallel to z, it will be found that

$$\left.\begin{array}{c} P = \rho \iint y\zeta\, dx\, dy, \qquad Q = -\rho \iint x\zeta\, dx\, dy, \\ N = \rho \iint (x^2 + y^2)\, \zeta\, dx\, dy \end{array}\right\} \quad \text{.........(1)}.$$

* See Greenhill, "On plane vortex-motion," *Quart. Journ. Math.*, t. xv. (1877), where some other interesting cases of motion of rectilinear vortex-filaments are discussed.

The literature of special problems in this part of the subject is somewhat extensive; for references see Hicks, *Brit. Ass. Rep.* 1882, pp. 41...; Love, "On Recent English Researches in Vortex Motion," *Math. Ann.*, t. xxx., p. 326 (1887); Winkelmann, *Handbuch der Physik*, t. i., pp. 446–451.

For instance, in the case of a single vortex-pair, the strengths of the two vortices being $\pm m$, and their distance apart c, the impulse is $2mc$, in a line bisecting c at right angles.

The constancy of the impulse gives

$$\left.\begin{array}{c}\Sigma mx = \text{const.}, \quad \Sigma my = \text{const.},\\ \Sigma m(x^2+y^2) = \text{const.}\end{array}\right\}\text{..............(2).}$$

It may also be shewn that the energy of the motion in the present case is given by

$$T = -\rho\iint\psi\zeta\,dx\,dy = -\rho\Sigma m\psi \text{..................(3).}$$

When Σm is not zero, the energy and the moment of the impulse are both infinite, as may be easily verified in the case of a single rectilinear vortex.

The theory of a system of isolated rectilinear vortices has been put in a very elegant form by Kirchhoff*.

Denoting the positions of the centres of the respective vortices by (x_1, y_1), (x_2, y_2), ... and their strengths by m_1, m_2, ..., it is evident from Art. 154 that we may write

$$\left.\begin{array}{ll} m_1\dfrac{dx_1}{dt} = -\dfrac{dW}{dy_1}, & m_1\dfrac{dy_1}{dt} = \dfrac{dW}{dx_1}, \\ m_2\dfrac{dx_2}{dt} = -\dfrac{dW}{dy_2}, & m_2\dfrac{dy_2}{dt} = \dfrac{dW}{dx_2}, \\ \text{.....................} & \end{array}\right\}\text{..................(i),}$$

where $$W = \frac{1}{\pi}\Sigma m_1 m_2 \log r_{12} \text{..........................(ii),}$$

if r_{12} denote the distance between the vortices m_1, m_2.

Since W depends only on the *relative* configuration of the vortices, its value is unaltered when $x_1, x_2, \ldots$ are increased by the same amount, whence $\Sigma dW/dx_1 = 0$, and, in the same way, $\Sigma dW/dy_1 = 0$. This gives the first two of equations (2), but the proof is not now limited to the case of $\Sigma m = 0$. The argument is in fact substantially the same as in Art. 154.

Again, we obtain from (i)

$$\Sigma m\left(x\frac{dx}{dt} + y\frac{dy}{dt}\right) = -\Sigma\left(x\frac{dW}{dy} - y\frac{dW}{dx}\right),$$

or if we introduce polar coordinates (r_1, θ_1), (r_2, θ_2), ... for the several vortices,

$$\Sigma mr\frac{dr}{dt} = -\Sigma\frac{dW}{d\theta} \text{..............................(iii).}$$

* *Mechanik*, c. xx.

Since W is unaltered by a rotation of the axes of coordinates in their own plane about the origin, we have $\Sigma dW/d\theta = 0$, whence

$$\Sigma mr^2 = \text{const.} \qquad \text{(iv)},$$

which agrees with the third of equations (2), but is free from the restriction there understood.

An additional integral of (i) is obtained as follows. We have

$$\Sigma m\left(x\frac{dy}{dt} - y\frac{dx}{dt}\right) = \Sigma\left(x\frac{dW}{dx} + y\frac{dW}{dy}\right),$$

or

$$\Sigma mr^2\frac{d\theta}{dt} = \Sigma r\frac{dW}{dr} \qquad \text{(v)}.$$

Now if every r be increased in the ratio $1+\epsilon$, where ϵ is infinitesimal, the increment of W is equal to $\Sigma\epsilon r \,.\, dW/dr$. The new configuration of the vortex-system is geometrically similar to the former one, so that the mutual distances r_{12} are altered in the same ratio $1+\epsilon$, and therefore, from (ii), the increment of W is $\epsilon\pi^{-1} \,.\, \Sigma m_1 m_2$. Hence

$$\Sigma mr^2\frac{d\theta}{dt} = \frac{1}{\pi}\Sigma m_1 m_2 \qquad \text{(vi)}.$$

157. The results of Art. 155 are independent of the form of the sections of the vortices, so long as the dimensions of these sections are small compared with the mutual distances of the vortices themselves. The simplest case is of course when the sections are circular, and it is of interest to inquire whether this form is stable. This question has been examined by Lord Kelvin*.

Let us suppose, as in Art. 28, that the space within a circle $r=a$, having the centre as origin, is occupied by fluid having a uniform rotation ζ, and that this is surrounded by fluid moving irrotationally. If the motion be continuous at this circle we have, for $r<a$

$$\psi = -\tfrac{1}{2}\zeta(a^2 - r^2) \qquad \text{(i)},$$

while for $r>a$,

$$\psi = -\zeta a^2 \log a/r \qquad \text{(ii)}.$$

To examine the effect of a slight irrotational disturbance, we assume, for $r<a$,

$$\psi = -\tfrac{1}{2}\zeta(a^2 - r^2) + A\frac{r^s}{a^s}\cos(s\theta - \sigma t),$$

and, for $r>a$,

$$\psi = -\zeta a^2 \log\frac{a}{r} + A\frac{a^s}{r^s}\cos(s\theta - \sigma t) \qquad \text{(iii)},$$

where s is integral, and σ is to be determined. The constant A must have the same value in these two expressions, since the radial component of the

* Sir W. Thomson, "On the Vibrations of a Columnar Vortex," *Phil. Mag.*, Sept. 1880.

velocity, $d\psi/rd\theta$, must be continuous at the boundary of the vortex, for which $r=a$, approximately. Assuming for the equation to this boundary

$$r=a+\alpha\cos(s\theta-\sigma t)\text{.......................(iv)},$$

we have still to express that the tangential component ($d\psi/dr$) of the velocity is continuous. This gives

$$\zeta r+s\frac{A}{a}\cos(s\theta-\sigma t)=\zeta\frac{a^2}{r}-s\frac{A}{a}\cos(s\theta-\sigma t).$$

Substituting from (iv), and neglecting the square of α, we find

$$\zeta\alpha=-sA/a\text{.......................(v)}.$$

So far the work is purely kinematical; the dynamical theorem that the vortex-lines move with the fluid shews that the normal velocity of a particle on the boundary must be equal to that of the boundary itself. This condition gives

$$\frac{dr}{dt}=-\frac{d\psi}{rd\theta}-\frac{d\psi}{dr}\frac{dr}{rd\theta},$$

where r has the value (iv), or

$$\sigma\alpha=s\frac{A}{a}+\zeta a.\frac{s\alpha}{a}\text{.......................(vi)}.$$

Eliminating the ratio A/α between (v) and (vi) we find

$$\sigma=(s-1)\zeta\text{.......................(vii)}.$$

Hence the disturbance represented by the plane harmonic in (iii) consists of a system of corrugations travelling round the circumference of the vortex with an angular velocity

$$\sigma/s=(s-1)/s.\zeta\text{.......................(viii)}.$$

This is the angular velocity in space; relative to the previously rotating fluid the angular velocity is

$$\sigma/s-\zeta=-\zeta/s\text{.......................(ix)},$$

the direction being opposite to that of the rotation.

When $s=2$, the disturbed section is an ellipse which rotates about its centre with angular velocity $\frac{1}{2}\zeta$.

The transverse and longitudinal oscillations of an isolated rectilinear vortex-filament have also been discussed by Lord Kelvin in the paper cited.

158. The particular case of an elliptic disturbance can be solved without approximation as follows*.

Let us suppose that the space within the ellipse

$$\frac{x^2}{a^2}+\frac{y^2}{b^2}=1\text{.......................(i)}$$

* Kirchhoff, *Mechanik*, c. xx., p. 261; Basset, *Hydrodynamics*, Cambridge, 1888, t. ii., p. 41.

is occupied by liquid having a uniform rotation ζ, whilst the surrounding fluid is moving irrotationally. It will appear that the conditions of the problem can all be satisfied if we imagine the elliptic boundary to rotate without change of shape with a constant angular velocity (n, say), to be determined.

The formula for the external space can be at once written down from Art. 72, 4°; viz. we have

$$\psi = \tfrac{1}{4} n (a+b)^2 e^{-2\xi} \cos 2\eta + \zeta ab \xi \text{ .... (ii)},$$

where ξ, η now denote the elliptic coordinates of Art. 71, 3°, and the cyclic constant κ has been put $= 2\pi ab\zeta$, in conformity with Art. 142.

The value of ψ for the internal space has to satisfy

$$\frac{d^2\psi}{dx^2} + \frac{d^2\psi}{dy^2} = 2\zeta \text{ .... (iii)},$$

with the boundary-condition

$$\frac{ux}{a^2} + \frac{vy}{b^2} = -ny \cdot \frac{x}{a^2} + nx \cdot \frac{y}{b^2} \text{ .... (iv)}.$$

These conditions are both fulfilled by

$$\psi = \zeta (Ax^2 + By^2) \text{ .... (v)},$$

provided

$$\left.\begin{aligned} A + B &= 1, \\ Aa^2 - Bb^2 &= \frac{n}{2\zeta}(a^2 - b^2) \end{aligned}\right\} \text{ .... (vi)}.$$

It remains to express that there is no tangential slipping at the boundary of the vortex; *i.e.* that the values of $d\psi/d\xi$ obtained from (ii) and (v) coincide. Putting $x = c \cosh \xi \cos \eta$, $y = c \sinh \xi \sin \eta$, where $c = (a^2 - b^2)^{\frac{1}{2}}$, differentiating, and equating coefficients of $\cos 2\eta$, we obtain the additional condition

$$-\tfrac{1}{2} n (a+b)^2 e^{-2\xi} = \zeta c^2 (A - B) \cosh \xi \sinh \xi,$$

which is equivalent to

$$A - B = -\frac{n}{2\zeta} \cdot \frac{a^2 - b^2}{ab} \text{ .... (vii)},$$

since, at points of the ellipse (i), $\cosh \xi = a/c$, $\sinh \xi = b/c$.

Combined with (vi) this gives

$$Aa = Bb = \frac{ab}{a+b} \text{ .... (viii)},$$

and

$$n = \frac{2ab}{(a+b)^2} \zeta \text{ .... (ix)}.$$

When $a = b$, this agrees with our former approximate result.

The component velocities $\dot{x}$, $\dot{y}$ of a particle of the vortex relative to the principal axes of the ellipse are given by

$$\dot{x} = -\frac{d\psi}{dy} + ny, \qquad \dot{y} = \frac{d\psi}{dx} - nx,$$

whence we find

$$\frac{\dot{x}}{a} = -n\frac{y}{b}, \qquad \frac{\dot{y}}{b} = n\frac{x}{a} \text{ .... (x)}.$$

Integrating, we find

$$x = ka \cos(nt + \epsilon), \qquad y = kb \sin(nt + \epsilon) \text{ .... (xi)},$$

where k, ϵ are arbitrary constants, so that the *relative* paths of the particles are ellipses similar to the section of the vortex, described according to the harmonic law. If x', y' be the coordinates relative to axes fixed in space, we find

$$\left.\begin{aligned} x' &= x\cos nt - y\sin nt = \frac{k}{2}(a+b)\cos(2nt+\epsilon) + \frac{k}{2}(a-b)\cos\epsilon, \\ y' &= x\sin nt + y\cos nt = \frac{k}{2}(a+b)\sin(2nt+\epsilon) - \frac{k}{2}(a-b)\sin\epsilon \end{aligned}\right\}\ldots\text{(xii)}.$$

The absolute paths are therefore circles described with angular velocity $2n$*.

159. It was pointed out in Art. 81 that the motion of an incompressible fluid in a curved stratum of small but uniform thickness is completely defined by a stream-function ψ, so that any kinematical problem of this kind may be transformed by projection into one relating to a plane stratum. If, further, the projection be 'orthomorphic,' the kinetic energy of corresponding portions of liquid, and the circulations in corresponding circuits, are the same in the two motions. The latter statement shews that vortices transform into vortices of equal strengths. It follows at once from Art. 142 that in the case of a *closed* simply-connected surface the algebraic sum of the strengths of all the vortices present is zero.

Let us apply this to motion in a spherical stratum. The simplest case is that of a pair of isolated vortices situate at antipodal points; the stream-lines are then parallel small circles, the velocity varying inversely as the radius of the circle. For a vortex-pair situate at *any* two points A, B, the stream-lines are coaxal circles as in Art. 81. It is easily found by the method of stereographic projection that the velocity at any point P is the resultant of two velocities $m/\pi a \,.\cot\frac{1}{2}\theta_1$ and $m/\pi a\,.\cot\frac{1}{2}\theta_2$, perpendicular respectively to the great-circle arcs AP, BP, where θ_1, θ_2 denote the lengths of these arcs, a the radius of the sphere, and $\pm m$ the strengths of the vortices. The centre† (see Art. 154)

* For further researches in this connection see Hill, "On the Motion of Fluid part of which is moving rotationally and part irrotationally," *Phil. Trans.*, 1884; and Love, "On the Stability of certain Vortex Motions," *Proc. Lond. Math. Soc.*, t. xxv., p. 18 (1893).

† To prevent possible misconception it may be remarked that the centres of corresponding vortices are not necessarily corresponding points. The paths of these centres are therefore not in general projective.

The problem of transformation *in plano* has been treated by Routh, "Some Applications of Conjugate Functions," *Proc. Lond. Math. Soc.*, t. xii., p. 73 (1881).

of either vortex moves perpendicular to AB with a velocity $m/\pi a . \cot \frac{1}{2}AB$. The two vortices therefore describe parallel and equal small circles, remaining at a constant distance from each other.

Circular Vortices.

160. Let us next take the case where all the vortices present in the liquid (supposed unlimited as before) are circular, having the axis of x as a common axis. Let ϖ denote the distance of any point P from this axis, ϑ the angle which ϖ makes with the plane xy, v the velocity in the direction of ϖ, and ω the angular velocity of the fluid at P. It is evident that u, v, ω are functions of x, ϖ only, and that the axis of the rotation ω is perpendicular to $x\varpi$. We have then

$$\left.\begin{aligned} y &= \varpi \cos \vartheta, & z &= \varpi \sin \vartheta, \\ v &= v \cos \vartheta, & w &= v \sin \vartheta, \\ \xi = 0, \quad \eta &= -\omega \sin \vartheta, & \zeta &= \omega \cos \vartheta \end{aligned}\right\} \text{..............(1).}$$

The impulse of the vortex-system now reduces to a force along Ox. Substituting from (1) in the first formula of Art. 150 (12) we find

$$P = \rho \iiint (y\zeta - z\eta)\, dx dy dz = 2\pi\rho \iint \varpi^2 \omega\, dx d\varpi \text{ ....(2),}$$

where the integration is to extend over the sections of all the vortices. If we denote by m the strength $\omega \delta x \delta \varpi$ of an elementary vortex-filament whose coordinates are x, ϖ, this may be written

$$P = 2\pi\rho \Sigma m \varpi^2 = 2\pi\rho \,.\, \Sigma m \,.\, \varpi_0^2 \text{.....................(3),}$$

if

$$\varpi_0^2 = \frac{\Sigma m \varpi^2}{\Sigma m} \text{ ....(4).}$$

The quantity ϖ_0, thus defined, may be called the 'mean-radius' of the whole system of circular vortices. Since m is constant for each vortex, the constancy of the impulse requires that the mean-radius shall be constant with respect to the time.

The formula for the kinetic energy (Art. 153 (4)) becomes, in the present case,

$$T = 4\pi\rho \iint (\varpi u - xv)\, \varpi\omega\, dx d\varpi = 4\pi\rho \Sigma m\, (\varpi u - xv)\, \varpi \text{ ......(5).}$$

Let us introduce a symbol x_0, defined by

$$x_0 = \frac{\Sigma m\varpi^2 x}{\Sigma m\varpi^2} \quad \text{.........................(6).}$$

It is plain that the position of the circle (x_0, ϖ_0) will depend only on the strengths and the configuration of the vortices, and not on the position of the origin on the axis of symmetry. This circle may be called the 'circular axis' of the whole system of vortex rings; we have seen that it remains constant in radius. To find its motion parallel to Ox, we have from (6) and (4),

$$\Sigma m \,.\, \varpi_0^2 \frac{dx_0}{dt} = \Sigma m\varpi^2 u + 2\Sigma m x\varpi v \quad \text{..............(7),}$$

since u and v are the rates of increase of x and ϖ for any particular vortex. By means of (5) we can put this in the form

$$\Sigma m \,.\, \varpi_0^2 \frac{dx_0}{dt} = \frac{T}{4\pi\rho} + 3\Sigma m (x - x_0)\varpi v \quad \text{...........(8),}$$

which will be of use to us later. The added term vanishes, since $\Sigma m\varpi v = 0$ on account of the constancy of the mean radius.

161. On account of the symmetry about Ox, there exists, in the cases at present under consideration, a stream-function ψ, defined as in Art. 93, viz. we have

$$u = -\frac{1}{\varpi}\frac{d\psi}{d\varpi}, \quad v = \frac{1}{\varpi}\frac{d\psi}{dx} \quad \text{.....................(1),}$$

whence
$$2\omega = \frac{dv}{dx} - \frac{du}{d\varpi} = \frac{1}{\varpi}\left(\frac{d^2\psi}{dx^2} + \frac{d^2\psi}{d\varpi^2} - \frac{1}{\varpi}\frac{d\psi}{d\varpi}\right) \quad \text{.........(2).}$$

It appears from Art. 148 (4) that at a great distance from the vortices u, v are of the order R^{-3}, and therefore ψ will be of the order R^{-1}.

The formula for the kinetic energy may therefore be written

$$\begin{aligned} T &= \pi\rho \iint (u^2 + v^2)\, \varpi\, dx\, d\varpi \\ &= \pi\rho \iint \left(v \frac{d\psi}{dx} - u \frac{d\psi}{d\varpi}\right) dx\, d\varpi \\ &= -2\pi\rho \iint \psi\omega\, dx\, d\varpi \quad \text{.............................(3),} \end{aligned}$$

by a partial integration, the terms at the limits vanishing.

To determine ψ in terms of the (arbitrary) distribution of angular velocity (ω), we may make use of the formulæ of Art. 145, which give

$$\left.\begin{aligned} F &= 0, \\ G &= -\frac{1}{2\pi}\iiint \frac{\omega' \sin \vartheta'}{r}\, \varpi' d\vartheta' dx' d\varpi', \\ H &= \frac{1}{2\pi}\iiint \frac{\omega' \cos \vartheta'}{r}\, \varpi' d\vartheta' dx' d\varpi' \end{aligned}\right\} \quad \ldots\ldots\ldots\ldots\ldots(4),$$

where $\quad r = \{(x-x')^2 + \varpi^2 + \varpi'^2 - 2\varpi\varpi' \cos(\vartheta - \vartheta')\}^{\frac{1}{2}}.$

Since $2\pi\psi$ denotes (Art. 93) the flux, in the direction of x-negative, through the circle (x, ϖ), we have

$$2\pi\psi = -\iint \left(\frac{dH}{dy} - \frac{dG}{dz}\right) dy dz \ldots\ldots\ldots\ldots\ldots(5),$$

where the integration extends over the area of this circle. By Stokes' Theorem, this gives

$$2\pi\psi = -\int (G dy + H dz) \ldots\ldots\ldots\ldots\ldots\ldots\ldots (6),$$

the integral being taken round the circumference, or, in terms of our present coordinates,

$$\begin{aligned} \psi &= -\frac{\varpi}{2\pi}\int_0^{2\pi} (H \cos\vartheta - G \sin\vartheta)\, d\vartheta \\ &= -\frac{\varpi}{2\pi}\iint f\begin{Bmatrix} x, & \varpi \\ x', & \varpi' \end{Bmatrix} \omega' \varpi' dx' d\varpi' \ldots\ldots\ldots\ldots\ldots\ldots (7)^*, \end{aligned}$$

provided

$$f\begin{Bmatrix} x, & \varpi \\ x', & \varpi' \end{Bmatrix} = \int_0^{2\pi} \frac{\cos\theta\, d\theta}{\{(x-x')^2 + \varpi^2 + \varpi'^2 - 2\varpi\varpi' \cos\theta\}^{\frac{1}{2}}} \quad \ldots\ldots(8),$$

where θ has been written for $\vartheta - \vartheta'$.

It is plain that the function here defined is symmetrical with respect to the two sets of variables x, ϖ and x', ϖ'. It can be expressed in terms of elliptic integrals, as follows. If we put

$$k^2 = \frac{4\varpi\varpi'}{(x-x')^2 + (\varpi + \varpi')^2} \ldots\ldots\ldots\ldots\ldots\ldots\ldots(9),$$

* The vector whose components are F, G, H is now perpendicular to the meridian plane $x\varpi$. If we denote it by S, we have $F=0$, $G=-S\sin\vartheta$, $H=S\cos\vartheta$, so that (7) is equivalent to

$$\psi = -\varpi S.$$

we find

$$\frac{\cos\theta}{\{(x-x')^2+\varpi^2+\varpi'^2-2\varpi\varpi'\cos\theta\}^{\frac{1}{2}}}=\frac{k}{2(\varpi\varpi')^{\frac{1}{2}}}\cdot\frac{2\cos^2\frac{1}{2}\theta-1}{(1-k^2\cos^2\frac{1}{2}\theta)^{\frac{1}{2}}}$$

$$=\frac{1}{2(\varpi\varpi')^{\frac{1}{2}}}\left\{\frac{A}{(1-k^2\cos^2\frac{1}{2}\theta)^{\frac{1}{2}}}+B(1-k^2\cos^2\tfrac{1}{2}\theta)^{\frac{1}{2}}\right\},$$

where, from comparison of coefficients,

$$A=2/k-k,\quad B=-2/k.$$

Hence

$$f\begin{Bmatrix}x, \varpi\\ x', \varpi'\end{Bmatrix}=\frac{2}{(\varpi\varpi')^{\frac{1}{2}}}\left\{\left(\frac{2}{k}-k\right)F_1(k)-\frac{2}{k}E_1(k)\right. \ldots(10),$$

where $F_1(k)$, $E_1(k)$ are the *complete* elliptic integrals of the first and second kinds, with respect to the modulus k, defined by (9).

162. The stream-function for points at a distance from an isolated circular vortex-filament, of strength m', whose coordinates are x', ϖ', is therefore given by

$$\psi=-\frac{m'}{\pi}(\varpi\varpi')^{\frac{1}{2}}\left\{\left(\frac{2}{k}-k\right)F_1(k)-\frac{2}{k}E_1(k)\right\} \ldots\ldots\ldots (1).$$

The forms of the stream-lines corresponding to equidistant values of ψ, at points whose distances from the filament are great in comparison with the dimensions of the cross-section, are shewn on the next page*.

At points of the infinitely small section the modulus k of the elliptic integrals in the value of ψ is nearly equal to unity. In this case we have†

$$F_1(k)=\log\frac{4}{k'},\qquad E_1(k)=1,$$

approximately, where k' denotes the complementary modulus $(1-k^2)^{\frac{1}{2}}$, so that in our case

$$k'^2=\frac{(x-x')^2+(\varpi-\varpi')^2}{(x-x')^2+(\varpi+\varpi')^2}=\frac{g^2}{4\varpi^2},$$

* For another elliptic-integral form of (1), and for the most convenient method of tracing the curves $\psi=$ const., see Maxwell, *Electricity and Magnetism*, Arts. 701, 702.

† See Cayley, *Elliptic Functions*, Cambridge, 1876, Arts. 72, 77; and Maxwell, *Electricity and Magnetism*, Arts. 704, 705.

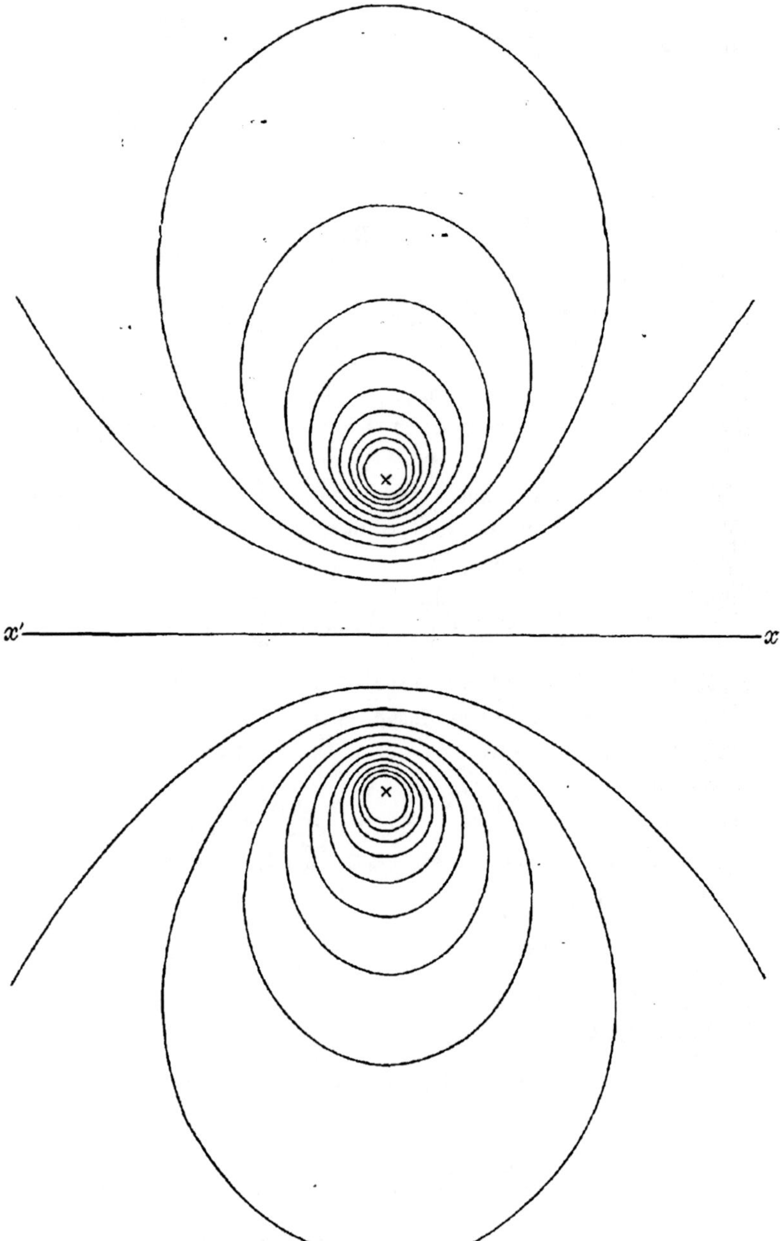
x′
x

nearly, if g denote the distance between two infinitely near points (x, ϖ), (x', ϖ') in the same meridian plane. Hence at points within the substance of the vortex the value of ψ is of the order $m'\varpi \log \varpi/\epsilon$, where ϵ is a small linear magnitude comparable with the dimensions of the section. The velocity at the same point, depending (Art. 93) on the differential coefficients of ψ, will be of the order m'/ϵ.

We can now estimate the magnitude of the velocity dx_0/dt of translation of the vortex-ring. By Art. 161 (3) T is of the order $\rho m'^2\varpi \log \varpi/\epsilon$, and v is, as we have seen, of the order m'/ϵ; whilst $x - x_0$ is of course of the order ϵ. Hence the second term on the right-hand side of the formula (8) of Art. 160 is, in this case, small compared with the first, and the velocity of translation of the ring is of the order $m'/\varpi \,.\log \varpi/\epsilon$, and approximately constant.

An isolated vortex-ring moves then, without sensible change of size, parallel to its rectilinear axis with nearly constant velocity. This velocity is small compared with that of the fluid in the immediate neighbourhood of the circular axis, but may be large compared with m'/ϖ_0, the velocity of the fluid at the centre of the ring, with which it agrees in direction.

For the case of a *circular* section more definite results can be obtained as follows. If we neglect the variations of ϖ' and ω' over the section, the formulæ (7) and (10) of Art. 161 give

$$\psi = -\frac{\omega}{\pi}\varpi_0 \iint \left(\log\frac{8\varpi_0}{g} - 2\right) dx'd\varpi',$$

or, if we introduce polar coordinates (s, χ) in the plane of the section,

$$\psi = -\frac{\omega'}{\pi}\varpi_0 \int_0^a\int_0^{2\pi} \left(\log\frac{8\varpi_0}{g} - 2\right) s'ds'd\chi' \quad\text{.....................(i)},$$

where a is the radius of the section. Now

$$\int_0^{2\pi} \log g\, d\chi' = \int_0^{2\pi} \log\{s^2 + s'^2 - 2ss'\cos(\chi - \chi')\}^{\frac{1}{2}} d\chi',$$

and this definite integral is known to be equal to $2\pi \log s'$, or $2\pi \log s$, according as $s' \gtrless s$. Hence, for points within the section,

$$\psi = -2\omega'\varpi_0 \int_0^s \left(\log\frac{8\varpi_0}{s} - 2\right) s'ds' - 2\omega'\varpi_0 \int_s^a \left(\log\frac{8\varpi_0}{s'} - 2\right) s'ds'$$

$$= -\omega'\varpi_0 a^2 \left\{\log\frac{8\varpi_0}{a} - \tfrac{3}{2} - \tfrac{1}{2}\frac{s^2}{a^2}\right\} \quad\text{...(ii)}.$$

The only variable part of this is the term $-\frac{1}{2}\omega'\varpi_0 s^2$; this shews that *to our order of approximation* the stream-lines within the section are concentric circles, the velocity at a distance s from the centre being $\omega' s$. Substituting in Art. 161 (3) we find

$$\frac{T}{4\pi\rho} = -\tfrac{1}{2}\omega' \int_0^a \int_0^{2\pi} \psi s\, ds\, d\chi = \frac{m'^2 \varpi_0}{2\pi} \left\{ \log \frac{8\varpi_0}{a} - \tfrac{7}{4} \right\} \text{..............(iii).}$$

The last term in Art. 160 (8) is equivalent to

$$3\varpi_0 \omega' \Sigma m (x - x_0)^2;$$

in our present notation, m' denoting the strength of the whole vortex, this is equal to $3m'^2\varpi_0/4\pi$. Hence the formula for the velocity of translation of the vortex becomes

$$\frac{dx_0}{dt} = \frac{m'}{2\pi\varpi_0} \left\{ \log \frac{8\varpi_0}{a} - \tfrac{1}{4} \right\} \text{.......................(iv)*.}$$

163. If we have any number of circular vortex-rings, coaxial or not, the motion of any one of these may be conceived as made up of two parts, one due to the ring itself, the other due to the influence of the remaining rings. The preceding considerations shew that the second part is insignificant compared with the first, except when two or more rings approach within a very small distance of one another. Hence each ring will move, without sensible change of shape or size, with nearly uniform velocity in the direction of its rectilinear axis, until it passes within a short distance of a second ring.

A general notion of the result of the encounter of two rings may, in particular cases, be gathered from the result of Art. 147 (3). Thus, let us suppose that we have two circular vortices having the same rectilinear axis. If the sense of the rotation be the same for both, the two rings will advance, on the whole, in the same direction. One effect of their mutual influence will be to increase the radius of the one in front, and to contract the radius of the one in the rear. If the radius of the one in front become larger than that of the one in the rear, the motion of the former ring will be retarded, whilst that of the latter is accelerated. Hence if the conditions as to relative size and strength of the two rings be favourable, it may happen that the second ring will overtake and pass through the first. The parts played by the two rings will then be reversed; the one which is now in

* This result was first obtained by Sir W. Thomson, *Phil. Mag.*, June, 1867.

the rear will in turn overtake and pass through the other, and so on, the rings alternately passing one through the other*.

If the rotations in the two rings be opposite, and such that the rings approach one another, the mutual influence will be to enlarge the radius of each ring. If the two rings be moreover equal in size and strength, the velocity of approach will continually diminish. In this case the motion at all points of the plane which is parallel to the two rings, and half-way between them, is tangential to this plane. We may therefore, if we please, regard this plane as a fixed boundary to the fluid on either side of it, and so obtain the case of a single vortex-ring moving directly towards a fixed rigid wall.

The foregoing remarks are taken from von Helmholtz' paper. He adds, in conclusion, that the mutual influence of vortex-rings may easily be studied experimentally in the case of the (roughly) semicircular rings produced by drawing rapidly the point of a spoon for a short space through the surface of a liquid, the spots where the vortex-filaments meet the surface being marked by dimples. (Cf. Art. 28.) The method of experimental illustration by means of smoke-rings† is too well-known to need description here. A beautiful variation of the experiment consists in forming the rings in water, the substance of the vortices being coloured‡.

For further theoretical researches on the motion of vortex-rings, including the question of stability, and the determination of the small oscillations, we must refer to the papers cited below§.

The motion of a vortex-ring in a fluid limited (whether internally or externally) by a fixed spherical surface, in the case

* The corresponding case in two dimensions appears to have been worked out very completely by Gröbli; see Winkelmann, *Handbuch der Physik*, t. i., p. 447. The same question has been discussed quite recently by Love, "On the Motion of Paired Vortices with a Common Axis," *Proc. Lond. Math. Soc.*, t. xxv., p. 185 (1894).

† Reusch, "Ueber Ringbildung der Flüssigkeiten," *Pogg. Ann.*, t. cx. (1860); see also Tait, *Recent Advances in Physical Science*, London, 1876, c. xii.

‡ Reynolds, "On the Resistance encountered by Vortex Rings &c.", *Brit. Ass. Rep.*, 1876, *Nature*, t. xiv., p. 477.

§ J. J. Thomson, *l. c. ante* p. 239, and *Phil. Trans.*, 1882.

W. M. Hicks, "On the Steady Motion and the Small Vibrations of a Hollow Vortex," *Phil. Trans.* 1884.

Dyson, *l. c. ante* p. 166.

The theory of 'Vortex-Atoms' which gave the impulse to some of these investigations was suggested by Sir W. Thomson, *Phil. Mag.*, July, 1867.

where the rectilinear axis of the ring passes through the centre of the sphere, has been investigated by Lewis*, by the method of 'images.'

The following simplified proof is due to Larmor†. The vortex-ring is equivalent (Art. 148) to a spherical sheet of double-sources of uniform density, concentric with the fixed sphere. The 'image' of this sheet will, by Art. 95, be another uniform concentric double-sheet, which is, again, equivalent to a vortex-ring coaxial with the first. It easily follows from the Art. last cited that the strengths (m', m'') and the radii (ϖ', ϖ'') of the vortex-ring and its image are connected by the relation

$$m'\varpi'^{\frac{1}{2}} + m''\varpi''^{\frac{1}{2}} = 0 \qquad \text{(i)}.$$

The argument obviously applies to the case of a reentrant vortex of any form, provided it lie on a sphere concentric with the boundary.

On the Conditions for Steady Motion.

164. In steady motion, *i.e.* when

$$\frac{du}{dt} = 0, \quad \frac{dv}{dt} = 0, \quad \frac{dw}{dt} = 0,$$

the equations (2) of Art. 6 may be written

$$u\frac{du}{dx} + v\frac{dv}{dx} + w\frac{dw}{dx} - 2(v\zeta - w\eta) = -\frac{d\Omega}{dx} - \frac{1}{\rho}\frac{dp}{dx}, \ldots, \ldots$$

Hence, if as in Art. 143 we put

$$\chi' = \int\frac{dp}{\rho} + \tfrac{1}{2}q^2 + \Omega \qquad (1),$$

we have

$$\frac{d\chi'}{dx} = 2(v\zeta - w\eta), \quad \frac{d\chi'}{dy} = 2(w\xi - u\zeta), \quad \frac{d\chi'}{dz} = 2(u\eta - v\xi).$$

It follows that

$$u\frac{d\chi'}{dx} + v\frac{d\chi'}{dy} + w\frac{d\chi'}{dz} = 0,$$

$$\xi\frac{d\chi'}{dx} + \eta\frac{d\chi'}{dy} + \zeta\frac{d\chi'}{dz} = 0,$$

* "On the Images of Vortices in a Spherical Vessel," *Quart. Journ. Math.*, t. xvi., p. 338 (1879).

† "Electro-magnetic and other Images in Spheres and Planes," *Quart. Journ. Math.*, t. xxiii., p. 94 (1889).

so that each of the surfaces $\chi' = \text{const.}$ contains both stream-lines and vortex-lines. If further δn denote an element of the normal at any point of such a surface, we have

$$\frac{d\chi'}{dn} = 2q\omega \sin\beta \quad\text{.......................} \quad (2),$$

where q is the current-velocity, ω the rotation, and β the angle between the stream-line and the vortex-line at that point.

Hence the conditions that a given state of motion of a fluid may be a possible state of steady motion are as follows. It must be possible to draw in the fluid an infinite system of surfaces each of which is covered by a network of stream-lines and vortex-lines, and the product $q\omega \sin\beta\, \delta n$ must be constant over each such surface, δn denoting the length of the normal drawn to a consecutive surface of the system.

These conditions may also be deduced from the considerations that the stream-lines are, in steady motion, the actual paths of the particles, that the product of the angular velocity into the cross-section is the same at all points of a vortex, and that this product is, for the same vortex, constant with regard to the time*.

The theorem that the function χ', defined by (1), is constant over each surface of the above kind is an extension of that of Art. 22, where it was shewn that χ' is constant along a stream-line.

The above conditions are satisfied identically in all cases of irrotational motion, provided of course the boundary-conditions be such as are consistent with the steady motion.

In the motion of a liquid in two dimensions (xy) the product $q\delta n$ is constant along a stream-line; the conditions in question then reduce to this, that the angular velocity ζ must be constant along each stream-line, or, by Art. 59,

$$\frac{d^2\psi}{dx^2} + \frac{d^2\psi}{dy^2} = f(\psi) \quad\text{.....................}\quad (3)\dagger,$$

where $f(\psi)$ is an arbitrary function of ψ.

* See a paper "On the Conditions for Steady Motion of a Fluid," *Proc. Lond. Math. Soc.*, t. ix., p. 91 (1878).

† Cf. Lagrange, *Nouv. Mém. de l'Acad. de Berlin*, 1781, *Oeuvres*, t. iv., p. 720; and Stokes, *l. c.* p. 264.

This condition is satisfied in all cases of motion in concentric circles about the origin. Another obvious solution of (3) is

$$\psi = \tfrac{1}{2}(Ax^2 + 2Bxy + Cy^2) \quad \text{.......................(i)},$$

in which case the stream-lines are similar and coaxial conics. The angular velocity at any point is $\tfrac{1}{2}(A + C)$, and is therefore uniform.

Again, if we put $f(\psi) = -k^2\psi$, where k is a constant, and transform to polar coordinates r, θ, we get

$$\frac{d^2\psi}{dr^2} + \frac{1}{r}\frac{d\psi}{dr} + \frac{1}{r^2}\frac{d^2\psi}{d\theta^2} + k^2\psi = 0 \quad \text{.......................(ii)},$$

which is satisfied by

$$\psi = CJ_s(kr) \left.\begin{matrix}\cos\\ \sin\end{matrix}\right\} s\theta \quad \text{.......................(iii)},$$

where J_s is a 'Bessel's Function.' This gives various solutions consistent with a fixed circular boundary of radius a, the admissible values of k being determined by

$$J_s(ka) = 0 \quad \text{.......................(iv)}.$$

The character of these solutions will be understood from the properties of Bessel's Functions, of which some indication will be given in Chapter VIII.

In the case of motion symmetrical about an axis (x), we have $q \,.\, 2\pi\varpi\delta n$ constant along a stream-line, ϖ denoting as in Art. 93 the distance of any point from the axis of symmetry. The condition for steady motion then is that the ratio ω/ϖ must be constant along any stream-line. Hence, if ψ be the stream-function, we must have, by Art. 161 (2),

$$\frac{d^2\psi}{dx^2} + \frac{d^2\psi}{d\varpi^2} - \frac{1}{\varpi}\frac{d\psi}{d\varpi} = \varpi^2 f(\psi) \quad \text{............ (4)*},$$

where $f(\psi)$ denotes an arbitrary function of ψ.

An interesting example of (4) is furnished by the case of Hill's 'Spherical Vortex†.' If we assume

$$\psi = \tfrac{1}{2}A\varpi^2(a^2 - r^2) \quad \text{.......................(v)},$$

where $r^2 = x^2 + \varpi^2$, for all points within the sphere $r = a$, the formula (2) of Art. 161 makes

$$\omega = -\tfrac{5}{2}A\varpi,$$

so that the condition of steady motion is satisfied. Again it is evident, on reference to Arts. 95, 96 that the irrotational flow of a stream with the

* This result is due to Stokes, "On the Steady Motion of Incompressible Fluids," *Camb. Trans.*, t. vii. (1842), *Math. and Phys. Papers*, t. i., p. 15.

† "On a Spherical Vortex," *Phil. Trans.*, 1894, A.

general velocity $-\mathbf{u}$ parallel to the axis, past a fixed spherical surface $r=a$, is given by

$$\psi=\tfrac{1}{2}\mathbf{u}\varpi^2\left(1-\frac{a^3}{r^3}\right) \quad\text{.................................(vi).}$$

The two values of ψ agree when $r=a$; this makes the normal velocity continuous. In order that the tangential velocity may be continuous, the values of $d\psi/dr$ must also agree. Remembering that $\varpi=r\sin\theta$, this gives $A=-\frac{3}{2}\mathbf{u}/a^2$, and therefore

$$\omega=\tfrac{15}{4}\mathbf{u}\varpi/a^2 \quad\text{.................................(vii).}$$

The sum of the strengths of the vortex-filaments composing the spherical vortex is $5\mathbf{u}a$.

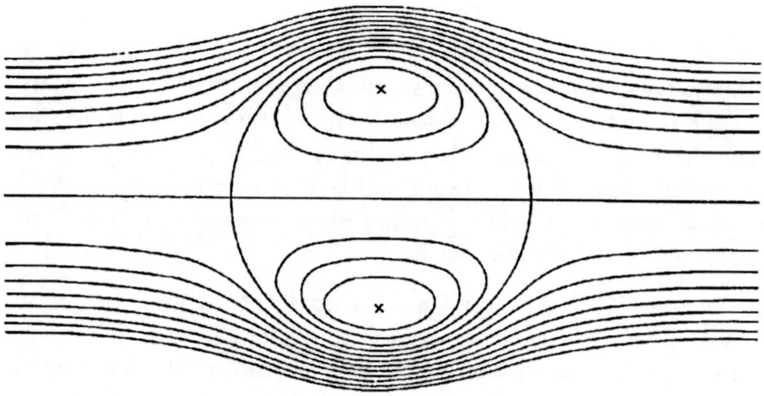

The figure shews the stream-lines, both inside and outside the vortex; they are drawn, as usual, for equidistant values of ψ.

If we impress on everything a velocity $\mathbf{u}$ parallel to x, we get a spherical vortex advancing with constant velocity $\mathbf{u}$ through a liquid which is at rest at infinity.

By the formulæ of Arts. 160, 161, we readily find that the square of the 'mean-radius' of the vortex is $\frac{2}{5}a^2$, the 'impulse' is $2\pi\rho a^3\mathbf{u}$, and the energy is $\frac{10}{7}\pi\rho a^3\mathbf{u}^2$.

CHAPTER VIII.

TIDAL WAVES.

165. ONE of the most interesting and successful applications of hydrodynamical theory is to the small oscillations, under gravity, of a liquid having a free surface. In certain cases, which are somewhat special as regards the theory, but very important from a practical point of view, these oscillations may combine to form progressive waves travelling with (to a first approximation) no change of form over the surface.

The term 'tidal,' as applied to waves, has been used in various senses, but it seems most natural to confine it to gravitational oscillations possessing the characteristic feature of the oceanic tides produced by the action of the sun and moon. We have therefore ventured to place it at the head of this Chapter, as descriptive of waves in which the motion of the fluid is mainly horizontal, and therefore (as will appear) sensibly the same for all particles in a vertical line. This latter circumstance greatly simplifies the theory.

It will be convenient to recapitulate, in the first place, some points in the general theory of small oscillations which will receive constant exemplification in the investigations which follow*.

Let $q_1, q_2, \ldots q_n$ be n generalized coordinates serving to specify the configuration of a dynamical system, and let them be so chosen as to vanish in the configuration of equilibrium. The kinetic

* For a fuller account of the general theory see Thomson and Tait, *Natural Philosophy*, Arts. 337,..., Lord Rayleigh, *Theory of Sound*, c. iv., Routh, *Elementary Rigid Dynamics* (5th ed.), London, 1891, c. ix.

energy T will, as explained in Art. 133, be a homogeneous quadratic function of the generalized velocities $\dot{q}_1, \dot{q}_2, \ldots$, say

$$2T = a_{11}\dot{q}_1^2 + a_{22}\dot{q}_2^2 + \ldots + 2a_{12}\dot{q}_1\dot{q}_2 + \ldots \qquad \text{.........(1)}.$$

The coefficients in this expression are in general functions of the coordinates $q_1, q_2, \ldots$, but in the application to *small* motions, we may suppose them to be constant, and to have the values corresponding to $q_1 = 0$, $q_2 = 0, \ldots$. Again, if (as we shall suppose) the system is 'conservative,' the potential energy V of a small displacement is a homogeneous quadratic function of the component displacements $q_1, q_2, \ldots$, with (on the same understanding) constant coefficients, say

$$2V = c_{11}q_1^2 + c_{22}q_2^2 + \ldots + 2c_{12}q_1q_2 + \ldots \qquad \text{.........(2)}.$$

By a real* linear transformation of the coordinates $q_1, q_2, \ldots$ it is possible to reduce T and V simultaneously to sums of squares; the new variables thus introduced are called the 'normal coordinates' of the system. In terms of these we have

$$2T = a_1\dot{q}_1^2 + a_2\dot{q}_2^2 + \ldots \qquad \text{..................(3)},$$

$$2V = c_1q_1^2 + c_2q_2^2 + \ldots \qquad \text{..................(4)}.$$

The coefficients $a_1, a_2, \ldots$ are called the 'principal coefficients of inertia'; they are necessarily positive. The coefficients $c_1, c_2, \ldots$ may be called the 'principal coefficients of stability'; they are all positive when the undisturbed configuration is stable.

When given extraneous forces act on the system, the work done by these during an arbitrary infinitesimal displacement $\Delta q_1, \Delta q_2, \ldots$ may be expressed in the form

$$Q_1\Delta q_1 + Q_2\Delta q_2 + \ldots \qquad \text{.....................(5)}.$$

The coefficients $Q_1, Q_2, \ldots$ are then called the 'normal components of external force.'

In terms of the normal coordinates, the equations of motion are given by Lagrange's equations (Art. 133 (17)), thus

$$\frac{d}{dt}\frac{dT}{d\dot{q}_s} - \frac{dT}{dq_s} = -\frac{dV}{dq_s} + Q_s.$$

* The algebraic proof of this involves the assumption that one at least of the functions T, V is essentially positive.

In the present application to infinitely small motions, these take the form

$$a_s\ddot{q}_s + c_s q_s = Q_s \quad \text{..........................(6).}$$

It is easily seen from this that the dynamical characteristics of the normal coordinates are (1°) that an impulse of any normal type produces an initial motion of that type only, and (2°) that a steady extraneous force of any type maintains a displacement of that type only.

To obtain the *free* motions of the system we put $Q_s = 0$ in (6). Solving we find

$$q_s = A_s \cos(\sigma_s t + \epsilon_s) \quad \text{......................(7),}$$

where

$$\sigma_s = (c_s/a_s)^{\frac{1}{2}} \quad \text{.......................... (8)*,}$$

and A_s, ϵ_s are arbitrary constants. Hence a mode of free motion is possible in which any normal coordinate q_s varies alone, and the motion of any particle of the system, since it depends linearly on q_s, will be simple-harmonic, of period $2\pi/\sigma_s$, and every particle will pass simultaneously through its equilibrium position. The several modes of this character are called the 'normal modes' of vibration of the system; their number is equal to that of the degrees of freedom, and any free motion whatever of the system may be obtained from them by superposition, with a proper choice of the 'amplitudes' (A_s) and 'epochs' (ϵ_s).

In certain cases, viz. when two or more of the free periods ($2\pi/\sigma$) of the system are equal, the normal coordinates are to a certain extent indeterminate, *i.e.* they can be chosen in an infinite number of ways. An instance of this is the spherical pendulum. Other examples will present themselves later; see Arts. 187, 191.

If two (or more) normal modes have the same period, then by compounding them, with arbitrary amplitudes and epochs, we obtain a small oscillation in which the motion of each particle is the resultant of simple-harmonic vibrations in different directions, and is therefore, in general, elliptic-harmonic, with the same period. This is exemplified in the conical pendulum; an important instance in our own subject is that of progressive waves in deep water (Chap. IX.).

* The ratio $\sigma/2\pi$ measures the 'frequency' of the oscillation. It is convenient, however, to have a name for the quantity σ itself; the term 'speed' has been used in this sense by Lord Kelvin and Prof. G. H. Darwin in their researches on the Tides.

If any of the coefficients of stability (c_s) be negative, the value of σ_s is pure imaginary. The circular function in (7) is then replaced by real exponentials, and an arbitrary displacement will in general increase until the assumptions on which the approximate equation (6) is based become untenable. The undisturbed configuration is then unstable. Hence the necessary and sufficient condition of stability is that the potential energy V should be a minimum in the configuration of equilibrium.

To find the effect of extraneous forces, it is sufficient to consider the case where Q_s varies as a simple-harmonic function of the time, say

$$Q_s = C_s \cos(\sigma t + \epsilon) \quad \text{.....................(9)},$$

where the value of σ is now prescribed. Not only is this the most interesting case in itself, but we know from Fourier's Theorem that, whatever the law of variation of Q_s with the time, it can be expressed by a series of terms such as (9). A particular integral of (9) is then

$$q_s = \frac{C_s}{c_s - \sigma^2 a_s} \cos(\sigma t + \epsilon) \quad \text{..... ....(10)}.$$

This represents the 'forced oscillation' due to the periodic force Q_s. In it the motion of every particle is simple-harmonic, of the prescribed period $2\pi/\sigma$, and the extreme displacements coincide in time with the maxima and minima of the force.

A constant force equal to the instantaneous value of the actual force (9) would maintain a displacement

$$\bar{q}_s = \frac{C_s}{c_s} \cos(\sigma t + \epsilon) \quad \text{.....................(11)},$$

the same, of course, as if the inertia-coefficient a_s were null. Hence (10) may be written

$$q_s = \frac{1}{1 - \sigma^2/\sigma_s^2} \bar{q}_s \quad \text{.....................(12)},$$

where σ_s has the value (8). This very useful formula enables us to write down the effect of a periodic force when we know that of a steady force of the same type. It is to be noticed that q_s and Q_s have the same or opposite phases according as $\sigma \lessgtr \sigma_s$, that is, according as the period of the disturbing force is greater or less than the free period. A simple example of this is furnished by a simple pendulum acted on by a periodic horizontal force. Other important illustrations will present themselves in the theory of the tides*.

When σ is very great in comparison with σ_s, the formula (10) becomes

$$q_s = -\frac{C_s}{\sigma^2 a_s} \cos(\sigma t + \epsilon) \quad \text{..............(13)};$$

the displacement is now always in the opposite phase to the force, and depends only on the *inertia* of the system.

If the period of the impressed force be nearly equal to that of the normal mode of order s, the amplitude of the forced oscillation, as given by (12), is very great compared with $\bar{q}_s$. In the case of exact equality, the solution (10) fails, and must be replaced by

$$q_s = Bt \sin(\sigma t + \epsilon) \quad \text{.....................(14)},$$

where, as is verified immediately on substitution, $B = C_s/2\sigma a_s$. This gives an oscillation of continually increasing amplitude, and can therefore only be accepted as a representation of the initial stages of the disturbance.

Another very important property of the normal modes may be noticed, although the use which we shall have occasion to make of it will be slight. If by the introduction of constraints the system be compelled to oscillate in any other manner, then if the character of this motion be known, the configuration at any instant can be specified by one variable, which we will denote by θ. In terms of this we shall have

$$q_s = B_s \theta,$$

where the quantities B_s are certain constants. This makes

$$2T = (B_1^2 a_1 + B_2^2 a_2 + \ldots)\dot{\theta}^2 \quad \text{.............................(i)},$$

$$2V = (B_1^2 c_1 + B_2^2 c_2 + \ldots)\,\theta^2 \quad \text{...........................(ii)}.$$

Hence if $\theta \propto \cos(\sigma t + \epsilon)$, the constancy of the energy $(T + V)$ requires

$$\sigma^2 = \frac{B_1^2 c_1 + B_2^2 c_2 + \ldots}{B_1^2 a_1 + B_2^2 a_2 + \ldots} \quad \text{...........................(iii)}.$$

Hence σ^2 is intermediate in value between the greatest and least of the quantities c_s/a_s; in other words, the frequency of the constrained oscillation is intermediate between the greatest and least frequencies corresponding to the normal modes of the system. In particular, when a system is modified by the introduction of any constraint, the frequency of the slowest natural oscillation is *increased*.

* Cf. T. Young, "A Theory of Tides," *Nicholson's Journal*, t. xxxv. (1813); *Miscellaneous Works*, London, 1854, t. ii., p. 262.

Moreover, if the constrained type differ but slightly from a normal type (s), σ^2 will differ from c_s/a_s by a small quantity *of the second order*. This gives a valuable method of estimating approximately the frequency in cases where the normal types cannot be accurately determined*.

The modifications which are introduced into the theory of small oscillations by the consideration of viscous forces will be noticed in Chapter XI.

Long Waves in Canals.

166. Proceeding now to the special problem of this Chapter, let us begin with the case of waves travelling along a straight canal, with horizontal bed, and parallel vertical sides. Let the axis of x be parallel to the length of the canal, that of y vertical and upwards, and let us suppose that the motion takes place in these two dimensions x, y. Let the ordinate of the free surface, corresponding to the abscissa x, at time t, be denoted by $\eta + y_0$, where y_0 is the ordinate in the undisturbed state.

As already indicated, we shall assume in all the investigations of this Chapter that the vertical acceleration of the fluid particles may be neglected, or (more precisely) that the pressure at any point (x, y) is sensibly equal to the statical pressure due to the depth below the free surface, viz.

$$p - p_0 = g\rho\,(y_0 + \eta - y) \quad\ldots\ldots\ldots\ldots(1),$$

where p_0 is the (uniform) external pressure.

Hence
$$\frac{dp}{dx} = g\rho\,\frac{d\eta}{dx} \quad\ldots\ldots\ldots\ldots(2).$$

This is independent of y, so that the horizontal acceleration is the same for all particles in a plane perpendicular to x. It follows that all particles which once lie in such a plane always do so; in other words, the horizontal velocity u is a function of x and t only.

The equation of horizontal motion, viz.

$$\frac{du}{dt} + u\,\frac{du}{dx} = -\frac{1}{\rho}\,\frac{dp}{dx},$$

is further simplified in the case of infinitely small motions by the

* These theorems are due to Lord Rayleigh, "Some General Theorems relating to Vibrations," *Proc. Lond. Math. Soc.*, t. iv., p. 357 (1873); *Theory of Sound*, c. iv.

omission of the term udu/dx, which is of the second order, so that

$$\frac{du}{dt} = -g\frac{d\eta}{dx} \quad\text{.........................(3).}$$

If we put

$$\xi = \int u dt,$$

then ξ measures the integral displacement of liquid past the point x, up to the time t; in the case of *small* motions it will, to the first order of small quantities, be equal to the displacement of the particle which originally occupied that position, or again to that of the particle which actually occupies it at time t. The equation (3) may now be written

$$\frac{d^2\xi}{dt^2} = -g\frac{d\eta}{dx} \quad\text{......................(4).}$$

The equation of continuity may be found by calculating the volume of fluid which has, up to time t, entered the space bounded by the planes x and $x+\delta x$; thus, if h be the depth and b the breadth of the canal,

$$-\frac{d}{dx}(\xi h b)\,\delta x = \eta b \delta x,$$

or

$$\eta = -h\frac{d\xi}{dx} \quad\text{.........................(5).}$$

The same result comes from the ordinary form of the equation of continuity, viz.

$$\frac{du}{dx} + \frac{dv}{dy} = 0 \quad\text{.................................(i).}$$

Thus

$$v = -\int_0^y \frac{du}{dx}dy = -y\frac{du}{dx} \quad\text{...........................(ii),}$$

if the origin be (for the moment) taken in the bottom of the canal. This formula is of interest as shewing that the vertical velocity of any particle is simply proportional to its height above the bottom. At the free surface we have $y = h + \eta$, $v = d\eta/dt$, whence (neglecting a product of small quantities)

$$\frac{d\eta}{dt} = -h\frac{d^2\xi}{dx\,dt} \quad\text{.............................. (iii).}$$

From this (5) follows by integration with respect to t.

Eliminating η between (4) and (5), we obtain

$$\frac{d^2\xi}{dt^2} = gh\frac{d^2\xi}{dx^2} \qquad\text{.......................(6).}$$

The elimination of ξ gives an equation of the same form, viz.

$$\frac{d^2\eta}{dt^2} = gh\frac{d^2\eta}{dx^2} \qquad\text{.......................(7).}$$

The above investigation can readily be extended to the case of a uniform canal of any form of section*. If the sectional area of the undisturbed fluid be S, and the breadth at the free surface b, the equation of continuity is

$$-\frac{d}{dx}(\xi S)\,\delta x = \eta b \delta x \qquad\text{..........................(iv),}$$

whence

$$\eta = -h\frac{d\xi}{dx} \qquad\text{..................................(v),}$$

as before, provided $h = S/b$, *i.e.* h now denotes the *mean* depth of the canal. The dynamical equation (4) is of course unaltered.

167. The equations (6) and (7) are of a well-known type which occurs in several physical problems, *e.g.* the transverse vibrations of strings, and the motion of sound-waves in one dimension.

To integrate them, let us write, for shortness,

$$c^2 = gh \qquad\text{............................(8),}$$

and

$$x - ct = x_1, \quad x + ct = x_2.$$

In terms of x_1 and x_2 as independent variables, the equation (6) takes the form

$$\frac{d^2\xi}{dx_1\,dx_2} = 0.$$

The complete solution is therefore

$$\xi = F(x - ct) + f(x + ct) \qquad\text{..................(9),}$$

where F, f are arbitrary functions.

The corresponding values of the particle-velocity and of the surface-elevation are given by

$$\left.\begin{aligned}\dot{\xi}/c &= -F'(x - ct) + f'(x + ct),\\ \eta/h &= -F'(x - ct) - f'(x + ct)\end{aligned}\right\} \qquad\text{............(10).}$$

* Kelland, *Trans. R. S. Edin.*, t. xiv. (1839).

The interpretation of these results is simple. Take first the motion represented by the first term in (9), alone. Since $F(x-ct)$ is unaltered when t and x are increased by τ and $c\tau$, respectively, it is plain that the disturbance which existed at the point x at time t has been transferred at time $t+\tau$ to the point $x+c\tau$. Hence the disturbance advances unchanged with a constant velocity c in space. In other words we have a 'progressive wave' travelling with constant velocity c in the direction of x-positive. In the same way the second term of (9) represents a progressive wave travelling with velocity c in the direction of x-negative. And it appears, since (9) is the *complete* solution of (6), that any motion whatever of the fluid, which is subject to the conditions laid down in the preceding Art., may be regarded as made up of waves of these two kinds.

The velocity (c) of propagation is, by (8), that 'due to' half the depth of the undisturbed fluid*.

The following table, giving in round numbers the velocity of wave-propagation for various depths, will be of interest, later, in connection with the theory of the tides.

h (feet)	c (feet per sec.)	c (sea-miles per hour)	$2\pi a/c$ (hours)
$312\frac{1}{2}$	100	60	360
1250	200	120	180
5000	400	240	90
11250†	600	360	60
20000	800	480	45

The last column gives the time a wave would take to travel over a distance equal to the earth's circumference ($2\pi a$). In order that a 'long' wave should traverse this distance in 24 hours, the depth would have to be about 14 miles. It must be borne in mind that these numerical results are only applicable to waves satisfying the conditions above postulated. The meaning of these conditions will be examined more particularly in Art. 169.

* Lagrange, *Nouv. mém. de l'Acad. de Berlin*, 1781, *Oeuvres*, t. i. p. 747.

† This is probably comparable in order of magnitude with the mean depth of the ocean.

168. To trace the effect of an arbitrary initial disturbance, let us suppose that when $t=0$ we have

$$\dot{\xi}/c=\phi(x), \qquad \eta/h=\psi(x) \text{..................} (11).$$

The functions F', f' which occur in (10) are then given by

$$\left.\begin{aligned} F'(x) &= -\tfrac{1}{2}\{\phi(x)+\psi(x)\}, \\ f'(x) &= \tfrac{1}{2}\{\phi(x)-\psi(x)\} \end{aligned}\right\} \text{..............} (12).$$

Hence if we draw the curves $y=\eta_1$, $y=\eta_2$, where

$$\left.\begin{aligned} \eta_1 &= \tfrac{1}{2}h\{\psi(x)+\phi(x)\}, \\ \eta_2 &= \tfrac{1}{2}h\{\psi(x)-\phi(x)\} \end{aligned}\right\} \text{..................} (13),$$

the form of the wave-profile at any subsequent instant t is found by displacing these curves parallel to x, through spaces $\pm ct$, respectively, and adding (algebraically) the ordinates. If, for example, the original disturbance be confined to a length l of the axis of x, then after a time $l/2c$ it will have broken up into two progressive waves of length l, travelling in opposite directions.

In the particular case where in the initial state $\dot{\xi}=0$, and therefore $\phi(x)=0$, we have $\eta_1=\eta_2$; the elevation in each of the derived waves is then exactly half what it was, at corresponding points, in the original disturbance.

It appears from (11) and (12) that if the initial disturbance be such that $\dot{\xi}=\pm\eta/h\,.\,c$, the motion will consist of a wave system travelling in one direction only, since one or other of the functions F' and f' is then zero. It is easy to trace the motion of a surface-particle as a progressive wave of either kind passes it. Suppose, for example, that

$$\xi=F(x-ct) \text{.......................} (14),$$

and therefore

$$\dot{\xi}=c\eta/h \text{..............................} (15).$$

The particle is at rest until it is reached by the wave; it then moves forward with a velocity proportional at each instant to the elevation above the mean level, the velocity being in fact less than the wave-velocity c, in the ratio of the surface-elevation to the depth of the water. The total displacement at any time is given by

$$\xi=\frac{1}{h}\int\eta c\,dt.$$

This integral measures the volume, per unit breadth of the canal, of the portion of the wave which has up to the instant in question passed the particle. Finally, when the wave has passed away, the particle is left at rest in advance of its original position at a distance equal to the total volume of the elevated water, divided by the sectional area of the canal.

169. We can now examine under what circumstances the solution expressed by (9) will be consistent with the assumptions made provisionally in Art. 166.

The restriction to infinitely small motions, made in equation (3), consisted in neglecting $u\,du/dx$ in comparison with du/dt. In a progressive wave we have $du/dt = \pm c\,du/dx$; so that u must be small compared with c, and therefore, by (15), η small compared with h.

Again, the exact equation of vertical motion, viz.

$$\rho \frac{Dv}{Dt} = -\frac{dp}{dz} - g\rho,$$

gives, on integration with respect to y,

$$p - p_0 = g\rho(y_0 + \eta - y) - \rho \int_y^{y_0+\eta} \frac{Dv}{Dt} dy \quad \text{...........} (16).$$

This may be replaced by the approximate equation (1), provided $\beta(h+\eta)$ be small compared with $g\eta$, where β denotes the maximum vertical acceleration. Now in a progressive wave, if λ denote the distance between two consecutive nodes (*i.e.* points at which the wave-profile meets the undisturbed level), the time which the corresponding portion of the wave takes to pass a particle is λ/c, and therefore the vertical velocity will be of the order $\eta c/\lambda$*, and the vertical acceleration of the order $\eta c^2/\lambda^2$, where η is the maximum elevation (or depression). Hence the neglect of the vertical acceleration is justified, provided h^2/λ^2 is a small quantity.

Waves whose slope is gradual, and whose length λ is large compared with the depth h of the fluid, are called 'long waves.'

* Hence, comparing with (15), we see that the ratio of the maximum vertical to the maximum horizontal velocity is of the order h/λ.

The requisite conditions will of course be satisfied in the general case represented by equation (9), provided they are satisfied for each of the two progressive waves into which the disturbance can be analysed.

170. There is another, although on the whole a less convenient, method of investigating the motion of 'long' waves, in which the Lagrangian plan is adopted, of making the coordinates refer to the individual particles of the fluid. For simplicity, we will consider only the case of a canal of rectangular section*. The fundamental assumption that the vertical acceleration may be neglected implies as before that the horizontal motion of all particles in a plane perpendicular to the length of the canal will be the same. We therefore denote by $x+\xi$ the abscissa at time t of the plane of particles whose undisturbed abscissa is x. If η denote the elevation of the free surface, in this plane, the equation of motion of unit breadth of a stratum whose thickness (in the undisturbed state) is δx, will be

$$\rho h \delta x \frac{d^2\xi}{dt^2} = -\frac{dp}{dx}\,\delta x\,(h+\eta),$$

where the factor $(dp/dx) . \delta x$ represents the pressure-difference for any two opposite particles x and $x+\delta x$ on the two faces of the stratum, while the factor $h+\eta$ represents the area of the stratum. Since the pressure about any particle depends only on its depth below the free surface we may write

$$\frac{dp}{dx} = g\rho\frac{d\eta}{dx},$$

so that our dynamical equation is

$$\frac{d^2\xi}{dt^2} = -g\left(1+\frac{\eta}{h}\right)\frac{d\eta}{dx} \qquad \text{.....................(1).}$$

The equation of continuity is obtained by equating the volumes of a stratum, consisting of the same particles, in the disturbed and undisturbed conditions respectively, viz. we have

$$\left(\delta x + \frac{d\xi}{dx}\,\delta x\right)(h+\eta) = h\delta x,$$

or

$$1+\frac{\eta}{h} = \left(1+\frac{d\xi}{dx}\right)^{-1} \qquad \text{.......................(2).}$$

* Airy, *Encyc. Metrop.*, "Tides and Waves," Art. 192 (1845); see also Stokes, "On Waves," *Camb. and Dub. Math. Journ.*, t. iv. (1849), *Math. and Phys. Papers*, t. ii., p. 222. The case of a canal with sloping sides has been treated by McCowan, "On the Theory of Long Waves...," *Phil. Mag.*, March, 1892.

Between equations (1) and (2) we may eliminate either η or ξ; the result in terms of ξ is the simpler, being

$$\frac{d^2\xi}{dt^2} = gh \frac{\dfrac{d^2\xi}{dx^2}}{\left(1 + \dfrac{d\xi}{dx}\right)^3} \quad \text{.....................(3)*.}$$

This is the general equation of 'long' waves in a uniform canal with vertical sides.

So far the only assumption is that the vertical acceleration of the particles may be neglected. If we now assume, in addition, that η/h is a small quantity, the equations (2) and (3) reduce to

$$\eta = -h \frac{d\xi}{dx} \quad \text{..........................(4),}$$

and

$$\frac{d^2\xi}{dt^2} = gh \frac{d^2\xi}{dx^2} \quad \text{..........................(5).}$$

The elevation η now satisfies the equation

$$\frac{d^2\eta}{dt^2} = gh \frac{d^2\eta}{dx^2} \quad \text{..........................(6).}$$

This is in conformity with our previous result; for the smallness of $d\xi/dx$ means that the relative displacement of any two particles is never more than a minute fraction of the distance between them, so that it is (to a first approximation) now immaterial whether the variable x be supposed to refer to a plane fixed in space, or to one moving with the fluid.

171. The potential energy of a wave, or system of waves, due to the elevation or depression of the fluid above or below the mean level is, per unit breadth, $g\rho \iint y\,dx\,dy$, where the integration with respect to y is to be taken between the limits 0 and η, and that with respect to x over the whole length of the waves. Effecting the former integration, we get

$$\tfrac{1}{2} g\rho \int \eta^2 dx \quad \text{.......................... (1).}$$

The kinetic energy is

$$\tfrac{1}{2} \rho h \int \dot{\xi}^2 dx \quad \text{.......................... (2).}$$

* Airy, *l. c.*

In a system of waves travelling in one direction only we have

$$\dot{\xi} = \pm \frac{c}{h}\eta,$$

so that the expressions (1) and (2) are equal; or the total energy is half potential, and half kinetic.

This result may be obtained in a more general manner, as follows*. Any progressive wave may be conceived as having been originated by the splitting up, into two waves travelling in opposite directions, of an initial disturbance in which the particle-velocity was everywhere zero, and the energy therefore wholly potential. It appears from Art. 168 that the two derived waves are symmetrical in every respect, so that each must contain half the original store of energy. Since, however, the elevation at corresponding points is for the derived waves exactly half that of the original disturbance, the potential energy of each will by (1) be one-fourth of the original store. The remaining (kinetic) part of the energy of each derived wave must therefore also be one-fourth of the original quantity.

172. If in any case of waves travelling in one direction only, without change of form, we impress on the whole mass a velocity equal and opposite to that of propagation, the motion becomes *steady*, whilst the forces acting on any particle remain the same as before. With the help of this artifice, the laws of wave-propagation can be investigated with great ease†. Thus, in the present case we shall have, by Art. 23 (4), at the free surface,

$$\frac{p}{\rho} = \text{const.} - g(h+\eta) - \tfrac{1}{2}q^2 \quad\text{..................(1)},$$

where q is the velocity. If the slope of the wave-profile be everywhere gradual, and the depth h small compared with the length of a wave, the horizontal velocity may be taken to be uniform throughout the depth, and approximately equal to q. Hence the equation of continuity is

$$q(h+\eta) = ch,$$

* Lord Rayleigh, "On Waves," *Phil. Mag.*, April, 1876.

† Lord Rayleigh, *l. c.*

c being the velocity, in the steady motion, at places where the depth of the stream is uniform and equal to h. Substituting for q in (1), we have

$$\frac{p}{\rho} = \text{const.} - gh\left(1 + \frac{\eta}{h}\right) - \tfrac{1}{2}c^2\left(1 + \frac{\eta}{h}\right)^{-2}.$$

Hence if η/h be small, the condition for a free surface, viz. $p = \text{const.}$, is satisfied approximately, provided

$$c^2 = gh,$$

which agrees with our former result.

173. It appears from the linearity of our equations that any number of independent solutions may be superposed. For example, having given a wave of any form travelling in one direction, if we superpose its *image* in the plane $x = 0$, travelling in the opposite direction, it is obvious that in the resulting motion the horizontal velocity will vanish at the origin, and the circumstances are therefore the same as if there were a fixed barrier at this point. We can thus understand the reflexion of a wave at a barrier; the elevations and depressions are reflected unchanged, whilst the horizontal velocity is reversed. The same results follow from the formula

$$\xi = F(ct - x) - F(ct + x) \quad\text{.................(1),}$$

which is evidently the most general value of ξ subject to the condition that $\xi = 0$ for $x = 0$.

We can further investigate without much difficulty the partial reflexion of a wave at a point where there is an abrupt change in the section of the canal. Taking the origin at the point in question, we may write, for the negative side,

$$\left.\begin{aligned} \eta_1 &= F\left(t - \frac{x}{c_1}\right) + f\left(t + \frac{x}{c_1}\right), \\ u_1 &= \frac{g}{c_1} F\left(t - \frac{x}{c_1}\right) - \frac{g}{c_1} f\left(t + \frac{x}{c_1}\right) \end{aligned}\right\} \quad\text{.....................(i),}$$

and for the positive side

$$\left.\begin{aligned} \eta_2 &= \phi\left(t - \frac{x}{c_2}\right), \\ u_2 &= \frac{g}{c_2} \phi\left(t - \frac{x}{c_2}\right) \end{aligned}\right\} \quad\text{...........................(ii),}$$

where the function F represents the original wave, and f, ϕ the reflected and transmitted portions respectively. The constancy of mass requires that at the point $x=0$ we should have $b_1h_1u_1=b_2h_2u_2$, where b_1, b_2 are the breadths at the surface, and h_1, h_2 are the mean depths. We must also have at the same point $\eta_1=\eta_2$, on account of the continuity of pressure*. These conditions give

$$\left.\begin{aligned}\frac{b_1h_1}{c_1}\{F(t)-f(t)\}&=\frac{b_2h_2}{c_2}\phi(t),\\ F(t)+f(t)&=\phi(t)\end{aligned}\right\}\quad\text{.......................(iii).}$$

We thence find that the ratio of the elevations in corresponding parts of the reflected and incident waves is

$$\frac{f}{F}=\frac{b_1c_1-b_2c_2}{b_1c_1+b_2c_2}\quad\text{..................................(iv).}$$

The similar ratio for the transmitted wave is

$$\frac{\phi}{F}=\frac{2b_1c_1}{b_1c_1+b_2c_2}\quad\text{....................................(v).}$$

The reader may easily verify that the energy contained in the reflected and transmitted waves is equal to that of the original incident wave.

174. Our investigations, so far, relate to cases of *free* waves. When, in addition to gravity, small disturbing forces X, Y act on the fluid, the equation of motion is obtained as follows.

We assume that within distances comparable with the depth h these forces vary only by a small fraction of their total value. On this understanding we have, in place of Art. 166 (1),

$$\frac{p-p_0}{\rho}=(g-Y)(y_0+\eta-y)\quad\text{................(1),}$$

and therefore

$$\frac{1}{\rho}\frac{dp}{dx}=(g-Y)\frac{d\eta}{dx}-(y_0+\eta-y)\frac{dY}{dx}.$$

The last term may be neglected for the reason just stated, and if

* It will be understood that the problem admits only of an approximate treatment, on account of the non-uniform character of the motion in the immediate neighbourhood of the point of discontinuity. The degree of approximation implied in the above assumptions will become more evident if we suppose the suffixes to refer to two sections S_1 and S_2, one on each side of the origin O, at distances from O which, though very small compared with the wave-length, are yet moderate multiples of the transverse dimensions of the canal. The motion of the fluid will be sensibly uniform over each of these sections, and parallel to the length. The conditions in the text then express that there is no sensible change of level between S_1 and S_2.

we further neglect the product of the small quantities Y and $d\eta/dx$, the equation reduces to

$$\frac{1}{\rho}\frac{dp}{dx} = g\frac{d\eta}{dx} \quad\text{..........................(2),}$$

as before. The equation of horizontal motion then takes the form

$$\frac{d^2\xi}{dt^2} = -g\frac{d\eta}{dx} + X \quad\text{.......................(3),}$$

where X may be regarded as a function of x and t only. The equation of continuity has the same form as in Art. 166, viz.

$$\eta = -h\frac{d\xi}{dx} \quad\text{..........................(4).}$$

Hence, on elimination of η,

$$\frac{d^2\xi}{dt^2} = gh\frac{d^2\xi}{dx^2} + X \quad\text{.......................(5).}$$

175. The oscillations of water in a canal of uniform section, closed at both ends, may, as in the corresponding problem of Acoustics, be obtained by superposition of progressive waves travelling in opposite directions. It is more instructive, however, with a view to subsequent more difficult investigations, to treat the problem as an example of the general theory sketched in Art. 165.

We have to determine ξ so as to satisfy

$$\frac{d^2\xi}{dt^2} = c^2\frac{d^2\xi}{dx^2} + X \quad\text{.......................(1),}$$

together with the terminal conditions that $\xi=0$ for $x=0$ and $x=l$, say. To find the free oscillations we put $X=0$, and assume that

$$\xi \propto \cos(\sigma t + \epsilon),$$

where σ is to be found. On substitution we obtain

$$\frac{d^2\xi}{dx^2} + \frac{\sigma^2}{c^2}\xi = 0 \quad\text{.......................(2),}$$

whence, omitting the time-factor,

$$\xi = A\sin\frac{\sigma x}{c} + B\cos\frac{\sigma x}{c}.$$

The terminal conditions give $B=0$, and

$$\sigma l/c = s\pi \text{.............................(3)},$$

where s is integral. Hence the normal mode of order s is given by

$$\xi = A_s \sin\frac{s\pi x}{l}\cos\left(\frac{s\pi ct}{l}+\epsilon_s\right) \text{..................(4)},$$

where the amplitude A_s and epoch ϵ_s are arbitrary.

In the slowest oscillation ($s=1$), the water sways to and fro, heaping itself up alternately at the two ends, and there is a node at the middle ($x=\frac{1}{2}l$). The period ($2l/c$) is equal to the time a progressive wave would take to traverse twice the length of the canal.

The periods of the higher modes are respectively $\frac{1}{2}, \frac{1}{3}, \frac{1}{4}, \ldots$ of this, but it must be remembered, in this and in other similar problems, that our theory ceases to be applicable when the length l/s of a semi-undulation becomes comparable with the depth h.

On comparison with the general theory of Art. 165, it appears that the normal coordinates of the present system are quantities $q_1, q_2, \ldots$ such that when the system is displaced according to any one of them, say q_s, we have

$$\xi = q_s \sin\frac{s\pi x}{l};$$

and we infer that the most general displacement of which the system is capable (subject to the conditions presupposed) is given by

$$\xi = \Sigma q_s \sin\frac{s\pi x}{l} \text{.................................(i)},$$

where $q_1, q_2, \ldots$ are arbitrary. This is in accordance with Fourier's Theorem.

When expressed in terms of the normal velocities and the normal coordinates, the expressions for T and V must reduce to sums of squares. This is easily verified, in the present case, from the formula (i). Thus if S denote the sectional area of the canal, we find

$$2T = \rho S\int_0^l \dot{\xi}^2 dx = \Sigma a_s \dot{q}_s^2 \text{.............................(ii)},$$

and

$$2V = g\rho\frac{S}{h}\int_0^l \eta^2 dx = \Sigma c_s q_s^2 \text{............................(iii)},$$

where

$$a_s = \tfrac{1}{2}\rho Sl, \quad c_s = \tfrac{1}{2}s^2\pi^2 g\rho hS/l \text{.......................(iv)}.$$

It is to be noted that the coefficients of stability (c_s) increase with the depth.

Conversely, if we assume from Fourier's theorem that (i) is a sufficiently general expression for the value of ξ at any instant, the calculation just indicated shews that the coefficients q_s are the normal coordinates; and the frequencies can then be found from the general formula (8) of Art. 165; viz. we have

$$\sigma_s = (c_s/a_s)^{\frac{1}{2}} = s\pi\,(gh)^{\frac{1}{2}}/l,$$

in agreement with (3).

176. As an example of forced waves we take the case of a *uniform* longitudinal force

$$X = f\cos(\sigma t + \epsilon) \qquad \text{.........................(5).}$$

This will illustrate, to a certain extent, the generation of tides in a land-locked sea of small dimensions. Assuming that ξ varies as $\cos(\sigma t + \epsilon)$, and omitting the time-factor, the equation (1) becomes

$$\frac{d^2\xi}{dx^2} + \frac{\sigma^2}{c^2}\xi = -\frac{f}{c^2},$$

the solution of which is

$$\xi = -\frac{f}{\sigma^2} + D\sin\frac{\sigma x}{c} + E\cos\frac{\sigma x}{c} \qquad \text{..................(6).}$$

The terminal conditions give

$$E = \frac{f}{\sigma^2}, \qquad D\sin\frac{\sigma l}{c} = \left(1 - \cos\frac{\sigma l}{c}\right)\frac{f}{\sigma^2} \qquad \text{............(7).}$$

Hence, unless $\sin\sigma l/c = 0$, we have $D = f/\sigma^2 . \tan\sigma l/2c$, so that

$$\left.\begin{aligned} \xi &= \frac{2f}{\sigma^2\cos\frac{\sigma l}{2c}}\sin\frac{\sigma x}{2c}\sin\frac{\sigma(l-x)}{2c}.\cos(\sigma t + \epsilon), \\ \text{and}\qquad \eta &= \frac{hf}{\sigma c\cos\frac{\sigma l}{2c}}\sin\frac{\sigma(2x-l)}{2c}.\cos(\sigma t + \epsilon) \end{aligned}\right\} \qquad \text{......(8).}$$

If the period of the disturbing force be large compared with that of the slowest free mode, $\sigma l/2c$ will be small, and the formula for the elevation becomes

$$\eta = \frac{f}{g}(x - \tfrac{1}{2}l)\cos(\sigma t + \epsilon) \qquad \text{.................. (9),}$$

approximately, exactly as if the water were devoid of inertia. The horizontal displacement of the water is always in the same phase with the force, so long as the period is greater than that of the slowest free mode, or $\sigma l/2c < \frac{1}{2}\pi$. If the period be diminished until it is less than the above value, the phase is reversed.

When the period is exactly equal to that of a free mode of *odd* order ($s = 1, 3, 5, \ldots$), the above expressions for ξ and η become infinite, and the solution fails. As pointed out in Art. 165, the interpretation of this is that, in the absence of dissipative forces (such as viscosity), the amplitude of the motion becomes so great that the foregoing approximations are no longer justified.

If, on the other hand, the period coincide with that of a free mode of *even* order ($s = 2, 4, 6, \ldots$), we have $\sin \sigma l/c = 0$, $\cos \sigma l/c = 1$, and the terminal conditions are satisfied independently of the value of D. The forced motion may then be represented by

$$\xi = -\frac{2f}{\sigma^2} \sin^2 \frac{\sigma x}{2c} \cos(\sigma t + \epsilon) \quad\ldots\ldots\ldots\ldots (10)^*.$$

The above example is simpler than many of its class in that it is possible to solve it without resolving the impressed force into its normal components. If we wish to effect this resolution, we must calculate the work done during an arbitrary displacement

$$\Delta\xi = \Sigma \Delta q_s \,.\, \sin \frac{s\pi x}{l}.$$

Since X denotes the force on unit mass, we have

$$\Sigma Q \Delta q = \rho S \int_0^l X \Delta\xi \, dx,$$

whence $$Q_s = C_s \cos(\sigma t + \epsilon) \quad\ldots\ldots\ldots\ldots (\text{i}),$$

provided $$C_s = \frac{1 - \cos s\pi}{s\pi} \,.\, \rho S l f \quad\ldots\ldots\ldots\ldots (\text{ii}).$$

This vanishes, as we should expect, for all even values of s. The solution of our problem then follows from the general formulae of Art. 165. The identification (by Fourier's Theorem) of the result thus obtained with that contained in the formulae (8) is left to the reader.

* In the language of the general theory, the impressed force has here no component of the particular type with which it synchronizes, so that a vibration of this type is not excited at all. In the same way a periodic pressure applied at any point of a stretched string will not excite any fundamental mode which has a *node* there, even though it synchronize with it.

Another very simple case of forced oscillations, of some interest in connection with tidal theory, is that of a canal closed at one end and communicating at the other with an open sea in which a periodic oscillation

$$\eta = a \cos(\sigma t + \epsilon) \quad\text{.......................}(11)$$

is maintained. If the origin be taken at the closed end, the solution is obviously

$$\eta = a \frac{\cos \dfrac{\sigma x}{c}}{\cos \dfrac{\sigma l}{c}} . \cos(\sigma t + \epsilon) \quad\text{..................}(12),$$

l denoting the length. If $\sigma l/c$ be small the tide has sensibly the same amplitude at all points of the canal. For particular values of l, (determined by $\cos \sigma l/c = 0$), the solution fails through the amplitude becoming infinite.

Canal Theory of the Tides.

177. The theory of forced oscillations in canals, or on open sheets of water, owes most of its interest to its bearing on the phenomena of the tides. The 'canal theory,' in particular, has been treated very fully by Airy*. We will consider one or two of the more interesting problems.

The calculation of the disturbing effect of a distant body on the waters of the ocean is placed for convenience in an Appendix at the end of this Chapter. It appears that the disturbing effect of the moon, for example, at a point P of the earth's surface, may be represented by a potential Ω whose approximate value is

$$\Omega = \tfrac{3}{2} \frac{\gamma M a^2}{D^3} \left(\tfrac{1}{3} - \cos^2 \vartheta\right) \quad\text{........................}(1),$$

where M denotes the mass of the moon, D its distance from the earth's centre, a the earth's radius, γ the 'constant of gravitation,' and ϑ the moon's zenith distance at the place P. This gives a horizontal acceleration $d\Omega/ad\vartheta$, or

$$f \sin 2\vartheta \quad\text{................................}(2),$$

* *Encycl. Metrop.*, "Tides and Waves," Section VI. (1845). Several of the leading features of the theory had been made out, by very simple methods, by Young in 1813 and 1823; *Miscellaneous Works*, t. ii. pp. 262, 291.

towards the point of the earth's surface which is vertically beneath the moon, provided

$$f = \tfrac{3}{2}\gamma Ma/D^3 \qquad (3).$$

If E be the earth's mass, we may write $g = \gamma E/a^2$, whence

$$\frac{f}{g} = \frac{3}{2} \cdot \frac{M}{E} \cdot \left(\frac{a}{D}\right)^3.$$

Putting $M/E = \frac{1}{81}$, $a/D = \frac{1}{60}$, this gives $f/g = 8{\cdot}57 \times 10^{-8}$. When the sun is the disturbing body, the corresponding ratio is $f/g = 3{\cdot}78 \times 10^{-8}$.

It is convenient, for some purposes, to introduce a linear magnitude H, defined by

$$H/a = f/g \qquad (4).$$

If we put $a = 21 \times 10^6$ feet, this gives, for the lunar tide, $H = 1{\cdot}80$ ft., and for the solar tide $H = {\cdot}79$ ft. It is shewn in the Appendix that H measures the maximum range of the tide, from high water to low water, on the 'equilibrium theory.'

178. Take now the case of a uniform canal coincident with the earth's equator, and let us suppose for simplicity that the moon describes a circular orbit in the same plane. Let ξ be the displacement, relative to the earth's surface, of a particle of water whose mean position is at a distance x, measured eastwards, from some fixed meridian. If n be the angular velocity of the earth's rotation, the actual displacement of the particle at time t will be $\xi + nt$, so that the tangential acceleration will be $d^2\xi/dt^2$. If we suppose the 'centrifugal force' to be as usual allowed for in the value of g, the processes of Arts. 166, 174 will apply without further alteration.

If n' denote the angular velocity of the moon relative to the fixed meridian*, we may write

$$\vartheta = n't + x/a + \epsilon,$$

so that the equation of motion is

$$\frac{d^2\xi}{dt^2} = c^2 \frac{d^2\xi}{dx^2} - f \sin 2\left(n't + \frac{x}{a} + \epsilon\right) \qquad (1).$$

The *free* oscillations are determined by the consideration that ξ is necessarily a periodic function of x, its value recurring whenever

* That is, $n' = n - n_1$, if n_1 be the angular velocity of the moon in her orbit.

x increases by $2\pi a$. It may therefore be expressed, by Fourier's Theorem, in the form

$$\xi = \Sigma_0^\infty \left(P_s \cos \frac{sx}{a} + Q_s \sin \frac{sx}{a}\right) \text{..................(2).}$$

Substituting in (1), with the last term omitted, it is found that P_s and Q_s must satisfy the equation

$$\frac{d^2 P_s}{dt^2} + \frac{s^2 c^2}{a^2} P_s = 0 \text{ .... (3).}$$

The motion, in any normal mode, is therefore simple-harmonic, of period $2\pi a/sc$.

For the *forced* waves, or tides, we find

$$\xi = -\tfrac{1}{4} \frac{fa^2}{c^2 - n'^2 a^2} \sin 2\left(n't + \frac{x}{a} + \epsilon\right) \text{ ....(4),}$$

whence

$$\eta = \tfrac{1}{2} \frac{c^2 H}{c^2 - n'^2 a^2} \cos 2\left(n't + \frac{x}{a} + \epsilon\right) \text{..............(5).}$$

The tide is therefore semi-diurnal (the *lunar* day being of course understood), and is 'direct' or 'inverted,' *i.e.* there is high or low water beneath the moon, according as $c \gtrless n'a$, in other words according as the velocity, relative to the earth's surface, of a point which moves so as to be always vertically beneath the moon, is less or greater than that of a free wave. In the actual case of the earth we have

$$c^2/n'^2 a^2 = (g/n'^2 a) \,.\, (h/a) = 311\, h/a,$$

so that unless the depth of the canal were to greatly exceed such depths as actually occur in the ocean, the tides would be inverted.

This result, which is sometimes felt as a paradox, comes under a general principle referred to in Art. 165. It is a consequence of the comparative slowness of the free oscillations in an equatorial canal of moderate depth. It appears from the rough numerical table on p. 274 that with a depth of 11250 feet a free wave would take about 30 hours to describe the earth's semi-circumference, whereas the period of the tidal disturbing force is only a little over 12 hours.

The formula (5) is, in fact, a particular case of Art. 165 (12), for it may be written

$$\eta = \frac{1}{1 - \sigma^2/\sigma_0^2} \bar{\eta} \text{ ....(6),}$$

where $\bar{\eta}$ is the elevation given by the 'equilibrium-theory,' viz.

$$\bar{\eta} = \tfrac{1}{2} H \cos 2\left(n't + \frac{x}{a} + \epsilon\right) \quad \text{.....................(7)},$$

and $\sigma = 2n'$, $\sigma_0 = 2c/a$.

For such moderate depths as 10000 feet and under, n'^2a^2 is large compared with gh; the amplitude of the horizontal motion, as given by (4), is then $f/4n'^2$, or $g/4n'^2a \,.\, H$, nearly, being approximately independent of the depth. In the case of the lunar tide this is equal to about 140 feet. The maximum elevation is obtained from this by multiplying by $2h/a$; this gives, for a depth of 10000 feet, a height of only ·133 of a foot.

For greater depths the tides would be higher, but still inverted, until we reach the critical depth n'^2a^2/g, which is about 13 miles. For depths beyond this limit, the tides become direct, and approximate more and more to the value given by the equilibrium theory*.

179. The case of a circular canal parallel to the equator can be worked out in a similar manner. If the moon's orbit be still supposed to lie in the plane of the equator, we find by spherical trigonometry

$$\cos \vartheta = \sin\theta \cos\left(n't + \frac{x}{a\sin\theta} + \epsilon\right) \quad \text{...............(1)},$$

where θ is the co-latitude, and x denotes the distance of any point P of the canal from the zero meridian. This leads to

$$X = -\frac{d\Omega}{dx} = -f \sin\theta \sin 2\left(n't + \frac{x}{a\sin\theta} + \epsilon\right) \quad \text{......(2)},$$

and thence to

$$\eta = \frac{1}{2}\frac{c^2 H \sin^2\theta}{c^2 - n'^2a^2\sin^2\theta} \cos 2\left(n't + \frac{x}{a\sin\theta} + \epsilon\right) \quad \text{......(3)}.$$

Hence if $n'a > c$ the tide will be direct or inverted according as $\theta \lessgtr \sin^{-1} c/n'a$. If the depth be so great that $c > n'a$, the tides will be direct for all values of θ.

If the moon be not in the plane of the equator, but have a co-declination Δ, the formula (1) is replaced by

$$\cos\vartheta = \cos\theta\cos\Delta + \sin\theta\sin\Delta\cos\alpha \quad \text{........................(i)},$$

* Cf. Young, *l. c. ante* p. 270.

where α is the hour-angle of the moon from the meridian of P. For simplicity, we will neglect the moon's motion in her orbit in comparison with the earth's angular velocity of rotation (n); thus we put

$$\alpha = nt + \frac{x}{a \sin\theta} + \epsilon,$$

and treat Δ as constant. The resulting expression for the component X of the disturbing force is found to be

$$X = -\frac{d\Omega}{dx} = -f \cos\theta \sin 2\Delta \sin\left(nt + \frac{x}{a\sin\theta} + \epsilon\right)$$

$$-f \sin\theta \sin^2\Delta \sin 2\left(nt + \frac{x}{a\sin\theta} + \epsilon\right) \text{ .... (ii).}$$

We thence obtain

$$\eta = \tfrac{1}{2}\frac{c^2 H}{c^2 - n^2a^2\sin^2\theta}\sin 2\theta \sin 2\Delta \cos\left(nt + \frac{x}{a\sin\theta} + \epsilon\right)$$

$$+\tfrac{1}{2}\frac{c^2 H}{c^2 - n^2a^2\sin^2\theta}\sin^2\theta \sin^2\Delta \cos 2\left(nt + \frac{x}{a\sin\theta} + \epsilon\right) \text{ ....(iii).}$$

The first term gives a 'diurnal' tide of period $2\pi/n$; this vanishes and changes sign when the moon crosses the equator, *i.e.* twice a month. The second term represents a semidiurnal tide of period π/n, whose amplitude is now less than before in the ratio of $\sin^2\Delta$ to 1.

180. In the case of a canal coincident with a meridian we should have to take account of the fact that the undisturbed figure of the free surface is one of relative equilibrium under gravity and centrifugal force, and is therefore not exactly circular. We shall have occasion later on to treat the question of displacements relative to a rotating globe somewhat carefully; for the present we will assume by anticipation that *in a narrow canal* the disturbances are sensibly the same as if the earth were at rest, and the disturbing body were to revolve round it with the proper relative motion.

If the moon be supposed to move in the plane of the equator, the hour-angle from the meridian of the canal may be denoted by $n't + \epsilon$, and if x be the distance of any point P on the canal from the equator, we find

$$\cos\vartheta = \cos\frac{x}{a} \,.\, \cos(n't + \epsilon) \text{ .... (1).}$$

Hence

$$X = -\frac{d\Omega}{dx} = -f \sin 2\frac{x}{a} \,.\, \cos^2(n't + \epsilon)$$

$$= -\tfrac{1}{2}f \sin 2\frac{x}{a} \,.\, \{1 + \cos 2(n't + \epsilon)\} \text{ .... (2).}$$

Substituting in the equation (5) of Art. 174, and solving, we find

$$\eta = \frac{1}{4} H \cos 2\frac{x}{a} + \frac{1}{4}\frac{c^2 H}{c^2 - n'^2 a^2} \cos 2\frac{x}{a} \,.\, \cos 2(n't + \epsilon) \text{ ...... (3).}$$

The first term represents a change of mean level to the extent

$$\eta = \frac{1}{4} H \cos 2\frac{x}{a} \text{ ....(4).}$$

The fluctuations above and below the disturbed mean level are given by the second term in (3). This represents a semi-diurnal tide; and we notice that if, as in the actual case of the earth, c be less than $n'a$, there will be high water in latitudes above 45°, and low water in latitudes below 45°, when the moon is in the meridian of the canal, and *vice versâ* when the moon is 90° from that meridian. These circumstances would be all reversed if c were greater than $n'a$.

When the moon is not on the equator, but has a given declination, the mean level, as indicated by the term corresponding to (4), has a coefficient depending on the declination, and the consequent variations in it indicate a fortnightly (or, in the case of the sun, a semi-annual) tide. There is also introduced a diurnal tide whose sign depends on the declination. The reader will have no difficulty in examining these points, by means of the general value of Ω given in the Appendix.

Wave-Motion in a Canal of Variable Section.

181. When the section (S, say) of the canal is not uniform, but varies gradually from point to point, the equation of continuity is, as in Art. 166 (iv),

$$\eta = -\frac{1}{b}\frac{d}{dx}(S\xi) \text{ ....(1),}$$

where b denotes the breadth at the surface. If h denote the mean depth over the width b, we have $S = bh$, and therefore

$$\eta = -\frac{1}{b}\frac{d}{dx}(hb\xi) \text{ .... (2),}$$

where h, b are now functions of x.

The dynamical equation has the same form as before, viz.

$$\frac{d^2\xi}{dt^2} = -g\frac{d\eta}{dx} \text{ .... (3).}$$

Between (2) and (3) we may eliminate either η or ξ; the equation in η is

$$\frac{d^2\eta}{dt^2} = \frac{g}{b}\frac{d}{dx}\left(hb\frac{d\eta}{dx}\right) \quad\text{(4).}$$

The laws of propagation of waves in a rectangular canal of gradually varying section were investigated by Green*. His results, freed from the restriction to a special form of section, may be obtained as follows.

If we introduce a variable θ defined by

$$dx/d\theta = (gh)^{\frac{1}{2}} \quad\text{(i),}$$

in place of x, the equation (4) transforms into

$$\frac{d^2\eta}{dt^2} = \eta'' + \left(\frac{b'}{b} + \frac{1}{2}\frac{h'}{h}\right)\eta' \quad\text{(ii),}$$

where the accents denote differentiations with respect to θ. If b and h were constants, the equation would be satisfied by $\eta = F(\theta - t)$, as in Art. 167; in the present case we assume, for trial,

$$\eta = \Theta \, . \, F(\theta - t) \quad\text{(iii),}$$

where Θ is a function of θ only. Substituting in (ii), we find

$$2\frac{\Theta'}{\Theta}\cdot\frac{F'}{F} + \frac{\Theta''}{\Theta} + \left(\frac{b'}{b} + \frac{1}{2}\frac{h'}{h}\right)\left(\frac{F'}{F} + \frac{\Theta'}{\Theta}\right) = 0 \quad\text{(iv).}$$

The terms of this which involve F will cancel provided

$$2\frac{\Theta'}{\Theta} + \frac{b'}{b} + \frac{1}{2}\frac{h'}{h} = 0,$$

or

$$\Theta = Cb^{-\frac{1}{2}}h^{-\frac{1}{4}} \quad\text{(v),}$$

C being a constant. Hence, provided the remaining terms in (iv) may be neglected, the equation (i) will be satisfied by (iii) and (v).

The above approximation is justified, provided we can neglect Θ''/Θ' and Θ'/Θ in comparison with F'/F. As regards Θ'/Θ, it appears from (v) and (iii) that this is equivalent to neglecting $b^{-1}.\,db/dx$ and $h^{-1}.\,dh/dx$ in comparison with $\eta^{-1}.\,d\eta/dx$. If, now, λ denote a wave-length, in the general sense of Art. 169, $d\eta/dx$ is of the order η/λ, so that the assumption in question is that $\lambda\, db/dx$ and $\lambda\, dh/dx$ are small compared with b and h, respectively. In other words, it is assumed that the transverse dimensions of the canal vary only by small fractions of themselves within the limits of a wave-length. It is easily seen, in like manner, that the neglect of Θ''/Θ' in comparison with F'/F implies a similar limitation to the rates of change of db/dx and dh/dx.

* "On the Motion of Waves in a Variable Canal of small depth and width." *Camb. Trans.*, t. vi. (1837), *Math. Papers*, p. 225; see also Airy, "Tides and Waves," Art. 260.

Since the equation (4) is unaltered when we reverse the sign of t, the complete solution, subject to the above restrictions, is

$$\eta = b^{-\frac{1}{2}} h^{-\frac{1}{4}} \{F(\theta - t) + f(\theta + t)\} \quad \text{.........................(vi)},$$

when F and f are arbitrary functions.

The first term in this represents a wave travelling in the direction of x-positive; the velocity of propagation is determined by the consideration that any particular phase is recovered when $\delta\theta$ and δt have equal values, and is therefore equal to $(gh)^{\frac{1}{2}}$, by (i), exactly as in the case of a uniform section. In like manner the second term in (vi) represents a wave travelling in the direction of x-negative. In each case the elevation of any particular part of the wave alters, as it proceeds, according to the law $b^{-\frac{1}{2}} h^{-\frac{1}{4}}$.

The reflection of a progressive wave at a point where the section of a canal suddenly changes has been considered in Art. 173. The formulæ there given shew, as we should expect, that the smaller the change in the dimensions of the section, the smaller will be the amplitude of the reflected wave. The case where the transition from one section to the other is continuous, instead of abrupt, comes under a general investigation of Lord Rayleigh's *. It appears that if the space within which the transition is completed be a moderate multiple of a wave-length there is practically no reflection; whilst in the opposite extreme the results agree with those of Art. 173.

If we assume, on the basis of these results, that when the change of section within a wave-length may be neglected a progressive wave suffers no disintegration by reflection, the law of amplitude easily follows from the principle of energy †. It appears from Art. 171 that the energy of the wave varies as the length, the breadth, and the square of the height, and it is easily seen that the length of the wave, in different parts of the canal, varies as the corresponding velocity of propagation ‡, and therefore as the square root of the mean depth. Hence, in the above notation, $\eta^2 b h^{\frac{1}{2}}$ is constant, or

$$\eta \propto b^{-\frac{1}{2}} h^{-\frac{1}{4}},$$

which is Green's law above found.

* "On Reflection of Vibrations at the Confines of two Media between which the Transition is gradual," *Proc. Lond. Math. Soc.*, t. xi. p. 51 (1880); *Theory of Sound*, 2nd ed., London, 1894, Art. 148 *b*.

† Lord Rayleigh, *l. c. ante* p. 279.

‡ For if P, Q be any two points of a wave, and P', Q' the corresponding points when it has reached another part of the canal, the time from P to P' is the same as from Q to Q', and therefore the time from P to Q is equal to that from P' to Q'. Hence the distances PQ, $P'Q'$ are proportional to the corresponding wave-velocities.

182. In the case of simple harmonic motion, assuming that $\eta \propto \cos(\sigma t + \epsilon)$, the equation (4) of the preceding Art. becomes

$$\frac{g}{b}\frac{d}{dx}\left(hb\frac{d\eta}{dx}\right) + \sigma^2\eta = 0 \qquad (1).$$

Some particular cases of considerable interest can be solved with ease.

1°. For example, let us take the case of a canal whose breadth varies as the distance from the end $x=0$, the depth being uniform; and let us suppose that at its mouth $(x=a)$ the canal communicates with an open sea in which a tidal oscillation

$$\eta = a\cos(\sigma t+\epsilon) \qquad (i),$$

is maintained. Putting $h=$const., $b \propto x$, in (1), we find

$$\frac{d^2\eta}{dx^2} + \frac{1}{x}\frac{d\eta}{dx} + k^2\eta = 0 \qquad (ii),$$

provided

$$k^2 = \sigma^2/gh \qquad (iii).$$

The solution of (ii) which is finite when $x=0$ is

$$\zeta = A\left(1 - \frac{k^2x^2}{2^2} + \frac{k^4x^4}{2^2.4^2} - \ldots\right) \qquad (iv),$$

or, in the notation of Bessel's Functions,

$$\zeta = AJ_0(kx) \qquad (v).$$

Hence the solution of our problem is evidently

$$\zeta = a\frac{J_0(kx)}{J_0(ka)}\cos(\sigma t+\epsilon) \qquad (vi).$$

The curve $y=J_0(x)$ is figured on p. 306; it indicates how the amplitude of the forced oscillation increases, whilst the wave length is practically constant, as we proceed up the canal from the mouth.

2°. Let us suppose that the variation is in the *depth* only, and that this increases uniformly from the end $x=0$ of the canal, to the mouth, the remaining circumstances being as before. If, in (1), we put $h=h_0x/a$, $\kappa=\sigma^2a/gh_0$, we obtain

$$\frac{d}{dx}\left(x\frac{d\eta}{dx}\right) + \kappa\eta = 0 \qquad (vii).$$

This solution of this which is finite for $x=0$ is

$$\eta = A\left(1 - \frac{\kappa x}{1^2} + \frac{\kappa^2x^2}{1^2.2^2} - \ldots\right) \qquad (viii),$$

or

$$\eta = AJ_0(2\kappa^{\frac{1}{2}}x^{\frac{1}{2}}) \qquad (ix),$$

whence finally, restoring the time-factor and determining the constant,

$$\eta = a\frac{J_0(2\kappa^{\frac{1}{2}}x^{\frac{1}{2}})}{J_0(2\kappa^{\frac{1}{2}}a^{\frac{1}{2}})}\cos(\sigma t+\epsilon) \qquad (x).$$

The annexed diagram of the curve $y = J_0(\sqrt{x})$, where, for clearness, the scale adopted for y is 200 times that of x, shews how the amplitude continually increases, and the wave-length diminishes, as we travel up the canal.

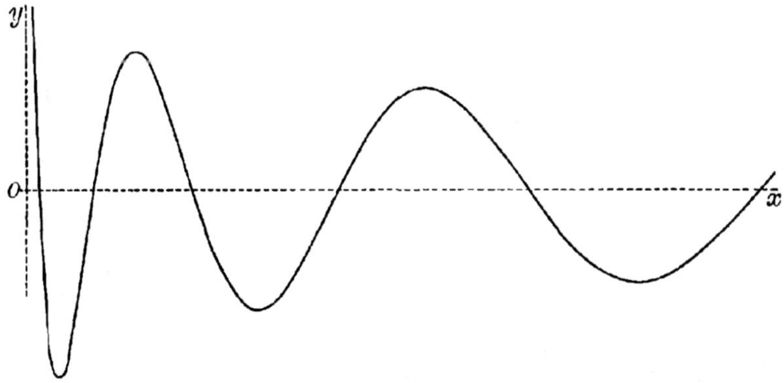

These examples may serve to illustrate the exaggeration of oceanic tides which takes place in shallow seas and in estuaries.

We add one or two simple problems of free oscillations.

3°. Let us take the case of a canal of uniform breadth, of length $2a$, whose bed slopes uniformly from either end to the middle. If we take the origin at one end, the motion in the first half of the canal will be determined, as above, by

$$\eta = AJ_0(2\kappa^{\frac{1}{2}} x^{\frac{1}{2}}) \quad \text{(xi)},$$

where $\kappa = \sigma^2 a/gh_0$, as before, h_0 denoting the depth at the middle.

It is evident that the normal modes will fall into two classes. In the first of these η will have opposite values at corresponding points of the two halves of the canal, and will therefore vanish at the centre ($x = a$). The values of σ are then determined by

$$J_0(2\kappa^{\frac{1}{2}} a^{\frac{1}{2}}) = 0 \quad \text{(xii)},$$

viz. κ being any root of this, we have

$$\sigma = \frac{(gh_0)^{\frac{1}{2}}}{a} \cdot (\kappa a)^{\frac{1}{2}} \quad \text{(xiii)}.$$

In the second class, the value of η is symmetrical with respect to the centre, so that $d\eta/dx = 0$ at the middle. This gives

$$J_0'(2\kappa^{\frac{1}{2}} a^{\frac{1}{2}}) = 0 \quad \text{(xiv)}.$$

Some account of Bessel's Functions will be given presently, in connection with another problem. It appears that the slowest oscillation is of the asymmetrical class, and so corresponds to the smallest root of (xii), which is $2\kappa^{\frac{1}{2}}a^{\frac{1}{2}} = \cdot 7655\pi$, whence

$$\frac{2\pi}{\sigma} = 1\cdot 306 \times \frac{4a}{(gh_0)^{\frac{1}{2}}}.$$

4°. Again, let us suppose that the depth of the canal varies according to the law

$$h = h_0\left(1 - \frac{x^2}{a^2}\right) \quad \text{.................................(xv),}$$

where x now denotes the distance from the middle. Substituting in (1), with b=const., we find

$$\frac{d}{dx}\left\{\left(1 - \frac{x^2}{a^2}\right)\frac{d\eta}{dx}\right\} + \frac{\sigma^2}{gh_0}\eta = 0 \quad \text{........................(xvi).}$$

If we put

$$\sigma^2 = n(n+1)\frac{gh_0}{a^2} \quad \text{...............................(xvii),}$$

this is of the same form as the general equation of zonal harmonics, Art. 85 (1).

In the present problem n is determined by the condition that ζ must be finite for $x/a = \pm 1$. This requires (Art. 86) that n should be integral; the normal modes are therefore of the types

$$\eta = CP_n\left(\frac{x}{a}\right).\cos(\sigma t + \epsilon) \quad \text{........................(xviii),}$$

where P_n is a Legendre's Function, the value of σ being determined by (xvii).

In the slowest oscillation ($n=1$), the profile of the free surface is a straight line. For a canal of *uniform* depth h_0, and of the same length ($2a$), the corresponding value of σ would be $\pi c/2a$, where $c = (gh_0)^{\frac{1}{2}}$. Hence in the present case the frequency is less, in the ratio $2\sqrt{2}/\pi$, or $\cdot 9003$.

The forced oscillations due to a uniform disturbing force

$$X = f\cos(\sigma t + \epsilon) \quad \text{.................................(xix),}$$

can be obtained by the rule of Art. 165 (12). The equilibrium form of the free surface is evidently

$$\bar{\eta} = \frac{f}{g}x\cos(\sigma t + \epsilon) \quad \text{.............................(xx),}$$

and, since the given force is of the normal type $n=1$, we have

$$\eta = \frac{f}{g(1 - \sigma^2/\sigma_0^2)}x\cos(\sigma t + \epsilon) \quad \text{........................(xxi),}$$

where

$$\sigma_0^2 = 2gh_0/a^2.$$

Waves of Finite Amplitude.

183. When the elevation η is not small compared with the mean depth h, waves, even in an uniform canal of rectangular section, are no longer propagated without change of type. This question was first investigated by Airy*, by methods of successive approximation. He found that in a progressive wave different parts will travel with different velocities, the wave-velocity corresponding to an elevation η being given approximately by

$$c\,(1+\tfrac{3}{2}\eta/h),$$

where c is the velocity corresponding to an infinitely small amplitude.

A more complete view of the matter can be obtained by the method employed by Riemann in treating the analogous problem in Acoustics, to which reference will be made in Chapter X.

The sole assumption on which we are now proceeding is that the vertical acceleration may be neglected. It follows, as explained in Art. 166, that the horizontal velocity may be taken to be uniform over any section of the canal. The dynamical equation is

$$\frac{du}{dt}+u\frac{du}{dx}=-g\frac{d\eta}{dx} \quad\text{.......................(1)},$$

as before, and the equation of continuity, in the case of a rectangular section, is easily seen to be

$$\frac{d}{dx}\{(h+\eta)\,u\}=-\frac{d\eta}{dt} \quad\text{...................... (2)},$$

where h is the depth. This may be written

$$\frac{d\eta}{dt}+u\frac{d\eta}{dx}=-(h+\eta)\frac{du}{dx} \quad\text{.....................(3)}.$$

Let us now write

$$2P=f(\eta)+u, \quad 2Q=f(\eta)-u \quad\text{.............. (4)},$$

where the function $f(\eta)$ is as yet at our disposal. If we multiply (3) by $f'(\eta)$, and add to (1), we get

$$\frac{dP}{dt}+u\frac{dP}{dx}=-\tfrac{1}{2}(h+\eta)f'(\eta)\frac{du}{dx}-\tfrac{1}{2}g\frac{d\eta}{dx}.$$

* "Tides and Waves," Art. 198.

If we now determine $f(\eta)$ so that

$$(h+\eta)f'(\eta)^2=g \qquad \text{(5)},$$

this may be written

$$\frac{dP}{dt}+u\frac{dP}{dx}=-(h+\eta)f'(\eta)\frac{dP}{dx} \qquad \text{(6)},$$

In the same way we find

$$\frac{dQ}{dt}+u\frac{dQ}{dx}=\quad(h+\eta)f'(\eta)\frac{dQ}{dx} \qquad \text{(7)}.$$

The condition (5) is satisfied by

$$f(\eta)=2c\left\{\left(1+\frac{\eta}{h}\right)^{\frac{1}{2}}-1\right\} \qquad \text{(8)},$$

where $c=(gh)^{\frac{1}{2}}$. The arbitrary constant has been chosen so as to make P and Q vanish in the parts of the canal which are free from disturbance, but this is not essential.

Substituting in (6) and (7) we find

$$\left.\begin{aligned} dP&=\left[dx-\left\{c\left(1+\frac{\eta}{h}\right)^{\frac{1}{2}}+u\right\}dt\right]\frac{dP}{dx},\\ dQ&=\left[dx+\left\{c\left(1+\frac{\eta}{h}\right)^{\frac{1}{2}}-u\right\}dt\right]\frac{dQ}{dx}\end{aligned}\right\} \qquad \text{(9)}.$$

It appears, therefore, that $dP=0$, *i.e.* P is constant, for a geometrical point moving with the velocity

$$\frac{dx}{dt}=c\left(1+\frac{\eta}{h}\right)^{\frac{1}{2}}+u \qquad \text{(10)},$$

whilst Q is constant for a point moving with the velocity

$$\frac{dx}{dt}=-c\left(1+\frac{\eta}{h}\right)^{\frac{1}{2}}+u \qquad \text{(11)}.$$

Hence any given value of P travels forwards, and any given value of Q travels backwards, with the velocities given by (10) and (11) respectively. The values of P and Q are determined by those of η and u, and conversely.

As an example, let us suppose that the initial disturbance is confined to the space between $x=a$ and $x=b$, so that P and Q are initially zero for $x<a$ and $x>b$. The region within which P

differs from zero therefore advances, whilst that within which Q differs from zero recedes, so that after a time these regions separate, and leave between them a space within which $P=0$, $Q=0$, and the fluid is therefore at rest. The original disturbance has now been resolved into two progressive waves travelling in opposite directions.

In the advancing wave we have

$$Q=0, \quad P=u=2c\left\{\left(1+\frac{\eta}{h}\right)^{\frac{1}{2}}-1\right\} \qquad \text{..........(12)},$$

so that the elevation and the particle-velocity are connected by a definite relation (cf. Art. 168). The wave-velocity is given by (10) and (12), viz. it is

$$c\left\{3\left(1+\frac{\eta}{h}\right)^{\frac{1}{2}}-2\right\} \qquad \text{.....................(13)}.$$

To the first order of η/h, this is in agreement with Airy's result.

Similar conclusions can be drawn in regard to the receding wave*.

Since the wave-velocity increases with the elevation, it appears that in a progressive wave-system the slopes will become continually steeper in front, and more gradual behind, until at length a state of things is reached in which we are no longer justified in neglecting the vertical acceleration. As to what happens after this point we have at present no guide from theory; observation shews, however, that the crests tend ultimately to curl over and 'break.'

184. In the application of the equations (1) and (3) to tidal phenomena, it is most convenient to follow the method of successive approximation. As an example, we will take the case of a canal communicating at one end ($x=0$) with an open sea, where the elevation is given by

$$\eta = a\cos\sigma t \qquad \text{.....................(14)}.$$

For a first approximation we have

$$\frac{du}{dt}=-g\frac{d\eta}{dx}, \quad \frac{d\eta}{dt}=-h\frac{du}{dx} \qquad \text{.........................(i)},$$

* The above results can also be deduced from the equation (3) of Art. 170, to which Riemann's method can be readily adapted.

the solution of which, consistent with (14), is

$$\eta = a\cos\sigma\left(t-\frac{x}{c}\right),\qquad u=\frac{ga}{c}\cos\sigma\left(t-\frac{x}{c}\right) \qquad\text{(ii)}.$$

For a second approximation we substitute these values of η and u in (1) and (3), and obtain

$$\left.\begin{aligned}\frac{du}{dt}&=-g\frac{d\eta}{dx}-\frac{g^2\sigma a^2}{2c^3}\sin 2\sigma\left(t-\frac{x}{c}\right),\\ \frac{d\eta}{dt}&=-h\frac{du}{dx}-\frac{g\sigma a^2}{c^2}\sin 2\sigma\left(t-\frac{x}{c}\right)\end{aligned}\right\} \qquad\text{(iii)}.$$

Integrating these by the usual methods, we find, as the solution consistent with (14),

$$\left.\begin{aligned}\eta&=a\cos\sigma\left(t-\frac{x}{c}\right)-\tfrac{3}{4}\frac{g\sigma a^2}{c^3}x\sin 2\sigma\left(t-\frac{x}{c}\right),\\ u&=\frac{ga}{c}\cos\sigma\left(t-\frac{x}{c}\right)-\tfrac{1}{8}\frac{g^2a^2}{c^3}\cos 2\sigma\left(t-\frac{x}{c}\right)\\ &\quad-\tfrac{3}{4}\frac{g^2\sigma a^2}{c^4}x\sin 2\sigma\left(t-\frac{x}{c}\right)\end{aligned}\right\} \qquad\text{(iv)}.$$

The figure shews, with, of course, exaggerated amplitude, the profile of the waves in a particular case, as determined by the first of these equations. It is to be noted that if we fix our attention on a particular point of the canal, the rise and fall of the water do not take place symmetrically, the fall occupying a longer time than the rise.

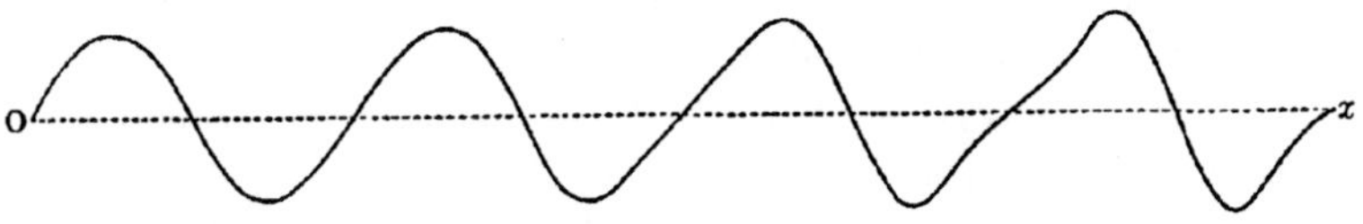

When analysed, as in (iv), into a series of simple-harmonic functions of the time, the expression for the elevation of the water at any particular place (x) consists of two terms, of which the second represents an 'over-tide,' or 'tide of the second order,' being proportional to a^2; its frequency is double that of the primary disturbance (14). If we were to continue the approximation we should obtain tides of higher orders, whose frequencies are 3, 4, ... times that of the primary.

If, in place of (14), the disturbance at the mouth of the canal were given by

$$\zeta = a\cos\sigma t + a'\cos(\sigma' t+\epsilon),$$

it is easily seen that in the second approximation we should obtain tides of periods $2\pi/(\sigma+\sigma')$ and $2\pi/(\sigma-\sigma')$; these are called 'compound tides.' They are closely analogous to the 'combination-tones' in Acoustics which were first investigated by von Helmholtz*.

* "Ueber Combinationstöne," *Berl. Monatsber.*, May 22, 1856, *Ges. Abh.*, t. i., p. 256, and "Theorie der Luftschwingungen in Röhren mit offenen Enden," *Crelle*, t. lvii., p. 14 (1859), *Ges. Abh.*, t. i., p. 318.

The occurrence of the factor x outside trigonometrical terms in (iv) shews that there is a limit beyond which the approximation breaks down. The condition for the success of the approximation is evidently that $g\sigma ax/c^3$ should be small. Putting $c^2 = gh$, $\lambda = 2\pi c/\sigma$, this fraction becomes equal to $2\pi(a/h).(x/\lambda)$. Hence however small the ratio of the original elevation (a) to the depth, the fraction ceases to be small when x is a sufficient multiple of the wave-length (λ).

It is to be noticed that the limit here indicated is already being overstepped in the right-hand portions of the figure above given; and that the peculiar features which are beginning to shew themselves on the rear slope are an indication rather of the imperfections of the analysis than of any actual property of the waves. If we were to trace the curve further, we should find a secondary maximum and minimum of elevation developing themselves on the rear slope. In this way Airy attempted to explain the phenomenon of a double high-water which is observed in some rivers; but, for the reason given, the argument cannot be sustained*.

The same difficulty does not necessarily present itself in the case of a canal closed by a fixed barrier at a distance from the mouth, or, again, in the case of the forced waves due to a periodic horizontal force in a canal closed at both ends (Art. 176). Enough has, however, been given to shew the general character of the results to be expected in such cases. For further details we must refer to Airy's treatise†.

Propagation in Two Dimensions.

185. Let us suppose, in the first instance, that we have a plane sheet of water of uniform depth h. If the vertical acceleration be neglected, the horizontal motion will as before be the same for all particles in the same vertical line. The axes of x, y being horizontal, let u, v be the component horizontal velocities at the point (x, y), and let ζ be the corresponding elevation of the free surface above the undisturbed level. The equation of continuity may be obtained by calculating the flux of matter into the columnar space which stands on the elementary rectangle $\delta x \delta y$; viz. we have, neglecting terms of the second order,

$$\frac{d}{dx}(uh\delta y)\,\delta x + \frac{d}{dy}(vh\delta x)\,\delta y = -\frac{d}{dt}\{(\zeta + h)\,\delta x\delta y\},$$

whence
$$\frac{d\zeta}{dt} = -h\left(\frac{du}{dx} + \frac{dv}{dy}\right) \quad\ldots\ldots\ldots\ldots\ldots\ldots\ldots (1).$$

* Cf. McCowan, *l. c. ante* p. 277.

† "Tides and Waves," Arts. 198, ...and 308. See also G. H. Darwin, "Tides," *Encyc. Britann.* (9th ed.) t. xxiii., pp. 362, 363 (1888).

The dynamical equations are, in the absence of disturbing forces,

$$\rho \frac{du}{dt} = -\frac{dp}{dx}, \qquad \rho \frac{dv}{dt} = -\frac{dp}{dy},$$

where we may write

$$p - p_0 = g\rho (z_0 + \zeta - z),$$

if z_0 denote the ordinate of the free surface in the undisturbed state, and so obtain

$$\frac{du}{dt} = -g \frac{d\zeta}{dx}, \qquad \frac{dv}{dt} = -g \frac{d\zeta}{dy} \quad \text{..............(2).}$$

If we eliminate u and v, we find

$$\frac{d^2\zeta}{dt^2} = c^2 \left(\frac{d^2\zeta}{dx^2} + \frac{d^2\zeta}{dy^2} \right) \quad \text{..................... (3),}$$

where $c^2 = gh$ as before.

In the application to simple-harmonic motion, the equations are shortened if we assume a 'complex' time-factor $e^{i(\sigma t + \epsilon)}$, and reject, in the end, the imaginary parts of our expressions. This is of course legitimate, so long as we have to deal solely with *linear* equations. We have then, from (2),

$$u = \frac{ig}{\sigma} \frac{d\zeta}{dx}, \qquad v = \frac{ig}{\sigma} \frac{d\zeta}{dy} \quad \text{.................. (4),}$$

whilst (3) becomes

$$\frac{d^2\zeta}{dx^2} + \frac{d^2\zeta}{dy^2} + k^2\zeta = 0 \quad \text{..................... (5),}$$

where

$$k^2 = \sigma^2/c^2 \quad \text{........................... (6).}$$

The condition to be satisfied at a vertical bounding wall is obtained at once from (4), viz. it is

$$\frac{d\zeta}{dn} = 0 \quad \text{.............................(7),}$$

if δn denote an element of the normal to the boundary.

When the fluid is subject to small disturbing forces whose variation within the limits of the depth may be neglected, the equations (2) are replaced by

$$\frac{du}{dt} = -g \frac{d\zeta}{dx} - \frac{d\Omega}{dx}, \qquad \frac{dv}{dt} = -g \frac{d\zeta}{dy} - \frac{d\Omega}{dy} \quad \text{.........(8),}$$

where Ω is the potential of these forces.

If we put $$\bar{\zeta} = -\Omega/g \qquad (9),$$

so that $\bar{\zeta}$ denotes the equilibrium-elevation corresponding to the potential Ω, these may be written

$$\frac{du}{dt} = -g\frac{d}{dx}(\zeta - \bar{\zeta}), \quad \frac{dv}{dt} = -g\frac{d}{dy}(\zeta - \bar{\zeta}) \qquad (10).$$

In the case of simple-harmonic motion, these take the forms

$$u = \frac{ig}{\sigma}\frac{d}{dx}(\zeta - \bar{\zeta}), \quad v = \frac{ig}{\sigma}\frac{d}{dy}(\zeta - \bar{\zeta}) \qquad (11),$$

whence, substituting in the equation of continuity (1), we obtain

$$(\nabla_1^2 + k^2)\,\zeta = \nabla_1^2\bar{\zeta} \qquad (12),$$

if $$\nabla_1^2 = d^2/dx^2 + d^2/dy^2, \qquad (13),$$

and $k^2 = \sigma^2/gh$, as before. The condition to be satisfied at a vertical boundary is now

$$\frac{d}{dn}(\zeta - \bar{\zeta}) = 0 \qquad (14).$$

186. The equation (3) of Art. 185 is identical in form with that which presents itself in the theory of the vibrations of a uniformly stretched membrane. A still closer analogy, when regard is had to the boundary conditions, is furnished by the theory of cylindrical waves of sound*. Indeed many of the results obtained in this latter theory can be at once transferred to our present subject.

Thus, to find the free oscillations of a sheet of water bounded by vertical walls, we require a solution of

$$(\nabla_1^2 + k^2)\,\zeta = 0 \qquad (1),$$

subject to the boundary condition

$$d\zeta/dn = 0 \qquad (2).$$

Just as in Art. 175 it will be found that such a solution is possible only for certain values of k, and thus the periods ($2\pi/kc$) of the several normal modes are determined.

* Lord Rayleigh, *Theory of Sound*, Art. 339.

Thus, in the case of a *rectangular* boundary, if we take the origin at one corner, and the axes of x, y along two of the sides, the boundary conditions are that $d\zeta/dx = 0$ for $x = 0$ and $x = a$, and $d\zeta/dy = 0$ for $y = 0$ and $y = b$, where a, b are the lengths of the edges parallel to x, y respectively. The general value of ζ subject to these conditions is given by the double Fourier's series

$$\zeta = \Sigma\Sigma A_{m,n} \cos\frac{m\pi x}{a} \cos\frac{n\pi y}{b} \quad\text{.................(3)},$$

where the summations include all integral values of m, n from 0 to ∞. Substituting in (1) we find

$$k^2 = \pi^2 (m^2/a^2 + n^2/b^2) \quad\text{.....................(4)}.$$

If $a > b$, the component oscillation of longest period is got by making $m = 1$, $n = 0$, whence $ka = \pi$. The motion is then everywhere parallel to the longer side of the rectangle. Cf. Art. 175.

187. In the case of a *circular* sheet of water, it is convenient to take the origin at the centre, and to transform to polar coordinates, writing

$$x = r\cos\theta, \quad y = r\sin\theta.$$

The equation (1) of the preceding Art. becomes

$$\frac{d^2\zeta}{dr^2} + \frac{1}{r}\frac{d\zeta}{dr} + \frac{1}{r^2}\frac{d^2\zeta}{d\theta^2} + k^2\zeta = 0 \quad\text{..................(1)}.$$

This might of course have been established independently.

As regards its dependance on θ, the value of ζ may, by Fourier's Theorem, be supposed expanded in a series of cosines and sines of multiples of θ; we thus obtain a series of terms of the form

$$f(r) \begin{matrix}\cos\\ \sin\end{matrix}\Big\} s\theta \quad\text{........................(2)}.$$

It is found on substitution in (1) that each of these terms must satisfy the equation independently, and that

$$f''(r) + \frac{1}{r}f'(r) + \left(k^2 - \frac{s^2}{r^2}\right) f(r) = 0 \quad\text{...........(3)}.$$

This is the differential equation of Bessel's Functions*. Its

* Forsyth, *Differential Equations*, Art. 100.

complete primitive consists, of course, of the sum of two definite functions of r, each multiplied by an arbitrary constant, but in the present problem we are restricted to a solution which shall be finite at the origin. This is easily obtained in the form of an ascending series; thus, in the ordinary notation of Bessel's Functions, we have

$$f(r) = AJ_s(kr),$$

where, on the usual convention as to the numerical factor,

$$J_s(z) = \frac{z^s}{2^s . s!}\left\{1 - \frac{z^2}{2(2s+2)} + \frac{z^4}{2.4(2s+2)(2s+4)} - \ldots\right\} \quad \ldots(4).$$

Hence the various normal modes are given by

$$\zeta = A_s J_s(kr) \begin{matrix}\cos\\ \sin\end{matrix}\Big\} s\theta . \cos(\sigma t + \epsilon) \quad \ldots\ldots\ldots\ldots\ldots(5),$$

where s may have any of the values 0, 1, 2, 3,..., and A_s is an arbitrary constant. The admissible values of k are determined by the condition that $d\zeta/dr = 0$ for $r = a$, or

$$J_s'(ka) = 0 \quad \ldots\ldots\ldots\ldots\ldots\ldots\ldots\ldots\ldots(6).$$

The corresponding 'speeds' (σ) of the oscillations are then given by $\sigma = k(gh)^{\frac{1}{2}}$.

The analytical theory of Bessel's Functions is treated more or less fully in various works to which reference is made below*. It appears that for large values of z we may put

$$J_s(z) = \left(\frac{2}{\pi z}\right)^{\frac{1}{2}}\left\{P\cos\left(z - \frac{2s+1}{4}\pi\right) + Q\sin\left(z - \frac{2s+1}{4}\pi\right)\right\} \quad \ldots\ldots\ldots(i),$$

where

$$\left.\begin{aligned} P &= 1 - \frac{(1^2-4s^2)(3^2-4s^2)}{1.2(8z)^2} + \ldots \\ Q &= \frac{1^2-4s^2}{1.8z} - \frac{(1^2-4s^2)(3^2-4s^2)(5^2-4s^2)}{1.2.3(8z)^3} + \ldots \end{aligned}\right\} \quad \ldots\ldots\ldots\ldots\ldots(ii).$$

The series P, Q are of the kind known as 'semi-convergent,' *i.e.* although for large values of z the successive terms may diminish for a time, they ultimately increase again, but if we stop at a small term we get an approximately correct result.

* Lommel, *Studien ueber die Bessel'schen Functionen*, Leipzig, 1868; Heine, *Kugelfunctionen*, Arts. 42,..., 57,...; Todhunter, *Functions of Laplace, Lamé, and Bessel*; Byerly, *On Fourier's Series, and Spherical, Cylindrical, and Ellipsoidal Harmonics*, Boston, U.S.A., 1893; see also Forsyth, *Differential Equations*, c. v. An ample account of the matter, from the physical point of view, will be found in Lord Rayleigh's *Theory of Sound*, cc. ix., xviii., with many interesting applications.

Numerical tables of the functions have been calculated by Bessel, and Hansen, and (more recently) by Meissel (*Berl. Abh.*, 1888). Hansen's tables are reproduced by Lommel, and (partially) by Lord Rayleigh and Byerly.

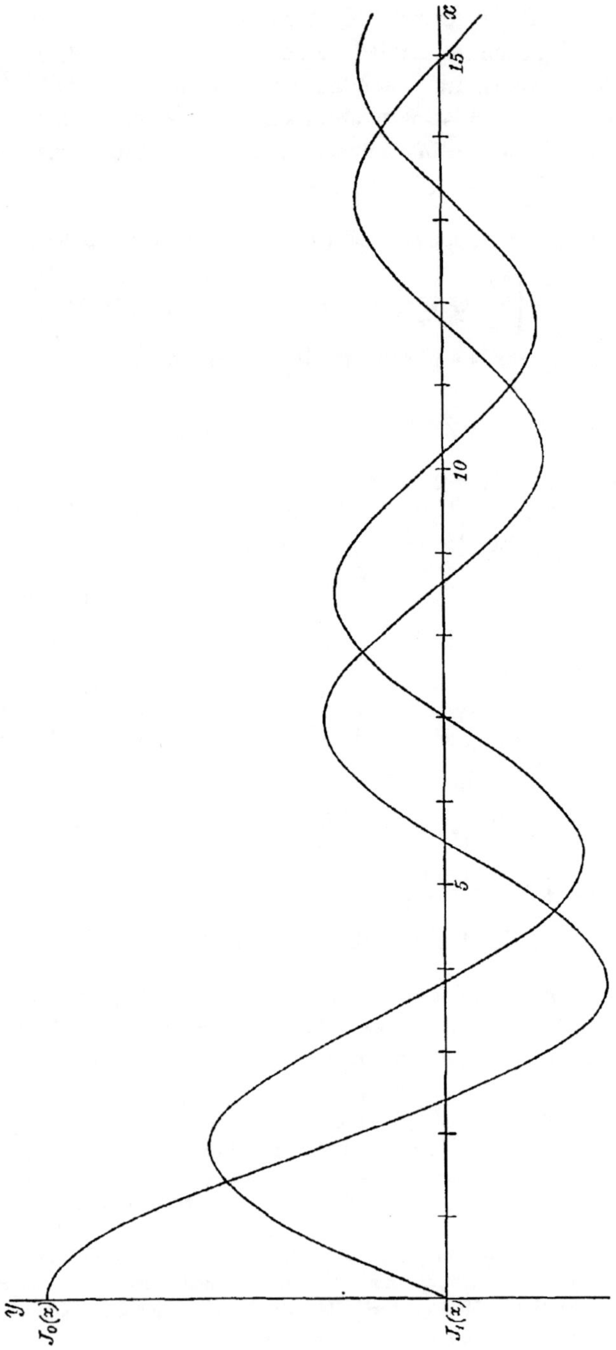
x
15
10
5
y
$J_0(x)$
$J_1(x)$

It appears from (i) that $J_s(z)$ belongs to the class of 'fluctuating functions,' viz. as z increases the value of the function oscillates on both sides of zero with a continually diminishing amplitude. The period of the oscillations is ultimately 2π.

The general march of the functions is illustrated to some extent by the curves $y=J_0(x)$, $y=J_1(x)$, which are figured on the opposite page. For the sake of clearness, the scale of the ordinates has been taken five times as great as that of the abscissæ.

In the case $s=0$, the motion is symmetrical about the origin, so that the waves have annular ridges and furrows. The lowest roots of

$$J_0'(ka)=0 \quad\quad (7)$$

are given by

$$ka/\pi = 1{\cdot}2197,\quad 2{\cdot}2330,\quad 3{\cdot}2383,\ \ldots \quad\quad (8)^*,$$

these values tending ultimately to the form $ka/\pi = m + \frac{1}{4}$, where m is integral. In the mth mode of the symmetrical class there are m nodal circles whose radii are given by $\zeta=0$ or

$$J_0(kr)=0 \quad\quad (9).$$

The roots of this are

$$kr/\pi = {\cdot}7655,\quad 1{\cdot}7571,\quad 2{\cdot}7546, \ldots \quad\quad (10)\dagger.$$

For example, in the first symmetrical mode there is one nodal circle $r={\cdot}628a$. The form of the section of the free surface by a plane through the axis of z, in any of these modes, will be understood from the drawing of the curve $y=J_0(x)$.

When $s>0$ there are s equidistant nodal diameters, in addition to the nodal circles

$$J_s(kr)=0 \quad\quad (11).$$

It is to be noticed that, owing to the equality of the frequencies of the two modes represented by (5), the normal modes are now to a certain extent indeterminate; viz. in place of $\cos s\theta$ or $\sin s\theta$ we might substitute $\cos s(\theta-\alpha_s)$, where α_s is arbitrary. The nodal diameters are then given by

$$\theta - \alpha_s = \frac{2m+1}{2s}\pi \quad\quad (12),$$

* Stokes, "On the Numerical Calculation of a class of Definite Integrals and Infinite Series," *Camb. Trans.* t. ix. (1850), *Math. and Phys. Papers*, t. ii. p. 355.

It is to be noticed that ka/π is equal to τ_0/τ, where τ is the actual period, and τ_0 is the time a progressive wave would take to travel with the velocity $(gh)^{\frac{1}{2}}$ over a space equal to the diameter $2a$.

† Stokes, *l. c.*

where $m = 0, 1, 2, \ldots, s-1$. The indeterminateness disappears, and the frequencies become unequal, if the boundary deviate, however slightly, from the circular form.

In the case of the circular boundary, we obtain by superposition of two fundamental modes of the same period, in different phases, a solution

$$\zeta = C_s J_s(kr) \cdot \cos(\sigma t \mp s\theta + \epsilon) \quad \ldots\ldots\ldots\ldots\ldots(13).$$

This represents a system of waves travelling unchanged round the origin with an angular velocity σ/s in the positive or negative direction of θ. The motion of the individual particles is easily seen from Art. 185 (4) to be elliptic-harmonic, one principal axis of each elliptic orbit being along the radius vector. All this is in accordance with the general theory referred to in Art. 165.

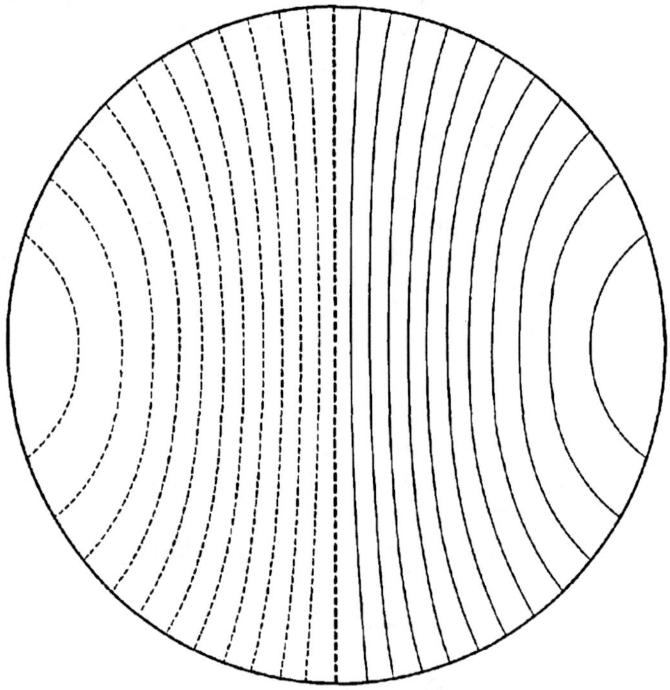

The most interesting modes of the unsymmetrical class are those corresponding to $s = 1$, *e.g.*

$$\zeta = A J_1(kr) \cos\theta \cdot \cos(\sigma t + \epsilon) \quad \ldots\ldots\ldots\ldots\ldots(14),$$

where k is determined by

$$J_1'(ka) = 0 \qquad \text{.............................(15).}$$

The roots of this are

$$ka/\pi = \cdot586, \quad 1\cdot697, \quad 2\cdot717, \ldots\ldots\ldots\ldots\ldots(16)^*.$$

We have now one nodal diameter ($\theta = \frac{1}{2}\pi$), whose position is, however, indeterminate, since the origin of θ is arbitrary. In the corresponding modes for an elliptic boundary, the nodal diameter would be fixed, viz. it would coincide with either the major or the minor axis, and the frequencies would be unequal.

The accompanying diagrams shew the contour-lines of the free surface in the first two modes of the present species. These lines meet the boundary at right angles, in conformity with the general boundary condition (Art. 186 (2)). The simple-harmonic vibrations

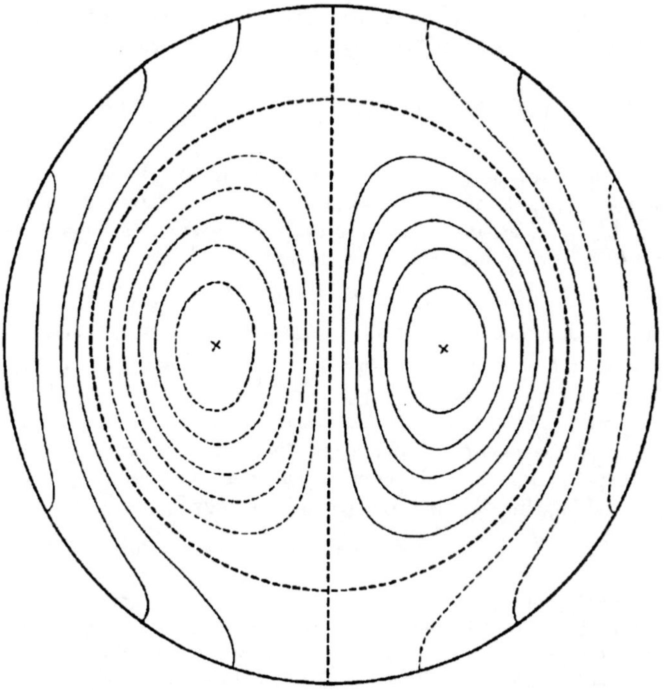

of the individual particles take place in straight lines perpendicular to the contour-lines, by Art. 185 (4). The form of the

* See Lord Rayleigh's treatise, Art. 339.

sections of the free surface by planes through the axis of z is given by the curve $y = J_1(x)$ on p. 306.

The first of the two modes here figured has the longest period of all the normal types. In it, the water sways from side to side, much as in the slowest mode of a canal closed at both ends (Art. 175). In the second mode there is a nodal circle, whose radius is given by the lowest root of $J_1(kr) = 0$; this makes $r = \cdot 719a$*.

A comparison of the preceding investigation with the general theory of small oscillations referred to in Art. 165 leads to several important properties of Bessel's Functions.

In the first place, since the total mass of water is unaltered, we must have

$$\int_0^{2\pi}\int_0^a \zeta r d\theta dr = 0 \quad\text{.............................. (iii),}$$

where ζ has any one of the forms given by (5). For $s>0$ this is satisfied in virtue of the trigonometrical factor $\cos s\theta$ or $\sin s\theta$; in the symmetrical case it gives

$$\int_0^a J_0(kr)\, rdr = 0 \quad\text{.................................(iv).}$$

Again, since the most general free motion of the system can be obtained by superposition of the normal modes, each with an arbitrary amplitude and epoch, it follows that any value whatever of ζ, which is subject to the condition (iii), can be expanded in a series of the form

$$\zeta = \Sigma\Sigma\,(A_s \cos s\theta + B_s \sin s\theta)\, J_s(kr) \quad\text{..................... (v),}$$

where the summations embrace all integral values of s (including 0) and, for each value of s, all the roots k of (6). If the coefficients A_s, B_s be regarded as functions of t, the equation (v) may be regarded as giving the value of the surface-elevation at any instant. The quantities A_s, B_s are then the normal coordinates of the present system (Art. 165); and in terms of them the formulæ for the kinetic and potential energies must reduce to sums of squares. Taking, for example, the potential energy

$$V = \tfrac{1}{2} g\rho \iint \zeta^2 dx dy \quad\text{.................................(vi),}$$

* The oscillations of a liquid in a circular basin of any uniform depth were discussed by Poisson, "Sur les petites oscillations de l'eau contenue dans un cylindre," *Ann. de Gergonne*, t. xix. p. 225 (1828–9); the theory of Bessel's Functions had not at that date been worked out, and the results were consequently not interpreted. The full solution of the problem, with numerical details, was given independently by Lord Rayleigh, *Phil. Mag.*, April, 1876.

The investigation in the text is limited, of course, to the case of a depth small in comparison with the radius a. Poisson's and Lord Rayleigh's solution for the case of finite depth will be noticed in the proper place in Chap. IX.

this requires that $$\int_0^{2\pi}\int_0^a w_1 w_2 r d\theta dr = 0 \qquad\text{(vii)},$$

where w_1, w_2 are any two terms of the expansion (v). If w_1, w_2 involve cosines or sines of different multiples of θ, this is verified at once by integrations with respect to θ; but if we take

$$w_1 \propto J_s(k_1 r)\cos s\theta, \quad w_2 \propto J_s(k_2 r)\cos s\theta,$$

where k_1, k_2 are any two distinct roots of (6), we get

$$\int_0^a J_s(k_1 r) \,.\, J_s(k_2 r)\, r dr = 0 \qquad\text{(viii)}.$$

The general results of which (iv) and (viii) are particular cases, are

$$\int_0^a J_0(kr)\, r dr = -\frac{a}{k} J_0'(ka) \qquad\text{(ix)},$$

and

$$\int_0^a J_s(k_1 r) J_s(k_2 r)\, r dr = \frac{1}{k_1^2 - k_2^2}\{k_2 a J_s'(k_2 a) J_s(k_1 a) - k_1 a J_s'(k_1 a) J_s(k_2 a)\} \qquad\text{(x)}.$$

In the case of $k_1 = k_2$ the latter expression becomes indeterminate; the evaluation in the usual manner gives

$$\int_0^a \{J_s(ka)\}^2 r dr = \frac{1}{2k^2}[k^2 a^2 \{J_s'(ka)\}^2 + (k^2 a^2 - s^2)\{J_s(ka)\}^2] \qquad\text{(xi)}.$$

For the analytical proofs of these formulæ we must refer to the treatises cited on p. 305.

The small oscillations of an *annular* sheet of water bounded by concentric circles are easily treated, theoretically, with the help of Bessel's Functions 'of the second kind.' The only case of any special interest, however, is when the two radii are nearly equal; we then have practically a re-entrant canal, and the solution follows more simply from Art. 178.

The analysis can also be applied to the case of a *circular sector* of any angle*, or to a sheet of water bounded by two concentric circular arcs and two radii.

188. As an example of *forced* vibrations, let us suppose that the disturbing forces are such that the equilibrium elevation would be

$$\bar{\zeta} = C\left(\frac{r}{a}\right)^s \cos s\theta \,.\, \cos(\sigma t + \epsilon) \qquad\text{(16)}.$$

* See Lord Rayleigh, *Theory of Sound*, Art. 339.

This makes $\nabla_1^2\bar{\zeta}=0$, so that the equation (12) of Art. 185 reduces to the form (1), above, and the solution is

$$\zeta = AJ_s(kr)\cos s\theta \,.\, \cos(\sigma t+\epsilon)\ldots\ldots\ldots\ldots\ldots(17),$$

where A is an arbitrary constant. The boundary-condition (Art. 185 (14)), gives

$$AkaJ_s'(ka) = sC,$$

whence
$$\zeta = C\frac{sJ_s(kr)}{kaJ_s'(ka)}\cos s\theta \,.\, \cos(\sigma t+\epsilon)\ldots\ldots\ldots\ldots(18).$$

The case $s=1$ is interesting as corresponding to a *uniform* horizontal force; and the result may be compared with that of Art. 176.

From the case $s = 2$ we could obtain a rough representation of the semi-diurnal tide in a polar basin bounded by a small circle of latitude, except that the rotation of the earth is not as yet taken into account.

We notice that the expression for the amplitude of oscillation becomes infinite when $J_s'(ka)=0$. This is in accordance with a general principle, of which we have already had several examples; the period of the disturbing force being now equal to that of one of the free modes investigated in the preceding Art.

189. When the sheet of water is of variable depth, the investigation at the beginning of Art. 185 gives, as the equation of continuity,

$$\frac{d\zeta}{dt} = -\frac{d(hu)}{dx} - \frac{d(hv)}{dy}\ldots\ldots\ldots\ldots\ldots\ldots\ldots(1).$$

The dynamical equations (Art. 185 (2)) are of course unaltered. Hence, eliminating ζ, we find, for the free oscillations,

$$\frac{d^2\zeta}{dt^2} = g\left\{\frac{d}{dx}\left(h\frac{d\zeta}{dx}\right) + \frac{d}{dy}\left(h\frac{d\zeta}{dy}\right)\right\}\ldots\ldots\ldots\ldots\ldots(2).$$

If the time-factor be $e^{i(\sigma t+\epsilon)}$, we obtain

$$\frac{d}{dx}\left(h\frac{d\zeta}{dx}\right) + \frac{d}{dy}\left(h\frac{d\zeta}{dy}\right) + \frac{\sigma^2}{g}\zeta = 0\ldots\ldots\ldots\ldots\ldots(3).$$

When h is a function of r, the distance from the origin, only, this may be written

$$h\nabla_1^2\zeta + \frac{dh}{dr}\frac{d\zeta}{dr} + \frac{\sigma^2}{g}\zeta = 0\ldots\ldots\ldots\ldots\ldots\ldots(4).$$

As a simple example we may take the case of a circular basin which shelves gradually from the centre to the edge, according to the law

$$h = h_0 \left(1 - \frac{r^2}{a^2}\right) \quad \text{.......................................(i).}$$

Introducing polar coordinates, and assuming that ζ varies as $\cos s\theta$ or $\sin s\theta$, the equation (4) takes the form

$$\left(1 - \frac{r^2}{a^2}\right)\left(\frac{d^2\zeta}{dr^2} + \frac{1}{r}\frac{d\zeta}{dr} - \frac{s^2}{r^2}\zeta\right) - \frac{2}{a^2} r \frac{d\zeta}{dr} + \frac{\sigma^2}{gh_0}\zeta = 0 \quad \text{............(ii).}$$

This can be integrated by series. Thus, assuming

$$\zeta = \Sigma A_m \left(\frac{r}{a}\right)^m \quad \text{..................................(iii),}$$

where the trigonometrical factors are omitted, for shortness, the relation between consecutive coefficients is found to be

$$(m^2 - s^2) A_m = \left\{m(m-2) - s^2 - \frac{\sigma^2 a^2}{gh_0}\right\} A_{m-2},$$

or, if we write

$$\frac{\sigma^2 a^2}{gh_0} = n(n-2) - s^2 \quad \text{..............................(iv),}$$

where n is not as yet assumed to be integral,

$$(m^2 - s^2) A_m = (m-n)(m+n-2) A_{m-2} \quad \text{.....................(v).}$$

The equation is therefore satisfied by a series of the form (iii), beginning with the term $A_s (r/a)^s$, the succeeding coefficients being determined by putting $m = s+2,\ s+4, \ldots$ in (v). We thus find

$$\zeta = A_s \left(\frac{r}{a}\right)^s \left\{1 - \frac{(n-s-2)(n+s)}{2(2s+2)} \frac{r^2}{a^2} + \frac{(n-s-4)(n-s-2)(n+s)(n+s+2)}{2 \cdot 4 (2s+2)(2s+4)} \frac{r^4}{a^4} - \ldots\right\} \quad \text{......(vi),}$$

or in the usual notation of hypergeometric series

$$\zeta = A_s \frac{r^s}{a^s} \cdot F\left(\alpha, \beta, \gamma, \frac{r^2}{a^2}\right) \quad \text{........................(vii),}$$

where

$$\alpha = \tfrac{1}{2}n + \tfrac{1}{2}s, \quad \beta = 1 + \tfrac{1}{2}s - \tfrac{1}{2}n, \quad \gamma = s+1.$$

Since these make $\gamma - \alpha - \beta = 0$, the series is not convergent for $r = a$, unless it terminate. This can only happen when n is integral, of the form $s + 2j$. The corresponding values of σ are then given by (iv).

In the symmetrical modes ($s = 0$) we have

$$\zeta = A_0 \left\{1 - \frac{j(j-1)}{1^2} \frac{r^2}{a^2} + \frac{(j+1)j(j-1)(j-2)}{1^2 \cdot 2^2} \frac{r^4}{a^4} - \ldots\right\} \quad \text{......(viii),}$$

where j may be any integer greater than unity. It may be shewn that this expression vanishes for $j-1$ values of r between 0 and a, indicating the existence of $j-1$ nodal circles. The value of σ is given by

$$\sigma^2 = 4j(j-1)\frac{gh_0}{a^2} \quad \text{..............................(ix).}$$

Thus the gravest symmetrical mode ($j=2$) has a nodal circle of radius ·707a; and its frequency is determined by $\sigma^2 = 8gh_0/a^2$.

Of the unsymmetrical modes, the slowest, for any given value of s, is that for which $n=s+2$, in which case we have

$$\zeta = A_s \frac{r^s}{a^s} \cos s\theta \cos(\sigma t + \epsilon),$$

the value of σ being given by

$$\sigma^2 = 2s \,.\, gh_0/a^2 \quad\text{.................................(x).}$$

The slowest mode of all is that for which $s=1$, $n=3$; the free surface is then always *plane*. It is found on comparison with Art. 187 (16) that the frequency is ·768 of that of the corresponding mode in a circular basin of *uniform* depth h_0, and of the same radius.

As in Art. 188 we could at once write down the formula for the tidal motion produced by a uniform horizontal periodic force; or, more generally, for the case when the disturbing potential is of the type

$$\Omega \propto r^s \cos s\theta \cos(\sigma t + \epsilon).$$

190. We proceed to consider the case of a spherical sheet, or ocean, of water, covering a solid globe. We will suppose for the present that the globe does not rotate, and we will also in the first instance neglect the mutual attraction of the particles of the water. The mathematical conditions of the question are then exactly the same as in the acoustical problem of the vibrations of spherical layers of air*.

Let a be the radius of the globe, h the depth of the fluid; we assume that h is small compared with a, but not (as yet) that it is uniform. The position of any point on the sheet being specified by the angular coordinates θ, ω, let u be the component velocity of the fluid at this point along the meridian, in the direction of θ increasing, and v the component along the parallel of latitude, in the direction of ω increasing. Also let ζ denote the elevation of the free surface above the undisturbed level. The horizontal motion being assumed, for the reasons explained in Art. 169, to be the same at all points in a vertical line, the condition of continuity is

$$\frac{d}{d\theta}(uha\sin\theta\delta\omega)\,\delta\theta + \frac{d}{d\omega}(vha\delta\theta)\,\delta\omega = -a\sin\theta\delta\omega \,.\, a\delta\theta \,.\, \frac{d\zeta}{dt},$$

where the left-hand side measures the flux out of the columnar

* Discussed in Lord Rayleigh's *Theory of Sound*, c. XVIII.

space standing on the element of area $a \sin\theta\delta\omega \,.\, a\delta\theta$, whilst the right-hand member expresses the rate of diminution of the volume of the contained fluid, owing to fall of the surface. Hence

$$\frac{d\zeta}{dt} = -\frac{1}{a\sin\theta}\left\{\frac{d(hu\sin\theta)}{d\theta} + \frac{d(hv)}{d\omega}\right\} \quad \text{..........(1).}$$

If we neglect terms of the second order in u, v, the dynamical equations are, on the same principles as in Arts. 166, 185,

$$\frac{du}{dt} = -g\frac{d\zeta}{ad\theta} - \frac{d\Omega}{ad\theta}, \qquad \frac{dv}{dt} = -g\frac{d\zeta}{a\sin\theta d\omega} - \frac{d\Omega}{a\sin\theta d\omega} \quad \text{...(2),}$$

where Ω denotes the potential of the extraneous forces.

If we put

$$\bar{\zeta} = -\Omega/g \quad \text{..........................(3),}$$

these may be written

$$\frac{du}{dt} = -\frac{g}{a}\frac{d}{d\theta}(\zeta - \bar{\zeta}), \qquad \frac{dv}{dt} = -\frac{g}{a\sin\theta}\frac{d}{d\omega}(\zeta - \bar{\zeta}) \quad \text{...... (4).}$$

Between (1) and (4) we can eliminate u, v, and so obtain an equation in ζ only.

In the case of simple-harmonic motion, the time-factor being $e^{i(\sigma t + \epsilon)}$, the equations take the forms

$$\zeta = \frac{i}{\sigma a\sin\theta}\left\{\frac{d(hu\sin\theta)}{d\theta} + \frac{d(hv)}{d\omega}\right\} \quad \text{........... (5),}$$

$$u = i\frac{g}{\sigma a}\frac{d}{d\theta}(\zeta - \bar{\zeta}), \quad v = i\frac{g}{\sigma a\sin\theta}\frac{d}{d\omega}(\zeta - \bar{\zeta}) \quad \text{...... (6).}$$

191. We will now consider more particularly the case of *uniform* depth. To find the free oscillations we put $\bar{\zeta} = 0$; the equations (5) and (6) of the preceding Art. then lead to

$$\frac{1}{\sin\theta}\frac{d}{d\theta}\left(\sin\theta\frac{d\zeta}{d\theta}\right) + \frac{1}{\sin^2\theta}\frac{d^2\zeta}{d\omega^2} + \frac{\sigma^2 a^2}{gh}\zeta = 0 \quad \text{...... (1).}$$

This is identical in form with the general equation of spherical surface-harmonics (Art. 84 (2)). Hence, if we put

$$\sigma^2 a^2/gh = n(n+1) \quad \text{......................(2),}$$

a solution of (1) will be

$$\zeta = S_n \quad \text{............................(3),}$$

where S_n is the general surface-harmonic of order n.

It was pointed out in Art. 87 that S_n will not be finite over the whole sphere unless n be integral. Hence, for an ocean covering the whole globe, the form of the free surface at any instant is, in any fundamental mode, that of a 'harmonic spheroid'

$$r = a + h + S_n \cos(\sigma t + \epsilon) \quad \text{..................(4)},$$

and the speed of the oscillation is given by

$$\sigma = \{n(n+1)\}^{\frac{1}{2}} \cdot (gh)^{\frac{1}{2}}/a \quad \text{.....................(5)},$$

the value of n being integral.

The characters of the various normal modes are best gathered from a study of the nodal lines ($S_n = 0$) of the free surface. Thus, it is shewn in treatises on Spherical Harmonics* that the zonal harmonic $P_n(\mu)$ vanishes for n real and distinct values of μ lying between ± 1, so that in this case we have n nodal circles of latitude. When n is odd one of these coincides with the equator. In the case of the tesseral harmonic

$$(1-\mu^2)^{\frac{1}{2}s} \frac{d^s P_n(\mu)}{d\mu^s} \begin{matrix}\cos\\ \sin\end{matrix}\Big\} s\omega,$$

the second factor vanishes for $n-s$ values of μ, and the trigonometrical factor for $2s$ equidistant values of ω. The nodal lines therefore consist of $n-s$ parallels of latitude and $2s$ meridians. Similarly the sectorial harmonic

$$(1-\mu^2)^{\frac{1}{2}n} \begin{matrix}\cos\\ \sin\end{matrix}\Big\} n\omega$$

has as nodal lines $2n$ meridians.

These are, however, merely special cases, for since there are $2n+1$ independent surface-harmonics of any integral order n, and since the frequency, determined by (5), is the same for each of these, there is a corresponding degree of indeterminateness in the normal modes, and in the configuration of the nodal lines†.

We can also, by superposition, build up various types of progressive waves; *e.g.* taking a sectorial harmonic we get a solution in which

$$\zeta \propto (1-\mu^2)^{\frac{1}{2}n} \cos(n\omega - \sigma t + \epsilon) \quad \text{..............(6)};$$

this gives a series of meridional ridges and furrows travelling

* For references, see p. 117.

† Some interesting varieties are figured in the plates to Maxwell's *Electricity and Magnetism*, t. i.

round the globe, the velocity of propagation, as measured at the equator, being

$$\sigma a/n = \left(\frac{n+1}{n}\right)^{\frac{1}{2}} . (gh)^{\frac{1}{2}} \quad \ldots\ldots\ldots\ldots\ldots\ldots (7).$$

It is easily verified, on examination, that the orbits of the particles are now ellipses having their principal axes in the directions of the meridians and parallels, respectively. At the equator these ellipses reduce to straight lines.

In the case $n = 1$, the harmonic is always of the zonal type. The harmonic spheroid (4) is then, to our order of approximation, a sphere excentric to the globe. It is important to remark, however, that this case is, strictly speaking, not included in our dynamical investigation, unless we imagine a constraint applied to the globe to keep it at rest; for the deformation in question of the free surface would involve a displacement of the centre of mass of the ocean, and a consequent reaction on the globe. A corrected theory for the case where the globe is free could easily be investigated, but the matter is hardly important, first because in such a case as that of the Earth the inertia of the solid globe is so enormous compared with that of the ocean, and secondly because disturbing forces which can give rise to a deformation of the type in question do not as a rule present themselves in nature. It appears, for example, that the first term in the expression for the tide-generating potential of the sun or moon is a spherical harmonic of the *second* order (see Appendix).

When $n = 2$, the free surface at any instant is approximately ellipsoidal. The corresponding period, as found from (5), is then ·816 of that belonging to the analogous mode in an equatorial canal (Art. 178).

For large values of n the distance from one nodal line to another is small compared with the radius of the globe, and the oscillations then take place much as on a plane sheet of water. For example, the velocity, at the equator, of the sectorial waves represented by (6) tends with increasing n to the value $(gh)^{\frac{1}{2}}$, in agreement with Art. 167.

From a comparison of the foregoing investigation with the general theory of Art. 165 we are led to infer, on physical grounds alone, the possibility of the expansion of any arbitrary value of ζ in a series of surface harmonics, thus

$$\zeta = \sum_0^\infty S_n,$$

the coefficients being the normal coordinates of the system. Again, since the products of these coefficients must disappear from the expressions for the kinetic and potential energies, we are led to the 'conjugate' properties of spherical harmonics quoted in Art. 88. The actual calculation of the potential and kinetic energies will be given in the next Chapter, in connection with an independent treatment of the same problem.

The effect of a simple-harmonic disturbing force can be written down at once from the formula (12) of Art. 165. If the surface-value of Ω be expanded in the form

$$\Omega = \Sigma \Omega_n \quad \text{.............................(8)},$$

where Ω_n is a surface-harmonic of integral order n, then the various terms are normal components of force, in the generalized sense of Art. 133; and the equilibrium value of ζ corresponding to any one term Ω_n is

$$\zeta_n = -\frac{1}{g}\Omega_n \quad \text{..........................(9)}.$$

Hence, for the forced oscillation due to this term, we have

$$\zeta_n = -\frac{1}{1 - \sigma^2/\sigma_n^2}\frac{\Omega_n}{g} \quad \text{.....................(10)},$$

where σ measures the 'speed' of the disturbing force, and σ_n that of the corresponding free oscillation, as given by (5). There is no difficulty, of course, in deducing (10) directly from the equations of the preceding Art.

192. We have up to this point neglected the mutual attraction of the parts of the liquid. In the case of an ocean covering the globe, and with such relations of density as we meet with in the actual earth and ocean, this is not insensible. To investigate its effect in the case of the free oscillations, we have only to substitute for Ω_n, in the last formula, the gravitation-potential of the displaced water. If the density of this be denoted by ρ, whilst ρ_0 represents the mean density of the globe and liquid combined, we have*

$$\Omega_n = -\frac{4\pi\gamma\rho a}{2n+1}\zeta_n \quad \text{.....................(11)},$$

and

$$g = \tfrac{4}{3}\gamma\pi a\rho_0 \quad \text{..........................(12)},$$

* See, for example, Routh, *Analytical Statics*, Cambridge 1892, t. ii. pp. 91–92.

γ denoting the gravitation-constant, whence

$$\Omega_n = -\frac{3}{2n+1} \cdot \frac{\rho}{\rho_0} \cdot g\zeta_n \quad\text{..................(13).}$$

Substituting in (10) we find

$$\frac{\sigma_n^2}{\sigma_n'^2} = \left(1 - \frac{3}{2n+1}\frac{\rho}{\rho_0}\right) \quad\text{..................(14),}$$

where σ_n is now used to denote the actual speed of the oscillation, and σ_n' the speed calculated on the former hypothesis of no mutual attraction. Hence the corrected speed is given by

$$\sigma_n^2 = n(n+1)\left(1 - \frac{3}{2n+1}\frac{\rho}{\rho_0}\right)\frac{gh}{a^2} \quad\text{..........(15)*.}$$

For an ellipsoidal oscillation ($n = 2$), and for $\rho/\rho_0 = \cdot 18$ (as in the case of the Earth), we find from (14) that the effect of the mutual attraction is to *lower* the frequency in the ratio of ·94 to 1.

The slowest oscillation would correspond to $n = 1$, but, as already indicated, it would be necessary, in this mode, to imagine a constraint applied to the globe to keep it at rest. This being premised, it appears from (15) that if $\rho > \rho_0$ the value of σ_1^2 is negative. The circular function of t is then replaced by real exponentials; this shews that the configuration in which the surface of the sea is a sphere concentric with the globe is one of unstable equilibrium. Since the introduction of a constraint tends in the direction of stability, we infer that when $\rho > \rho_0$ the equilibrium is *a fortiori* unstable when the globe is free. In the extreme case when the globe itself is supposed to have no gravitative power at all, it is obvious that the water, if disturbed, would tend ultimately, under the influence of dissipative forces, to collect itself into a spherical mass, the nucleus being expelled.

It is obvious from Art. 165, or it may easily be verified independently, that the forced vibrations due to a given periodic disturbing force, when the gravitation of the water is taken into account, will be given by the formula (10), provided Ω_n now denote the potential of the extraneous forces only, and σ_n have the value given by (15).

* This result was given by Laplace, *Mécanique Céleste*, Livre 1er, Art. 1 (1799). The free and the forced oscillations of the type $n=2$ had been previously investigated in his "Recherches sur quelques points du système du monde," *Mém. de l'Acad. roy. des Sciences*, 1775 [1778]; *Oeuvres Complètes*, t. ix., pp. 109,....

193. The oscillations of a sea bounded by meridians, or parallels of latitude, or both, can also be treated by the same method*. The spherical harmonics involved are however, as a rule, no longer of integral order, and it is accordingly difficult to deduce numerical results.

In the case of a zonal sea bounded by two parallels of latitude, we assume

$$\zeta = \{Ap(\mu) + Bq(\mu)\} \begin{matrix}\cos \\ \sin\end{matrix}\Big\} s\omega \qquad \text{(i)},$$

where $\mu = \cos\theta$, and $p(\mu)$, $q(\mu)$ are the two functions of μ, containing $(1-\mu^2)^{\frac{1}{2}s}$ as a factor, which are given by the formula (2) of Art. 87. It will be noticed that $p(\mu)$ is an *even*, and $q(\mu)$ an *odd* function of μ.

If we distinguish the limiting parallels by suffixes, the boundary conditions are that $u=0$ for $\mu=\mu_1$ and $\mu=\mu_2$. For the free oscillations this gives, by Art. 190 (6),

$$Ap'(\mu_1) + Bq'(\mu_1) = 0 \qquad \text{(ii)},$$

$$Ap'(\mu_2) + Bq'(\mu_2) = 0 \qquad \text{(iii)},$$

whence

$$\begin{vmatrix} p'(\mu_1), & q'(\mu_1) \\ p'(\mu_2), & q'(\mu_2) \end{vmatrix} = 0 \qquad \text{(iv)},$$

which is the equation to determine the admissible values of n. The speeds (σ) corresponding to the various roots are given as before by Art. 191 (5).

If the two boundaries are equidistant from the equator, we have $\mu_2 = -\mu_1$. The above solutions then break up into two groups; viz. for one of these we have

$$B=0, \qquad p'(\mu_1) = 0 \qquad \text{(v)},$$

and for the other

$$A=0, \qquad q'(\mu_1) = 0 \qquad \text{(vi)}.$$

In the former case ζ has the same value at two points symmetrically situated on opposite sides of the equation; in the latter the values at these points are numerically equal, but opposite in sign.

If we imagine one of the boundaries to be contracted to a point (say $\mu_2 = 1$), we pass to the case of a circular basin. The values of $p'(1)$ and $q'(1)$ are infinite, but their ratio can be evaluated by means of formulæ given in Art. 85. This gives, by (iii), the ratio $A : B$, and substituting in (ii) we get the equation to determine n. A more interesting method of treating this case consists, however, in obtaining, directly from the differential equation of surface-harmonics, a solution which shall be finite at the pole $\mu = 1$. This involves a change of variable, as to which there is some latitude of choice. Perhaps the simplest plan is to write, for a moment,

$$z = \tfrac{1}{2}(1-\mu) = \sin^2 \tfrac{1}{2}\theta \qquad \text{(vii)}.$$

* Cf. Lord Rayleigh, *l. c. ante* p. 314.

Assuming $$S_n = (1-\mu^2)^{\frac{1}{2}s} w \left.\begin{matrix}\cos\\ \sin\end{matrix}\right\} s\omega \quad\text{.........................(viii)},$$

the differential equation in w, which is given in Art. 87, becomes, in terms of the new variable,

$$z(1-z)\frac{d^2w}{dz^2} + (s+1)(1-2z)\frac{dw}{dz} + (n-s)(n+s+1)w = 0 \quad\text{...... (ix)}.$$

The solution of this which is finite for $z=0$ is given by the ascending series

$$w = A\left\{1 - \frac{(n-s)(n+s+1)}{1.(s+1)}z + \frac{(n-s-1)(n-s)(n+s+1)(n+s+2)}{1.2.(s+1)(s+2)}z^2 - \ldots\right\}$$

$$= AF(s-n,\ s+n+1,\ s+1,\ z) \quad\text{.........(x)}.$$

Hence the expression adapted to our case is

$$\zeta = A\sin^s\theta\left\{1 - \frac{(n-s)(n+s+1)}{1.(s+1)}\sin^2\tfrac{1}{2}\theta + \frac{(n-s-1)(n-s)(n+s+1)(n+s+2)}{1.2.(s+1)(s+2)}\sin^4\tfrac{1}{2}\theta - \ldots\right\}\left.\begin{matrix}\cos\\ \sin\end{matrix}\right\} s\omega \quad\text{... (xi)*},$$

where the admissible values of n are to be determined from the condition that $d\zeta/d\theta = 0$ for $\theta = \theta_1$.

The actual calculation of the roots of the equation in n, for any arbitrary value of θ_1, would be difficult. The main interest of the investigation consists, in fact, in the transition to the plane problem of Art. 187, and in the connection which we can thus trace between Bessel's Functions and Spherical Harmonics. If we put $a=\infty$, $a\theta = r$, we get the case of a plane sheet of water, referred to polar coordinates r, ω. Making, in addition, $n\theta = kr$, so that n is now infinite, the formula (xi) gives

$$\zeta \propto r^s\left\{1 - \frac{k^2r^2}{2(2s+2)} + \frac{k^4r^4}{2.4(2s+2)(2s+4)} - \ldots\right\}\left\{\begin{matrix}\cos\\ \sin\end{matrix}\right\} s\omega,$$

or $$\zeta \propto J_s(kr)\left.\begin{matrix}\cos\\ \sin\end{matrix}\right\} s\omega \quad\text{.............................(xii)},$$

in the notation of Art. 187 (4). We thus obtain Bessel's Functions as limiting forms of Spherical Harmonics of infinite order†.

* When n (as well as s) is integral, the series terminates, and the expression differs only by a numerical factor from the tesseral harmonic denoted by $T_n^s(\mu)\left.\begin{matrix}\cos\\ \sin\end{matrix}\right\} s\omega$, in Art. 87. In the case $s=0$ we obtain one of the expansions of the zonal harmonic given by Murphy, *Elementary Principles of the Theories of Electricity...*, Cambridge, 1833, p. 7. (The investigation is reproduced by Thomson and Tait, Art. 782.)

† This connection appears to have been first explicitly noticed by Mehler, "Ueber die Vertheilung der statischen Elektricität in einem von zwei Kugelkalotten begrenzten Körper," *Crelle*, t. lxviii. (1868). It was investigated independently by Lord Rayleigh, "On the Relation between the Functions of Laplace and Bessel," *Proc. Lond. Math. Soc.*, t. ix., p. 61 (1878); see also the same author's *Theory of Sound*, Arts. 336, 338.

If the sheet of water considered have as boundaries two meridians (with or without parallels of latitude), say $\omega = 0$ and $\omega = \alpha$, the condition that $v = 0$ at these restricts us to the factor $\cos s\omega$, and gives $s\alpha = m\pi$, where m is integral. This determines the admissible values of s, which are not in general integral*.

Tidal Oscillations of a Rotating Sheet of Water.

194. The theory of the tides on an open sheet of water is seriously complicated by the fact of the earth's rotation. If, indeed, we could assume that the periods of the free oscillations, and of the disturbing forces, were small compared with a day, the preceding investigations would apply as a first approximation, but these conditions are far from being fulfilled in the actual circumstances of the Earth.

The difficulties which arise when we attempt to take the rotation into account have their origin in this, that a particle having a motion in latitude tends to keep its angular momentum about the earth's axis unchanged, and so to alter its motion in longitude. This point is of course familiar in connection with Hadley's theory of the trade-winds†. Its bearing on tidal theory seems to have been first recognised by Maclaurin‡.

195. Owing to the enormous inertia of the solid body of the earth compared with that of the ocean, the effect of tidal reactions in producing periodic changes of the angular velocity is quite insensible. This angular velocity will therefore for the present be treated as constant§.

The theory of the small oscillations of a dynamical system about a state of equilibrium relative to a solid body which rotates with constant angular velocity about a fixed axis differs in some important particulars from the theory of small oscillations about a state of absolute equilibrium, of which some account was given

* The reader who wishes to carry the study of the problem further in this direction is referred to Thomson and Tait, *Natural Philosophy* (2nd ed.), Appendix B, "Spherical Harmonic Analysis."

† "Concerning the General Cause of the Trade Winds," *Phil. Trans.* 1735.

‡ *De Causâ Physicâ Fluxus et Refluxus Maris*, Prop. vii.: "Motus aquæ turbatur ex inæquali velocitate quâ corpora circa axem Terræ motu diurno deferuntur" (1740).

§ The *secular* effect of tidal friction in this respect will be noticed later (Chap. XI.).

in Art. 165. It is therefore worth while to devote a little space to it before entering on the consideration of special problems.

Let us take a set of rectangular axes x, y, z, fixed relatively to the solid, of which the axis of z coincides with the axis of rotation, and let n be the angular velocity of the rotation. The equations of motion of a particle m relative to these moving axes are known to be

$$\left.\begin{aligned} m(\ddot{x} - 2n\dot{y} - n^2x) &= X, \\ m(\ddot{y} + 2n\dot{x} - n^2y) &= Y, \\ m\ddot{z} &= Z \end{aligned}\right\} \quad\text{..................} \quad (1),$$

where X, Y, Z are the impressed forces on the particle. Let us now suppose that the relative coordinates (x, y, z) of any particle can be expressed in terms of a certain number of independent quantities $q_1, q_2, \ldots$. If we multiply the above equations by dx/dq_s, dy/dq_s, dz/dq_s, and add, and denote by Σ a summation embracing all the particles of the system, we obtain

$$\Sigma m\left(\ddot{x}\frac{dx}{dq_s} + \ddot{y}\frac{dy}{dq_s} + \ddot{z}\frac{dz}{dq_s}\right) + 2n\Sigma m\left(\dot{x}\frac{dy}{dq_s} - \dot{y}\frac{dx}{dq_s}\right)$$

$$= \tfrac{1}{2}n^2\frac{d}{dq_s}\Sigma m(x^2 + y^2) + \Sigma\left(X\frac{dx}{dq_s} + Y\frac{dy}{dq_s} + Z\frac{dz}{dq_s}\right) \ldots (2).$$

There is a similar equation for each of the generalized coordinates q_s.

Now, exactly as in Hamilton's proof* of Lagrange's equations, the first term in (2) may be replaced by

$$\frac{d}{dt}\frac{d\mathfrak{T}}{d\dot{q}_s} - \frac{d\mathfrak{T}}{dq_s},$$

where $$\mathfrak{T} = \tfrac{1}{2}\Sigma m(\dot{x}^2 + \dot{y}^2 + \dot{z}^2) \quad\text{..................}\quad (3),$$

i.e. $\mathfrak{T}$ denotes the energy of the *relative* motion, supposed expressed in terms of the generalized coordinates q_s, and the generalized velocities $\dot{q}_s$. Again, we may write

$$\Sigma\left(X\frac{dx}{dq_s} + Y\frac{dy}{dq_s} + Z\frac{dz}{dq_s}\right) = -\frac{dV}{dq_s} + Q_s \quad\text{.........}\quad (4),$$

where V is the potential energy, and Q_s is the generalized com-

* See *ante* p. 201 (footnote).

ponent of extraneous force corresponding to the coordinate q_s. Also, since

$$\dot{x} = \frac{dx}{dq_1}\dot{q}_1 + \frac{dx}{dq_2}\dot{q}_2 + \ldots,$$

$$\dot{y} = \frac{dy}{dq_1}\dot{q}_1 + \frac{dy}{dq_2}\dot{q}_2 + \ldots,$$

we have

$$\Sigma m\left(\dot{x}\frac{dy}{dq_s} - \dot{y}\frac{dx}{dq_s}\right) = \Sigma m\left\{\frac{d(x,y)}{d(q_1,q_s)}\dot{q}_1 + \frac{d(x,y)}{d(q_2,q_s)}\dot{q}_2 + \ldots\right\}.$$

We will write, for shortness,

$$2n\,.\,\Sigma m\frac{d(x,y)}{d(q_r,q_s)} = [s,r] \quad\ldots\ldots\ldots\ldots\ldots\ldots (5).$$

Finally, we put

$$T_0 = \tfrac{1}{2}n^2\Sigma m(x^2+y^2)\ldots\ldots\ldots\ldots\ldots\ldots\ldots (6),$$

viz. T_0 denotes the energy of the system when rotating with the solid, without relative motion, in the configuration $(q_1, q_2, \ldots)$.

With these notations, the typical equation (2) takes the form

$$\frac{d}{dt}\frac{d\mathfrak{T}}{d\dot{q}_s} - \frac{d\mathfrak{T}}{dq_s} + [s,1]\dot{q}_1 + [s,2]\dot{q}_2 + \ldots = -\frac{d}{dq_s}(V-T_0) + Q_s \ldots (7)^*,$$

and it is to be particularly noticed that the coefficients $[r, s]$ are subject to the relations

$$[r,s] = -[s,r], \quad [s,s] = 0 \ldots\ldots\ldots\ldots\ldots\ldots (8).$$

The conditions for relative equilibrium, in the absence of extraneous forces, are found by putting $\dot{q}_1 = 0$, $\dot{q}_2 = 0$, ... in (7), or more simply from (2). In either way we obtain

$$\frac{d}{dq_s}(V-T_0) = 0 \ldots\ldots\ldots\ldots\ldots\ldots\ldots\ldots (9),$$

which shews that the equilibrium value of the expression $V - T_0$ is 'stationary.'

196. We will now suppose the coordinates q_s to be chosen so as to vanish in the undisturbed state. In the case of a *small* disturbance, we may then write

$$2\mathfrak{T} = a_{11}\dot{q}_1^2 + a_{22}\dot{q}_2^2 + \ldots + 2a_{12}\dot{q}_1\dot{q}_2 + \ldots \quad \ldots (1),$$

$$2(V-T_0) = c_{11}q^2 + c_{22}q^2 + \ldots + 2c_{12}q_1q_2 + \ldots \quad \ldots (2),$$

* Cf. Thomson and Tait, *Natural Philosophy* (2nd ed.), Part I. p. 319. It should be remarked that these equations are a particular case of Art. 139 (14), obtained, with the help of the relations (7) of Art. 141, by supposing the rotating solid to be free, but to have an infinite moment of inertia.

where the coefficients may be treated as constants. The terms of the first degree in $V - T_0$ have been omitted, on account of the 'stationary' property.

In order to simplify the equations as much as possible, we will further suppose that, by a linear transformation, each of these expressions is reduced, as in Art. 165, to a sum of squares; viz.

$$2\mathfrak{T} = a_1\dot{q}_1^2 + a_2\dot{q}_2^2 + \ldots \ldots\ldots\ldots\ldots(3),$$

$$2(V - T_0) = c_1 q_1^2 + c_2 q_2^2 + \ldots \ldots\ldots\ldots\ldots(4).$$

The quantities $q_1, q_2, \ldots$ may be called the 'principal coordinates' of the system, but we must be on our guard against assuming that the same simplicity of properties attaches to them as in the case of no rotation. The coefficients $a_1, a_2, \ldots$ and $c_1, c_2, \ldots$ may be called the 'principal coefficients' of inertia and of stability, respectively. The latter coefficients are the same as if we were to ignore the rotation, and to introduce fictitious 'centrifugal' forces $(mn^2x, mn^2y, 0)$ acting on each particle in the direction outwards from the axis.

If we further write, for convenience, β_{rs} in place of $[r, s]$, then, in terms of the new coordinates, the equation (7) of the preceding Art. gives, in the case of infinitely small motions,

$$\left.\begin{array}{l} a_1\ddot{q}_1 + c_1q_1 \qquad\qquad + \beta_{12}\dot{q}_2 + \beta_{13}\dot{q}_3 + \ldots = Q_1, \\ a_2\ddot{q}_2 + c_2q_2 + \beta_{21}\dot{q}_1 \qquad\qquad + \beta_{23}\dot{q}_3 + \ldots = Q_2, \\ a_3\ddot{q}_3 + c_3q_3 + \beta_{31}\dot{q}_1 + \beta_{32}\dot{q}_2 \qquad\qquad + \ldots = Q_3, \\ \ldots\ldots\ldots\ldots\ldots\ldots\ldots\ldots\ldots\ldots\ldots\ldots \end{array}\right\} \ldots\ldots(5).$$

If we multiply these equations by $\dot{q}_1, \dot{q}_2, \ldots$ in order, and add, then taking account of the relation

$$\beta_{rs} = -\beta_{sr} \ldots\ldots\ldots\ldots\ldots\ldots\ldots\ldots(6),$$

we find
$$\frac{d}{dt}(\mathfrak{T} + V - T_0) = Q_1\dot{q}_1 + Q_2\dot{q}_2 + \ldots \quad \ldots\ldots\ldots\ldots(7).$$

This might have been obtained without approximation from the exact equations (7) of Art. 195. It may also be deduced directly from first principles.

197. To investigate the *free* motions of the system, we put $Q_1 = 0$, $Q_2 = 0, \ldots$ in (5), and assume, in accordance with the usual method of treating linear equations,

$$q_1 = A_1e^{\lambda t}, \quad q_2 = A_2e^{\lambda t}, \ldots, \ldots\ldots\ldots\ldots\ldots\ldots(8).$$

Substituting, we find

$$\left.\begin{array}{llll}(a_1\lambda^2+c_1)A_1 & +\beta_{12}\lambda A_2 & +\beta_{13}\lambda A_3+\ldots=0, \\ \beta_{21}\lambda A_1+(a_2\lambda^2+c_2)A_2 & & +\beta_{23}\lambda A_3+\ldots=0, \\ \beta_{31}\lambda A_1 & +\beta_{32}\lambda A_2+(a_3\lambda^2+c_3)A_3+\ldots=0, & & \\ \ldots\ldots\ldots\ldots\ldots\ldots\ldots\ldots\ldots\ldots & & & \end{array}\right\} \ldots (9).$$

Eliminating the ratios $A_1 : A_2 : A_3 : \ldots$, we get the equation

$$\begin{vmatrix} a_1\lambda^2+c_1, & \beta_{12}\lambda, & \beta_{13}\lambda, \ldots \\ \beta_{21}\lambda, & a_2\lambda^2+c_2, & \beta_{23}\lambda, \ldots \\ \beta_{31}\lambda, & \beta_{32}\lambda, & a_3\lambda^2+c_3, \ldots \\ \ldots\ldots\ldots & \ldots\ldots\ldots & \ldots\ldots\ldots \end{vmatrix} = 0 \ldots\ldots (10),$$

or, as we shall occasionally write it, for shortness,

$$\Delta(\lambda)=0 \ldots\ldots\ldots\ldots (11).$$

The determinant $\Delta(\lambda)$ comes under the class called by Cayley 'skew-determinants,' in virtue of the relation (6). If we reverse the sign of λ, the rows and columns are simply interchanged, and the value of the determinant therefore unaltered. Hence, when expanded, the equation (10) will involve only *even* powers of λ, and the roots will be in pairs of the form

$$\lambda = \pm(\rho + i\sigma).$$

In order that the configuration of relative equilibrium should be stable it is essential that the values of ρ should all be zero, for otherwise terms of the forms $e^{\pm\rho t}\cos\sigma t$ and $e^{\pm\rho t}\sin\sigma t$ would present themselves in the realized expression for any coordinate q_s. This would indicate the possibility of an oscillation of continually increasing amplitude.

In the theory of absolute equilibrium, sketched in Art. 165, the necessary and sufficient condition of stability is simply that the potential energy must be a minimum in the configuration of equilibrium. In the present case the conditions are more complicated*, but we may readily shew that if the expression for $V-T_0$ be essentially positive, in other words if the coefficients $c_1, c_2, \ldots$ in (4) be all positive, the equilibrium will be stable. This follows at once from the equation (7), which gives, in the case of free motion,

$$\mathfrak{T}+(V-T_0)=\text{const.} \ldots\ldots\ldots\ldots (12),$$

* They have been investigated by Routh, *On the Stability of a Given State of Motion*; see also his *Advanced Rigid Dynamics* (4th ed.), London, 1884.

shewing that under the present supposition neither $\mathfrak{T}$ nor $V - T_0$ can increase beyond a certain limit depending on the initial circumstances.

Hence stability is assured if $V - T_0$ is a minimum in the configuration of relative equilibrium. But this condition is not essential, and there may even be stability with $V - T_0$ a maximum, as will be shewn presently in the particular case of two degrees of freedom. It is to be remarked, however, that if the system be subject to dissipative forces, however slight, affecting the relative coordinates $q_1, q_2, \ldots$, the equilibrium will be permanently or 'secularly' stable only if $V - T_0$ is a minimum. It is the characteristic of such forces that the work done by them on the system is always negative. Hence, by (7), the expression $\mathfrak{T} + (V - T_0)$ will, so long as there is any relative motion of the system, continually diminish, in the algebraical sense. Hence if the system be started from relative rest in a configuration such that $V - T_0$ is negative, the above expression, and therefore *à fortiori* the part $V - T_0$, will assume continually increasing negative values, which can only take place by the system deviating more and more from its equilibrium-configuration.

This important distinction between 'ordinary' or kinetic, and 'secular' or practical stability was first pointed out by Thomson and Tait*. It is to be observed that the above investigation presupposes a constant angular velocity (n) maintained, if necessary, by a proper application of force to the rotating solid. When the solid is *free*, the condition of secular stability takes a somewhat different form, to be referred to later (Chap. XII.).

To examine the character of a free oscillation, in the case of stability, we remark that if λ be any root of (10), the equations (9) give

$$\frac{A_1}{\Delta_{r1}(\lambda)} = \frac{A_2}{\Delta_{r2}(\lambda)} = \frac{A_3}{\Delta_{r3}(\lambda)} = \ldots = C \quad \text{.........} (13),$$

where $\Delta_{r1}, \Delta_{r2}, \Delta_{r3}, \ldots$ are the minors of any row in the determinant Δ, and C is arbitrary. It is to be noticed that these minors will as a rule involve odd as well as even powers of λ, and so

* *Natural Philosophy* (2nd ed.), Part I. p. 391. See also Poincaré, "Sur l'équilibre d'une masse fluide animée d'un mouvement de rotation," *Acta Mathematica*, t. vii. (1885).

assume unequal values for the two oppositely signed roots ($\pm\lambda$) of any pair. If we put $\lambda = \pm i\sigma$, the general symbolical value of q_s corresponding to any such pair of roots may be written

$$q_s = C\Delta_{rs}(i\sigma)\, e^{i\sigma t} + C'\Delta_{rs}(-i\sigma)\, e^{-i\sigma t}.$$

If we put

$$2\Delta_{rs}(i\sigma) = F_s(\sigma^2) + i\sigma f_s(\sigma^2),$$
$$C = Ke^{i\epsilon}, \quad C' = Ke^{-i\epsilon},$$

we get a solution of our equations in real form, involving two arbitrary constants K, ϵ; thus

$$\left.\begin{array}{l} q_1 = F_1(\sigma^2) . K\cos(\sigma t + \epsilon) - \sigma f_1(\sigma^2) . K\sin(\sigma t + \epsilon), \\ q_2 = F_2(\sigma^2) . K\cos(\sigma t + \epsilon) - \sigma f_2(\sigma^2) . K\sin(\sigma t + \epsilon), \\ q_3 = F_3(\sigma^2) . K\cos(\sigma t + \epsilon) - \sigma f_3(\sigma^2) . K\sin(\sigma t + \epsilon), \\ \dots\dots\dots\dots\dots\dots\dots\dots\dots\dots\dots\dots \end{array}\right\} \dots(14)^*.$$

The formulæ (14) express what may be called a 'natural mode' of oscillation of the system. The number of such possible modes is of course equal to the number of pairs of roots of (10), *i.e.* to the number of degrees of freedom of the system.

If ξ, η, ζ denote the component displacements of any particle from its equilibrium position, we have

$$\left.\begin{array}{l} \xi = \dfrac{dx}{dq_1} q_1 + \dfrac{dx}{dq_2} q_2 + \dots, \\ \eta = \dfrac{dy}{dq_1} q_1 + \dfrac{dy}{dq_2} q_2 + \dots, \\ \zeta = \dfrac{dz}{dq_1} q_1 + \dfrac{dz}{dq_2} q_2 + \dots \end{array}\right\} \dots\dots\dots\dots(15).$$

Substituting from (15), we obtain a result of the form

$$\left.\begin{array}{l} \xi = P . K\cos(\sigma t + \epsilon) + P' . K\sin(\sigma t + \epsilon), \\ \eta = Q . K\cos(\sigma t + \epsilon) + Q' . K\sin(\sigma t + \epsilon), \\ \zeta = R . K\cos(\sigma t + \epsilon) + R' . K\sin(\sigma t + \epsilon) \end{array}\right\} \dots\dots(16),$$

where P, P', Q, Q', R, R' are determinate functions of the mean position of the particle, involving also the value of σ, and therefore different for the different normal modes, but independent of the arbitrary constants K, ϵ. These formulæ represent an elliptic-

* We might have obtained the same result by assuming, in (5),

$$q_1 = A_1 e^{i(\sigma t+\epsilon)}, \quad q_2 = A_2 e^{i(\sigma t+\epsilon)}, \quad q_3 = A_3 e^{i(\sigma t+\epsilon)}, \dots\dots,$$

where A_1, A_2, A_3, ... are real, and rejecting, in the end, the imaginary parts.

harmonic motion of period $2\pi/\sigma$; the directions

$$\xi/P = \eta/Q = \zeta/R, \text{ and } \xi/P' = \eta/Q' = \zeta/R' \quad \text{.........(17)},$$

being those of two semi-conjugate diameters of the elliptic orbit, of lengths $(P^2+Q^2+R^2)^{\frac{1}{2}}.K$, and $(P'^2+Q'^2+R'^2)^{\frac{1}{2}}.K$, respectively. The positions and forms and relative dimensions of the elliptic orbits, as well as the relative phases of the particles in them, are in each natural mode determinate, the absolute dimensions and epochs being alone arbitrary.

198. The symbolical expressions for the *forced* oscillations due to a periodic disturbing force can easily be written down. If we assume that $Q_1, Q_2, \ldots$ all vary as $e^{i\sigma t}$, where σ is prescribed, the equations (5) give, omitting the time-factors,

$$\left.\begin{aligned} q_1 &= \frac{\Delta_{11}(i\sigma)}{\Delta(i\sigma)} Q_1 + \frac{\Delta_{12}(i\sigma)}{\Delta(i\sigma)} Q_2 + \ldots, \\ q_2 &= \frac{\Delta_{21}(i\sigma)}{\Delta(i\sigma)} Q_1 + \frac{\Delta_{22}(i\sigma)}{\Delta(i\sigma)} Q_2 + \ldots, \\ &\ldots\ldots\ldots\ldots\ldots\ldots\ldots\ldots\ldots\ldots \end{aligned}\right\} \quad \text{..........(18)}.$$

The most important point of contrast with the theory of the 'normal modes' in the case of no rotation is that the displacement of any one type is no longer affected solely by the disturbing force of that type. As a consequence, the motions of the individual particles are, as is easily seen from (15), now in general elliptic-harmonic.

As in Art. 165, the displacement becomes very great when $\Delta(i\sigma)$ is very small, *i.e.* whenever the 'speed' σ of the disturbing force approximates to that of one of the natural modes of free oscillation.

When the period of the disturbing forces is infinitely long, the displacements tend to the 'equilibrium-values'

$$q_1 = Q_1/c_1, \quad q_2 = Q_2/c_2, \ldots, \quad \text{..............(19)},$$

as is found by putting $\sigma = 0$ in (18), or more simply from the fundamental equations (5). This conclusion must be modified, however, when any one or more of the coefficients of stability $c_1, c_2, \ldots$ is zero. If, for example, $c_1 = 0$, the first row and column of the determinant $\Delta(\lambda)$ are both divisible by λ, so that the determinantal equation (10) has a pair of zero roots. In other words we have a possible free motion of infinitely long period. The coefficients of Q_2, Q_3, ... on the right-hand side of (18) then become indeterminate for $\sigma = 0$, and the evaluated results do not as a rule coincide with (19). This point is of some importance, because in the hydrodynamical applications, as we shall see, steady circulatory motions of the fluid, with a constant deformation of the free surface, are possible when no extraneous forces act; and as a consequence forced tidal oscillations of long period do not necessarily approximate to the values given by the equilibrium theory of the tides. Cf. Arts. 207, 210.

In order to elucidate the foregoing statements we may consider more in detail the case of two degrees of freedom. The equations of motion are then of the forms

$$\left.\begin{aligned} a_1\ddot{q}_1 + c_1 q_1 + \beta\dot{q}_2 = Q_1, \\ a_2\ddot{q}_2 + c_2 q_2 - \beta\dot{q}_1 = Q_2 \end{aligned}\right\} \quad \text{(i)}.$$

The equation determining the periods of the free oscillations is

$$(a_1\lambda^2 + c_1)(a_2\lambda^2 + c_2) + \beta^2\lambda^2 = 0 \quad \text{(ii)},$$

or

$$a_1 a_2\lambda^4 + (a_1 c_2 + a_2 c_1 + \beta^2)\lambda^2 + c_1 c_2 = 0 \quad \text{(iii)}.$$

For 'ordinary' stability it is sufficient that the roots of this quadratic in λ^2 should be real and negative. Since a_1, a_2 are essentially positive, it is easily seen that this condition is in any case fulfilled if c_1, c_2 are both positive, and that it will also be satisfied even when c_1, c_2 are both negative, provided β^2 be sufficiently great. It will be shewn later, however, that in the latter case the equilibrium is rendered unstable by the introduction of dissipative forces.

To find the forced oscillations when Q_1, Q_2 vary as $e^{i\sigma t}$, we have, omitting the time-factor,

$$\left.\begin{aligned} (c_1 - \sigma^2 a_1) q_1 + i\sigma\beta q_2 = Q_1, \\ -i\sigma\beta q_1 + (c_2 - \sigma^2 a_2) q_2 = Q_2 \end{aligned}\right\} \quad \text{(iv)},$$

whence

$$\left.\begin{aligned} q_1 &= \frac{(c_2 - \sigma^2 a_2) Q_1 - i\sigma\beta Q_2}{(c_1 - \sigma^2 a_1)(c_2 - \sigma^2 a_2) - \sigma^2\beta^2}, \\ q_2 &= \frac{i\sigma\beta Q_1 + (c_1 - \sigma^2 a_1) Q_2}{(c_1 - \sigma^2 a_1)(c_2 - \sigma^2 a_2) - \sigma^2\beta^2} \end{aligned}\right\} \quad \text{(v)}$$

Let us now suppose that $c_2 = 0$, or, in other words, that the displacement q_2 does not affect the value of $V - T_0$. We will also suppose that $Q_2 = 0$, *i.e.* that the extraneous forces do no work during a displacement of the type q_2. The above formulæ then give

$$\left.\begin{aligned} q_1 &= \frac{a_2}{a_2(c_1 - \sigma^2 a_1) + \beta^2} Q_1, \\ \dot{q}_2 &= \frac{\beta}{a_2(c_1 - \sigma^2 a_1) + \beta^2} Q_1 \end{aligned}\right\} \quad \text{(vi)}.$$

In the case of a disturbance of long period we have $\sigma=0$, approximately, and therefore

$$\left.\begin{aligned} q_1 &= \frac{1}{c_1+\beta^2/a_2} Q_1, \\ \dot{q}_2 &= -\frac{\beta}{a_2c_1+\beta^2} Q_1 \end{aligned}\right\} \quad\text{.......................... (vii).}$$

The displacement q_1 is therefore *less* than its equilibrium-value, in the ratio $1 : 1+\beta^2/a_2c_1$; and it is accompanied by a motion of the type q_2 although there is no extraneous force of the latter type (cf. Art. 210). We pass, of course, to the case of absolute equilibrium, considered in Art. 165, by putting $\beta=0$.

199. Proceeding to the hydrodynamical examples, we begin with the case of a plane horizontal sheet of water having in the undisturbed state a motion of uniform rotation about a vertical axis*. The results will apply without serious qualification to the case of a polar or other basin, of not too great dimensions, on a rotating globe.

Let the axis of rotation be taken as axis of z. The axes of x and y being now supposed to rotate in their own plane with the prescribed angular velocity n, let us denote by u, v, w the velocities at time t, *relative to these axes*, of the particle which then occupies the position (x, y, z).

The actual velocities of the same particle, parallel to the instantaneous positions of the axes, will be $u - ny$, $v + nx$, w.

After a time δt, the particle in question will occupy, relatively to the axes, the position $(x + u\delta t,\ y + v\delta t,\ z + w\delta t)$, and therefore the values of its actual component velocities parallel to the new positions of the axes will be

$$u + \frac{Du}{Dt}\delta t - n(y + v\delta t),$$

$$v + \frac{Dv}{Dt}\delta t + n(x + u\delta t),$$

$$w + \frac{Dw}{Dt}\delta t,$$

* Sir W. Thomson, "On Gravitational Oscillations of Rotating Water," *Phil. Mag.*, Aug. 1880.

where

$$\frac{D}{Dt} = \frac{d}{dt} + u\frac{d}{dx} + v\frac{d}{dy} + w\frac{d}{dz} \text{..............} (1),$$

as usual. These are in directions making with the original axis of x angles whose cosines are 1, $-n\delta t$, 0, respectively, so that the velocity parallel to this axis at time $t + \delta t$ is

$$u + \frac{Du}{Dt}\delta t - n(y + v\delta t) - (v + nx)n\delta t.$$

Hence, and by similar reasoning, we obtain, for the component accelerations in space, the expressions

$$\frac{Du}{Dt} - 2nv - n^2x, \quad \frac{Dv}{Dt} + 2nu - n^2y, \quad \frac{Dw}{Dt} \text{........} (2)^*.$$

In the present application, the relative motion is assumed to be infinitely small, so that we may replace D/Dt by d/dt.

200. Now let z_0 be the ordinate of the free surface when there is relative equilibrium under gravity alone, so that

$$z_0 = \tfrac{1}{2}\frac{n^2}{g}(x^2 + y^2) + \text{const.} \text{..................} (3),$$

as in Art. 27. For simplicity we will suppose that the slope of this surface is everywhere very small, in other words, if r be the greatest distance of any part of the sheet from the axis of rotation, n^2r/g is assumed to be small.

If $z_0 + \zeta$ denote the ordinate of the free surface when disturbed, then on the usual assumption that the vertical acceleration of the water is small compared with g, the pressure at any point (x, y, z) will be given by

$$p - p_0 = g\rho(z_0 + \zeta - z) \text{.....................} (4),$$

whence $$-\frac{1}{\rho}\frac{dp}{dx} = -n^2x - g\frac{d\zeta}{dx}, \quad -\frac{1}{\rho}\frac{dp}{dy} = -n^2y - g\frac{d\zeta}{dy}.$$

The equations of horizontal motion are therefore

$$\left.\begin{aligned} \frac{du}{dt} - 2nv &= -g\frac{d\zeta}{dx} - \frac{d\Omega}{dx}, \\ \frac{dv}{dt} + 2nu &= -g\frac{d\zeta}{dy} - \frac{d\Omega}{dy} \end{aligned}\right\} \text{..............} (5),$$

where Ω denotes the potential of the disturbing forces.

* These are obviously equivalent to the expressions for the component accelerations which appear on the left-hand sides of Art. 195 (1).

If we write
$$\bar{\zeta} = -\Omega/g \qquad (6),$$
these become
$$\left.\begin{aligned} \frac{du}{dt} - 2nv &= -g\frac{d}{dx}(\zeta - \bar{\zeta}), \\ \frac{dv}{dt} + 2nu &= -g\frac{d}{dy}(\zeta - \bar{\zeta}) \end{aligned}\right\} \qquad (7).$$

The equation of continuity has the same form as in Art. 189 viz.
$$\frac{d\zeta}{dt} = -\frac{d(hu)}{dx} - \frac{d(hv)}{dy} \qquad (8),$$
where h denotes the depth, from the free surface to the bottom, in the undisturbed condition. This depth will not, of course, be uniform unless the bottom follows the curvature of the free surface as given by (3).

If we eliminate $\zeta - \bar{\zeta}$ from the equations (7), by cross-differentiation, we find
$$\frac{d}{dt}\left(\frac{dv}{dx} - \frac{du}{dy}\right) + 2n\left(\frac{du}{dx} + \frac{dv}{dy}\right) = 0 \qquad (i),$$
or, writing
$$u = d\xi/dt, \quad v = d\eta/dt,$$
and integrating with respect to t,
$$\frac{dv}{dx} - \frac{du}{dy} + 2n\left(\frac{d\xi}{dx} + \frac{d}{dy}\right) = \text{const.} \qquad (ii).$$
This is merely the expression of von Helmholtz' theorem that the product of the angular velocity
$$n + \tfrac{1}{2}\left(\frac{dv}{dx} - \frac{du}{dy}\right)$$
and the cross-section
$$\left(1 + \frac{d\xi}{dx} + \frac{d\eta}{dy}\right)\delta x\,\delta y,$$
of a vortex-filament, is constant.

In the case of a simple-harmonic disturbance, the time-factor being $e^{i\sigma t}$, the equations (7) and (8) become
$$\left.\begin{aligned} i\sigma u - 2nv &= -g\frac{d}{dx}(\zeta - \bar{\zeta}), \\ i\sigma v + 2nu &= -g\frac{d}{dy}(\zeta - \bar{\zeta}) \end{aligned}\right\} \qquad (9),$$
and
$$i\sigma\zeta = -\frac{d(hu)}{dx} - \frac{d(hv)}{dy} \qquad (10).$$

From (9) we find

$$\left.\begin{aligned} u &= \frac{g}{\sigma^2 - 4n^2}\left(i\sigma\frac{d}{dx} + 2n\frac{d}{dy}\right)(\zeta - \bar{\zeta}), \\ v &= \frac{g}{\sigma^2 - 4n^2}\left(i\sigma\frac{d}{dy} - 2n\frac{d}{dx}\right)(\zeta - \bar{\zeta}) \end{aligned}\right\} \quad \text{.........} (11),$$

and if we substitute from these in (10), we obtain an equation in ζ only.

In the case of *uniform* depth the result takes the form

$$\nabla_1^2\zeta + \frac{\sigma^2 - 4n^2}{gh}\zeta = \nabla_1^2\bar{\zeta} \quad \text{..............} (12),$$

where $\nabla_1^2 = d^2/dx^2 + d^2/dy^2$, as before.

When $\bar{\zeta} = 0$, the equations (7) and (8) can be satisfied by *constant* values of u, v, ζ provided certain conditions are satisfied. We must have

$$u = -\frac{g}{2n}\frac{d\zeta}{dy}, \qquad v = \frac{g}{2n}\frac{d\zeta}{dx} \quad \text{.....................} (\text{iii}),$$

and therefore

$$\frac{d(h, \zeta)}{d(x, y)} = 0 \quad \text{...............................} (\text{iv}).$$

The latter condition shews that the contour-lines of the free surface must be everywhere parallel to the contour-lines of the bottom, but that the value of ζ is otherwise arbitrary. The flow of the fluid is everywhere parallel to the contour-lines, and it is therefore further necessary for the possibility of such steady motions that the depth should be uniform along the boundary (supposed to be a vertical wall). When the depth is everywhere the same, the condition (iv) is satisfied identically, and the only limitation on the value of ζ is that it should be constant along the boundary.

201. A simple application of these equations is to the case of free waves in an infinitely long uniform straight canal *.

If we assume $\zeta = ae^{ik(ct-x)+my}, \; v = 0$.....................(1),

the axis of x being parallel to the length of the canal, the equations (7) of the preceding Art., with the terms in $\bar{\zeta}$ omitted, give

$$cu = g\zeta, \quad 2nu = -gm\zeta \quad \text{....................} (2),$$

whilst, from the equation of continuity (Art. 200 (8)),

$$c\zeta = hu \quad \text{.............................} (3).$$

* Sir W. Thomson, *l.c. ante* p. 331.

We thence derive

$$c^2 = gh, \quad m = -2n/c \qquad (4).$$

The former of these results shews that the wave-velocity is unaffected by the rotation.

When expressed in real form, the value of ζ is

$$\zeta = ae^{-2ny/c} \cos \{k(ct - x) + \epsilon\} \qquad (5).$$

The exponential factor indicates that the wave-height increases as we pass from one side of the canal to the other, being least on the side which is *forward*, in respect of the rotation. If we take account of the directions of motion of a water-particle, at a crest and at a trough, respectively, this result is easily seen to be in accordance with the tendency pointed out in Art. 194*.

The problem of determining the free oscillations in a rotating canal of *finite* length, or in a rotating rectangular sheet of water, has not yet been solved.

202. We take next the case of a *circular* sheet of water rotating about its centre†.

If we introduce polar coordinates r, θ, and employ the symbols R, Θ to denote displacements along and perpendicular to the radius vector, then since $\dot{R} = i\sigma R$, $\dot{\Theta} = i\sigma\Theta$, the equations (9) of Art. 200 are equivalent to

$$\left.\begin{aligned} \sigma^2 R + 2in\sigma\Theta &= g\frac{d}{dr}(\zeta - \bar{\zeta}), \\ \sigma^2\Theta - 2in\sigma R &= g\frac{d}{rd\theta}(\zeta - \bar{\zeta}) \end{aligned}\right\} \qquad (1),$$

whilst the equation of continuity (10) becomes

$$\zeta = -\frac{d(hRr)}{rdr} - \frac{d(h\Theta)}{rd\theta} \qquad (2).$$

Hence

$$\left.\begin{aligned} R &= \frac{g}{\sigma^2 - 4n^2}\left(\frac{d}{dr} - \frac{2in}{\sigma}\frac{d}{rd\theta}\right)(\zeta - \bar{\zeta}), \\ \Theta &= \frac{ig}{\sigma^2 - 4n^2}\left(\frac{2n}{\sigma}\frac{d}{dr} - i\frac{d}{rd\theta}\right)(\zeta - \bar{\zeta}) \end{aligned}\right\} \qquad (3),$$

and substituting in (2) we get the differential equation in ζ.

* For applications to tidal phenomena see Sir W. Thomson, *Nature*, t. xix. pp. 154, 571 (1879).

† The investigation which follows is a development of some indications given by Lord Kelvin in the paper referred to.

In the case of *uniform* depth, we find

$$(\nabla_1^2+\kappa)\,\zeta=\nabla_1^2\bar{\zeta}\quad\text{.......................(4)},$$

where

$$\nabla_1^2=\frac{d^2}{dr^2}+\frac{1}{r}\frac{d}{dr}+\frac{1}{r^2}\frac{d^2}{d\theta^2}\quad\text{.................(5)},$$

and

$$\kappa=(\sigma^2-4n^2)/gh\quad\text{.....................(6)}.$$

This might have been written down at once from Art. 200 (12).

The condition to be satisfied at the boundary ($r=a$, say) is $R=0$, or

$$\left(r\frac{d}{dr}-\frac{2in}{\sigma}\frac{d}{d\theta}\right)(\zeta-\bar{\zeta})=0\quad\text{.................(7)}.$$

203. In the case of the *free* oscillations we have $\bar{\zeta}=0$. The way in which the imaginary i enters into the above equations, taken in conjunction with Fourier's theorem, suggests that θ occurs in the form of a factor $e^{is\theta}$, where s is integral. On this supposition, the differential equation (4) becomes

$$\frac{d^2\zeta}{dr^2}+\frac{1}{r}\frac{d\zeta}{dr}+\left(\kappa-\frac{s^2}{r^2}\right)\zeta=0\quad\text{..............(8)},$$

and the boundary-condition (7) gives

$$r\frac{d\zeta}{dr}+\frac{2sn}{\sigma}\zeta=0\quad\text{.......................(9)},$$

for $r=a$.

The equation (8) is of Bessel's form, except that κ is not, in the present problem, necessarily positive. The solution which is finite for $r=0$ may be written

$$\zeta=Af_s(\kappa,r)\quad\text{..........................(10)},$$

where

$$f_s(\kappa,r)=r^s\left\{1-\frac{\kappa r^2}{2(2s+2)}+\frac{\kappa^2r^4}{2.4(2s+2)(2s+4)}-\dots\right\}\text{...(11)}.$$

According as κ is positive or negative, this differs only by a numerical factor from $J_s(\kappa^{\frac{1}{2}}r)$ or $I_s(\kappa'^{\frac{1}{2}}r)$, where κ' is written for $-\kappa$, and $I_s(z)$ denotes the function obtained by making all the signs + on the right-hand side of Art. 187 (4)*.

* The functions $I_s(z)$ have been tabulated by Prof. A. Lodge, *Brit. Ass. Rep.* 1889.

In the case of symmetry about the axis ($s=0$), we have, in real form,

$$\zeta = AJ_0(\kappa^{\frac{1}{2}}r) \,.\, \cos(\sigma t+\epsilon) \text{..................(12),}$$

where κ is determined by

$$J_0'(\kappa^{\frac{1}{2}}a)=0 \text{..........................(13).}$$

The corresponding values of σ are then given by (6). The free surface has, in the various modes, the same forms as in Art. 187, but the frequencies are now greater, viz. we have

$$\sigma^2 = \sigma_0^2 + 4n^2 \text{ ....(14),}$$

where σ_0 is the corresponding value of σ when there is no rotation. It is easily seen, however, on reference to (3), that the relative motions of the fluid particles are no longer purely radial; the particles describe, in fact, ellipses whose major axes are in the direction of the radius vector.

When $s>0$ we have

$$\zeta = Af_s(\kappa, r) \,.\, \cos(\sigma t + s\theta + \epsilon) \text{ ....(15),}$$

where the admissible values of κ, and thence of σ, are determined by (9), which gives

$$a\frac{d}{da}f_s(\kappa, a) + \frac{2sn}{\sigma}f_s(\kappa, a) = 0 \text{ ....(16).}$$

The formula (15) represents a wave rotating relatively to the water with an angular velocity σ/s, the rotation of the wave being in the same direction with that of the water, or the opposite, according as σ/n is negative or positive.

Some indications as to the values of σ may be gathered from a graphical construction. If we put $\kappa a^2 = x$, we have, from (6),

$$\sigma/2n = \pm(1+x/\beta)^{\frac{1}{2}} \text{ .... (i),}$$

where

$$\beta = 4n^2a^2/gh \text{...................................(ii).}$$

It is easily seen that the quotient of

$$sf_s(\kappa, a) \text{ by } a\frac{d}{da}f_s(\kappa, a)$$

is a function of κa^2, or x, only. Denoting this function by $\phi(x)$, the equation (16) may be written

$$\phi(x) \pm (1+x/\beta)^{\frac{1}{2}} = 0 \text{.............................(iii).}$$

The curve

$$y = -\phi(x) \text{ ....(iv)}$$

can be readily traced by means of the tables of the functions $J_s(z)$, $I_s(z)$, and its intersections with the parabola

$$y^2 = 1 + x/\beta \quad\text{..............................(v)},$$

will give, by their ordinates, the values of $\sigma/2n$. The constant β, on which the positions of the roots depend, is equal to the square of the ratio $2na/(gh)^{\frac{1}{2}}$ which the period of a wave travelling round a circular canal of depth h and perimeter $2\pi a$ bears to the half-period (π/n) of the rotation of the water.

The accompanying figures indicate the relative magnitudes of the lower roots, in the cases $s=1$ and $s=2$, when β has the values 2, 6, 40, respectively*.

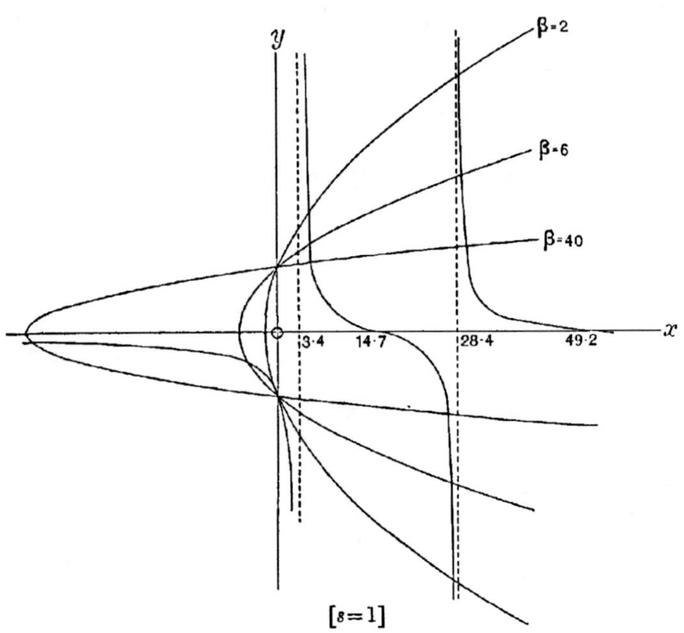

[$s=1$]

With the help of these figures we can trace, in a general way, the changes in the character of the free modes as β increases from zero. The results may be interpreted as due either to a continuous increase of n, or to a continuous diminution of h. We will use the terms 'positive' and 'negative' to distinguish waves which travel, relatively to the water, in the same direction as the rotation and the opposite.

When β is infinitely small, the values of x are given by $J_s'(x^{\frac{1}{2}})=0$; these correspond to the vertical asymptotes of the curve (iv). The values of σ then occur in pairs of equal and oppositely-signed quantities, indicating that there is now no difference between the velocity of positive and negative waves. The case is, in fact, that of Art. 187 (13).

* For clearness the scale of y has been taken to be 10 times that of x.

As β increases, the two values of σ forming a pair become unequal in magnitude, and the corresponding values of x separate, that being the greater for which $\sigma/2n$ is positive. When $\beta = s(s+1)$ the curve (iv) and the parabola (v) *touch* at the point $(0, -1)$, the corresponding value of σ being $-2n$. As β increases beyond this critical value, one value of x becomes negative, and the corresponding (negative) value of $\sigma/2n$ becomes smaller and smaller.

Hence, as β increases from zero, the relative angular velocity becomes greater for a negative than for a positive wave of (approximately) the same type; moreover the value of σ for a negative wave is always greater than $2n$.

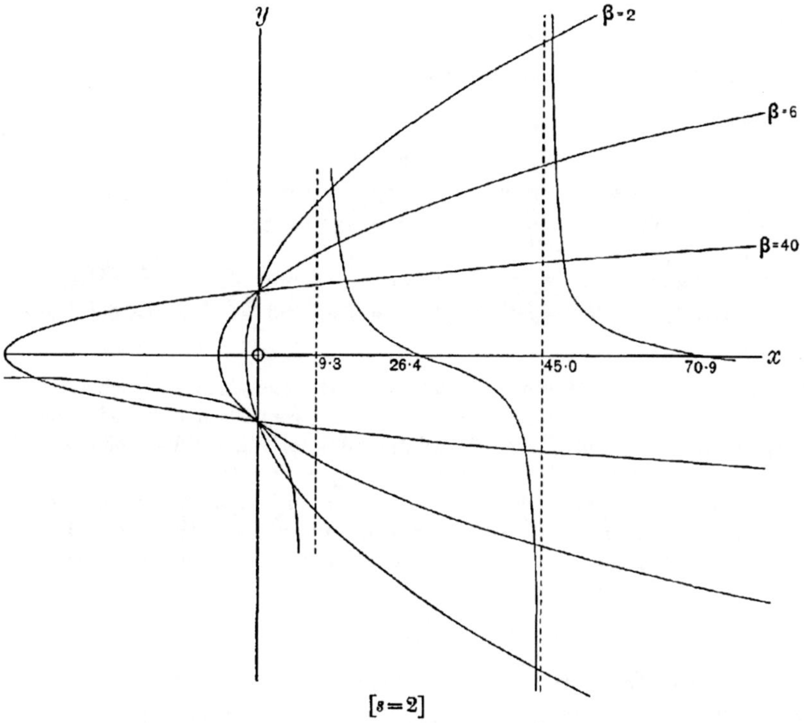

[$s=2$]

As the rotation increases, the two kinds of wave become more and more distinct in character as well as in 'speed.' With a sufficiently great value of β we may have one, but never more than one, positive wave for which σ is numerically less than $2n$. Finally, when β is very great, the value of σ corresponding to this wave becomes very small compared with n, whilst the remaining values tend all to become more and more nearly equal to $\pm 2n$.

If we use a zero suffix to distinguish the case of $n=0$, we find

$$\frac{\sigma^2}{\sigma_0^2} = \frac{\kappa + 4n^2/gh}{\kappa_0} = \frac{x+\beta}{x_0} \quad \text{..........................} \quad \text{(vi)},$$

where x_0 refers to the proper asymptote of the curve (iv). This gives the 'speed' of any free mode in terms of that of the corresponding mode when there is no rotation.

204. As a sufficient example of *forced* oscillations we may assume

$$\bar{\zeta} = C\left(\frac{r}{a}\right)^s e^{i(\sigma t + s\theta + \epsilon)} \quad \ldots\ldots\ldots\ldots\ldots\ldots(17),$$

where the value of σ is now prescribed.

This makes $\nabla^2 \bar{\zeta} = 0$, and the equation (4) then gives

$$\zeta = A f_s(\kappa, r)\, e^{i(\sigma t + s\theta + \epsilon)} \ldots\ldots\ldots\ldots\ldots\ldots(18),$$

where A is to be determined by the boundary-condition (7), whence

$$A = \frac{s\left(1 + \frac{2n}{\sigma}\right)}{a\frac{d}{da} f_s(\kappa, a) + \frac{2sn}{\sigma} f_s(\kappa, a)} \cdot C \quad \ldots\ldots\ldots(19).$$

This becomes very great when the frequency of the disturbance is nearly coincident with that of a free mode of corresponding type.

From the point of view of tidal theory the most interesting cases are those of $s = 1$ with $\sigma = n$, and $s = 2$ with $\sigma = 2n$, respectively. These would represent the diurnal and semidiurnal tides due to a distant disturbing body whose proper motion may be neglected in comparison with the rotation n.

In the case of $s = 1$ we have a *uniform* horizontal disturbing force. Putting, in addition, $\sigma = n$, we find without difficulty that the amplitude of the tide-elevation at the edge ($r = a$) of the basin has to its 'equilibrium-value' the ratio

$$\frac{3I_1(z)}{I_1(z) + zI_0(z)} \ldots\ldots\ldots\ldots\ldots\ldots\ldots\ldots\ldots\ldots\ldots\ldots\ldots\ldots(i),$$

where $z = \frac{1}{2}\sqrt{(3\beta)}$. With the help of Lodge's tables we find that this ratio has the values

	1·000,	·638,	·396,	
for $\beta =$	0,	12,	48,	respectively.

When $\sigma = 2n$, we have $\kappa = 0$, $f_s(\kappa, r) = r^s$, and thence, by (17), (18), (19),

$$\zeta = \bar{\zeta} \ldots\ldots\ldots\ldots\ldots\ldots\ldots\ldots\ldots\ldots\ldots\ldots\ldots(ii),$$

i.e. the tidal elevation has exactly the equilibrium-value.

This remarkable result can be obtained in a more general manner; it holds whenever the disturbing force is of the type

$$\bar{\zeta} = \chi(r)\, e^{i(2nt + s\theta + \epsilon)} \ldots\ldots\ldots\ldots\ldots\ldots\ldots\ldots\ldots(iii),$$

provided the depth h be a function of r only. If we revert to the equations

(1), we notice that when $\sigma=2n$ they are satisfied by $\zeta=\bar{\zeta}$, $\Theta=iR$. To determine R as a function of r, we substitute in the equation of continuity (2), which gives

$$\frac{d(hR)}{dr}-\frac{s-1}{r}hR=-\chi(r)\qquad\text{(iv)}.$$

The arbitrary constant which appears on integration of this equation is to be determined by the boundary-condition.

In the present case we have $\chi(r)=Cr^s/a^s$. Integrating, and making $R=0$ for $r=a$, we find,

$$hR=\frac{Cr^{s-1}}{2a^s}(a^2-r^2)\,e^{i(2nt+s\theta+\epsilon)}\qquad\text{(v)}.$$

The relation $\Theta=iR$ shews that the amplitudes of R and Θ are equal, while their phases differ always by 90°; the relative orbits of the fluid particles are in fact circles of radii

$$\mathrm{r}=\frac{Cr^{s-1}}{2ha^s}(a^2-r^2)\qquad\text{(vi)},$$

described each about its centre with angular velocity $2n$ in the negative direction. We may easily deduce that the path of any particle *in space* is an ellipse of semi-axes $r\pm\mathrm{r}$ described about the origin with harmonic motion in the positive direction, the period being $2\pi/n$. This accounts for the peculiar features of the case. For if ζ have always the equilibrium-value, the horizontal forces due to the elevation exactly balance the disturbing force, and there remain only the forces due to the undisturbed form of the free surface (Art. 200 (3)). These give an acceleration $g\,dz_0/dr$, or n^2r, to the centre, where r is the radius-vector of the particle in its actual position. Hence all the conditions of the problem are satisfied by elliptic-harmonic motion of the individual particles, provided the positions, the dimensions, and the 'epochs' of the orbits can be adjusted so as to satisfy the condition of continuity, with the assumed value of ζ. The investigation just given resolves this point.

205. We may also briefly notice the case of a circular basin of variable depth, the law of depth being the same as in Art. 189, viz.

$$h=h_0\left(1-\frac{r^2}{a^2}\right)\qquad\text{(1)}.$$

Assuming that R, Θ, ζ all vary as $e^{i(\sigma t+s\theta+\epsilon)}$, and that h is a function of r only, we find, from Art. 202 (2), (3),

$$(\sigma^2-4n^2)\zeta+g\frac{dh}{dr}\left(\frac{d}{dr}+\frac{2ns}{\sigma r}\right)(\zeta-\bar{\zeta})$$
$$+gh\left(\frac{d^2}{dr^2}+\frac{1}{r}\frac{d}{dr}-\frac{s^2}{r^2}\right)(\zeta-\bar{\zeta})=0\qquad\text{(i)}.$$

Introducing the value of h from (1), we have, for the *free* oscillations

$$\left(1-\frac{r^2}{a^2}\right)\left(\frac{d^2\zeta}{dr^2}+\frac{1}{r}\frac{d\zeta}{dr}-\frac{s^2}{r^2}\zeta\right)-\frac{2}{a^2}\left(r\frac{d\zeta}{dr}+\frac{2ns}{\sigma}\zeta\right)+\frac{\sigma^2-4n^2}{gh_0}\zeta=0\qquad\text{(ii)}.$$

This is identical with Art. 189 (ii), except that we now have

$$\frac{\sigma^2-4n^2}{gh_0}-\frac{4ns}{\sigma a^2}$$

in place of σ^2/gh_0. The solution can therefore be written down from the results of that Art., viz. if we put

$$\frac{(\sigma^2-4n^2)\,a^2}{gh_0}-\frac{4ns}{\sigma}=k\,(k-2)-s^2 \quad\text{.....................(iii)},$$

we have
$$\zeta=A_s\left(\frac{r}{a}\right)^s F\left(\alpha,\,\beta,\,\gamma,\,\frac{r^2}{a^2}\right)e^{i\,(\sigma t+s\theta+\epsilon)} \quad\text{.................(iv)},$$

where
$$\alpha=\tfrac{1}{2}k+\tfrac{1}{2}s,\quad \beta=1+\tfrac{1}{2}s-\tfrac{1}{2}k,\quad \gamma=s+1\,;$$

and the condition of convergence at the boundary $r=a$ requires that

$$k=s+2j \quad\text{.......................................(v)},$$

where j is some positive integer. The values of σ are then given by (iii).

The forms of the free surface are therefore the same as in the case of no rotation, but the motion of the water-particles is different. The relative orbits are in fact now ellipses having their principal axes along and perpendicular to the radius vector; this follows easily from Art. 202 (3).

In the symmetrical modes ($s=0$), the equation (iii) gives

$$\sigma^2=\sigma_0^{\,2}+4n^2 \quad\text{...................................(vi)},$$

where σ_0 denotes the 'speed' of the corresponding mode in the case of no rotation, as found in Art. 189.

For any value of s other than zero, the most important modes are those for which $k=s+2$. The equation (iii) is then divisible by $\sigma+2n$, but this is an extraneous factor; discarding it, we have the quadratic

$$\sigma^2-2n\sigma=2sgh_0/a^2 \quad\text{.............................(vii)},$$

whence
$$\sigma=n\pm(n^2+2sgh_0/a^2)^{\frac{1}{2}} \quad\text{.......................(viii)}.$$

This gives two waves rotating round the origin, the relative wave-velocity being greater for the negative than for the positive wave, as in the case of uniform depth (Art. 203). With the help of (vii) the formulæ reduce to

$$\zeta=A_s\left(\frac{r}{a}\right)^s,\quad R=\tfrac{1}{2}\frac{a}{h_0}A_s\left(\frac{r}{a}\right)^{s-1},\quad \Theta=\tfrac{1}{2}i\frac{a}{h_0}A_s\left(\frac{r}{a}\right)^{s-1} \quad\text{.........(ix)},$$

the factor $e^{i\,(\sigma t+s\theta+\epsilon)}$ being of course understood in each case. Since $\Theta=iR$, the relative orbits are all circles. The case $s=1$ is noteworthy; the free surface is then always *plane*, and the circular orbits have all the same radius.

When $k>s+2$, we have nodal circles. The equation (iii) is then a *cubic* in $\sigma/2n$; it is easily seen that its roots are all real, lying between $-\infty$ and

-1, -1 and 0, and $+1$ and $+\infty$, respectively. As a numerical example, in the case of $s=1$, $k=5$, corresponding to the values

$$2, \qquad 6, \qquad 40$$

of $4n^2a^2/gh_0$, we find

$$\sigma/2n = \begin{cases} +2{\cdot}889 & +1{\cdot}874 & +1{\cdot}180, \\ 0{\cdot}125 & -0{\cdot}100 & -0{\cdot}037, \\ -2{\cdot}764 & -1{\cdot}774 & -1{\cdot}143. \end{cases}$$

The first and last root of each triad give positive and negative waves of a somewhat similar character to those already obtained in the case of uniform depth. The smaller negative root gives a comparatively slow oscillation which, when the angular velocity n is infinitely small, becomes a *steady* rotational motion, without elevation or depression of the surface.

The most important type of *forced* oscillations is such that

$$\bar{\zeta} = C\left(\frac{r}{a}\right)^s e^{i(\sigma t + s\theta + \epsilon)} \quad \text{.............................(x).}$$

We readily verify, on substitution in (ii), that

$$\zeta = \frac{2sgh_0}{2sgh_0 - (\sigma^2 - 2n\sigma)a^2}\bar{\zeta} \quad \text{...........................(xi).}$$

We notice that when $\sigma = 2n$ the tide-height has exactly the equilibrium-value, in agreement with Art. 204.

If σ_1, σ_2 denote the two roots of (vii), the last formula may be written

$$\zeta = \frac{1}{(1-\sigma/\sigma_1)(1-\sigma/\sigma_2)}\bar{\zeta} \quad \text{..........................(xii).}$$

Tides on a Rotating Globe.

206. We proceed to give some account of Laplace's problem of the tidal oscillations of an ocean of (comparatively) small depth covering a rotating globe*. In order to bring out more clearly the nature of the approximations which are made on various grounds, we shall adopt a method of establishing the fundamental equations somewhat different from that usually followed.

When in relative equilibrium, the free surface is of course a level-surface with respect to gravity and centrifugal force; we shall assume it to be a surface of revolution about the polar axis, but the ellipticity will not in the first instance be taken to be small.

* "Recherches sur quelques points du système du monde," *Mém. de l'Acad. roy. des Sciences*, 1775 [1778] and 1776 [1779]; *Oeuvres Complètes*, t. ix. pp. 88, 187. The investigation is reproduced, with various modifications, in the *Mécanique Céleste*, Livre 4me, c. i. (1799).

We adopt this equilibrium-form of the free surface as a surface of reference, and denote by θ and ω the co-latitude (*i.e.* the angle which the normal makes with the polar axis) and the longitude, respectively, of any point upon it. We shall further denote by z the altitude, measured outwards along a normal, of any point above this surface.

The relative position of any particle of the fluid being specified by the three orthogonal coordinates θ, ω, z, the kinetic energy of unit mass is given by

$$2T = (R+z)^2\dot{\theta}^2 + \varpi^2(n+\dot{\omega})^2 + \dot{z}^2 \quad \text{..............(1)},$$

where R is the radius of curvature of the meridian-section of the surface of reference, and ϖ is the distance of the particle from the polar axis. It is to be noticed that R is a function of θ only, whilst ϖ is a function of both θ and z; and it easily follows from geometrical considerations that

$$d\varpi/(R+z)\,d\theta = \cos\theta, \qquad d\varpi/dz = \sin\theta \quad \text{.........(2)}.$$

The component accelerations are obtained at once from (1) by Lagrange's formula. Omitting terms of the second order, on account of the restriction to infinitely small motions, we have

$$\left.\begin{aligned}
\frac{1}{R+z}\left(\frac{d}{dt}\frac{dT}{d\dot{\theta}} - \frac{dT}{d\theta}\right) &= (R+z)\ddot{\theta} - \frac{1}{R+z}(n^2+2n\dot{\omega})\,\varpi\,\frac{d\varpi}{d\theta}, \\
\frac{1}{\varpi}\left(\frac{d}{dt}\frac{dT}{d\dot{\omega}} - \frac{dT}{d\omega}\right) &= \varpi\ddot{\omega} + 2n\left(\frac{d\varpi}{d\theta}\dot{\theta} + \frac{d\varpi}{dz}\dot{z}\right), \\
\frac{d}{dt}\frac{dT}{d\dot{z}} - \frac{dT}{dz} &= \ddot{z} - (n^2+2n\dot{\omega})\,\varpi\,\frac{d\varpi}{dz}
\end{aligned}\right\} \text{...(3)}.$$

Hence, if we write u, v, w for the component relative velocities of a particle, viz.

$$u = (R+z)\dot{\theta}, \qquad v = \varpi\dot{\omega}, \qquad w = \dot{z} \quad \text{............(4)},$$

and make use of (2), the hydrodynamical equations may be put in the forms

$$\left.\begin{aligned}
\frac{du}{dt} - 2nv\cos\theta &= -\frac{1}{R+z}\frac{d}{d\theta}\left(\frac{p}{\rho} + \Psi - \tfrac{1}{2}n^2\varpi^2 + \Omega\right), \\
\frac{dv}{dt} + 2nu\cos\theta + 2nw\sin\theta &= -\frac{1}{\varpi}\frac{d}{d\omega}\left(\frac{p}{\rho} + \Psi - \tfrac{1}{2}n^2\varpi^2 + \Omega\right), \\
\frac{dw}{dt} - 2nv\sin\theta &= -\frac{d}{dz}\left(\frac{p}{\rho} + \Psi - \tfrac{1}{2}n^2\varpi^2 + \Omega\right)
\end{aligned}\right\}$$

$$\text{.........................(5)},$$

where Ψ is the gravitation-potential due to the earth's attraction, whilst Ω denotes the potential of the extraneous forces.

So far the only approximation consists in the omission of terms of the second order in u, v, w. In the present application, the depth of the sea being small compared with the dimensions of the globe, we may replace $R+z$ by R. We will further assume that the effect of the *relative* vertical acceleration on the pressure may be neglected, and that the vertical velocity is small compared with the horizontal velocity. The last of the equations (5) then reduces to

$$\frac{d}{dz}\left(\frac{p}{\rho}+\Psi-\tfrac{1}{2}n^2\varpi^2+\Omega\right)=0 \quad\ldots\ldots\ldots\ldots\ldots\ldots(6).$$

Let us integrate this between the limits z and ζ, where ζ denotes the elevation of the disturbed surface above the surface of reference. At the surface of reference ($z=0$) we have

$$\Psi-\tfrac{1}{2}n^2\varpi^2=\text{const.},$$

by hypothesis, and therefore at the free surface ($z=\zeta$)

$$\Psi-\tfrac{1}{2}n^2\varpi^2=\text{const.}+g\zeta,$$

provided

$$g=\left[\frac{d}{dz}(\Psi-\tfrac{1}{2}n^2\varpi^2)\right]_{z=0} \quad\ldots\ldots\ldots\ldots\ldots\ldots(7).$$

Here g denotes the value of *apparent* gravity at the surface of reference; it is of course, in general, a function of θ. The integration in question then gives

$$\frac{p}{\rho}+\Psi-\tfrac{1}{2}n^2\varpi^2+\Omega=\text{const.}+g\zeta+\Omega \quad\ldots\ldots\ldots\ldots(8),$$

the variation of Ω with z being neglected. Substituting from (8) in the first two of equations (5), we obtain, with the approximations above indicated,

$$\left.\begin{aligned}\frac{du}{dt}-2nv\cos\theta&=-g\frac{d}{Rd\theta}(\zeta-\bar{\zeta}),\\ \frac{dv}{dt}+2nu\cos\theta&=-g\frac{d}{\varpi d\omega}(\zeta-\bar{\zeta})\end{aligned}\right\} \quad\ldots\ldots\ldots\ldots(9),$$

where

$$\bar{\zeta}=-\Omega/g \quad\ldots\ldots\ldots\ldots\ldots\ldots\ldots\ldots\ldots(10).$$

These equations are independent of z, so that the horizontal motion may be assumed to be sensibly the same for all particles in the same vertical line.

As in Art. 190, this last result greatly simplifies the equation of continuity. In the present case we find without difficulty

$$\frac{d\zeta}{dt}=-\frac{1}{\varpi}\left\{\frac{d(h\varpi u)}{Rd\theta}+\frac{d(hv)}{d\omega}\right\}\dots\dots\dots\dots(11).$$

207. It is important to notice that these equations involve no assumptions beyond those expressly laid down; in particular, there is no restriction as to the ellipticity of the meridian, which may be of any degree of oblateness.

In order, however, to simplify the question as far as possible, without sacrificing any of its essential features, we will now take advantage of the circumstance that in the actual case of the earth the ellipticity is a small quantity, being in fact comparable with the ratio (n^2a/g) of centrifugal force to gravity at the equator, which is known to be about $\frac{1}{289}$. Subject to an error of this order of magnitude, we may put $R=a$, $\varpi=a\sin\theta$, $g=$ const., where a is the earth's mean radius. We thus obtain*

$$\left.\begin{aligned}\frac{du}{dt}-2nv\cos\theta&=-\frac{g}{a}\frac{d}{d\theta}(\zeta-\bar{\zeta}),\\ \frac{dv}{dt}+2nu\cos\theta&=-\frac{g}{a}\frac{d}{\sin\theta d\omega}(\zeta-\bar{\zeta})\end{aligned}\right\}\dots\dots\dots(1),$$

with

$$\frac{d\zeta}{dt}=-\frac{1}{a\sin\theta}\left\{\frac{d(hu\sin\theta)}{d\theta}+\frac{d(hv)}{d\omega}\right\}\dots\dots\dots(2),$$

this last equation being identical with Art. 190 (1).

Two conclusions of some interest in connection with our previous work follow at once from the *form* of the equations (1). In the first place, if $\mathbf{u}$, $\mathbf{v}$ denote the velocities along and perpendicular to *any* horizontal direction s, we easily find, by transformation of coordinates

$$\frac{d\mathbf{u}}{dt}-2n\mathbf{v}\cos\theta=-g\frac{d}{ds}(\zeta-\bar{\zeta})\dots\dots\dots\dots\dots(\text{i}).$$

In the case of a narrow canal, the transverse velocity $\mathbf{v}$ is zero, and the equation (i) takes the same form as in the case of no rotation; this has been assumed by anticipation in Art. 180. The only effect of the rotation in such cases is to produce a slight slope of the wave-crests and furrows in the direction *across* the canal, as investigated in Art. 201.

Again, by comparison of (1) with Art. 200 (7), we see that the oscillations of a sheet of water of relatively small dimensions, in colatitude θ, will take place according to the same laws as those of a *plane* sheet rotating about a normal to its plane with angular velocity $n\cos\theta$.

* Laplace, *l.c. ante* p. 343.

As in Art. 200, free steady motions are possible, subject to certain conditions. Putting $\bar{\zeta}=0$, we find that the equations (1) and (2) are satisfied by constant values of u, v, ζ, provided

$$u=-\frac{g}{2na\sin\theta\cos\theta}\frac{d\zeta}{d\omega},\quad v=\frac{g}{2na\cos\theta}\frac{d\zeta}{d\theta}\quad\text{.................. (ii),}$$

and

$$\frac{d(h\sec\theta,\,\zeta)}{d(\theta,\,\omega)}=0\quad\text{.......................... (iii).}$$

The latter condition is satisfied by any assumption of the form

$$\zeta=f(h\sec\theta)\quad\text{..................................(iv),}$$

and the equations (ii) then give the values of u, v. It appears from (ii) that the velocity in these steady motions is everywhere parallel to the contour-lines of the disturbed surface.

If h is constant, or a function of the latitude only, the only condition imposed on ζ is that it should be independent of ω; in other words the elevation must be symmetrical about the polar axis.

208. We will now suppose that the depth h is a function of θ only, and that the barriers to the sea, if any, coincide with parallels of latitude. Assuming, further, that Ω, u, v, ζ all vary as $e^{i(\sigma t+s\omega+\epsilon)}$, where s is integral, we find

$$\left.\begin{aligned} i\sigma u-2nv\cos\theta&=-\frac{g}{a}\frac{d}{d\theta}(\zeta-\bar{\zeta}),\\ i\sigma v+2nu\cos\theta&=-\frac{isg}{a\sin\theta}(\zeta-\bar{\zeta})\end{aligned}\right\}\quad\text{..............(3),}$$

with

$$i\sigma\zeta=-\frac{1}{a\sin\theta}\left\{\frac{d(hu\sin\theta)}{d\theta}+ishv\right\}\quad\text{............(4).}$$

Solving for u, v, we get

$$\left.\begin{aligned} u&=\frac{ig/a}{\sigma^2-4n^2\cos^2\theta}\left(\sigma\frac{d}{d\theta}+2sn\cot\theta\right)(\zeta-\bar{\zeta}),\\ v&=-\frac{g/a}{\sigma^2-4n^2\cos^2\theta}\left(2n\cos\theta\frac{d}{d\theta}+s\sigma\operatorname{cosec}\theta\right)(\zeta-\bar{\zeta})\end{aligned}\right\}\quad\text{...(5).}$$

If we put, for shortness,

$$\zeta-\bar{\zeta}=\zeta',\qquad \sigma/2n=f,\qquad n^2a/g=m\quad\text{...........(6),}$$

these may be written

$$\left.\begin{aligned} u&=\frac{i\sigma}{4m(f^2-\cos^2\theta)}\left(\frac{d\zeta'}{d\theta}+\frac{s}{f}\zeta'\cot\theta\right),\\ v&=-\frac{\sigma}{4m(f^2-\cos^2\theta)}\left(\frac{\cos\theta}{f}\frac{d\zeta'}{d\theta}+s\zeta'\operatorname{cosec}\theta\right)\end{aligned}\right\}\quad\text{...(7).}$$

The formulæ for the component displacements (ξ, η, say), can be written down from the relations $u = \dot{\xi}$, $v = \dot{\eta}$, or $u = i\sigma\xi$, $v = i\sigma\eta$. It appears that in all cases of periodic disturbing forces the fluid particles describe ellipses having their principal axes along the meridians and the parallels of latitude, respectively.

Substituting from (7) in (4) we obtain the differential equation in ζ':

$$\frac{1}{\sin\theta}\frac{d}{d\theta}\left\{\frac{h\sin\theta}{f^2-\cos^2\theta}\left(\frac{d\zeta'}{d\theta}+\frac{s}{f}\zeta'\cot\theta\right)\right\}$$

$$-\frac{h}{f^2-\cos^2\theta}\left(\frac{s}{f}\cot\theta\frac{d\zeta'}{d\theta}+s^2\zeta'\operatorname{cosec}^2\theta\right)+4ma\zeta'=-4ma\bar{\zeta}$$

$$\ldots\ldots\ldots\ldots\ldots\ldots(8).$$

In the case of the *free* oscillations we have $\bar{\zeta}=0$. The manner in which the boundary-conditions (if any), or the conditions of finiteness, then determine the admissible values of f, and thence of σ, will be understood by analogy, in a general way, from Arts. 191, 193. For further details we must refer to the paper cited below*. A practical solution of the problem, even in the case ($s=0$) of symmetry about the axis, with uniform depth, has not yet been worked out.

The more important problem of the *forced* oscillations, though difficult, can be solved for certain laws of depth, and for certain special values of σ which correspond more or less closely to the main types of tidal disturbance. To this we now proceed.

209. It is shewn in the Appendix to this Chapter that the tide-generating potential, when expanded in simple-harmonic functions of the time, consists of terms of three distinct types.

The first type is such that the equilibrium tide-height would be given by

$$\bar{\zeta}=H'(\tfrac{1}{3}-\cos^2\theta)\,.\cos(\sigma t+\epsilon)\ldots\ldots\ldots\ldots\ldots(1)\dagger.$$

The corresponding forced waves are called by Laplace the 'Oscillations of the First Species'; they include the lunar fortnightly

* Sir W. Thomson, "On the General Integration of Laplace's Differential Equation of the Tides," *Phil. Mag.*, Nov. 1875.

† In strictness, θ here denotes the *geocentric* latitude, but the difference between this and the geographical latitude may be neglected in virtue of the assumptions introduced in Art. 207.

and the solar semi-annual tides, and, generally, all the tides of long period. Their characteristic is symmetry about the polar axis.

Putting $s=0$ in the formulæ of the preceding Art. we have

$$\left.\begin{aligned} u &= \frac{i\sigma}{4m(f^2-\cos^2\theta)}\frac{d\zeta'}{d\theta}, \\ v &= -\frac{\sigma}{4m(f^2-\cos^2\theta)}\frac{\cos\theta}{f}\frac{d\zeta'}{d\theta} \end{aligned}\right\} \text{............ (2),}$$

and

$$i\sigma\zeta = -\frac{1}{a\sin\theta}\frac{d(hu\sin\theta)}{d\theta} \text{..................(3).}$$

The equations (2) shew that the axes of the elliptic orbit of any particle are in the ratio of $f : \cos\theta$. Since f is small, the ellipses are very elongated, the greatest length being from E. to W., except in the neighbourhood of the equator. At the equator itself the motion of the particles vanishes.

Eliminating u, v between (2) and (3), or putting $s=0$ in Art. 208 (8), we find

$$\frac{1}{a\sin\theta}\frac{d}{d\theta}\left(\frac{h\sin\theta}{f^2-\cos^2\theta}\frac{d\zeta'}{d\theta}\right)+4m\zeta' = -4mH'(\tfrac{1}{3}-\cos^2\theta)\text{...(4).}$$

We shall consider only the case of uniform depth ($h=$ const.). Writing μ for $\cos\theta$, the equation then becomes

$$\frac{d}{d\mu}\left(\frac{1-\mu^2}{f^2-\mu^2}\frac{d\zeta'}{d\mu}\right)+\beta\zeta' = -\beta H'(\tfrac{1}{3}-\mu^2) \text{ ...... (5),}$$

where

$$\beta = 4ma/h = 4n^2a^2/gh\text{.....................(6).}$$

The complete primitive of this equation is necessarily of the form

$$\zeta' = \phi(\mu) + AF(\mu) + Bf(\mu)\text{..................(7),}$$

where $\phi(\mu)$, $F(\mu)$ are even functions, and $f(\mu)$ is an odd function, of μ, and the constants A, B are arbitrary. In the case of an ocean completely covering the globe, it is not obvious at first sight that there is any limitation to the values of A and B, although on physical grounds we are assured that the solution of the problem is uniquely determinate, except for certain special values of the ratio $f(=\sigma/2n)$, which imply a coincidence between the 'speed' of the disturbing force and that of one of the free oscillations of symmetrical type. The difficulty disappears if we consider first, for a moment, the case of a zonal sea bounded by two parallels of latitude. The constants A, B are then determined by the conditions that $u=0$ at each of these parallels. If the boundaries in question are symmetrically situated on opposite sides of the equator, the constant B will be zero, and the odd function $f(\mu)$ may be disregarded *ab initio*. By supposing the boundaries to contract to points at the poles we pass to the case of an unlimited ocean. If we address ourselves in the first instance to this latter form of the problem, the one arbitrary constant (A) which it is necessary to introduce is determined by the condition that the motion must be finite at the poles.

210. The integration of the equation (5) has been treated by Lord Kelvin* and Prof. G. H. Darwin†.

We assume

$$\frac{1}{\mu^2-f^2}\frac{d\zeta'}{d\mu}=B_1\mu+B_3\mu^3+\ldots+B_{2j+1}\mu^{2j+1}+\ldots \quad\ldots\ldots(8).$$

This leads to

$$\zeta'=A-\tfrac{1}{2}f^2B_1\mu^2+\tfrac{1}{4}(B_1-f^2B_3)\mu^4+\ldots$$
$$+\frac{1}{2j}(B_{2j-3}-f^2B_{2j-1})\mu^{2j}+\ldots \quad\ldots\ldots(9),$$

where A is arbitrary; and makes

$$\frac{d}{d\mu}\left(\frac{1-\mu^2}{\mu^2-f^2}\frac{d\zeta'}{d\mu}\right)=B_1+3(B_3-B_1)\mu^2+\ldots$$
$$+(2j+1)(B_{2j+1}-B_{2j-1})\mu^{2j}+\ldots \quad\ldots\ldots(10).$$

Substituting in (5), and equating coefficients of the several powers of μ, we find

$$B_1-\tfrac{1}{3}\beta H'-\beta A=0\ldots\ldots\ldots\ldots\ldots\ldots\ldots(11),$$

$$B_3-\left(1-\frac{\beta f^2}{2.3}\right)B_1+\tfrac{1}{3}\beta H'=0\ldots\ldots\ldots\ldots\ldots(12),$$

and thenceforward

$$B_{2j+1}-\left(1-\frac{\beta f^2}{2j(2j+1)}\right)B_{2j-1}-\frac{\beta}{2j(2j+1)}B_{2j-3}=0\ldots(13).$$

* Sir W. Thomson, "On the 'Oscillations of the First Species' in Laplace's Theory of the Tides," *Phil. Mag.*, Oct. 1875.

† "On the Dynamical Theory of the Tides of Long Period," *Proc. Roy. Soc.*, Nov. 5, 1886; *Encyc. Britann.*, Art. "Tides."

It is to be noticed that (12) may be included under the typical form (13), provided we write $B_{-1} = -2H'$.

These equations determine $B_1, B_3, \ldots B_{2j+1}, \ldots$ in succession, in terms of A, and the solution thus obtained would be appropriate, as already explained, to the case of a zonal sea bounded by two parallels in equal N. and S. latitudes. In the case of an ocean covering the globe, it would, as we shall prove, give infinite velocities at the poles, except for one definite value of A, to be determined.

Let us write

$$B_{2j+1}/B_{2j-1} = N_{j+1} \qquad (14);$$

we shall shew, in the first place, that as j increases N_j must tend either to the limit 0 or to the limit 1. The equation (13) may be written

$$N_{j+1} = 1 - \frac{\beta f^2}{2j(2j+1)} + \frac{\beta}{2j(2j+1)} \frac{1}{N_j} \qquad (15).$$

Hence, when j is large, either

$$N_j = -\frac{\beta}{2j(2j+1)} \qquad (16),$$

approximately, or N_{j+1} is not small, in which case N_{j+2} will be nearly equal to 1, and the values of $N_{j+3}, N_{j+4}, \ldots$ will tend more and more nearly to 1, the approximate formula being

$$N_{j+1} = 1 - \frac{\beta(f^2-1)}{2j(2j+1)} \qquad (17).$$

Hence, with increasing j, N_j tends to one or other of the forms (16) and (17).

In the former case (16), the series (8) will be convergent for $\mu = \pm 1$, and the solution is valid over the whole globe.

In the other event (17), the product $N_1 . N_2 . \ldots N_{j+1}$, and therefore the coefficient B_{2j+1}, tends with increasing j to a finite limit other than zero. The series (8) will then, after some finite number of terms, become comparable with $1 + \mu^2 + \mu^4 + \ldots$, or $(1-\mu^2)^{-1}$, so that we may write

$$\frac{1}{\mu^2 - f^2} \frac{d\zeta'}{d\mu} = L + \frac{M}{1-\mu^2} \qquad (18),$$

where L and M are functions of μ which remain finite when $\mu = \pm 1$. Hence, from (2),

$$u = -\frac{i\sigma}{4m}\frac{(1-\mu^2)^{\frac{1}{2}}}{\mu^2 - f^2}\frac{d\zeta'}{d\mu} = -\frac{i\sigma}{4m}\{(1-\mu^2)^{\frac{1}{2}} L + (1-\mu^2)^{-\frac{1}{2}} M\} \quad \text{...(19)},$$

which makes u infinite at the poles.

It follows that the conditions of our problem can only be satisfied if N_j tends to the limit zero; and this consideration, as we shall see, restricts us to a determinate value of the hitherto arbitrary constant A.

The relation (15) may be put in the form

$$N_j = \frac{-\dfrac{\beta}{2j(2j+1)}}{1 - \dfrac{\beta f^2}{2j(2j+1)} - N_{j+1}} \quad \text{..............(20)},$$

and by successive applications of this we find

$$N_j = \frac{-\dfrac{\beta}{2j(2j+1)}}{1 - \dfrac{\beta f^2}{2j(2j+1)} +} \; \frac{\dfrac{\beta}{(2j+2)(2j+3)}}{1 - \dfrac{\beta f^2}{(2j+2)(2j+3)} +} \; \frac{\dfrac{\beta}{(2j+4)(2j+5)}}{1 - \dfrac{\beta f^2}{(2j+4)(2j+5)} + \&c.} \quad \text{..................(21)},$$

on the present supposition that N_{j+k} tends with increasing k to the limit 0, in the manner indicated by (16). In particular, this formula determines the value of N_1. Now

$$B_1 = N_1 B_{-1} = -2N_1 H',$$

and the equation (11) then gives

$$A = -\tfrac{1}{3}H' - \frac{2}{\beta}N_1 H' \quad \text{..................(22)};$$

in other words, this is the only value of A which is consistent with a zero limit of N_j, and therefore with a finite motion at the poles. Any other value of A, differing by however little, if adopted as a starting-point for the successive calculation of B_1, B_3, ... will inevitably lead at length to values of N_j which approximate to the limit 1.

For this reason it is not possible, as a matter of practical Arithmetic, to calculate B_1, B_3, ... in succession in the above manner; for this would require us to start with *exactly* the right value of A, and to observe absolute accuracy in the subsequent stages of the work. The only practical method is to use the formulæ

$$B_1/H' = -2N_1, \qquad B_3 = N_2 B_1, \qquad B_5 = N_3 B_3, \ldots,$$

$$\text{or } B_1/H' = -2N_1, \quad B_3/H' = -2N_1 N_2, \quad B_5/H' = -2N_1 N_2 N_3, \ldots \qquad (23),$$

where the values of N_1, N_2, N_3, ... are to be computed from the continued fraction (21). It is evident *a posteriori* that the solution thus obtained will satisfy all the conditions of the problem, and that the series (9) will converge with great rapidity. The most convenient plan of conducting the calculation is to assume a roughly approximate value, suggested by (16), for one of the ratios N_j of sufficiently high order, and thence to compute

$$N_{j-1},\ N_{j-2}, \ldots\ N_2,\ N_1$$

in succession by means of the formula (20). The values of the constants A, B_1, B_3, ..., in (9), are then given by (22) and (23). For the tidal elevation we find

$$\zeta/H' = -2N_1/\beta - (1 - f^2 N_1)\mu^2 - \tfrac{1}{2}N_1(1 - f^2 N_2)\mu^4 - \ldots$$
$$- \frac{1}{j} N_1 N_2 \ldots N_{j-1}(1 - f^2 N_j)\mu^{2j} - \ldots\ldots \quad (24).$$

In the case of the lunar fortnightly tide, f is the ratio of a sidereal day to a lunar month, and is therefore equal to about $\frac{1}{28}$, or more precisely ·0365. This makes $f^2 = {\cdot}00133$. It is evident that a fairly accurate representation of this tide, and *à fortiori* of the solar semi-annual tide, and of the remaining tides of long period, will be obtained by putting $f = 0$; this materially shortens the calculations.

The results will involve the value of β, $= 4n^2a^2/gh$. For $\beta = 40$, which corresponds to a depth of 7260 feet, we find in this way

$$\zeta/H' = {\cdot}1515 - 1{\cdot}0000\mu^2 + 1{\cdot}5153\mu^4 - 1{\cdot}2120\mu^6 + {\cdot}6063\mu^8 - {\cdot}2076\mu^{10}$$
$$+ {\cdot}0516\mu^{12} - {\cdot}0097\mu^{14} + {\cdot}0018\mu^{16} - {\cdot}0002\mu^{18} \ldots\ldots (25)^*,$$

whence, at the poles ($\mu = \pm 1$),

$$\zeta = -\tfrac{2}{3}H' \times {\cdot}154,$$

* The coefficients in (25) and (26) differ only slightly from the numerical values obtained by Prof. Darwin for the case $f = {\cdot}0365$.

and, at the equator ($\mu=0$),

$$\zeta=\tfrac{1}{3}H'\times\cdot455.$$

Again, for $\beta=10$, or a depth of 29040 feet, we get

$$\zeta/H=\cdot2359-1\cdot0000\mu^2+\cdot5898\mu^4-\cdot1623\mu^6$$
$$+\cdot0258\mu^8-\cdot0026\mu^{10}+\cdot0002\mu^{12}\ \ldots\ldots\ (26).$$

This makes, at the poles,

$$\zeta=-\tfrac{2}{3}H'\times\cdot470,$$

and, at the equator,

$$\zeta=\ \tfrac{1}{3}H'\times\cdot708.$$

For $\beta=5$, or a depth of 58080 feet, we find

$$\zeta/H'=\cdot2723-1\cdot0000\mu^2+\cdot3404\mu^4.$$
$$-\cdot0509\mu^6+\cdot0043\mu^8-\cdot0004\mu^{10}\ \ldots\ldots\ldots\ (27).$$

This gives, at the poles,

$$\zeta=-\tfrac{2}{3}H'\times\cdot651,$$

and, at the equator,

$$\zeta=\ \tfrac{1}{3}H'\times\cdot817.$$

Since the polar and equatorial values of the equilibrium tide are $-\tfrac{2}{3}H'$ and $\tfrac{1}{3}H'$, respectively, these results shew that for the depths in question the long-period tides are, on the whole, *direct*, though the nodal circles will, of course, be shifted more or less from the positions assigned by the equilibrium theory. It appears, moreover, that, for depths comparable with the actual depth of the sea, the tide has less than half the equilibrium value. It is easily seen from the form of equation (5), that with increasing depth, and consequent diminution of β, the tide height will approximate more and more closely to the equilibrium value. This tendency is illustrated by the above numerical results.

It is to be remarked that the kinetic theory of the long-period tides was passed over by Laplace, under the impression that practically, owing to the operation of dissipative forces, they would have the values given by the equilibrium theory. He proved, indeed, that the tendency of frictional forces must be in this direction, but it has been pointed out by Darwin* that in the case of the fortnightly tide, at all events, it is doubtful whether the effect would be nearly so great as Laplace supposed. We shall return to this point later.

* *l.c. ante* p. 350.

211. It remains to notice how the free oscillations are determined. In the case of symmetry with respect to the equator, we have only to put $H' = 0$ in the foregoing analysis. The conditions of convergency for $\mu = \pm 1$ determine $N_2, N_3, N_4, \ldots$ exactly as before; whilst equation (12) gives $N_2 = 1 - \beta f^2/2.3$, and therefore, by (20),

$$1 - \frac{\beta f^2}{2.3} + \frac{\dfrac{\beta}{4.5}}{1 - \dfrac{\beta f^2}{4.5} +} \, \frac{\dfrac{\beta}{6.7}}{1 - \dfrac{\beta f^2}{6.7} + \&c.} = 0 \ldots\ldots (28),$$

which is equivalent to $N_1 = \infty$. This equation determines the admissible values of $f \,(= \sigma/2n)$. The constants in (9) are then given by

$$B_1 = \beta A, \quad B_3 = N_2 \beta A, \quad B_5 = N_2 N_3 \beta A, \ldots,$$

where A is arbitrary.

The corresponding theory for the asymmetrical oscillations may be left to the reader. The right-hand side of (8) must now be replaced by an *even* function of μ.

212. In the next class of tidal motions (Laplace's 'Oscillations of the Second Species') which we shall consider, we have

$$\bar{\zeta} = H'' \sin\theta \cos\theta \,.\, \cos(\sigma t + \omega + \epsilon) \ldots\ldots\ldots\ldots\ldots (1),$$

where σ differs not very greatly from n. This includes the lunar and solar diurnal tides.

In the case of a disturbing body whose proper motion could be neglected, we should have $\sigma = n$, exactly, and therefore $f = \frac{1}{2}$. In the case of the moon, the orbital motion is so rapid that the actual period of the principal lunar diurnal tide is very appreciably longer than a sidereal day*; but the supposition that $f = \frac{1}{2}$ simplifies the formulæ so materially that we adopt it in the following

* It is to be remarked, however, that there is an important term in the harmonic development of Ω for which $\sigma = n$ exactly, provided we neglect the changes in the plane of the disturbing body's orbit. This period is the same for the sun as for the moon, and the two partial tides thus produced combine into what is called the 'luni-solar' diurnal tide.

investigation*. We shall find that it enables us to calculate the forced oscillations when the depth follows the law

$$h = (1 - q\cos^2\theta)\, h_0 \quad\text{.......................(2)},$$

where q is any given constant.

Taking an exponential factor $e^{i(nt+\omega+\epsilon)}$, and therefore putting $s=1$, $f=\frac{1}{2}$, in Art. 208 (7), and assuming

$$\zeta' = C\sin\theta\cos\theta \quad\text{........................(3)},$$

we find $$u = -i\sigma C/m, \quad v = \sigma C/m \,.\, \cos\theta \quad\text{..............(4)}.$$

Substituting in the equation of continuity (Art. 208 (4)), we get

$$\zeta' + \bar{\zeta} = \frac{C}{ma}\frac{dh}{d\theta} \quad\text{........................ (5)},$$

which is consistent with the law of depth (2), provided

$$C = -\frac{1}{1 - 2qh_0/ma} H'' \quad\text{................. (6)}.$$

This gives $$\zeta = -\frac{2qh_0/ma}{1 - 2qh_0/ma}\bar{\zeta} \quad\text{..................... (7)}.$$

One remarkable consequence of this formula is that in the case of uniform depth ($q = 0$) there is no diurnal tide, so far as the rise and fall of the surface is concerned. This result was first established (in a different manner) by Laplace, who attached great importance to it as shewing that his kinetic theory is able to account for the relatively small values of the diurnal tide which are given by observation, in striking contrast to what would be demanded by the equilibrium-theory.

But, although with a uniform depth there is no rise and fall, there are tidal currents. It appears from (4) that every particle describes an ellipse whose major axis is in the direction of the meridian, and of the same length in all latitudes. The ratio of the minor to the major axis is $\cos\theta$, and so varies from 1 at the poles to 0 at the equator, where the motion is wholly N. and S.

213. Finally, we have to consider Laplace's 'Oscillations of the Third Species,' which are such that

$$\bar{\zeta} = H''' \sin^2\theta \,.\, \cos(\sigma t + 2\omega + \epsilon) \quad\text{..............(1)},$$

* Taken with very slight alteration from Airy ("Tides and Waves," Arts. 95...), and Darwin (*Encyc. Britann.*, t. xxiii., p. 359).

where σ is nearly equal to $2n$. This includes the most important of all the tidal oscillations, viz. the lunar and solar semi-diurnal tides.

If the orbital motion of the disturbing body were infinitely slow we should have $\sigma = 2n$, and therefore $f = 1$; for simplicity we follow Laplace in making this approximation, although it is a somewhat rough one in the case of the principal lunar tide*.

A solution similar to that of the preceding Art. can be obtained for the special law of depth

$$h = h_0 \sin^2\theta \quad\text{.........................(2)}\dagger.$$

Adopting an exponential factor $e^{i(2nt+2\omega+\epsilon)}$, and putting therefore $f = 1$, $s = 2$, we find that if we assume

$$\zeta' = C \sin^2\theta \quad\text{.........................(3)}$$

the equations (7) of Art. 208 give

$$u = \frac{i\sigma}{m} C \cot\theta, \quad v = -\frac{\sigma}{2m} C \frac{1+\cos^2\theta}{\sin\theta} \quad\text{...........(4),}$$

whence, substituting in Art. 208 (4),

$$\zeta = 2h_0/ma \,.\, C \sin^2\theta \quad\text{.....................(5).}$$

Putting $\zeta = \zeta' + \bar{\zeta}$, and substituting from (1) and (3), we find

$$C = -\frac{1}{1 - 2h_0/ma} H''' \quad\text{.....................(6),}$$

and therefore

$$\zeta = -\frac{2h_0/ma}{1 - 2h_0/ma} \bar{\zeta} \quad\text{.......................(7).}$$

For such depths as actually occur in the ocean we have $2h_0 < ma$, and the tide is therefore inverted.

It may be noticed that the formulæ (4) make the velocity infinite at the poles.

214. For any other law of depth a solution can only be obtained in the form of an infinite series.

In the case of *uniform* depth we find, putting $s = 2$, $f = 1$, $4ma/h = \beta$ in Art. 208 (8),

$$(1-\mu^2)^2 \frac{d^2\zeta'}{d\mu^2} + \{\beta(1-\mu^2)^2 - 2\mu^2 - 6\}\zeta' = -\beta(1-\mu^2)^2\bar{\zeta} \quad\text{...(8),}$$

* There is, however, a 'luni-solar' semi-diurnal tide whose speed is exactly $2n$ if we neglect the changes in the planes of the orbits. Cf. p. 355, footnote.

† Cf. Airy and Darwin, *ll. cc.*

where μ is written for $\cos\theta$. In this form the equation is somewhat intractable, since it contains terms of four different dimensions in μ. It simplifies a little, however, if we transform to

$$\nu, = (1-\mu^2)^{\frac{1}{2}}, = \sin\theta,$$

as independent variable; viz. we find

$$\nu^2(1-\nu^2)\frac{d^2\zeta'}{d\nu^2} - \nu\frac{d\zeta'}{d\nu} - (8-2\nu^2-\beta\nu^4)\zeta' = -\beta\nu^4\zeta = -\beta H'''\nu^6 \ldots (9),$$

which is of *three* different dimensions in ν.

To obtain a solution for the case of an ocean covering the globe, we assume

$$\zeta' = B_0 + B_2\nu^2 + B_4\nu^4 + \ldots + B_{2j}\nu^{2j} + \ldots \ldots\ldots (10).$$

Substituting in (9), and equating coefficients, we find

$$B_0 = 0, \quad B_2 = 0, \quad 0 \,.\, B_4 = 0 \ldots\ldots\ldots\ldots (11),$$

$$16B_6 - 10B_4 + \beta H''' = 0 \ldots\ldots\ldots\ldots (12),$$

and thenceforward

$$2j(2j+6)B_{2j+4} - 2j(2j+3)B_{2j+2} + \beta B_{2j} = 0 \ldots\ldots (13).$$

These equations give $B_6, B_8, \ldots B_{2j}, \ldots$ in succession, in terms of B_4, which is so far undetermined. It is obvious, however, from the nature of the problem, that, except for certain special values of h (and therefore of β), which are such that there is a free oscillation of corresponding type ($s=2$) having the speed $2n$, the solution must be unique. We shall see, in fact, that unless B_4 have a certain definite value the solution above indicated will make the meridian component (u) of the velocity discontinuous at the equator*.

The argument is in some respects similar to that of Art. 210. If we denote by N_j the ratio B_{2j+2}/B_{2j} of consecutive coefficients, we have, from (13),

$$N_{j+1} = \frac{2j+3}{2j+6} - \frac{\beta}{2j(2j+6)}\frac{1}{N_j} \ldots\ldots\ldots\ldots (14),$$

from which it appears that, with increasing j, N_j must tend to one or other of the limits 0 and 1. More precisely, unless the limit of N_j be zero, the limiting form of N_{j+1} will be

$$(2j+3)/(2j+6), \text{ or } 1 - 3/2j,$$

* In the case of a polar sea bounded by a small circle of latitude whose angular radius is $<\frac{1}{2}\pi$, the value of B_4 is determined by the condition that $u=0$, or $d\zeta'/d\nu=0$, at the boundary.

approximately. This is the same as the limiting form of the ratio of the coefficients of ν^{2j} and ν^{2j-2} in the expansion of $(1-\nu^2)^{\frac{1}{2}}$. We infer that, unless B_4 have such a value as to make $N_\infty = 0$, the terms of the series (10) will become ultimately comparable with those of $(1-\nu^2)^{\frac{1}{2}}$, so that we may write

$$\zeta' = L + (1-\nu^2)^{\frac{1}{2}} M \quad\text{.....................(15)},$$

where L, M are functions of ν which do not vanish for $\nu = 1$. Near the equator ($\nu = 1$) this makes

$$\frac{d\zeta'}{d\theta} = \pm(1-\nu^2)^{\frac{1}{2}} \frac{d\zeta'}{d\nu} = \mp M \quad\text{.............. (16)}.$$

Hence, by Art. 208 (7), u would change from a certain finite value to an equal but opposite value as we cross the equator.

It is therefore essential, for our present purpose, to choose the value of B_4 so that $N_\infty = 0$. This is effected by the same method as in Art. 210. Writing (13) in the form

$$N_j = \frac{\dfrac{\beta}{2j(2j+6)}}{\dfrac{2j+3}{2j+6} - N_{j+1}} \quad\text{.....................(17)},$$

we see that N_j must be given by the converging continued fraction

$$N_j = \frac{\dfrac{\beta}{2j(2j+6)}}{\dfrac{2j+3}{2j+6} -}\;\frac{\dfrac{\beta}{(2j+2)(2j+8)}}{\dfrac{2j+5}{2j+8} -}\;\frac{\dfrac{\beta}{(2j+4)(2j+10)}}{\dfrac{2j+7}{2j+10} - \&c.} \quad\text{... (18)}.$$

This holds from $j = 2$ upwards, but it appears from (12) that it will give also the value of N_1 (not hitherto defined), provided we use this symbol for B_4/H'''. We have then

$$B_4 = N_1 H''', \quad B_6 = N_2 B_4, \quad B_8 = N_3 B_6, \; \ldots.$$

Finally, writing $\zeta = \bar{\zeta} + \zeta'$, we obtain

$$\zeta/H''' = \nu^2 + N_1\nu^4 + N_1N_2\nu^6 + N_1N_2N_3\nu^8 + \ldots \quad\text{......(19)}.$$

As in Art. 210, the practical method of conducting the calculation is to assume an approximate value for N_{j+1}, where j is a moderately large number, and then to deduce N_j, $N_{j-1}, \ldots N_2$, N_1 in succession by means of the formula (17).

The above investigation is taken substantially from the very remarkable paper written by Lord Kelvin* in vindication of Laplace's treatment of the problem, as given in the *Mécanique Céleste*. In the passage more especially in question, Laplace determines the constant B_4 by means of the continued fraction for N_1, without, it must be allowed, giving any adequate justification of the step; and the soundness of this procedure had been disputed by Airy†, and after him by Ferrel‡.

Laplace, unfortunately, was not in the habit of giving specific references, so that few of his readers appear to have become acquainted with the original presentment§ of the kinetic theory, where the solution for the case in question is put in a very convincing, though somewhat different, form. Aiming in the first instance at an approximate solution by means of a *finite* series, thus:

$$\zeta' = B_4\nu^4 + B_6\nu^6 + \ldots + B_{2k+2}\nu^{2k+2} \quad\ldots\ldots\ldots\ldots\text{(i)},$$

Laplace remarks‖ that in order to satisfy the differential equation, the coefficients would have to fulfil the conditions

$$\left.\begin{aligned} &16B_6 - 10B_4 + \beta H''' = 0,\\ &40B_8 - 28B_6 + \beta B_4 = 0,\\ &\ldots\ldots\ldots\ldots\ldots\ldots\\ &(2k-2)(2k+4)\,B_{2k+2} - (2k-2)(2k+1)\,B_{2k} + \beta B_{2k-2} = 0,\\ &\qquad\qquad - 2k\,(2k+3)\,B_{2k+2} + \beta B_{2k} = 0,\\ &\qquad\qquad\qquad\qquad \beta B_{2k+2} = 0 \end{aligned}\right\}\ldots\ldots\text{(ii)},$$

as is seen at once by putting $B_{2k+4} = 0$, $B_{2k+6} = 0, \ldots$ in the general relation (13).

We have here $k+1$ equations between k constants. The method followed is to determine the constants by means of the first k relations; we thus obtain an exact solution, not of the proposed differential equation (9), but of the equation as modified by the addition of a term $\beta B_{2k+2}\nu^{2k+6}$ to the right-hand side. This is equivalent to an alteration of the disturbing force, and if we can obtain a solution such that the required alteration is very small, we may accept it as an approximate solution of the problem in its original form¶.

Now, taking the first k relations of the system (ii) in reverse order, we obtain B_{2k+2} in terms of B_{2k}, thence B_{2k} in terms of B_{2k-1}, and so on, until, finally, B_4 is expressed in terms of H'''; and it is obvious that if k be large enough the value of B_{2k+2}, and the consequent adjustment of the disturbing

* Sir W. Thomson, "On an Alleged Error in Laplace's Theory of the Tides," *Phil. Mag.*, Sept. 1875.

† "Tides and Waves," Art. 111.

‡ "Tidal Researches," *U.S. Coast Survey Rep.*, 1874, p. 154.

§ "Recherches sur quelques points du système du monde," *Mém. de l'Acad. roy. des Sciences*, 1776 [1779]; *Oeuvres Complètes*, t. ix., pp. 187....

‖ *Oeuvres*, t. ix., p. 218. The notation has been altered.

¶ It is remarkable that this argument is of a kind constantly employed by Airy himself in his researches on waves.

force which is required to make the solution exact, will be very small. This will be illustrated presently, after Laplace, by a numerical example.

The process just given is plainly equivalent to the use of the continued fraction (17) in the manner already explained, starting with $j+1=k$, and $N_k=\beta/2k(2k+3)$. The continued fraction, as such, does not, however, make its appearance in the memoir here referred to, but was introduced in the *Mécanique Céleste*, probably as an after-thought, as a condensed expression of the method of computation originally employed.

The following table gives the numerical values of the coefficients of the several powers of ν in the formula (19) for ζ/H''', in the cases $\beta=40, 20, 10, 5, 1$, which correspond to depths of 7260, 14520, 29040, 58080, 290400, feet, respectively*. The last line gives the value of ζ/H''' for $\nu=1$, *i.e.* the ratio of the amplitude at the equator to its equilibrium-value. At the poles ($\nu=0$), the tide has in all cases the equilibrium-value zero.

	$\beta=40$	$\beta=20$	$\beta=10$	$\beta=5$	$\beta=1$
ν^2	+ 1·0000	+1·0000	+1·0000	+1·0000	+1·0000
ν^4	+20·1862	−0·2491	+6·1960	+0·7504	+0·1062
ν^6	+10·1164	−1·4056	+3·2474	+0·1566	+0·0039
ν^8	−13·1047	−0·8594	+0·7238	+0·0157	+0·0001
ν^{10}	−15·4488	−0·2541	+0·0919	+0·0009	
ν^{12}	− 7·4581	−0·0462	+0·0076		
ν^{14}	− 2·1975	−0·0058	+0·0004		
ν^{16}	− 0·4501	−0·0006			
ν^{18}	− 0·0687				
ν^{20}	− 0·0082				
ν^{22}	− 0·0008				
ν^{24}	− 0·0001				
	− 7·434	−1·821	+11·267	+1·924	+1·110

We may use the above results to estimate the closeness of the approximation in each case. For example, when $\beta=40$, Laplace finds $B_{28}=-\cdot000004H'''$; the addition to the disturbing force which is necessary to make the solution exact would then be $-\cdot00002H'''\nu^{30}$, and would therefore bear to the actual force the ratio $-\cdot00002\,\nu^{28}$.

It appears from (19) that near the poles, where ν is small, the tides are in all cases direct. For sufficiently great depths, β will

* The first three cases were calculated by Laplace, *l.c. ante* p. 360; the last by Lord Kelvin. The results have been roughly verified by the present writer.

be very small, and the formulæ (17) and (19) then shew that the tide has everywhere sensibly the equilibrium value, all the coefficients being small except the first, which is unity. As h is diminished, β increases, and the formula (17) shews that each of the ratios N_j will continually increase, except when it changes sign from + to − by passing through the value ∞. No singularity in the solution attends this passage of N_j through ∞, except in the case of N_1, since, as is easily seen, the product $N_{j-1} N_j$ remains finite, and the coefficients in (19) are therefore all finite. But when $N_1 = \infty$, the expression for ζ becomes infinite, shewing that the depth has then one of the critical values already referred to.

The table above given indicates that for depths of 29040 feet, and upwards, the tides are everywhere direct, but that there is some critical depth between 29040 feet and 14520 feet, for which the tide at the equator changes from direct to inverted. The largeness of the second coefficient in the case $\beta = 40$ indicates that the depth could not be reduced much below 7260 feet before reaching a second critical value.

Whenever the equatorial tide is inverted, there must be one or more pairs of nodal circles ($\zeta = 0$), symmetrically situated on opposite sides of the equator. In the case of $\beta = 40$, the position of the nodal circles is given by $\nu = \cdot 95$, or $\theta = 90° \pm 18°$, approximately*.

215. We close this chapter with a brief notice of the question of the stability of the ocean, in the case of rotation.

It has been shewn in Art. 197 that the condition of secular stability is that $V - T_0$ should be a minimum in the equilibrium configuration. If we neglect the mutual attraction of the elevated water, the application to the present problem is very simple. The excess of the quantity $V - T_0$ over its undisturbed value is evidently

$$\iint\left\{\int_0^\zeta (\Psi - \tfrac{1}{2}n^2\varpi^2)\, dz\right\} dS \quad \text{.................} \quad (1),$$

where Ψ denotes the potential of the earth's attraction, δS is an element of the oceanic surface, and the rest of the notation is as

* For a fuller discussion of these points reference may be made to the original investigation of Laplace, and to Lord Kelvin's papers.

before. Since $\Psi - \frac{1}{2}n^2\varpi^2$ is constant over the undisturbed level ($z = 0$), its value at a small altitude z may be taken to be $gz +$ const., where, as in Art. 206,

$$g = \left[\frac{d}{dz}(\Psi - \tfrac{1}{2}n^2\varpi^2)\right]_{z=0} \quad\text{..................}\quad (2).$$

Since $\iint\zeta dS = 0$, on account of the constancy of volume, we find from (1) that the increment of $V - T_0$ is

$$\tfrac{1}{2}\iint g\zeta^2 dS \quad\text{............................}\quad (3).$$

This is essentially positive, and the equilibrium is therefore secularly stable*.

It is to be noticed that this proof does not involve any restriction as to the depth of the fluid, or as to smallness of the ellipticity, or even as to symmetry of the undisturbed surface with respect to the axis of rotation.

If we wish to take into account the mutual attraction of the water, the problem can only be solved without difficulty when the undisturbed surface is nearly spherical, and we neglect the variation of g. The question (as to secular stability) is then exactly the same as in the case of no rotation. The calculation for this case will find an appropriate place in the next chapter. The result, as we might anticipate from Art. 192, is that the ocean is stable if, and only if, its density be less than the mean density of the Earth*.

* Cf. Laplace, *Mécanique Céleste*, Livre 4me, Arts. 13, 14.

APPENDIX.

ON TIDE-GENERATING FORCES.

a. IF, in the annexed figure, O and C be the centres of the earth and of the disturbing body (say the moon), the potential of the moon's attraction at a point P near the earth's surface will be $-\gamma M/CP$, where M denotes the

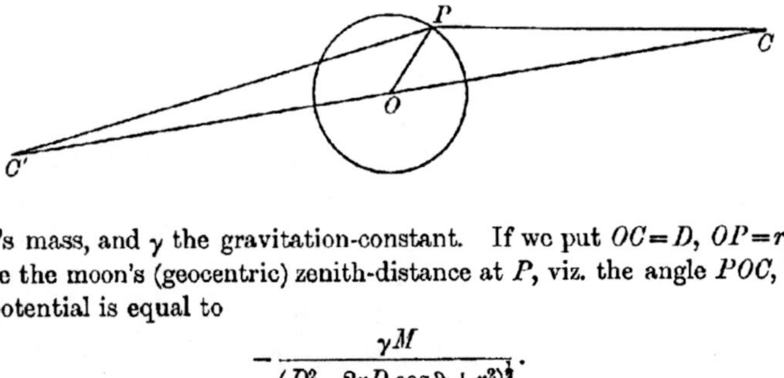

moon's mass, and γ the gravitation-constant. If we put $OC=D$, $OP=r$, and denote the moon's (geocentric) zenith-distance at P, viz. the angle POC, by ϑ, this potential is equal to

$$-\frac{\gamma M}{(D^2-2rD\cos\vartheta+r^2)^{\frac{1}{2}}}.$$

We require, however, not the absolute accelerative effect on P, but the acceleration relative to the earth. Now the moon produces in the whole mass of the earth an acceleration $\gamma M/D^2$* parallel to OC, and the potential of a uniform field of force of this intensity is evidently

$$-\frac{\gamma M}{D^2}\cdot r\cos\vartheta.$$

Subtracting this from the former result we get, for the potential of the relative attraction on P,

$$\Omega=-\frac{\gamma M}{(D^2-2rD\cos\vartheta+r^2)^{\frac{1}{2}}}+\frac{\gamma M}{D^2}\cdot r\cos\vartheta \qquad \text{(i)}.$$

This function Ω is identical with the 'disturbing-function' of planetary theory.

* The effect of this is to produce a monthly inequality in the motion of the earth's centre about the sun. The amplitude of the inequality in radius vector is about 3000 miles; that of the inequality in longitude is about 7″. Laplace, *Mécanique Céleste*, Livre 6me, Art. 30, and Livre 13me, Art. 10.

Expanding in powers of r/D, which is in our case a small quantity, and retaining only the most important term, we find

$$\Omega = \tfrac{3}{2}\frac{\gamma M r^2}{D^3}(\tfrac{1}{3} - \cos^2\vartheta) \qquad \text{(ii)}.$$

Considered as a function of the position of P, this is a zonal harmonic of the second degree, with OC as axis.

The reader will easily verify that, to the order of approximation adopted, Ω is equal to the joint potential of two masses, each equal to $\tfrac{1}{2}M$, placed, one at C, and the other at a point C' in CO produced such that $OC' = OC$*.

b. In the 'equilibrium-theory' of the tides it is assumed that the free surface takes at each instant the equilibrium-form which might be maintained if the disturbing body were to retain unchanged its actual position relative to the rotating earth. In other words, the free surface is assumed to be a level-surface under the combined action of gravity, of centrifugal force, and of the disturbing force. The equation to this level-surface is

$$\Psi - \tfrac{1}{2}n^2\varpi^2 + \Omega = \text{const.} \qquad \text{(iii)},$$

where n is the angular velocity of the rotation, ϖ denotes the distance of any point from the earth's axis, and Ψ is the potential of the earth's attraction. If we use square brackets [ ] to distinguish the values of the enclosed quantities at the undisturbed level, and denote by $\bar{\zeta}$ the elevation of the water above this level due to the disturbing potential Ω, the above equation is equivalent to

$$[\Psi - \tfrac{1}{2}n^2\varpi^2] + \left[\frac{d}{dz}(\Psi - \tfrac{1}{2}n^2\varpi^2)\right]\bar{\zeta} + \Omega = \text{const.} \qquad \text{(iv)},$$

approximately, where d/dz is used to indicate a space-differentiation along the normal outwards. The first term is of course constant, and we therefore have

$$\bar{\zeta} = -\Omega/g + C \qquad \text{(v)},$$

where, as in Art. 206,

$$g = \left[\frac{d}{dz}(\Psi - \tfrac{1}{2}n^2\varpi^2)\right] \qquad \text{(vi)}.$$

Evidently, g denotes the value of 'apparent gravity'; it will of course vary more or less with the position of P on the earth's surface.

It is usual, however, in the theory of the tides, to ignore the slight variations in the value of g, and the effect of the ellipticity of the undisturbed level on the surface-value of Ω. Putting, then, $r = a$, $g = \gamma E/a^2$, where E denotes the earth's mass, and a the mean radius of the surface, we have, from (ii) and (v),

$$\bar{\zeta} = H(\cos^2\vartheta - \tfrac{1}{3}) + C \qquad \text{(vii)},$$

where

$$H = \tfrac{3}{2}\cdot\frac{M}{E}\cdot\left(\frac{a}{D}\right)^3\cdot a \qquad \text{(viii)},$$

as in Art. 177. Hence the equilibrium-form of the free surface is a harmonic

* Thomson and Tait, *Natural Philosophy*, Art. 804.

spheroid of the second order, of the zonal type, having its axis passing through the disturbing body.

c. Owing to the diurnal rotation, and also to the orbital motion of the disturbing body, the position of the tidal spheroid relative to the earth is continually changing, so that the level of the water at any particular place will continually rise and fall. To analyse the character of these changes, let θ be the co-latitude, and ω the longitude, measured eastward from some fixed meridian, of any place P, and let Δ be the north-polar-distance, and α the hour-angle west of the same meridian, of the disturbing body. We have, then,

$$\cos\vartheta = \cos\Delta\cos\theta + \sin\Delta\sin\theta\cos(\alpha+\omega) \quad \text{(ix)},$$

and thence, by (vii),

$$\begin{aligned}\bar{\zeta} &= \tfrac{3}{2}H(\cos^2\Delta - \tfrac{1}{3})(\cos^2\theta - \tfrac{1}{3}) \\ &+ \tfrac{1}{2}H\sin 2\Delta\sin 2\theta\cos(\alpha+\omega) \\ &+ \tfrac{1}{2}H\sin^2\Delta\sin^2\theta\cos 2(\alpha+\omega) + C \quad \text{(x)}.\end{aligned}$$

Each of these terms may be regarded as representing a partial tide, and the results superposed.

Thus, the *first* term is a zonal harmonic of the second order, and gives a tidal spheroid symmetrical with respect to the earth's axis, having as nodal lines the parallels for which $\cos^2\theta = \frac{1}{3}$, or $\theta = 90° \pm 35° 16'$. The amount of the tidal elevation in any particular latitude varies as $\cos^2\Delta - \frac{1}{3}$. In the case of the moon the chief fluctuation in this quantity has a period of about a fortnight; we have here the origin of the 'lunar fortnightly' or 'declinational' tide. When the sun is the disturbing body, we have a 'solar semi-annual' tide. It is to be noticed that the mean value of $\cos^2\Delta - \frac{1}{3}$ with respect to the time is not zero, so that the inclination of the orbit of the disturbing body to the equator involves as a consequence a permanent change of mean level. Cf. Art. 180.

The *second* term in (x) is a spherical harmonic of the type obtained by putting $n=2$, $s=1$ in Art. 87 (6). The corresponding tidal spheroid has as nodal lines the meridian which is distant 90° from that of the disturbing body, and the equator. The disturbance of level is greatest in the meridian of the disturbing body, at distances of 45° N. and S. of the equator. The oscillation at any one place goes through its period with the hour-angle α, *i.e.* in a lunar or solar day. The amplitude is, however, not constant, but varies slowly with Δ, changing sign when the disturbing body crosses the equator. This term accounts for the lunar and solar 'diurnal' tides.

The *third* term is a sectorial harmonic ($n=2$, $s=2$), and gives a tidal spheroid having as nodal lines the meridians which are distant 45° E. and W. from that of the disturbing body. The oscillation at any place goes through its period with 2α, *i.e.* in half a (lunar or solar) day, and the amplitude varies as $\sin^2\Delta$, being greatest when the disturbing body is on the equator. We have here the origin of the lunar and solar 'semi-diurnal' tides.

The 'constant' C is to be determined by the consideration that, on account of the invariability of volume, we must have

$$\iint \bar{\zeta} dS = 0 \quad \text{(xi)},$$

where the integration extends over the surface of the ocean. If the ocean cover the whole earth we have $C=0$, by the general property of spherical surface-harmonics quoted in Art. 88. It appears from (vii) that the greatest elevation above the undisturbed level is then at the points $\vartheta=0$, $\vartheta=180^\circ$, *i.e.* at the points where the disturbing body is in the zenith or nadir, and the amount of this elevation is $\frac{2}{3}H$. The greatest depression is at places where $\vartheta=90^\circ$, *i.e.* the disturbing body is on the horizon, and is $\frac{1}{3}H$. The greatest possible range is therefore equal to H.

In the case of a limited ocean, C does not vanish, but has at each instant a definite value depending on the position of the disturbing body relative to the earth. This value may be easily written down from equations (x) and (xi); it is a sum of spherical harmonic functions of Δ, a, of the second order, with constant coefficients in the form of surface-integrals whose values depend on the distribution of land and water over the globe. The changes in the value of C, due to relative motion of the disturbing body, give a *general* rise and fall of the free surface, with (in the case of the moon) fortnightly, diurnal, and semi-diurnal periods. This 'correction to the equilibrium-theory,' as usually presented, was first fully investigated by Thomson and Tait*. The necessity for a correction of the kind, in the case of a limited sea, had however been recognized by D. Bernoulli†.

d. We have up to this point neglected the mutual attraction of the particles of the water. To take this into account, we must add to the disturbing potential Ω the gravitation-potential of the elevated water. In the case of an ocean covering the earth, the correction can be easily applied, as in Art. 192. Putting $n=2$ in the formulæ of that Art., the addition to the value of Ω is $-\frac{3}{5}\rho/\rho_0 \cdot g\bar{\zeta}$; and we thence find without difficulty

$$\bar{\zeta} = \frac{H}{1-\frac{3}{5}\rho/\rho_0}(\cos^2\vartheta - \tfrac{1}{3}) \quad \text{(xii)}.$$

It appears that all the tides are *increased*, in the ratio $(1-\frac{3}{5}\rho/\rho_0)^{-1}$. If we assume $\rho/\rho_0 = \cdot18$, this ratio is 1·12.

e. So much for the equilibrium-theory. For the purposes of the kinetic theory of Arts. 206—214, it is necessary to suppose the value (x) of $\bar{\zeta}$ to be expanded in a series of simple-harmonic functions of the time. The actual

* *Natural Philosophy*, Art. 808; see also Prof. G. H. Darwin, "On the Correction to the Equilibrium Theory of the Tides for the Continents," *Proc. Roy. Soc.*, April 1, 1886. It appears as the result of a numerical calculation by Prof. H. H. Turner, appended to this paper, that with the actual distribution of land and water the correction is of little importance.

† *Traité sur le Flux et Reflux de la Mer*, c. xi. (1740). This essay, as well as the one by Maclaurin cited on p. 322, and another on the same subject by Euler, is reprinted in Le Seur and Jacquier's edition of Newton's *Principia*.

expansion, taking account of the variations of Δ and a, and of the distance D of the disturbing body, (which enters into the value of H), is a somewhat complicated problem of Physical Astronomy, into which we do not enter here*.

Disregarding the constant C, which disappears in the dynamical equations (1) of Art. 207, the constancy of volume being now secured by the equation of continuity (2), it is easily seen that the terms in question will be of three distinct types.

First, we have the tides of long period, for which

$$\bar{\zeta} = H' (\cos^2 \theta - \tfrac{1}{3}) . \cos (\sigma t + \epsilon) \quad \text{.....................} \quad \text{(xiii)}.$$

The most important tides of this class are the 'lunar fortnightly' for which, in degrees per mean solar hour, $\sigma = 1^\circ \cdot 098$, and the 'solar semi-annual' for which $\sigma = 0^\circ \cdot 082$.

Secondly, we have the diurnal tides, for which

$$\bar{\zeta} = H'' \sin \theta \cos \theta . \cos (\sigma t + \omega + \epsilon) \quad \text{.....................} \quad \text{(xiv)},$$

where σ differs but little from the angular velocity n of the earth's rotation. These include the 'lunar diurnal' [$\sigma = 13^\circ \cdot 943$], the 'solar diurnal' [$\sigma = 14^\circ \cdot 959$], and the 'luni-solar diurnal' [$\sigma = n = 15^\circ \cdot 041$].

Lastly, we have the semi-diurnal tides, for which

$$\bar{\zeta} = H''' \sin^2 \theta . \cos (\sigma t + 2\omega + \epsilon) \quad \text{.....................} \quad \text{(xv)} \dagger,$$

where σ differs but little from $2n$. These include the 'lunar semi-diurnal' [$\sigma = 28^\circ \cdot 984$], the 'solar semi-diurnal' [$\sigma = 30^\circ$], and the 'luni-solar semi-diurnal' [$\sigma = 2n = 30^\circ \cdot 082$].

For a complete enumeration of the more important partial tides, and for the values of the coefficients H', H'', H''' in the several cases, we must refer to the papers by Lord Kelvin and Prof. G. H. Darwin, already cited. In the Harmonic Analysis of Tidal Observations, which is the special object of these investigations, the only result of dynamical theory which is made use of is the general principle that the tidal elevation at any place must be equal to the sum of a series of simple-harmonic functions of the time, whose periods are the same as those of the several terms in the development of the disturbing potential, and are therefore known *à priori*. The amplitudes and phases of the various partial tides, for any particular port, are then determined by comparison with tidal observations extending over a sufficiently long period‡.

* Reference may be made to Laplace, *Mécanique Céleste*, Livre 13me, Art. 2; to the investigations of Lord Kelvin and Prof. G. H. Darwin in the *Brit. Ass. Reports* for 1868, 1872, 1876, 1883, 1885; and to the Art. on "Tides," by the latter author, in the *Encyc. Britann.* (9th ed.).

† It is evident that over a small area, near the poles, which may be treated as sensibly plane, the formulæ (xiv) and (xv) make

$$\bar{\zeta} \propto r \cos (\sigma t + \omega + \epsilon), \quad \text{and} \quad \bar{\zeta} \propto r^2 \cos (\sigma t + 2\omega + \epsilon),$$

respectively, where r, ω are plane polar coordinates. These forms have been used by anticipation in Arts. 188, 204.

‡ It is of interest to note, in connection with Art. 184, that the tide-gauges, being situated in relatively shallow water, are sensibly affected by certain tides of the second order, which therefore have to be taken account of in the general scheme of Harmonic Analysis.

We thus obtain a practically complete expression which can be used for the systematic prediction of the tides at the port in question.

f. One point of special interest in the Harmonic Analysis is the determination of the long-period tides. It has been already stated that owing to the influence of dissipative forces these must tend to approximate more or less closely to their equilibrium values. Unfortunately, the only long-period tide, whose coefficient can be inferred with any certainty from the observations, is the lunar fortnightly, and it is at least doubtful whether the dissipative forces are sufficient to produce in this case any great effect in the direction indicated. Hence the observed fact that the fortnightly tide has less than its equilibrium value does not entitle us to make any inference as to elastic yielding of the solid body of the earth to the tidal distorting forces exerted by the moon*.

* Prof. G. H. Darwin, *l.c. ante* p. 350.

CHAPTER IX.

SURFACE WAVES.

216. WE have now to investigate, as far as possible, the laws of wave-motion in liquids when the restriction that the vertical acceleration may be neglected is no longer imposed. The most important case not covered by the preceding theory is that of waves on relatively deep water, where, as will be seen, the agitation rapidly diminishes in amplitude as we pass downwards from the surface; but it will be understood that there is a continuous transition to the state of things investigated in the preceding chapter, where the horizontal motion of the fluid was sensibly the same from top to bottom.

We begin with the oscillations of a horizontal sheet of water, and we will confine ourselves in the first instance to cases where the motion is in two dimensions, of which one (x) is horizontal, and the other (y) vertical. The elevations and depressions of the free surface will then present the appearance of a series of parallel straight ridges and furrows, perpendicular to the plane xy.

The motion, being assumed to have been generated originally from rest by the action of ordinary forces, will be necessarily irrotational, and the velocity-potential ϕ will satisfy the equation

$$\frac{d^2\phi}{dx^2} + \frac{d^2\phi}{dy^2} = 0 \qquad (1),$$

with the condition

$$\frac{d\phi}{dn} = 0 \qquad (2)$$

at a fixed boundary.

To find the condition which must be satisfied at the free surface ($p = \text{const.}$), let the origin O be taken at the undisturbed level, and let Oy be drawn vertically upwards. The motion being assumed to be infinitely small, we find, putting $\Omega = gy$ in the formula (4) of Art. 21, and neglecting the square of the velocity (q),

$$\frac{p}{\rho} = \frac{d\phi}{dt} - gy + F(t) \quad \text{.....................} \quad (3).$$

Hence if η denote the elevation of the surface at time t above the point (x, 0), we shall have, since the pressure there is uniform,

$$\eta = \frac{1}{g}\left[\frac{d\phi}{dt}\right]_{y=\eta} \quad \text{..........................} (4),$$

provided the function $F(t)$, and the additive constant, be supposed merged in the value of $d\phi/dt$. Subject to an error of the order already neglected, this may be written

$$\eta = \frac{1}{g}\left[\frac{d\phi}{dt}\right]_{y=0} \quad \text{..........................} (5).$$

Since the normal to the free surface makes an infinitely small angle ($d\eta/dx$) with the vertical, the condition that the normal component of the fluid velocity at the free surface must be equal to the normal velocity of the surface itself gives, with sufficient approximation,

$$\frac{d\eta}{dt} = -\left[\frac{d\phi}{dy}\right]_{y=0} \quad \text{......................} \quad (6).$$

This is in fact what the general surface condition (Art. 10 (3)) becomes, if we put $F(x, y, z, t) \equiv y - \eta$, and neglect small quantities of the second order.

Eliminating η between (5) and (6), we obtain the condition

$$\frac{d^2\phi}{dt^2} + g\frac{d\phi}{dy} = 0 \quad \text{......................} \quad (7),$$

to be satisfied when $y = 0$.

In the case of simple-harmonic motion, the time-factor being $e^{i(\sigma t + \epsilon)}$, this condition becomes

$$\sigma^2\phi = g\frac{d\phi}{dy} \quad \text{..........................} (8).$$

217. Let us apply this to the free oscillations of a sheet of water, or a straight canal, of uniform depth h, and let us suppose for the present that there are no limits to the fluid in the direction of x, the fixed boundaries, if any, being vertical planes parallel to xy.

Since the conditions are uniform in respect to x, the simplest supposition we can make is that ϕ is a simple-harmonic function of x; the most general case consistent with the above assumptions can be derived from this by superposition, in virtue of Fourier's Theorem.

We assume then

$$\phi = P \cos kx \, . \, e^{i(\sigma t + \epsilon)} \qquad \text{.......................(1)},$$

where P is a function of y only. The equation (1) of Art. 216 gives

$$\frac{d^2P}{dy^2} - k^2P = 0 \qquad \text{....................... (2)},$$

whence

$$P = Ae^{ky} + Be^{-ky} \qquad \text{.......................(3)}.$$

The condition of no vertical motion at the bottom is $d\phi/dy = 0$ for $y = -h$, whence

$$Ae^{-kh} = Be^{kh}, \ = \tfrac{1}{2}C, \text{ say.}$$

This leads to

$$\phi = C \cosh k(y+h) \cos kx \, . \, e^{i(\sigma t + \epsilon)} \qquad \text{...............(4)}.$$

The value of σ is then determined by Art. 216 (8), which gives

$$\sigma^2 = gk \tanh kh \qquad \text{.......................(5)}.$$

Substituting from (4) in Art. 216 (5), we find

$$\eta = \frac{i\sigma C}{g} \cosh kh \cos kx \, . \, e^{i(\sigma t + \epsilon)} \qquad \text{.............. (6)},$$

or, writing

$$a = -\sigma C/g \, . \cosh kh,$$

and retaining only the real part of the expression,

$$\eta = a \cos kx \, . \sin (\sigma t + \epsilon) \qquad \text{.................. (7)}.$$

This represents a system of 'standing waves,' of wave-length $\lambda = 2\pi/k$, and vertical amplitude a. The relation between the period $(2\pi/\sigma)$ and the wave-length is given by (5). Some numerical examples of this dependence will be given in Art. 218.

In terms of a we have

$$\phi = -\frac{ga}{\sigma}\frac{\cosh k(y+h)}{\cosh kh}\cos kx \,.\, \cos(\sigma t+\epsilon) \qquad (8),$$

and it is easily seen from Art. 62 that the corresponding value of the stream-function is

$$\psi = \frac{ga}{\sigma}\frac{\sinh k(y+h)}{\cosh kh}\sin kx \,.\, \cos(\sigma t+\epsilon) \qquad (9).$$

If $\mathbf{x}$, $\mathbf{y}$ be the coordinates of a particle relative to its mean position (x, y), we have

$$\frac{d\mathbf{x}}{dt} = -\frac{d\phi}{dx}, \quad \frac{d\mathbf{y}}{dt} = -\frac{d\phi}{dy} \qquad (10),$$

if we neglect the differences between the component velocities at the points (x, y) and $(x+\mathbf{x},\ y+\mathbf{y})$, as being small quantities of the second order.

Substituting from (8), and integrating with respect to t, we find

$$\left.\begin{aligned} \mathbf{x} &= -a\frac{\cosh k(y+h)}{\sinh kh}\sin kx \,.\, \sin(\sigma t+\epsilon), \\ \mathbf{y} &= a\frac{\sinh k(y+h)}{\sinh kh}\cos kx \,.\, \sin(\sigma t+\epsilon) \end{aligned}\right\} \qquad (11),$$

where a slight reduction has been effected by means of (5). The motion of each particle is rectilinear, and simple-harmonic, the direction of motion varying from vertical, beneath the crests and hollows ($kx = m\pi$), to horizontal, beneath the nodes ($kx = (m+\frac{1}{2})\pi$). As we pass downwards from the surface to the bottom the amplitude of the vertical motion diminishes from $a\cos kx$ to 0, whilst that of the horizontal motion diminishes in the ratio $\cosh kh : 1$.

When the wave-length is very small compared with the depth, kh is large, and therefore $\tanh kh = 1$. The formulæ (11) then reduce to

$$\left.\begin{aligned} \mathbf{x} &= -ae^{ky}\sin kx \,.\, \sin(\sigma t+\epsilon), \\ \mathbf{y} &= ae^{ky}\cos kx \,.\, \sin(\sigma t+\epsilon) \end{aligned}\right\} \qquad (12),$$

with

$$\sigma^2 = gk \qquad (13)^*.$$

The motion now diminishes rapidly from the surface down-

* This case may of course be more easily investigated independently.

wards; thus at a depth of a wave-length the diminution of amplitude is in the ratio $e^{-2\pi}$ or 1/535. The forms of the lines of (oscillatory) motion (ψ = const.), for this case, are shewn in the annexed figure.

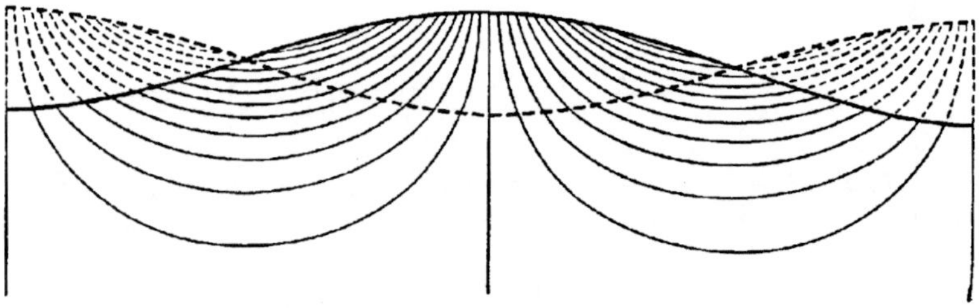

In the above investigation the fluid is supposed to extend to infinity in the direction of x, and there is consequently no restriction to the value of k. The formulæ also, give, however, the longitudinal oscillations in a canal of finite length, provided k have the proper values. If the fluid be bounded by the vertical planes $x=0$, $x=l$ (say), the condition $d\phi/dx=0$ is satisfied at both ends provided $\sin kl=0$, or $kl=m\pi$, where $m=1, 2, 3, \ldots$. The wave-lengths of the normal modes are therefore given by the formula $\lambda=2l/m$. Cf. Art. 175.

218. The investigation of the preceding Art. relates to the case of 'standing' waves; it naturally claims the first place, as a straightforward application of the usual method of treating the free oscillations of a system about a state of equilibrium.

In the case, however, of a sheet of water, or a canal, of uniform depth, extending to infinity in both directions, we can, by superposition of two systems of standing waves of the same wave-length, obtain a system of progressive waves which advance unchanged with constant velocity. For this, it is necessary that the crests and troughs of one component system should coincide (horizontally) with the nodes of the other, that the amplitudes of the two systems should be equal, and that their phases should differ by a quarter-period.

Thus if we put $$\eta = \eta_1 \pm \eta_2 \qquad (1),$$

where $$\eta_1 = a \sin kx \cos \sigma t, \quad \eta_2 = a \cos kx \sin \sigma t \qquad (2),$$

we get $$\eta = a \sin (kx \pm \sigma t) \qquad (3),$$

which represents (Art. 167) an infinite train of waves travelling in the negative or positive direction of x, respectively, with the velocity c given by

$$c = \frac{\sigma}{k} = \left(\frac{g}{k}\tanh kh\right)^{\frac{1}{2}} \quad \text{......................} \quad (4),$$

where the value of σ has been substituted from Art. 217 (5). In terms of the wave-length (λ) we have

$$c = \left(\frac{g\lambda}{2\pi}\tanh\frac{2\pi h}{\lambda}\right)^{\frac{1}{2}} \quad \text{......................} (5).$$

When the wave-length is anything less than double the depth, we have $\tanh kh = 1$, sensibly, and therefore

$$c = \left(\frac{g}{k}\right)^{\frac{1}{2}} = \left(\frac{g\lambda}{2\pi}\right)^{\frac{1}{2}} \quad \text{......................} \quad (6)*.$$

On the other hand when λ is moderately large compared with h we have $\tanh kh = kh$, nearly, so that the velocity is independent of the wave-length, being given by

$$c = (gh)^{\frac{1}{2}} \text{..............................} (7),$$

as in Art. 167. This formula is here obtained on the assumption that the wave-profile is a curve of sines, but Fourier's theorem shews that this restriction is now unnecessary.

It appears, on tracing the curve $y = (\tanh x)/x$, or from the numerical table to be given presently, that for a given depth h the wave-velocity increases constantly with the wave-length, from zero to the asymptotic value (7).

Let us now fix our attention, for definiteness, on a train of simple-harmonic waves travelling in the positive direction, *i.e.* we take the lower sign in (1) and (3). It appears, on comparison with Art. 217 (7), that the value of η_1 is deduced by putting $\epsilon = \frac{1}{2}\pi$, and subtracting $\frac{1}{2}\pi$ from the value of kx†, and that of η_2 by putting $\epsilon = 0$, simply. This proves a statement made above as to the relation between the component systems of standing waves,

* Green, "Note on the Motion of Waves in Canals," *Camb. Trans.*, t. vii. (1839); *Mathematical Papers*, p. 279.

† This is of course merely equivalent to a change of the origin from which x is measured.

and also enables us to write down at once the proper modifications of the remaining formulæ of the preceding Art.

Thus, we find, for the component displacements of a particle,

$$\left.\begin{aligned}\mathbf{x} = \mathbf{x}_1 - \mathbf{x}_2 = a\,\frac{\cosh k(y+h)}{\sinh kh}\cos(kx - \sigma t),\\ \mathbf{y} = \mathbf{y}_1 - \mathbf{y}_2 = a\,\frac{\sinh k(y+h)}{\sinh kh}\sin(kx-\sigma t)\end{aligned}\right\}\quad\ldots\ldots(8).$$

This shews that the motion of each particle is elliptic-harmonic, the period ($2\pi/\sigma$, $=\lambda/c$,) being of course that in which the disturbance travels over a wave-length. The semi-axes, horizontal and vertical, of the elliptic orbits are

$$a\,\frac{\cosh k(y+h)}{\sinh kh}\quad\text{and}\quad a\,\frac{\sinh k(y+h)}{\sinh kh},$$

respectively. These both diminish from the surface to the bottom ($y=-h$), where the latter vanishes. The distance between the foci is the same for all the ellipses, being equal to a cosech kh. It easily appears, on comparison of (8) with (3), that a surface-particle is moving in the direction of wave-propagation when it is at a crest, and in the opposite direction when it is in a trough*.

When the depth exceeds half a wave-length, e^{-kh} is very small, and the formulæ (8) reduce to

$$\left.\begin{aligned}\mathbf{x} = ae^{ky}\cos(kx-\sigma t),\\ \mathbf{y} = ae^{ky}\sin(kx-\sigma t)\end{aligned}\right\}\quad\ldots\ldots\ldots\ldots\ldots\ldots(9),$$

so that each particle describes a circle, with constant angular velocity σ, $=(g\lambda/2\pi)^{\frac{1}{2}}$†. The radii of these circles are given by the formula ae^{ky}, and therefore diminish rapidly downwards.

In the following table, the second column gives the values of sech kh corresponding to various values of the ratio h/λ. This quantity measures the ratio of the horizontal motion at the bottom to that at the surface. The third column gives the ratio of the vertical to the horizontal diameter of the elliptic orbit of a surface particle. The fourth and fifth columns give the ratios of the wave-velocity to that of waves of the same length on water of infinite depth, and to that of 'long' waves on water of the actual depth, respectively.

* The results of Arts. 217, 218, for the case of finite depth, were given, substantially, by Airy, "Tides and Waves," Arts. 160... (1845).

† Green, *l. c. ante* p. 375.

h/λ	sech kh	tanh kh	$c/(gk^{-1})^{\frac{1}{2}}$	$c/(gh)^{\frac{1}{2}}$
0·00	1·000	0·000	0·000	1·000
·01	·998	·063	·250	·999
·02	·992	·125	·354	·997
·03	·983	·186	·432	·994
·04	·969	·246	·496	·990
·05	·953	·304	·552	·984
·06	·933	·360	·600	·977
·07	·911	·413	·643	·970
·08	·886	·464	·681	·961
·09	·859	·512	·715	·951
·10	·831	·557	·746	·941
·20	·527	·850	·922	·823
·30	·297	·955	·977	·712
·40	·161	·987	·993	·627
·50	·086	·996	·998	·563
·60	·046	·999	·999	·515
·70	·025	1·000	1·000	·477
·80	·013	1·000	1·000	·446
·90	·007	1·000	1·000	·421
1·00	·004	1·000	1·000	·399
∞	·000	1·000	1·000	·000

The annexed tables of absolute values of periods and wave-velocities are abridged from Airy's treatise*. The value of g adopted by him is 32·16 f.s.s.

Depth of water, in feet	Length of wave, in feet: 1	10	100	1000	10,000
	Period of wave, in seconds				
1	0·442	1·873	17·645	176·33	1763·3
10	0·442	1·398	5·923	55·80	557·62
100	0·442	1·398	4·420	18·73	176·45
1000	0·442	1·398	4·420	13·98	59·23
10,000	0·442	1·398	4·420	13·98	44·20

Depth of water, in feet	Length of wave, in feet: 1	10	100	1000	10,000	∞
	Wave-velocity, in feet per second					
1	2·262	5·339	5·667	5·671	5·671	5·671
10	2·262	7·154	16·88	17·92	17·93	17·93
100	2·262	7·154	22·62	53·39	56·67	56·71
1000	2·262	7·154	22·62	71·54	168·8	179·3
10,000	2·262	7·154	22·62	71·54	226·2	567·1

* "Tides and Waves," Arts. 169, 170.

The possibility of progressive waves advancing with unchanged form is of course limited, theoretically, to the case of uniform depth; but the foregoing numerical results shew that practically a variation in the depth will have no appreciable influence, provided the depth everywhere exceeds (say) half the wave-length.

We remark, finally, that the theory of progressive waves may be obtained, without the intermediary of standing waves, by assuming at once, in place of Art. 217 (1),

$$\phi = Pe^{i(\sigma t - kx)} \quad \text{.........................(10).}$$

The conditions to be satisfied by P are exactly the same as before, and we easily find, in real form,

$$\eta = a \sin(kx - \sigma t) \quad \text{.......................(11),}$$

$$\phi = \frac{ga}{\sigma} \frac{\cosh k(y+h)}{\cosh kh} \cos(kx - \sigma t) \quad \text{........... (12),}$$

with the same determination of σ as before. From (12) all the preceding results as to the motion of the individual particles can be inferred without difficulty.

219. The *energy* of a system of standing waves of the simple-harmonic type is easily found. If we imagine two vertical planes to be drawn at unit distance apart, parallel to xy, the potential energy per wave-length of the fluid between these planes is, as in Art. 171,

$$\tfrac{1}{2} g\rho \int_0^\lambda \eta^2 \, dx.$$

Substituting the value of η from Art. 217 (7), we obtain

$$\tfrac{1}{4} g\rho a^2 \lambda \,.\, \sin^2(\sigma t + \epsilon) \quad \text{....................(1).}$$

The kinetic energy is, by the formula (1) of Art. 61,

$$\tfrac{1}{2} \rho \int_0^\lambda \left[\phi \frac{d\phi}{dy} \right]_{y=0} dx.$$

Substituting from Art. 217 (8), and remembering the relation between σ and k, we obtain

$$\tfrac{1}{4} g\rho a^2 \lambda \,.\, \cos^2(\sigma t + \epsilon) \quad \text{....................(2).}$$

The total energy, being the sum of (1) and (2), is constant, and equal to $\frac{1}{4}g\rho a^2\lambda$. We may express this by saying that the total energy per unit area of the water-surface is $\frac{1}{4}g\rho a^2$.

A similar calculation may be made for the case of progressive waves, or we may apply the more general method explained in Art. 171. In either way we find that the energy at any instant is half potential and half kinetic, and that the total amount, per unit area, is $\frac{1}{2}g\rho a^2$. In other words, the energy of a progressive wave-system of amplitude a is equal to the work which would be required to raise a stratum of the fluid, of thickness a, through a height $\frac{1}{2}a$.

220. So long as we confine ourselves to a first approximation all our equations are linear; so that if ϕ_1, ϕ_2, ... be the velocity-potentials of distinct systems of waves of the simple-harmonic type above considered, then

$$\phi = \phi_1 + \phi_2 + \ldots \qquad (1)$$

will be the velocity-potential of a possible form of wave-motion, with a free surface. Since, when ϕ is determined, the equation of the free surface is given by Art. 216 (5), the elevation above the mean level at any point of the surface, in the motion given by (1), will be equal to the algebraic sum of the elevations due to the separate systems of waves ϕ_1, ϕ_2, ... Hence each of the latter systems is propagated exactly as if the others were absent, and produces its own elevation or depression at each point of the surface.

We can in this way, by adding together terms of the form given in Art. 218 (12), with properly chosen values of a, build up an analytical expression for the free motion of the water in an infinitely long canal, due to any arbitrary initial conditions. Thus, let us suppose that, when $t=0$, the equation of the free surface is

$$\eta = f(x), \qquad \text{(i)},$$

and that the normal velocity at the surface is then $F(x)$, or, to our order of approximation,

$$-\left[\frac{d\phi}{dy}\right]_{y=0} = F(x). \qquad \text{(ii)}.$$

The value of ϕ is found to be

$$\phi = \int_0^\infty \frac{dk}{\pi}\frac{g}{kc}\frac{\cosh k(y+h)}{\cosh kh}\left[\left\{\int_{-\infty}^{\infty} d\lambda\, f(\lambda)\cos k(\lambda - x)\right\}\sin kct \right.$$
$$\left. - \frac{1}{kc}\left\{\int_{-\infty}^{\infty} d\lambda\, F(\lambda)\cos k(\lambda - x)\right\}\cos kct\right], \qquad \text{(iii)},$$

and the equation of the free surface is

$$\eta = \int_0^\infty \frac{dk}{\pi} \left[\left\{ \int_{-\infty}^{\infty} d\lambda\, f(\lambda) \cos k(\lambda - x) \right\} \cos kct + \frac{1}{kc} \left\{ \int_{-\infty}^{\infty} d\lambda\, F(\lambda) \cos k(\lambda - x) \right\} \sin kct \right] \text{.............(iv).}$$

These formulæ, in which c is a function of k given by Art. 218 (4), may be readily verified by means of Fourier's expression for an arbitrary function as a definite integral, viz.

$$f(x) = \frac{1}{\pi} \int_0^\infty dk \left\{ \int_{-\infty}^{\infty} d\lambda\, f(\lambda) \cos k(\lambda - x) \right\} \text{ .... (v).}$$

When the initial conditions are arbitrary, the subsequent motion is made up of systems of waves, of all possible lengths, travelling in either direction, each with the velocity proper to its own wave-length. Hence, in general, the form of the free surface is continually altering, the only exception being when the wave-length of every component system which is present in sensible amplitude is large compared with the depth of the fluid. In this case the velocity of propagation $(gh)^{\frac{1}{2}}$ is independent of the wave-length, so that, if we have waves travelling in one direction only, the wave-profile remains unchanged in form as it advances, as in Art. 167.

In the case of infinite depth, the formulæ (iii), (iv) take the simpler forms

$$\phi = \int_0^\infty \frac{dk}{\pi} \frac{e^{ky}}{k} \left[(gk)^{\frac{1}{2}} \left\{ \int_{-\infty}^{\infty} d\lambda\, f(\lambda) \cos k(\lambda - x) \right\} \sin g^{\frac{1}{2}} k^{\frac{1}{2}} t - \left\{ \int_{-\infty}^{\infty} d\lambda\, F(\lambda) \cos k(\lambda - x) \right\} \cos g^{\frac{1}{2}} k^{\frac{1}{2}} t \right] \text{...........(vi),}$$

$$\eta = \int_0^\infty \frac{dk}{\pi} \left[\left\{ \int_{-\infty}^{\infty} d\lambda\, f(\lambda) \cos k(\lambda - x) \right\} \cos g^{\frac{1}{2}} k^{\frac{1}{2}} t + \frac{1}{g^{\frac{1}{2}} k^{\frac{1}{2}}} \left\{ \int_{-\infty}^{\infty} d\lambda\, F(\lambda) \cos k(\lambda - x) \right\} \sin g^{\frac{1}{2}} k^{\frac{1}{2}} t \right] \text{...... (vii).}$$

The problem of tracing out the consequences of a limited initial disturbance, in this case, received great attention at the hands of the earlier investigators in the subject, to the neglect of the more important and fundamental properties of simple-harmonic trains. Unfortunately, the results, even on the simplest suppositions which we may make as to the nature and extent of the original disturbance, are complicated and difficult of interpretation. We shall therefore content ourselves with the subjoined references, which will enable the reader to make himself acquainted with what has been achieved in this branch of the subject*.

* Poisson, "Mémoire sur la Théorie des Ondes," *Mém. de l'Acad. roy. des Sciences*, 1816.

Cauchy, *l. c. ante* p. 18.

Sir W. Thomson, "On the Waves produced by a Single Impulse in Water of any Depth, or in a Dispersive Medium," *Proc. Roy. Soc.*, Feb. 3, 18 7.

W. Burnside, "On Deep-Water Waves resulting from a Limited Original Disturbance," *Proc. Lond. Math. Soc.*, t. xx., p. 22 (1888).

221. A remarkable result of the dependence of the velocity of propagation on the wave-length is furnished by the theory of group-velocity. It has often been noticed that when an isolated group of waves, of sensibly the same length, is advancing over relatively deep water, the velocity of the group as a whole is less than that of the waves composing it. If attention be fixed on a particular wave, it is seen to advance through the group, gradually dying out as it approaches the front, whilst its former position in the group is occupied in succession by other waves which have come forward from the rear.

The simplest analytical representation of such a group is obtained by the superposition of two systems of waves of the same amplitude, and of nearly but not quite the same wave-length. The corresponding equation of the free surface will be of the form

$$\eta = a \sin k (x - ct) + a \sin k' (x - c't)$$

$$= 2a \cos\left(\frac{k-k'}{2} x - \frac{kc - k'c'}{2} t\right) \sin\left(\frac{k+k'}{2} x - \frac{kc+k'c'}{2} t\right) \ldots (1).$$

If k, k' be very nearly equal, the cosine in this expression varies very slowly with x; so that the wave-profile at any instant has the form of a curve of sines in which the amplitude alternates gradually between the values 0 and $2a$. The surface therefore presents the appearance of a series of groups of waves, separated at equal intervals by bands of nearly smooth water. The motion of each group is then sensibly independent of the presence of the others. Since the interval between the centres of two successive groups is $2\pi/(k-k')$, and the time occupied by the system in shifting through this space is $2\pi/(kc - k'c')$, the group-velocity is $(kc - k'c')/(k-k')$, or $d(kc)/dk$, ultimately. In terms of the wave-length $\lambda \,(= 2\pi/k)$, the group-velocity is

$$\frac{d(kc)}{dk} = c - \lambda \frac{dc}{d\lambda} \ldots\ldots\ldots\ldots\ldots\ldots\ldots\ldots (2).$$

This result holds for any case of waves travelling through a uniform medium. In the present application we have

$$c = \left(\frac{g}{k} \tanh kh\right)^{\frac{1}{2}} \ldots\ldots\ldots\ldots\ldots\ldots\ldots\ldots (3),$$

and therefore, for the group-velocity,

$$\frac{d(kc)}{dk} = \tfrac{1}{2}c\left(1 + \frac{2kh}{\sinh 2kh}\right) \quad\text{..................(4).}$$

The ratio which this bears to the wave-velocity c increases as kh diminishes, being $\frac{1}{2}$ when the depth is very great, and unity when it is very small, compared with the wave-length.

The above explanation seems to have been first suggested by Stokes*. The question was attacked from another point of view by Prof. Osborne Reynolds†, by a calculation of the energy propagated across a vertical plane of particles. In the case of infinite depth, the velocity-potential corresponding to a simple-harmonic train of waves

$$\eta = a \sin k(x - ct) \quad\text{.......................(5),}$$

is

$$\phi = ace^{ky} \cos k(x - ct) \quad\text{.....................(6),}$$

as may be verified by the consideration that for $y = 0$ we must have $d\eta/dt = -d\phi/dy$. The variable part of the pressure is $\rho d\phi/dt$, if we neglect terms of the second order, so that the rate at which work is being done on the fluid to the right of the plane x is

$$-\int_{-\infty}^{0} p\frac{d\phi}{dx}dy = \rho a^2k^2c^3\sin^2 k(x-ct)\int_{-\infty}^{0} e^{2ky}dy$$

$$= \tfrac{1}{2}g\rho a^2 c \sin^2 k(x - ct) \quad\text{............(7),}$$

since $c^2 = g/k$. The mean value of this expression is $\frac{1}{4}g\rho a^2 c$. It appears on reference to Art. 219 that this is exactly one-half of the energy of the waves which cross the plane in question per unit time. Hence in the case of an isolated group the supply of energy is sufficient only if the group advance with *half* the velocity of the individual waves.

It is readily proved in the same manner that in the case

* Smith's Prize Examination, 1876. See also Lord Rayleigh, *Theory of Sound*, Art. 191.

† "On the Rate of Progression of Groups of Waves, and the Rate at which Energy is Transmitted by Waves," *Nature*, t. xvi., p. 343 (1877). Professor Reynolds has also constructed a model which exhibits in a very striking manner the distinction between wave-velocity and group-velocity in the case of the transverse oscillations of a row of equal pendulums whose bobs are connected by a string.

of a finite depth h the average energy transmitted per unit time is

$$\tfrac{1}{4}g\rho a^2 c\left(1+\frac{2kh}{\sinh 2kh}\right) \quad\text{.................. (8)*,}$$

which is, by (4), the same as

$$\tfrac{1}{2}g\rho a^2 \times \frac{d(kc)}{dk} \quad\text{........................ (9).}$$

Hence the rate of transmission of energy is equal to the group-velocity, $d(kc)/dk$, found independently by the former line of argument.

These results have a bearing on such questions as the 'wave-resistance' of ships. It appears from Art. 227, below, in the two-dimensional form of the problem, that a local disturbance of pressure advancing with velocity c [$< (gh)^{\frac{1}{2}}$] over still water of depth h is followed by a simple-harmonic train of waves of the length $(2\pi/k)$ appropriate to the velocity c, and determined therefore by (3); whilst the water in front of the disturbance is sensibly at rest. If we imagine a fixed vertical plane to be drawn in the rear of the disturbance, the space in front of this plane gains, per unit time, the additional wave-energy $\tfrac{1}{2}g\rho a^2 c$, where a is the amplitude of the waves generated. The energy transmitted across the plane is given by (8). The difference represents the work done by the disturbing force. Hence if R denote the horizontal resistance experienced by the disturbing body, we have

$$R=\tfrac{1}{4}g\rho a^2\left(1-\frac{2kh}{\sinh 2kh}\right) \quad\text{............... (10).}$$

As c increases from zero to $(gh)^{\frac{1}{2}}$, kh diminishes from ∞ to 0, and therefore R diminishes from $\tfrac{1}{4}g\rho a^2$ to 0†.

When $c > (gh)^{\frac{1}{2}}$, the water is unaffected beyond a certain small distance on either side, and the wave-resistance R is then zero‡.

* Lord Rayleigh, "On Progressive Waves," *Proc. Lond. Math. Soc.*, t. ix., p. 21 (1877); *Theory of Sound*, t. i., Appendix.

† It must be remarked, however, that the amplitude a due to a disturbance of given character will also vary with c.

‡ Cf. Sir W. Thomson "On Ship Waves," *Proc. Inst. Mech. Eng.*, Aug. 3, 1887; *Popular Lectures and Addresses*, London, 1889–94, t. iii., p. 450. A formula equivalent to (10) was given in a paper by the same author, "On Stationary Waves in Flowing Water," *Phil. Mag.*, Nov. 1886.

222. The theory of progressive waves may be investigated, in a very compact manner, by the method of Art. 172*.

Thus if ϕ, ψ be the velocity- and stream-functions when the problem has been reduced to one of steady motion, we assume

$$(\phi + i\psi)/c = -(x + iy) + i\alpha e^{ik(x+iy)} + i\beta e^{-ik(x+iy)},$$

whence
$$\left.\begin{aligned}\phi/c &= -x - (\alpha e^{-ky} - \beta e^{ky}) \sin kx, \\ \psi/c &= -y + (\alpha e^{-ky} + \beta e^{ky}) \cos kx\end{aligned}\right\} \qquad (1).$$

This represents a motion which is periodic in respect to x, superposed on a uniform current of velocity c. We shall suppose that $k\alpha$ and $k\beta$ are small quantities; in other words that the amplitude of the disturbance is small compared with the wave-length.

The profile of the free surface must be a stream-line; we will take it to be the line $\psi = 0$. Its form is then given by (1), viz. to a first approximation we have

$$y = (\alpha + \beta) \cos kx \qquad (2),$$

shewing that the origin is at the mean level of the surface. Again, at the bottom $(y = -h)$ we must also have $\psi = \text{const.}$; this requires

$$\alpha e^{kh} + \beta e^{-kh} = 0.$$

The equations (1) may therefore be put in the forms

$$\left.\begin{aligned}\phi/c &= -x + C \cosh k(y + h) \sin kx, \\ \psi/c &= -y + C \sinh k(y + h) \cos kx\end{aligned}\right\} \qquad (3).$$

The formula for the pressure is

$$\frac{p}{\rho} = \text{const.} - gy - \tfrac{1}{2}\left\{\left(\frac{d\phi}{dx}\right)^2 + \left(\frac{d\phi}{dy}\right)^2\right\}$$

$$= \text{const.} - gy - \frac{c^2}{2}\{1 - 2kC \cosh k(y + h) \cos kx\},$$

neglecting k^2C^2. Since the equation to the stream-line $\psi = 0$ is

$$y = C \sinh kh \cos kx \qquad (4),$$

approximately, we have, along this line,

$$\frac{p}{\rho} = \text{const.} + (kc^2 \coth kh - g)\, y.$$

* Lord Rayleigh, *l. c. ante* p. 279.

The condition for a free surface is therefore satisfied, provided

$$c^2 = gh \cdot \frac{\tanh kh}{kh} \quad \text{.......................} \quad (5).$$

This determines the wave-length ($2\pi/k$) of possible stationary undulations on a stream of given uniform depth h, and velocity c. It is easily seen that the value of kh is real or imaginary according as c is less or greater than $(gh)^{\frac{1}{2}}$.

If, on the other hand, we impress on everything the velocity $-c$ parallel to x, we get progressive waves on still water, and (5) is then the formula for the wave-velocity, as in Art. 218.

When the ratio of the depth to the wave-length is sufficiently great, the formulæ (1) become

$$\left.\begin{aligned}\phi/c &= -x + \beta e^{ky} \sin kx, \\ \psi/c &= -y + \beta e^{ky} \cos kx\end{aligned}\right\} \quad \text{..........................} \quad \text{(i)},$$

leading to $$\frac{p}{\rho} = \text{const.} - gy - \frac{c^2}{2}\{1 - 2k\beta e^{ky} \cos kx + k^2\beta^2 e^{2ky}\} \text{...............(ii)}.$$

If we neglect $k^2\beta^2$, the latter equation may be written

$$\frac{p}{\rho} = \text{const.} + (kc^2 - g)\, y + kc\psi \text{........................(iii)}.$$

Hence if $$c^2 = g/k \text{....................................(iv)},$$

the pressure will be uniform not only at the upper surface, but along *every* stream-line $\psi = \text{const.}$* This point is of some importance; for it shews that the solution expressed by (i) and (iv) can be extended to the case of any number of liquids of different densities, arranged one over the other in horizontal strata, provided the uppermost surface be free, and the total depth infinite. And, since there is no limitation to the thinness of the strata, we may even include the case of a heterogeneous liquid whose density varies continuously with the depth.

223. The method of the preceding Art. can be readily adapted to a number of other problems.

For example, to find the velocity of propagation of waves over the common horizontal boundary of two masses of fluid which are otherwise unlimited, we may assume

$$\left.\begin{aligned}\psi/c &= -y + \beta e^{ky} \cos kx, \\ \psi'/c &= -y + \beta e^{-ky} \cos kx\end{aligned}\right\} \text{.................(1)},$$

where the accent relates to the upper fluid. For these satisfy the

* This conclusion, it must be noted, is limited to the case of infinite depth. It was first remarked by Poisson, *l.c. ante*, p. 380.

condition of irrotational motion, $\nabla^2\psi=0$; and they give a uniform velocity c at a great distance above and below the common surface, at which we have $\psi=\psi'=0$, say, and therefore $y=\beta\cos kx$, approximately.

The pressure-equations are

$$\frac{p}{\rho}=\text{const.}-gy-\frac{c^2}{2}(1-2k\beta e^{ky}\cos kx),$$

$$\frac{p'}{\rho'}=\text{const.}-gy-\frac{c^2}{2}(1+2k\beta e^{-ky}\cos kx),$$

which give, at the common surface,

$$p/\rho=\text{const.}-(g-kc^2)\,y,$$

$$p'/\rho'=\text{const.}-(g+kc^2)\,y,$$

the usual approximations being made. The condition $p=p'$ thus leads to

$$c^2=\frac{g}{k}\cdot\frac{\rho-\rho'}{\rho+\rho'}\quad\text{.........................(2)},$$

a result first obtained by Stokes.

The presence of the upper fluid has therefore the effect of diminishing the velocity of propagation of waves of any given length in the ratio $\{(1-s)/(1+s)\}^{\frac{1}{2}}$, where s is the ratio of the density of the upper to that of the lower fluid. This diminution has a two-fold cause; the potential energy of a given deformation of the common surface is diminished, whilst the inertia is increased. As a numerical example, in the case of water over mercury ($s^{-1}=13\cdot6$) the above ratio comes out equal to $\cdot929$.

It is to be noticed, in this problem, that there is a discontinuity of motion at the common surface. The normal velocity $(d\psi/dx)$ is of course continuous, but the tangential velocity $(-d\psi/dy)$ changes from $c(1-k\beta\cos kx)$ to $c(1+k\beta\cos kx)$ as we cross the surface; in other words we have (Art. 149) a *vortex-sheet* of strength $-kc\beta\cos kx$. This is an extreme illustration of the remark, made in Art. 18, that the free oscillations of a liquid of variable density are not necessarily irrotational.

If $\rho<\rho'$, the value of c is imaginary. The undisturbed equilibrium-arrangement is then of course unstable.

The case where the two fluids are bounded by rigid horizontal planes $y=-h$, $y=h'$, is almost equally simple. We have, in place of (1),

$$\left.\begin{aligned}\psi/c &= -y+\beta\frac{\sinh k(y+h)}{\sinh kh}\cos kx,\\ \psi'/c &= -y-\beta\frac{\sinh k(y-h')}{\sinh kh'}\cos kx\end{aligned}\right\}\text{..........(i),}$$

leading to

$$c^2=\frac{g}{k}\cdot\frac{\rho-\rho'}{\rho\coth kh+\rho'\coth kh'}\text{..........(ii).}$$

When kh and kh' are both very great, this reduces to the form (2). When kh' is large, and kh small, we have

$$c^2=\left(1-\frac{\rho'}{\rho}\right)gh\text{..........(iii),}$$

the main effect of the presence of the upper fluid being now the change in the potential energy of a given deformation.

When the upper surface of the upper fluid is *free*, we may assume

$$\left.\begin{aligned}\psi/c &= -y+\beta\frac{\sinh k(y+h)}{\sinh kh}\cos kx,\\ \psi'/c &= -y+(\beta\cosh ky+\gamma\sinh ky)\cos kx\end{aligned}\right\}\text{..........(iv),}$$

and the conditions that $\psi=\psi'$, $p=p'$ at the free surface then lead to the equation

$$c^4(\rho\coth kh\coth kh'+\rho')-c^2\rho(\coth kh'+\coth kh)\frac{g}{k}+(\rho-\rho')\frac{g^2}{k^2}=0\text{......(v).}$$

Since this is a quadratic in c^2, there are *two* possible systems of waves of any given length $(2\pi/k)$. This is as we should expect, since when the wave-length is prescribed the system has virtually two degrees of freedom, so that there are two independent modes of oscillation about the state of equilibrium. For example, in the extreme case where ρ'/ρ is small, one mode consists mainly in an oscillation of the upper fluid which is almost the same as if the lower fluid were solidified, whilst the other mode may be described as an oscillation of the lower fluid which is almost the same as if its upper surface were free.

The ratio of the amplitudes at the upper and lower surfaces is found to be

$$\frac{kc^2}{kc^2\cosh kh'-g\sinh kh'}\text{..........(vi).}$$

Of the various special cases that may be considered, the most interesting is that in which kh is large; *i.e.* the depth of the lower fluid is great compared with the wave-length. Putting $\coth kh=1$, we see that one root of (v) is now

$$c^2=g/k\text{..........(vii),}$$

exactly as in the case of a single fluid of infinite depth, and that the ratio of the amplitudes is $e^{kh'}$. This is merely a particular case of the general result stated at the end of Art. 222; it will in fact be found on examination that there is now no slipping at the common boundary of the two fluids. The second root of (v) is

$$c^2 = \frac{\rho - \rho'}{\rho \coth kh' + \rho'} \cdot \frac{g}{k} \ldots\ldots\ldots\ldots\ldots\ldots\ldots\ldots\text{(viii)};$$

and for this the ratio (vi) assumes the value

$$-\left(\frac{\rho}{\rho'} - 1\right) e^{-kh'} \ldots\ldots\ldots\ldots\ldots\ldots\ldots\ldots\ldots\ldots\text{(ix)}.$$

If in (viii) and (ix) we put $kh' = \infty$, we fall back on a former case; whilst if we make kh' small, we find

$$c^2 = \left(1 - \frac{\rho'}{\rho}\right) gh' \ldots\ldots\ldots\ldots\ldots\ldots\ldots\ldots\ldots\ldots \text{(x)},$$

and the ratio of the amplitudes is

$$-\left(\frac{\rho}{\rho'} - 1\right) \ldots\ldots\ldots\ldots\ldots\ldots\ldots\ldots\ldots\ldots\text{(xi)}.$$

These problems were first investigated by Stokes*. The case of any number of superposed strata of different densities has been treated by Webb† and Greenhill‡. For investigations of the possible *rotational* oscillations in a heterogeneous liquid the reader may consult the papers cited below§.

224. As a further example of the method of Art. 222, let us suppose that two fluids of densities ρ, ρ', one beneath the other, are moving parallel to x with velocities U, U', respectively, the common surface (when undisturbed) being of course plane and horizontal. This is virtually a problem of small oscillations about a state of steady motion.

The fluids being supposed unlimited vertically, we assume, for the lower fluid

$$\psi = -U\{y - \beta e^{ky} \cos kx\} \ldots\ldots\ldots\ldots\ldots\ldots\text{(1)},$$

and for the upper fluid

$$\psi' = -U'\{y - \beta e^{-ky} \cos kx\} \ldots\ldots\ldots\ldots\ldots\ldots \text{(2)},$$

* "On the Theory of Oscillatory Waves," *Camb. Trans.* t. viii. (1847); *Math. and Phys. Papers*, t. i., pp. 212—219.

† *Math. Tripos Papers*, 1884.

‡ "Wave Motion in Hydrodynamics," *Amer. Journ. Math.*, t. ix. (1887).

§ Lord Rayleigh, "Investigation of the Character of the Equilibrium of an Incompressible Heavy Fluid of Variable Density." *Proc. Lond. Math. Soc.*, t. xiv., p. 170 (1883).

Burnside, "On the small Wave-Motions of a Heterogeneous Fluid under Gravity." *Proc. Lond. Math. Soc.*, t. xx., p. 392 (1889).

Love, "Wave-Motion in a Heterogeneous Heavy Liquid." *Proc. Lond. Math. Soc.*, t. xxii., p. 307 (1891).

the origin being at the mean level of the common surface, which is assumed to be stationary, and to have the form

$$y = \beta \cos kx \qquad\text{.........................(3).}$$

The pressure-equations give

$$\left.\begin{aligned}\frac{p}{\rho} &= \text{const.} - gy - \tfrac{1}{2}U^2(1 - 2k\beta e^{ky}\cos kx),\\ \frac{p'}{\rho'} &= \text{const.} - gy - \tfrac{1}{2}U'^2(1 + 2k\beta e^{-ky}\cos kx)\end{aligned}\right\}\text{......(4),}$$

whence, at the common surface,

$$\left.\begin{aligned}\frac{p}{\rho} &= \text{const.} + (kU^2 - g)\,y,\\ \frac{p'}{\rho'} &= \text{const.} - (kU'^2 + g)\,y\end{aligned}\right\}\text{.................. (5).}$$

Since we must have $p = p'$ over this surface, we get

$$\rho U^2 + \rho' U'^2 = \frac{g}{k}(\rho - \rho')\text{.....................(6).}$$

This is the condition for stationary waves on the common surface of the two currents U, U'.

If we put $U' = U$, we fall back on the case of Art. 223. Again if we put

$$U = -c, \quad U' = -c + \mathbf{u},$$

we get the case where the upper fluid has a velocity $\mathbf{u}$ relative to the lower; c then denotes the velocity (relative to the lower fluid) of waves on the common surface. An interesting application of this is to the effect of wind on the velocity of water-waves.

The equation (6) now takes the form

$$\rho c^2 + \rho'(c - \mathbf{u})^2 = \frac{g}{k}(\rho - \rho')\text{.................(7),}$$

or, if we write s for ρ'/ρ, and put c_0 for the wave-velocity in the absence of wind, as given by Art. 223 (2),

$$c^2 - \frac{2s\mathbf{u}}{1+s}c = c_0^2 - \frac{s\mathbf{u}^2}{1+s}\text{ .... (8).}$$

The roots of this quadratic in c are

$$c = \frac{s\mathbf{u}}{1+s} \pm \left\{c_0^2 - \frac{s\mathbf{u}^2}{(1+s)^2}\right\}^{\frac{1}{2}}\text{..................(9).}$$

These are both real, provided

$$\mathbf{u} < \frac{1+s}{s^{\frac{1}{2}}} \,.\, c_0 \text{.........................(10)},$$

and they have, moreover, opposite signs, if

$$\mathbf{u} < \left(\frac{1+s}{s}\right)^{\frac{1}{2}} . \, c_0 \text{.......................(11)}.$$

In this latter case waves of the prescribed length ($2\pi/k$) may travel with or against the wind, but the velocity is greater with the wind than against it. If $\mathbf{u}$ lie *between* the limits (10) and (11), waves of the given length cannot travel against the wind. Finally when $\mathbf{u}$ exceeds the limit (10), the values of c are imaginary. This indicates that the plane form of the common surface is now unstable. Any disturbance whose wave-length is less than

$$\frac{2\pi s}{1-s^2} \cdot \frac{\mathbf{u}^2}{g} \text{ .... (12)}$$

tends to increase indefinitely.

Hence, if there were no modifying circumstances, the slightest breath of wind would suffice to ruffle the surface of water. We shall give, later, a more complete investigation of the present problem, taking account of capillary forces, which act in the direction of stability.

It appears from (6) that if $\rho = \rho'$, or if $g = 0$, the plane form of the surface is unstable for *all* wave-lengths.

These results illustrate the statement, as to the instability of surfaces of discontinuity in a liquid, made in Art. 80*.

When the currents are confined by fixed horizontal planes $y = -h$, $y = h'$, we assume

$$\psi = -U \left\{ y - \beta \frac{\sinh k(y+h)}{\sinh kh} \cos kx \right\} \text{.....................(i)},$$

$$\psi' = -U' \left\{ y + \beta \frac{\sinh k(y-h')}{\sinh kh'} \cos kx \right\} \text{ .... (ii)}.$$

The condition for stationary waves on the common surface is then found to be

$$\rho U^2 \coth kh + \rho' U'^2 \coth kh' = \frac{g}{k}(\rho - \rho') \text{ ....(iii)†}.$$

* This instability was first remarked by von Helmholtz, *l.c. ante*, p. 24.

† Greenhill, *l.c. ante*, p. 388.

It appears on examination that the undisturbed motion is stable or unstable, according as

$$\mathbf{u} \lessgtr \frac{\rho \coth kh + \rho' \coth kh'}{(\rho\rho' \coth kh \coth kh')^{\frac{1}{2}}} \cdot c_0 \text{ .... (iv)},$$

where $\mathbf{u}$ is the velocity of the upper current relative to the lower, and c_0 is the wave-velocity when there are no currents (Art. 223 (ii)). When h and h' both exceed half the wave-length, this reduces practically to the former result (10).

225. These questions of stability are so important that it is worth while to give the more direct method of treatment*.

If ϕ be the velocity-potential of a slightly disturbed stream flowing with the general velocity U parallel to x, we may write

$$\phi = -Ux + \phi_1 \text{ ....(1)},$$

where ϕ_1 is small. The pressure-formula is, to the first order,

$$\frac{p}{\rho} = \frac{d\phi_1}{dt} - gy + U\frac{d\phi_1}{dx} + \dots \text{ .... (2)};$$

and the condition to be satisfied at a bounding surface $y = \eta$, where η is small, is

$$\frac{d\eta}{dt} + U\frac{d\eta}{dx} = -\frac{d\phi_1}{dy} \text{ ....(3)}.$$

To apply this to the problem stated at the beginning of Art. 224, we assume, for the lower fluid,

$$\phi_1 = Ce^{ky+i(kx+\sigma t)} \text{ ....(4)};$$

for the upper fluid

$$\phi_1' = C'e^{-ky+i(kx+\sigma t)} \text{ .... (5)};$$

with, as the equation of the common surface,

$$\eta = ae^{i(kx+\sigma t)} \text{ ....(6)}.$$

The continuity of the pressure at this surface requires, by (2),

$$\rho\{i(\sigma + kU)C - ga\} = \rho'\{i(\sigma + kU')C' - ga\} \text{......(7)};$$

whilst the surface-condition (3) gives

$$\left.\begin{aligned} i(\sigma + kU)a &= -kC, \\ i(\sigma + kU')a &= kC' \end{aligned}\right\} \text{ ....(8)}.$$

* Sir W. Thomson, "Hydrokinetic Solutions and Observations," *Phil. Mag.*, Nov. 1871; Lord Rayleigh, "On the Instability of Jets," *Proc. Lond. Math. Soc.*, t. x., p. 4 (1878).

Eliminating a, C, C', we get

$$\rho(\sigma + kU)^2 + \rho'(\sigma + kU')^2 = gk(\rho - \rho') \quad \text{..........(9).}$$

It is obvious that whatever the values of U, U', other than zero, the values of σ will become imaginary when k is sufficiently great.

Nothing essential is altered in the problem if we impress on both fluids an arbitrary velocity in the direction of x. Hence, putting $U = 0$, $U' = \mathbf{u}$, we get

$$\rho\sigma^2 + \rho'(\sigma + k\mathbf{u})^2 = gk(\rho - \rho') \quad \text{..............(10),}$$

which is equivalent to Art. 224 (7).

If $\rho = \rho'$, it is evident from (9) that σ will be imaginary for all values of k. Putting $U' = -U$, we get

$$\sigma = \pm ikU \quad \text{..........................(11).}$$

Hence, taking the real part of (6), we find

$$\eta = ae^{\pm kUt} \cos kx \quad \text{......................(12).}$$

The upper sign gives a system of standing waves whose height continually increases with the time, the rate of increase being greater, the shorter the wave-length.

The case of $\rho = \rho'$, with $U = U'$, is of some interest, as illustrating the flapping of sails and flags*. We may conveniently simplify the question by putting $U = U' = 0$; any common velocity may be superposed afterwards if desired.

On the present suppositions, the equation (9) reduces to $\sigma^2 = 0$. On account of the double root the solution has to be completed by the method explained in books on Differential Equations. In this way we obtain the two independent solutions

$$\left.\begin{aligned} \eta &= ae^{ikx}, \\ \phi_1 = 0, &\quad \phi_1' = 0 \end{aligned}\right\} \quad \text{..................................(i),}$$

and

$$\left.\begin{aligned} \eta &= ate^{ikx}, \\ \phi_1 = -\frac{a}{k}e^{ky}.e^{ikx}, &\quad \phi_1' = \frac{a}{k}e^{-ky}.e^{ikx} \end{aligned}\right\} \quad \text{..................(ii).}$$

The former solution represents a state of equilibrium; the latter gives a system of stationary waves with amplitude increasing proportionally to the time.

In this problem there is no physical surface of separation to begin with; but if a slight discontinuity of motion be artificially produced, *e.g.* by impulses

* Lord Rayleigh, *l.c.*

applied to a thin membrane which is afterwards dissolved, the discontinuity will persist, and, as we have seen, the height of the corrugations will continually increase.

The above method, when applied to the case where the fluids are confined between two rigid horizontal planes $y=-h$, $y=h'$, leads to

$$\rho(\sigma+kU)^2\coth kh+\rho'(\sigma+kU')^2\coth kh'=gk(\rho-\rho')\text{.........(iii)},$$

which is equivalent to Art. 224 (iii).

226. We may next calculate the effect of an arbitrary, but steady, application of pressure to the surface of a stream flowing with uniform velocity c in the direction of x positive*.

It is to be noted that, in the absence of dissipative forces, this problem is to a certain extent indeterminate, for on any motion satisfying the prescribed pressure-conditions we may superpose a train of free waves, of arbitrary amplitude, whose length is such that their velocity relative to the water is equal and opposite to that of the stream, and which therefore maintain a fixed position in space.

To remove this indeterminateness we may suppose that the deviation of any particle of the fluid from the state of uniform flow is resisted by a force proportional to the relative velocity. This law of resistance is not that which actually obtains in nature, but it will serve to represent in a rough way the effect of small dissipative forces; and it has the great mathematical convenience that it does not interfere with the irrotational character of the motion. For if we write, in the equations of Art. 6,

$$X=-\mu(u-c),\quad Y=-g-\mu v,\quad Z=-\mu w\text{.........(1)},$$

where the axis of y is supposed drawn vertically upwards, and c denotes the velocity of the stream, the investigation of Art. 34, when applied to a closed circuit, gives

$$\left(\frac{D}{Dt}+\mu\right)\int(udx+vdy+wdz)=0\text{............(2)},$$

whence

$$\int(udx+vdy+wdz)=Ce^{-\mu t}\text{..................(3)}.$$

* The first steps of the following investigation are adapted from a paper by Lord Rayleigh, "On the Form of Standing Waves on the Surface of Running Water," *Proc. Lond. Math. Soc.*, t. xv., p. 69 (1883), being simplified by the omission, for the present, of all reference to Capillarity. The definite integrals involved are treated, however, in a somewhat more general manner, and the discussion of the results necessarily follows a different course.

Hence the circulation in a circuit moving with the fluid, if once zero, is always zero.

If ϕ be the velocity-potential, the equations of motion have now the integral

$$\frac{p}{\rho} = \frac{d\phi}{dt} - gy + \mu (cx + \phi) - \tfrac{1}{2}q^2 \quad \text{...............} (4),$$

this being, in fact, the form assumed by Art. 21 (4) when we write

$$\Omega = gy - \mu (cx + \phi) \quad \text{.....................} (5),$$

in accordance with (1) above.

To calculate, in the first place, the effect of a simple-harmonic distribution of pressure we assume

$$\left.\begin{aligned} \phi/c &= -x + \beta e^{ky} \sin kx, \\ \psi/c &= -y + \beta e^{ky} \cos kx \end{aligned}\right\} \quad \text{..................} (6).$$

The equation (4) becomes, on neglecting as usual the square of $k\beta$,

$$\frac{p}{\rho} = \ldots - gy + \beta e^{ky} (kc^2 \cos kx + \mu c \sin kx) \quad \text{.........} (7).$$

This gives for the variable part of the pressure at the upper surface ($\psi = 0$)

$$\frac{\Delta p}{\rho} = \beta \{(kc^2 - g) \cos kx + \mu c \sin kx\} \quad \text{...........} (8),$$

which is equal to the real part of

$$\beta (kc^2 - g - i\mu c) e^{ikx}.$$

If we equate the coefficient to P, we may say that to the pressure

$$\frac{\Delta p}{\rho} = P e^{ikx} \quad \text{........................} (9)$$

corresponds the surface-form

$$y = \frac{P}{kc^2 - g - i\mu c} e^{ikx} \quad \text{...................} (10).$$

Hence taking the real parts, we find that the surface-pressure

$$\frac{\Delta p}{\rho} = P \cos kx \quad \text{.......................} (11)$$

produces the wave-form

$$y = P \cdot \frac{(kc^2 - g) \cos kx - \mu c \sin kx}{(kc^2 - g)^2 + \mu^2 c^2} \quad \text{...........} (12).$$

If we write $\kappa = g/c^2$, so that $2\pi/\kappa$ is the wave-length of the free waves which could maintain their position in space against the flow of the stream, the last formula may be written

$$y = \frac{P}{c^2} \cdot \frac{(k-\kappa)\cos kx - \mu_1 \sin kx}{(k-\kappa)^2 + {\mu_1}^2} \quad \text{.............}(13),$$

where $\mu_1 = \mu/c$.

This shews that if μ be small the wave-crests will coincide in position with the maxima, and the troughs with the minima, of the applied pressure, when the wave-length is less than $2\pi/\kappa$; whilst the reverse holds in the opposite case. This is in accordance with a general principle. If we impress on everything a velocity $-c$ parallel to x, the result obtained by putting $\mu_1 = 0$ in (13) is seen to be merely a special case of Art. 165 (12).

In the critical case of $k = \kappa$, we have

$$y = -\frac{P}{\mu c} \cdot \sin kx,$$

shewing that the excess of pressure is now on the slopes which face down the stream. This explains roughly how a system of progressive waves may be maintained against our assumed dissipative forces by a properly adjusted distribution of pressure over their slopes.

227. The solution expressed by (13) may be generalized, in the first place by the addition of an arbitrary constant to x, and secondly by a summation with respect to k. In this way we may construct the effect of any arbitrary distribution of pressure, say

$$\frac{\Delta p}{\rho} = f(x) \quad \text{..........................}(14),$$

using Fourier's expression

$$f(x) = \frac{1}{\pi}\int_0^\infty dk \int_{-\infty}^{\infty} f(\lambda) \cos k(x-\lambda)\, d\lambda \quad \text{........}(15).$$

It will be sufficient to consider the case where the imposed pressure is confined to an infinitely narrow strip of the surface, since the most general case can be derived from this by integration. We will suppose then that $f(\lambda)$ vanishes for all but infinitely small values of λ, so that (15) becomes

$$f(x) = \frac{1}{\pi}\int_0^\infty dk \cos kx \, . \int_{-\infty}^{\infty} f(\lambda)\, d\lambda \quad \text{.........} (16)^*.$$

* The indeterminateness of this expression may be avoided by the temporary use of Poisson's formula

$$f(x) = \mathop{\mathrm{Lt}}_{\alpha=0} \frac{1}{\pi}\int_0^\infty e^{-\alpha k} dk \int_{-\infty}^{\infty} f(\lambda) \cos k(x-\lambda)\, d\lambda$$

in place of (15).

Hence in (13) we must replace P by $Q/\pi.\delta k$, where

$$Q=\int_{-\infty}^{\infty} f(\lambda)\, d\lambda \quad\text{.........................(17)},$$

and integrate with respect to k between the limits 0 and ∞; thus

$$\frac{\pi c^2}{Q}\cdot y=\int_0^{\infty}\frac{(k-\kappa)\cos kx-\mu_1\sin kx}{(k-\kappa)^2+\mu_1^2}\,dk\quad\text{.........(18)}.$$

If we put $\zeta=k+im$, where k, m are taken to be the rectangular coordinates of a variable point in a plane, the properties of the expression (18) are contained in those of the complex integral

$$\int\frac{e^{ix\zeta}}{\zeta-c}\,d\zeta \quad\text{.....................................(i)}.$$

It is known (Art. 62) that the value of this integral, taken round the boundary of any area which does not include the singular point ($\zeta=c$), is zero. In the present case we have $c=\kappa+i\mu_1$, where κ and μ_1 are both positive.

Let us first suppose that x is positive, and let us apply the above theorem to the region which is bounded externally by the line $m=0$ and by an infinite semicircle, described with the origin as centre on the side of this line for which m is positive, and internally by a small circle surrounding the point (κ, μ_1). The part of the integral due to the infinite semicircle obviously vanishes, and it is easily seen, putting $\zeta-c=re^{i\theta}$, that the part due to the small circle is

$$-2\pi i e^{i(\kappa+i\mu_1)x},$$

if the direction of integration be chosen in accordance with the rule of Art. 33. We thus obtain

$$\int_{-\infty}^{0}\frac{e^{ikx}}{k-(\kappa+i\mu_1)}\,dk+\int_0^{\infty}\frac{e^{ikx}}{k-(\kappa+i\mu_1)}\,dk-2\pi i e^{i(\kappa+i\mu_1)x}=0,$$

which is equivalent to

$$\int_0^{\infty}\frac{e^{ikx}}{k-(\kappa+i\mu_1)}\,dk=2\pi i e^{i(\kappa+i\mu_1)x}+\int_0^{\infty}\frac{e^{-ikx}}{k+(\kappa+i\mu_1)}\,dk \quad\text{............(ii)}.$$

On the other hand, when x is negative we may take the integral (i) round the contour made up of the line $m=0$ and an infinite semicircle lying on the side for which m is negative. This gives the same result as before, with the omission of the term due to the singular point, which is now external to the contour. Thus, for x negative,

$$\int_0^{\infty}\frac{e^{ikx}}{k-(\kappa+i\mu_1)}\,dk=\int_0^{\infty}\frac{e^{-ikx}}{k+(\kappa+i\mu_1)}\,dk \quad\text{..................(iii)}.$$

An alternative form of the last term in (ii) may be obtained by integrating round the contour made up of the negative portion of the axis of k, and the positive portion of the axis of m, together with an infinite quadrant. We thus find

$$\int_{-\infty}^{0} \frac{e^{ikx}}{k-(\kappa+i\mu_1)}\,dk + \int_0^\infty \frac{e^{-mx}}{im-(\kappa+i\mu_1)}\,idm = 0,$$

which is equivalent to

$$\int_0^\infty \frac{e^{-ikx}}{k+(\kappa+i\mu_1)}\,dk = \int_0^\infty \frac{e^{-mx}}{m-\mu_1+i\kappa}\,dm \quad\text{..................(iv).}$$

This is for x positive. In the case of x negative, we must take as our contour the negative portions of the axes of k, m, and an infinite quadrant. This leads to

$$\int_0^\infty \frac{e^{-ikx}}{k+(\kappa+i\mu_1)}\,dk = \int_0^\infty \frac{e^{mx}}{m+\mu_1-i\kappa}\,dm \quad\text{.................. (v),}$$

as the transformation of the second member of (iii).

In the foregoing argument μ_1 is positive. The corresponding results for the integral

$$\int \frac{e^{ix\zeta}}{\zeta-(\kappa-i\mu_1)}\,d\zeta \quad\text{..................................(vi)}$$

are not required for our immediate purpose, but it will be convenient to state them for future reference. For x positive, we find

$$\int_0^\infty \frac{e^{ikx}}{k-(\kappa-i\mu_1)}\,dk = \int_0^\infty \frac{e^{-ikx}}{k+(\kappa-i\mu_1)}\,dk = \int_0^\infty \frac{e^{-mx}}{m+\mu_1+i\kappa}\,dm \quad\text{... (vii);}$$

whilst, for x negative,

$$\int_0^\infty \frac{e^{ikx}}{k-(\kappa-i\mu_1)}\,dk = -2\pi i e^{i(\kappa-i\mu_1)x} + \int_0^\infty \frac{e^{-ikx}}{k+(\kappa-i\mu_1)}\,dk$$

$$= -2\pi i e^{i(\kappa-i\mu_1)x} + \int_0^\infty \frac{e^{mx}}{m-\mu_1-i\kappa}\,dm \quad\text{......(viii).}$$

The verification is left to the reader.

If we take the real parts of the formulæ (ii), (iv), and (iii), (v), respectively, we obtain the results which follow.

The formula (18) is equivalent, for x positive, to

$$\frac{\pi c^2}{Q}\cdot y = -2\pi e^{-\mu_1 x}\sin\kappa x + \int_0^\infty \frac{(k+\kappa)\cos kx - \mu_1\sin kx}{(k+\kappa)^2+\mu_1^2}\,dk$$

$$= -2\pi e^{-\mu_1 x}\sin\kappa x + \int_0^\infty \frac{(m-\mu_1)\,e^{-mx}\,dm}{(m-\mu_1)^2+\kappa^2} \quad\text{......... (19),}$$

and, for x negative, to

$$\frac{\pi c^2}{Q}\cdot y = \int_0^\infty \frac{(m+\mu_1)\,e^{mx}\,dm}{(m+\mu_1)^2+\kappa^2} \quad\text{..................(20).}$$

The interpretation of these results is simple. The first term of (19) represents a train of simple-harmonic waves, on the down-stream side of the origin, of wave-length $2\pi c^2/g$, with amplitudes gradually diminishing according to the law $e^{-\mu_1 x}$. The remaining part of the deformation of the free-surface, expressed by the definite integrals in (19) and (20), though very great for small values of x, diminishes very rapidly as x increases, however small the value of the frictional coefficient μ_1.

When μ_1 is infinitesimal, our results take the simpler forms

$$\frac{\pi c^2}{Q} \cdot y = -2\pi \sin \kappa x + \int_0^\infty \frac{\cos kx}{k+\kappa} dk$$

$$= -2\pi \sin \kappa x + \int_0^\infty \frac{me^{-mx}}{m^2+\kappa^2} dm \text{ .... (21)},$$

for x positive, and

$$\frac{\pi c^2}{Q} \cdot y = \int_0^\infty \frac{\cos kx}{k+\kappa} dk = \int_0^\infty \frac{me^{mx}}{m^2+\kappa^2} dm \text{............(22)},$$

for x negative. The part of the disturbance of level which is represented by the definite integrals in these expressions is now symmetrical with respect to the origin, and diminishes constantly as the distance from the origin increases. It is easily found, by usual methods, that when κx is moderately large

$$\int_0^\infty \frac{me^{-mx}}{m^2+\kappa^2} dm = \frac{1}{\kappa^2 x^2} - \frac{3\,!}{\kappa^4 x^4} + \frac{5\,!}{\kappa^6 x^6} - \text{... ......(23)},$$

the series being of the kind known as 'semi-convergent.' It appears that at a distance of about half a wave-length from the origin, on the down-stream side, the simple-harmonic wave-system is fully established.

The definite integrals in (21) and (22) can be reduced to known functions as follows. If we put $(k+\kappa)x=u$, we have, for x positive,

$$\int_0^\infty \frac{\cos kx}{k+\kappa} dk = \int_{\kappa x}^\infty \frac{\cos(\kappa x - u)}{u} du$$

$$= -\mathrm{Ci}\,\kappa x \cos \kappa x + (\tfrac{1}{2}\pi - \mathrm{Si}\,\kappa x)\sin \kappa x \text{......(ix)},$$

where, in the usual notation,

$$\mathrm{Ci}\,u = -\int_u^\infty \frac{\cos u}{u} du, \qquad \mathrm{Si}\,u = \int_0^u \frac{\sin u}{u} du \text{ .... (x)}.$$

The functions Ci u and Si u have been tabulated by Glaisher*. It appears that as u increases from zero they tend very rapidly to their asymptotic values 0 and $\frac{1}{2}\pi$, respectively. For small values of u we have

$$\left.\begin{aligned} \mathrm{Ci}\, u &= \gamma + \log u - \frac{u^2}{2\,.\,2\,!} + \frac{u^4}{4\,.\,4\,!} - \ldots, \\ \mathrm{Si}\, u &= u - \frac{u^3}{3\,.\,3\,!} + \frac{u^5}{5\,.\,5\,!} - \ldots \end{aligned}\right\} \quad \text{(xi)};$$

where γ is Euler's constant ·5772....

The expressions (19), (20) and (21), (22) alike make the elevation infinite at the origin, but this difficulty disappears when the pressure, which we have supposed concentrated on a mathematical line of the surface, is diffused over a band of finite breadth. In fact, to calculate the effect of a distributed pressure, it is only necessary to write $x - x'$ for x, in (21) and (22), to replace Q by $\Delta p/\rho\,.\,\delta x'$, where $\Delta p/\rho$ is any given function of x', and to integrate with respect to x' between the proper limits. It follows from known principles of the Integral Calculus that, if Δp be finite, the resulting integrals are finite for all values of x.

If we write $$\chi(u) = \mathrm{Ci}\, u \sin u + (\tfrac{1}{2}\pi - \mathrm{Si}\, u)\cos u \quad \text{(xii)},$$
it is easily found from (19) and (20) that, when μ_1 is infinitesimal, we have, for positive values of x,

$$\frac{\pi g}{Q}\int_x^\infty y\,dx = -2\pi\cos\kappa x + \chi(\kappa x) \quad \text{(xiii)},$$

and for negative values of x

$$\frac{\pi g}{Q}\int_x^\infty y\,dx = -\pi - \chi(-\kappa x) \quad \text{(xiv)}.$$

In particular, the integral depression of the free surface is given by

$$-\int_{-\infty}^{\infty} y\,dx = Q/g \quad \text{(xv)},$$

and is therefore independent of the velocity of the stream.

By means of a rough table of the function $\chi(u)$, it is easy to construct the wave-profile corresponding to a uniform pressure applied over a band of any given breadth. It may be noticed that if the breadth of the band be an exact multiple of the wave-length ($2\pi/\kappa$), we have zero elevation of the surface at a distance, on the down-stream as well as on the up-stream side of the seat of disturbance.

* "Tables of the Numerical Values of the Sine-Integral, Cosine-Integral, and Exponential-Integral," *Phil. Trans.*, 1870. The expression of the last integral in (22) in terms of the sine- and cosine-integrals, was obtained, in a different manner from the above, by Schlömilch, "Sur l'intégrale définie $\int_0^\infty \frac{d\theta}{\theta^2 + a^2} e^{-x\theta}$," *Crelle*, t. xxxiii. (1846); see also De Morgan, *Differential and Integral Calculus*, London, 1842, p. 654.

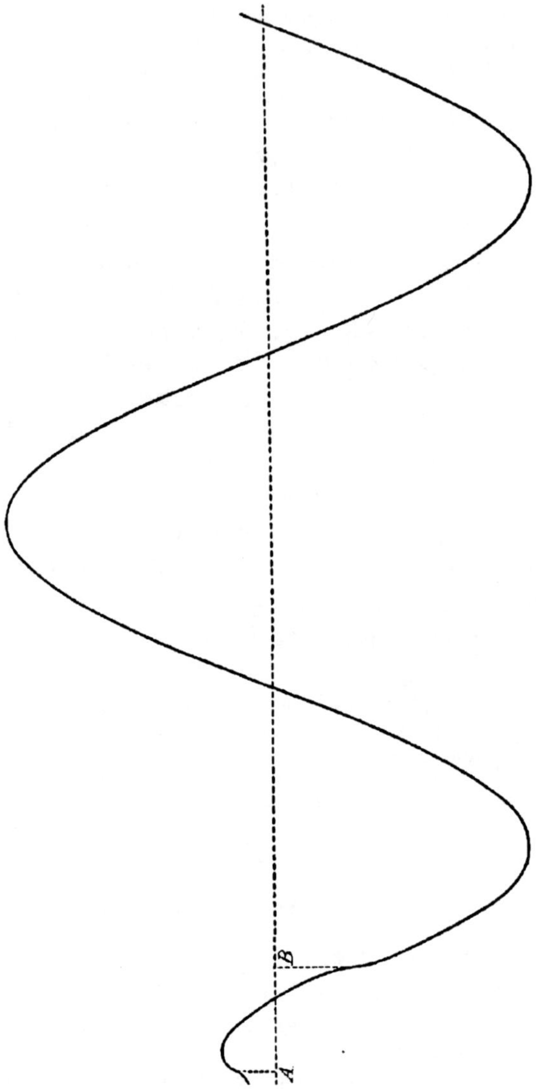
B
A

The figure on p. 400 shews, with a somewhat extravagant vertical scale, the case where the band (AB) has a breadth κ^{-1}, or ·159 of the length of a standing wave.

The circumstances in any such case might be realized approximately by dipping the edge of a slightly inclined board into the surface of a stream, except that the pressure on the wetted area of the board would not be uniform, but would diminish from the central parts towards the edges. To secure a uniform pressure, the board would have to be curved towards the edges, to the shape of the portion of the wave-profile included between the points A, B in the figure.

If we impress on everything a velocity $-c$ parallel to x, we get the case of a pressure-disturbance advancing with constant velocity c over the surface of otherwise still water. In this form of the problem it is not difficult to understand, in a general way, the origin of the train of waves following the disturbance. It is easily seen from the theory of forced oscillations referred to in Art. 165 that the only motion which can be maintained against small dissipative forces will consist of a train of waves of the velocity c, equal to that of the disturbance, and therefore of the wave-length $2\pi c^2/g$. And the theory of 'group-velocity' explained in Art. 221 shews that a train of waves cannot be maintained *ahead* of the disturbance, since the supply of energy is insufficient.

228. The main result of the preceding investigation is that a line of pressure athwart a stream flowing with velocity c produces a disturbance consisting of a train of waves, of length $2\pi c^2/g$, lying on the down-stream side. To find the effect of a line of pressure *oblique* to the stream, making (say) an angle $\frac{1}{2}\pi - \theta$ with its direction, we have only to replace the velocity of the stream by its two components, $c\cos\theta$ and $c\sin\theta$, perpendicular and parallel to the line. If the former component existed alone, we should have a train of waves of length $2\pi c^2/g \,.\, \cos^2\theta$, and the superposition of the latter component does not affect the configuration. Hence the waves are now shorter, in the ratio $\cos^2\theta : 1$. It appears also from Art. 227 (21) that, for the same integral pressure, the amplitude is *greater*, varying as $\sec^2\theta$, but against this must be set the increased dissipation to which the shorter waves are subject*.

To infer the effect of a pressure localized about a *point* of the

* On the special hypothesis made above this is indicated by the factor $e^{-\mu_1 x}$ in Art. 227 (19), where $\mu_1 = \mu/c \,.\, \sec\theta$.

surface, we have only to take the mean result of a series of lines of pressure whose inclinations θ are distributed uniformly between the limits $\pm \frac{1}{2}\pi$*. This result is expressed by a definite integral whose interpretation would be difficult; but a general idea of the forms of the wave-ridges may be obtained by a process analogous to that introduced by Huyghens in Physical Optics, viz. by tracing the envelopes of the straight lines which represent them in the component systems. It appears on reference to (21) that the perpendicular distance p of any particular ridge from the origin is given by

$$\kappa p = (2s - \tfrac{1}{2})\,\pi,$$

where s is integral, and $\kappa = g/c^2 \cos^2 \theta$. The tangential polar equation of the envelopes in question is therefore

$$p = a \cos^2 \theta \qquad\qquad (1),$$

where, for consecutive crests or hollows, a differs by $2\pi c^2/g$. The

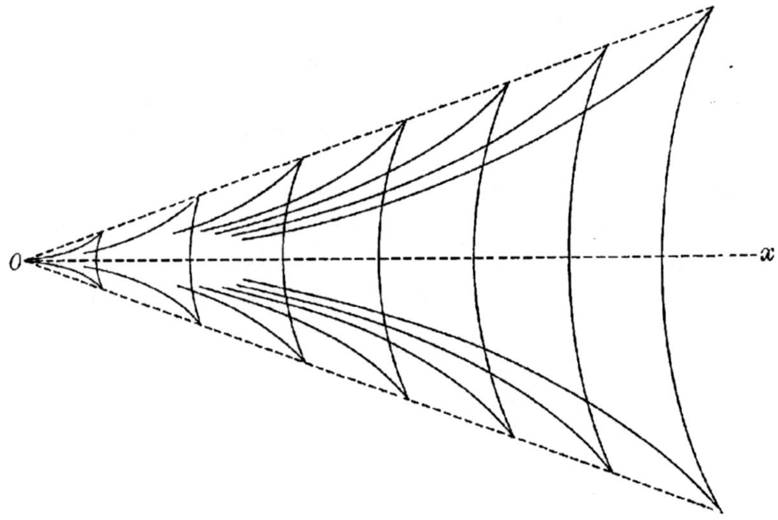

forms of the curves are shewn in the annexed figure, traced from the equations

$$\left.\begin{aligned} x &= p\cos\theta - \frac{dp}{d\theta}\sin\theta = \tfrac{1}{4}a\,(5\cos\theta - \cos 3\theta), \\ y &= p\sin\theta + \frac{dp}{d\theta}\cos\theta = -\tfrac{1}{4}a\,(\sin\theta + \sin 3\theta) \end{aligned}\right\} \qquad (2).$$

* This artifice is taken from Lord Rayleigh's paper, cited on p. 393.

The values of x and y are both stationary when $\sin^2\theta = \frac{1}{3}$; this gives a series of cusps lying on the straight lines

$$y/x = \pm 2^{-\frac{3}{2}} = \pm \tan^{-1} 19^\circ\ 28'\,*.$$

We have here an explanation, at all events as to the main features, of the peculiar system of waves which accompanies a ship in sufficiently rapid motion through the water. To an observer on board the problem is of course one of steady motion; and although the mode of disturbance is somewhat different, the action of the bows of the ship may be roughly compared to that of a pressure-point of the kind we have been considering. The preceding figure accounts clearly for the two systems of transverse and diverging waves which are in fact observed, and for the specially conspicuous 'echelon' waves at the cusps, where these two systems coalesce. These are well shewn in the annexed drawing† by Mr. R. E. Froude of the waves produced by a model.

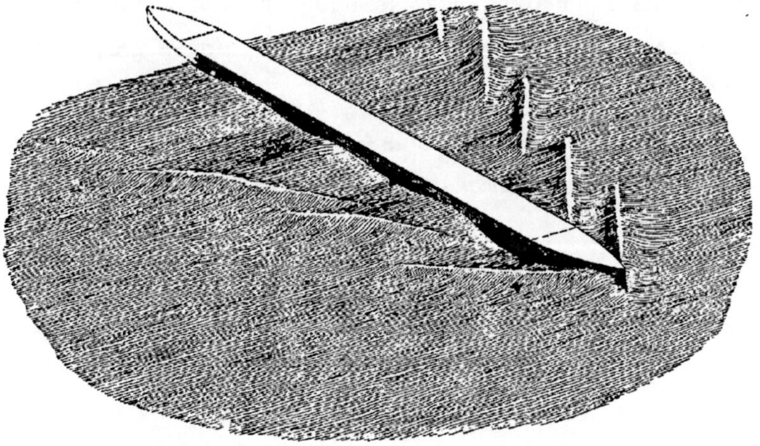

A similar system of waves is generated at the stern of the ship, which may roughly be regarded as a negative pressure-point.

* Cf. Sir W. Thomson, "On Ship Waves," *Proc. Inst. Mech. Eng.*, Aug. 3, 1887, *Popular Lectures*, t. iii., p. 482, where a similar drawing is given. The investigation there referred to, based apparently on the theory of 'group-velocity,' has unfortunately not been published. See also R. E. Froude, "On Ship Resistance," *Papers of the Greenock Phil. Soc.*, Jan. 19, 1894.

† Copied, by the kind permission of Mr Froude and the Council of the Institute of Naval Architects, from a paper by the late W. Froude, "On the Effect on the Wave-Making Resistance of Ships of Length of Parallel Middle Body," *Trans. Inst. Nav. Arch.*, t. xvii. (1877).

With varying speeds of the ship the stern-waves may tend partially to annul, or to exaggerate, the effect of the bow-waves, and consequently the wave-resistance to the ship as a whole for a given speed may fluctuate up and down as the length of the ship is increased*.

229. If in the problem of Art. 226 we suppose the depth to be finite and equal to h, there will be, in the absence of dissipation, indeterminateness or not, according as the velocity c of the stream is less or greater than $(gh)^{\frac{1}{2}}$, the maximum wave-velocity for the given depth. See Art. 222. The difficulty presented by the former case can be evaded as before by the introduction of small frictional forces; but it may be anticipated from the investigation of Art. 227 that the main effect of these will be to annul the elevation of the surface at a distance on the up-stream side of the region of disturbed pressure†, and if we assume this at the outset we need not complicate our equations by retaining the frictional terms.

For the case of a simple-harmonic distribution of pressure we assume

$$\left.\begin{aligned}\phi/c &= -x + \beta \cosh k(y+h) \sin kx,\\ \psi/c &= -y + \beta \sinh k(y+h) \cos kx\end{aligned}\right\} \quad\text{(1)},$$

as in Art. 222 (3). Hence, at the surface

$$y = \beta \sinh kh \cos kx \quad\text{(2)},$$

we have

$$\frac{\Delta p}{\rho} = -gy - \tfrac{1}{2}(q^2 - c^2) = \beta\,(kc^2 \cosh kh - g \sinh kh) \cos kx \ldots \text{(3)},$$

so that to the imposed pressure

$$\frac{\Delta p}{\rho} = P \cos kx \quad\text{(4)},$$

will correspond the surface-form

$$y = P\frac{\sinh kh}{kc^2 \cosh kh - g \sinh kh} \cos kx \quad\text{(5)}.$$

* See W. Froude, *l.c.*, and R. E. Froude, "On the Leading Phenomena of the Wave-Making Resistance of Ships," *Trans. Inst. Nav. Arch.*, t. xxii. (1881), where drawings of actual wave-patterns under varied conditions of speed are given, which are, as to their main features, in striking agreement with the results of the above theory. Some of these drawings are reproduced in Lord Kelvin's paper in the *Proc. Inst. Mech. Eng.*, above cited.

† There is no difficulty in so modifying the investigation as to take the frictional forces into account, when these are very small.

As in Art. 226, the pressure is greatest over the troughs, and least over the crests, of the waves, or *vice versâ*, according as the wave-length is greater or less than that corresponding to the velocity c, in accordance with general theory.

The generalization of (5) by Fourier's method gives, with the help and in the notation of Art. 227 (15) and (17),

$$y=\frac{Q}{\pi}\int_0^\infty \frac{\sinh kh \cos kx}{kc^2\cosh kh - g\sinh kh}\,dk \quad\text{.......................(i)},$$

as the representation of the effect of a pressure of integral amount ρQ applied to a narrow band of the surface at the origin. This may be written

$$\frac{\pi c^2}{Q}\cdot y=\int_0^\infty \frac{\cos(xu/h)}{u\coth u - gh/c^2}\,du \quad\text{.......................(ii)}.$$

Now consider the complex integral

$$\int \frac{e^{ix\zeta/h}}{\zeta\coth\zeta - gh/c^2}\,d\zeta \quad\text{.............................(iii)},$$

where $\zeta=u+iv$. The function under the integral sign has a singular point at $\zeta=\mp i\infty$, according as x is positive or negative, and the remaining singular points are given by the roots of

$$(\tanh\zeta)/\zeta=c^2/gh \quad\text{...............................(iv)}.$$

Since (i) is an even function of x, it will be sufficient to take the case of x positive.

Let us first suppose that $c^2>gh$. The roots of (iv) are then all pure imaginaries; viz. they are of the form $\pm i\beta$, where β is a root of

$$(\tan\beta)/\beta=c^2/gh \quad\text{..................................(v)}.$$

The smallest positive root of this lies between 0 and $\frac{1}{2}\pi$, and the higher roots approximate with increasing closeness to the values $(s+\frac{1}{2})\pi$, where s is integral. We will denote these roots in order by $\beta_0, \beta_1, \beta_2, \ldots$. Let us now take the integral (iii) round the contour made up of the axis of u, an infinite semicircle on the positive side of this axis, and a series of small circles surrounding the singular points $\zeta=i\beta_0, i\beta_1, i\beta_2, \ldots$. The part due to the infinite semicircle obviously vanishes. Again, it is known that if α be a simple root of $f(\zeta)=0$ the value of the integral

$$\int\frac{F(\zeta)}{f(\zeta)}\,d\zeta$$

taken in the positive direction round a small circle enclosing the point $\zeta=\alpha$ is equal to

$$2\pi i\frac{F(\alpha)}{f'(\alpha)} \quad\text{..................................(vi)*}.$$

* Forsyth, *Theory of Functions*, Art. 24.

Now in the case of (iii) we have,

$$f'(\alpha)=\coth \alpha-\alpha(\coth^2 \alpha-1)=\frac{1}{\alpha}\left\{\frac{gh}{c^2}\left(1-\frac{gh}{c^2}\right)+\alpha^2\right\} \qquad \text{(vii)},$$

whence, putting $\alpha=i\beta_s$, the expression (vi) takes the form

$$2\pi B_s e^{-\beta_s x/h} \qquad \text{(viii)},$$

where

$$B_s=\frac{\beta_s}{\beta_s^2-\frac{gh}{c^2}\left(1-\frac{gh}{c^2}\right)} \qquad \text{(ix)}.$$

The theorem in question then gives

$$\int_{-\infty}^0 \frac{e^{ixu/h}}{u\coth u-gh/c^2}\,du+\int_0^\infty \frac{e^{ixu/h}}{u\coth u-gh/c^2}\,du-2\pi\sum_0^\infty B_s e^{-\beta_s x/h}=0 \qquad \text{(x)}.$$

If in the former integral we write $-u$ for u, this becomes

$$\int_0^\infty \frac{\cos(xu/h)}{u\coth u-gh/c^2}\,du=\pi\sum_0^\infty B_s e^{-\beta_s x/h} \qquad \text{(xi)}.$$

The surface-form is then given by

$$y=\frac{Q}{c^2}\cdot\sum_0^\infty B_s e^{-\beta_s x/h} \qquad \text{(xii)}.$$

It appears that the surface-elevation (which is symmetrical with respect to the origin) is insensible beyond a certain distance from the seat of disturbance.

When, on the other hand, $c^2 < gh$, the equation (iv) has a pair of real roots ($\pm\alpha$, say), the lowest roots ($\pm\beta_0$) of (v) having now disappeared. The integral (ii) is then indeterminate, owing to the function under the integral sign becoming infinite within the range of integration. One of its values, viz. the 'principal value,' in Cauchy's sense, can however be found by the same method as before, provided we exclude the points $\zeta=\pm\alpha$ from the contour by drawing semicircles of small radius ϵ round them, on the side for which v is positive. The parts of the complex integral (iii) due to these semicircles will be

$$-i\pi\frac{e^{\pm i\alpha x/h}}{f'(\pm\alpha)},$$

where $f'(\alpha)$ is given by (vii); and their sum is therefore equal to

$$2\pi A \sin \alpha x/h \qquad \text{(xiii)},$$

where

$$A=\frac{\alpha}{\alpha^2-\frac{gh}{c^2}\left(\frac{gh}{c^2}-1\right)} \qquad \text{(xiv)}.$$

The equation corresponding to (xi) now takes the form

$$\left\{\int_0^{\alpha-\epsilon}+\int_{\alpha+\epsilon}^\infty\right\}\frac{\cos xu/h}{u\coth u-gh/c^2}\,du=-\pi A\sin \alpha x/h+\pi\sum_1^\infty B_s e^{-\beta_s x/h} \qquad \text{(xv)},$$

so that, if we take the principal value of the integral in (ii), the surface-form on the side of x-positive is

$$y = -\frac{Q}{c^2} A \sin ax/h + \frac{Q}{c^2} \Sigma_1^\infty B_s e^{-\beta_s x/h} \quad \text{.................(xvi).}$$

Hence at a distance from the origin the deformation of the surface consists of the simple-harmonic train of waves indicated by the first term, the wave-length $2\pi h/a$ being that corresponding to a velocity of propagation c relative to still water.

Since the function (ii) is symmetrical with respect to the origin, the corresponding result for negative values of x is

$$y = \frac{Q}{c^2} A \sin ax/h + \frac{Q}{c^2} \Sigma_1^\infty B_s e^{\beta_s x/h} \quad \text{.....................(xvii).}$$

The general solution of our indeterminate problem is completed by adding to (xvi) and (xvii) terms of the form

$$C \cos ax/h + D \sin ax/h \quad \text{.......................(xviii).}$$

The practical solution including the effect of infinitely small dissipative forces is obtained by so adjusting these terms as to make the deformation of the surface insensible at a distance on the up-stream side. We thus get, finally, for positive values of x,

$$y = -\frac{2Q}{c^2} A \sin ax/h + \frac{Q}{c^2} \Sigma_1^\infty B_s e^{-\beta_s x/h} \quad \text{.................(xix),}$$

and, for negative values of x,

$$y = \frac{Q}{c^2} \Sigma_1^\infty B_s e^{\beta_s x/h} \quad \text{.............................. (xx).}$$

For a different method of reducing the definite integral in this problem we must refer to the paper by Lord Kelvin cited below.

230. The same method can be employed to investigate the effect on a uniform stream of slight inequalities in the bed.*

Thus, in the case of a simple-harmonic corrugation given by

$$y = -h + \gamma \cos kx \quad \text{......................(1),}$$

the origin being as usual in the undisturbed surface, we assume

$$\left.\begin{aligned} \phi/c &= -x + (\alpha \cosh ky + \beta \sinh ky) \sin kx, \\ \psi/c &= -y + (\alpha \sinh ky + \beta \cosh ky) \cos kx \end{aligned}\right\} \quad \text{.........(2).}$$

The condition that (1) should be a stream-line is

$$\gamma = -\alpha \sinh kh + \beta \cosh kh \quad \text{.............. (3).}$$

* Sir W. Thomson, "On Stationary Waves in Flowing Water," *Phil. Mag.*, Oct. Nov. and Dec. 1886, and Jan. 1887.

The pressure-formula is

$$\frac{p}{\rho} = \text{const.} - gy + kc^2 (\alpha \cosh ky + \beta \sinh ky) \cos kx \ \ldots \ (4),$$

approximately, and therefore along the stream-line $\psi = 0$

$$\frac{p}{\rho} = \text{const.} + (kc^2\alpha - g\beta) \cos kx,$$

so that the condition for a free surface gives

$$kc^2\alpha - g\beta = 0 \ldots\ldots\ldots\ldots\ldots\ldots\ldots\ldots (5).$$

The equations (3) and (5) determine α and β. The profile of the free surface is then given by

$$y = \beta \cos kx$$
$$= \frac{\gamma}{\cosh kh - g/kc^2 . \sinh kh} \cos kx \ldots\ldots\ldots\ldots (6).$$

If the velocity of the stream be less than that of waves in still water of uniform depth h, of the same length as the corrugations, as determined by Art. 218 (4), the denominator is negative, so that the undulations of the free surface are inverted relatively to those of the bed. In the opposite case, the undulations of the surface follow those of the bed, but with a different vertical scale. When c has precisely the value given by Art. 218 (4), the solution fails, as we should expect, through the vanishing of the denominator. To obtain an intelligible result in this case we should be compelled to take special account of dissipative forces.

The above solution may be generalized, by Fourier's Theorem, so as to apply to the case where the inequalities of the bed follow any arbitrary law. Thus, if the profile of the bed be given by

$$y = -h + f(x) = -h + \frac{1}{\pi}\int_0^\infty dk \int_{-\infty}^\infty f(\lambda) \cos k(x - \lambda)\, d\lambda \ldots\ldots\ldots (\text{i}),$$

that of the free surface will be obtained by superposition of terms of the type 6) due to the various elements of the Fourier-integral; thus

$$y = \frac{1}{\pi}\int_0^\infty dk \int_{-\infty}^\infty \frac{f(\lambda) \cos k(x-\lambda)}{\cosh kh - g/kc^2 . \sinh kh} d\lambda \ldots\ldots\ldots\ldots\ldots (\text{ii}).$$

In the case of a single isolated inequality at the point of the bed vertically beneath the origin, this reduces to

$$y = \frac{Q}{\pi}\int_0^\infty \frac{\cos kx}{\cosh kh - g/kc^2 . \sinh kh} dk$$
$$= \frac{Q}{\pi h}\int_0^\infty \frac{u \cos (xu/h)}{u \cosh u - gh/c^2 . \sinh u} du \ldots\ldots\ldots\ldots\ldots\ldots (\text{iii}),$$

where Q represents the area included by the profile of the inequality above the general level of the bed. For a depression Q will of course be negative.

The discussion of the integral

$$\int \frac{\zeta e^{ix\zeta/h} d\zeta}{\zeta \cosh \zeta - gh/c^2 . \sinh \zeta} \quad \text{.........................(iv)}$$

can be conducted exactly as in the last Art. The function to be integrated differs in fact only by the factor $\zeta/\sinh \zeta$; the singular points therefore are the same as before, and we can at once write down the results.

Thus when $c^2 > gh$ we find, for the surface-form,

$$y = \frac{Q}{h} \Sigma_0^\infty B_s \frac{\beta_s}{\sin \beta_s} e^{\mp \beta_s x/h} \quad \text{..............................(v),}$$

the upper or the lower sign being taken according as x is positive or negative.

When $c^2 < gh$, the 'practical' solution is, for x positive,

$$y = -\frac{2Q}{h} A \frac{a}{\sinh a} \sin ax/h + \frac{Q}{h} \Sigma_1^\infty B_s \frac{\beta_s}{\sin \beta_s} e^{-\beta_s x/h} \quad \text{...........(vi),}$$

and, for x negative,

$$y = \frac{Q}{h} \Sigma_1^\infty B_s \frac{\beta_s}{\sin \beta_s} e^{\beta_s x/h} \quad \text{..........................(vii).}$$

The symbols a, β_s, A, B_s have here exactly the same meanings as in Art. 230*.

Waves of Finite Amplitude.

231. The restriction to 'infinitely small' motions, in the investigations of Arts. 216,... implies that the ratio (a/λ) of the maximum elevation to the wave-length must be small. The determination of the wave-forms which satisfy the conditions of uniform propagation without change of type, when this restriction is abandoned, forms the subject of a classical research by Sir G. Stokes†.

The problem is, of course, most conveniently treated as one of steady motion. If we neglect small quantities of the order

* A very interesting drawing of the wave-profile produced by an isolated inequality in the bed is given in Lord Kelvin's paper, *Phil. Mag.*, Dec. 1886.

† "On the theory of Oscillatory Waves," *Camb. Trans.*, t. viii. (1847); reprinted, with a "Supplement," *Math. and Phys. Papers*, t. i., pp. 197, 314.

The outlines of a more general investigation, including the case of permanent waves on the common surface of two horizontal currents, have been given by von Helmholtz, "Zur Theorie von Wind und Wellen," *Berl. Monatsber.*, July 25, 1889.

a^3/λ^3, the solution of the problem in the case of infinite depth is contained in the formulæ

$$\left.\begin{aligned}\phi/c &= -x + \beta e^{ky}\sin kx,\\ \psi/c &= -y + \beta e^{ky}\cos kx\end{aligned}\right\} \quad\text{.................. (1)*.}$$

The equation of the wave-profile $\psi = 0$ is found by successive approximations to be

$$\begin{aligned}y &= \beta e^{ky}\cos kx = \beta\,(1 + ky + \tfrac{1}{2}k^2y^2 + \ldots)\cos kx\\ &= \tfrac{1}{2}k\beta^2 + \beta\,(1 + \tfrac{3}{8}k^2\beta^2)\cos kx + \tfrac{1}{2}k\beta^2\cos 2kx + \tfrac{3}{8}k^2\beta^3\cos 3kx + \ldots\end{aligned}$$
$$\text{............(2);}$$

or, if we put $\qquad \beta\,(1 + k^2\beta^2) = a,$

$$y - \tfrac{1}{2}ka^2 = a\cos kx + \tfrac{1}{2}ka^2\cos 2kx + \tfrac{3}{8}k^2a^3\cos 3kx + \ldots \text{......(3).}$$

So far as we have developed it, this coincides with the equation of a trochoid, the circumference of the rolling circle being $2\pi/k$, or λ, and the length of the arm of the tracing point being a.

We have still to shew that the condition of uniform pressure along this stream-line can be satisfied by a suitably chosen value of c. We have, from (1), without approximation

$$\frac{p}{\rho} = \text{const.} - gy - \tfrac{1}{2}c^2\{1 - 2k\beta e^{ky}\cos kx + k^2\beta^2 e^{2ky}\}\text{.....(4),}$$

and therefore, at points of the line $y = \beta e^{ky}\cos kx$,

$$\begin{aligned}\frac{p}{\rho} &= \text{const.} + (kc^2 - g)\,y - \tfrac{1}{2}k^2c^2\beta^2e^{2ky}\\ &= \text{const.} + (kc^2 - g - k^3c^2\beta^2)\,y + \ldots \text{ ....(5).}\end{aligned}$$

Hence the condition for a free surface is satisfied, to the present order of approximation, provided

$$c^2 = \frac{g}{k} + k^2c^2\beta^2 = \frac{g}{k}(1 + k^2a^2)\text{..................(6).}$$

This determines the velocity of progressive waves of permanent type, and shews that it increases somewhat with the amplitude a.

For methods of proceeding to a higher approximation, and for the treatment of the case of finite depth, we must refer to the original investigations of Stokes.

* Lord Rayleigh, *l. c. ante* p. 279.

The figure shews the wave-profile, as given by (3), in the case of $ka = \frac{1}{2}$, or $a/\lambda = \cdot 0796$.

The approximately trochoidal form gives an outline which is sharper near the crests, and flatter in the troughs, than in the case of the simple-harmonic waves of infinitely small amplitude investigated in Art. 218, and these features become accentuated as the amplitude is increased. If the trochoidal form were exact, instead of merely approximate, the limiting form would have cusps at the crests, as in the case of Gerstner's waves to be considered presently. In the actual problem, which is one of irrotational motion, the extreme form has been shewn by Stokes*, in a very simple manner, to have sharp angles of 120°.

The problem being still treated as one of steady motion, the motion near the angle will be given by the formulæ of Art. 63; viz. if we introduce polar coordinates r, θ with the crest as origin, and the initial line of θ drawn vertically downwards, we have

$$\psi = Cr^m \cos m\theta \quad \text{.................................} \quad \text{(i)},$$

with the condition that $\psi = 0$ when $\theta = \pm\alpha$ (say), so that $m\alpha = \frac{1}{2}\pi$. This formula leads to

$$q = mCr^{m-1} \quad \text{.................................} \quad \text{(ii)},$$

where q is the resultant fluid velocity. But since the velocity vanishes at the crest, its value at a neighbouring point of the free surface will be given by

$$q^2 = 2gr \cos \alpha \quad \text{.................................} \quad \text{(iii)},$$

as in Art. 25 (2). Comparing (ii) and (iii), we see that we must have $m = \frac{3}{2}$, and therefore $\alpha = \frac{1}{3}\pi$†.

In the case of progressive waves advancing over still water, the particles at the crests, when these have their extreme forms, are moving forwards with exactly the velocity of the wave.

Another point of interest in connection with these waves of permanent type is that they possess, relatively to the undisturbed water, a certain

* *Math. and Phys. Papers*, t. i., p. 227.

† The wave-profile has been investigated and traced, for the neighbourhood of the crest, by Michell, "The Highest Waves in Water," *Phil. Mag.*, Nov. 1893. He finds that the extreme height is $\cdot 142\,\lambda$, and that the wave-velocity is greater than in the case of infinitely small height in the ratio of 1·2 to 1.

momentum in the direction of wave-propagation. The momentum, per wave-length, of the fluid contained between the free surface and a depth h (beneath the level of the origin) which we will suppose to be great compared with λ, is

$$-\rho \iint \frac{d\psi}{dy} dx dy = \rho c h \lambda \text{ .... (iv),}$$

since $\psi = 0$, by hypothesis, at the surface, and $= ch$, by (1), at the great depth h. In the absence of waves, the equation to the upper surface would be $y = \frac{1}{2}ka^2$, by (3), and the corresponding value of the momentum would therefore be

$$\rho c (h + \tfrac{1}{2}ka^2) \lambda \text{ .... (v).}$$

The difference of these results is equal to

$$\pi \rho a^2 c \text{ .... (vi),}$$

which gives therefore the momentum, per wave-length, of a system of progressive waves of permanent type, moving over water which is at rest at a great depth.

To find the vertical distribution of this momentum, we remark that the equation of a stream-line $\psi = ch'$ is found from (2) by writing $y + h'$ for y, and $\beta e^{-kh'}$ for β. The mean-level of this stream-line is therefore given by

$$y = -h' + \tfrac{1}{2}k\beta^2 e^{-2kh'} \text{ .... (vii).}$$

Hence the momentum, in the case of undisturbed flow, of the stratum of fluid included between the surface and the stream-line in question would be, per wave-length,

$$\rho c \lambda \{h' + \tfrac{1}{2}k\beta^2 (1 - e^{-2kh'})\} \text{ .... (viii).}$$

The actual momentum being $\rho c h' \lambda$, we have, for the momentum of the same stratum in the case of waves advancing over still water,

$$\pi \rho a^2 c (1 - e^{-2kh'}) \text{ .... (ix).}$$

It appears therefore that the motion of the individual particles, in these progressive waves of permanent type, is not purely oscillatory, and that there is, on the whole, a slow but continued advance in the direction of wave-propagation*. The rate of this flow at a depth h' is found approximately by differentiating (ix) with respect to h', and dividing by $\rho\lambda$, viz. it is

$$k^2 a^2 c e^{-2kh'} \text{ .... (x).}$$

This diminishes rapidly from the surface downwards.

232. A system of *exact* equations, expressing a possible form of wave-motion when the depth of the fluid is infinite, was given so long ago as 1802 by Gerstner†, and at a later period independently by Rankine. The circumstance, however, that the motion

* Stokes, *l. c. ante*, p. 409. Another very simple proof of this statement has been given by Lord Rayleigh, *l. c. ante*, p. 279.

† Professor of Mathematics at Prague, 1789—1823.

in these waves is not irrotational detracts somewhat from the physical interest of the results.

If the axis of x be horizontal, and that of y be drawn vertically upwards, the formulæ in question may be written

$$\left.\begin{aligned} x &= a + \frac{1}{k} e^{kb} \sin k (a + ct), \\ y &= b - \frac{1}{k} e^{kb} \cos k (a + ct) \end{aligned}\right\} \qquad \text{(1)},$$

where the specification is on the Lagrangian plan (Art. 16), viz., a, b are two parameters serving to identify a particle, and x, y are the coordinates of this particle at time t. The constant k determines the wave-length, and c is the velocity of the waves, which are travelling in the direction of x-negative.

To verify this solution, and to determine the value of c, we remark, in the first place, that

$$\frac{d(x, y)}{d(a, b)} = 1 - e^{2kb} \qquad \text{(2)},$$

so that the Lagrangian equation of continuity (Art. 16 (2)) is satisfied. Again, substituting from (1) in the equations of motion (Art. 13), we find

$$\left.\begin{aligned} \frac{d}{da}\left(\frac{p}{\rho} + gy\right) &= \quad kc^2 e^{kb} \sin k (a + ct), \\ \frac{d}{db}\left(\frac{p}{\rho} + gy\right) &= -kc^2 e^{kb} \cos k (a + ct) + kc^2 e^{2kb} \end{aligned}\right\} \qquad \text{(3)};$$

whence

$$\frac{p}{\rho} = \text{const.} - g\left\{b - \frac{1}{k} e^{kb} \cos k (a + ct)\right\}$$
$$- c^2 e^{kb} \cos k (a + ct) + \tfrac{1}{2} c^2 e^{2kb} \qquad \text{(4)}.$$

For a particle on the free surface the pressure must be constant; this requires

$$c^2 = g/k \qquad \text{(5)};$$

cf. Art. 218. This makes

$$\frac{p}{\rho} = \text{const.} - gb + \tfrac{1}{2} c^2 e^{2kb} \qquad \text{(6)}.$$

It is obvious from (1) that the path of any particle (a, b) is a circle of radius $k^{-1}e^{kb}$.

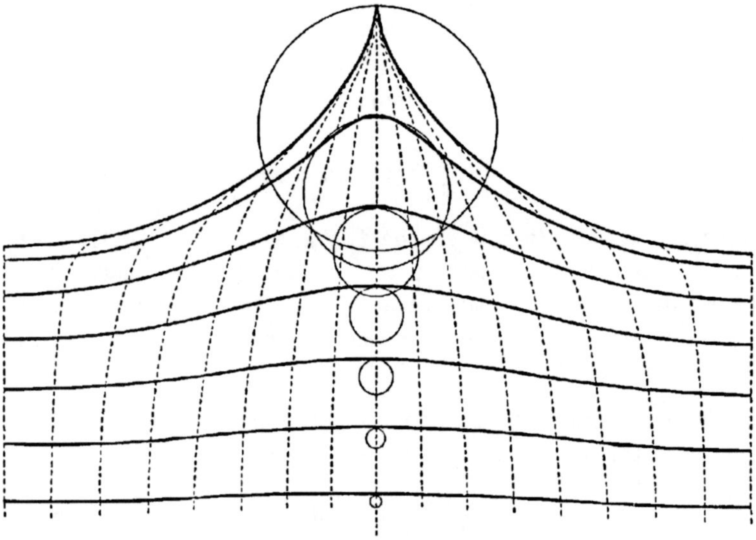

The figure shews the forms of the lines of equal pressure $b = \text{const.}$, for a series of equidistant values of b*. These curves are trochoids, obtained by rolling circles of radii k^{-1} on the under sides of the lines $y = b + k^{-1}$, the distances of the tracing points from the respective centres being $k^{-1}e^{kb}$. Any one of these lines may be taken as representing the free surface, the extreme admissible form being that of the cycloid. The dotted lines represent the successive forms taken by a line of particles which is vertical when it passes through a crest or a trough.

It has been already stated that the motion of the fluid in these waves is rotational. To prove this, we remark that

$$u\delta x + v\delta y = \left(\dot{x}\frac{dx}{da} + \dot{y}\frac{dy}{da}\right)\delta a + \left(\dot{x}\frac{dx}{db} + \dot{y}\frac{dy}{db}\right)\delta b$$

$$= \frac{c}{k}\,\delta\,\{e^{kb}\sin k\,(a + ct)\} + ce^{2kb}\,\delta a \quad \text{(i)},$$

which is not an exact differential.

* The diagram is very similar to the one given originally by Gerstner, and copied more or less closely by subsequent writers.

The circulation in the boundary of the parallelogram whose vertices coincide with the particles

$$(a, b),\ (a+\delta a, b),\ (a, b+\delta b),\ (a+\delta a, b+\delta b)$$

is, by (i),
$$-\frac{d}{db}(ce^{2kb}\delta a)\,\delta b,$$

and the area of the circuit is

$$\frac{d(x, y)}{d(a, b)}\delta a\,\delta b=(1-e^{2kb})\,\delta a\,\delta b.$$

Hence the angular velocity (ω) of the element (a, b) is

$$\omega=-\frac{kce^{2kb}}{1-e^{2kb}}\text{.......................................(ii).}$$

This is greatest at the surface, and diminishes rapidly with increasing depth. Its *sense* is opposite to that of the revolution of the particles in their circular orbits.

A system of waves of the present type cannot therefore be originated from rest, or destroyed, by the action of forces of the kind contemplated in the general theorem of Arts. 18, 34. We may however suppose that by properly adjusted pressures applied to the surface of the waves the liquid is gradually reduced to a state of flow in horizontal lines, in which the velocity (u') is a function of the ordinate (y') only*. In this state we shall have $x'=a$, while y' is a function of b determined by the condition

$$\frac{d(x', y')}{d(a, b)}=\frac{d(x, y)}{d(a, b)}\text{..............................(iii),}$$

or
$$\frac{dy'}{db}=1-e^{2kb}\text{....................................(iv).}$$

This makes
$$\frac{du'}{db}=\frac{du'}{dy'}\frac{dy'}{db}=-2\omega\frac{dy'}{db}=2kce^{2kb}\text{ .... (v),}$$

and therefore
$$u'=ce^{2kb}\text{ .... (vi).}$$

Hence, for the genesis of the waves by ordinary forces, we require as a foundation an initial horizontal motion, in the direction *opposite* to that of propagation of the waves ultimately set up, which diminishes rapidly from the surface downwards, according to the law (vi), where b is a function of y' determined by

$$y'=b-\tfrac{1}{2}k^{-1}e^{2kb}\text{ .... (vii).}$$

It is to be noted that these rotational waves, when established, have zero momentum.

* For a fuller statement of the argument see Stokes, *Math. and Phys. Papers*, t. i., p. 222.

233. Rankine's results were obtained by him by a synthetic process for which we must refer to his paper*.

Gerstner's procedure†, again, is different. He assumed, erroneously, that when the problem is reduced to one of steady motion the pressure must be uniform, not only along that particular stream-line which coincides with the free surface, but also along every other stream-line. Considered, however, as a determination of the only type of steady motion, under gravity, which possesses this property, his investigation is perfectly valid, and, especially when regard is had to its date, very remarkable.

The argument, somewhat condensed with the help of the more modern invention of the stream-function, is as follows.

Fixing our attention at first on any one stream-line, and choosing the origin on it at a point of minimum altitude, let the axis of x be taken horizontal, in the general direction of the flow, and let that of y be drawn vertically upwards. If v be the velocity at any point, and v_0 the velocity at the origin, we have, resolving along the arc s,

$$v\frac{dv}{ds} = -g\frac{dy}{ds} \qquad \text{(i)},$$

on account of the assumed uniformity of pressure. Hence

$$v^2 = v_0^2 - 2gy \qquad \text{(ii)},$$

as in Art. 25. Again, resolving along the normal,

$$\frac{v^2}{R} = -\frac{1}{\rho}\frac{dp}{dn} - g\frac{dx}{ds} \qquad \text{(iii)},$$

where δn is an element of the normal, and R is the radius of curvature.

Now $v = -d\psi/dn$, where ψ is the stream-function, so that if we write σ for $dp/\rho d\psi$, which is, by hypothesis, constant along the stream-line, we have

$$\frac{v^2}{R} = \sigma v - g\frac{dx}{ds} \qquad \text{(iv)}.$$

Putting

$$1/R = -\frac{d^2x}{ds^2}\Big/\frac{dy}{ds},$$

multiplying by dy/ds, and making use of (i), we obtain

$$v\frac{d^2x}{ds^2} + \frac{dv}{ds}\frac{dx}{ds} = -\sigma\frac{dy}{ds} \qquad \text{(v)},$$

whence, on integration,

$$v\frac{dx}{ds} = v_0 - \sigma y \qquad \text{(vi)},$$

* "On the Exact Form of Waves near the Surface of Deep Water," *Phil. Trans.*, 1863.

† "Theorie der Wellen," *Abh. der k. böhm. Ges. der Wiss.*, 1802; Gilbert's *Annalen der Physik*, t. xxxii. (1809).

which is a formula for the horizontal velocity. Combined with (ii), this gives

$$v^2\left(\frac{dy}{ds}\right)^2 = v_0^2 - 2gy - (v_0 - \sigma y)^2 = \sigma^2 y\,(2\beta - y) \qquad \text{(vii)},$$

provided

$$\beta = v_0/\sigma - g/\sigma^2 \qquad \text{(viii)}.$$

Hence, for the vertical velocity, we have

$$v\frac{dy}{ds} = \sigma\,\{y\,(2\beta - y)\}^{\frac{1}{2}} \qquad \text{(ix)}.$$

If the coordinates x, y of any particle on the stream-line be regarded as functions of t, we have, then,

$$\frac{dx}{dt} = v_0 - \sigma y, \qquad \frac{dy}{dt} = \sigma\,\{y\,(2\beta - y)\}^{\frac{1}{2}} \qquad \text{(x)},$$

whence

$$x = \frac{g}{\sigma}t + \beta \sin \sigma t, \quad y = \beta\,(1 - \cos \sigma t) \qquad \text{(xi)},$$

if the time be reckoned from the instant at which the particle passes through the origin of coordinates. The equations (xi) determine a trochoid; the radius of the rolling circle is g/σ^2, and the distance of the tracing point from the centre is β. The wave-length of the curve is $\lambda = 2\pi g/\sigma^2$.

It remains to shew that the trochoidal paths can be so adjusted that the condition of constancy of volume is satisfied. For this purpose we must take an origin of y which shall be independent of the particular path considered, so that the paths are now given by

$$x = \frac{g}{\sigma}t + \beta \sin \sigma t, \quad y = b - \beta \cos \sigma t \qquad \text{(xii)},$$

where b is a function of β, and conversely. It is evident that σ must be an absolute constant, since it determines the wave-length. Now consider two particles P, P', on two consecutive stream-lines, which are in the same phase of their motions. The projections of PP' on the coordinate axes are

$$\delta\beta \sin \sigma t \text{ and } \delta b - \delta\beta \cos \sigma t.$$

The flux (Art. 59) across a line fixed in space which coincides with the instantaneous position of PP' is obtained by multiplying these projections by

$$dy/dt \text{ and } -dx/dt,$$

respectively, and adding; viz. we find

$$\delta\psi = -\frac{g}{\sigma}\delta b + \sigma\beta\delta\beta + \left(\frac{g}{\sigma}\delta\beta - \sigma\beta\delta b\right)\cos \sigma t \qquad \text{(xiii)}.$$

In order that this may be independent of t, we must have

$$\delta\beta/\beta = \sigma^2/g \,.\, \delta b,$$

or
$$\beta = Ce^{kb} \quad \text{(xiv)},$$
where
$$k = \sigma^2/g = 2\pi/\lambda \quad \text{(xv)}.$$

Hence, finally,
$$x = ct + Ce^{kb}\sin kct, \quad y = b - Ce^{kb}\cos kct \quad \text{(xvi)},$$
where
$$c = \frac{g}{\sigma} = \left(\frac{g}{2\pi}\right)^{\frac{1}{2}} \quad \text{(xvii)}.$$

The addition of a constant to b merely changes the position of the origin and the value of C; we may therefore suppose that $b=0$ for the limiting cycloidal form of the path. This makes $C=k^{-1}$.

If the time be reckoned from some instant other than that of passage through a lowest point, we must in the above formulæ write $a+ct$ for ct, where a is arbitrary. If we further impress on the whole mass a velocity c in the direction of x-negative, we obtain the formulæ (1) of Art. 232.

234. Scott Russell, in his interesting experimental investigations*, was led to pay great attention to a particular type which he calls the 'solitary wave.' This is a wave consisting of a single elevation, of height not necessarily small compared with the depth of the fluid, which, if properly started, may travel for a considerable distance along a uniform canal, with little or no change of type. Waves of depression, of similar relative amplitude, were found not to possess the same character of permanence, but to break up into series of shorter waves.

The solitary type may be regarded as an extreme case of Stokes' oscillatory waves of permanent type, the wave-length being great compared with the depth of the canal, so that the widely separated elevations are practically independent of one another. The methods of approximation employed by Stokes become, however, unsuitable when the wave-length much exceeds the depth; and the only successful investigations of the solitary wave which have yet been given proceed on different lines.

The first of these was given independently by Boussinesq† and Lord Rayleigh‡. The latter writer, treating the problem as one of steady motion, starts virtually from the formula
$$\phi + i\psi = F(x+iy) = e^{iy\frac{d}{dx}}F(x) \quad \text{(i)},$$
where $F(x)$ is real. This is especially appropriate to cases, such as the

* "Report on Waves," *Brit. Ass. Rep.*, 1844.

† *Comptes Rendus*, June 19, 1871.

‡ "On Waves," *Phil. Mag.*, April, 1876.

present, where one of the family of stream-lines is straight. We derive from (i)

$$\left.\begin{aligned}\phi &= F - \frac{y^2}{2\,!}F'' + \frac{y^4}{4\,!}F^{\text{iv}} - \ldots,\\ \psi &= yF' - \frac{y^3}{3\,!}F''' + \frac{y^5}{5\,!}F^{\text{v}} - \ldots\end{aligned}\right\}\ldots\ldots\ldots\ldots\ldots\ldots\text{(ii)},$$

where the accents denote differentiations with respect to x. The stream-line $\psi=0$ here forms the bed of the canal, whilst at the free surface we have $\psi=-ch$, where c is the uniform velocity, and h the depth, in the parts of the fluid at a distance from the wave, whether in front or behind.

The condition of uniform pressure along the free surface gives

$$u^2+v^2=c^2-2g\,(y-h)\ldots\ldots\ldots\ldots\ldots\ldots\text{(iii)},$$

or, substituting from (ii),

$$F'^2-y^2F'F'''+y^2F''^2+\ldots=c^2-2g\,(y-h)\ldots\ldots\ldots\ldots\text{(iv)}.$$

But, from (ii), we have, along the same surface,

$$yF'-\frac{y^3}{3\,!}F'''+\ldots=-ch\ldots\ldots\ldots\ldots\ldots\ldots\text{(v)}.$$

It remains to eliminate F between (iv) and (v); the result will be a differential equation to determine the ordinate y of the free surface. If (as we will suppose) the function $F'(x)$ and its differential coefficients vary slowly with x, so that they change only by a small fraction of their values when x increases by an amount comparable with the depth h, the terms in (iv) and (v) will be of gradually diminishing magnitude, and the elimination in question can be carried out by a process of successive approximation.

Thus, from (v),

$$F'=-\frac{ch}{y}+\frac{1}{6}y^2F'''+\ldots=-ch\left\{\frac{1}{y}+\frac{1}{6}y^2\left(\frac{1}{y}\right)''+\ldots\right\}\ldots\ldots\text{(vi)};$$

and if we retain only terms up to the order last written, the equation (iv) becomes

$$\frac{1}{y^2}-\frac{2}{3}y\left(\frac{1}{y}\right)''+y^2\left\{\left(\frac{1}{y}\right)'\right\}^2=\frac{1}{h^2}-\frac{2g\,(y-h)}{c^2h^2},$$

or, on reduction,

$$\frac{1}{y^2}+\frac{2}{3}\frac{y''}{y}-\frac{1}{3}\frac{y'^2}{y^2}=\frac{1}{h^2}-\frac{2g\,(y-h)}{c^2h^2}\ldots\ldots\ldots\ldots\text{(vii)}.$$

If we multiply by y', and integrate, determining the arbitrary constant so as to make $y'=0$ for $y=h$, we obtain

$$-\frac{1}{y}+\frac{1}{3}\frac{y'^2}{y}=-\frac{1}{h}+\frac{y-h}{h^2}-\frac{g\,(y-h)^2}{c^2h^2},$$

or

$$y'^2=3\frac{(y-h)^2}{h^2}\left(1-\frac{gy}{c^2}\right)\ldots\ldots\ldots\ldots\ldots\ldots\text{(viii)}.$$

Hence y' vanishes only for $y=h$ and $y=c^2/g$, and since the last factor must be positive, it appears that c^2/g is a *maximum* value of y. Hence the wave is necessarily one of elevation only, and denoting by a the maximum height above the undisturbed level, we have

$$c^2 = g(h+a) \qquad \text{(ix)},$$

which is exactly the empirical formula for the wave-velocity adopted by Russell.

The extreme form of the wave will, as in Art. 231, have a sharp crest of 120°; and since the fluid is there at rest we shall have $c^2 = 2ga$. If the formula (ix) were applicable to such an extreme case, it would follow that $a = h$.

If we put, for shortness,

$$y - h = \eta, \quad h^2(h+a)/3a = b^2 \qquad \text{(x)},$$

we find, from (viii)

$$\eta' = \pm \frac{\eta}{b}\left(1 - \frac{\eta}{a}\right)^{\frac{1}{2}} \qquad \text{(xi)},$$

the integral of which is

$$\eta = a \operatorname{sech}^2 x/2b \qquad \text{(xii)},$$

if the origin of x be taken beneath the summit.

There is no definite 'length' of the wave, but we may note, as a rough indication of its extent, that the elevation has one-tenth of its maximum value when $x/b = 3{\cdot}636$.

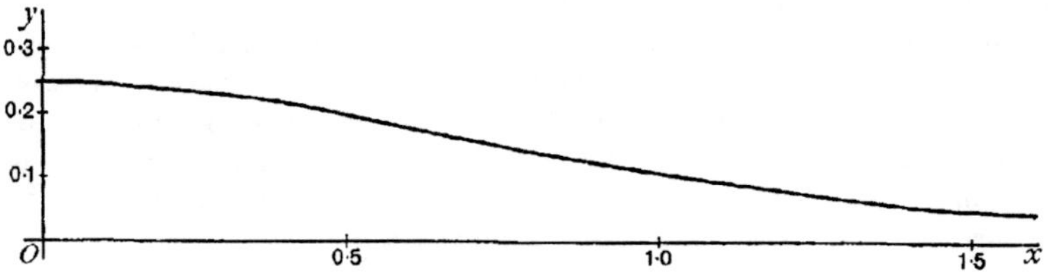

The annexed drawing of the curve

$$y = \tfrac{1}{4}\operatorname{sech}^2 x$$

represents the wave-profile in the case $a = \frac{1}{2}h$. For lower waves the scale of y must be contracted, and that of x enlarged, as indicated by the annexed table giving the ratio b/h, which determines the horizontal scale, for various values of a/h.

a/h	b/h
·1	1·915
·2	1·414
·3	1·202
·4	1·080
·5	1·000
·6	·943
·7	·900
·8	·866
·9	·839
1·0	·816

It will be found, on reviewing the above investigation, that the approximations consist in neglecting the fourth power of the ratio $(h+a)/2b$.

If we impress on the fluid a velocity $-c$ parallel to x we get the case of a progressive wave on still water. It is not difficult to shew that, when the ratio a/h is small, the path of each particle is an arc of a parabola having its axis vertical and apex upwards*.

It might appear, at first sight, that the above theory is inconsistent with the results of Art. 183, where it was shewn that a wave whose length is great compared with the depth

* Boussinesq, *l. c.*

must inevitably suffer a continual change of form as it advances, the changes being the more rapid the greater the elevation above the undisturbed level. The investigation referred to postulates, however, a length so great that the vertical acceleration may be neglected, with the result that the horizontal velocity is sensibly uniform from top to bottom (Art. 169). The numerical table above given shews, on the other hand, that the longer the 'solitary wave' is, the lower it is. In other words, the more nearly it approaches to the character of a 'long' wave, in the sense of Art. 169, the more easily is the change of type averted by a slight adjustment of the particle-velocities*.

The motion at the outskirts of the solitary wave can be represented by a very simple formula†. Considering a progressive wave travelling in the direction of x-positive, and taking the origin in the bottom of the canal, at a point in the front part of the wave, we assume

$$\phi = Ae^{-m(x-ct)} \cos my \quad \text{.........................(xiii).}$$

This satisfies $\nabla^2\phi = 0$, and the surface-condition

$$\frac{d^2\phi}{dt^2} + g\frac{d\phi}{dy} = 0 \quad \text{.................................(xiv)}$$

will also be satisfied for $y = h$, provided

$$c^2 = gh\frac{\tan mh}{mh} \quad \text{.................................(xv).}$$

This will be found to agree approximately with Lord Rayleigh's investigation if we put $m = b^{-1}$.

235. The theory of waves of permanent type has been brought into relation with general dynamical principles by von Helmholtz‡.

If in the equations of motion of a 'gyrostatic' system, Art. 139 (14), we put

$$Q_1 = -\frac{dV}{dq_1}, \quad Q_2 = -\frac{dV}{dq_2}, \ldots, \quad \text{...............(1),}$$

* Stokes, "On the Highest Wave of Uniform Propagation," *Proc. Camb. Phil. Soc.*, t. iv., p. 361 (1883).

For another method of investigation see McCowan "On the Solitary Wave," *Phil. Mag.*, July 1891; and "On the Highest Wave of Permanent Type," *Phil. Mag.*, Oct. 1894. The latter paper gives an approximate determination of the extreme form of the wave, when the crest has a sharp angle of 120°. The limiting value for the ratio a/h is found to be ·78.

† Kindly communicated by Sir George Stokes.

‡ "Die Energie der Wogen und des Windes," *Berl. Monatsber.*, July 17, 1890; *Wied. Ann.*, t. xli., p. 641.

where V is the potential energy, it appears that the conditions for steady motion, with $q_1, q_2, \ldots$ constant, are

$$\frac{d}{dq_1}(V+K)=0,\ \frac{d}{dq_2}(V+K)=0, \ldots, \qquad \ldots\ldots\ldots\ldots(2),$$

where K is the energy of the motion corresponding to any given values of the coordinates $q_1, q_2, \ldots$, when these are prevented from varying by the application of suitable extraneous forces.

This energy is here supposed expressed in terms of the constant momenta $C, C', \ldots$ corresponding to the ignored coordinates $\chi, \chi', \ldots$, and of the palpable coordinates $q_1, q_2, \ldots$. It may however also be expressed in terms of the velocities $\dot{\chi}, \dot{\chi}', \ldots$ and the coordinates $q_1, q_2, \ldots$; in this form we denote it by T_0. It may be shewn, exactly as in Art. 141, that $dT_0/dq_r = -dK/dq_r$, so that the conditions (2) are equivalent to

$$\frac{d}{dq_1}(V-T_0)=0,\ \frac{d}{dq_2}(V-T_0)=0 \ldots, \qquad \ldots\ldots\ldots (3).$$

Hence the condition for free steady motion with any assigned constant values of $q_1, q_2, \ldots$ is that the corresponding value of $V+K$, or of $V-T_0$, should be stationary. Cf. Art. 195.

Further, if in the equations of Art. 139 we write $-dV/dq_s + Q_s$ for Q_s, so that Q_s now denotes a component of extraneous force, we find, on multiplying by $\dot{q}_1, \dot{q}_2, \ldots$ in order, and adding,

$$\frac{d}{dt}(\mathfrak{T} + V + K) = Q_1\dot{q}_1 + Q_2\dot{q}_2 + \ldots \qquad \ldots\ldots\ldots\ldots (4),$$

where $\mathfrak{T}$ is the part of the energy which involves the velocities $\dot{q}_1, \dot{q}_2, \ldots$. It follows, by the same argument as in Art. 197, that the condition for 'secular' stability, when there are dissipative forces affecting the coordinates $q_1, q_2, \ldots$, but not the ignored coordinates $\chi, \chi', \ldots$, is that $V+K$ should be a minimum.

In the application to the problem of stationary waves, it will tend to clearness if we eliminate all infinities from the question by imagining that the fluid circulates in a ring-shaped canal of uniform rectangular section (the sides being horizontal and vertical), of very large radius. The generalized velocity $\dot{\chi}$ corresponding to the ignored coordinate may be taken to be the flux per unit breadth of the channel, and the constant momentum of the circulation may be replaced by the cyclic constant κ. The coordinates $q_1, q_2, \ldots$ of the general theory are now represented by the value of the surface-elevation (η) considered as a function of the longitudinal space-coordinate x. The corresponding components of extraneous force are represented by arbitrary pressures applied to the surface.

If l denote the whole length of the circuit, then considering unit breadth of the canal we have

$$V = \tfrac{1}{2} g\rho \int_0^l \eta^2 dx \quad\ldots\ldots(5),$$

where η is subject to the condition

$$\int_0^l \eta\, dx = 0 \quad\ldots\ldots(6).$$

If we could with the same ease obtain a general expression for the kinetic energy of the steady motion corresponding to any prescribed form of the surface, the minimum condition in either of the forms above given would, by the usual processes of the Calculus of Variations, lead to a determination of the possible forms, if any, of stationary waves*.

Practically, this is not feasible, except by methods of successive approximation, but we may illustrate the question by reproducing, on the basis of the present theory, the results already obtained for 'long' waves of infinitely small amplitude.

If h be the depth of the canal, the velocity in any section when the surface is maintained at rest, with arbitrary elevation η, is $\dot{\chi}/(h+\eta)$, where $\dot{\chi}$ is the flux. Hence, for the cyclic constant,

$$\kappa = \dot{\chi}\int_0^l (h+\eta)^{-1} dx = \frac{l\dot{\chi}}{h}\left(1 + \frac{1}{h^2 l}\int_0^l \eta^2 dx\right) \quad\ldots\ldots(\text{i}),$$

* For some general considerations bearing on the problem of stationary waves on the common surface of two currents reference may be made to von Helmholtz' paper. This also contains, at the end, some speculations, based on calculations of energy and momentum, as to the length of the waves which would be excited in the first instance by a wind of given velocity. These appear to involve the assumption that the waves will necessarily be of permanent type, since it is only on some such hypothesis that we get a determinate value for the momentum of a train of waves of small amplitude.

approximately, where the term of the first order in η has been omitted, in virtue of (6).

The kinetic energy, $\frac{1}{2}\rho\kappa\dot{\chi}$, may be expressed in terms of either $\dot{\chi}$ or κ. We thus obtain the forms

$$T_0 = \tfrac{1}{2}\frac{\rho l \dot{\chi}^2}{h}\left(1 + \frac{1}{h^2 l}\int_0^l \eta^2 dx\right) \quad\text{(ii)},$$

$$K = \tfrac{1}{2}\frac{\rho h \kappa^2}{l}\left(1 - \frac{1}{h^2 l}\int_0^l \eta^2 dx\right) \quad\text{(iii)}.$$

The variable part of $V - T_0$ is

$$\tfrac{1}{2}\rho\left(g - \frac{\dot{\chi}^2}{h^3}\right)\int_0^l \eta^2 dx \quad\text{(iv)},$$

and that of $V + K$ is

$$\tfrac{1}{2}\rho\left(g - \frac{\kappa^2}{hl^2}\right)\int_0^l \eta^2 dx \quad\text{(v)}.$$

It is obvious that these are both stationary for $\eta = 0$; and that they will be stationary for *any* infinitely small values of η, provided $\dot{\chi}^2 = gh^3$, or $\kappa^2 = ghl^2$. If we put $\dot{\chi} = Uh$, or $\kappa = Ul$, this condition gives

$$U^2 = gh \quad\text{(vi)},$$

in agreement with Art. 172.

It appears, moreover, that $\eta = 0$ makes $V + K$ a maximum or a minimum according as U^2 is greater or less than gh. In other words, the plane form of the surface is secularly stable if, and only if, $U < (gh)^{\frac{1}{2}}$. It is to be remarked, however, that the dissipative forces here contemplated are of a special character, viz. they affect the *vertical* motion of the surface, but not (directly) the flow of the liquid. It is otherwise evident from Art. 172 that if pressures be applied to maintain any given constant form of the surface, then if $U^2 > gh$ these pressures must be greatest over the elevations and least over the depressions. Hence if the pressures be removed, the inequalities of the surface will tend to increase.

Standing Waves in Limited Masses of Water.

236. The problem of wave-motion in *two* horizontal dimensions (x, y), in the case where the depth is uniform and the fluid is bounded laterally by vertical walls, can be reduced to the same analytical form as in Art. 185*.

If the origin be taken in the undisturbed surface, and if ζ denote the elevation at time t above this level, the pressure-

* For references to the original investigations of Poisson and Lord Rayleigh see p. 310. The problem was also treated by Ostrogradsky, "Mémoire sur la propagation des ondes dans un bassin cylindrique," *Mém. des Sav. Étrang.*, t. iii. (1832).

condition to be satisfied at the surface is, in the case of infinitely small motions,

$$\zeta = \frac{1}{g}\left[\frac{d\phi}{dt}\right]_{z=0} \text{ .... (1),}$$

and the kinematical surface-condition is

$$\frac{d\zeta}{dt} = -\left[\frac{d\phi}{dz}\right]_{z=0} \text{ .... (2).}$$

Hence, for $z = 0$, we must have

$$\frac{d^2\phi}{dt^2} + g\frac{d\phi}{dz} = 0 \text{ .... (3);}$$

or, in the case of simple-harmonic motion,

$$\sigma^2\phi = g\frac{d\phi}{dz} \text{ .... (4),}$$

if the time-factor be $e^{i(\sigma t+\epsilon)}$. The proof is the same as in Art. 216.

The equation of continuity, $\nabla^2\phi = 0$, and the condition of zero vertical motion at the depth $z = -h$, are both satisfied by

$$\phi = \phi_1 \cosh k(z+h) \text{ .... (5),}$$

where ϕ_1 is a function of x, y, provided

$$\frac{d^2\phi_1}{dx^2} + \frac{d^2\phi_1}{dy^2} + k^2\phi_1 = 0 \text{ .... (6).}$$

The form of ϕ_1 and the admissible values of k are determined by this equation, and by the condition that

$$\frac{d\phi_1}{dn} = 0 \text{ .... (7),}$$

at the vertical walls. The corresponding values of the 'speed' (σ) of the oscillations are then given by the surface-condition (4), viz. we have

$$\sigma^2 = gk \tanh kh \text{ .... (8).}$$

From (2) and (5) we obtain

$$\zeta = \frac{ik}{\sigma} \sinh kh \,.\, \phi_1 \text{ .... (9).}$$

The conditions (6) and (7) are of the same form as in the case of small depth, and we could therefore at once write down the results for a rectangular or a circular tank. The values of k, and the forms of the free surface, in the various fundamental modes, are the same as in Arts. 186, 187*, but the amplitude of the oscillation now diminishes with increasing depth below the surface, according to the law (5); whilst the speed of any particular mode is given by (8).

When kh is small, we have $\sigma^2 = k^2gh$, as in the Arts. referred to.

237. The number of cases of motion with a *variable* depth, of which the solution has been obtained, is very small.

1°. We may notice, first, the two-dimensional oscillations of water across a channel whose section consists of two straight lines inclined at 45° to the vertical†.

The axes of y, z being respectively horizontal and vertical, in the plane of the cross-section, we assume

$$\phi + i\psi = A\,\{\cosh k(y+iz) + \cos k(y+iz)\} \qquad \text{(i)},$$

the time-factor $e^{i(\sigma t+\epsilon)}$ being understood. This gives

$$\left.\begin{aligned}\phi &= A\,(\cosh ky \cos kz + \cos ky \cosh kz),\\ \psi &= A\,(\sinh ky \sin kz - \sin ky \sinh kz)\end{aligned}\right\} \qquad \text{(ii)}.$$

The latter formula shews at once that the lines $y = \pm z$ constitute the stream-line $\psi = 0$, and may therefore be taken as fixed boundaries.

The condition to be satisfied at the free surface is, as in Art. 216,

$$\sigma^2\phi = g\,d\phi/dz \qquad \text{(iii)}.$$

Substituting from (ii) we find, if h denote the height of the surface above the origin,

$$\sigma^2(\cosh ky \cos kh + \cos ky \cosh kh) = gk(-\cosh ky \sin kh + \cos ky \sinh kh).$$

This will be satisfied for all values of y, provided

$$\left.\begin{aligned}\sigma^2 \cos kh &= -gk \sin kh,\\ \sigma^2 \cosh kh &= gk \sinh kh\end{aligned}\right\} \qquad \text{(iv)},$$

whence

$$\tanh kh = -\tan kh \qquad \text{(v)}.$$

This determines the admissible values of k; the corresponding values of σ are then given by either of the equations (iv).

Since (ii) makes ϕ an *even* function of y, the oscillations which it represents are symmetrical with respect to the medial plane $y = 0$.

* It may be remarked that either of the two modes figured on pp. 308, 309 may be easily excited by properly-timed horizontal agitation of a tumbler containing water.

† Kirchhoff, "Ueber stehende Schwingungen einer schweren Flüssigkeit," *Berl. Monatsber.*, May 15, 1879; *Ges. Abh.*, p. 428. Greenhill, *l. c. ante* p. 388.

The asymmetrical oscillations are given by

$$\phi + i\psi = iA\,\{\cosh k\,(y+iz) - \cos k\,(y+iz)\} \quad\text{.............. (vi)},$$

or

$$\left.\begin{aligned}\phi &= -A\,(\sinh ky \sin kz + \sin ky \sinh kz),\\ \psi &= A\,(\cosh ky \cos kz - \cos ky \cosh kz)\end{aligned}\right\} \quad\text{............ (vii)}.$$

The stream-line $\psi=0$ consists, as before, of the lines $y=\pm z$; and the surface-condition (iii) gives

$$\sigma^2(\sinh ky \sin kh + \sin ky \sinh kh) = gk\,(\sinh ky \cos kh + \sin ky \cosh kh).$$

This requires

$$\left.\begin{aligned}\sigma^2 \sin kh &= gk \cos kh,\\ \sigma^2 \sinh kh &= gk \cosh kh\end{aligned}\right\} \quad\text{......................(viii)},$$

whence

$$\tanh kh = \tan kh \quad\text{..................................(ix)}.$$

The equations (v) and (ix) present themselves in the theory of the lateral vibrations of a bar free at both ends; viz. they are both included in the equation

$$\cos m \cosh m = 1 \quad\text{.............................. (x)*},$$

where $m=2kh$.

The root $kh=0$, of (ix), which is extraneous in the theory referred to, is now important; it corresponds in fact to the slowest mode of oscillation in the present problem. Putting $Ak^2=B$, and making k infinitesimal, the formulæ (vii) become, on restoring the time-factor, and taking the real parts,

$$\left.\begin{aligned}\phi &= -2Byz\,.\cos(\sigma t+\epsilon),\\ \psi &= B\,(y^2-z^2)\,.\cos(\sigma t+\epsilon)\end{aligned}\right\} \quad\text{........................ (xi)},$$

whilst from (viii)

$$\sigma^2 = g/h \quad\text{.................................... (xii)}.$$

The corresponding form of the free surface is

$$\zeta = \frac{1}{g}\left[\frac{d\phi}{dt}\right]_{z=h} = 2\sigma Bhy\,.\sin(\sigma t+\epsilon) \quad\text{..................(xiii)}.$$

The surface in this mode is therefore always plane.

The annexed figure shews the lines of motion (ψ=const.) for a series of equidistant values of ψ.

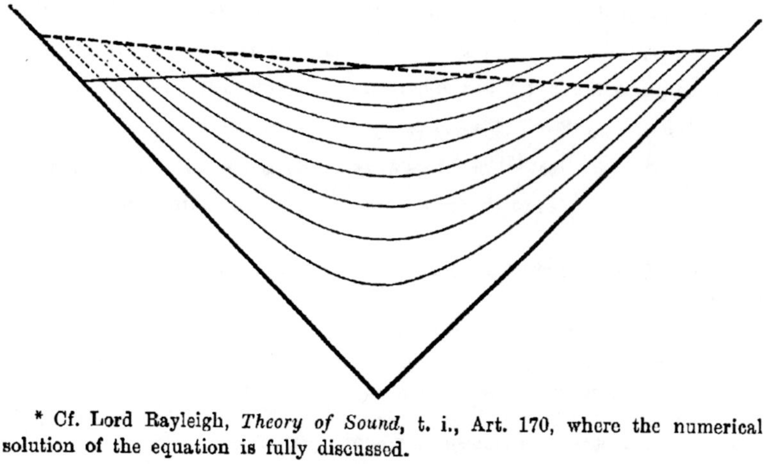

* Cf. Lord Rayleigh, *Theory of Sound*, t. i., Art. 170, where the numerical solution of the equation is fully discussed.

The next gravest mode is symmetrical, and is given by the lowest finite root of (v), which is $kh=2{\cdot}3650$, whence $\sigma=1{\cdot}5244\,(g/h)^{\frac{1}{2}}$.

In this mode, the profile of the surface has two nodes, whose positions are determined by putting $\phi=0$, $z=h$, in (ii); whence it is found that

$$x/h=\pm{\cdot}5516^*.$$

The next mode corresponds to the lowest finite root of (ix), and so on†.

2°. Greenhill, in the paper already cited, has investigated the *symmetrical* oscillations of the water across a channel whose section consists of two straight lines inclined at 60° to the vertical. In the (analytically) simplest mode of this kind we have, omitting the time-factor,

$$\phi+i\psi=iA\,(y+iz)^3+B \qquad \text{(xiv)},$$

or

$$\phi=Az\,(z^2-3y^2)+B,\quad \psi=Ay\,(y^2-3z^2) \qquad \text{(xv)},$$

the latter formula making $\psi=0$ along the boundary $y=\pm\sqrt{3}\,.\,z$. The surface-condition (iii) is satisfied for $z=h$, provided

$$\sigma^2=g/h,\quad B=2Ah^3 \qquad \text{(xvi)}.$$

The corresponding form of the free surface is

$$\zeta=\frac{1}{g}\left[\frac{d\phi}{dt}\right]_{z=h}=-\frac{3A}{\sigma}\,(h^2-x^2)\sin(\sigma t+\epsilon) \qquad \text{(xvii)},$$

a parabolic cylinder, with two nodes at distances of ·5774 of the half-breadth from the centre. Unfortunately, this is not the slowest mode, which must evidently be of asymmetrical type.

3°. If in any of the above cases we transfer the origin to either edge of the canal, and then make the breadth infinite, we get a system of standing waves on a sea bounded by a sloping bank. This may be regarded as made up of an incident and a reflected system. The reflection is complete, but there is in general a change of phase.

When the inclination of the bank is 45° the solution is

$$\phi=H\{e^{kz}(\cos ky-\sin ky)+e^{-ky}(\cos kz+\sin kz)\}\cos(\sigma t+\epsilon) \qquad \text{(xviii)}.$$

For an inclination of 30° to the horizontal we have

$$\phi=H\{e^{kz}\sin ky+e^{-\frac{1}{2}k(\sqrt{3}y+z)}\sin\tfrac{1}{2}k\,(y-\sqrt{3}z)$$
$$-\sqrt{3}e^{-\frac{1}{2}k(\sqrt{3}y-z)}\cos\tfrac{1}{2}k\,(y+\sqrt{3}z)\}\cos(\sigma t+\epsilon) \qquad \text{(xix)}.$$

In each case $\sigma^2=gk$, as in the case of waves on an unlimited sheet of deep water.

These results, which may easily be verified *ab initio*, were given by Kirchhoff (*l. c.*).

* Lord Rayleigh, *Theory of Sound*, Art. 178.

† An experimental verification of the frequencies, and of the positions of the loops (places of maximum vertical amplitude), in various fundamental modes, has been made by Kirchhoff and Hansemann, "Ueber stehende Schwingungen des Wassers," *Wied. Ann.*, t. x. (1880); Kirchhoff, *Ges. Abh.*, p. 442.

238. An interesting problem which presents itself in this connection is that of the transversal oscillations of water contained in a canal of *circular* section. This has not yet been solved, but it may be worth while to point out that an approximate determination of the frequency of the slowest mode, in the case where the free surface is at the level of the axis, can be effected by Lord Rayleigh's method, explained in Art. 165.

If we assume as an 'approximate type' that in which the free surface remains always plane, making a small angle θ (say) with the horizontal, it appears, from Art. 72, 3°, that the kinetic energy T is given by

$$2T = \left(\frac{4}{\pi} - \frac{\pi}{4}\right) \rho a^4 \dot{\theta}^2 \quad\ldots\ldots\ldots\ldots\ldots\ldots\ldots (1),$$

where a is the radius, whilst for the potential energy V we have

$$2V = \tfrac{2}{3} g \rho a^3 \theta^2 \quad\ldots\ldots\ldots\ldots\ldots\ldots\ldots\ldots (2).$$

If we assume that $\theta \propto \cos(\sigma t + \epsilon)$, this gives

$$\sigma^2 = \frac{8\pi}{48 - 3\pi^2} \frac{g}{a} \quad\ldots\ldots\ldots\ldots\ldots\ldots\ldots\ldots (3),$$

whence $\sigma = 1{\cdot}169\, (g/a)^{\frac{1}{2}}$.

In the case of a rectangular section of breadth $2a$, and depth a, the speed is given by Art. 236 (8), where we must put $k = \pi/2a$ from Art. 186, and $h = a$. This gives

$$\sigma^2 = \tfrac{1}{2}\pi \tanh \tfrac{1}{2}\pi \,.\, \frac{g}{a} \ldots\ldots\ldots\ldots\ldots\ldots\ldots\ldots (4),$$

or $\sigma = 1{\cdot}200\, (g/a)^{\frac{1}{2}}$. The frequency in the actual problem is less, since the kinetic energy due to a given motion of the surface is greater, whilst the potential energy for a given deformation is the same. Cf. Art. 45.

239. We may next consider the free oscillations of the water included between two transverse partitions in a uniform horizontal canal. It will be worth while, before proceeding to particular cases, to examine for a moment the nature of the analytical problem, with the view of clearing up some misunderstandings which have arisen as to the general question of wave-propagation in a uniform canal of unlimited length.

If the axis of x be parallel to the length, and the origin be taken in one of the ends, the velocity potential in any one of the fundamental modes referred to may, by Fourier's theorem, be supposed expressed in the form

$$\phi = (P_0 + P_1 \cos kx + P_2 \cos 2kx + \ldots$$
$$+ P_s \cos skx + \ldots) \cos (\sigma t + \epsilon) \quad \text{.........(1)},$$

where $k = \pi/l$, if l denote the length of the compartment. The coefficients P_s are here functions of y, z. If the axis of z be drawn vertically upwards, and that of y be therefore horizontal and transverse to the canal, the forms of these functions, and the admissible values of σ, are to be determined from the equation of continuity

$$\nabla^2 \phi = 0 \quad \text{.........................(2)},$$

with the conditions that

$$d\phi/dn = 0 \quad \text{.........................(3)}$$

at the sides, and that

$$\sigma^2 \phi = g d\phi/dz \quad \text{.........................(4)}$$

at the free surface. Since $d\phi/dx$ must vanish for $x = 0$ and $x = l$, it follows from known principles* that each term in (1) must satisfy the conditions (2), (3), (4) independently; viz. we must have

$$\frac{d^2 P_s}{dy^2} + \frac{d^2 P_s}{dz^2} - s^2 k^2 P_s = 0 \quad \text{.................(5)},$$

with

$$dP_s/dn = 0 \quad \text{.........................(6)}$$

at the lateral boundary, and

$$\sigma^2 P_s = g dP_s/dz \quad \text{.........................(7)}$$

at the free surface.

The term P_0 gives purely transverse oscillations such as have been discussed in Art. 237. Any other term $P_s \cos skx$ gives a series of fundamental modes with s nodal lines transverse to the canal, and 0, 1, 2, 3,... nodal lines parallel to the length.

It will be sufficient for our purpose to consider the term $P_1 \cos kx$. It is evident that the assumption

$$\phi = P_1 \cos kx \,.\, \cos (\sigma t + \epsilon) \quad \text{.................(8)},$$

with a proper form of P_1 and the corresponding value of σ deter-

* See Stokes, "On the Critical Values of the Sums of Periodic Series," *Camb. Trans.*, t. viii. (1847); *Math. and Phys. Papers*, t. i., p. 236.

mined as above, gives the velocity-potential of a possible system of standing waves, of arbitrary wave-length $2\pi/k$, in an unlimited canal of the given form of section. Now, as explained in Art. 218, by superposition of two properly adjusted systems of standing waves of this type we can build up a system of progressive waves

$$\phi = P_1 \cos (kx \mp \sigma t) \qquad (9).$$

Hence, contrary to what has been sometimes asserted, progressive waves of simple-harmonic profile, of any assigned wave-length, are possible in an infinitely long canal of any uniform section.

We might go further, and assert the possibility of an infinite number of types, of any given wave-length, with wave-velocities ranging from a certain lowest value to infinity. The types, however, in which there are longitudinal nodes at a distance from the sides are from the present point of view of subordinate interest.

Two extreme cases call for special notice, viz. where the wave-length is very great or very small compared with the dimensions of the transverse section.

The most interesting types of the former class have no longitudinal nodes, and are covered by the general theory of 'long' waves given in Arts. 166, 167. The only additional information we can look for is as to the shapes of the 'wave-ridges' in the direction transverse to the canal.

In the case of relatively short waves, the most important type is one in which the ridges extend across the canal with gradually varying height, and the wave-velocity is that of free waves on deep-water as given by Art. 218 (6).

There is another type of short waves which may present itself when the banks are inclined, and which we may distinguish by the name of 'edge-waves,' since the amplitude diminishes exponentially as the distance from the bank increases. In fact, if the amplitude at the edges be within the limits imposed by our approximations, it will become altogether insensible at a distance whose projection on the slope exceeds a wave-length. The wave-velocity is *less* than that of waves of the same length on deep water. It does not appear that the type of motion here referred to is of any physical importance.

A general formula for these edge-waves has been given by Stokes*. Taking the origin in one edge, the axis of z vertically upwards, and that of y transverse to the canal, and treating the breadth as relatively infinite, the formula in question is

$$\phi = He^{-k(y\cos\beta - z\sin\beta)}\cos k(x-ct) \qquad \text{(i)},$$

where β is the slope of the bank to the horizontal, and

$$c = \left(\frac{g}{k}\sin\beta\right)^{\frac{1}{2}} \qquad \text{(ii)}.$$

The reader will have no difficulty in verifying this result.

240. We proceed to the consideration of some special cases. We shall treat the question as one of standing waves in an infinitely long canal, or in a compartment bounded by two transverse partitions whose distance apart is a multiple of half the arbitrary wave-length $(2\pi/k)$, but the investigations can be easily modified as above so as to apply to progressive waves, and we shall occasionally state results in terms of the wave-velocity.

1°. The solution for the case of a rectangular section, with horizontal bed and vertical sides, could be written down at once from the results of Arts. 186, 236. The nodal lines are transverse and longitudinal, except in the case of a coincidence in period between two distinct modes, when more complex forms are possible. This will happen, for instance, in the case of a square tank.

2°. In the case of a canal whose section consists of two straight lines inclined at 45° to the vertical we have, first, the type discovered by Kelland†; viz. if the axis of x coincide with the bottom line of the canal,

$$\phi = A\cosh\frac{ky}{\sqrt{2}}\cosh\frac{kz}{\sqrt{2}}\cos kx \,.\, \cos(\sigma t + \epsilon) \qquad \text{(i)}.$$

This evidently satisfies $\nabla^2\phi = 0$, and makes

$$d\phi/dy = \pm d\phi/dz \qquad \text{(ii)},$$

for $y = \pm z$, respectively. The surface-condition (7) then gives

$$\sigma^2 = \frac{gk}{\sqrt{2}}\tanh\frac{kh}{\sqrt{2}} \qquad \text{(iii)},$$

where h is the height of the free surface above the bottom line. If we put $\sigma = kc$, the wave-velocity c is given by

$$c^2 = \frac{g}{\sqrt{2}k}\tanh\frac{kh}{\sqrt{2}} \qquad \text{(iv)},$$

where $k = 2\pi/\lambda$, if λ be the wave-length.

* "Report on Recent Researches in Hydrodynamics," *Brit. Ass. Rep.*, 1846; *Math. and Phys. Papers*, t. i., p. 167.

† "On Waves," *Trans. R. S. Edin.*, t. xiv. (1839).

When h/λ is small, this reduces to

$$c = (\tfrac{1}{2}gh)^{\frac{1}{2}} \quad \text{(v)},$$

in agreement with Art. 167 (8), since the mean depth is now denoted by $\frac{1}{2}h$.

When, on the other hand, h/λ is moderately large, we have

$$c^2 = g/k\sqrt{2} \quad \text{(vi)}.$$

The formula (i) indicates now a rapid increase of amplitude towards the sides. We have here, in fact, an instance of 'edge-waves,' and the wave-velocity agrees with that obtained by putting $\beta = 45°$ in Stokes' formula.

The remaining types of oscillation which are symmetrical with respect to the medial plane $y=0$ are given by the formula

$$\phi = C(\cosh \alpha y \cos \beta z + \cos \beta y \cosh \alpha z) \cos kx \,.\, \cos(\sigma t + \epsilon) \quad \text{(vii)},$$

provided α, β, σ are properly determined. This evidently satisfies (ii), and the equation of continuity gives

$$\alpha^2 - \beta^2 = k^2 \quad \text{(viii)}.$$

The surface-condition, Art. 239 (4), to be satisfied for $z = h$, requires

$$\left.\begin{aligned} \sigma^2 \cosh \alpha h &= g\alpha \sinh \alpha h, \\ \sigma^2 \cos \beta h &= -g\beta \sin \beta h \end{aligned}\right\} \quad \text{(ix)}.$$

Hence
$$\alpha h \tanh \alpha h + \beta h \tan \beta h = 0 \quad \text{(x)}.$$

The values of α, β are determined by (viii) and (x), and the corresponding values of σ are then given by either of the equations (ix).

If, for a moment, we write

$$x = \alpha h, \quad y = \beta h \quad \text{(xi)},$$

the roots are given by the intersections of the curve

$$x \tanh x + y \tan y = 0 \quad \text{(xii)},$$

whose general form can be easily traced, with the hyperbola

$$x^2 - y^2 = k^2h^2 \quad \text{(xiii)}.$$

There are an infinite number of real solutions, with values of βh lying in the second, fourth, sixth, ... quadrants. These give respectively 2, 4, 6, ... longitudinal nodes of the free surface. When h/λ is moderately large, we have $\tanh \alpha h = 1$, nearly, and βh is (in the simplest mode of this class) a little greater than $\frac{1}{2}\pi$. The two longitudinal nodes in this case approach very closely to the edges as λ is diminished, whilst the wave-velocity becomes practically equal to that of waves of length λ on deep water. As a numerical example, assuming $\beta h = 1{\cdot}1 \times \frac{1}{2}\pi$, we find

$$\alpha h = 10{\cdot}910, \quad kh = 10{\cdot}772, \quad c = 1{\cdot}0064 \times (g/k)^{\frac{1}{2}}.$$

The distance of either nodal line from the nearest edge is then $\cdot 12h$.

We may next consider the asymmetrical modes. The solution of this type which is analogous to Kelland's was noticed by Greenhill (*l. c.*). It is

$$\phi = A \sinh \frac{ky}{\sqrt{2}} \sinh \frac{kz}{\sqrt{2}} \cos kx \,.\, \cos(\sigma t + \epsilon) \quad \text{.............. (xiv)},$$

with

$$\sigma^2 = \frac{gk}{\sqrt{2}} \coth \frac{kh}{\sqrt{2}} \quad \text{.............................. (xv)}.$$

When kh is small, this makes $\sigma^2 = g/h$, so that the 'speed' is very great compared with that given by the theory of 'long' waves. The oscillation is in fact mainly transversal, with a very gradual variation of phase as we pass along the canal. The middle line of the surface is of course nodal.

When kh is great, we get 'edge-waves,' as before.

The remaining asymmetrical oscillations are given by

$$\phi = A(\sinh \alpha y \sin \beta z + \sin \beta y \sinh \alpha z) \cos kx \,.\, \cos(\sigma t + \epsilon) \quad \text{...... (xvi)}.$$

This leads in the same manner as before to

$$\alpha^2 - \beta^2 = k^2 \quad \text{................................ (xvii)},$$

and

$$\left.\begin{aligned} \sigma^2 \sinh \alpha h &= g\alpha \cosh \alpha h, \\ \sigma^2 \sin \beta h &= g\beta \cos \beta h \end{aligned}\right\} \quad \text{..................... (xviii)},$$

whence

$$\alpha h \coth \alpha h = \beta h \cot \beta h \quad \text{.......................... (xix)}.$$

There are an infinite number of solutions, with values of βh in the third, fifth, seventh, ... quadrants, giving 3, 5, 7, ... longitudinal nodes, one of which is central.

3°. The case of a canal with plane sides inclined at 60° to the vertical has been recently treated by Macdonald*. He has discovered a very comprehensive type, which may be verified as follows.

The assumption

$$\phi = P \cos kx \,.\, \cos(\sigma t + \epsilon) \quad \text{........................... (xx)},$$

where

$$P = A \cosh kz + B \sinh kz + \cosh \frac{ky\sqrt{3}}{2} \left(C \cosh \frac{kz}{2} + D \sinh \frac{kz}{2} \right) \quad \text{... (xxi)},$$

evidently satisfies the equation of continuity; and it is easily shewn that it makes

$$d\phi/dy = \pm\sqrt{3}\, d\phi/dz$$

for $y = \pm\sqrt{3}z$, provided

$$C = 2A, \quad D = -2B \quad \text{.......................... (xxii)}.$$

The surface-condition, Art. 239 (4), is then satisfied, provided

$$\left.\begin{aligned} \frac{\sigma^2}{gk}(A \cosh kh + B \sinh kh) &= A \sinh kh + B \cosh kh, \\ \frac{2\sigma^2}{gk}\left(A \cosh \frac{kh}{2} - B \sinh \frac{kh}{2} \right) &= A \sinh \frac{kh}{2} - B \cosh \frac{kh}{2} \end{aligned}\right\} \quad \text{...... (xxiii)}.$$

* "Waves in Canals," *Proc. Lond. Math. Soc.*, t. xxv., p. 101 (1894).

The former of these is equivalent to

$$\left.\begin{aligned} A &= H\left(\cosh kh - \frac{\sigma^2}{gk}\sinh kh\right), \\ B &= H\left(\frac{\sigma^2}{gk}\cosh kh - \sinh kh\right) \end{aligned}\right\} \quad \text{..............} (\text{xxiv}),$$

and the latter then leads to

$$2\left(\frac{\sigma^2}{gk}\right)^2 - 3\frac{\sigma^2}{gk}\coth 3\frac{kh}{2} + 1 = 0 \quad \text{....................} (\text{xxv}).$$

Also, substituting from (xxii) and (xxiv) in (xxi), we find

$$P = H\left\{\cosh k(z-h) + \frac{\sigma^2}{gk}\sinh k(z-h)\right\} \\ + 2H\cosh\frac{ky\sqrt{3}}{2}\left\{\cosh k\left(\frac{z}{2}+h\right) - \frac{\sigma^2}{gk}\sinh k\left(\frac{z}{2}+h\right)\right\} \text{...} (\text{xxvi}).$$

The equations (xxv) and (xxvi) are those arrived at by Macdonald, by a different process. The surface-value of P is

$$P = H\left\{1 + 2\cosh\frac{ky\sqrt{3}}{2}\left(\cosh\frac{3kh}{2} - \frac{\sigma^2}{gk}\sinh\frac{3kh}{2}\right)\right\} \text{......} (\text{xxvii}).$$

The equation (xxv) is a quadratic in σ^2/gk. In the case of a wave whose length ($2\pi/k$) is great compared with h, we have

$$\coth\frac{3kh}{2} = \frac{2}{3kh},$$

nearly, and the roots of (xxv) are then

$$\sigma^2/gk = \tfrac{1}{2}kh, \text{ and } \sigma^2/gk = 1/kh \quad \text{.................} (\text{xxviii}),$$

approximately. If we put $\sigma = kc$, the former result gives $c^2 = \frac{1}{2}gh$, in accordance with the usual theory of 'long' waves (Arts. 166, 167). The formula (xxvii) now makes $P = 3H$, approximately; this is independent of y, so that the wave ridges are nearly straight. The second of the roots (xxviii) makes $\sigma^2 = g/h$, giving a much greater wave-velocity; but the considerations adduced above shew that there is nothing paradoxical in this*. It will be found on examination that the cross-sections of the waves are parabolic in form, and that there are two nodal lines parallel to the length of the canal. The period is, in fact, almost exactly that of the symmetrical transverse oscillation discussed in Art. 237, 2°.

When, on the other hand, the wave-length is short compared with the transverse dimensions of the canal, kh is large, and $\coth \frac{3}{2}kh = 1$, nearly. The roots of (xxv) are then

$$\sigma^2/gk = 1 \text{ and } \sigma^2/gk = \tfrac{1}{2} \quad \text{........................} (\text{xxix}),$$

approximately. The former result makes $P = H$, nearly, so that the wave-ridges are straight, experiencing only a slight change of altitude towards the

* There is some divergence here, and elsewhere in the text, from the views maintained by Greenhill and Macdonald in the papers cited.

sides. The speed, $\sigma=(gk)^{\frac{1}{2}}$, is exactly what we should expect from the general theory of waves on relatively deep water.

If in this case we transfer the origin to one edge of the water-surface, writing $z+h$ for z, and $y-\sqrt{3}h$ for y, and then make h infinite, we get the case of a system of waves travelling parallel to a shore which slopes downwards at an angle of 30° to the horizon. The result is

$$\phi=H\{e^{kz}+e^{-\frac{1}{2}k(\sqrt{3}y+z)}-3e^{-\frac{1}{2}k(\sqrt{3}y-z)}\}\cos kx \,.\, \cos(\sigma t+\epsilon) \quad\text{......(xxx)},$$

where $c=(g/k)^{\frac{1}{2}}$. This admits of immediate verification. At a distance of a wave-length or so from the shore, the value of ϕ, near the surface, reduces to

$$\phi=He^{kz}\cos kx \,.\, \cos(\sigma t+\epsilon) \quad\text{......................(xxxi)},$$

practically, as in Art. 217 *. Near the edge the elevation changes sign, there being a longitudinal node for which

$$\frac{\sqrt{3}}{2}ky=\log_e 2 \quad\text{.......................... (xxxii)},$$

or $y/\lambda=\cdot 127$.

The second of the two roots (xxix) gives a system of edge-waves, the results being equivalent to those obtained by making $\beta=30°$ in Stokes' formula.

Oscillations of a Spherical Mass of Liquid.

241. The theory of the gravitational oscillations of a mass of liquid about the spherical form has been given by Lord Kelvin †.

Taking the origin at the centre, and denoting the radius vector at any point of the surface by $a+\zeta$, where a is the radius in the undisturbed state, we assume

$$\zeta=\Sigma_1^\infty \zeta_n \quad\text{.............................(1)},$$

where ζ_n is a surface-harmonic of integral order n. The equation of continuity $\nabla^2\phi=0$ is satisfied by

$$\phi=\Sigma_1^\infty \frac{r^n}{a^n} S_n \quad\text{.......................... (2)},$$

where S_n is a surface-harmonic, and the kinematical condition

$$\frac{d\zeta}{dt}=-\frac{d\phi}{dr} \quad\text{.......................... (3)},$$

* The result contained in (xxx) does not appear to have been hitherto noticed.

† Sir W. Thomson, "Dynamical Problems regarding Elastic Spheroidal Shells and Spheroids of Incompressible Liquid," *Phil. Trans.*, 1863; *Math. and Phys. Papers*, t. iii., p. 384.

to be satisfied when $r = a$, gives

$$\frac{d\zeta_n}{dt} = -\frac{n}{a} S_n \qquad\qquad (4).$$

The gravitation-potential at the free surface is, by Art. 192,

$$\Omega = -\frac{4\pi\gamma\rho a^3}{3r} - \Sigma_1^\infty \frac{4\pi\gamma\rho a}{2n+1} \zeta_n \qquad\qquad (5),$$

where γ is the gravitation-constant. Putting

$$g = \tfrac{4}{3}\pi\gamma\rho a, \quad r = a + \Sigma\zeta_n,$$

we find

$$\Omega = \text{const.} + g\Sigma_1^\infty \frac{2(n-1)}{2n+1} \zeta_n \qquad\qquad (6).$$

Substituting from (2) and (6) in the pressure equation

$$\frac{p}{\rho} = \frac{d\phi}{dt} - \Omega + \text{const.} \qquad\qquad (7),$$

we find, since p must be constant over the surface,

$$\frac{dS_n}{dt} = \frac{2(n-1)}{2n+1} g\zeta_n \qquad\qquad (8).$$

Eliminating S_n between (4) and (8), we obtain

$$\frac{d^2\zeta_n}{dt^2} + \frac{2n(n-1)}{2n+1} \frac{g}{a} \zeta_n = 0 \qquad\qquad (9).$$

This shews that $\zeta_n \propto \cos(\sigma_n t + \epsilon)$, where

$$\sigma_n^2 = \frac{2n(n-1)}{2n+1} \frac{g}{a} \qquad\qquad (10).$$

For the same density of liquid, $g \propto a$, and the frequency is therefore independent of the dimensions of the globe.

The formula makes $\sigma_1 = 0$, as we should expect, since in the deformation expressed by a surface-harmonic of the first order the surface remains spherical, and the period is therefore infinitely long.

"For the case $n = 2$, or an ellipsoidal deformation, the length of the isochronous simple pendulum becomes $\frac{5}{4}a$, or one and a quarter times the earth's radius, for a homogeneous liquid globe of the same mass and diameter as the earth; and therefore for this case, or for any homogeneous liquid globe of about $5\frac{1}{2}$ times the density of water, the half-period is 47 m. 12 s.*"

"A steel globe of the same dimensions, without mutual gravitation of its parts, could scarcely oscillate so rapidly, since the velocity of plane waves of distortion in steel is only about 10,140 feet per second, at which rate a space equal to the earth's diameter would not be travelled in less than 1 h. 8 m. 40 s.†"

When the surface oscillates in the form of a *zonal* harmonic spheroid of the second order, the equation of the lines of motion is $x\varpi^2 = \text{const.}$, where ϖ denotes the distance of any point from the axis of symmetry, which is taken as axis of x (see Art. 94 (11)). The forms of these lines, for a series of equidistant values of the constant, are shewn in the annexed figure.

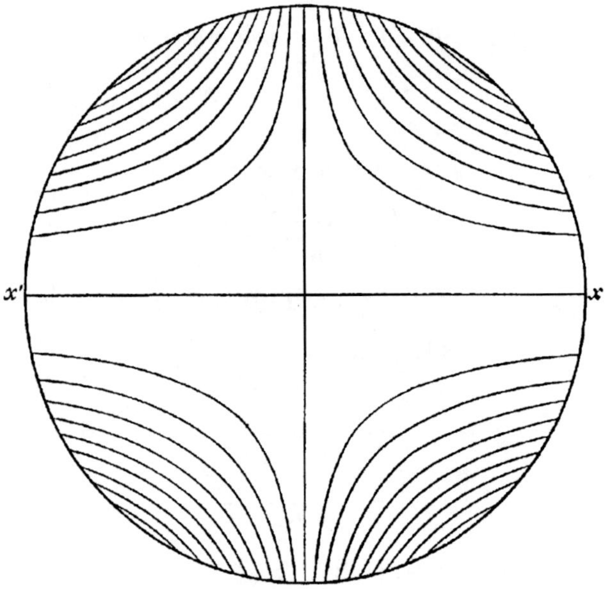

242. This problem may also be treated very compactly by the method of 'normal coordinates' (Art. 165).

The kinetic energy is given by the formula

$$T = \tfrac{1}{2}\rho \iint \phi \frac{d\phi}{dr} dS \quad\text{.....................}\quad (11),$$

* Sir W. Thomson, *l. c.*

† Sir W. Thomson. The exact theory of the vibrations of an elastic sphere gives, for the slowest oscillation of a steel globe of the dimensions of the earth, a period of 1 h. 18 m. *Proc. Lond. Math. Soc.*, t. xiii., p. 212 (1882).

where δS is an element of the surface $r=a$. Hence, when the surface oscillates in the form $r=a+\zeta_n$, we find, on substitution from (2) and (4),

$$T=\tfrac{1}{2}\frac{\rho a}{n}\iint \zeta_n^2 dS \quad\text{..................... (12).}$$

To find the potential energy, we may suppose that the external surface is constrained to assume in succession the forms $r=a+\theta\zeta_n$, where θ varies from 0 to 1. At any stage of this process, the gravitation potential at the surface is, by (6),

$$\Omega=\text{const.}+\frac{2(n-1)}{2n+1}g\theta\zeta_n \quad\text{.............. (13).}$$

Hence the work required to add a film of thickness $\zeta_n\delta\theta$ is

$$\theta\delta\theta\,.\,\frac{2(n-1)}{2n+1}g\rho\iint\zeta_n^2 dS \quad\text{..................(14).}$$

Integrating this from $\theta=0$ to $\theta=1$, we find

$$V=\frac{n-1}{2n+1}g\rho\iint\zeta_n^2 dS \quad\text{.................. (15).}$$

The results corresponding to the general deformation (1) are obtained by prefixing the sign Σ of summation with respect to n, in (12) and (15); since the terms involving products of surface-harmonics of different orders vanish, by Art. 88.

The fact that the general expressions for T and V thus reduce to sums of squares shews that any spherical-harmonic deformation is of a 'normal type.' Also, assuming that $\zeta_n \propto \cos(\sigma_n t+\epsilon)$, the consideration that the total energy $T+V$ must be constant leads us again to the result (10).

In the case of the forced oscillations due to a disturbing potential $\Omega'\cos(\sigma t+\epsilon)$ which satisfies the equation $\nabla^2\Omega'=0$ at all points of the fluid, we must suppose Ω' to be expanded in a series of solid harmonics. If $\bar{\zeta}_n$ be the equilibrium-elevation corresponding to the term of order n, we have, by Art. 165 (12), for the forced oscillation,

$$\zeta_n=\frac{1}{1-\sigma^2/\sigma_n^2}\bar{\zeta}_n \quad\text{..................... (16),}$$

where σ is the imposed speed, and σ_n that of the free oscillations of the same type, as given by (10).

The numerical results given above for the case $n=2$ shew that, in a non-rotating liquid globe of the same dimensions and mean density as the earth, forced oscillations having the characters and periods of the actual lunar and solar tides, would practically have the amplitudes assigned by the equilibrium-theory.

243. The investigation is easily extended to the case of an ocean of any uniform depth, covering a symmetrical spherical nucleus.

Let b be the radius of the nucleus, a that of the external surface. The surface-form being

$$r=a+\Sigma_1^\infty \zeta_n \quad \text{..................................... (i),}$$

we assume, for the velocity-potential,

$$\phi=\left\{(n+1)\frac{r^n}{b^n}+n\frac{b^{n+1}}{r^{n+1}}\right\} S_n \quad \text{............................(ii),}$$

where the coefficients have been adjusted so as to make $d\phi/dr=0$ for $r=b$.

The condition that

$$\frac{d\zeta}{dt}=-\frac{d\phi}{dr} \quad \text{..................................(iii),}$$

for $r=a$, gives

$$\frac{d\zeta_n}{dt}=-n(n+1)\left\{\left(\frac{a}{b}\right)^n-\left(\frac{b}{a}\right)^{n+1}\right\}\frac{S_n}{a} \quad \text{......................(iv).}$$

For the gravitation-potential at the free surface (i) we have

$$\Omega=-\frac{4\pi\gamma\rho_0 a^3}{3r}-\Sigma_1^\infty \frac{4\pi\gamma\rho a}{2n+1}\zeta_n \quad \text{..........................(v),}$$

where ρ_0 is the mean density of the whole mass. Hence, putting $g=\frac{4}{3}\pi\gamma\rho_0 a$, we find

$$\Omega=\text{const.}+g\Sigma_1^\infty\left(1-\frac{3}{2n+1}\frac{\rho}{\rho_0}\right)\zeta_n \quad \text{........................(vi).}$$

The pressure-condition at the free surface then gives

$$\left\{(n+1)\left(\frac{a}{b}\right)^n+n\left(\frac{b}{a}\right)^{n+1}\right\}\frac{dS_n}{dt}=\left(1-\frac{3}{2n+1}\frac{\rho}{\rho_0}\right)g\zeta_n \quad \text{.........(vii).}$$

The elimination of S_n between (iv) and (vii) then leads to

$$\frac{d^2\zeta_n}{dt^2}+\sigma_n^2\zeta_n=0 \quad \text{.............................(viii),}$$

where

$$\sigma_n^2=\frac{n(n+1)\left\{\left(\frac{a}{b}\right)^n-\left(\frac{b}{a}\right)^{n+1}\right\}}{(n+1)\left(\frac{a}{b}\right)^n+n\left(\frac{b}{a}\right)^{n+1}}\left(1-\frac{3}{2n+1}\frac{\rho}{\rho_0}\right)\frac{g}{a} \quad \text{...........(ix).}$$

If $\rho=\rho_0$, we have $\sigma_1=0$ as we should expect. When $\rho>\rho_0$ the value of σ_1 is imaginary; the equilibrium configuration in which the external surface of the fluid is concentric with the nucleus is then unstable. (Cf. Art. 192.)

If in (ix) we put $b=0$, we reproduce the result of the preceding Art. If, on the other hand, the depth of the ocean be small compared with the radius, we find, putting $b=a-h$, and neglecting the square of h/a,

$$\sigma_n^2=n(n+1)\left(1-\frac{3}{2n+1}\frac{\rho}{\rho_0}\right)\frac{gh}{a^2} \quad\text{.....................(x)},$$

provided n be small compared with a/h. This agrees with Laplace's result, obtained in a more direct manner in Art. 192.

But if n be comparable with a/h, we have, putting $n=ka$,

$$(a/b)^n=(1-h/a)^{-ka}=e^{kh},$$

so that (ix) reduces to

$$\sigma^2=gk\tanh kh \quad\text{................................(xi)},$$

as in Art. 217. Moreover, the expression (ii) for the velocity-potential becomes, if we write $r=a+z$,

$$\phi=\phi_1\cosh k(z+h) \quad\text{.............................(xii)},$$

where ϕ_1 is a function of the coordinates in the surface, which may now be treated as plane. Cf. Art. 236.

The formulæ for the kinetic and potential energies, in the general case, are easily found by the same method as in the preceding Art. to be

$$T=\tfrac{1}{2}\rho a\Sigma_1^\infty\frac{(n+1)\left(\frac{a}{b}\right)^n+n\left(\frac{b}{a}\right)^{n+1}}{n(n+1)\left\{\left(\frac{a}{b}\right)^n-\left(\frac{b}{a}\right)^{n+1}\right\}}\iint\dot{\zeta}_n^2\,dS \quad\text{............ (xiii)},$$

and

$$V=\tfrac{1}{2}g\rho\Sigma_1^\infty\left(1-\frac{3}{2n+1}\frac{\rho}{\rho_0}\right)\iint\zeta_n^2\,dS \quad\text{.....................(xiv)}.$$

The latter result shews, again, that the equilibrium configuration is one of minimum potential energy, and therefore thoroughly stable, provided $\rho<\rho_0$.

In the case where the depth is relatively small, whilst n is finite, we obtain, putting $b=a-h$,

$$T=\tfrac{1}{2}\frac{\rho a^2}{h}\Sigma_1^\infty\frac{1}{n(n+1)}\iint\dot{\zeta}_n^2\,dS \quad\text{........................ (xv)},$$

whilst the expression for V is of course unaltered.

If the amplitudes of the harmonics ζ_n be regarded as generalized coordinates (Art. 165), the formula (xv) shews that for relatively small depths the 'inertia-coefficients' vary inversely as the depth. We have had frequent illustrations of this principle in our discussions of tidal waves.

Capillarity.

244. The part played by Cohesion in certain cases of fluid motion has long been recognized in a general way, but it is only within recent years that the question has been subjected to exact mathematical treatment. We proceed to give some account of the remarkable investigations of Lord Kelvin and Lord Rayleigh in this field.

It is, of course, beyond our province to discuss the physical theory of the matter*. It is sufficient, for our purpose, to know that the free surface of a liquid, or, more generally, the common surface of two fluids which do not mix, behaves as if it were in a state of uniform *tension*, the stress between two adjacent portions of the surface, estimated at per unit length of the common boundary-line, depending only on the nature of the two fluids and on the temperature. We shall denote this 'surface-tension,' as it is called, by the symbol T_1. Its value in C.G.S. units (dynes per linear centimetre) appears to be about 74 for a water-air surface at 20° C.†; it diminishes somewhat with rise of temperature. The corresponding value for a mercury-air surface is about 540.

An equivalent statement is that the potential energy of any system, of which the surface in question forms part, contains a term proportional to the area of the surface, the amount of this 'superficial energy' per unit area being equal to T_1§. Since the condition of stable equilibrium is that the energy should be a minimum, the surface tends to contract as much as is consistent with the other conditions of the problem.

The chief modification which the consideration of surface-tension will introduce into our previous methods is contained in the theorem that the fluid pressure is now discontinuous at a surface of separation, viz. we have

$$p - p' = T_1\left(\frac{1}{R_1} + \frac{1}{R_2}\right) \quad\text{.....................(1)},$$

* For this, see Maxwell, *Encyc. Britann.*, Art. "Capillary Action"; *Scientific Papers*, Cambridge, 1890, t. ii., p. 541, where references to the older writers are given. Also, Lord Rayleigh, "On the Theory of Surface Forces," *Phil. Mag.*, Oct. and Dec., 1890, and Feb. and May, 1892.

† Lord Rayleigh "On the Tension of Water-Surfaces, Clean and Contaminated, investigated by the method of Ripples," *Phil. Mag.* Nov. 1890.

§ See Maxwell, *Theory of Heat*, London, 1871, c. xx.

where p, p' are the pressures close to the surface on the two sides, and R_1, R_2 are the principal radii of curvature of the surface, to be reckoned negative when the corresponding centres of curvature lie on the side to which the accent refers. This formula is readily obtained by resolving along the normal the forces acting on a rectangular element of a superficial film, bounded by lines of curvature; but it seems unnecessary to give here the proof, which may be found in most recent treatises on Hydrostatics.

245. The simplest problem we can take, to begin with, is that of waves on a plane surface forming the common boundary of two fluids at rest.

If the origin be taken in this plane, and the axis of y normal to it, the velocity-potentials corresponding to a simple-harmonic deformation of the common surface may be assumed to be

$$\left.\begin{aligned}\phi &= Ce^{ky}\cos kx\,.\cos(\sigma t+\epsilon),\\ \phi' &= C'e^{-ky}\cos kx\,.\cos(\sigma t+\epsilon)\end{aligned}\right\}\quad\ldots\ldots\ldots\ldots\ldots\ldots(1),$$

where the former equation relates to the side on which y is negative, and the latter to that on which y is positive. For these values satisfy $\nabla^2\phi=0$, $\nabla^2\phi'=0$, and make the velocity zero for $y=\mp\infty$, respectively.

The corresponding displacement of the surface in the direction of y will be of the type

$$\eta = a\cos kx\,.\sin(\sigma t+\epsilon)\ldots\ldots\ldots\ldots\ldots\ldots(2);$$

and the conditions that

$$d\eta/dt = -d\phi/dy = -d\phi'/dy,$$

for $y=0$, give

$$\sigma a = -kC = kC'\ldots\ldots\ldots\ldots\ldots\ldots\ldots\ldots(3).$$

If, for the moment, we ignore gravity, the variable part of the pressure is given by

$$\left.\begin{aligned}\frac{p}{\rho} &= \frac{d\phi}{dt} = \frac{\sigma^2 a}{k}e^{ky}\cos kx\,.\sin(\sigma t+\epsilon),\\ \frac{p'}{\rho'} &= \frac{d\phi'}{dt} = -\frac{\sigma^2 a}{k}e^{-ky}\cos kx\,.\sin(\sigma t+\epsilon)\end{aligned}\right\}\quad\ldots\ldots\ldots(4).$$

To find the pressure-condition at the common surface, we may calculate the forces which act in the direction of y on a strip of breadth δx. The fluid pressures on the two sides have a resultant $(p'-p)\,\delta x$, and the difference of the tensions parallel to y on the two edges gives $\delta(T_1\, d\eta/dx)$. We thus get the equation

$$p - p' + T_1 \frac{d^2\eta}{dx^2} = 0 \quad\text{.....................(5)},$$

to be satisfied when $y=0$ approximately. This might have been written down at once as a particular case of the general surface-condition (Art. 244 (1)). Substituting in (5) from (2) and (4), we find

$$\sigma^2 = \frac{T_1 k^3}{\rho+\rho'} \quad\text{.........................(6)},$$

which determines the speed of the oscillations of wave-length $2\pi/k$.

The energy of motion, per wave-length, of the fluid included between two planes parallel to xy, at unit distance apart, is

$$T = \tfrac{1}{2}\rho \int_0^\lambda \left[\phi \frac{d\phi}{dy}\right]_{y=0} dx - \tfrac{1}{2}\rho' \int_0^\lambda \left[\phi' \frac{d\phi'}{dy}\right]_{y=0} dx \quad\text{...........(i)}.$$

If we assume $\eta = a\cos kx$ ....(ii),

where a depends on t only, and therefore, having regard to the kinematical conditions,

$$\phi = -k^{-1}\dot{a}e^{ky}\cos kx, \quad \phi' = k^{-1}\dot{a}e^{-ky}\cos kx \quad\text{..............(iii)},$$

we find $T = \tfrac{1}{4}(\rho+\rho')\,k^{-1}\dot{a}^2 . \lambda$ ....(iv).

Again, the energy of extension of the surface of separation is

$$V = T_1 \int^\lambda \left\{1 + \left(\frac{d\eta}{dx}\right)^2\right\}^{\frac{1}{2}} dx - T_1\lambda = \tfrac{1}{2}T_1 \int_0^\lambda \left(\frac{d\eta}{dx}\right)^2 dx \quad\text{.........(v)}.$$

Substituting from (ii), this gives

$$V = \tfrac{1}{4}T_1 k^2 a^2 . \lambda \quad\text{..............................(vi)}.$$

To find the mean energy, of either kind, per unit length of the axis of x, we must omit the factor λ.

If we assume that $a \propto \cos(\sigma t + \epsilon)$, where σ is determined by (6), we verify that the total energy $T + V$ is constant.

Conversely, if we assume that

$$\eta = \Sigma(a\cos kx + \beta\sin kx) \quad\text{..........................(vii)},$$

it is easily seen that the expressions for T and V will reduce to sums of squares of $\dot{a}$, $\dot{\beta}$ and a, β, respectively, with constant coefficients, so that the quantities a, β are 'normal coordinates.' The general theory of Art. 165 then leads independently to the formula (6) for the speed.

By compounding two systems of standing waves, as in Art. 218, we obtain a progressive wave-system

$$\eta = a \cos (kx \mp \sigma t) \quad \text{.......................(7)},$$

travelling with the velocity

$$c = \frac{\sigma}{k} = \left(\frac{T_1 k}{\rho + \rho'}\right)^{\frac{1}{2}} \quad \text{....................... (8)},$$

or, in terms of the wave-length,

$$c = \left(\frac{2\pi T_1}{\rho + \rho'}\right)^{\frac{1}{2}} . \lambda^{-\frac{1}{2}} \quad \text{.......................(9)}.$$

The contrast with Art. 218 is noteworthy; as the wave-length is diminished, the period diminishes in a more rapid ratio, so that the wave-velocity *increases*.

Since c varies as $\lambda^{-\frac{1}{2}}$, the group-velocity, Art. 221 (2), is in the present case

$$c - \lambda \frac{dc}{d\lambda} = \tfrac{3}{2} c \quad \text{.......................(10)}.$$

The fact that the group-velocity for capillary waves exceeds the wave-velocity helps to explain some interesting phenomena to be referred to later (Art. 249).

For numerical illustration we may take the case of a free water-surface; thus, putting $\rho = 1$, $\rho' = 0$, $T_1 = 74$, we have the following results, the units being the centimetre and second*.

Wave-length.	Wave-velocity.	Frequency.
·50	30	61
·10	68	680
·05	96	1930

246. When gravity is to be taken into account, the common surface, in equilibrium, will of course be horizontal. Taking the

* Cf. Sir W. Thomson, *Math. and Phys. Papers*, t. iii., p. 520.

The above theory gives the explanation of the 'crispations' observed on the surface of water contained in a finger-bowl set into vibration by stroking the rim with a wetted finger. It is to be observed, however, that the frequency of the capillary waves in this experiment is *double* that of the vibrations of the bowl; see Lord Rayleigh, "On Maintained Vibrations," *Phil. Mag.*, April, 1883.

positive direction of y upwards, the pressure at the disturbed surface will be given by

$$\left.\begin{aligned} \frac{p}{\rho} &= \frac{d\phi}{dt} - gy = \left(\frac{\sigma^2}{k} - g\right) a \cos kx \,.\, \sin(\sigma t + \epsilon), \\ \frac{p'}{\rho'} &= \frac{d\phi'}{dt} - gy = -\left(\frac{\sigma^2}{k} + g\right) a \cos kx \,.\, \sin(\sigma t + \epsilon) \end{aligned}\right\} \quad \ldots (1),$$

approximately. Substituting in Art. 245 (5), we find

$$\sigma^2 = \frac{\rho - \rho'}{\rho + \rho'} gk + \frac{T_1 k^3}{\rho + \rho'}, \quad \ldots\ldots\ldots\ldots\ldots\ldots (2).$$

Putting $\sigma = kc$, we find, for the velocity of a train of progressive waves,

$$c^2 = \frac{\rho - \rho'}{\rho + \rho'} \frac{g}{k} + \frac{T_1}{\rho + \rho'} k$$

$$= \frac{1 - s}{1 + s} \left(\frac{g}{k} + T'k\right) \quad \ldots\ldots\ldots\ldots\ldots\ldots (3),$$

where we have written

$$\rho'/\rho = s, \quad T_1/(\rho - \rho') = T' \quad \ldots\ldots\ldots\ldots\ldots (4).$$

In the particular cases of $T_1 = 0$ and $g = 0$, respectively, we fall back on the results of Arts. 223, 245.

There are several points to be noticed with respect to the formula (3). In the first place, although, as the wave-length ($2\pi/k$) diminishes from ∞ to 0, the speed (σ) continually increases, the wave-velocity, after falling to a certain minimum, begins to increase again. This minimum value (c_m, say) is given by

$$c_m^2 = \frac{1 - s}{1 + s} \,.\, 2 (gT')^{\frac{1}{2}} \quad \ldots\ldots\ldots\ldots\ldots\ldots (5),$$

and corresponds to a wave-length

$$\lambda_m = 2\pi/k_m = 2\pi (T'/g)^{\frac{1}{2}} \ldots\ldots\ldots\ldots\ldots\ldots (6)^*.$$

In terms of λ_m and c_m the formula (3) may be written

$$\frac{c^2}{c_m^2} = \frac{1}{2}\left(\frac{\lambda}{\lambda_m} + \frac{\lambda_m}{\lambda}\right) \quad \ldots\ldots\ldots\ldots\ldots\ldots (7),$$

* The theory of the minimum wave-velocity, together with most of the substance of Arts. 245, 246, was given by Sir W. Thomson, "Hydrokinetic Solutions and Observations," *Phil. Mag.*, Nov. 1871; see also *Nature*, t. v., p. 1 (1871).

shewing that for any prescribed value of c, greater than c_m, there are two admissible values (reciprocals) of λ/λ_m. For example, corresponding to

$$c/c_m = 1\cdot2 \qquad 1\cdot4 \qquad 1\cdot6 \qquad 1\cdot8 \qquad 2\cdot0$$

we have

$$\lambda/\lambda_m = \begin{cases} 2\cdot476 \quad 3\cdot646 \quad 4\cdot917 \quad 6\cdot322 \quad 7\cdot873 \\ \cdot404 \quad \cdot274 \quad \cdot203 \quad \cdot158 \quad \cdot127, \end{cases}$$

to which we add, for future reference,

$$\sin^{-1} c_m/c = 56^\circ\, 26' \qquad 45^\circ\, 35' \qquad 38^\circ\, 41' \qquad 33^\circ\, 45' \qquad 30^\circ.$$

For sufficiently large values of λ the first term in the formula (3) for c^2 is large compared with the second; the force governing the motion of the waves being mainly that of gravity. On the other hand, when λ is very small, the second term preponderates, and the motion is mainly governed by cohesion, as in Art. 245. As an indication of the actual magnitudes here in question, we may note that if $\lambda/\lambda_m > 10$, the influence of cohesion on the wave-velocity amounts only to about 5 per cent., whilst gravity becomes relatively ineffective to a like degree if $\lambda/\lambda_m < \frac{1}{10}$.

It has been proposed by Lord Kelvin to distinguish by the name of 'ripples' waves whose length is less than λ_m.

The relative importance of gravity and cohesion, as depending on the value of λ, may be traced to the form of the expression for the potential energy of a deformation of the type

$$\eta = a \cos kx \qquad \text{(i)}.$$

The part of this energy due to the extension of the bounding surface is, per unit area,

$$\pi^2 T_1 a^2/\lambda^2 \qquad \text{(ii)},$$

whilst the part due to gravity is

$$\tfrac{1}{4} g (\rho - \rho') a^2 \qquad \text{(iii)}.$$

As λ diminishes, the former becomes more and more important compared with the latter.

For a water-surface, using the same data as before, with $g = 981$, we find from (5) and (6),

$$\lambda_m = 1\cdot73, \quad c_m = 23\cdot2,$$

the units being the centimetre and the second. That is to say, roughly, the minimum wave-velocity is about nine inches per second, or ·45 sea-miles per hour, with a wave-length of two-thirds of an inch. Combined with the numerical results already obtained, this gives,

for	$c=$	27·8	32·5	37·1	41·8	46·4
the values	$\lambda=$	4·3	6·3	8·5	10·9	13·6
		·70	·47	·35	·27	·22

in centimetres and seconds.

If we substitute from (7) in the general formula (Art. 221 (2)) for the group-velocity, we find

$$c-\lambda\frac{dc}{d\lambda}=c\left(1-\tfrac{1}{2}\frac{\lambda^2-\lambda_m^2}{\lambda^2+\lambda_m^2}\right) \quad\ldots\ldots\ldots\ldots\ldots\ldots (8).$$

Hence the group-velocity is greater or less than the wave-velocity, according as $\lambda \lessgtr \lambda_m$. For sufficiently long waves the group-velocity is practically equal to $\frac{1}{2}c$, whilst for very short waves it tends to the value $\frac{3}{2}c$*.

A further consequence of (2) is to be noted. We have hitherto tacitly supposed that the lower fluid is the denser (*i.e.* $\rho>\rho'$), as is indeed necessary for stability when T_1 is neglected. The formula referred to shows, however, that there is stability even when $\rho<\rho'$, provided

$$\lambda<2\pi\left(\frac{T_1}{g(\rho'-\rho)}\right)^{\frac{1}{2}} \quad\ldots\ldots\ldots\ldots\ldots\ldots\ldots\ldots (\text{iv}),$$

i.e. provided λ be less than the wave-length λ_m of minimum velocity when the denser fluid is below. Hence in the case of water above and air below the maximum wave-length consistent with stability is 1·73 cm. If the fluids be included between two parallel vertical walls, this imposes a superior limit to the admissible wave-length, and we learn that there is stability (in the two-dimensional problem) provided the interval between the walls does not exceed ·86 cm. We have here an explanation, in principle, of a familiar experiment in which water is retained by atmospheric pressure in an inverted tumbler, or other vessel, whose mouth is covered by a gauze with sufficiently fine meshes †.

247. We next consider the case of waves on a horizontal surface forming the common boundary of two parallel currents U, U'.

* Cf. Lord Rayleigh, *l. c. ante* p. 383.

† The case where the fluids are contained in a cylindrical tube has been solved by Maxwell, *Encyc. Britann.*, Art. "Capillary Action," t. v., p. 69, *Scientific Papers*, t. ii., p. 585, and compared with some experiments of Duprez. The agreement is better than might have been expected when we consider that the special condition to be satisfied at the line of contact of the surface with the wall of the tube has been left out of account.

If we apply the method of Art. 224, we find without difficulty that the condition for stationary waves is now

$$\rho U^2 + \rho' U'^2 = \frac{g}{k}(\rho - \rho') + kT_1 \text{.................}(1),$$

the last term being due to the altered form of the pressure-condition which has to be satisfied at the surface. Putting

$$U = -c, \quad U' = -c + \mathbf{u}, \quad \rho'/\rho = s,$$

we get

$$c = \frac{s}{1+s}\mathbf{u} \pm \left\{c_0^2 - \frac{s}{(1+s)^2}\mathbf{u}^2\right\}^{\frac{1}{2}} \text{..............}(2),$$

where

$$c_0^2 = \frac{1-s}{1+s}\left(\frac{g}{k} + T'k\right) \text{....................}(3),$$

i.e. c_0 is the velocity of waves of the given length $(2\pi/k)$ when there are no currents.

The various inferences to be drawn from (2) are much as in Art. 224, with the important qualification that, since c_0 has now a minimum value, viz. the c_m of Art. 246 (5), the equilibrium of the surface when plane is stable for disturbances of all wave-lengths so long as

$$\mathbf{u} < \frac{1+s}{s^{\frac{1}{2}}} \cdot c_m \text{.......................} (4).$$

When the relative velocity $\mathbf{u}$ of the two currents exceeds this value, c becomes imaginary for wave-lengths lying between certain limits. It is evident that in the alternative method of Art. 225 the time-factor $e^{i\sigma t}$ will now take the form $e^{\pm\alpha t + i\beta t}$, where

$$\alpha = \left\{\frac{s}{(1+s)^2}\mathbf{u}^2 - c_0^2\right\}^{\frac{1}{2}} k, \qquad \beta = \frac{s}{1+s} k\mathbf{u} \text{...........} (5).$$

The real part of the exponential indicates the possibility of a disturbance of continually increasing amplitude.

For the case of air over water we have $s = \cdot 00129$, $c_m = 23 \cdot 2$ (c.s.), whence the maximum value of $\mathbf{u}$ consistent with stability is about 646 centimetres per second, or (roughly) 12·5 sea-miles per hour*. For slightly greater values of $\mathbf{u}$ the instability will manifest itself by the formation, in the first in-

* The wind-velocity at which the surface of water actually begins to be ruffled by the formation of capillary waves, so as to lose the power of distinct reflection, is much less than this, and is determined by other causes. We shall revert to this point later (Art. 302).

stance, of wavelets of about two-thirds of an inch in length, which will continually increase in amplitude until they transcend the limits implied in our approximation.

248. We resume the investigation of the effect of a steady pressure-disturbance on the surface of a running stream, by the method of Arts. 226, 227, including now the effect of capillary forces. This will give, in addition to the former results, the explanation (in principle) of the fringe of ripples which is seen in advance of a solid moving at a moderate speed through still water, or on the up-stream side of any disturbance in a uniform current.

Beginning with a simple-harmonic distribution of pressure, we assume

$$\left.\begin{aligned}\phi/c &= -x+\beta e^{ky}\sin kx,\\ \psi/c &= -y+\beta e^{ky}\cos kx\end{aligned}\right\}\quad\text{..................}\quad(1),$$

the upper surface coinciding with the stream-line $\psi=0$, whose equation is

$$y=\beta\cos kx\text{..........................}(2),$$

approximately. At a point just beneath this surface we find, as in Art. 226 (8), for the variable part of the pressure,

$$\frac{\Delta p}{\rho}=\beta\,\{(kc^2-g)\cos kx+\mu c\sin kx\}\text{ ....}(3),$$

where μ is the frictional coefficient. At an adjacent point just above the surface we must have

$$\begin{aligned}\frac{\Delta p'}{\rho}&=\frac{\Delta p}{\rho}+T'\frac{d^2y}{dx^2}\\ &=\beta\,\{(kc^2-g-k^2T')\cos kx+\mu c\sin kx\}\text{.........}(4),\end{aligned}$$

where T' is now written for T_1/ρ. This is equal to the real part of

$$\beta\,(kc^2-g-k^2T'-i\mu c)\,e^{ikx}.$$

Writing P for the coefficient, we find that to the imposed pressure

$$\frac{\Delta p'}{\rho}=P\cos kx\text{ ....}(5)$$

will correspond the surface-form

$$y=P\,\frac{(kc^2-g-k^2T')\cos kx-\mu c\sin kx}{(kc^2-g-k^2T')^2+\mu^2c^2}\text{.........}(6).$$

Let us first suppose that the velocity c of the stream exceeds the minimum wave-velocity (c_m) investigated in Art. 246. We may then write

$$kc^2 - g - k^2T' = T'(k-\kappa_1)(\kappa_2 - k) \quad \ldots\ldots\ldots\ldots\ldots\ldots (7),$$

where κ_1, κ_2 are the two values of k corresponding to the wave-velocity c on still water; in other words, $2\pi/\kappa_1$, $2\pi/\kappa_2$ are the lengths of the two systems of free waves which could maintain a stationary position in space, on the surface of the flowing stream. We will suppose that $\kappa_2 > \kappa_1$.

In terms of these quantities, the formula (6) may be written

$$y = \frac{P}{T'} \cdot \frac{(k-\kappa_1)(\kappa_2 - k)\cos kx - \mu' \sin kx}{(k-\kappa_1)^2(\kappa_2-k)^2 + \mu'^2} \quad \ldots\ldots (8),$$

where $\mu' = \mu c/T'$. This shews that if μ' be small the pressure is least over the crests, and greatest over the troughs of the waves when k is greater than κ_2 or less than κ_1, whilst the reverse is the case when k is intermediate to κ_1, κ_2. In the case of a progressive disturbance advancing over still water, these results are seen to be in accordance with Art. 165 (12).

249. From (8) we can infer as in Art. 227 the effect of a pressure of integral amount Q concentrated on a line of the surface at the origin, viz. we find

$$y = \frac{Q}{\pi T_1} \cdot \int_0^\infty \frac{(k-\kappa_1)(\kappa_2-k)\cos kx - \mu' \sin kx}{(k-\kappa_1)^2(\kappa_2-k)^2+\mu'^2}\, dk \quad \ldots\ldots. (9).$$

This definite integral is the real part of

$$\int_0^\infty \frac{e^{ikx}dk}{(k-\kappa_1)(\kappa_2-k) - i\mu'} \quad \ldots\ldots\ldots\ldots\ldots\ldots\ldots\ldots (i).$$

The dissipation-coefficient μ' has been introduced solely for the purpose of making the problem determinate; we may therefore avail ourselves of the slight gain in simplicity obtained by supposing μ' to be infinitesimal. In this case the two roots of the denominator in (i) are

$$k = \kappa_1 + i\nu, \quad k = \kappa_2 - i\nu,$$

where

$$\nu = \mu'/(\kappa_2 - \kappa_1).$$

Since $\kappa_2 > \kappa_1$, ν is positive. The integral (i) is therefore equivalent to

$$\frac{1}{\kappa_2 - \kappa_1 - 2i\nu}\left\{\int_0^\infty \frac{e^{ikx}dk}{k-(\kappa_1+i\nu)} - \int_0^\infty \frac{e^{ikx}dk}{k-(\kappa_2-i\nu)}\right\} \quad \ldots\ldots\ldots\ldots (ii).$$

These integrals are of the forms discussed in Art. 227. It appears that when x is positive the former integral is equal to

$$2\pi i e^{i\kappa_1 x} + \int_0^\infty \frac{e^{-ikx}}{k+\kappa_1}\,dk \quad\text{.........................(iii)},$$

and the latter to

$$\int_0^\infty \frac{e^{-ikx}}{k+\kappa_2}\,dk \quad\text{...............................(iv)}.$$

On the other hand, when x is negative, the former reduces to

$$\int_0^\infty \frac{e^{-ikx}}{k+\kappa_1}\,dk \quad\text{..................................(v)},$$

and the latter to

$$-2\pi i e^{i\kappa_2 x} + \int_0^\infty \frac{e^{-ikx}}{k+\kappa_2}\,dk \quad\text{.......................(vi)}.$$

We have here simplified the formulæ by putting $\nu=0$ *after* the transformations.

If we now discard the imaginary parts of our expressions, we obtain the results which immediately follow.

When μ' is infinitesimal, the equation (9) gives, for x positive,

$$\frac{\pi T_1}{Q} \,.\, y = -\frac{2\pi}{\kappa_2 - \kappa_1} \sin \kappa_1 x + F(x) \quad\text{..............(10)},$$

and, for x negative,

$$\frac{\pi T_1}{Q} \,.\, y = -\frac{2\pi}{\kappa_2 - \kappa_1} \sin \kappa_2 x + F(x) \quad\text{..............(11)},$$

where

$$F(x) = \frac{1}{\kappa_2 - \kappa_1} \left\{ \int_0^\infty \frac{\cos kx}{k+\kappa_1}\,dk - \int_0^\infty \frac{\cos kx}{k+\kappa_2}\,dk \right\} \quad\text{.......(12)}.$$

This function $F(x)$ can be expressed in terms of the known functions $\mathrm{Ci}\,\kappa_1 x$, $\mathrm{Si}\,\kappa_1 x$, $\mathrm{Ci}\,\kappa_2 x$, $\mathrm{Si}\,\kappa_2 x$, by Art. 227 (ix). The disturbance of level represented by it is very small for values of x, whether positive or negative, which exceed, say, half the greater wave-length ($2\pi/\kappa_1$).

Hence, beyond some such distance, the surface is covered on the down-stream side by a regular train of simple-harmonic waves of length $2\pi/\kappa_1$, and on the up-stream side by a train of the shorter wave-length $2\pi/\kappa_2$. It appears from the numerical results of Art. 246 that when the velocity c of the stream much exceeds the minimum wave-velocity (c_m) the former system of waves is governed mainly by gravity, and the latter by cohesion.

It is worth notice that, in contrast with the case of Art. 227, the elevation is now finite when $x=0$, viz. we have

$$\frac{\pi T_1}{Q}\cdot y = \frac{1}{\kappa_2-\kappa_1}\log\frac{\kappa_2}{\kappa_1} \;\ldots\; (13).$$

This follows easily from (10).

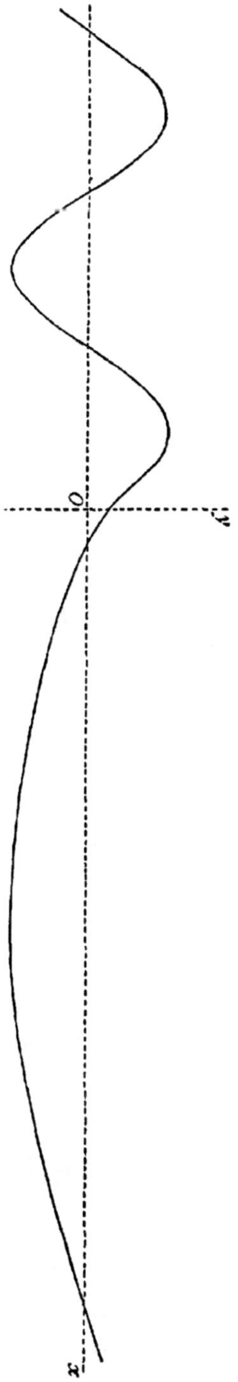

The figure shews the transition between the two sets of waves, in the case of $\kappa_2 = 5\kappa_1$.

The general explanation of the effects of an isolated pressure-disturbance advancing over still water, indicated near the end of Art. 227, is now modified by the fact that there are *two* wave-lengths corresponding to the given velocity c. For one of these (the shorter) the group-velocity is greater, whilst for the other it is less, than c. We can thus understand why the waves of shorter wave-length should be found ahead, and those of longer wave-length in the rear, of the disturbing pressure.

It will be noticed that the formulæ (10), (11) make the height of the up-stream capillary waves the same as that of the down-stream gravity waves; but this result will be greatly modified when the pressure is diffused over a band of finite breadth, instead of being concentrated on a mathematical line. If, for example, the breadth of the band do not exceed one-fourth of the wave-length on the down-stream side, whilst it considerably exceeds the wave-length of the up-stream ripples, as may happen with a very moderate velocity, the different parts of the breadth will on the whole reinforce one another as regards their action on the down-stream side, whilst on the up-stream side we shall have 'interference,' with a comparatively small residual amplitude.

When the velocity c of the stream is less than the minimum wave-velocity, the factors of

$$kc^2 - g - k^2T'$$

are imaginary. There is now no indeterminateness caused by putting $\mu = 0$ *ab initio*. The surface-form is given by

$$y = -\frac{Q}{\pi\rho}\int_0^\infty \frac{\cos kx}{k^2T' - kc^2 + g}\,dk \qquad \text{..............(14).}$$

The integral might be transformed by the previous method, but it is evident *à priori* that its value tends rapidly, with increasing x, to zero, on account of the more and more rapid fluctuations in sign of $\cos kx$. The disturbance of level is now confined to the neighbourhood of the origin. For $x = 0$ we find

$$y = -\frac{Q}{(c_m{}^4 - c^4)^{\frac{1}{2}}\rho}\left(1 + \frac{2}{\pi}\sin^{-1}\frac{c^2}{c_m{}^2}\right) \qquad \text{............(15).}$$

Finally we have the critical case where c is exactly equal to the minimum wave-velocity, and therefore $\kappa_2 = \kappa_1$. The first term in (10) or (11) is now infinite, whilst the remainder of the expression, when evaluated, is finite. To get an intelligible result in this case it is necessary to retain the frictional coefficient μ'.

If we put $\mu' = 2\varpi^2$, we have

$$(k-\kappa)^2 + i\mu' = \{k - (\kappa + \varpi - i\varpi)\}\{k - (\kappa - \varpi + i\varpi)\} \qquad \text{...........(vii),}$$

so that the integral (i) may now be equated to

$$\frac{1+i}{4\varpi}\left\{\int_0^\infty \frac{e^{ikx}}{k - (\kappa - \varpi + i\varpi)}\,dk - \int_0^\infty \frac{e^{ikx}}{k - (\kappa + \varpi - i\varpi)}\,dk\right\} \qquad \text{......(viii).}$$

The formulæ of Art. 227 shew that when ϖ is small the most important part of this expression, for points at a distance from the origin on either side,

is

$$\frac{1+i}{4\varpi}\,.\,2\pi i e^{i\kappa x} \qquad \text{.....................................(ix).}$$

It appears that the surface-elevation is now given by

$$\frac{\pi T_1}{Q}\,.\,y = -\frac{\pi}{\mu'^{\frac{1}{2}}}\cos\left(\kappa x - \tfrac{1}{4}\pi\right) \qquad \text{..............(16).}$$

The examination of the effect of inequalities in the bed of a stream, by the method of Art. 230, must be left to the reader.

250. The investigation by Lord Rayleigh*, from which the foregoing differs principally in the manner of treating the definite integrals, was undertaken with a view to explaining more fully some phenomena described by Scott Russell† and Lord Kelvin‡.

"When a small obstacle, such as a fishing line, is moved forward slowly through still water, or (which of course comes to the same thing) is held stationary in moving water, the surface is covered with a beautiful wave-pattern, fixed relatively to the obstacle. On the up-stream side the wave-length is short, and, as Thomson has shewn, the force governing the vibrations is principally cohesion. On the down-stream side the waves are longer, and are governed principally by gravity. Both sets of waves move with the same velocity relatively to the water; namely, that required in order that they may maintain a fixed position relatively to the obstacle. The same condition governs the velocity, and therefore the wave-length, of those parts of the pattern where the fronts are oblique to the direction of motion. If the angle between this direction and the normal to the wave-front be called θ, the velocity of propagation of the waves must be equal to $v_0 \cos\theta$, where v_0 represents the velocity of the water relatively to the fixed obstacle.

"Thomson has shewn that, whatever the wave-length may be, the velocity of propagation of waves on the surface of water cannot be less than about 23 centimetres per second. The water must run somewhat faster than this in order that the wave-pattern may be formed. Even then the angle θ is subject to a limit defined by $v_0 \cos\theta = 23$, and the curved wave-front has a corresponding asymptote.

"The immersed portion of the obstacle disturbs the flow of the liquid independently of the deformation of the surface, and renders the problem in its original form one of great difficulty. We may however, without altering the essence of the matter, suppose that the disturbance is produced by the application to one point of the surface of a slightly abnormal pressure, such as might be produced by electrical attraction, or by the impact of a small jet of air.

* *l. c. ante* p. 393.

† "On Waves," *Brit. Ass. Rep.*, 1844.

‡ *l. c. ante* p. 446.

Indeed, either of these methods—the latter especially—gives very beautiful wave-patterns*."

The solution of the problem here stated is to be derived from the results of the last Art. in the manner explained in Art. 228.

For a line of pressure making an angle $\frac{1}{2}\pi - \theta$ with the direction of the stream, the distances (p) of the successive wave-ridges from the origin are given by

$$kp = (2m - \tfrac{1}{2})\,\pi,$$

where m is an integer, and the values of k are determined by

$$k^2T' - kc^2\cos^2\theta + g = 0 \qquad (1).$$

If we put

$$c_m = (4gT')^{\frac{1}{4}} \qquad (2),$$

and

$$\cos\alpha = c_m/c, \quad a = (m - \tfrac{1}{4})\,\pi c^2/g \qquad (3),$$

this gives

$$\frac{p^2}{a^2} - 2\frac{p}{a}\cos^2\theta + \cos^4\alpha = 0 \qquad (4),$$

whence

$$p/a = \cos^2\theta \pm (\cos^4\theta - \cos^4\alpha)^{\frac{1}{2}} \qquad (5).$$

The greater of these two values of p corresponds to the down-stream and the smaller to the up-stream side of the seat of disturbance.

The general form of the wave-ridges due to a *pressure-point* at the origin is then given, on Huyghens' principle, by (5), considered as a 'tangential-polar' equation between p and θ. The four lines for which $\theta = \pm\alpha$ are asymptotes. The values of $\frac{1}{2}\pi - \alpha$ for several values of c/c_m have been tabulated in Art. 246.

The figure opposite shews the wave-system thus obtained, in the particular case where the ratio of the wave-lengths in the line of symmetry is 4 : 1. This corresponds to $\alpha = 26° \, 34'$†.

In the outlying parts of the wave-pattern, where the ridges are nearly straight, the wave-lengths of the two systems are nearly equal, and we have then the abnormal amplitude indicated by equation (16) of the preceding Art.

When the ratio c/c_m is at all considerable, α is nearly equal to $\frac{1}{2}\pi$, and the asymptotes make a very acute angle with the axis. The wave-envelope

* Lord Rayleigh, *l. c.*

† The figure may be compared with the drawing, from observation, given by Scott Russell, *l. c.*

on the down-stream side then approximates to the form investigated in Art. 228, except that the curve, after approaching the axis of x near the origin, runs back along the asymptotes. On the up-stream side we have approximately

$$p = b \sec^2 \theta \qquad \text{(i)},$$

where $b = \frac{1}{2} a \cos^4 \alpha$. This gives

$$\left.\begin{aligned} x &= a \sec \theta \,(1 - 2 \tan^2 \theta), \\ y &= 3a \sec \theta \tan \theta \end{aligned}\right\} \qquad \text{(ii)}.$$

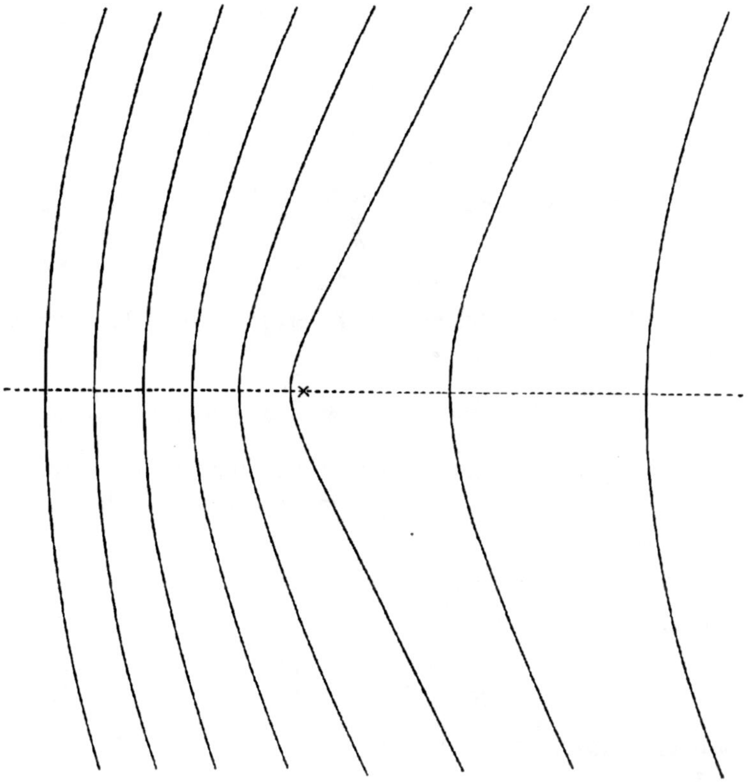

251. Another problem of great interest is the determination of the nature of the equilibrium of a cylindrical column of liquid, of circular section. This contains the theory of the well-known experiments of Bidone, Savart, and others, on the behaviour of a jet issuing under pressure from a small orifice in the wall of a containing vessel. It is obvious that the uniform velocity in the direction of the axis of the jet does not affect the dynamics of the question, and may be disregarded in the analytical treatment.

We will take first the two-dimensional vibrations of the column, the motion being supposed to be the same in each section. Using polar coordinates r, θ in the plane of a section, with the origin in the axis, we may write, in accordance with Art. 63,

$$\phi = A\frac{r^s}{a^s}\cos s\theta \,.\, \cos(\sigma t+\epsilon) \quad\ldots\ldots\ldots\ldots\ldots(1),$$

where a is the mean radius. The equation of the boundary at any instant will then be

$$r = a+\zeta \quad\ldots\ldots\ldots\ldots\ldots\ldots\ldots\ldots\ldots(2),$$

where

$$\zeta = -\frac{sA}{\sigma a}\cos s\theta \,.\, \sin(\sigma t+\epsilon) \quad\ldots\ldots\ldots\ldots\ldots(3),$$

the relation between the coefficients being determined by

$$\frac{d\zeta}{dt} = -\frac{d\phi}{dr}, \quad\ldots\ldots\ldots\ldots\ldots\ldots\ldots\ldots(4),$$

for $r=a$. For the variable part of the pressure inside the column, close to the surface, we have

$$\frac{p}{\rho} = \frac{d\phi}{dt} = -\sigma A\cos s\theta \,.\, \sin(\sigma t+\epsilon) \quad\ldots\ldots\ldots\ldots(5).$$

The curvature of a curve which differs infinitely little from a circle having its centre at the origin is found by elementary methods to be

$$\frac{1}{R} = \frac{1}{r} - \frac{1}{r^2}\frac{d^2 r}{d\theta^2},$$

or, in the notation of (2),

$$\frac{1}{R} = \frac{1}{a} - \frac{1}{a^2}\left(\zeta + \frac{d^2\zeta}{d\theta^2}\right) \quad\ldots\ldots\ldots\ldots\ldots\ldots(6),$$

Hence the surface condition

$$p = T_1/R + \text{const.}, \quad\ldots\ldots\ldots\ldots\ldots\ldots(7),$$

gives, on substitution from (5),

$$\sigma^2 = s(s^2-1)\frac{T_1}{\rho a^3} \quad\ldots\ldots\ldots\ldots\ldots\ldots (8)^*.$$

* For the original investigation, by the method of energy, see Lord Rayleigh, "On the Instability of Jets," *Proc. Lond. Math. Soc.*, t. x., p. 4 (1878); "On the Capillary Phenomena of Jets," *Proc. Roy. Soc.*, May 5, 1879. The latter paper contains a comparison of the theory with experiment.

For $s=1$, we have $\sigma=0$; to our order of approximation the section remains circular, being merely displaced, so that the equilibrium is neutral. For all other integral values of s, σ^2 is positive, so that the equilibrium is thoroughly stable for two-dimensional deformations. This is evident *à priori*, since the circle is the form of least perimeter, and therefore least potential energy, for given sectional area.

In the case of a jet issuing from an orifice in the shape of an ellipse, an equilateral triangle, or a square, prominence is given to the disturbance of the type $s=2, 3$, or 4, respectively. The motion being steady, the jet exhibits a system of stationary waves, whose length is equal to the velocity of the jet multiplied by the period $(2\pi/\sigma)$.

252. Abandoning now the restriction to two dimensions, we assume that

$$\phi = \phi_1 \cos kz \,.\, \cos(\sigma t + \epsilon) \qquad \text{(9)},$$

where the axis of z coincides with that of the cylinder, and ϕ_1 is a function of the remaining coordinates x, y. Substituting in the equation of continuity, $\nabla^2\phi = 0$, we get

$$(\nabla_1^2 - k^2)\,\phi_1 = 0 \qquad \text{(10)},$$

where $\nabla_1^2 = d^2/dx^2 + d^2/dy^2$. If we put $x = r\cos\theta$, $y = r\sin\theta$, this may be written

$$\frac{d^2\phi_1}{dr^2} + \frac{1}{r}\frac{d\phi_1}{dr} + \frac{1}{r^2}\frac{d^2\phi_1}{d\theta^2} - k^2\phi_1 = 0 \qquad \text{(11)}.$$

This equation is of the form considered in Art. 187, except for the sign of k^2; the solutions which are finite for $r=0$ are therefore of the type

$$\phi_1 = BI_s(kr) \begin{Bmatrix}\cos\\ \sin\end{Bmatrix} s\theta \qquad \text{(12)},$$

where

$$I_s(z) = \frac{z^s}{2^s\,.\,s!}\left(1 + \frac{z^2}{2(2s+2)} + \frac{z^4}{2\,.\,4\,(2s+2)(2s+4)} + \ldots\right) \qquad \text{(13)}.$$

Hence, writing

$$\phi = BI_s(kr)\cos s\theta \cos kz \,.\, \cos(\sigma t + \epsilon) \qquad \text{(14)},$$

we have, by (4),

$$\zeta = -B\frac{kaI_s'(ka)}{\sigma a}\cos s\theta \cos kz \,.\, \sin(\sigma t + \epsilon) \qquad \text{(15)}.$$

To find the sum of the principal curvatures, we remark that, as an obvious consequence of Euler's and Meunier's theorems on curvature of surfaces, the curvature of any section differing infinitely little from a principal normal section is, to the first order of small quantities, the same as that of the principal section itself. It is sufficient therefore in the present problem to calculate the curvatures of a transverse section of the cylinder, and of a section through the axis. These are the principal sections in the undisturbed state, and the principal sections of the deformed surface will make infinitely small angles with them. For the transverse section the formula (6) applies, whilst for the axial section the curvature is $-d^2\zeta/dz^2$; so that the required sum of the principal curvatures is

$$\frac{1}{R_1}+\frac{1}{R_2}=\frac{1}{a}-\frac{1}{a^2}\left(\zeta+\frac{d^2\zeta}{d\theta^2}\right)-\frac{d^2\zeta}{dz^2}$$

$$=\frac{1}{a}-B\frac{kaI_s'(ka)}{\sigma a^3}(k^2a^2+s^2-1)\cos s\theta\cos kz\,.\sin(\sigma t+\epsilon)\ldots(16).$$

Also, at the surface,

$$\frac{p}{\rho}=\frac{d\phi}{dt}=-\sigma B\,I_s(ka)\cos s\theta\cos kz\,.\sin(\sigma t+\epsilon)\ldots(17).$$

The surface-condition Art. 244 (1) then gives

$$\sigma^2=\frac{ka\,I_s'(ka)}{I_s(ka)}(k^2a^2+s^2-1)\,.\frac{T_1}{\rho a^3}\quad\ldots\ldots\ldots\ldots(18).$$

For $s>0$, σ^2 is positive; but in the case ($s=0$) of symmetry about the axis σ^2 will be negative if $ka<1$; that is, the equilibrium is unstable for disturbances whose wave-length ($2\pi/k$) exceeds the circumference of the jet. To ascertain the type of disturbance for which the instability is greatest, we require to know the value of ka which makes

$$\frac{kaI_0'(ka)}{I_0(ka)}(k^2a^2-1),$$

a maximum. For this Lord Rayleigh finds $k^2a^2=\cdot4858$, whence, for the wave-length of maximum instability,

$$2\pi/k=4\cdot508\times2a.$$

There is a tendency therefore to the production of bead-like swellings and contractions of this wave-length, with continually increasing amplitude, until finally the jet breaks up into detached drops*.

253. This leads naturally to the discussion of the small oscillations of a drop of liquid about the spherical form†. We will slightly generalize the question by supposing that we have a sphere of liquid, of density ρ, surrounded by an infinite mass of other liquid of density ρ'.

Taking the origin at the centre, let the shape of the common surface at any instant be given by

$$r = a + \zeta = a + S_n \,.\, \sin(\sigma t + \epsilon) \qquad\qquad (1),$$

where a is the mean radius, and S_n is a surface-harmonic of order n. The corresponding values of the velocity-potential will be, at internal points,

$$\phi = -\frac{\sigma a}{n}\frac{r^n}{a^n} S_n \,.\, \cos(\sigma t + \epsilon) \qquad\qquad (2),$$

and at external points

$$\phi' = \frac{\sigma a}{n+1}\frac{a^{n+1}}{r^{n+1}} S_n \,.\, \cos(\sigma t + \epsilon) \qquad\qquad (3),$$

since these make

$$\frac{d\zeta}{dt} = -\frac{d\phi}{dr} = -\frac{d\phi'}{dr},$$

for $r = a$. The variable parts of the internal and external pressures at the surface are then given by

$$p = \ldots + \frac{\rho\sigma^2 a}{n} S_n \,.\, \sin(\sigma t + \epsilon), \quad p' = \ldots - \frac{\rho'\sigma^2 a}{n+1} S_n \,.\, \sin(\sigma t + \epsilon) \ldots (4).$$

To find the sum of the curvatures we make use of the theorem

* The argument here is that if we have a series of possible types of disturbance, with time-factors $e^{\alpha_1 t}$, $e^{\alpha_2 t}$, $e^{\alpha_3 t}$,..., where $\alpha_1 > \alpha_2 > \alpha_3 > \ldots$, and if these be excited simultaneously, the amplitude of the first will increase relatively to those of the other components in the ratios $e^{(\alpha_1 - \alpha_2)t}$, $e^{(\alpha_1 - \alpha_3)t}$,.... The component with the greatest α will therefore ultimately predominate.

The instability of a cylindrical jet surrounded by other fluid has been discussed by Lord Rayleigh, "On the Instability of Cylindrical Fluid Surfaces," *Phil. Mag.*, Aug. 1892. For a jet of air in water the wave-length of maximum instability is found to be $6{\cdot}48 \times 2a$.

† Lord Rayleigh, *l. c. ante* p. 458; Webb, *Mess. of Math.*, t. ix. p. 177 (1880).

of Solid Geometry, that if λ, μ, ν be the direction-cosines of the normal at any point of a surface $F(x, y, z)=0$, viz.

$$\lambda, \mu, \nu = F_x, F_y, F_z \div (F_x^2 + F_y^2 + F_z^2)^{\frac{1}{2}},$$

then
$$\frac{1}{R_1} + \frac{1}{R_2} = \frac{d\lambda}{dx} + \frac{d\mu}{dy} + \frac{d\nu}{dz} \quad \text{..................(5)}.$$

Since the square of ζ is to be neglected, the equation (1) of the harmonic spheroid may also be written

$$r = a + \zeta_n, \quad \text{..........................(6)},$$

where
$$\zeta_n = \frac{r^n}{a^n} S_n \,.\, \sin(\sigma t + \epsilon) \quad \text{...................(7)},$$

i.e. ζ_n is a *solid* harmonic of degree n. We thus find

$$\left.\begin{aligned} \lambda &= \frac{x}{r} - \frac{d\zeta_n}{dx} + n\frac{x}{r^2}\zeta_n, \\ \mu &= \frac{y}{r} - \frac{d\zeta_n}{dy} + n\frac{y}{r^2}\zeta_n, \\ \nu &= \frac{z}{r} - \frac{d\zeta_n}{dz} + n\frac{z}{r^2}\zeta_n \end{aligned}\right\} \quad \text{....................(8)},$$

whence

$$\begin{aligned} \frac{1}{R_1} + \frac{1}{R_2} &= \frac{2}{r} + \frac{n(n+1)}{r^2}\zeta_n \\ &= \frac{2}{a} + \frac{(n-1)(n+2)}{a^2} S_n \,.\, \sin(\sigma t + \epsilon) \text{......(9)}. \end{aligned}$$

Substituting from (4) and (9) in the general surface-condition of Art. 244, we find

$$\sigma^2 = n(n+1)(n-1)(n+2)\frac{T_1}{\{(n+1)\rho + n\rho'\}\, a^3} \text{......(10)}.$$

If we put $\rho' = 0$, this gives

$$\sigma^2 = n(n-1)(n+2)\frac{T_1}{\rho a^3} \quad \text{..............(11)}.$$

The most important mode of vibration is the ellipsoidal one, for which $n = 2$; we then have

$$\sigma^2 = 8T_1/\rho a^3.$$

Hence for a drop of water, putting $T_1 = 74$, $\rho = 1$, we find, for the frequency,

$$\sigma/2\pi = 3{\cdot}87a^{-\frac{3}{2}} \text{ seconds,}$$

if a be the radius in centimetres. The radius of the sphere which would vibrate seconds is $a = 2{\cdot}47$ cm. or a little less than an inch.

The case of a spherical bubble of air, surrounded by liquid, is obtained by putting $\rho = 0$ in (10), viz. we have

$$\sigma^2 = (n+1)(n-1)(n+2)\frac{T_1}{\rho' a^3} \qquad \text{............(12).}$$

For the same density of the liquid, the frequency of any given mode is greater than in the case represented by (11), on account of the diminished inertia; cf. Art. 90 (6), (7).

CHAPTER X.

WAVES OF EXPANSION.

254. A TREATISE on Hydrodynamics would hardly be complete without some reference to this subject, if merely for the reason that all actual fluids are more or less compressible, and that it is only when we recognize this compressibility that we escape such apparently paradoxical results as that of Art. 21, where a change of pressure was found to be propagated *instantaneously* through a liquid mass.

We shall accordingly investigate in this Chapter the general laws of propagation of small disturbances, passing over, however, for the most part, such details as belong more properly to the Theory of Sound.

In most cases which we shall consider, the changes of pressure are small, and may be taken to be proportional to the changes in density, thus

$$\Delta p = \kappa \, . \, \frac{\Delta \rho}{\rho} \quad \text{.........................} \quad (1),$$

where κ $(= \rho \, dp/d\rho)$ is a certain coefficient, called the 'elasticity of volume.' For a given liquid the value of κ varies with the temperature, and (very slightly) with the pressure. For water at 15° C., $\kappa = 2 \cdot 22 \times 10^{10}$ dynes per square centimetre; for mercury at the same temperature $\kappa = 5 \cdot 42 \times 10^{11}$. The case of gases will be considered presently.

Plane Waves.

255. We take first the case of plane waves in a uniform medium.

The motion being in one dimension (x), the dynamical equation is, in the absence of extraneous forces,

$$\frac{du}{dt} + u \frac{du}{dx} = -\frac{1}{\rho} \frac{dp}{dx} = -\frac{1}{\rho} \frac{dp}{d\rho} \frac{d\rho}{dx} \quad \text{..............} \quad (1),$$

whilst the equation of continuity, Art. 8 (4), reduces to

$$\frac{d\rho}{dt} + \frac{d}{dx}(\rho u) = 0 \quad \text{.......................(2).}$$

If we put

$$\rho = \rho_0 (1 + s) \quad \text{..........................(3),}$$

where ρ_0 is the density in the undisturbed state, s may be called the 'condensation' in the plane x. Substituting in (1) and (2), we find, on the supposition that the motion is infinitely small,

$$\frac{du}{dt} = -\frac{\kappa}{\rho_0}\frac{ds}{dx} \quad \text{..........................(4),}$$

and

$$\frac{ds}{dt} = -\frac{du}{dx} \quad \text{....... .... (5),}$$

if

$$\kappa = [\rho \, dp/d\rho]_{\rho=\rho_0} \quad \text{.......................(6),}$$

as above. Eliminating s we have

$$\frac{d^2u}{dt^2} = c^2 \frac{d^2u}{dx^2} \quad \text{.......................... (7),}$$

where

$$c^2 = \kappa/\rho_0 = [dp/d\rho]_{\rho=\rho_0} \quad \text{........... ....(8).}$$

The equation (7) is of the form treated in Art. 167, and the complete solution is

$$u = F(ct - x) + f(ct + x) \quad \text{................. (9),}$$

representing two systems of waves travelling with the constant velocity c, one in the positive and the other in the negative direction of x. It appears from (5) that the corresponding value of s is given by

$$cs = F(ct - x) - f(ct + x) \quad \text{.............. (10).}$$

For a single wave we have

$$u = \pm cs \quad \text{........................... (11),}$$

since one or other of the functions F, f is zero. The upper or the lower sign is to be taken according as the wave is travelling in the positive or the negative direction.

There is an exact correspondence between the above approximate theory and that of 'long' gravity-waves on water. If we write η/h for s, and gh for κ/ρ_0, the equations (4) and (5), above, become identical with Art. 166 (3), (5).

256. With the value of κ given in Art. 254, we find for water at 15° C.

$$c = 1490 \text{ metres per second.}$$

The number obtained directly by Colladon and Sturm in their experiments on the lake of Geneva was 1437, at a temperature of 8° C.*

In the case of a gas, if we assume that the temperature is constant, the value of κ is determined by Boyle's Law

$$p/p_0 = \rho/\rho_0 \qquad (1),$$

viz.

$$\kappa = p_0 \qquad (2),$$

so that

$$c = (p_0/\rho_0)^{\frac{1}{2}} \qquad (3).$$

This is known as the 'Newtonian' velocity of sound†. If we denote by **H** the height of a 'homogeneous atmosphere' of the gas, we have $p_0 = g\rho_0\mathbf{H}$, and therefore

$$c = (g\mathbf{H})^{\frac{1}{2}} \qquad (4),$$

which may be compared with the formula (8) of Art. 167 for the velocity of 'long' gravity-waves in liquids. For air at 0° C. we have as corresponding values‡

$$p_0 = 76 \times 13{\cdot}60 \times 981, \quad \rho_0 = {\cdot}00129,$$

in absolute C.G.S. units; whence

$$c = 280 \text{ metres per second.}$$

This is considerably below the value found by direct observation.

The reconciliation of theory and fact is due to Laplace§. When a gas is suddenly compressed, its temperature rises, so that the pressure is increased more than in proportion to the diminution of volume; and a similar statement applies of course to the case of a sudden expansion. The formula (1) is appropriate only to the case where the expansions and rarefactions are so gradual that there is ample time for equalization of temperature by thermal conduction and radiation. In most cases of interest, the alternations of density are exceedingly rapid; the flow of heat

* *Ann. de Chim. et de Phys.*, t. xxxvi. (1827).

† *Principia*, Lib. ii., Sect. viii., Prop. 48.

‡ Everett, *Units and Physical Constants.*

§ "Sur la vitesse du son dans l'air et dans l'eau, *Ann. de Chim. et de Phys.*, t. iii. (1816); *Mécanique Céleste*, Livre 12me, c. iii. (1823).

from one element to another has hardly set in before its direction is reversed, so that practically each element behaves as if it neither gained nor lost heat.

On this view we have, in place of (1), the 'adiabatic' law

$$p/p_0 = (\rho/\rho_0)^\gamma \quad \text{.......................} \quad (5),$$

where, as explained in books on Thermodynamics, γ is the ratio of the two specific heats of the gas. This makes

$$\kappa = \gamma p_0 \quad \text{.................................} \quad (6),$$

and therefore

$$c = (\gamma p_0/\rho_0)^{\frac{1}{2}} \quad \text{............................} \quad (7).$$

If we put $\gamma = 1{\cdot}410$*, the former result is to be multiplied by 1·187, whence

$$c = 332 \text{ metres per second,}$$

which agrees very closely with the best direct determinations.

The confidence felt by physicists in the soundness of Laplace's view is so complete that it is now usual to apply the formula (7) in the inverse manner, and to infer the values of γ for various gases and vapours from observation of wave-velocities in them.

In strictness, a similar distinction should be made between the 'adiabatic' and 'isothermal' coefficients of elasticity of a liquid or a solid, but practically the difference is unimportant. Thus in the case of water the ratio of the two volume-elasticities is calculated to be 1·0012†.

The effects of thermal radiation and conduction on air-waves have been studied theoretically by Stokes ‡ and Lord Rayleigh §. When the oscillations are too rapid for equalization of temperature, but not so rapid as to exclude communication of heat between adjacent elements, the waves diminish in amplitude as they advance, owing to the dissipation of energy which takes place in the thermal processes.

According to the law of Charles and Gay Lussac

$$p_0/\rho_0 \propto 1 + {\cdot}00366\,\theta,$$

where θ is the temperature Centigrade. Hence the velocity of sound will vary as the square root of the absolute temperature. For several of the more permanent gases, which have sensibly the same value of γ, the formula (7) shews that the velocity varies

of Sound?

* The value found by direct experiment.

† Everett, *Units and Physical Constants.*

‡ "An Examination of the possible effect of the Radiation of Heat on the Propagation of Sound," *Phil. Mag.*, April, 1851.

§ *Theory of Sound*, Art. 247.

cf. p. 29

inversely as the square root of the density, provided the relative densities be determined under the same conditions of pressure and temperature.

257. The theory of plane waves can also be treated very simply by the Lagrangian method.

If ξ denote the displacement at time t of the particles whose undisturbed abscissa is x, the stratum of matter originally included between the planes x and $x+\delta x$ is at the time $t+\delta t$ bounded by the planes

$$x+\xi \text{ and } x+\xi+\left(1+\frac{d\xi}{dx}\right)\delta x,$$

so that the equation of continuity is

$$\rho\left(1+\frac{d\xi}{dx}\right)=\rho_0 \quad\text{.......................}\quad (1),$$

where ρ_0 is the density in the undisturbed state. Hence if s denote the 'condensation' $(\rho-\rho_0)/\rho_0$, we have

$$s=-\frac{\dfrac{d\xi}{dx}}{1+\dfrac{d\xi}{dx}} \quad\text{.......................}\quad (2).$$

The dynamical equation obtained by considering the forces acting on unit area of the above stratum is

$$\rho_0\frac{d^2\xi}{dt^2}=-\frac{dp}{dx} \quad\text{.......................}\quad (3).$$

These equations are exact, but in the case of *small* motions we may write

$$p=p_0+\kappa s \quad\text{.......................}\quad (4),$$

and

$$s=-\frac{d\xi}{dx} \quad\text{.......................}\quad (5).$$

Substituting in (3) we find

$$\frac{d^2\xi}{dt^2}=c^2\frac{d^2\xi}{dx^2} \quad\text{.......................}\quad (6),$$

where

$$c^2=\kappa/\rho_0 \quad\text{.......................}\quad (7).$$

The interpretation of (6) is the same as in Arts. 167, 255.

258. The *kinetic energy* of a system of plane waves is given by

$$T = \tfrac{1}{2}\rho_0 \iiint u^2 dxdydz \quad\text{..................... (1)},$$

where u is the velocity at the point (x, y, z) at time t.

The calculation of the *intrinsic energy* requires a little care. If v be the volume of unit mass, the work which this gives out in expanding from its actual volume to the normal volume v_0 is

$$\int_v^{v_0} pdv \quad\text{............................ (2).}$$

Putting $v = v_0/(1+s)$, $p = p_0 + \kappa s$, we find, for the intrinsic energy (E) of unit mass

$$E = \{p_0 s + (\tfrac{1}{2}\kappa - p_0) s^2\} v_0 \quad\text{.................. (3),}$$

if we neglect terms of higher order. Hence, for the intrinsic energy of the fluid which in the disturbed condition occupies any given region, we have the expression

$$W = \iiint E\rho\, dxdydz = \rho_0 \iiint E(1+s)\, dxdydz$$
$$= \iiint (p_0 s + \tfrac{1}{2}\kappa s^2)\, dxdydz \quad\text{.................. (4),}$$

since $\rho_0 v_0 = 1$. If we consider a region so great that the condensations and rarefactions balance, we have

$$\iiint s\, dxdydz = 0 \quad\text{....................... (5),}$$

and therefore

$$W = \tfrac{1}{2}\kappa \iiint s^2 dxdydz \quad\text{..................... (6).}$$

In a progressive plane wave we have $cs = \pm u$, and therefore $T = W$. The equality of the two kinds of energy, in this case, may also be inferred from the more general line of argument given in Art. 171.

In the theory of Sound special interest attaches, of course, to the case of simple-harmonic vibrations. If a be the amplitude of a progressive wave of period $2\pi/\sigma$, we may assume, in conformity with Art. 257 (6),

$$\xi = a\cos(kx - \sigma t + \epsilon) \quad\text{.................... (7),}$$

where $k = \sigma/c$. The formulæ (1) and (6) then give, for the energy contained in a prismatic space of sectional area unity and length λ (in the direction x),

$$T + W = \tfrac{1}{2}\rho_0 \sigma^2 a^2 \lambda \quad\text{....................... (8),}$$

the same as the kinetic energy of the whole mass when animated with the maximum velocity σa.

The rate of transmission of energy across unit area of a plane moving with the particles situate in it is

$$p\frac{d\xi}{dt}=p\sigma a\sin(kx-\sigma t+\epsilon)\ldots\ldots(\text{i}).$$

The work done by the constant part of the pressure in a complete period is zero. For the variable part we have

$$\Delta p=\kappa s=-\kappa\frac{d\xi}{dx}=\kappa ka\sin(kx-\sigma t+\epsilon)\ldots\ldots(\text{ii}).$$

Substituting in (i), we find, for the mean rate of transmission of energy,

$$\tfrac{1}{2}\kappa\sigma ka^2=\tfrac{1}{2}\rho_0\sigma^2a^2\times c\ldots\ldots(\text{iii}).$$

Hence the energy transmitted in any number of complete periods is exactly that corresponding to the waves which pass the plane in the same time. This is in accordance with the general theory of Art. 221, since, c being independent of λ, the group-velocity is identical with the wave-velocity.

Waves of Finite Amplitude.

259. If p be a function of ρ only, the equations (1) and (3) of Art. 257, give, without approximation,

$$\frac{d^2\xi}{dt^2}=\frac{\rho^2}{\rho_0^2}\frac{dp}{d\rho}\cdot\frac{d^2\xi}{dx^2}\ldots\ldots(1).$$

On the 'isothermal' hypothesis that

$$p/p_0=\rho/\rho_0,\ldots\ldots(2),$$

this becomes

$$\frac{d^2\xi}{dt^2}=\frac{p_0}{\rho_0}\cdot\frac{\dfrac{d^2\xi}{dx^2}}{\left(1+\dfrac{d\xi}{dx}\right)^2}\ldots\ldots(3).$$

In the same way, the 'adiabatic' relation

$$p/p_0=(\rho/\rho_0)^\gamma\ldots\ldots(4),$$

leads to

$$\frac{d^2\xi}{dt^2}=\frac{\gamma p_0}{\rho_0}\cdot\frac{\dfrac{d^2\xi}{dx^2}}{\left(1+\dfrac{d\xi}{dx}\right)^{\gamma+1}}\ldots\ldots(5).$$

These exact equations (3) and (4) may be compared with the similar equation for 'long' waves in a uniform canal, Art. 170 (3).

It appears from (1) that the equation (6) of Art. 257 could be regarded as exact if the relation between p and ρ were such that

$$\rho^2 \frac{dp}{d\rho} = \rho_0^2 c^2 \quad \text{.................................(i).}$$

Hence plane waves of finite amplitude can be propagated without change of type if, and only if,

$$p - p_0 = \rho_0 c^2 \left(1 - \frac{\rho_0}{\rho}\right) \quad \text{...........................(ii).}$$

A relation of this form does not hold for any known substance, whether at constant temperature or when free from gain or loss of heat by conduction and radiation. Hence sound-waves of finite amplitude must inevitably undergo a change of type as they proceed.

260. The laws of propagation of waves of finite amplitude have been investigated, independently and by different methods, by Earnshaw and Riemann. It is proposed to give here a brief account of these investigations, referring for further details to the original papers, and to the very full discussion of the matter by Lord Rayleigh *.

Riemann's method † has already been applied in this treatise to the discussion of the corresponding question in the theory of 'long' gravity-waves on liquids (Art. 183). He starts from the Eulerian equations of Art. 255, which may be written

$$\frac{du}{dt} + u\frac{du}{dx} = -\frac{1}{\rho}\frac{dp}{d\rho}\frac{d\rho}{dx} \quad \text{..................(1),}$$

$$\frac{d\rho}{dt} + u\frac{d\rho}{dx} = -\rho\frac{du}{dx} \quad \text{........................(2).}$$

If we put

$$P = f(\rho) + u, \quad Q = f(\rho) - u \quad \text{..............(3),}$$

where $f(\rho)$ is as yet undetermined, we find, multiplying (2) by $f'(\rho)$, and adding to (1),

$$\frac{dP}{dt} + u\frac{dP}{dx} = -\frac{1}{\rho}\frac{dp}{d\rho}\frac{d\rho}{dx} - \rho f'(\rho)\frac{du}{dx}.$$

If we now determine $f(\rho)$ so that

$$\{f'(\rho)\}^2 = \frac{1}{\rho^2}\frac{dp}{d\rho} \quad \text{......................(4),}$$

* *Theory of Sound*, c. xi.

† "Ueber die Fortpflanzung ebener Luftwellen von endlicher Schwingungsweite," *Gött. Abh.*, t. viii. (1860); *Werke*, Leipzig, 1876, p. 145.

this may be written

$$\frac{dP}{dt} + u\frac{dP}{dx} = -\rho f'(\rho)\frac{dP}{dx} \text{ ....(5).}$$

In the same way we obtain

$$\frac{dQ}{dt} + u\frac{dQ}{dx} = \rho f'(\rho)\frac{dQ}{dx} \text{ ....(6).}$$

The condition (4) is satisfied by

$$f(\rho) = \int_{\rho_0}^{\rho} \left(\frac{dp}{d\rho}\right)^{\frac{1}{2}} \frac{d\rho}{\rho} \text{ ....(7).}$$

Substituting in (5) and (6), we find

$$\left. \begin{aligned} dP &= \left[dx - \left\{ \left(\frac{dp}{d\rho}\right)^{\frac{1}{2}} + u \right\} dt \right] \frac{dP}{dx}, \\ dQ &= \left[dx + \left\{ \left(\frac{dp}{d\rho}\right)^{\frac{1}{2}} - v \right\} dt \right] \frac{dQ}{dx} \end{aligned} \right\} \text{ ....(8),}$$

Hence $dP = 0$, or P is constant, for a geometrical point moving with the velocity

$$\frac{dx}{dt} = \left(\frac{dp}{d\rho}\right)^{\frac{1}{2}} + u \text{ ....(9),}$$

whilst Q is constant for a point whose velocity is

$$\frac{dx}{dt} = -\left(\frac{dp}{d\rho}\right)^{\frac{1}{2}} + u \text{ ....(10).}$$

Hence, any given value of P moves forward, and any value of Q moves backward, with the velocity given by (9) or (10), as the case may be.

These results enable us to understand, in a general way, the nature of the motion in any given case. Thus if the initial disturbance be confined to the space between the two planes $x = a$, $x = b$, we may suppose that P and Q both vanish for $x > a$ and for $x < b$. The region within which P is variable will advance, and that within which Q is variable will recede, until after a time these regions separate and leave between them a space for which $P = 0$, $Q = 0$, and in which the fluid is therefore at rest. The original disturbance has thus been split up into two progressive waves travelling in opposite directions. In the advancing wave we have $Q = 0$, and therefore

$$u = f(\rho) \text{ ....(11),}$$

so that both the density and the particle-velocity are propagated forwards at the rate given by (9). Whether we adopt the isothermal or the adiabatic law of expansion, this velocity of propagation will be found to be greater, the greater the value of ρ. The law of progress of the wave may be illustrated by drawing a curve with x as abscissa and ρ as ordinate, and making each point of this curve move forward with the appropriate velocity, as given by (9) and (11). Since those parts move faster which have the greater ordinates, the curve will eventually become at some point perpendicular to x. The quantities du/dx, $d\rho/dx$ are then infinite; and the preceding method fails to yield any information as to the subsequent course of the motion. Cf. Art. 183.

261. Similar results can be deduced from Earnshaw's investigation *, which is, however, somewhat less general in that it applies only to a progressive wave supposed already established.

For simplicity we will suppose p and ρ to be connected by Boyle's Law

$$p=c^2\rho \qquad \text{(i)}.$$

If we write $y=x+\xi$, so that y denotes the absolute coordinate at time t of the particle whose undisturbed abscissa is x, the equation (3) of Art. 259 becomes

$$\frac{d^2y}{dt^2}=c^2\frac{d^2y}{dx^2}\Big/\left(\frac{dy}{dx}\right)^2 \qquad \text{(ii)}.$$

This is satisfied by

$$\frac{dy}{dt}=f\left(\frac{dy}{dx}\right) \qquad \text{(iii)},$$

provided

$$\left\{f'\left(\frac{dy}{dx}\right)\right\}^2=c^2\Big/\left(\frac{dy}{dx}\right)^2 \qquad \text{(iv)}.$$

Hence a first integral of (ii) is

$$\frac{dy}{dt}=C\pm c\log\frac{dy}{dx} \qquad \text{(v)}.$$

To obtain the 'general integral' of (v) we must eliminate a between the equations

$$\left.\begin{aligned} y&=ax+(C\pm c\log a)\,t+\phi(a),\\ 0&=ax\pm ct+a\phi'(a)\end{aligned}\right\} \qquad \text{(vi)†},$$

where ϕ is arbitrary. Now

$$dy/dx=\rho_0/\rho,$$

* "On the Mathematical Theory of Sound," *Phil. Trans.*, 1860.

† See Forsyth, *Differential Equations*, c. ix.

so that, if u be the velocity of the particle x, we have

$$u=\frac{dy}{dt}=C\pm c\log\frac{\rho_0}{\rho} \qquad \text{(vii)}.$$

On the outskirts of the wave we shall have $u=0$, $\rho=\rho_0$. It follows that $C=0$, and therefore

$$\rho=\rho_0 e^{\mp u/c} \qquad \text{(viii)}.$$

Hence in a progressive wave ρ and u must be connected by this relation. If this be satisfied initially, the function ϕ which occurs in (vi) is to be determined from the conditions at time $t=0$ by the equation

$$\phi'(\rho_0/\rho)=-x \qquad \text{(ix)}.$$

To obtain results independent of the particular form of the wave, consider two particles (which we will distinguish by suffixes) so related that the value of ρ which obtains for the first particle at time t_1 is found at the second particle at time t_2.

The value of a $(=\rho_0/\rho)$ is the same for both, and therefore by (vi), with $C=0$,

$$\left.\begin{aligned} y_2-y_1&=a(x_2-x_1)\pm c(t_2-t_1)\log a, \\ 0&=a(x_2-x_1)\pm c(t_2-t_1) \end{aligned}\right\} \qquad \text{(x)}.$$

The latter equation may be written

$$\frac{\Delta x}{\Delta t}=\mp c\frac{\rho}{\rho_0} \qquad \text{(xi)},$$

shewing that the value of ρ is propagated *from particle to particle* at the rate $\rho/\rho_0 . c$. The rate of propagation *in space* is given by

$$\frac{\Delta y}{\Delta t}=\mp c\pm c\log a$$

$$=\mp c+u \qquad \text{(xii)}.$$

This is in agreement with Riemann's results, since on the 'isothermal' hypothesis $(dp/d\rho)^{\frac{1}{2}}=c$.

For a wave travelling in the positive direction we must take the lower signs. If it be one of condensation $(\rho>\rho_0)$, u is positive, by (viii). It follows that the denser parts of the wave are continually gaining on the rarer, and at length overtake them; the subsequent motion is then beyond the scope of our analysis.

Eliminating x between the equations (vi), and writing for $c\log a$ its value $-u$, we find for a wave travelling in the positive direction,

$$y=(c+u)t+F(a) \qquad \text{(xiii)}.$$

In virtue of (viii) this is equivalent to

$$u=f\{y-(c+u)t\} \qquad \text{(xiv)}.$$

This formula is due to Poisson*. Its interpretation, leading to the same results as above, for the mode of alteration of the wave as it proceeds, forms the subject of a paper by Stokes†.

262. The conditions for a wave of permanent type have been investigated in a very simple manner by Rankine‡.

If, as in Art. 172, we impress on everything a velocity c equal and opposite to that of the waves, we reduce the problem to one of steady motion.

Let A, B be two points of an ideal tube of unit section drawn in the direction of propagation, and let the values of the pressure, the density, and the particle-velocity at A and B be denoted by p_1, ρ_1, u_1 and p_2, ρ_2, u_2, respectively.

Since the same amount of matter now crosses in unit time each section of the tube, we have

$$\rho_1 (c - u_1) = \rho_2 (c - u_2), = m, \quad \text{..............(1)},$$

say; where m denotes the mass swept past in unit time by a plane moving with the wave, in the original form of the problem. This quantity m is called by Rankine the 'mass-velocity' of the wave.

Again, the total force acting on the mass included between A and B is $p_2 - p_1$, and the rate at which this mass is gaining momentum is

$$m (c - u_1) - m (c - u_2).$$

Hence $$p_2 - p_1 = m (u_2 - u_1) \quad \text{....................(2)}.$$

Combined with (1) this gives

$$p_1 + m^2/\rho_1 = p_2 + m^2/\rho_2 \text{....................(3)}.$$

Hence a wave of finite amplitude cannot be propagated unchanged except in a medium such that

$$p + m^2/\rho = \text{const.} \text{........................(4)}.$$

This conclusion has already been arrived at, in a different manner, in Art. 259.

* "Mémoire sur la Théorie du Son," *Journ. de l'École Polytechn.*, t. vii., p. 319 (1808).

† "On a Difficulty in the Theory of Sound," *Phil. Mag.*, Nov. 1848; *Math. and Phys. Papers*, t. ii., p. 51.

‡ "On the Thermodynamic Theory of Waves of Finite Longitudinal Disturbance," *Phil. Trans.*, 1870.

If the variation of density be slight, the relation (4) may, however, be regarded as holding approximately for actual fluids, provided m have the proper value. Putting

$$\rho = \rho_0 (1 + s), \quad p = p_0 + \kappa s, \quad m = \rho_0 c \text{ ....(5)},$$

we find
$$c^2 = \kappa/\rho_0 \text{ ....(6)},$$

as in Art. 255.

The fact that in actual fluids a progressive wave of finite amplitude continually alters its type, so that the variations of density towards the front become more and more abrupt, has led various writers to speculate on the possibility of a wave of discontinuity, analogous to a 'bore' in water-waves.

It has been shewn, first by Stokes*, and afterwards by several other writers, that the conditions of constancy of mass and of constancy of momentum can both be satisfied for such a wave. The simplest case is when there is no variation in the values of ρ and u except at the plane of discontinuity. If, in Rankine's argument, the sections A, B be taken, one in front of, and the other behind this plane, we find

$$m = \left(\frac{p_1 - p_2}{\rho_1 - \rho_2} \cdot \rho_1 \rho_2\right)^{\frac{1}{2}} \text{ ....(7)},$$

and, if we further suppose that $u_2 = 0$, so that the medium is at rest in front of the wave,

$$c = \frac{m}{\rho_2} = \left(\frac{p_1 - p_2}{\rho_1 - \rho_2} \cdot \frac{\rho_1}{\rho_2}\right)^{\frac{1}{2}} \text{ ....(8)},$$

and
$$u_1 = c - \frac{m}{\rho_1} = \pm \left(\frac{(p_1 - p_2)(\rho_1 - \rho_2)}{\rho_1 \rho_2}\right)^{\frac{1}{2}} \text{ ....(9)}.$$

The upper or the lower sign is to be taken according as ρ_1 is greater or less than ρ_2, *i.e.* according as the wave is one of condensation or of rarefaction.

These results have, however, lost some of their interest since it has been pointed out by Lord Rayleigh † that the equation of energy cannot be satisfied consistently with (1) and (2). Considering the excess of the work done on the fluid entering the

* *l. c. ante* p. 475.

† *Theory of Sound*, Art. 253.

space AB at B over that done by the fluid leaving at A, we find

$$p_2(c-u_2)-p_1(c-u_1)=\tfrac{1}{2}m\{(c-u_1)^2-(c-u_2)^2\} \\ +m(E_1-E_2)\ldots\ldots(10),$$

where the first term on the right-hand represents the gain of kinetic, and the second that of intrinsic energy; cf. Art. 23. As in Art. 11 (7), we have

$$E=\int_\rho^{\rho_0} pd\left(\frac{1}{\rho}\right)\ldots\ldots\ldots\ldots\ldots\ldots\ldots\ldots(11).$$

It is easily shewn that (10) is inconsistent with (2) unless

$$E_1-E_2=\frac{1}{2m^2}(p_1^2-p_2^2)\ \ldots\ldots\ldots\ldots\ldots\ldots(12),$$

which is only satisfied provided the relation between p and ρ be that given by (4). In words, the conditions for a wave of discontinuity can only be satisfied in the case of a medium whose intrinsic energy varies as the square of the pressure.

In the above investigation no account has been taken of dissipative forces, such as viscosity and thermal conduction and radiation. Practically, a wave such as we have been considering would imply a finite difference of temperature between the portions of the fluid on the two sides of the plane of discontinuity, so that, to say nothing of viscosity, there would necessarily be a dissipation of energy due to thermal action at the junction. Whether this dissipation would be of such an amount as to be consistent, approximately, with the relation (12) is a physical question, involving considerations which lie outside the province of theoretical Hydrodynamics.

Spherical Waves.

263. Let us next suppose that the disturbance is symmetrical with respect to a fixed point, which we take as origin. The motion is necessarily irrotational, so that a velocity-potential ϕ exists, which is here a function of r, the distance from the origin, and t, only. If as before we neglect the squares of small quantities, we have by Art. 21 (3)

$$\int\frac{dp}{\rho}=\frac{d\phi}{dt}.$$

In the notation of Arts. 254, 255 we may write

$$\int \frac{dp}{\rho} = \int \frac{\kappa ds}{\rho_0} = c^2 s,$$

whence
$$c^2 s = \frac{d\phi}{dt} \qquad \text{.........................(1).}$$

To form the equation of continuity we remark that, owing to the difference of flux across the inner and outer surfaces, the space included between the spheres r and $r + \delta r$ is gaining mass at the rate

$$\frac{d}{dr}\left(4\pi r^2 \rho \frac{d\phi}{dr}\right) \delta r.$$

Since the same rate is also expressed by $d\rho/dt \,.\, 4\pi r^2 \delta r$ we have

$$r^2 \frac{d\rho}{dt} = \frac{d}{dr}\left(\rho r^2 \frac{d\phi}{dr}\right) \qquad \text{....................(2).}$$

This might also have been arrived at by direct transformation of the general equation of continuity, Art. 8 (4). In the case of infinitely small motions, (2) gives

$$\frac{ds}{dt} = \frac{1}{r^2}\frac{d}{dr}\left(r^2 \frac{d\phi}{dr}\right) \qquad \text{....................(3),}$$

whence, substituting from (1),

$$\frac{d^2\phi}{dt^2} = \frac{c^2}{r^2}\frac{d}{dr}\left(r^2 \frac{d\phi}{dr}\right) \qquad \text{....................(4).}$$

This may be put into the more convenient form

$$\frac{d^2 \,.\, r\phi}{dt^2} = c^2 \frac{d^2 \,.\, r\phi}{dr^2} \qquad \text{......................(5),}$$

so that the solution is

$$r\phi = F(r - ct) + f(r + ct) \qquad \text{.................(6).}$$

Hence the motion is made up of two systems of spherical waves, travelling, one outwards, the other inwards, with velocity c. Considering for a moment the first system alone, we have

$$s = -\frac{c}{r} F'(r - ct),$$

which shews that a condensation is propagated outwards with velocity c, but diminishes as it proceeds, its amount varying inversely as the distance from the origin. The velocity due to the same train of waves is

$$-\frac{d\phi}{dr} = -\frac{1}{r}F'(r-ct) + \frac{1}{r^2}F(r-ct).$$

As r increases the second term becomes less and less important compared with the first, so that ultimately the velocity is propagated according to the same law as the condensation.

264. The determination of the functions F and f in terms of the initial conditions, for an unlimited space, can be effected as follows. Let us suppose that the initial distributions of velocity and condensation are determined by the formulæ

$$\phi = \psi(r), \quad \frac{d\phi}{dt} = \chi(r) \quad \text{.................(7)},$$

where ψ, χ are arbitrary functions, of which the former must fulfil the condition $\psi'(0) = 0$, since otherwise the equation of continuity would not be satisfied at the origin. Both functions are given, *primâ facie*, only for positive values of the variable; but all our equations are consistent with the view that r changes sign as the point to which it refers passes through the origin. On this understanding we have, on account of the symmetry of the circumstances with respect to the origin,

$$\psi(-r) = \psi(r), \quad \chi(-r) = \chi(r) \text{..............(8)},$$

that is, ψ and χ are *even* functions. From (6) and (7) we have

$$\left.\begin{aligned} F(r) + f(r) &= r\psi(r), \\ -F'(r) + f'(r) &= \frac{r}{c}\chi(r) \end{aligned}\right\} \quad \text{..................(9)}.$$

If we put

$$\int_0^r r\chi(r)\,dr = \chi_1(r) \text{.....................(10)},$$

the latter equation may be written

$$-F(r) + f(r) = \frac{1}{c}\chi_1(r) \text{..................(11)},$$

the constant of integration being omitted, as it will disappear from the final result. We notice that

$$\chi_1(-r) = \chi(r) \text{ .... (12)}.$$

Hence, we have

$$\left.\begin{aligned} F(r) &= \tfrac{1}{2} r\psi(r) - \frac{1}{2c}\chi_1(r) \\ f(r) &= \tfrac{1}{2} r\psi(r) + \frac{1}{2c}\chi_1(r) \end{aligned}\right\} \quad \text{...............(13).}$$

The complete value of ϕ is then given by (6), viz.

$$\left.\begin{aligned} r\phi = \tfrac{1}{2}(r-ct)\,\psi(r-ct) &- \frac{1}{2c}\chi_1(r-ct) \\ +\tfrac{1}{2}(r+ct)\,\psi(r+ct) &+ \frac{1}{2c}\chi_1(r+ct) \end{aligned}\right\} \quad \text{......(14).}$$

As a very simple example, we may suppose that the air is initially at rest, and that the disturbance consists of a uniform condensation s_0 extending through a sphere of radius a. The formulæ then shew that after a certain time the disturbance is confined to a spherical shell whose internal and external radii are $ct-a$ and $ct+a$, and that the condensation at any point within the thickness of this shell is given by

$$s/s_0 = (r-ct)/2r.$$

The condensation is therefore positive through the outer half, and negative through the inner half, of the thickness. This is a particular case of a general result stated long ago by Stokes*, according to which a diverging spherical wave must necessarily contain both condensed and rarefied portions.

We shall require shortly the form which the general value (14) of ϕ assumes at the origin. This is found most simply by differentiating both sides of (14) with respect to r and then making $r=0$. The result is, if we take account of the relations (8), (10), (12),

$$[\phi]_{r=0} = \frac{d}{dt}\cdot t\psi(ct) + t\chi(ct) \quad \text{...............(15).}$$

General Equation of Sound Waves.

265. We proceed to the general case of propagation of expansion-waves. We neglect, as before, the squares of small quantities, so that the dynamical equation is as in Art. 263,

$$c^2 s = \frac{d\phi}{dt} \quad \text{.......................... (1).}$$

* "On Some Points in the Received Theory of Sound," *Phil. Mag.*, Jan. 1849; *Math. and Phys. Papers*, t. ii., p. 82.

Also, writing $\rho = \rho_0 (1 + s)$ in the general equation of continuity, Art. 8 (4), we have, with the same approximation,

$$\frac{ds}{dt} = \frac{d^2\phi}{dx^2} + \frac{d^2\phi}{dy^2} + \frac{d^2\phi}{dz^2} \quad \text{......................(2).}$$

The elimination of s between (1) and (2) gives

$$\frac{d^2\phi}{dt^2} = c^2 \left(\frac{d^2\phi}{dx^2} + \frac{d^2\phi}{dy^2} + \frac{d^2\phi}{dz^2} \right) \quad \text{................(3)}$$

or, in our former notation,

$$\frac{d^2\phi}{dt^2} = c^2 \nabla^2 \phi \quad \text{..........................(4).}$$

Since this equation is linear, it will be satisfied by the arithmetic mean of any number of separate solutions $\phi_1, \phi_2, \phi_3, \ldots$. As in Art. 39, let us imagine an infinite number of systems of rectangular axes to be arranged uniformly about any point P as origin, and let $\phi_1, \phi_2, \phi_3, \ldots$ be the velocity-potentials of motions which are the same with respect to these systems as the original motion ϕ is with respect to the system x, y, z. In this case the arithmetic mean ($\bar{\phi}$, say), of the functions $\phi_1, \phi_2, \phi_3, \ldots$ will be the velocity-potential of a motion symmetrical with respect to the point P, and will therefore come under the investigation of Art. 264, provided r denote the distance of any point from P. In other words, if $\bar{\phi}$ be a function of r and t, defined by the equation

$$\bar{\phi} = \frac{1}{4\pi} \iint \phi \, d\varpi \quad \text{........................ (5),}$$

where ϕ is any solution of (4), and $\delta\varpi$ is the solid angle subtended at P by an element of the surface of a sphere of radius r having this point as centre, then

$$\frac{d^2 . r\bar{\phi}}{dt^2} = c^2 \frac{d^2 . r\bar{\phi}}{dr^2} \quad \text{......................(6)*.}$$

Hence $$r\bar{\phi} = F(r - ct) + f(r + ct) \quad \text{................. (7).}$$

The mean value of ϕ over a sphere having any point P of the medium as centre is therefore subject to the same laws as the

* This result was obtained, in a different manner, by Poisson, "Mémoire sur la théorie du son," *Journ. de l'École Polytechn.*, t. vii. (1807), pp. 334—338. The remark that it leads at once to the complete solution of (4) is due to Liouville, *Journ. de Math.*, 1856, pp. 1—6.

velocity-potential of a symmetrical spherical disturbance. We see at once that the value of ϕ at P at the time t depends on the mean initial values of ϕ and $d\phi/dt$ over a sphere of radius ct described about P as centre, so that the disturbance is propagated in all directions with uniform velocity c. Thus if the original disturbance extend only through a finite portion Σ of space, the disturbance at any point P external to Σ will begin after a time r_1/c, will last for a time $(r_2 - r_1)/c$, and will then cease altogether; r_1, r_2 denoting the radii of two spheres described with P as centre, the one just excluding, the other just including Σ.

To express the solution of (4), already virtually obtained, in an analytical form, let the values of ϕ and $d\phi/dt$, when $t = 0$, be

$$\phi = \psi(x, y, z), \quad \frac{d\phi}{dt} = \chi(x, y, z) \quad \text{..............(8).}$$

The mean initial values of these quantities over a sphere of radius r described about (x, y, z) as centre are

$$\bar{\phi} = \frac{1}{4\pi}\iint \psi(x + lr, y + mr, z + nr)\, d\varpi,$$

$$\frac{d\bar{\phi}}{dt} = \frac{1}{4\pi}\iint \chi(x + lr, y + mr, z + nr)\, d\varpi,$$

where l, m, n denote the direction-cosines of any radius of this sphere, and $\delta\varpi$ the corresponding elementary solid angle. If we put

$$l = \sin\theta\cos\omega, \quad m = \sin\theta\sin\omega, \quad n = \cos\theta,$$

we shall have

$$\delta\varpi = \sin\theta\,\delta\theta\,\delta\omega.$$

Hence, comparing with Art. 264 (15), we see that the value of ϕ at the point (x, y, z), at any subsequent time t, is

$$\phi = \frac{1}{4\pi}\frac{d}{dt}\cdot t\iint \psi(x + ct\sin\theta\cos\omega,\ y + ct\sin\theta\sin\omega,\ z + ct\cos\theta)\sin\theta\, d\theta\, d\omega$$
$$+ \frac{t}{4\pi}\iint \chi(x + ct\sin\theta\cos\omega,\ y + ct\sin\theta\sin\omega,\ z + ct\cos\theta)\sin\theta\, d\theta\, d\omega \quad \text{... (9),}$$

which is the form given by Poisson*.

* "Mémoire sur l'intégration de quelques équations linéaires aux différences partielles, et particulièrement de l'équation générale du mouvement des fluides élastiques," *Mém. de l'Acad. des Sciences*, t. iii., 1818–19.

266. In the case of simple-harmonic motion, the time-factor being $e^{i\sigma t}$, the equation (4) of Art. 265 takes the form

$$(\nabla^2 + k^2)\,\phi = 0 \quad\text{......................}\quad (1),$$

where

$$k = \sigma/c \quad\text{..........................}\quad (2).$$

It appears on comparison with Art. 258 (7) that $2\pi/k$ is the wave-length of plane waves of the same period $(2\pi/\sigma)$.

There is little excuse for trespassing further on the domain of Acoustics; but we may briefly notice the solutions of (1) which are appropriate when the boundary-conditions have reference to spherical surfaces, as this will introduce us to some results of analysis which will be of service in the next Chapter.

In the case of symmetry with respect to the origin, we have by Art. 263 (5), or by direct transformation of (1),

$$\frac{d^2 . r\phi}{dt^2} + k^2 . r\phi = 0 \quad\text{...................}\quad (3),$$

the solution of which is

$$\phi = A\frac{\sin kr}{kr} + B\frac{\cos kr}{kr} \quad\text{...................}\quad (4).$$

When the motion is finite at the origin we must have $B = 0$.

1°. This may be applied to the radial vibrations of air contained in a spherical cavity. The condition that $d\phi/dr = 0$ at the surface $r = a$ gives

$$\tan ka = ka \quad\text{..................................}\quad (i),$$

which determines the frequencies of the normal modes. The roots of this equation, which presents itself in various physical problems, can be calculated without much difficulty, either by means of a series*, or by a method devised by Fourier†. The values obtained by Schwerd‡ for the first few roots are

$$ka/\pi = 1{\cdot}4303,\ \ 2{\cdot}4590,\ \ 3{\cdot}4709,\ \ 4{\cdot}4774,\ \ 5{\cdot}4818,\ \ 6{\cdot}4844 \quad\text{.........}\quad (ii),$$

approximating to the form $m + \frac{1}{2}$, where m is integral. These numbers give the ratio $(2a/\lambda)$ of the diameter of the sphere to the wave-length. Taking the reciprocals we find

$$\lambda/2a = {\cdot}6992,\ \ {\cdot}4067,\ \ {\cdot}2881,\ \ {\cdot}2233,\ \ {\cdot}1824,\ \ {\cdot}1542 \quad\text{..............}\quad (iii).$$

In the case of the second and higher roots of (i) the roots of lower order give

* Euler, *Introductio in Analysin Infinitorum*, Lausannæ, 1748, t. ii., p. 319; Rayleigh, *Theory of Sound*, Art. 207.

† *Théorie analytique de la Chaleur*, Paris, 1822, Art. 286.

‡ Quoted by Verdet, *Optique Physique*, t. i., p. 266.

the positions of the spherical nodes ($d\phi/dr=0$). Thus in the second mode there is a spherical node whose radius is given by

$$r/a=(1\cdot4303)/(2\cdot4590)=\cdot5817.$$

2°. In the case of waves propagated outwards into infinite space from a spherical surface, it is more convenient to use the solution of (3), including the time-factor, in the form

$$\phi=C\frac{e^{i(\sigma t-kr)}}{r}\quad\text{..................................(iv).}$$

If the motion of the gas be due to a prescribed radial motion

$$\dot{r}=ae^{i\sigma t}\quad\text{...................................... (v)}$$

of a sphere of radius a, C is determined by the condition that $\dot{r}=-d\phi/dr$ for $r=a$. This gives

$$C=\frac{a^2 a}{1+k^2a^2}(1-ika)\,e^{ika}\quad\text{........................ (vi),}$$

whence, taking the real parts, we have, corresponding to a prescribed normal motion

$$\dot{r}=a\cos\sigma t\text{....................................(vii),}$$

$$\phi=\frac{a^2a}{1+k^2a^2}\left\{\frac{\cos\{\sigma t-k(r-a)\}}{r}+ka\frac{\sin\{\sigma t-k(r-a)\}}{r}\right\}\text{......(viii).}$$

When ka is infinitesimal, this reduces to

$$\phi=\frac{A}{4\pi}\frac{\cos(\sigma t-kr)}{r}\quad\text{.............................(ix),}$$

where $A=4\pi a^2 a$. We have here the conception of the 'simple source' of sound, which plays so great a part in the modern treatment of Acoustics.

The rate of emission of energy may be calculated from the result of Art. 258. At a great distance r from the origin, the waves are approximately plane, of amplitude $A/4\pi cr$. Putting this value of a in the expression $\frac{1}{2}\rho_0\sigma^2a^2c$ for the energy transmitted across unit area, and multiplying by $4\pi r^2$, we obtain for the energy emitted per second

$$\frac{\rho_0\sigma^2A^2}{8\pi c}\quad\text{......................................(x).}$$

267. When the restriction as to symmetry is abandoned, we may suppose the value of ϕ over any sphere of radius r, having its centre at the origin, to be expanded in a series of surface-harmonics whose coefficients are functions of r. We therefore assume

$$\phi=\Sigma R_n\phi_n\quad\text{.......................... (5),}$$

where ϕ_n is a solid harmonic of degree n, and R_n is a function of r only. Now

$$\nabla^2(R_n\phi_n)=\nabla^2R_n\,.\,\phi_n+2\left(\frac{dR_n}{dx}\frac{d\phi_n}{dx}+\frac{dR_n}{dy}\frac{d\phi_n}{dy}+\frac{dR_n}{dz}\frac{d\phi_n}{dz}\right)+R_n\nabla^2\phi_n$$

$$=\nabla^2R_n\,.\,\phi_n+\frac{2}{r}\frac{dR_n}{dr}\left(x\frac{d\phi_n}{dx}+y\frac{d\phi_n}{dy}+z\frac{d\phi_n}{dz}\right)+R_n\nabla^2\phi_n \quad \text{......(6).}$$

And, by the definition of a solid harmonic, we have

$$\nabla^2\phi_n=0,$$

and

$$x\frac{d\phi_n}{dx}+y\frac{d\phi_n}{dy}+z\frac{d\phi_n}{dz}=n\phi_n.$$

Hence

$$\nabla^2(R_n\phi_n)=\left(\nabla^2R_n+\frac{2n}{r}\frac{dR_n}{dr}\right)\phi_n$$

$$=\left(\frac{d^2R_n}{dr^2}+\frac{2(n+1)}{r}\frac{dR_n}{dr}\right)\phi_n \quad \text{............ (7).}$$

If we substitute in (1), the terms in ϕ_n must satisfy the equation independently, whence

$$\frac{d^2R_n}{dr^2}+\frac{2(n+1)}{r}\frac{dR_n}{dr}+k^2R_n=0 \quad \text{............ (8),}$$

which is the differential equation in R_n.

This can be integrated by series. Thus, assuming that

$$R_n=\Sigma A_m(kr)^m,$$

the relation between consecutive coefficients is found to be

$$m(2n+1+m)A_m+A_{m-2}=0.$$

This gives two ascending series, one beginning with $m=0$, and the other with $m=-2n-1$; thus

$$R_n=A\left(1-\frac{k^2r^2}{2(2n+3)}+\frac{k^4r^4}{2.4(2n+3)(2n+5)}-\dots\right)$$

$$+Br^{-2n-1}\left(1-\frac{k^2r^2}{2(1-2n)}+\frac{k^4r^4}{2.4(1-2n)(3-2n)}-\dots\right),$$

where A, B are arbitrary constants. Hence putting $\phi_n=r^nS_n$, so that S_n is a surface-harmonic of order n, the general solution of (1) may be written

$$\phi=\Sigma\{A\psi_n(kr)+B\Psi_n(kr)\}r^nS_n \quad \text{............ (9),}$$

where

$$\left.\begin{aligned}\psi_n(\zeta) &= \frac{1}{1.3\ldots(2n+1)}\left(1-\frac{\zeta^2}{2(2n+3)}+\frac{\zeta^4}{2.4(2n+3)(2n+5)}-\ldots\right)\\ \Psi_n(\zeta) &= \frac{1.3\ldots(2n-1)}{\zeta^{2n+1}}\left(1-\frac{\zeta^2}{2(1-2n)}+\frac{\zeta^4}{2.4(1-2n)(3-2n)}-\ldots\right)\end{aligned}\right\} \quad \ldots\ldots\ldots(10)^*.$$

The first term of (9) is alone to be retained when the motion is finite at the origin.

The functions $\psi_n(\zeta)$, $\Psi_n(\zeta)$ can also be expressed in finite terms, as follows:

$$\left.\begin{aligned}\psi_n(\zeta) &= (-)^n\left(\frac{d}{\zeta d\zeta}\right)^n\frac{\sin\zeta}{\zeta},\\ \Psi_n(\zeta) &= (-)^n\left(\frac{d}{\zeta d\zeta}\right)^n\frac{\cos\zeta}{\zeta}\end{aligned}\right\} \quad \ldots\ldots\ldots\ldots (11).$$

These are readily identified with (10) by expanding $\sin\zeta$, $\cos\zeta$, and performing the differentiations. As particular cases we have

$$\psi_0(\zeta) = \frac{\sin\zeta}{\zeta},$$

$$\psi_1(\zeta) = \frac{\sin\zeta}{\zeta^3} - \frac{\cos\zeta}{\zeta^2},$$

$$\psi_2(\zeta) = \left(\frac{3}{\zeta^5}-\frac{1}{\zeta^3}\right)\sin\zeta - \frac{3\cos\zeta}{\zeta^4}.$$

The formulæ (9) and (11) shew that the general solution of the equation

$$\frac{d^2R_n}{d\zeta^2} + \frac{2(n+1)}{\zeta}\frac{dR_n}{d\zeta} + R_n = 0 \quad \ldots\ldots\ldots\ldots (12),$$

which is obtained by writing ζ for kr in (8), is

$$R_n = \left(\frac{d}{\zeta d\zeta}\right)^n \frac{Ae^{i\zeta}+Be^{-i\zeta}}{\zeta} \quad \ldots\ldots\ldots\ldots\ldots (13).$$

This is easily verified; for if R_n be any solution of (12), we find that the corresponding equation for R_{n+1} is satisfied by

$$R_{n+1} = \frac{dR_n}{\zeta d\zeta},$$

* There is a slight deviation here from the notation adopted by Heine, *Kugelfunctionen*, p. 82.

and by repeated applications of this result it appears that (12) is satisfied by

$$R_n = \left(\frac{d}{\zeta d\zeta}\right)^n R_0 \quad\text{.............................(i),}$$

where R_0 is the solution of

$$\frac{d^2(\zeta R_0)}{d\zeta^2} + \zeta R_0 = 0,$$

that is

$$R_0 = \frac{Ae^{i\zeta} + Be^{-i\zeta}}{\zeta} \quad\text{..........................(ii)*.}$$

268. A simple application of the foregoing analysis is to the vibrations of air contained in a spherical envelope.

1°. Let us first consider the free vibrations when the envelope is rigid.

Since the motion is finite at the origin, we have, by (9),

$$\phi = A\psi_n(kr)\, r^n S_n \,.\, e^{i\sigma t} \quad\text{..............................(i),}$$

with the boundary-condition

$$ka\psi_n'(ka) + n\psi_n(ka) = 0 \quad\text{..........................(ii),}$$

a being the radius. This determines the admissible values of k and thence of $\sigma\,(=kc)$.

It is evident from Art. 267 (11) that this equation reduces always to the form

$$\tan ka = f(ka) \quad\text{..............................(iii),}$$

where $f(ka)$ is a rational algebraic function. The roots can then be calculated without difficulty by Fourier's method, referred to in Art. 266.

In the case $n=1$, if we take the axis of x coincident with that of the harmonic S_1, and write $x = r\cos\theta$, we have

$$\phi = A\left(\frac{\sin kr}{k^2r^2} - \frac{\cos kr}{kr}\right)\cos\theta \,.\, e^{i\sigma t} \quad\text{................ (iv);}$$

and the equation (ii) becomes

$$\tan ka = \frac{2ka}{2 - k^2a^2} \quad\text{..............................(v).}$$

The zero root is irrelevant. The next root gives, for the ratio of the diameter to the wave-length,

$$ka/\pi = \cdot 6625,$$

and the higher values of this ratio approximate to the successive integers 2, 3, 4.... In the case of the lowest root, we have, inverting,

$$\lambda/2a = 1\cdot 509.$$

* The above analysis, which has a wide application in mathematical physics, has been given, in one form or another, by various writers, from Poisson (*Théorie mathématique de la Chaleur*, Paris, 1835) downwards. For references to the history of the matter, considered as a problem in Differential Equations, see Glaisher, "On Riccati's Equation and its Transformations," *Phil. Trans.*, 1881.

In this, the gravest of all the normal modes, the air sways to and fro much in the same manner as in a doubly-closed pipe. In the case of any one of the higher roots, the roots of lower order give the positions of the spherical nodes ($d\phi/dr=0$). For the further discussion of the problem we must refer to the investigation by Lord Rayleigh*.

2°. To find the motion of the enclosed air due to a prescribed normal motion of the boundary, say

$$\frac{d\phi}{dr}=S_n \cdot e^{i\sigma t} \qquad \text{(viii)},$$

we have,

$$\phi=A\psi_n(kr)\, r^n S_n \cdot e^{i\sigma t} \qquad \text{(ix)},$$

with the condition

$$A\,\{ka\psi_n'(ka)+n\psi_n(ka)\}a^{n-1}=1,$$

and therefore

$$\phi=\frac{\psi_n(kr)}{ka\psi_n'(ka)+n\psi_n(ka)}\cdot a\left(\frac{r}{a}\right)^n S_n \cdot e^{i\sigma t} \qquad \text{(x)}.$$

This expression becomes infinite, as we should expect, whenever ka is a root of (ii); i.e. whenever the period of the imposed vibration coincides with that of one of the natural periods, of the same spherical-harmonic type.

By putting $ka=0$ we pass to the case of an incompressible fluid. The formula (x) then reduces to

$$\phi=\frac{a}{n}\left(\frac{r}{a}\right)^n S_n \cdot e^{i\sigma t} \qquad \text{(xi)},$$

as in Art. 90. It is important to notice that the same result holds approximately, even in the case of a gas, whenever ka is small, *i.e.* whenever the wave-length ($2\pi/k$) corresponding to the actual period is large compared with the circumference of the sphere. This is otherwise evident from the mere form of the fundamental equation, Art. 266 (1), since as k diminishes the equation tends more and more to the form $\nabla^2\phi=0$ appropriate to an incompressible fluid†.

* "On the Vibrations of a Gas contained within a Rigid Spherical Envelope," *Proc. Lond. Math. Soc.*, t. iv., p. 93 (1872); *Theory of Sound*, Art. 331.

† In the transverse oscillations of the air contained in a *cylindrica* vessel we have

$$(\nabla_1^2+k^2)\phi=0,$$

where $\nabla_1^2=d^2/dx^2+d^2/dy^2$. In the case of a circular section, transforming to polar coordinates r, θ, we have, for the free oscillations,

$$\phi \propto J_s(kr)\begin{matrix}\cos\\ \sin\end{matrix}\Big\}\, s\theta \cdot e^{i\sigma t},$$

with k determined by

$$J_s'(ka)=0,$$

a being the radius. The nature of the results will be understood from Art. 187, where the mathematical problem is identical. The figures on pp. 308, 309 shew the forms of the lines of equal pressure, to which the motion of the particle is orthogonal, in two of the more important modes. The problem is fully discussed in Lord Rayleigh's *Theory of Sound*, Art. 339.

269. To determine the motion of a gas within a space bounded by two concentric spheres, we require the complete formula (9) of Art. 267. The only interesting case, however, is where the two radii are nearly equal; and this can be solved more easily by an independent process*.

In terms of polar coordinates r, θ, ω, the equation $(\nabla^2+k^2)\,\phi=0$ becomes

$$\frac{d^2\phi}{dr^2}+\frac{2}{r}\frac{d\phi}{dr}+\frac{1}{r^2}\left[\frac{d}{d\mu}\left\{(1-\mu^2)\frac{d\phi}{d\mu}\right\}+\frac{1}{1-\mu^2}\frac{d^2\phi}{d\omega^2}\right]+k^2\phi=0 \text{ ....(i).}$$

If, now, $d\phi/dr=0$ for $r=a$ and $r=b$, where a and b are nearly equal, we may neglect the radial motion altogether, so that the equation reduces to

$$\frac{d}{d\mu}\left\{(1-\mu^2)\frac{d\phi}{d\mu}\right\}+\frac{1}{1-\mu^2}\frac{d^2\phi}{d\omega^2}+k^2a^2\phi=0 \text{..................(ii).}$$

It appears, exactly as in Art. 191, that the only solutions which are finite over the whole spherical surface are of the type

$$\phi \propto S_n \text{......................................(iii),}$$

where S_n is a surface-harmonic of integral order n, and that the corresponding values of k are given by

$$k^2a^2=n(n+1) \text{..................................(iv).}$$

In the gravest mode $(n=1)$, the gas sways to and fro across the equator of the harmonic S_1, being, in the extreme phases of the oscillation, condensed at one pole and rarefied at the other. Since $ka=\sqrt{2}$ in this case, we have for the equivalent wave-length $\lambda/2a=2\cdot221$.

In the next mode $(n=2)$, the type of the vibration depends on that of the harmonic S_2. If this be zonal, the equator is a node. The frequency is determined by $ka=\sqrt{6}$, or $\lambda/2a=1\cdot283$.

270. We may next consider the propagation of waves *outwards* from a spherical surface into an unlimited medium.

If at the surface $(r=a)$ we have a prescribed normal velocity

$$\dot{r}=S_n\,.\,e^{i\sigma t} \text{ .... (i),}$$

the appropriate solution of $(\nabla^2+k^2)\,\phi=0$ is

$$\phi=Ck^n r^n\left\{\frac{d}{kr\,d(kr)}\right\}^n\frac{e^{i(\sigma t-kr)}}{kr}\,.\,S_n \text{ ....(ii),}$$

for this is included in the general formula (13) of Art. 207, and evidently represents a system of waves travelling outwards†.

* Lord Rayleigh, *Theory of Sound*, Art. 333.

† This problem was solved, in a somewhat different manner, by Stokes, "On the Communication of Vibrations from a Vibrating Body to a surrounding Gas," *Phil. Trans.*, 1868.

We shall here only follow out in detail the case of $n=1$, which corresponds to an oscillation of the sphere, as rigid, to and fro in a straight line. Putting

$$S_1 = a\cos\theta \qquad\text{(iii)},$$

where θ is the angle which r makes with the line in which the centre oscillates, the formula (ii) reduces to

$$\phi = -C\frac{1+ikr}{k^2r^2}e^{i(\sigma t-kr)}\,a\cos\theta \qquad\text{(iv)}.$$

The value of C is determined by the surface-condition

$$-\frac{d\phi}{dr} = ae^{i\sigma t}\cos\theta \qquad\text{(v)},$$

for $r=a$. This gives

$$C = -\frac{k^2a^2(2-k^2a^2-2ika)}{4+k^4a^4}\,ae^{ika} \qquad\text{(vi)}.$$

The resultant pressure on the sphere is

$$X = -\int_0^\pi \Delta p\cos\theta \,.\, 2\pi a^2\sin\theta d\theta \qquad\text{(vii)},$$

where

$$\Delta p = c^2\rho_0 s = \rho_0\, d\phi/dt = i\sigma\rho_0\phi \qquad\text{(viii)}.$$

Substituting from (iv) and (vi), and performing the integration, we find

$$X = -\tfrac{4}{3}\pi\rho_0 a^3 \,.\, \frac{2+k^2a^2-ik^3a^3}{4+k^4a^4}\,i\sigma ae^{i\sigma t} \qquad\text{(ix)}.$$

This may be written in the form

$$X = -\tfrac{4}{3}\pi\rho_0 a^3 \,.\, \frac{2+k^2a^2}{4+k^4a^4}\,.\,\frac{du}{dt} - \tfrac{4}{3}\pi\rho_0 a^3 \,.\, \frac{k^3a^3}{4+k^4a^4}\,.\,\sigma u \qquad\text{(x)*},$$

where $u(=ae^{i\sigma t})$ denotes the velocity of the sphere.

The first term of this expression is the same as if the inertia of the sphere were increased by the amount

$$\frac{2+k^2a^2}{4+k^4a^4}\times\tfrac{4}{3}\pi\rho_0 a^3 \qquad\text{(xi)};$$

whilst the second is the same as if the sphere were subject to a frictional force varying as the velocity, the coefficient being

$$\frac{k^3a^3}{4+k^4a^4}\times\tfrac{4}{3}\pi\rho_0 a^3\sigma \qquad\text{(xii)}.$$

In the case of an incompressible fluid, and, more generally, whenever the wave-length $2\pi/k$ is large compared with the circumference of the sphere, we may put $ka=0$. The addition to the inertia is then *half* that of the fluid displaced; whilst the frictional coefficient vanishes†. Cf. Art. 91.

The frictional coefficient is in any case of high order in ka, so that the vibrations of a sphere whose circumference is moderately small compared with

* This formula is given by Lord Rayleigh, *Theory of Sound*, Art. 325. For another treatment of the problem of the vibrating sphere, see Poisson, "Sur les mouvements simultanés d'un pendule et de l'air environnant," *Mém. de l'Acad. des Sciences*, t. xi. (1832), and Kirchhoff, *Mechanik*, c. xxiii.

† Poisson, *l. c.*

the wave-length are only slightly affected in this way. To find the energy expended per unit time in generating waves in the surrounding medium, we must multiply the frictional term in (x), now regarded as an equation in real quantities, by u, and take the mean value; this is found to be

$$\tfrac{2}{3}\pi\rho_0 a^3 \cdot \frac{k^3 a^3}{4+k^4a^4} \cdot \sigma a^2 \text{ .... (xiii).}$$

In other words, if ρ_1 be the mean density of the sphere, the fraction of its energy which is expended in one period is

$$2\pi\frac{\rho_0}{\rho_1} \cdot \frac{k^3a^3}{4+k^4a^4} \text{ .... (xiv).}$$

It has been tacitly assumed in the foregoing investigation that the amplitude of vibration of the sphere is small compared with the radius. This restriction may however be removed, if we suppose the symbols u, v, w to represent the component velocities of the fluid, not at a fixed point of space, but at a point whose coordinates relative to a system of axes originating at the centre of the sphere, and moving with it, are x, y, z. The only change which this will involve is that we must, in our fundamental equations, replace

$$\frac{d}{dt} \text{ by } \frac{d}{dt} - \mathrm{u}\frac{d}{dx}.$$

The additional terms thus introduced are of the second order in the velocities, and may consistently be neglected*.

271. The theory of such questions as the large-scale oscillations of the earth's atmosphere, where the equilibrium-density cannot be taken to be uniform, has received little attention at the hands of mathematicians.

Let us suppose that we have a gas in equilibrium under certain constant forces having a potential Ω, and let us denote by ρ_0 and p_0 the values of ρ and p in this state, these quantities being in general functions of the coordinates x, y, z. We have, then,

$$dp_0 = -\rho_0 d\Omega \text{ .... (1).}$$

The equations of small motion, under the influence (it may be) of disturbing forces having a potential Ω', may therefore be written

$$\left.\begin{aligned} \rho_0\frac{du}{dt} &= -\frac{dp}{dx} + \frac{\rho}{\rho_0}\frac{dp_0}{dx} - \rho_0\frac{d\Omega'}{dx}, \\ \rho_0\frac{dv}{dt} &= -\frac{dp}{dy} + \frac{\rho}{\rho_0}\frac{dp_0}{dy} - \rho_0\frac{d\Omega'}{dy}, \\ \rho_0\frac{dw}{dt} &= -\frac{dp}{dz} + \frac{\rho}{\rho_0}\frac{dp_0}{dz} - \rho_0\frac{d\Omega'}{dz} \end{aligned}\right\} \text{ .... (2).}$$

* Cf. Stokes, *Camb. Trans.*, t. ix., p. [50]. The assumption is that the maximum velocity of the sphere is small compared with the velocity of sound.

The case that lends itself most readily to mathematical treatment is where the equilibrium-temperature is uniform*, and the expansions and contractions are assumed to follow the 'isothermal' law, so that

$$p = c^2\rho \quad\text{.............................(3)},$$

c denoting the Newtonian velocity of sound. If we write

$$\rho = \rho_0(1+s), \qquad p = p_0(1+s),$$

the equations (2) reduce to the forms

$$\left.\begin{aligned} \frac{du}{dt} &= -c^2\frac{d}{dx}(s-\bar{s}), \\ \frac{dv}{dt} &= -c^2\frac{d}{dy}(s-\bar{s}), \\ \frac{dw}{dt} &= -c^2\frac{d}{dz}(s-\bar{s}) \end{aligned}\right\} \quad\text{.................. (4)},$$

where

$$\bar{s} = -\Omega'/c^2 \quad\text{.......................... (5)},$$

that is, $\bar{s}$ denotes the 'equilibrium-value' of the condensation due to the disturbing-potential Ω'.

The general equation of continuity, Art. 8 (4), gives, with the same approximation,

$$\rho_0\frac{ds}{dt} = -\frac{d}{dx}(\rho_0 u) - \frac{d}{dy}(\rho_0 v) - \frac{d}{dz}(\rho_0 w) \quad\text{......... (6)}.$$

We find, by elimination of u, v, w between (5) and (6),

$$\frac{d^2s}{dt^2} = c^2\nabla^2(s-\bar{s}) + \frac{c^2}{\rho_0}\left(\frac{d\rho_0}{dx}\frac{d}{dx} + \frac{d\rho_0}{dy}\frac{d}{dy} + \frac{d\rho_0}{dz}\frac{d}{dz}\right)(s-\bar{s})\text{...(7)}.$$

272. If we neglect the curvature of the earth, and suppose the axis of z to be drawn vertically upwards, ρ_0 will be a function of z only, determined by

$$\frac{dp_0}{dz} = -g\rho_0 \quad\text{.......................... (1)}.$$

On the present hypothesis of uniform temperature, we have, by Boyle's Law,

$$p_0 = g\rho_0\mathbf{H} \quad\text{.......................... (2)},$$

* The motion is in this case irrotational, and might have been investigated in terms of the velocity-potential.

where $\mathbf{H}$ denotes as in Art. 256 the height of a 'homogeneous atmosphere' at the given temperature. Hence

$$\rho_0 \propto e^{-z/\mathbf{H}} \qquad\qquad (3).$$

Substituting in Art. 271 (7), and putting $\bar{s}=0$, we find, in the case of no disturbing forces,

$$\frac{d^2 s}{dt^2} = c^2 \left(\nabla^2 s - \frac{1}{\mathbf{H}} \frac{ds}{dz}\right) \qquad\qquad (4).$$

For plane waves travelling in a vertical direction, s will be a function of z only, and therefore

$$\frac{d^2 s}{dt^2} = c^2 \left(\frac{d^2 s}{dz^2} - \frac{1}{\mathbf{H}} \frac{ds}{dz}\right) \qquad\qquad (\text{i}).$$

If we assume a time-factor $e^{i\sigma t}$, this is satisfied by

$$\phi = A e^{mz} \qquad\qquad (\text{ii}),$$

provided

$$m^2 - m/\mathbf{H} + \sigma^2/c^2 = 0 \qquad\qquad (\text{iii}),$$

or

$$m = 1/2\mathbf{H} \pm ik' \qquad\qquad (\text{iv}),$$

where

$$k' = \frac{\sigma}{c}\left(1 - \frac{c^2}{4\sigma^2 \mathbf{H}^2}\right)^{\frac{1}{2}} \qquad\qquad (\text{v}).$$

The lower sign gives the case of waves propagated upwards. Expressed in real form the solution for this case is

$$s = C e^{z/2\mathbf{H}} \cos(\sigma t - k'z) \qquad\qquad (\text{vi}).$$

The wave-velocity (σ/k') varies with the frequency, but so long as σ is large compared with $c/2\mathbf{H}$ it is approximately constant, differing from c by a small quantity of the second order. The main effect of the variation of density is on the amplitude, which increases as the waves ascend upwards into the rarer regions, according to the law indicated by the exponential factor. This increase might have been foreseen without calculation; for when the variation of density within the limits of a wave-length is small, there is no sensible reflection, and the energy per wave-length, which varies as $a^2 \rho_0$ (a being the amplitude), must therefore remain unaltered as the waves proceed. Since $\rho_0 \propto e^{-z/\mathbf{H}}$, this shews that $a \propto e^{z/2\mathbf{H}}$.

When $\sigma < c/2\mathbf{H}$, the form of the solution is changed, viz. we have

$$s = (A_1 e^{m_1 z} + A_2 e^{m_2 z}) \cos \sigma t \qquad\qquad (\text{vii}),$$

where m_1, m_2 (the two roots of (iii)) are real and positive. This represents a standing oscillation, with one nodal and one 'loop' plane. For example, if the nodal plane be that of $z=0$, we have $m_1 A_1 + m_2 A_2 = 0$, and the position of the loop ($s=0$) is given by

$$z = \frac{1}{m_1 - m_2} \log \frac{m_1}{m_2} \qquad\qquad (\text{viii}).$$

For plane waves travelling *horizontally*, the equation (4) takes the form

$$\frac{d^2s}{dt^2}=c^2\frac{d^2s}{dx^2} \text{ ....} \quad \text{(ix).}$$

The waves are therefore propagated unchanged with velocity c, as we should expect, since on the present hypothesis of uniform equilibrium-temperature the wave-velocity is independent of the altitude*.

273. We may next consider the large-scale oscillations of an atmosphere of uniform temperature covering a globe at rest.

If we introduce angular coordinates θ, ω as in Art. 190, and denote by u, v the velocities along and perpendicular to the meridian, the equations (4) of Art. 271 give

$$\frac{du}{dt}=-\frac{c^2}{a}\frac{d}{d\theta}(s-\bar{s}), \quad \frac{dv}{dt}=-\frac{c^2}{a\sin\theta}\frac{d}{d\omega}(s-\bar{s})\text{......}(1),$$

where a is the radius. If we assume that the vertical motion (w) is zero, the equation of continuity, Art. 271 (6), becomes

$$\frac{ds}{dt}=-\frac{1}{a\sin\theta}\left\{\frac{d(u\sin\theta)}{d\theta}+\frac{dv}{d\omega}\right\}\text{...............}(2).$$

The equations (1) and (2) shew that u, v, s may be regarded as independent of the altitude. The formulæ are in fact the same as in Art. 190, except that s takes the place of ζ/h, and c^2 of gh. Since, in our present notation, we have $c^2=g\mathbf{H}$, it appears that the free and the forced oscillations will follow exactly the same laws as those of a liquid of uniform depth **H** covering the same globe.

Thus for the free oscillations we shall have

$$s=S_n\,.\cos(\sigma t+\epsilon)\text{.....................}(3),$$

where S_n is a surface-harmonic of integral order n, and

$$\sigma^2=n(n+1)\frac{c^2}{a^2}\text{ .... } (4).$$

As a numerical example, putting $c=2{\cdot}80\times10^4$, $2\pi a=4\times10^9$ [c. s.], we find, in the cases $n=1$, $n=2$, periods of 28·1 and 16·2 hours, respectively.

* The substance of this Art. is from a paper by Lord Rayleigh, "On Vibrations of an Atmosphere," *Phil. Mag.*, Feb. 1890. For a discussion of the effects of upward variation of temperature on propagation of sound-waves, see the same author's *Theory of Sound*, Art. 288.

The tidal variations of pressure due to the gravitational action of the sun and moon are very minute. It appears from the above analogy that the equilibrium value $\bar{s}$ of the condensation will be comparable with $H/\mathbf{H}$, where H is the quantity defined in Art. 177. Taking $H = 1{\cdot}80$ ft. (for the lunar tide), and $\mathbf{H} = 25000$ feet, this gives for the amplitude of $\bar{s}$ the value $7{\cdot}2 \times 10^{-5}$. If the normal height of the barometer be 30 inches, this means an oscillation of only ·00216 of an inch.

It will be seen on reference to Art. 206 that the analogy with the oscillations of a liquid of depth $\mathbf{H}$ is not disturbed when we proceed to the tidal oscillations on a *rotating* globe. The height $\mathbf{H}$ of the homogeneous atmosphere does not fall very far short of one of the values (29040 ft.) of the depth of the ocean for which the semi-diurnal tides were calculated by Laplace*. The tides in this case were found to be direct, and to have at the equator 11·267 times their equilibrium value. Even with this factor the corresponding barometric oscillation would only amount to ·0243 of an inch†.

274. The most regular oscillations of the barometer have solar diurnal and semi-diurnal periods, and cannot be due to gravitational action, since in that case the corresponding lunar tides would be 2·28 times as great, whereas they are practically insensible.

The observed oscillations must be ascribed to the daily variation in temperature, which, when analyzed into simple-harmonic constituents, will have components whose periods are respectively $1, \frac{1}{2}, \frac{1}{3}, \frac{1}{4}, \ldots$ of a solar day. It is very remarkable that the second (viz. the semi-diurnal) component has a considerably greater amplitude than the first. It has been suggested by Lord Kelvin that the explanation of this peculiarity is to be sought for in the closer agreement of the period of the semi-diurnal component with a free period of the earth's atmosphere than is the case with the diurnal component. This question has been made the subject of an elaborate investigation by Margules‡, taking into account the earth's rotation. The further consideration of atmospheric problems is, however, outside our province.

* See the table on p. 361, above.

† Cf. Laplace, "Recherches sur plusieurs points du système du monde," *Mém. de l'Acad. roy. des Sciences*, 1776 [1779], *Oeuvres*, t. ix., p. 283. Also *Mécanique Céleste*, Livre 4me, chap. v.

‡ This paper, with several others cited in the course of this work, is included in a very useful collection edited and (where necessary) translated by Prof. Cleveland Abbe, under the title: "Mechanics of the Earth's Atmosphere," *Smithsonian Miscellaneous Collections*, Washington, 1891.

CHAPTER XI.

VISCOSITY.

275. THE main theme of this Chapter is the resistance to distortion, known as 'viscosity' or 'internal friction,' which is exhibited more or less by all real fluids, but which we have hitherto neglected.

It will be convenient, following a plan already adopted on several occasions, to recall briefly the outlines of the general theory of a dynamical system subject to dissipative forces which are linear functions of the generalized velocities*. This will not only be useful as tending to bring under one point of view most of the special investigations which follow; it will sometimes indicate the general character of the results to be expected in cases which are as yet beyond our powers of calculation.

We begin with the case of one degree of freedom. The equation of motion is of the type

$$a\ddot{q} + b\dot{q} + cq = Q \quad \text{.....................(1).}$$

Here q is a generalized coordinate specifying the deviation from a position of equilibrium; a is the coefficient of inertia, and is necessarily positive; c is the coefficient of stability, and is positive in the applications which we shall consider; b is a coefficient of friction, and is positive.

If we put

$$T = \tfrac{1}{2}a\dot{q}^2, \quad V = \tfrac{1}{2}cq^2, \quad F = \tfrac{1}{2}b\dot{q}^2 \quad \text{..............(2),}$$

the equation may be written

$$\frac{d}{dt}(T + V) = -2F + Q\dot{q} \quad \text{...................(3).}$$

* For a fuller account of the theory reference may be made to Lord Rayleigh, *Theory of Sound*, cc. iv., v.; Thomson and Tait, *Natural Philosophy* (2nd ed.) Arts. 340–345; Routh, *Advanced Rigid Dynamics*, cc. vi., vii.

This shews that the energy $T+V$ is increasing at a rate less than that at which the extraneous force is doing work on the system. The difference $2F$ represents the rate at which energy is being dissipated; this is always positive.

In *free* motion we have

$$a\ddot{q}+b\dot{q}+cq=0 \qquad\qquad (4).$$

If we assume that $q \propto e^{\lambda t}$, the solution takes different forms according to the relative importance of the frictional term. If $b^2<4ac$, we have

$$\lambda=-\tfrac{1}{2}\frac{b}{a}\pm i\left(\frac{c}{a}-\tfrac{1}{4}\frac{b^2}{a^2}\right)^{\frac{1}{2}} \qquad\qquad (5),$$

or, say,

$$\lambda=-\tau^{-1}\pm i\sigma \qquad\qquad (6).$$

Hence the full solution, expressed in real form, is

$$q=Ae^{-t/\tau}\cos(\sigma t+\epsilon) \qquad\qquad (7),$$

where A, ϵ are arbitrary. The type of motion which this represents may be described as a simple-harmonic vibration, with amplitude diminishing asymptotically to zero, according to the law $e^{-t/\tau}$. The time τ in which the amplitude sinks to $1/e$ of its original value is sometimes called the 'modulus of decay' of the oscillations.

If $b/2a$ be small compared with $(c/a)^{\frac{1}{2}}$, $b^2/4ac$ is a small quantity of the second order, and the 'speed' σ is then practically unaffected by the friction. This is the case whenever the time $(2\pi\tau)$ in which the amplitude sinks to $e^{-2\pi}\,(=\frac{1}{535})$ of its initial value is large compared with the period $(2\pi/\sigma)$.

When, on the other hand, $b^2>4ac$, the values of λ are real and negative. Denoting them by $-\alpha_1$, $-\alpha_2$, we have

$$q=A_1e^{-\alpha_1 t}+A_2e^{-\alpha_2 t} \qquad\qquad (8).$$

This represents 'aperiodic motion'; viz. the system never passes more than once through its equilibrium position, towards which it finally creeps asymptotically.

In the critical case $b^2=4ac$, the two values of λ are equal; we then find by usual methods

$$q=(A+Bt)e^{-\alpha t} \qquad\qquad (9),$$

which may be similarly interpreted.

As the frictional coefficient b is increased, the two quantities α_1, α_2 become more and more unequal; viz. one of them (α_2, say) tends to the value b/a, and the other to the value c/b. The effect of the second term in (8) then rapidly disappears, and the residual motion is the same as if the inertia-coefficient (a) were zero.

276. We consider next the effect of a periodic extraneous force. Assuming that

$$Q \propto e^{i(\sigma t+\epsilon)} \qquad \text{.........................(10)},$$

the equation (1) gives

$$q = \frac{Q}{c - \sigma^2 a + i\sigma b} \qquad \text{.........................(11)}.$$

If we put

$$\left. \begin{aligned} 1 - \sigma^2 a/c &= R\cos\epsilon_1, \\ \sigma b/c &= R\sin\epsilon_1 \end{aligned} \right\} \qquad \text{.........................(12)},$$

where ϵ_1 lies between 0 and 180°, we have

$$q = \frac{Q}{Rc} e^{-i\epsilon_1} \qquad \text{.........................(13)}.$$

Taking real parts, we may say that the force

$$Q = C\cos(\sigma t + \epsilon) \qquad \text{.........................(14)}$$

will maintain the oscillation

$$q = \frac{C}{Rc}\cos(\sigma t + \epsilon - \epsilon_1) \qquad \text{.........................(15)}.$$

Since

$$R^2 = (1 - \sigma^2 a/c)^2 + \sigma^2 b^2/c^2 \qquad \text{.........................(16)},$$

it is easily found that if $b^2 < 4ac$ the amplitude is greatest when

$$\sigma = \left(\frac{c}{a}\right)^{\frac{1}{2}} \cdot \left(1 - \tfrac{1}{2}\frac{b^2}{ac}\right)^{\frac{1}{2}} \qquad \text{.........................(17)},$$

its value being then

$$\frac{C}{b}\left(\frac{a}{c}\right)^{\frac{1}{2}}\left(1 - \tfrac{1}{4}\frac{b^2}{ac}\right)^{-\frac{1}{2}} \qquad \text{.........................(18)}.$$

In the case of relatively small friction, where $b^2/4ac$ may be treated as of the second order, the amplitude is greatest when the period of the imposed force coincides with that of the free oscillation (cf. Art. 165). The formula (18) then shews that the amplitude when a maximum bears to its 'equilibrium-value' (C/c) the ratio $(ac)^{\frac{1}{2}}/b$, which is by hypothesis large.

On the other hand, when $b^2 > 4ac$ the amplitude continually increases as the speed σ diminishes, tending ultimately to the 'equilibrium-value' C/c.

It also appears from (15) and (12) that the maximum displacement follows the maximum of the force at an interval of phase equal to ϵ_1, where

$$\tan \epsilon_1 = \frac{\sigma b}{c - \sigma^2 a} \qquad\qquad (19).$$

If the period be longer than the free-period in the absence of friction this difference of phase lies between 0 and 90°; in the opposite case it lies between 90° and 180°. If the frictional coefficient b be relatively small, the interval differs very little from 0 or 180°, as the case may be.

The rate of dissipation is $b\dot{q}^2$, the mean value of which is easily found to be

$$\tfrac{1}{2} \frac{bC^2}{(\sigma a - c/\sigma)^2 + b^2} \qquad\qquad (20).$$

This is greatest when $\sigma = (c/a)^{\frac{1}{2}}$.

As in Art. 165, when the oscillations are very rapid the formula (11) gives

$$q = -Q/\sigma^2 a \qquad\qquad (21),$$

approximately; the *inertia* only of the system being operative.

On the other hand when σ is small, the displacement has very nearly the equilibrium-value

$$q = Q/c \qquad\qquad (22).$$

277. An interesting example is furnished by the tides in an equatorial canal*.

The equation of motion, as modified by the introduction of a frictional term, is

$$\frac{d^2\xi}{dt^2} = -\mu \frac{d\xi}{dt} + c^2 \frac{d^2\xi}{dx^2} + X \qquad\qquad (1),$$

where the notation is as in Art. 178†.

* Airy, "Tides and Waves," Arts. 315...

† In particular, c^2 now stands for gh, where h is the depth.

In the case of *free* waves, putting $X = 0$ and assuming that

$$\xi \propto e^{\lambda t + ikx} \quad\text{.........................(2),}$$

we find

$$\lambda^2 + \mu\lambda + k^2c^2 = 0,$$

whence

$$\lambda = -\tfrac{1}{2}\mu \pm i\,(k^2c^2 - \tfrac{1}{4}\mu^2) \quad\text{.................(3).}$$

If we neglect the square of μ/kc, this gives, in real form,

$$\xi = Ae^{-\frac{1}{2}\mu t} \cos\{k\,(ct \pm x) + \epsilon\} \quad\text{.................(4).}$$

The modulus of decay is $2\mu^{-1}$, and the wave-velocity is (to the first order) unaffected by the friction.

To find the forced waves due to the attraction of the moon we write, in conformity with Art. 178,

$$X = ife^{2i(n't + x/a + \epsilon)} \quad\text{.......................(5),}$$

where n' is the angular velocity of the moon relative to a fixed point on the canal, and a is the earth's radius. We find, assuming the same time-factor,

$$\xi = \tfrac{1}{4}\,\frac{ifa^2}{c^2 - n'^2a^2 + \tfrac{1}{2}i\mu n'a^2}\,e^{2i(n't + x/a + \epsilon)} \quad\text{............(6).}$$

Hence, for the surface-elevation, we have

$$\eta = -h\,\frac{d\xi}{dx} = \tfrac{1}{2}\,\frac{Hc^2}{c^2 - n'^2a^2 + \tfrac{1}{2}i\mu n'a^2}\,e^{2i(n't + x/a + \epsilon)} \quad\text{.........(7),}$$

where $H/a = f/g$, as in Art. 177.

To put these expressions in real form, we write

$$\tan 2\chi = \tfrac{1}{2}\,\frac{\mu n'a^2}{c^2 - n'^2a^2} \quad\text{.......................(8),}$$

where $0 < \chi < 90°$. We thus find that to the tidal disturbing force

$$X = -f \sin 2\left(n't + \frac{x}{a} + \epsilon\right) \quad\text{....................(9)}$$

corresponds the horizontal displacement

$$\xi = -\tfrac{1}{4}\,\frac{fa^2}{\{(c^2 - n'^2a^2)^2 + \tfrac{1}{4}\mu^2n'^2a^4\}^{\frac{1}{2}}} \sin 2\left(n't + \frac{x}{a} + \epsilon - \chi\right) \text{...(10),}$$

and the surface-elevation

$$\eta = \tfrac{1}{2}\,\frac{Hc^2}{\{(c^2 - n'^2a^2)^2 + \tfrac{1}{4}\mu^2n'^2a^4\}^{\frac{1}{2}}} \cos 2\left(n't + \frac{x}{a} + \epsilon - \chi\right) \text{...(11).}$$

Since in these expressions $n't + x/a + \epsilon$ measures the hour-angle of the moon past the meridian of any point (x) on the canal, it appears that high-water will follow the moon's transit at an interval t_1 given by $n't_1 = \chi$.

If $c^2 < n'^2a^2$, or $h/a < n'^2a/g$, we should in the case of infinitesimal friction have $\chi = 90^\circ$, *i.e.* the tides would be *inverted* (cf. Art. 178). With sensible friction, χ will lie between 90° and 45°, and the time of high-water is *accelerated* by the time-equivalent of the angle $90^\circ - \chi$.

On the other hand, when $h/a > n'^2a/g$, so that in the absence of friction the tides would be *direct*, the value of χ lies between 0° and 45°, and the time of high-water is *retarded* by the time-equivalent of this angle.

The figures shew the two cases. The letters M, M' indicate the positions of the moon and 'anti-moon' (see p. 365) supposed situate in the plane of the equator, and the curved arrows shew the direction of the earth's rotation.

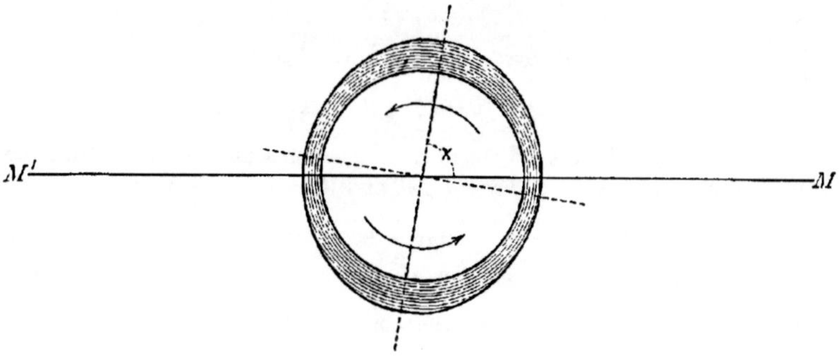

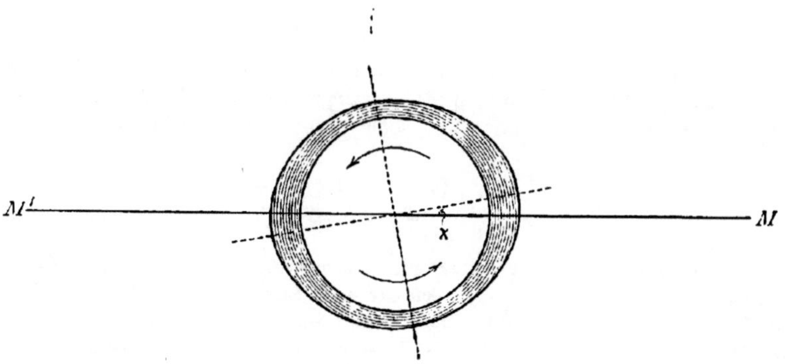

It is evident that in each case the attraction of the disturbing system on the elevated water is equivalent to a couple tending to *diminish* the angular momentum of the system composed of the earth and sea.

In the present problem the amount of the couple can be easily calculated. We find, from (9) and (11), for the integral tangential force on the elevated water

$$\int_0^{2\pi a} \rho X \eta \, dx = -\pi \rho a \mathbf{h} f \sin 2\chi \quad \text{..............(12)},$$

where $\mathbf{h}$ is the vertical amplitude. Since the positive direction of X is eastwards, this shews that there is on the whole a balance of westward force. If we multiply by a we get the amount of the retarding couple, per unit breadth of the canal*.

Another more obvious phenomenon, viz. the retardation of the time of spring tides behind the days of new and full moon, can be illustrated on the same principles. The composition of two simple-harmonic oscillations of nearly equal speed gives

$$\eta = A\cos(\sigma t + \epsilon) + A'\cos(\sigma' t + \epsilon')$$

$$= (A + A'\cos\phi)\cos(\sigma t + \epsilon) + A'\sin\phi\sin(\sigma t + \epsilon) \quad \text{.............. (i)},$$

where

$$\phi = (\sigma - \sigma')t + \epsilon - \epsilon' \quad \text{.............................. (ii)}.$$

If the first term in the second member of (i) represents the lunar, and the second the solar tide, we shall have $\sigma < \sigma'$, and $A > A'$. If we write

$$A + A'\cos\phi = C\cos\alpha, \qquad A'\sin\phi = C\sin\alpha \quad \text{...............(iii)},$$

we get

$$\eta = C\cos(\sigma t + \epsilon - \alpha) \quad \text{.............................(iv)},$$

where

$$C = (A^2 + 2AA'\cos\phi + A'^2)^{\frac{1}{2}} \quad \text{........................ (v)},$$

and

$$\alpha = \tan^{-1}\frac{A'\sin\phi}{A + A'\cos\phi} \quad \text{.......................... (vi)}.$$

This may be described as a simple-harmonic vibration of slowly varying amplitude and phase. The amplitude ranges between the limits $A \pm A'$, whilst α lies always between $\pm\frac{1}{2}\pi$. The 'speed' must also be regarded as variable, viz. we find

$$\sigma - \frac{d\alpha}{dt} = \frac{\sigma A^2 + (\sigma + \sigma')AA'\cos\phi + \sigma' A'^2}{A^2 + 2AA'\cos\phi + A'^2} \quad \text{.............. (vii)}.$$

* Cf. Delaunay, "Sur l'existence d'une cause nouvelle ayant une influence sensible sur la valeur de l'équation séculaire de la Lune," *Comptes Rendus*, t. lxi. (1865); Sir W. Thomson, "On the Observations and Calculations required to find the Tidal Retardation of the Earth's Rotation," *Phil. Mag.*, June (supplement) 1866, *Math. and Phys. Papers*, t. iii., p. 337. The first direct numerical estimate of tidal retardation appears to have been made by Ferrel, in 1853.

This ranges between $\frac{A\sigma + A'\sigma'}{A + A'}$ and $\frac{A\sigma - A'\sigma'}{A - A'}$ ....(viii)*.

The above is the well-known explanation of the phenomena of the spring- and neap-tides†; but we are now concerned further with the question of phase. In the absence of friction, the maxima of the amplitude C would occur whenever

$$(\sigma' - \sigma)\,t = 2m\pi + \epsilon - \epsilon',$$

where m is integral. Owing to the friction, ϵ and ϵ' are replaced by quantities of the form $\epsilon - \epsilon_1$ and $\epsilon' - \epsilon_1'$, and the corresponding times of maximum are given by

$$(\sigma' - \sigma)\,t - (\epsilon_1' - \epsilon_1) = 2m\pi + \epsilon - \epsilon',$$

i.e. they occur *later* by an interval $(\epsilon_1' - \epsilon_1)/(\sigma' - \sigma)$. If the difference between σ' and σ were infinitesimal, this would be equal to $d\epsilon_1/d\sigma$.

In the case of the semi-diurnal tides in an equatorial canal we have $\sigma = 2n'$, $\epsilon_1 = 2\chi$, whence

$$\frac{d\epsilon_1}{d\sigma} = \frac{d\chi}{dn'} = \frac{\mu a^2 (c^2 + n'^2 a^2)}{4(c^2 - n'^2 a^2)^2 + \mu^2 n'^2 a^4} \quad\text{......................(ix)‡.}$$

278. Returning to the general theory, let $q_1, q_2, \ldots$ be the coordinates of a dynamical system, which we will suppose subject to conservative forces depending on its configuration, to 'motional' forces varying as the velocities, and to given extraneous forces. The equations of small motion of such a system, on the most general assumptions we can make, will be of the type

$$\frac{d}{dt}\frac{dT}{d\dot{q}_r} + B_{r1}\dot{q}_1 + B_{r2}\dot{q}_2 + \ldots = -\frac{dV}{dq_r} + Q_r \quad\text{..........(1),}$$

where the kinetic and potential energies T, V are given by expressions of the forms

$$2T = a_{11}\dot{q}_1^2 + a_{22}\dot{q}_2^2 + \ldots + 2a_{12}\dot{q}_1\dot{q}_2 + \ldots \quad\text{.........(2),}$$

$$2V = c_{11}q_1^2 + c_{22}q_2^2 + \ldots + 2c_{12}q_1q_2 + \ldots \quad\text{.........(3).}$$

It is to be remembered that

$$a_{rs} = a_{sr}, \quad c_{rs} = c_{sr} \quad\text{........................(4),}$$

but we do not assume the equality of B_{rs} and B_{sr}.

If we now write

$$b_{rs} = b_{sr} = \tfrac{1}{2}(B_{rs} + B_{sr}) \quad\text{....................(5),}$$

* Helmholtz, *Lehre von den Tonempfindungen* (2° Aufl.), Braunschweig, 1870, p. 622.

† Cf. Thomson and Tait, *Natural Philosophy*, Art. 60.

‡ Cf. Airy, "Tides and Waves," Arts. 328...

and
$$\beta_{rs} = -\beta_{sr} = \tfrac{1}{2}(B_{rs} - B_{sr}) \quad\text{.................(6)},$$
the typical equation (1) takes the form
$$\frac{d}{dt}\frac{dT}{d\dot{q}_r} + \frac{dF}{d\dot{q}_r} + \beta_{r1}\dot{q}_1 + \beta_{r2}\dot{q}_2 + \ldots = -\frac{dV}{dq_r} + Q_r \quad\text{.......(7)},$$
provided
$$2F = b_{11}\dot{q}_1^2 + b_{22}\dot{q}_2^2 + \ldots + 2b_{12}\dot{q}_1\dot{q}_2 + \ldots \quad\text{............(8)}.$$

From the equations in this form we derive
$$\frac{d}{dt}(T + V) + 2F = \Sigma Q_r \dot{q}_r \quad\text{...................(9)}.$$

The right-hand side expresses the rate at which the extraneous forces are doing work. Part of this work goes to increase the total energy $T + V$ of the system; the remainder is dissipated, at the rate $2F$. In the application to natural problems the function F is essentially positive; it is called by Lord Rayleigh*, by whom it was first formally employed, the 'Dissipation-Function.'

The terms in (7) which are due to F may be distinguished as the 'frictional terms.' The remaining terms in $\dot{q}_1, \dot{q}_2, \ldots$, with coefficients subject to the relation $\beta_{rs} = -\beta_{sr}$, are of the type we have already met with in the general equations of a 'gyrostatic' system (Art. 139); they may therefore be referred to as the 'gyrostatic terms.'

279. When the gyrostatic terms are absent, the equation (7) reduces to
$$\frac{d}{dt}\frac{dT}{d\dot{q}_r} + \frac{dF}{d\dot{q}_r} + \frac{dV}{dq_r} = Q_r \quad\text{...................(10)}.$$

As in Art. 165, we may suppose that by transformation of coordinates the expressions for T and V are reduced to sums of squares, thus:
$$2T = a_1\dot{q}_1^2 + a_2\dot{q}_2^2 + \ldots \quad\text{..................(11)},$$
$$2V = c_1\dot{q}_1^2 + c_2\dot{q}_2^2 + \ldots \quad\text{..................(12)}.$$

It frequently, but not necessarily, happens that the same transformation also reduces F to this form, say
$$2F = b_1\dot{q}_1^2 + b_2\dot{q}_2^2 + \ldots \quad\text{..................(13)}.$$

* "Some General Theorems relating to Vibrations," *Proc. Lond. Math. Soc.*, t. iv., p. 363 (1873); *Theory of Sound*, Art. 81.

The typical equation (10) then assumes the simple form

$$a_r\ddot{q}_r + b_r\dot{q}_r + c_r q_r = Q_r \qquad \text{(14)},$$

which has been discussed in Art. 275. Each coordinate q_r now varies independently of the rest.

When F is not reduced by the same transformation as T and V, the equations of small motion are

$$\left.\begin{array}{l} a_1\ddot{q}_1 + b_{11}\dot{q}_1 + b_{12}\dot{q}_2 + \ldots + c_1 q_1 = Q_1, \\ a_2\ddot{q}_2 + b_{21}\dot{q}_1 + b_{22}\dot{q}_2 + \ldots + c_2 q_2 = Q_2, \\ \ldots\ldots\ldots\ldots\ldots\ldots\ldots\ldots\ldots\ldots \end{array}\right\} \qquad \text{(i)},$$

where $b_{rs} = b_{sr}$.

The motion is now more complicated; for example, in the case of free oscillations about stable equilibrium, each particle executes (in any fundamental type) an elliptic-harmonic vibration, with the axes of the orbit contracting according to the law e^{-at}.

The question becomes somewhat simpler when the frictional coefficients b_{rs} are *small*, since the modes of motion will then be almost the same as in the case of no friction. Thus it appears from (i) that a mode of free motion is possible in which the main variation is in *one* coordinate, say q_r. The rth equation then reduces to

$$a_r\ddot{q}_r + b_{rr}\dot{q}_r + c_r q_r = 0 \qquad \text{(ii)},$$

where we have omitted terms in which the relatively small quantities $\dot{q}_1, \dot{q}_2, \ldots$ (other than $\dot{q}_r$) are multiplied by the small coefficients $b_{r1}, b_{r2}, \ldots$ We have seen in Art. 275 that if b_{rr} be small the solution of (ii) is of the type

$$q_r = Ae^{-t/\tau}\cos(\sigma t + \epsilon) \qquad \text{(iii)},$$

where

$$\tau^{-1} = \tfrac{1}{2}b_{rr}/a_r, \quad \sigma = (c_r/a_r)^{\frac{1}{2}} \qquad \text{(iv)}.$$

The relatively small variations of the remaining coordinates are then given by the remaining equations of the system (i). For example, with the same approximations,

$$a_s\ddot{q}_s + b_{rs}\dot{q}_r + c_s q_s = 0 \qquad \text{(v)},$$

whence

$$q_s = \frac{\sigma b_{rs}}{c_s - \sigma^2 a_s} Ae^{-t/\tau}\sin(\sigma t + \epsilon) \qquad \text{(vi)}.$$

Except in the case of approximate equality of period between two fundamental modes, the elliptic orbits of the particles will on the present suppositions be very flat.

If we were to assume that

$$q_r = a\cos(\sigma t + \epsilon) \qquad \text{(vii)},$$

where σ has the same value as in the case of no friction, whilst a varies slowly with the time, and that the variations of the other coordinates are relatively small, we should find

$$T+V=\tfrac{1}{2}a_r\dot{q}_r^2+\tfrac{1}{2}c_rq_r^2=\tfrac{1}{2}\sigma^2a_ra^2 \quad\text{.................. (viii)},$$

nearly. Again, the dissipation is

$$2F=b_{rr}\dot{q}_r^2,$$

the mean value of which is $\tfrac{1}{2}\sigma^2b_{rr}a^2$ .... (ix),

approximately. Hence equating the rate of decay of the energy to the mean value of the dissipation, we get

$$\frac{da}{dt}=-\tfrac{1}{2}\frac{b_{rr}}{a_r}a \quad\text{.................................. (x)},$$

whence $a=a_0e^{-t/\tau}$ .... (xi),

if $\tau^{-1}=\tfrac{1}{2}b_{rr}/a_r$ .... (xii),

as in Art. 275. This method of ascertaining the rate of decay of the oscillations is sometimes useful when the complete determination of the character of the motion, as affected by friction, would be difficult.

When the frictional coefficients are relatively great, the inertia of the system becomes ineffective; and the most appropriate system of coordinates is that which reduces F and V simultaneously to sums of squares, say

$$\left.\begin{aligned}2F&=b_1\dot{q}_1^2+b_2\dot{q}_2^2+\ldots,\\ 2V&=c_1q_1^2+c_2q_2^2+\ldots\end{aligned}\right\} \quad\text{......................... (xiii)}.$$

The equations of free-motion are then of the type

$$b_r\dot{q}_r+c_rq_r=0 \quad\text{.................................(xiv)},$$

whence $q_r=Ce^{-t/\tau}$ .... (xv),

if $\tau=b_r/c_r$ .... (xvi).

280. When gyrostatic as well as frictional terms are present in the fundamental equations, the theory is naturally more complicated. It will be sufficient here to consider the case of *two* degrees of freedom, by way of supplement to the investigation of Art. 198.

The equations of motion are now of the types

$$\left.\begin{aligned}a_1\ddot{q}_1+b_{11}\dot{q}_1+(b_{12}+\beta)\,\dot{q}_2+c_1q_1&=Q_1,\\ a_2\ddot{q}_2+(b_{21}-\beta)\,\dot{q}_1+b_{22}\dot{q}_2+c_2q_2&=Q_2\end{aligned}\right\} \quad\text{.................. (i)}.$$

To determine the modes of free motion we put $Q_1=0$, $Q_2=0$, and assume that q_1 and q_2 vary as $e^{\lambda t}$. This leads to the biquadratic in λ:

$$a_1a_2\lambda^4+(a_2b_{11}+a_1b_{22})\lambda^3+(a_2c_1+a_1c_2+\beta^2+b_{11}b_{22}-b_{12}^2)\lambda^2$$
$$+(b_{11}c_2+b_{22}c_1)\lambda+c_1c_2=0 \quad\text{......(ii)}.$$

There is no difficulty in shewing, with the help of criteria given by Routh*, that if, as in our case, the quantities

$$a_1,\ a_2,\ b_{11},\ b_{22},\ b_{11}b_{22}-b_{12}^2$$

are all positive, the necessary and sufficient conditions that this biquadratic should have the real parts of its roots all negative are that c_1, c_2 should both be positive.

If we neglect terms of the second order in the frictional coefficients, the same conclusion may be attained more directly as follows. On this hypothesis the roots of (ii) are, approximately,

$$\lambda = -\alpha_1 \pm i\sigma_1,\quad -\alpha_2 \pm i\sigma_2 \qquad\text{(iii)},$$

where σ_1, σ_2 are, to the first order, the same as in the case of no friction, viz. they are the roots of

$$a_1a_2\sigma^4-(a_2c_1+a_1c_2+\beta^2)\,\sigma^2+c_1c_2=0 \qquad\text{(iv)},$$

whilst α_1, α_2 are determined by

$$\left.\begin{aligned}\alpha_1+\alpha_2&=\tfrac{1}{2}\left(\frac{b_{11}}{a_1}+\frac{b_{22}}{a_2}\right),\\ \frac{\alpha_1}{\sigma_1^2}+\frac{\alpha_2}{\sigma_2^2}&=\tfrac{1}{2}\left(\frac{b_{11}}{c_1}+\frac{b_{22}}{c_2}\right)\end{aligned}\right\} \qquad\text{(v)}.$$

It is evident that, if σ_1 and σ_2 are to be real, c_1, c_2 must have the same sign, and that if α_1, α_2 are to be positive, this sign must be $+$. Conversely, if c_1, c_2 are both positive, the values of σ_1^2, σ_2^2 are real and positive, and the quantities c_1/a_1, c_2/a_2 both lie in the interval between them. It then easily follows from (v) that α_1, α_2 are both positive†.

If one of the coefficients c_1, c_2 (say c_2) be zero, one of the values of σ (say σ_2) is zero, indicating a free mode of infinitely long period. We then have

$$\sigma_1^2=\frac{c_1}{a_1}+\frac{\beta^2}{a_1a_2} \qquad\text{(vi)},$$

$$\alpha_2=\frac{b_{22}c_1}{a_2c_1+\beta^2} \qquad\text{(vii)}.$$

* *Advanced Rigid Dynamics*, Art. 287.

† A simple example of the above theory is supplied by the case of a particle in an ellipsoidal bowl rotating about a principal axis, which is vertical. If the bowl be frictionless, the equilibrium of the particle when at the lowest point will be stable unless the period of the rotation lie *between* the periods of the two fundamental modes of oscillation (one in each principal plane) of the particle when the bowl is at rest. But if there be friction of motion between the particle and the bowl, there will be 'secular' stability only so long as the speed of the rotation is less than that of the slower of the two modes referred to. If the rotation be more rapid, the particle will gradually work its way outwards into a position of relative equilibrium in which it rotates with the bowl like the bob of a conical pendulum. In this state the system made up of the particle and the bowl has *less* energy for the same angular momentum than when the particle was at the bottom. Cf. Art. 235.

As in Art. 198 we could easily write down the expressions for the forced oscillations in the general case where Q_1, Q_2 vary as $e^{i\sigma t}$, but we shall here consider more particularly the case where $c_2=0$ and $Q_2=0$. The equations (i) then give

$$\left.\begin{aligned}(c_1-\sigma^2 a_1+i\sigma b_{11})\, q_1+(b_{12}+\beta)\, \dot{q}_2=Q_1,\\ i\sigma\,(b_{12}-\beta)\, q_1+(i\sigma a_2+b_{22})\, \dot{q}_2=0\end{aligned}\right\} \quad\text{(viii)}.$$

Hence

$$q_1=\frac{i\sigma a_2+b_{22}}{-a_1 a_2 i\sigma^3-(a_2 b_{11}+a_1 b_{22})\,\sigma^2+(a_2 c_1+\beta^2+b_{11}b_{22}-b_{12}^2)\, i\sigma+b_{22}c_1}\, Q_1 \quad\text{(ix)}.$$

This may also be written

$$q_1=\frac{i\sigma a_2+b_{22}}{a_1 a_2\{(i\sigma+a_1)^2+\sigma_1^2\}\,(i\sigma+a_2)}\, Q_1 \quad\text{(x)}.$$

Our main object is to examine the case of a disturbing force of long period, for the sake of its bearing on Laplace's argument as to the fortnightly tide (Art. 210). We will therefore suppose that the ratio σ_1/σ, as well as σ_1/a_1, is large. The formula then reduces to

$$q_1=\frac{i\sigma a_2+b_{22}}{a_1 a_2 \sigma_1^2\,(i\sigma+a_2)}\, Q_1=\frac{i\sigma a_2+b_{22}}{b_{22}c_1\,(i\sigma/a_2+1)}\, Q_1 \quad\text{(xi)}.$$

Everything now turns on the values of the ratios σ/a_2 and $\sigma a_2/b_{22}$. If σ be so small that these may be both neglected, we have

$$q_1=Q_1/c_1 \quad\text{(xii)},$$

in agreement with the equilibrium theory. The assumption here made is that the period of the imposed force is long compared with the time in which free motions would, owing to friction, fall to $e^{-2\pi}$ of their initial amplitudes. This condition is evidently far from being fulfilled in the case of the fortnightly tide. If, as is more in agreement with the actual state of things, we assume σ/a_2 and $\sigma a_2/b_{22}$ to be large, we obtain

$$q_1=\frac{a_2 a_2}{b_{22}c_1}\, Q_1=\frac{a_2}{a_2 c_1+\beta^2}\, Q_1 \quad\text{(xiii)},$$

as in Art. 198 (vii).

Viscosity.

281. We proceed to consider the special kind of resistance which is met with in fluids. The methods we shall employ are of necessity the same as are applicable to the resistance to distortion, known as 'elasticity,' which is characteristic of solid bodies. The two classes of phenomena are of course physically distinct, the latter depending on the actual changes of shape produced, the former on the *rate* of change of shape, but the mathematical methods appropriate to them are to a great extent identical.

If we imagine three planes to be drawn through any point P

perpendicular to the axes of x, y, z, respectively, the three components of the stress, per unit area, exerted across the first of these planes may be denoted by p_{xx}, p_{xy}, p_{xz}, respectively; those of the stress across the second plane by p_{yx}, p_{yy}, p_{yz}; and those of the stress across the third plane by p_{zx}, p_{zy}, p_{zz}*. If we fix our attention on an element $\delta x \delta y \delta z$ having its centre at P, we find, on taking moments, and dividing by $\delta x \delta y \delta z$,

$$p_{yz} = p_{zy}, \quad p_{zx} = p_{xz}, \quad p_{xy} = p_{yx} \quad \ldots\ldots\ldots\ldots\ldots(1),$$

the extraneous forces and the kinetic reactions being omitted, since they are of a higher order of small quantities than the surface tractions. These equalities reduce the nine components of stress to six; in the case of a viscous fluid they will also follow independently from the expressions for p_{yz}, p_{zx}, p_{xy} in terms of the rates of distortion, to be given presently (Art. 283).

282. It appears from Arts. 1, 2 that in a fluid the deviation of the state of stress denoted by $p_{xx}, p_{xy}, \ldots$ from one of pressure uniform in all directions depends entirely on the motion of distortion in the neighbourhood of P, *i.e.* on the six quantities a, b, c, f, g, h by which this distortion was in Art. 31 shewn to be specified. Before endeavouring to express $p_{xx}, p_{xy}, \ldots$ as functions of these quantities, it will be convenient to establish certain formulæ of transformation.

Let us draw Px', Py', Pz' in the directions of the principal axes of distortion at P, and let a', b', c' be the rates of extension along these lines. Further let the mutual configuration of the two sets of axes, x, y, z and x', y', z', be specified in the usual manner by the annexed scheme of direction-cosines. We have, then,

	x	y	z
x'	$l_1,$	$m_1,$	$n_1,$
y'	$l_2,$	$m_2,$	$n_2,$
z'	$l_3,$	$m_3,$	$n_3.$

$$\frac{du}{dx} = \left(l_1 \frac{d}{dx'} + l_2 \frac{d}{dy'} + l_3 \frac{d}{dz'}\right)(l_1 u' + l_2 v' + l_3 w')$$

$$= l_1^2 \frac{du'}{dx'} + l_2^2 \frac{dv'}{dy'} + l_3^2 \frac{dw'}{dz'}.$$

* In conformity with the usual practice in the theory of Elasticity, we reckon a *tension* as positive, a *pressure* as negative. Thus in the case of a frictionless fluid we have

$$p_{xx} = p_{yy} = p_{zz} = -p.$$

Hence
$$\left.\begin{aligned} a &= l_1^2a' + l_2^2b' + l_3^2c', \\ b &= m_1^2a' + m_2^2b' + m_3^2c', \\ c &= n_1^2a' + n_2^2b' + n_3^2c' \end{aligned}\right\} \quad\text{..................}\quad (1),$$

the last two relations being written down from symmetry. We notice that

$$a + b + c = a' + b' + c' \quad\text{.....................}(2),$$

an invariant, as it should be, by Art. 7.

Again

$$\frac{dw}{dy} + \frac{dv}{dz} = \left(m_1\frac{d}{dx'} + m_2\frac{d}{dy'} + m_3\frac{d}{dz'}\right)(n_1u' + n_2v' + n_3w')$$
$$+ \left(n_1\frac{d}{dx'} + n_2\frac{d}{dy'} + n_3\frac{d}{dz'}\right)(m_1u' + m_2v' + m_3w');$$

and this, with the two corresponding formulæ, gives

$$\left.\begin{aligned} f &= m_1n_1a' + m_2n_2b' + m_3n_3c', \\ g &= n_1l_1a' + n_2l_2b' + n_3l_3c', \\ h &= l_1m_1a' + l_2m_2b' + l_3m_3c' \end{aligned}\right\} \quad\text{..............}\quad (3).$$

283. From the symmetry of the circumstances it is plain that the stresses exerted at P across the planes $y'z'$, $z'x'$, $x'y'$ must be wholly perpendicular to these planes. Let us denote them by p_1, p_2, p_3 respectively. In the figure of Art. 2 let ABC now represent a plane drawn perpendicular to x, infinitely close to P, meeting the axes of x', y', z' in A, B, C, respectively; and let Δ denote the area ABC. The areas of the remaining faces of the tetrahedron $PABC$ will then be $l_1\Delta$, $l_2\Delta$, $l_3\Delta$. Resolving parallel to x the forces acting on the tetrahedron, we find

$$p_{xx}\Delta = p_1l_1\Delta \,.\, l_1 + p_2l_2\Delta \,.\, l_2 + p_3l_3\Delta \,.\, l_3;$$

the external impressed forces and the resistances to acceleration being omitted for the same reason as before. Hence, and by similar reasoning,

$$\left.\begin{aligned} p_{xx} &= p_1l_1^2 + p_2l_2^2 + p_3l_3^2, \\ p_{yy} &= p_1m_1^2 + p_2m_2^2 + p_3m_3^2, \\ p_{zz} &= p_1n_1^2 + p_2n_2^2 + p_3n_3^2 \end{aligned}\right\} \quad\text{..................}(1).$$

We notice that

$$p_{xx} + p_{yy} + p_{zz} = p_1 + p_2 + p_3 \quad\text{..................}\quad (2).$$

Hence the arithmetic mean of the normal pressures on any three mutually perpendicular planes through the point P is the same. We shall denote this mean pressure by p.

Again, resolving parallel to y, we obtain the third of the following symmetrical system of equations:

$$\left.\begin{aligned} p_{yz} &= p_1 m_1 n_1 + p_2 m_2 n_2 + p_3 m_3 n_3, \\ p_{zx} &= p_1 n_1 l_1 \ + p_2 n_2 l_2 \ + p_3 n_3 l_3, \\ p_{xy} &= p_1 l_1 m_1 \ + p_2 l_2 m_2 \ + p_3 l_3 m_3 \end{aligned}\right\} \quad \ldots\ldots\ldots\ldots\ldots(3).$$

These shew that

$$p_{yz} = p_{zy}, \quad p_{zx} = p_{xz}, \quad p_{xy} = p_{yx},$$

as in Art. 281.

If in the same figure we suppose PA, PB, PC to be drawn parallel to x, y, z respectively, whilst ABC is any plane drawn near P, whose direction-cosines are l, m, n, we find in the same way that the components (p_{hx}, p_{hy}, p_{hz}) of the stress exerted across this plane are

$$\left.\begin{aligned} p_{hx} &= lp_{xx} + mp_{xy} + np_{xz}, \\ p_{hy} &= lp_{yx} + mp_{yy} + np_{yz}, \\ p_{hz} &= lp_{zx} + mp_{zy} + np_{zz} \end{aligned}\right\} \quad \ldots\ldots\ldots\ldots\ldots\ldots(4).$$

284. Now p_1, p_2, p_3 differ from $-p$ by quantities depending on the motion of distortion, which must therefore be functions of a', b', c', only. The simplest hypothesis we can frame on this point is that these functions are linear. We write therefore

$$\left.\begin{aligned} p_1 &= -p + \lambda(a' + b' + c') + 2\mu a', \\ p_2 &= -p + \lambda(a' + b' + c') + 2\mu b', \\ p_3 &= -p + \lambda(a' + b' + c') + 2\mu c' \end{aligned}\right\} \quad \ldots\ldots\ldots\,..(1),$$

where λ, μ are constants depending on the nature of the fluid, and on its physical state, this being the most general assumption consistent with the above suppositions, and with symmetry. Substituting these values of p_1, p_2, p_3 in (1) and (3) of Art. 283, and making use of the results of Art. 282, we find

$$\left.\begin{aligned} p_{xx} &= -p + \lambda(a + b + c) + 2\mu a, \\ p_{yy} &= -p + \lambda(a + b + c) + 2\mu b, \\ p_{zz} &= -p + \lambda(a + b + c) + 2\mu c \end{aligned}\right\} \quad \ldots\ldots\ldots\ldots\ldots(2),$$

$$p_{yz} = 2\mu f, \quad p_{zx} = 2\mu g, \quad p_{xy} = 2\mu h \quad \ldots\ldots\ldots\ldots\ldots(3).$$

The definition of p adopted in Art. 283 implies the relation

$$3\lambda + 2\mu = 0,$$

whence, finally, introducing the values of $a, b, c, f, g, h,$ from Art. 31,

$$\left.\begin{aligned} p_{xx} &= -p - \tfrac{2}{3}\mu\left(\frac{du}{dx} + \frac{dv}{dy} + \frac{dw}{dz}\right) + 2\mu\frac{du}{dx}, \\ p_{yy} &= -p - \tfrac{2}{3}\mu\left(\frac{du}{dx} + \frac{dv}{dy} + \frac{dw}{dz}\right) + 2\mu\frac{dv}{dy}, \\ p_{zz} &= -p - \tfrac{2}{3}\mu\left(\frac{du}{dx} + \frac{dv}{dy} + \frac{dw}{dz}\right) + 2\mu\frac{dw}{dz} \end{aligned}\right\}\quad\ldots\ldots\ldots(4),$$

$$\left.\begin{aligned} p_{yz} &= \mu\left(\frac{dw}{dy} + \frac{dv}{dz}\right) = p_{zy}, \\ p_{zx} &= \mu\left(\frac{du}{dz} + \frac{dw}{dx}\right) = p_{xz}, \\ p_{xy} &= \mu\left(\frac{dv}{dx} + \frac{du}{dy}\right) = p_{yx} \end{aligned}\right\}\quad\ldots\ldots\ldots\ldots\ldots\ldots(5).$$

The constant μ is called the 'coefficient of viscosity.' Its physical meaning may be illustrated by reference to the case of a fluid in what is called 'laminar' motion (Art. 31); *i.e.* the fluid moves in a system of parallel planes, the velocity being in direction everywhere the same, and in magnitude proportional to the distance from some fixed plane of the system. Each stratum of fluid will then exert on the one next to it a tangential traction, opposing the relative motion, whose amount per unit area is μ times the variation of velocity per unit distance perpendicular to the planes. In symbols, if $u = \alpha y$, $v = 0$, $w = 0$, we have

$$p_{xx} = p_{yy} = p_{zz} = -p, \quad p_{yz} = 0, \quad p_{zx} = 0, \quad p_{xy} = \alpha.$$

If $[M]$, $[L]$, $[T]$ denote the units of mass, length, and time, the dimensions of the p's are $[ML^{-1}T^{-2}]$, and those of the rates of distortion $(a, b, c, \ldots)$ are $[T^{-1}]$, so that the dimensions of μ are $[ML^{-1}T^{-1}]$.

The stresses in different fluids, under similar circumstances of motion, will be proportional to the corresponding values of μ; but if we wish to compare their effects in modifying the existing motion we have to take account of the ratio of these stresses to the inertia of the fluid. From this point of view, the determining quantity is the ratio μ/ρ; it is therefore usual to denote this by a special symbol ν, called by Maxwell the 'kinematic coefficient' of viscosity. The dimensions of ν are $[L^2T^{-1}]$.

The hypothesis made above that the stresses $p_{xx}, p_{xy}, \ldots$ are linear functions of the rates of strain $a, b, c, \ldots$ is of a purely tentative character, and although there is considerable *à priori* probability that it will represent the facts accurately for the case of infinitely small motions, we have so far no assurance that it will hold generally. It has however been pointed out by Prof. Osborne Reynolds* that the equations based on this hypothesis have been put to a very severe test in the experiments of Poiseuille and others, to be referred to presently (Art. 289). Considering the very wide range of values of the rates of distortion over which these experiments extend, we can hardly hesitate to accept the equations in question as a complete statement of the laws of viscosity. In the case of gases we have additional grounds for this assumption in the investigations of the kinetic theory by Maxwell†.

The practical determination of μ (or ν) is a matter of some difficulty. Without entering into the details of experimental methods, we quote a few of the best-established results. The calculations of von Helmholtz‡, based on Poiseuille's observations, give for water

$$\mu = \frac{\cdot 0178}{1 + \cdot 0337\theta + \cdot 000221\theta^2},$$

in C.G.S. units, where θ is the temperature Centigrade. The viscosity, as in the case of all liquids as yet investigated, diminishes rapidly as the temperature rises; thus at 17° C. the value is

$$\mu_{17} = \cdot 0109.$$

For mercury Koch§ found

$$\mu_0 = \cdot 01697, \text{ and } \mu_{10} = \cdot 01633,$$

respectively.

In gases, the value of μ is found to be sensibly independent of the pressure, within very wide limits, but to *increase* somewhat with rise of temperature. Maxwell found as the result of his experiments‖,

$$\mu = \cdot 0001878\,(1 + \cdot 00366\,\theta);$$

this makes μ proportional to the absolute temperature as measured by the air-thermometer. Subsequent observers have found a somewhat smaller value for the first factor, and a less rapid increase with temperature. We may take perhaps as a fairly established value

$$\mu_0 = \cdot 000170$$

* "On the Theory of Lubrication, &c.," *Phil. Trans.*, 1886, Pt. I., p. 165.

† "On the Dynamical Theory of Gases," *Phil. Trans.*, 1867; *Scientific Papers*, t. ii., p. 26.

‡ "Ueber Reibung tropfbarer Flüssigkeiten," *Wien. Sitzungsber.*, t. xl. (1860); *Ges. Abh.*, t. i., p. 172.

§ *Wied. Ann.*, t. xiv. (1881).

‖ "On the Viscosity or Internal Friction of Air and other Gases," *Phil. Trans.*, 1866; *Scientific Papers*, t. ii., p. 1.

for the temperature 0° C. For air at atmospheric pressure, assuming $\rho = \cdot 00129$ this gives

$$\nu_0 = \cdot 132.$$

The value of ν varies inversely as the pressure*.

285. We have still to inquire into the dynamical conditions to be satisfied at the boundaries.

At a free surface, or at the surface of contact of two dissimilar fluids, the three components of stress across the surface must be continuous†. The resulting conditions can easily be written down with the help of Art. 283 (4).

A more difficult question arises as to the state of things at the surface of contact of a fluid with a solid. It appears probable that in all ordinary cases there is no motion, relative to the solid, of the fluid immediately in contact with it. The contrary supposition would imply an infinitely greater resistance to the sliding of one portion of the fluid past another than to the sliding of the fluid over a solid§.

If however we wish, temporarily, to leave this point open, the most natural supposition to make is that the slipping is resisted by a tangential force proportional to the relative velocity. If we consider the motion of a small film of fluid, of thickness infinitely small compared with its lateral dimensions, in contact with the solid, it is evident that the tangential traction on its inner surface must ultimately balance the force exerted on its outer surface by the solid. The former force may be calculated from Art. 283 (4); the latter is in a direction opposite to the relative velocity, and proportional to it. The constant (β, say) which expresses the ratio of the tangential force to the relative velocity may be called the 'coefficient of sliding friction.'

286. The equations of motion of a viscous fluid are obtained by considering, as in Art. 6, a rectangular element $\delta x \delta y \delta z$ having its centre at P. Taking, for instance, the resolution parallel to x, the difference of the normal tractions on the two yz-faces gives $(dp_{xx}/dx)\,\delta x \,.\, \delta y \delta z$. The tangential tractions on the two zx-faces contribute $(dp_{yx}/dy)\,\delta y \,.\, \delta z \delta x$, and the two xy-faces give

* A very full account of the results obtained by various experimenters is given in Winkelmann's *Handbuch der Physik*, t. i., Art. 'Reibung.'

† This statement requires an obvious modification when capillarity is taken into account. Cf. Art. 302.

§ Stokes, *l. c.* p. 518.

in like manner $(dp_{zx}/dz)\,\delta z\,.\,\delta x\delta y$. Hence, with our usual notation,

$$\left.\begin{aligned}\rho\frac{Du}{Dt}&=\rho X+\frac{dp_{xx}}{dx}+\frac{dp_{yx}}{dy}+\frac{dp_{zx}}{dz},\\ \rho\frac{Dv}{Dt}&=\rho Y+\frac{dp_{xy}}{dx}+\frac{dp_{yy}}{dy}+\frac{dp_{zy}}{dz},\\ \rho\frac{Dw}{Dt}&=\rho Z+\frac{dp_{xz}}{dx}+\frac{dp_{yz}}{dy}+\frac{dp_{zz}}{dz}\end{aligned}\right\}\quad\text{..............(1).}$$

Substituting the values of p_{xx}, p_{xy}, ... from Art. 284 (4), (5), we find

$$\left.\begin{aligned}\rho\frac{Du}{Dt}&=\rho X-\frac{dp}{dx}+\tfrac{1}{3}\mu\frac{d\theta}{dx}+\mu\nabla^2 u,\\ \rho\frac{Dv}{Dt}&=\rho Y-\frac{dp}{dy}+\tfrac{1}{3}\mu\frac{d\theta}{dy}+\mu\nabla^2 v,\\ \rho\frac{Dw}{Dt}&=\rho Z-\frac{dp}{dz}+\tfrac{1}{3}\mu\frac{d\theta}{dz}+\mu\nabla^2 w\end{aligned}\right\}\quad\text{...........(2),}$$

where

$$\theta=\frac{du}{dx}+\frac{dv}{dy}+\frac{dw}{dz}\quad\text{......................(3),}$$

and ∇^2 has its usual meaning.

When the fluid is incompressible, these reduce to

$$\left.\begin{aligned}\rho\frac{Du}{Dt}&=\rho X-\frac{dp}{dx}+\mu\nabla^2 u,\\ \rho\frac{Dv}{Dt}&=\rho Y-\frac{dp}{dy}+\mu\nabla^2 v,\\ \rho\frac{Dw}{Dt}&=\rho Z-\frac{dp}{dz}+\mu\nabla^2 w\end{aligned}\right\}\quad\text{..................(4).}$$

These dynamical equations were first obtained by Navier* and Poisson† on various considerations as to the mutual action of the ultimate molecules of fluids. The method above adopted, which is free from all hypothesis of this kind, appears to be due in principle to de Saint-Venant and Stokes‡.

* "Mémoire sur les Lois du Mouvement des Fluides," *Mém. de l'Acad. des Sciences*, t. vi. (1822).

† "Mémoire sur les Équations générales de l'Équilibre et du Mouvement des Corps solides élastiques et des Fluides," *Journ. de l'École Polytechn.*, t. xiii. (1829).

‡ "On the Theories of the Internal Friction of Fluids in Motion, &c.," *Camb. Trans.*, t. viii. (1845); *Math. and Phys. Papers*, t. i., p. 88.

The equations (4) admit of an interesting interpretation. The first of them, for example, may be written

$$\frac{Du}{Dt}=X-\frac{1}{\rho}\frac{dp}{dx}+\nu\nabla^2 u \quad\text{.............................. (i).}$$

The first two terms on the right hand express the rate of variation of u in consequence of the external forces and of the instantaneous distribution of pressure, and have the same forms as in the case of a frictionless liquid. The remaining term $\nu\nabla^2 u$, due to viscosity, gives an additional variation following the same law as that of temperature in Thermal Conduction, or of density in the theory of Diffusion. This variation is in fact proportional to the (positive or negative) excess of the mean value of u through a small sphere of given radius surrounding the point (x, y, z) over its value at that point*. In connection with this analogy it is interesting to note that the value of ν for water is of the same order of magnitude as that (·01249) found by Dr Everett for the thermometric conductivity of the Greenwich gravel.

When the forces X, Y, Z have a potential Ω, the equations (4) may be written

$$\left.\begin{aligned}\frac{du}{dt}-2v\zeta+2w\eta&=-\frac{d\chi'}{dx}+\nu\nabla^2 u,\\ \frac{dv}{dt}-2w\xi+2u\zeta&=-\frac{d\chi'}{dy}+\nu\nabla^2 v,\\ \frac{dw}{dt}-2u\eta+2v\xi&=-\frac{d\chi'}{dz}+\nu\nabla^2 w\end{aligned}\right\}\quad\text{..................... (ii),}$$

where

$$\chi'=\frac{p}{\rho}+\tfrac{1}{2}q^2+\Omega \quad\text{................................ (iii),}$$

q denoting the resultant velocity, and ξ, η, ζ the components of the angular velocity of the fluid. If we eliminate χ' by cross-differentiation, we find,

$$\left.\begin{aligned}\frac{D\xi}{Dt}&=\xi\frac{du}{dx}+\eta\frac{du}{dy}+\zeta\frac{du}{dz}+\nu\nabla^2\xi,\\ \frac{D\eta}{Dt}&=\xi\frac{dv}{dx}+\eta\frac{dv}{dy}+\zeta\frac{dv}{dz}+\nu\nabla^2\eta,\\ \frac{D\zeta}{Dt}&=\xi\frac{dw}{dx}+\eta\frac{dw}{dy}+\zeta\frac{dw}{dz}+\nu\nabla^2\zeta\end{aligned}\right\}\quad\text{..................... (iv).}$$

The first three terms on the right hand of each of these equations express, as in Art. 143, the rates at which ξ, η, ζ vary for a particle, when the vortex-lines move with the fluid, and the strengths of the vortices remain constant. The additional variation of these quantities, due to viscosity, is given by the last terms, and follows the law of conduction of heat. It is evident from this analogy that vortex-motion cannot originate in the interior of a viscous liquid, but must be diffused inwards from the boundary.

* Maxwell, *Proc. Lond. Math. Soc.*, t. iii., p. 230; *Electricity and Magnetism*, Art. 26.

287. To compute the rate of dissipation of energy, due to viscosity, we consider first the portion of fluid which at time t occupies a rectangular element $\delta x \delta y \delta z$ having its centre at (x, y, z). Calculating the differences of the rates at which work is being done by the tractions on the pairs of opposite faces, we obtain

$$\left\{\frac{d}{dx}(p_{xx}u + p_{xy}v + p_{xz}w) + \frac{d}{dy}(p_{yx}u + p_{yy}v + p_{yz}w) + \frac{d}{dz}(p_{zx}u + p_{zy}v + p_{zz}w)\right\}\delta x \delta y \delta z \quad \text{.............(1).}$$

The terms

$$\left\{\left(\frac{dp_{xx}}{dx} + \frac{dp_{yx}}{dy} + \frac{dp_{zx}}{dz}\right)u + \left(\frac{dp_{xy}}{dx} + \frac{dp_{yy}}{dy} + \frac{dp_{zy}}{dz}\right)v + \left(\frac{dp_{xz}}{dx} + \frac{dp_{yz}}{dy} + \frac{dp_{zz}}{dz}\right)w\right\}\delta x \delta y \delta z \quad \text{...... (2)}$$

express, by Art. 286 (1), the rate at which the tractions on the faces are doing work on the element as a whole, in increasing its kinetic energy and in compensating the work done against the extraneous forces X, Y, Z. The remaining terms express the rate at which work is being done in changing the volume and shape of the element. They may be written

$$(p_{xx}a + p_{yy}b + p_{zz}c + 2p_{yz}f + 2p_{zx}g + 2p_{xy}h)\,\delta x \delta y \delta z \quad \text{...(3),}$$

where a, b, c, f, g, h have the same meanings as in Arts. 31, 284. Substituting from Art. 284 (2), (3), we get

$$-p(a+b+c)\,\delta x \delta y \delta z$$
$$+\{-\tfrac{2}{3}\mu(a+b+c)^2 + 2\mu(a^2+b^2+c^2+2f^2+2g^2+2h^2)\}\,\delta x \delta y \delta z \quad \text{......(4).}$$

If p be a function of ρ only, the first line of this is equal to

$$DE/Dt\,.\,\rho\delta x \delta y \delta z,$$

provided

$$E = -\int p\,d\left(\frac{1}{\rho}\right) \quad \text{........................(5),}$$

i.e. E denotes, as in Art. 11, the intrinsic energy per unit mass. Hence the second line of (4) represents the rate at which energy is being dissipated. On the principles established by Joule, the mechanical energy thus lost takes the form of heat, developed in the element.

If we integrate over the whole volume of the fluid, we find, for the total rate of dissipation,

$$2F = \iiint \Phi \, dx\,dy\,dz \quad\text{.......................(6)},$$

where

$$\Phi = -\tfrac{2}{3}\mu\left(\frac{du}{dx}+\frac{dv}{dy}+\frac{dw}{dz}\right)^2$$
$$+\mu\left\{2\left(\frac{du}{dx}\right)^2+2\left(\frac{dv}{dy}\right)^2+2\left(\frac{dw}{dz}\right)^2\right.$$
$$\left.+\left(\frac{dw}{dy}+\frac{dv}{dz}\right)^2+\left(\frac{du}{dz}+\frac{dw}{dx}\right)^2+\left(\frac{dv}{dx}+\frac{du}{dy}\right)^2\right\}\text{.....(7)*}.$$

If we write this in the form

$$\Phi = \tfrac{2}{3}\mu\{(b-c)^2+(c-a)^2+(a-b)^2\}+4\mu(f^2+g^2+h^2)\text{...........(i)},$$

it appears that F cannot vanish unless

$$a=b=c, \text{ and } f=g=h=0,$$

at every point of the fluid. In the case of an incompressible fluid it is necessary that the quantities a, b, c, f, g, h should all vanish. It easily follows, on reference to Art. 31, that the only condition under which a liquid can be in motion without dissipation of energy by viscosity is that there must be nowhere any extension or contraction of linear elements; in other words, the motion must be composed of a translation and a pure rotation, as in the case of a rigid body. In the case of a gas there may be superposed on this an expansion or contraction which is the same in all directions.

We now consider specially the case when the fluid is incompressible, so that

$$\Phi = \left\{2\left(\frac{du}{dx}\right)^2+2\left(\frac{dv}{dy}\right)^2+2\left(\frac{dw}{dz}\right)^2\right.$$
$$\left.+\left(\frac{dw}{dy}+\frac{dv}{dz}\right)^2+\left(\frac{du}{dz}+\frac{dw}{dx}\right)^2+\left(\frac{dv}{dx}+\frac{du}{dy}\right)^2\right\}\text{.........(ii)}.$$

If we subtract from this the expression

$$2\mu\left(\frac{du}{dx}+\frac{dv}{dy}+\frac{dw}{dz}\right)^2,$$

which is zero, we obtain

$$\Phi = \mu\left\{\left(\frac{dw}{dy}-\frac{dv}{dz}\right)^2+\left(\frac{du}{dz}-\frac{dw}{dx}\right)^2+\left(\frac{dv}{dx}-\frac{du}{dy}\right)^2\right\}$$
$$-4\mu\left(\frac{dv}{dy}\frac{dw}{dz}-\frac{dv}{dz}\frac{dw}{dy}+\frac{dw}{dz}\frac{du}{dx}-\frac{dw}{dx}\frac{du}{dz}+\frac{du}{dx}\frac{dv}{dy}-\frac{du}{dy}\frac{dv}{dx}\right)\text{... (iii)}.$$

* Stokes, "On the Effect of the Internal Friction of Fluids on the Motion of Pendulums," *Camb. Trans.*, t. ix., p. [58] (1851).

If we integrate this over a region such that u, v, w vanish at every point of the boundary, as in the case of a liquid filling a closed vessel, on the hypothesis of no slipping, the terms due to the second line vanish (after a partial integration), and we obtain

$$2F = \iiint \Phi\, dx\, dy\, dz = 4\mu \iiint (\xi^2 + \eta^2 + \zeta^2)\, dx\, dy\, dz \qquad \text{(iv)*}.$$

In the general case, when no limitation is made as to the boundary conditions, the formula (iii) leads to

$$2F = 4\mu \iiint (\xi^2 + \eta^2 + \zeta^2)\, dx\, dy\, dz - \mu \iint \frac{d \cdot q^2}{dn} dS$$

$$+ 4\mu \iiint \begin{vmatrix} l, & m, & n, \\ u, & v, & w, \\ \xi, & \eta, & \zeta, \end{vmatrix} dS \qquad \text{(v)},$$

where, in the former of the two surface-integrals, δn denotes an element of the normal, and, in the latter, l, m, n are the direction-cosines of the normal, drawn inwards in each case from the surface-element δS.

When the motion considered is irrotational, this formula reduces to

$$2F = -\mu \iint \frac{d \cdot q^2}{dn} dS \qquad \text{(vi)},$$

simply. In the particular case of a spherical boundary this expression follows independently from Art. 44 (i).

Problems of Steady Motion.

288. The first application which we shall consider is to the steady motion of liquid, under pressure, between two fixed parallel planes, the flow being supposed to take place in parallel lines.

Let the origin be taken half-way between the planes, and the axis of y perpendicular to them. We assume that u is a function of y only, and that v, $w = 0$. Since the traction parallel to x on any plane perpendicular to y is equal to $\mu\, du/dy$, the difference of the tractions on the two faces of a stratum of unit area and thickness δy gives a resultant $\mu\, d^2u/dy^2 \cdot \delta y$. This must be balanced by the normal pressures, which give a resultant $-dp/dx$ per unit volume of the stratum. Hence

$$\mu \frac{d^2u}{dy^2} = \frac{dp}{dx} \qquad \text{(1)}.$$

* Bobyleff, "Einige Betrachtungen über die Gleichungen der Hydrodynamik," *Math. Ann.*, t. vi. (1873); Forsyth, "On the Motion of a Viscous Incompressible Fluid," *Mess. of Math.*, t. ix. (1880).

Also, since there is no motion parallel to y, dp/dy must vanish. These results might of course have been obtained immediately from the general equations of Art. 286.

It follows that the pressure-gradient dp/dx is an absolute constant. Hence (1) gives

$$u = A + By + \frac{1}{2\mu} y^2 \frac{dp}{dx} \quad \text{.................} \quad (2),$$

and determining the constants so as to make $u = 0$ for $y = \pm h$, we find

$$u = -\frac{1}{2\mu}(h^2 - y^2)\frac{dp}{dx} \quad \text{.....................} (3).$$

Hence

$$\int_{-h}^{h} u\,dy = -\frac{2h^3}{3\mu}\frac{dp}{dx} \quad \text{....................} \quad (4).$$

289. The investigation of the steady flow of a liquid through a straight pipe of uniform circular section is equally simple, and physically more important.

If we take the axis of z coincident with the axis of the tube, and assume that the velocity is everywhere parallel to z, and a function of the distance (r) from this axis, the tangential stress across a plane perpendicular to r will be $\mu dw/dr$. Hence, considering a cylindrical shell of fluid, whose bounding radii are r and $r + \delta r$, and whose length is l, the difference of the tangential tractions on the two curved surfaces gives a retarding force

$$-\frac{d}{dr}\left(\mu \frac{dw}{dr} \, . \, 2\pi r l\right) \delta r.$$

On account of the steady character of the motion, this must be balanced by the normal pressures on the ends of the shell. Since $dw/dz = 0$, the difference of these normal pressures is equal to

$$(p_1 - p_2)\, 2\pi r \delta r,$$

where p_1, p_2 are the values of p (the mean pressure) at the two ends. Hence

$$\frac{d}{dr}\left(r\frac{dw}{dr}\right) = -\frac{p_1 - p_2}{\mu l} \, . \, r \quad \text{.................} (1).$$

Again, if we resolve along the radius the forces acting on a rectangular element, we find $dp/dr = 0$, so that the mean pressure is uniform over each section of the pipe.

The equation (1) might have been obtained from Art. 286 (4) by direct transformation of coordinates, putting

$$r = (x^2 + y^2)^{\frac{1}{2}}.$$

The integral of (1) is

$$w = -\frac{p_1 - p_2}{4\mu l} r^2 + A \log r + B \text{ .... } (2).$$

Since the velocity must be finite at the axis, we must have $A = 0$; and if we determine B on the hypothesis that there is no slipping at the wall of the pipe ($r = a$, say), we obtain

$$w = \frac{p_1 - p_2}{4\mu l}(a^2 - r^2) \text{ .... } (3).$$

This gives, for the flux across any section,

$$\int_0^a w \, . \, 2\pi r dr = \frac{\pi a^4}{8\mu} \, . \, \frac{p_1 - p_2}{l} \text{ .... } (4).$$

It has been assumed, for shortness, that the flow takes place under pressure only. If we have an extraneous force X acting parallel to the length of the pipe, the flux will be

$$\frac{\pi a^4}{8\mu}\left(\frac{p_1 - p_2}{l} + \rho X\right) \text{ .... } (5).$$

In practice, X is the component of gravity in the direction of the length.

The formula (4) contains exactly the laws found experimentally by Poiseuille* in his researches on the flow of water through capillary tubes; viz. that the time of efflux of a given volume of water is directly as the length of the tube, inversely as the difference of pressure at the two ends, and inversely as the fourth power of the diameter.

This last result is of great importance as furnishing a conclusive proof that there is in these experiments no appreciable slipping of the fluid in contact with the wall. If we were to assume a slipping-coefficient β, as explained in Art. 285, the surface-condition would be

$$-\mu dw/dr = \beta w,$$

or

$$w = -\lambda dw/dr \text{ .... } \text{(i)},$$

* "Recherches expérimentales sur le mouvement des liquides dans les tubes de très petits diamètres," *Comptes Rendus*, tt. xi., xii. (1840–1), *Mém. des Sav. Étrangers*, t. ix. (1846).

if $\lambda=\mu/\beta$. This determines B, in (2), so that

$$w=\frac{p_1-p_2}{4\mu l}(a^2-r^2+2\lambda a)\qquad\text{(ii)}.$$

If λ/a be small, this gives sensibly the same law of velocity as in a tube of radius $a+\lambda$, on the hypothesis of no slipping. The corresponding value of the flux is

$$\frac{\pi a^4}{8\mu}\cdot\frac{p_1-p_2}{l}\cdot\left(1+4\frac{\lambda}{a}\right)\qquad\text{(iii)}.$$

If λ were more than a very minute fraction of a in the narrowest tubes employed by Poiseuille [$a=\cdot0015$ cm.] a deviation from the law of the fourth power of the diameter, which was found to hold very exactly, would become apparent. This is sufficient to exclude the possibility of values of λ such as $\cdot235$ cm., which were inferred by Helmholtz and Piotrowski from their experiments on the torsional oscillations of a metal globe filled with water, described in the paper already cited*.

The assumption of no slipping being thus justified, the comparison of the formula (4) with experiment gives a very direct means of determining the value of the coefficient μ for various fluids.

It is easily found from (3) and (4) that the rate of shear close to the wall of the tube is equal to $4w_0/a$, where w_0 is the mean velocity over the cross-section. As a numerical example, we may take a case given by Poiseuille, where a mean velocity of 126·6 c. s. was obtained in a tube of ·01134 cm. diameter. This makes $4w_0/a=89300$ radians per second of time.

290. Some theoretical results for sections other than circular may be briefly noticed.

1°. The solution for a channel of *annular* section is readily deduced from equation (2) of the preceding Art., with A retained. Thus if the boundary-conditions be that $w=0$ for $r=a$ and $r=b$, we find

$$w=\frac{p_1-p_2}{4\mu l}\left\{a^2-r^2+\frac{b^2-a^2}{\log b/a}\log\frac{r}{a}\right\}\qquad\text{(i)},$$

giving a flux

$$\int_a^b w\,.\,2\pi r dr=\frac{\pi}{8\mu}\cdot\frac{p_1-p_2}{l}\cdot\left\{b^4-a^4-\frac{(b^2-a^2)^2}{\log b/a}\right\}\qquad\text{(ii)}.$$

2°. It has been pointed out by Greenhill† that the analytical conditions of the present problem are similar to those which determine the motion of a frictionless liquid in a rotating prismatic vessel of the same form of section

* For a fuller discussion of this point see Whetham, "On the Alleged Slipping at the Boundary of a Liquid in Motion," *Phil. Trans.*, 1890, A.

† "On the Flow of a Viscous Liquid in a Pipe or Channel," *Proc. Lond. Math. Soc.*, t. xiii. p. 43 (1881).

(Art. 72). If the axis of z be parallel to the length of the pipe, and if we assume that w is a function of x, y only, then in the case of steady motion the equations reduce to

$$\left.\begin{array}{l} dp/dx=0, \quad dp/dy=0, \\ \mu\nabla_1^2 w = dp/dz \end{array}\right\} \qquad \text{(iii)},$$

where $\nabla_1^2 = d^2/dx^2 + d^2/dy^2$. Hence, denoting by P the constant pressure-gradient $(-dp/dz)$, we have

$$\nabla_1^2 w = -P/\mu \qquad \text{(iv)},$$

with the condition that $w=0$ at the boundary. If we write $\psi - \frac{1}{2}\omega(x^2+y^2)$ for w, and 2ω for P/μ, we reproduce the conditions of the Art. referred to. This proves the analogy in question.

In the case of an elliptic section of semi-axes a, b, we assume

$$w = C\left(1 - \frac{x^2}{a^2} - \frac{y^2}{b^2}\right) \qquad \text{(v)},$$

which will satisfy (iv) provided

$$C = \frac{P}{2\mu} \cdot \frac{a^2b^2}{a^2+b^2} \qquad \text{(vi)}.$$

The discharge per second is therefore

$$\iint w\,dx\,dy = \frac{P}{4\mu} \cdot \frac{\pi a^3 b^3}{a^2+b^2} \qquad \text{(vii)*}.$$

This bears to the discharge through a circular pipe of the same sectional area the ratio $2ab/(a^2+b^2)$. For small values of the eccentricity (e) this fraction differs from unity by a quantity of the order e^4. Hence considerable variations may exist in the shape of the section without seriously affecting the discharge, provided the sectional area be unaltered. Even when $a : b = 8 : 7$, the discharge is diminished by less than one per cent.

291. We consider next some simple cases of steady rotatory motion.

The first is that of two-dimensional rotation about the axis of z, the angular velocity being a function of the distance (r) from this axis. Writing

$$u = -\omega y, \quad v = \omega x, \qquad \text{(1)}$$

we find that the rates of extension along and perpendicular to the radius vector are zero, whilst the rate of shear in the plane xy is $r d\omega/dr$. Hence the moment, about the origin, of the tangential forces on a cylindrical surface of radius r, is per unit length of the axis, $= \mu r d\omega/dr \,.\, 2\pi r \,.\, r$. On account of the steady motion, the fluid included between two coaxial cylinders is neither gaining

* This, with corresponding results for other forms of section, appears to have been obtained by Boussinesq in 1868; see Hicks, *Brit. Ass. Rep.*, 1882, p. 63.

nor losing angular momentum, so that the above expression must be independent of r. This gives

$$\omega = A/r^2 + B \qquad\qquad (2).$$

If the fluid extend to infinity, while the internal boundary is that of a solid cylinder of radius a, whose angular velocity is ω_0, we have

$$\omega = \omega_0 a^2/r^2 \qquad\qquad (3).$$

The frictional couple on the cylinder is therefore

$$-4\pi\mu a^4\omega_0 \qquad\qquad (4).$$

If the fluid were bounded externally by a fixed coaxial cylindrical surface of radius b we should find

$$\omega = \frac{a^2}{r^2}\cdot\frac{b^2-r^2}{b^2-a^2}\cdot\omega_0 \qquad\qquad (5),$$

which gives a frictional couple

$$-4\pi\mu\,.\,\frac{a^4b^2}{b^2-a^2}\cdot\omega_0 \qquad\qquad (6)^*.$$

292. A similar solution, restricted however to the case of infinitely small motions, can be obtained for the steady motion of a fluid surrounding a solid sphere which is made to rotate uniformly about a diameter. Taking the centre as origin, and the axis of rotation as axis of x, we assume

$$u = -\omega y, \quad v = \omega x, \quad w = 0 \qquad\qquad (1),$$

where ω is a function of the radius vector r, only. If we put

$$P = \int \omega r dr \qquad\qquad (2),$$

these equations may be written

$$u = -dP/dy, \quad v = dP/dx, \quad w = 0 \qquad\qquad (3);$$

and it appears on substitution in Art. 286 (4) that, provided we neglect the terms of the second order in the velocities, the equations are satisfied by

$$p = \text{const.}, \quad \nabla^2 P = \text{const.} \qquad\qquad (4).$$

* This problem was first treated, not quite accurately, by Newton, *Principia*, Lib. II., Prop. 51. The above results were given substantially by Stokes, *l. c. ante*, p. 515.

The latter equation may be written

$$\frac{d^2P}{dr^2}+\frac{2}{r}\frac{dP}{dr}=\text{const.},$$

or

$$r\frac{d\omega}{dr}+3\omega=\text{const.} \quad\text{.................... (5),}$$

whence

$$\omega=A/r^3+B \quad\text{.................... (6).}$$

If the fluid extend to infinity and is at rest there, whilst ω_0 is the angular velocity of the rotating sphere ($r=a$), we have

$$\omega=\frac{a^3}{r^3}\,\omega_0 \quad\text{.................... (7).}$$

If the external boundary be a fixed concentric sphere of radius b the solution is

$$\omega=\frac{a^3}{r^3}\cdot\frac{b^3-r^3}{b^3-a^3}\cdot\omega_0 \quad\text{.................... (8).}$$

The retarding couple on the sphere may be calculated directly by means of the formulæ of Art. 284, or, perhaps more simply, by means of the Dissipation Function of Art. 287. We find without difficulty that the rate of dissipation of energy

$$=\mu\iiint(x^2+y^2)\left(\frac{d\omega}{dr}\right)^2 dx\,dy\,dz$$

$$=\tfrac{8}{3}\pi\mu\int_a^b r^4\left(\frac{d\omega}{dr}\right)^2 dr$$

$$=8\pi\mu\frac{a^3b^3}{b^3-a^3}\,\omega_0^2 \quad\text{.................... (9).}$$

If N denote the couple which must be applied to the sphere to maintain the rotation, this expression must be equivalent to $N\omega_0$, whence

$$N=8\pi\mu\frac{a^3b^3}{b^3-a^3}\,\omega_0 \quad\text{.................... (10),}$$

or, in the case corresponding to (7), where $b=\infty$,

$$N=8\pi\mu a^3\omega_0 \quad\text{.................... (11).*}$$

The neglect of the terms of the second order in this problem involves a more serious limitation of its practical value than might be expected. It is not difficult to ascertain that the assumption virtually made is that the ratio

* Kirchhoff, *Mechanik*, c. xxvi.

$\omega_0 a^2/\nu$ is small. If we put $\nu = \cdot 018$ (water), and $a = 10$, we find that the equatorial velocity $\omega_0 a$ must be small compared with ·0018 (c. s.)*.

When the terms of the second order are sensible, no steady motion of this kind is possible. The sphere then acts like a centrifugal fan, the motion at a distance from the sphere consisting of a flow outwards from the equator and inwards towards the poles, superposed on a motion of rotation†.

It appears from Art. 286 that the equations of motion may be written

$$\frac{du}{dt} - 2v\zeta + 2w\eta = X - \frac{d\chi'}{dx} + \nu\nabla^2 u, \text{ \&c., \&c.} \qquad \text{(i)},$$

where

$$\chi' = p/\rho + \tfrac{1}{2}q^2 \qquad \text{(ii)}.$$

Hence a steady motion which satisfies the conditions of any given problem, when the terms of the second order are neglected, will hold when these are retained, provided we introduce the constraining forces

$$X = 2(w\eta - v\zeta), \quad Y = 2(u\zeta - w\xi), \quad Z = 2(v\xi - u\eta) \qquad \text{(iii)‡}.$$

The only change is that the pressure p is diminished by $\frac{1}{2}\rho q^2$. These forces are everywhere perpendicular to the stream-lines and to the vortex-lines, and their intensity is given by the product $2q\omega \sin\chi$, where ω is the angular velocity of the fluid element, and χ is the angle between the direction of q and the axis of ω.

In the problem investigated in this Art. it is evident *à priori* that the constraining forces

$$X = -\omega^2 x, \quad Y = -\omega^2 y, \quad Z = 0 \qquad \text{(iv)}.$$

would make the solution rigorous. It may easily be verified that these expressions differ from (iii) by terms of the forms $-d\Omega/dx$, $-d\Omega/dy$, $-d\Omega/dz$, respectively, which will only modify the pressure.

293. The motion of a viscous incompressible fluid, when the effects of inertia are insensible, can be treated in a very general manner, in terms of spherical harmonic functions.

It will be convenient, in the first place, to investigate the general solution of the following system of equations:

$$\nabla^2 u' = 0, \quad \nabla^2 v' = 0, \quad \nabla^2 w' = 0 \qquad \text{(1)},$$

$$\frac{du'}{dx} + \frac{dv'}{dy} + \frac{dw'}{dz} = 0 \qquad \text{(2)}.$$

* Cf. Lord Rayleigh, "On the Flow of Viscous Liquids, especially in Two Dimensions," *Phil. Mag.*, Oct. 1893.

† Stokes, *l. c. ante*, p. 515.

‡ Lord Rayleigh, *l. c.*

The functions u', v', w' may be expanded in series of solid harmonics, and it is plain that the terms of algebraical degree n in these expansions, say u_n', v_n', w_n', must separately satisfy (2). The equations $\nabla^2 u_n' = 0$, $\nabla^2 v_n' = 0$, $\nabla^2 w_n' = 0$ may therefore be put in the forms

$$\left.\begin{aligned} \frac{d}{dy}\left(\frac{dv_n'}{dx} - \frac{du_n'}{dy}\right) &= \frac{d}{dz}\left(\frac{du_n'}{dz} - \frac{dw_n'}{dx}\right), \\ \frac{d}{dz}\left(\frac{dw_n'}{dy} - \frac{dv_n'}{dz}\right) &= \frac{d}{dx}\left(\frac{dv_n'}{dx} - \frac{du_n'}{dy}\right), \\ \frac{d}{dx}\left(\frac{du_n'}{dz} - \frac{dw_n'}{dx}\right) &= \frac{d}{dy}\left(\frac{dw_n'}{dy} - \frac{dv_n'}{dz}\right) \end{aligned}\right\} \quad \text{.........} \ (3).$$

Hence

$$\frac{dw_n'}{dy} - \frac{dv_n'}{dz} = \frac{d\chi_n}{dx}, \quad \frac{du_n'}{dz} - \frac{dw_n'}{dx} = \frac{d\chi_n}{dy}, \quad \frac{dv_n'}{dx} - \frac{du_n'}{dy} = \frac{d\chi_n}{dz} \ \ldots(4),$$

where χ_n is some function of x, y, z; and it further appears from these relations that $\nabla^2 \chi_n = 0$, so that χ_n is a solid harmonic of degree n.

From (4) we also obtain

$$z\frac{d\chi_n}{dy} - y\frac{d\chi_n}{dz} = x\frac{du_n'}{dx} + y\frac{du_n'}{dy} + z\frac{du_n'}{dz} + u_n'$$
$$- \frac{d}{dx}(xu_n' + yv_n' + zw_n') \ldots (5),$$

with two similar equations. Now it follows from (1) and (2) that

$$\nabla^2 (xu_n' + yv_n' + zw_n') = 0 \ \ldots\ldots\ldots\ldots\ldots\ldots \ (6),$$

so that we may write

$$xu_n' + yv_n' + zw_n' = \phi_{n+1} \ \ldots\ldots\ldots\ldots\ldots\ldots \ (7),$$

where ϕ_{n+1} is a solid harmonic of degree $n+1$. Hence (5) may be written

$$(n+1)\,u_n' = \frac{d\phi_{n+1}}{dx} + z\frac{d\chi_n}{dy} - y\frac{d\chi_n}{dz} \ \ldots\ldots\ldots\ldots \ (8).$$

The factor $n+1$ may be dropped without loss of generality; and we obtain as the solution of the proposed system of equations:

$$\left.\begin{aligned}u' &= \Sigma\left(\frac{d\phi_n}{dx} + z\frac{d\chi_n}{dy} - y\frac{d\chi_n}{dz}\right),\\ v' &= \Sigma\left(\frac{d\phi_n}{dy} + x\frac{d\chi_n}{dz} - z\frac{d\chi_n}{dx}\right),\\ w' &= \Sigma\left(\frac{d\phi_n}{dz} + y\frac{d\chi_n}{dx} - x\frac{d\chi_n}{dy}\right)\end{aligned}\right\} \quad\ldots\ldots\ldots\ldots (9),$$

where the harmonics ϕ_n, χ_n are arbitrary*.

294. If we neglect the inertia-terms, the equations of motion of a viscous liquid reduce, in the absence of extraneous forces, to the forms

$$\mu\nabla^2 u = \frac{dp}{dx}, \quad \mu\nabla^2 v = \frac{dp}{dy}, \quad \mu\nabla^2 w = \frac{dp}{dz} \ldots\ldots\ldots\ldots (1),$$

with

$$\frac{du}{dx} + \frac{dv}{dy} + \frac{dw}{dz} = 0 \ldots\ldots\ldots\ldots (2).$$

By differentiation we obtain

$$\nabla^2 p = 0 \ldots\ldots\ldots\ldots (3),$$

so that p can be expanded in a series of solid harmonics, thus

$$p = \Sigma p_n \ldots\ldots\ldots\ldots (4).$$

The terms of the solution involving harmonics of different algebraical degrees will be independent. To obtain the terms in p_n we assume

$$\left.\begin{aligned}u &= Ar^2\frac{dp_n}{dx} + Br^{2n+3}\frac{d}{dx}\frac{p_n}{r^{2n+1}},\\ v &= Ar^2\frac{dp_n}{dy} + Br^{2n+3}\frac{d}{dy}\frac{p_n}{r^{2n+1}},\\ w &= Ar^2\frac{dp_n}{dz} + Br^{2n+3}\frac{d}{dz}\frac{p_n}{r^{2n+1}}\end{aligned}\right\} \ldots\ldots\ldots\ldots (5),$$

where $r^2 = x^2 + y^2 + z^2$. The terms multiplied by B are solid harmonics of degree $n + 1$, by Arts. 82, 84. Now

$$\nabla^2\left(r^2\frac{dp_n}{dx}\right) = r^2\nabla^2\frac{dp_n}{dx} + 4\left(x\frac{d}{dx} + y\frac{d}{dy} + z\frac{d}{dz}\right)\frac{dp_n}{dx} + \frac{dp_n}{dx}\nabla^2 r^2$$

$$= 2(2n+1)\frac{dp_n}{dx}.$$

* Cf. Borchardt, "Untersuchungen über die Elasticität fester Körper unter Berücksichtigung der Wärme," *Berl. Monatsber.*, Jan. 9, 1873; *Gesammelte Werke*, Berlin, 1888, p. 245. The investigation in the text is from a paper "On the Oscillations of a Viscous Spheroid," *Proc. Lond. Math. Soc.*, t. xiii., p. 51 (1881).

Hence the equations (1) are satisfied, provided

$$A = \frac{1}{2(2n+1)\mu} \quad \ldots\ldots\ldots\ldots\ldots\ldots\ldots\ldots(6).$$

Also, substituting in (2), we find

$$2nA - (n+1)(2n+3)B = 0,$$

whence

$$B = \frac{n}{(n+1)(2n+1)(2n+3)\mu} \quad \ldots\ldots\ldots\ldots\ldots\ldots(7).$$

Hence the general solution of the system (1) and (2) is

$$\left.\begin{aligned} u &= \frac{1}{\mu}\Sigma\left\{\frac{r^2}{2(2n+1)}\frac{dp_n}{dx} + \frac{nr^{2n+3}}{(n+1)(2n+1)(2n+3)}\frac{d}{dx}\frac{p_n}{r^{2n+1}}\right\} + u', \\ v &= \frac{1}{\mu}\Sigma\left\{\frac{r^2}{2(2n+1)}\frac{dp_n}{dy} + \frac{nr^{2n+3}}{(n+1)(2n+1)(2n+3)}\frac{d}{dy}\frac{p_n}{r^{2n+1}}\right\} + v', \\ w &= \frac{1}{\mu}\Sigma\left\{\frac{r^2}{2(2n+1)}\frac{dp_n}{dz} + \frac{nr^{2n+3}}{(n+1)(2n+1)(2n+3)}\frac{d}{dz}\frac{p_n}{r^{2n+1}}\right\} + w' \end{aligned}\right\} \quad \ldots\ldots\ldots(8)^*,$$

where u', v', w' have the forms given in (9) of the preceding Art.

The formulæ (8) make

$$xu + yv + zw = \frac{1}{\mu}\Sigma\frac{nr^2}{2(2n+3)}p_n + \Sigma n\phi_n \quad \ldots\ldots\ldots\ldots(9).$$

Also, if we denote by ξ, η, ζ the components of the angular velocity of the fluid (Art. 31), we find

$$\left.\begin{aligned} 2\xi &= \frac{1}{\mu}\Sigma\frac{1}{(n+1)(2n+1)}\left(y\frac{dp_n}{dz} - z\frac{dp_n}{dy}\right) + \Sigma(n+1)\frac{d\chi_n}{dx}, \\ 2\eta &= \frac{1}{\mu}\Sigma\frac{1}{(n+1)(2n+1)}\left(z\frac{dp_n}{dx} - x\frac{dp_n}{dz}\right) + \Sigma(n+1)\frac{d\chi_n}{dy}, \\ 2\zeta &= \frac{1}{\mu}\Sigma\frac{1}{(n+1)(2n+1)}\left(x\frac{dp_n}{dy} - y\frac{dp_n}{dx}\right) + \Sigma(n+1)\frac{d\chi_n}{dz} \end{aligned}\right\} \ldots(10).$$

These make $$2(x\xi + y\eta + z\zeta) = \Sigma n(n+1)\chi_n \quad \ldots\ldots\ldots\ldots\ldots(11).$$

* This investigation is derived, with some modifications, from various sources. Cf. Thomson and Tait, *Natural Philosophy*, Art. 736; Borchardt, *l. c.*; Oberbeck, "Ueber stationäre Flüssigkeitsbewegungen mit Berücksichtigung der inneren Reibung," *Crelle*, t. lxxxi., p. 62 (1876).

295. The results of Arts. 293, 294 can be applied to the solution of a number of problems where the boundary conditions have relation to spherical surfaces. The most interesting cases fall under one or other of two classes, viz. we either have

$$xu + yv + zw = 0 \qquad (1)$$

everywhere, and therefore $p_n = 0$, $\phi_n = 0$; or

$$x\xi + y\eta + z\zeta = 0 \qquad (2),$$

and therefore $\chi_n = 0$.

1°. Let us investigate the steady motion of a liquid past a fixed spherical obstacle. If we take the origin at the centre, and the axis of x parallel to the flow, the boundary conditions are that $u=0$, $v=0$, $w=0$ for $r=a$ (the radius), and $u=\mathrm{u}$, $v=0$, $w=0$ for $r=\infty$. It is obvious that the vortex-lines will be circles about the axis of x, so that the relation (2) will be fulfilled. Again, the equation (9) of Art. 294, taken in conjunction with the condition to be satisfied at infinity, shews that as regards the functions p_n and ϕ_n we are limited to surface-harmonics of the first order, and therefore to the cases $n=1$, $n=-2$. Also, we must evidently have $p_1=0$. Assuming, then,

$$p_{-2} = A\frac{x}{r^3}, \quad \phi_1 = \mathrm{u}x, \quad \phi_{-2} = B\frac{x}{r^3} \qquad \text{(i)},$$

we find

$$\left.\begin{aligned} u &= -\frac{A}{6\mu r^3}(r^2-3x^2) + \frac{2A}{3\mu r} + \frac{B}{r^5}(r^2-3x^2) + \mathrm{u}, \\ v &= \frac{A}{2\mu r^3}xy - \frac{3B}{r^5}xy, \\ w &= \frac{A}{2\mu r^3}xz - \frac{3B}{r^5}xz \end{aligned}\right\} \qquad \text{(ii)}.$$

The condition of no slipping at the surface $r=a$ gives

$$\tfrac{1}{2}\frac{A}{\mu a} + \frac{B}{a^3} + \mathrm{u} = 0, \qquad \frac{A}{2\mu a} - \frac{3B}{a^3} = 0,$$

whence

$$A = -\tfrac{3}{2}\mu\mathrm{u}a, \quad B = -\tfrac{1}{4}\mathrm{u}a^3 \qquad \text{(iii)}.$$

Hence

$$\left.\begin{aligned} u &= -\tfrac{3}{4}\frac{\mathrm{u}a}{r^3}\left(1-\frac{a^2}{r^2}\right)x^2 + \mathrm{u}\left(1-\tfrac{3}{4}\frac{a}{r}-\tfrac{1}{4}\frac{a^3}{r^3}\right), \\ v &= -\tfrac{3}{4}\frac{\mathrm{u}a}{r^3}\left(1-\frac{a^2}{r^2}\right)xy, \\ w &= -\tfrac{3}{4}\frac{\mathrm{u}a}{r^3}\left(1-\frac{a^2}{r^2}\right)xz \end{aligned}\right\} \qquad \text{(iv)}.$$

These make

$$xu + yv + zw = \mathrm{u}\left(1-\tfrac{3}{2}\frac{a}{r}+\tfrac{1}{2}\frac{a^3}{r^3}\right)x \qquad \text{(v)},$$

$$\xi = 0, \quad \eta = -\tfrac{1}{2}\frac{\mathrm{u}a}{r^3}z, \quad \zeta = \tfrac{1}{2}\frac{\mathrm{u}a}{r^3}y \qquad \text{(vi)}.$$

The components of stress across the surface of a sphere of radius r are, by Art. 283,

$$\left.\begin{aligned} p_{rx} &= \frac{x}{r}p_{xx} + \frac{y}{r}p_{xy} + \frac{z}{r}p_{xz}, \\ p_{ry} &= \frac{x}{r}p_{yx} + \frac{y}{r}p_{yy} + \frac{z}{r}p_{yz}, \\ p_{rz} &= \frac{x}{r}p_{zx} + \frac{y}{r}p_{zy} + \frac{z}{r}p_{zz} \end{aligned}\right\} \quad\text{.........................(vii).}$$

If we substitute the values of $p_{xx}, p_{xy}, p_{xz}, \ldots$, from Art. 284, we find

$$\left.\begin{aligned} xp_{xx} + yp_{xy} + zp_{xz} &= -xp + \mu\left(r\frac{d}{dr} - 1\right)u + \mu\frac{d}{dx}(xu + yv + zw), \\ xp_{yx} + yp_{yy} + zp_{yz} &= -yp + \mu\left(r\frac{d}{dr} - 1\right)v + \mu\frac{d}{dy}(xu + yv + zw), \\ xp_{zx} + yp_{zy} + zp_{zz} &= -zp + \mu\left(r\frac{d}{dr} - 1\right)w + \mu\frac{d}{dz}(xu + yv + zw) \end{aligned}\right\} \quad\text{...(viii)}$$

In the present case we have

$$p = p_0 + p_{-2} = p_0 - \tfrac{3}{2}\frac{\mu \mathrm{u} a}{r^3}x \quad\text{...........................(ix).}$$

We thus obtain, for the component tractions on the sphere $r=a$,

$$p_{rx} = -\frac{x}{a}p_0 + \tfrac{3}{2}\frac{\mu \mathrm{u}}{a}, \quad p_{ry} = -\frac{y}{a}p_0, \quad p_{rz} = -\frac{z}{a}p_0 \quad\text{............ (x).}$$

If δS denote an element of the surface, we find

$$\iint p_{rx}\,dS = 6\pi\mu \mathrm{u} a, \quad \iint p_{ry}\,dS = 0, \quad \iint p_{rz}\,dS = 0 \quad\text{...............(xi).}$$

The resultant force on the sphere is therefore parallel to x, and equal to $6\pi\mu a \mathrm{u}$.

The character of the motion may be most concisely expressed by means of the stream-function of Art. 93. If we put $x = r\cos\theta$, the flux $(2\pi\psi)$ through a circle with Ox as axis, whose radius subtends an angle θ at O is given by

$$\psi = -\tfrac{1}{2}\mathrm{u}\left(1 - \tfrac{3}{2}\frac{a}{r} + \tfrac{1}{2}\frac{a^3}{r^3}\right)r^2\sin^2\theta \quad\text{.................. (xii),}$$

as is evident at once from (v).

If we impress on everything a velocity $-\mathrm{u}$ in the direction of x, we get the case of a sphere moving steadily through a viscous fluid which is at rest at infinity. The stream-function is then

$$\psi = \tfrac{3}{4}\mathrm{u} a r\left(1 - \tfrac{1}{3}\frac{a^2}{r^2}\right)\sin^2\theta \quad\text{.......................(xiii)*.}$$

The diagram on p. 532, shews the stream-lines $\psi = \text{const.}$, in this case, for a series of equidistant values of ψ. The contrast with the case of a frictionless liquid, depicted on p. 137, is remarkable, but it must be remembered that the

* This problem was first solved by Stokes, in terms of the stream-function, *l.c. ante* p. 518.

fundamental assumptions are very different. In the former case inertia was predominant, and viscosity neglected; in the present problem these circumstances are reversed.

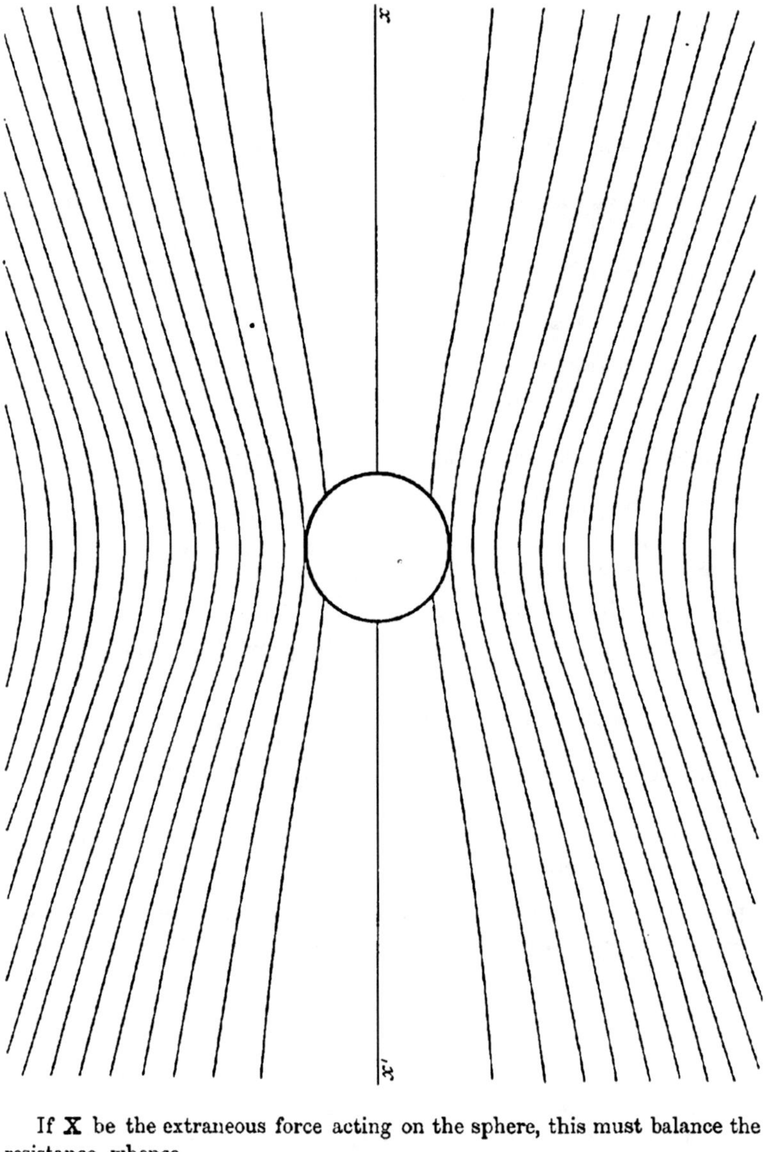

If **X** be the extraneous force acting on the sphere, this must balance the resistance, whence

$$\mathbf{X} = 6\pi\mu a \mathrm{u} \quad \text{.................................... (xiv).}$$

It is to be noticed that the formula (xiii) makes the momentum and the energy of the fluid both infinite*. The steady motion here investigated could therefore only be fully established by a constant force **X** acting on the sphere through an infinite distance.

The whole of this investigation is based on the assumption that the inertia-terms $u\,du/dx, \ldots$ in the fundamental equations (4) of Art. 286 may be neglected in comparison with $\nu\nabla^2 u, \ldots$. It easily follows from (iv) above that $\mathbf{u}a$ must be small compared with ν. This condition can always be realized by making $\mathbf{u}$ or a sufficiently small, but in the case of mobile fluids like water, this restricts us to velocities or dimensions which are, from a practical point of view, exceedingly minute. Thus even for a sphere of a millimetre radius moving through water ($\nu = \cdot 018$), the velocity must be considerably less than ·18 cm. per sec.†.

We might easily apply the formula (xiv) to find the 'terminal velocity' of a sphere falling vertically in a fluid. The force **X** is then the excess of the gravity of the sphere over its buoyancy, viz.

$$\mathbf{X} = \tfrac{4}{3}\pi(\rho_0 - \rho)\,a^3 g \quad\ldots\ldots\ldots\ldots (\text{xv}),$$

where ρ denotes the density of the fluid, and ρ_0 the mean density of the sphere. This gives

$$\mathbf{u} = \tfrac{2}{9}\frac{\rho_0 - \rho}{\mu}\,g a^2 \quad\ldots\ldots\ldots\ldots (\text{xvi}).$$

This will only apply, as already stated, provided $\mathbf{u}a/\nu$ is small. For a particle of sand descending in water, we may put (roughly)

$$\rho_0 = 2\rho, \quad \nu = \cdot 018, \quad g = 981,$$

whence it appears that a must be small compared with ·0114 cm. Subject to this condition, the terminal velocity is $\mathbf{u} = 12000\,a^2$.

For a globule of water falling through the air, we have

$$\rho_0 = 1, \quad \rho = \cdot 00129, \quad \mu = \cdot 00017.$$

This gives a terminal velocity $\mathbf{u} = 1280000\,a^2$, subject to the condition that a is small compared with ·006 cm.

2°. The problem of a rotating sphere in an infinite mass of liquid is solved by assuming

$$\left.\begin{aligned} u &= z\frac{d\chi_{-2}}{dy} - y\frac{d\chi_{-2}}{dz}, \\ v &= x\frac{d\chi_{-2}}{dz} - z\frac{d\chi_{-2}}{dx}, \\ w &= y\frac{d\chi_{-2}}{dx} - x\frac{d\chi_{-2}}{dy} \end{aligned}\right\} \quad\ldots\ldots\ldots\ldots (\text{xvii}),$$

where

$$\chi_{-2} = Az/r^3 \quad\ldots\ldots\ldots\ldots (\text{xviii}),$$

* Lord Rayleigh, *Phil. Mag.*, May 1886.

† Lord Rayleigh, *l. c. ante* p. 526.

the axis of z being that of rotation. At the surface $r=a$ we must have

$$u=-\omega y,\quad v=\omega x,\quad w=0,$$

if ω be the angular velocity of the sphere. This gives $A=\omega a^3$; cf. Art. 292.

296. The solutions of the corresponding problems for an ellipsoid can be obtained in terms of the gravitation-potential of the solid, regarded as homogeneous and of unit density.

The equation of the surface being

$$\frac{x^2}{a^2}+\frac{y^2}{b^2}+\frac{z^2}{c^2}=1 \quad\text{.................................}\quad \text{(i)},$$

the gravitation-potential is given, at external points, by Dirichlet's formula*

$$\Omega=\pi abc\int_\lambda^\infty\left(\frac{x^2}{a^2+\lambda}+\frac{y^2}{b^2+\lambda}+\frac{z^2}{c^2+\lambda}-1\right)\frac{d\lambda}{\Delta}\text{...............(ii)},$$

where

$$\Delta=\{(a^2+\lambda)(b^2+\lambda)(c^2+\lambda)\}^{\frac{1}{2}}\text{.........................(iii)},$$

and the lower limit is the positive root of

$$\frac{x^2}{a^2+\lambda}+\frac{y^2}{b^2+\lambda}+\frac{z^2}{c^2+\lambda}=1\text{...........................(iv)}.$$

This makes

$$\frac{d\Omega}{dx}=2\pi\alpha x,\quad \frac{d\Omega}{dy}=2\pi\beta y,\quad \frac{d\Omega}{dz}=2\pi\gamma z \quad\text{..................}\quad \text{(v)},$$

where

$$\alpha=abc\int_\lambda^\infty\frac{d\lambda}{(a^2+\lambda)\Delta},\quad \beta=abc\int_\lambda^\infty\frac{d\lambda}{(b^2+\lambda)\Delta},\quad \gamma=\int_\lambda^\infty\frac{d\lambda}{(c^2+\lambda)\Delta}\text{...(vi)}.$$

We will also write

$$\chi=abc\int_\lambda^\infty\frac{d\lambda}{\Delta}\quad\text{...............................}\quad \text{(vii)};$$

it has been shewn in Art. 110 that this satisfies $\nabla^2\chi=0$.

If the fluid be streaming past the ellipsoid, regarded as fixed, with the general velocity $\mathbf{u}$ in the direction of x, we assume†

$$\left.\begin{aligned}u&=A\frac{d^2\Omega}{dx^2}+B\left(x\frac{d\chi}{dx}-\chi\right)+\mathbf{u},\\ v&=A\frac{d^2\Omega}{dxdy}+Bx\frac{d\chi}{dy},\\ w&=A\frac{d^2\Omega}{dxdz}+Bx\frac{d\chi}{dz}\end{aligned}\right\}\quad\text{......................}\quad \text{(viii)}.$$

These satisfy the equation of continuity, in virtue of the relations

$$\nabla^2\Omega=0,\quad \nabla^2\chi=0;$$

* *Crelle*, t. xxxii. (1846); see also Kirchhoff, *Mechanik*, c. xviii., and Thomson and Tait, *Natural Philosophy* (2nd ed.), Art. 494 *m*.

† Oberbeck, *l.c. ante* p. 529.

and they evidently make $u=\mathrm{u}$, $v=0$, $w=0$ at infinity. Again, they make

$$\nabla^2 u = 2B\frac{d^2\chi}{dx^2},\quad \nabla^2 v = 2B\frac{d^2\chi}{dxdy},\quad \nabla^2 w = 2Bx\frac{d^2\chi}{dxdz} \quad\text{.........}\quad \text{(ix)},$$

so that the equations (1) of Art. 294 are satisfied by

$$p = 2B\mu\frac{d\chi}{dx} + \text{const.} \quad\text{..............................}\quad \text{(x)}.$$

It remains to shew by a proper choice of A, B we can make u, v, $w=0$ at the surface (i). The conditions $v=0$, $w=0$ require

$$\left[2\pi A\frac{d\alpha}{d\lambda} + B\frac{d\chi}{d\lambda}\right]_{\lambda=0} = 0,$$

or

$$2\pi A/a^2 + B = 0, \quad\text{..............................}\quad \text{(xi)}.$$

With the help of this relation, the condition $u=0$ reduces to

$$2\pi A\alpha_0 - B\chi_0 + \mathrm{u} = 0 \quad\text{..............................}\quad \text{(xii)},$$

where the suffix denotes that the lower limit in the integrals (vi) and (vii) is to be replaced by zero. Hence

$$\left.\begin{aligned} \pi A &= -\tfrac{1}{2}Ba^2, \\ B &= \frac{\mathrm{u}}{\chi_0 + \alpha_0 a^2} \end{aligned}\right\} \quad\text{..............................}\quad \text{(xiii)}.$$

At a great distance r from the origin we have

$$\Omega = -\tfrac{4}{3}\pi abc/r,\quad \chi = 2abc/r,$$

whence it appears, on comparison with the equations (iv) of the preceding Art., that the disturbance is the same as would be produced by a sphere of radius a, determined by

$$\tfrac{3}{4}\mathrm{ua} = 2abcB \quad\text{..............................}\quad \text{(xiv)},$$

or

$$\mathrm{a} = \tfrac{8}{3}\frac{abc}{\chi_0 + \alpha_0 a^2} \quad\text{..............................}\quad \text{(xv)}.$$

The resistance experienced by the ellipsoid will therefore be

$$6\pi\mu\mathrm{au} \quad\text{..............................}\quad \text{(xvi)}.$$

In the case of a circular disk moving broadside-on, we have $a=0$, $b=c$; whence $\alpha_0=2$, $\chi_0=\pi ac$, so that

$$\mathrm{a} = \frac{8}{3\pi}c = \cdot 85\,c.$$

We must not delay longer over problems which, for reasons already given, have hardly any real application except to fluids of extremely great viscosity. We can therefore only advert to the mathematically very elegant investigations which have been given of the steady rotation of an ellipsoid*, and of the flow

* Edwardes, *Quart. Journ. Math.*, t. xxvi., pp. 70, 157 (1892).

through a channel bounded by a hyperboloid of revolution (of one sheet)*.

Some examples of a different kind, relating to two-dimensional steady motions in a circular cylinder, due to sources and sinks in various positions on the boundary, have been recently discussed by Lord Rayleigh†.

297. Some general theorems relating to the dissipation of energy in the steady motion of a liquid under constant extraneous forces have been given by von Helmholtz and Korteweg. They involve the assumption that the terms of the second order in the velocities may be neglected.

1°. Considering the motion in a region bounded by any closed surface Σ, let u, v, w be the component velocities in the steady motion, and $u+u'$, $v+v'$, $w+w'$ the values of the same components in any other motion subject only to the condition that u', v', w' vanish at all points of the boundary Σ. By Art. 287 (3), the dissipation in the altered motion is equal to

$$\iiint\{(p_{xx}+p'_{xx})(a+a')+\ldots+\ldots+2(p_{yz}+p'_{yz})(f+f')+\ldots+\ldots\}\,dx\,dy\,dz \ldots\text{(i)},$$

where the accent attached to any symbol indicates the value which the function in question assumes when u, v, w are replaced by u', v', w'. Now the formulæ (2), (3) of Art. 284 shew that, in the case of an incompressible fluid,

$$p_{xx}a'+p_{yy}b'+p_{zz}c'+2p_{yz}f'+2p_{zx}g'+2p_{xy}h'$$
$$=p'_{xx}a+p'_{yy}b+p'_{zz}c+2p'_{yz}f+2p'_{zx}g+2p'_{xy}h \ldots\ldots\text{(ii)},$$

each side being a symmetric function of a, b, c, f, g, h and a', b', c', f', g', h'. Hence, and by Art. 287, the expression (i) reduces to

$$\iiint\Phi\,dx\,dy\,dz+\iiint\Phi'\,dx\,dy\,dz+2\iiint(p_{xx}a'+p_{yy}b'+p_{zz}c'$$
$$+2p_{yz}f'+2p_{zx}g'+2p_{xy}h')\,dx\,dy\,dz \ldots\ldots\text{(iii)}.$$

The last integral may be written

$$\iiint\left(p_{xx}\frac{du'}{dx}+p_{xy}\frac{du'}{dy}+p_{xz}\frac{du'}{dz}+\ldots+\ldots\right)dx\,dy\,dz \ldots\ldots\ldots \text{(iv)};$$

and by a partial integration, remembering that u', v', w' vanish at the boundary, this becomes

$$-\iiint\left\{u'\left(\frac{dp_{xx}}{dx}+\frac{dp_{xy}}{dy}+\frac{dp_{xz}}{dz}\right)+\ldots+\ldots\right\}dx\,dy\,dz \ldots\ldots\ldots \text{(v)},$$

or

$$\iiint\rho\,(Xu'+Yv'+Zw')\,dx\,dy\,dz \ldots\ldots\ldots\ldots\ldots\ldots\ldots\ldots \text{(vi)},$$

* Sampson, *l. c. ante* p. 134.

† "On the Flow of Viscous Liquids, especially in Two Dimensions," *Phil. Mag.*, Oct. 1893.

by Art. 286. If the extraneous forces X, Y, Z have a single-valued potential, this vanishes, in virtue of the equation of continuity, by Art. 42 (4).

Under these conditions the dissipation in the altered motion is equal to

$$\iiint \Phi \, dx\,dy\,dz + \iiint \Phi' \, dx\,dy\,dz \qquad \text{(vii)},$$

or $2(F+F')$. That is, it exceeds the dissipation in the steady motion by the essentially positive quantity $2F'$ which represents the dissipation in the motion u', v', w'.

In other words, provided the terms of the second order in the velocities may be neglected, the steady motion of a liquid under constant forces having a single-valued potential is characterized by the property that the dissipation in any region is less than in any other motion consistent with the same values of u, v, w at the boundary.

It follows that, with prescribed velocities over the boundary, there is only one type of steady motion in the region*.

2°. If u, v, w refer to any motion whatever in the given region, we have

$$2\dot{F} = \iiint \dot{\Phi} \, dx\,dy\,dz$$
$$= 2\iiint (p_{xx}\dot{a} + p_{yy}\dot{b} + p_{zz}\dot{c} + 2p_{yz}\dot{f} + 2p_{zx}\dot{g} + 2p_{xy}\dot{h}) \, dx\,dy\,dz \qquad \text{(viii)},$$

since the formula (ii) holds when dots take the place of accents.

The treatment of this integral is the same as before. If we suppose that $\dot{u}$, $\dot{v}$, $\dot{w}$ vanish over the bounding surface Σ, we find

$$\dot{F} = -\iiint \left\{ \dot{u} \left(\frac{dp_{xx}}{dx} + \frac{dp_{xy}}{dy} + \frac{dp_{xz}}{dz} \right) + \ldots + \ldots \right\} dx\,dy\,dz$$
$$= -\rho \iiint (\dot{u}^2 + \dot{v}^2 + \dot{w}^2) \, dx\,dy\,dz + \rho \iiint (X\dot{u} + Y\dot{v} + Z\dot{w}) \, dx\,dy\,dz \qquad \text{(ix)}.$$

The latter integral vanishes when the extraneous forces have a single-valued potential, so that

$$\dot{F} = -\rho \iiint (\dot{u}^2 + \dot{v}^2 + \dot{w}^2) \, dx\,dy\,dz \qquad \text{(x)}.$$

This is essentially negative, so that F continually diminishes, the process ceasing only when $\dot{u}=0$, $\dot{v}=0$, $\dot{w}=0$, that is, when the motion has become steady.

Hence when the velocities over the boundary Σ are maintained constant, the motion in the interior will tend to become steady. The type of steady motion ultimately attained is therefore stable, as well as unique†.

It has been shewn by Lord Rayleigh‡ that the above theorem can be extended so as to apply to any dynamical system devoid of potential energy,

* Helmholtz, "Zur Theorie der stationären Ströme in reibenden Flüssigkeiten," *Verh. d. naturhist.-med. Vereins*, Oct. 30, 1868; *Wiss. Abh.*, t. i., p. 223.

† Korteweg, "On a General Theorem of the Stability of the Motion of a Viscous Fluid," *Phil. Mag.*, Aug. 1883.

‡ *l.c. ante* p. 526.

in which the kinetic energy (T) and the dissipation-function (F) can be expressed as quadratic functions of the generalized velocities, with constant coefficients.

If the extraneous forces have not a single-valued potential, or if instead of given velocities we have given tractions over the boundary, the theorems require a slight modification. The excess of the dissipation over *double* the rate at which work is being done by the extraneous forces (including the tractions on the boundary) tends to a unique minimum, which is only attained when the motion is steady*.

Periodic Motion.

298. We next examine the influence of viscosity in various problems of small oscillations.

We begin with the case of 'laminar' motion, as this will enable us to illustrate some points of great importance, without elaborate mathematics. If we assume that $v=0$, $w=0$, whilst u is a function of y only, the equations (4) of Art. 286 require that $p=$ const., and

$$\frac{du}{dt}=\nu\frac{d^2u}{dy^2}\qquad\qquad(1).$$

This has the same form as the equation of linear motion of heat. In the case of simple-harmonic motion, assuming a time-factor $e^{i(\sigma t+\epsilon)}$, we have

$$\frac{d^2u}{dy^2}=\frac{i\sigma}{\nu}u\qquad\qquad(2),$$

the solution of which is

$$u=Ae^{(1+i)\beta y}+Be^{-(1+i)\beta y}\qquad\qquad(3),$$

provided

$$\beta=(\sigma/2\nu)^{\frac{1}{2}}\qquad\qquad(4).$$

Let us first suppose that the fluid lies on the positive side of the plane xz, and that the motion is due to a prescribed oscillation

$$u=ae^{i(\sigma t+\epsilon)}\qquad\qquad(5)$$

of a rigid surface coincident with this plane. If the fluid extend to infinity in the direction of y-positive, the first term in (3) is excluded, and determining B by the boundary-condition (5), we have

$$u=ae^{-(1+i)\beta y+i(\sigma t+\epsilon)}\qquad\qquad(6),$$

* Cf. Helmholtz, *l. c.*

or, taking the real part,

$$u = ae^{-\beta y} \cos (\sigma t - \beta y + \epsilon) \quad \text{.................(7)},$$

corresponding to a prescribed motion

$$u = a \cos (\sigma t + \epsilon) \quad \text{.......................(8)}$$

at the boundary*.

The formula (7) represents a wave of transversal vibrations propagated inwards from the boundary with the velocity σ/β, but with rapidly diminishing amplitude, the falling off within a wave-length being in the ratio $e^{-2\pi}$, or $\frac{1}{535}$.

The linear magnitude

$$2\pi/\beta \text{ or } (4\pi\nu \,.\, 2\pi/\sigma)^{\frac{1}{2}}$$

is of great importance in all problems of oscillatory motion which do not involve changes of density, as indicating the extent to which the effects of viscosity penetrate into the fluid. In the case of air ($\nu = \cdot 13$) its value is $1{\cdot}28P^{\frac{1}{2}}$ centimetres, if P be the period of oscillation in seconds. For water the corresponding value is $\cdot 47P^{\frac{1}{2}}$. We shall have further illustrations, presently, of the fact that the influence of viscosity extends only to a short distance from the surface of a body performing small oscillations with sufficient frequency.

The retarding force on the rigid plane is, per unit area,

$$-\mu \left[\frac{du}{dy}\right]_{y=0} = \mu\beta a \left\{\cos(\sigma t + \epsilon) - \sin(\sigma t + \epsilon)\right\}$$

$$= \rho\nu^{\frac{1}{2}}\sigma^{\frac{1}{2}} a \cos(\sigma t + \epsilon + \tfrac{1}{4}\pi) \quad \text{..............(9)}.$$

The force has its maxima at intervals of one-eighth of a period before the oscillating plane passes through its mean position.

On the forced oscillation above investigated we may superpose any of the normal modes of free motion of which the system is capable. If we assume that

$$u \propto A \cos my + B \sin my \quad \text{..........................(i)},$$

and substitute in (1), we find

$$\frac{du}{dt} = -\nu m^2 u \quad \text{..................................(ii)},$$

whence we obtain the solution

$$u = \Sigma (A \cos my + B \sin my)\, e^{-\nu m^2 t} \quad \text{....................(iii)}.$$

* Stokes, *l.c. ante* p. 518.

The admissible values of m, and the ratios $A : B$ are as a rule determined by the boundary conditions. The arbitrary constants which remain are then to be found in terms of the initial conditions, by Fourier's methods.

In the case of a fluid extending from $y = -\infty$ to $y = +\infty$, all real values of m are admissible. The solution, in terms of the initial conditions, can in this case be immediately written down by Fourier's Theorem (Art. 227 (15)). Thus

$$u = \frac{1}{\pi}\int_0^\infty dm \int_{-\infty}^{\infty} f(\lambda) \cos m(y-\lambda) e^{-\nu m^2 t} d\lambda \quad \text{.............. (iv),}$$

if

$$u = f(y) \quad \text{.. (v)}$$

be the arbitrary initial distribution of velocity.

The integration with respect to m can be effected by the known formula

$$\int_0^\infty e^{-\alpha x^2} \cos \beta x \, dx = \tfrac{1}{2}\left(\frac{\pi}{\alpha}\right)^{\frac{1}{2}} e^{-\beta^2/4\alpha} \quad \text{..................... (vi).}$$

We thus find

$$u = \frac{1}{2(\pi\nu t)^{\frac{1}{2}}}\int_{-\infty}^{\infty} e^{-(y-\lambda)^2/4\nu t} f(\lambda)\, d\lambda \quad \text{.................... (vii).}$$

As a particular case, let us suppose that $f(y) = \pm U$, where the upper or lower sign is to be taken according as y is positive or negative. This will represent the case of an initial surface of discontinuity coincident with the plane $y=0$. After the first instant, the velocity at this surface will be zero on both sides. We find

$$u = \frac{U}{2(\pi\nu t)^{\frac{1}{2}}}\int_0^\infty \{e^{-(y-\lambda)^2/4\nu t} - e^{-(y+\lambda)^2/4\nu t}\} d\lambda \quad \text{........... (viii).}$$

By a change of variables, and easy reductions, this can be brought to the form

$$u = 2\frac{U}{\pi^{\frac{1}{2}}} \operatorname{Erf} \frac{y}{2\nu^{\frac{1}{2}} t^{\frac{1}{2}}} \quad \text{.......................... (ix)*,}$$

where in Glaisher's (revised) notation †

$$\operatorname{Erf} x = \int_0^x e^{-x^2} dx \quad \text{............................ (x).}$$

The function $2\pi^{-\frac{1}{2}} \operatorname{Erf} x$ was tabulated by Encke ‡. It appears that u will equal $\frac{1}{2}U$ when $y/2\nu^{\frac{1}{2}}t^{\frac{1}{2}} = \cdot 4769$. For water, this gives, in seconds and centimetres,

$$t = 61 \cdot 8\, y^2.$$

* Lord Rayleigh, "On the Stability, or Instability, of certain Fluid Motions," *Proc. Lond. Math. Soc.*, t. xi., p. 57 (1880).

† See *Phil. Mag.*, Dec. 1871, and *Encyc. Britann.*, Art. "Tables."

‡ *Berl. Ast. Jahrbuch*, 1834. The table has been reprinted by De Morgan, *Encyc. Metrop.*, Art. "Probabilities," and Lord Kelvin, *Math. and Phys. Papers*, t. iii., p. 434.

The corresponding result for air is

$$t = 8{\cdot}3\, y^2.$$

These results indicate how rapidly a surface of discontinuity, if it could ever be formed, would be obliterated in a viscous fluid.

The angular velocity (ω) of the fluid is given by

$$2\omega = -\frac{du}{dy} = \frac{U}{(\pi\nu t)^{\frac{1}{2}}} e^{-y^2/4\nu t} \quad\text{.......................... (xi).}$$

This represents the diffusion of the angular velocity, which is initially confined to a vortex-sheet coincident with the plane $y=0$, into the fluid on either side.

299. When the fluid does not extend to infinity, but is bounded by a fixed rigid plane $y = h$, then in determining the motion due to a forced oscillation of the plane $y = 0$ both terms of (3) are required, and the boundary conditions give

$$\left.\begin{aligned} A + B &= a, \\ Ae^{(1+i)\beta h} + Be^{-(1+i)\beta h} &= 0 \end{aligned}\right\} \quad\text{............... (10),}$$

whence $$u = a\,\frac{\sinh(1+i)\beta(h-y)}{\sinh(1+i)\beta h}\,.\,e^{i(\sigma t+\epsilon)} \quad\text{............ (11),}$$

as is easily verified. This gives for the retarding force per unit area on the oscillating plane

$$-\mu\left[\frac{du}{dy}\right]_{y=0} = \mu(1+i)\,\beta a \coth(1+i)\,\beta h\,.\,e^{i(\sigma t+\epsilon)} \quad\text{...(12).}$$

The real part of this may be reduced to the form

$$\sqrt{2}\mu\beta a\,\frac{\sinh 2\beta h\cos(\sigma t+\epsilon+\frac{1}{4}\pi)+\sin 2\beta h\sin(\sigma t+\epsilon+\frac{1}{4}\pi)}{\cosh 2\beta h-\cos 2\beta h} \quad\text{.........(13).}$$

When βh is moderately large this is equivalent to (9) above; whilst for small values of βh it reduces to

$$\mu a/h\,.\cos(\sigma t+\epsilon) \quad\text{..................... (14),}$$

as might have been foreseen.

This example contains the theory of the modification introduced by Maxwell* into Coulomb's method† of investigating the viscosity of liquids by the rotational oscillation of a circular disk in its own (horizontal) plane. The

* *l. c. ante* p. 513.

† *Mém. de l'Inst.*, t. iii. (1800).

addition of fixed parallel disks at a short distance above and below greatly increases the effect of viscosity.

The free modes of motion are expressed by (iii), with the conditions that $u=0$ for $y=0$ and $y=h$. This gives $A=0$ and $mh=s\pi$, where s is integral. The corresponding moduli of decay are then given by $\tau=1/\nu m^2$.

300. As a further example, let us take the case of a force

$$X=f\cos(\sigma t+\epsilon) \qquad (1),$$

acting uniformly on an infinite mass of water of uniform depth h.

The equation (1) of Art. 298 is now replaced by

$$\frac{du}{dt}=\nu\frac{d^2u}{dy^2}+X \qquad (2).$$

If the origin be taken in the bottom, the boundary-conditions are $u=0$ for $y=0$, and $du/dy=0$ for $y=h$; this latter condition expressing the absence of tangential force on the free surface. Replacing (1) by

$$X=fe^{i(\sigma t+\epsilon)} \qquad (3),$$

we find

$$u=-\frac{if}{\sigma}\left\{1-\frac{\cosh(1+i)\beta(h-y)}{\cosh(1+i)\beta h}\right\}e^{i(\sigma t+\epsilon)} \qquad (4),$$

if $\beta=(\sigma/2\nu)^{\frac{1}{2}}$, as before.

When βh is large, the expression in { } reduces practically to its first term for all points of the fluid whose height above the bottom exceeds a moderate multiple of β^{-1}. Hence, taking the real part,

$$u=\frac{f}{\sigma}\sin(\sigma t+\epsilon) \qquad (5).$$

This shews that the bulk of the fluid, with the exception of a stratum at the bottom, oscillates exactly like a free particle, the effect of viscosity being insensible. For points near the bottom the formula (4) becomes

$$u=-\frac{if}{\sigma}\left(1-e^{-(1+i)\beta y}\right)e^{i(\sigma t+\epsilon)} \qquad (6),$$

or, on rejecting the imaginary part,

$$u=\frac{f}{\sigma}\sin(\sigma t+\epsilon)-\frac{f}{\sigma}e^{-\beta y}\sin(\sigma t-\beta y+\epsilon) \qquad (7).$$

This might have been obtained directly, as the solution of (2) satisfying the conditions that $u = 0$ for $y = 0$, and

$$u = f/\sigma \,.\, \sin(\sigma t + \epsilon)$$

for large values of βy.

The curves A, B, C, D, E, F in the accompanying figure represent successive forms assumed by the same line of particles at intervals of one-tenth of a period. To complete the series it would be necessary to add the *images* of E, D, C, B with respect to the vertical through O. The whole system of curves may be regarded as successive aspects of a properly shaped spiral revolving uniformly about a vertical axis through O. The vertical range of the diagram is one wave-length ($2\pi/\beta$) of the laminar disturbance.

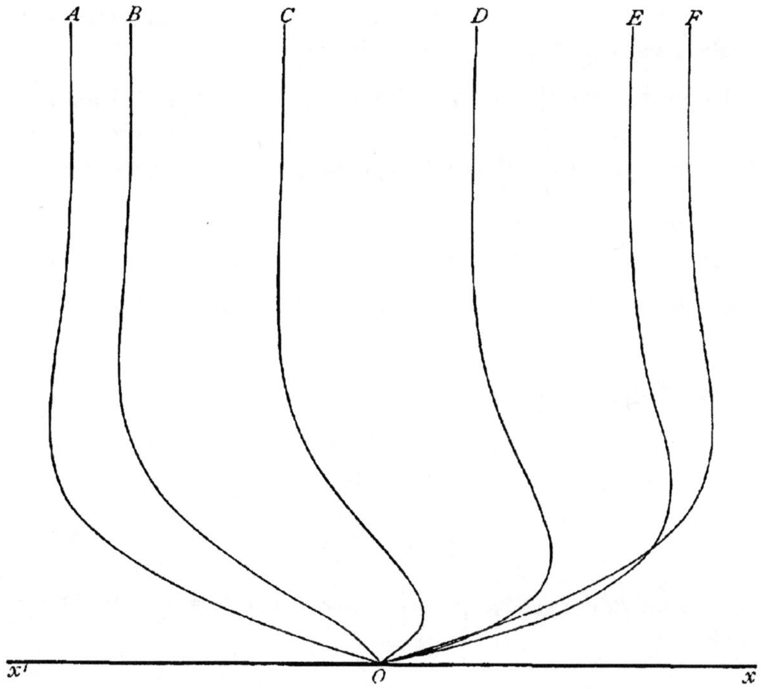

As a numerical illustration we note that if $\nu = \cdot 0178$, and $2\pi/\sigma = 12$ hours, we find $\beta^{-1} = 15\cdot 6$ centimetres. This indicates how utterly insensible must be the *direct* action of viscosity on oceanic tides. There can be no doubt that the dissipation of energy by 'tidal friction' takes place mainly through the eddying motion produced by the exaggeration of tidal currents in shallow water. Cf. Art. 310.

When βh is small the real part of (4) gives

$$u = \frac{f}{2\nu} y (2h - y) . \cos (\sigma t + \epsilon) \quad \text{.............. (8),}$$

the velocity being in the same phase with the force, and varying inversely as ν.

301. To find the effect of viscosity on free waves on deep water we may make use of the Dissipation-Function of Art. 287, in any of the forms there given, the simplest for our purpose being

$$2F = -\mu \iint \frac{d . q^2}{dn} dS \quad \text{....................(1),}$$

since, by Art. 279, the dissipation may, under a certain restriction, be calculated as if the motion were irrotational.

To put the calculation in a form which shall apply at once to the case where capillary as well as gravitational forces are taken into account, we recall that, corresponding to the surface-elevation

$$\eta = \alpha \sin k (x - ct) \quad \text{.................... (2),}$$

we have

$$\phi = \alpha c e^{ky} \cos k (x - ct) \quad \text{....................(3),}$$

since this makes $d\eta/dt = -d\phi/dy$ for $y = 0$. Hence

$$q^2 = u^2 + v^2 = k^2 c^2 e^{2ky} \alpha^2 \quad \text{................. (4),}$$

and the dissipation is, by (1),

$$2\mu k^3 c^2 \alpha^2 \quad \text{..............................(5),}$$

per unit area of the surface. The kinetic energy,

$$\tfrac{1}{2}\rho \iint \phi \frac{d\phi}{dy} dS \quad \text{........................(6),}$$

has a mean value $\frac{1}{4}\rho k c^2 \alpha^2$ per unit area. The total energy, being double of this, is

$$\tfrac{1}{2}\rho k c^2 \alpha^2 \quad \text{..............................(7).}$$

Hence, equating the rate of decay of the energy to the dissipation, we have

$$\frac{d}{dt}(\tfrac{1}{2}\rho k c^2 \alpha^2) = -2\mu k^3 c^2 \alpha^2 \quad \text{................. (8),}$$

or

$$\frac{d\alpha}{dt} = -2\nu k^2 \alpha \quad \text{....................... (9),}$$

whence $$\alpha = \alpha_0 e^{-2\nu k^2 t} \qquad\qquad (10).$$

The 'modulus of decay,' τ, is therefore given by $\tau = 1/2\nu k^2$, or, in terms of the wave-length (λ),

$$\tau = \lambda^2/8\pi^2\nu \qquad\qquad (11)^*.$$

In the case of water, this gives

$$\tau = \cdot 712\,\lambda^2 \text{ seconds},$$

if λ be expressed in centimetres. It follows that capillary waves are very rapidly extinguished by viscosity; whilst for a wave-length of one metre τ would be about 2 hours.

The above method rests on the assumption that $\sigma\tau$ is moderately large, where $\sigma\,(=kc)$ denotes the 'speed.' In mobile fluids such as water this condition is fulfilled for all but excessively minute wave-lengths.

The method referred to fails for another reason when the depth is less than (say) half the wave-length. Owing to the practically infinite resistance to slipping at the bottom, the dissipation can no longer be calculated as if the motion were irrotational.

302. The direct calculation of the effect of viscosity on water waves can be conducted as follows.

If the axis of y be drawn vertically upwards, and if we assume that the motion is confined to the two dimensions x, y, we have

$$\left.\begin{aligned} \frac{du}{dt} &= -\frac{1}{\rho}\frac{dp}{dx} + \nu\nabla^2 u, \\ \frac{dv}{dt} &= -\frac{1}{\rho}\frac{dp}{dy} - g + \nu\nabla^2 v \end{aligned}\right\} \qquad\qquad (1).$$

with $$\frac{du}{dx} + \frac{dv}{dy} = 0 \qquad\qquad (2).$$

These are satisfied by

$$u = -\frac{d\phi}{dx} - \frac{d\psi}{dy}, \quad v = -\frac{d\phi}{dy} + \frac{d\psi}{dx} \qquad\qquad (3),$$

and $$\frac{p}{\rho} = \frac{d\phi}{dt} - gy \qquad\qquad (4),$$

* Stokes, *l. c. ante* p. 518. (Through an oversight in the calculation the value obtained for τ was too small by one-half.)

provided

$$\left.\begin{aligned}\nabla_1^2\phi &= 0,\\ \frac{d\psi}{dt} &= \nu\nabla_1^2\psi\end{aligned}\right\} \quad\text{.......................} \quad (5),$$

where

$$\nabla_1^2 = d^2/dx^2 + d^2/dy^2.$$

To determine the 'normal modes' which are periodic in respect of x, with a prescribed wave-length $2\pi/k$, we assume a time-factor $e^{\alpha t}$ and a space-factor e^{ikx}. The solutions of (5) are then

$$\left.\begin{aligned}\phi &= (Ae^{ky} + Be^{-ky})\, e^{ikx+\alpha t}\\ \psi &= (Ce^{my} + De^{-my})\, e^{ikx+\alpha t}\end{aligned}\right\} \quad\text{..................} \quad (6),$$

with

$$m^2 = k^2 + \alpha/\nu \quad\text{..........................} \quad (7).$$

The boundary-conditions will supply equations which are sufficient to determine the nature of the various modes, and the corresponding values of α.

In the case of infinite depth one of these conditions takes the form that the motion must be finite for $y = -\infty$. Excluding for the present the cases where m is pure-imaginary, this requires that $B = 0$, $D = 0$, provided m denote that root of (7) which has its real part positive. Hence

$$\left.\begin{aligned}u &= -(ikAe^{ky} + mCe^{my})\, e^{ikx+\alpha t},\\ v &= -(kAe^{ky} - ikCe^{my})\, e^{ikx+\alpha t}\end{aligned}\right\} \quad\text{...............} \quad (8).$$

If η denote the elevation at the free surface, we must have $d\eta/dt = v$. If the origin of y be taken in the undisturbed level, this gives

$$\eta = -\frac{k}{\alpha}(A - iC)\, e^{ikx+\alpha t} \quad\text{..................} \quad (9).$$

If T_1 denote the surface-tension, the stress-conditions at the surface are evidently

$$p_{yy} = T_1\frac{d^2\eta}{dx^2}, \quad p_{xy} = 0 \quad\text{..................} \quad (10),$$

to the first order, since the inclination of the surface to the horizontal is assumed to be infinitely small. Now

$$p_{yy} = -p + 2\mu\frac{dv}{dy}, \quad p_{xy} = \mu\left(\frac{dv}{dx} + \frac{du}{dy}\right) \quad\text{......} \quad (11),$$

whence, by (4) and (6) we find, at the surface,

$$\frac{p_{yy}}{\rho} - T'\frac{d^2\eta}{dx^2} = -\frac{d\phi}{dt} + (g + T'k^2)\,\eta + 2\nu\frac{dv}{dy}$$

$$= -\frac{1}{\alpha}\{(\alpha^2 + 2\nu k^2\alpha + gk + T'k^3)\,A - i\,(gk + T'k^3 + 2\nu km\alpha)\,C\}\ \text{....(12)},$$

$$\frac{p_{xy}}{\rho} = -\{2i\nu k^2 A + (\alpha + 2\nu k^2)\,C\}\ \text{...............(13)},$$

where $T' = T_1/\rho$, the common factor $e^{ikx+\alpha t}$ being understood. Substituting in (10), and eliminating the ratio $A : C$, we obtain

$$(\alpha + 2\nu k^2)^2 + gk + T'k^3 = 4\nu k^3 m\ \text{............ (14)}.$$

If we eliminate m by means of (7), we get a biquadratic in α, but only those roots are admissible which give a positive value to the real part of the left-hand member of (14), and so make the real part of m positive.

If we write, for shortness,

$$gk + T'k^3 = \sigma^2, \quad \nu k^2/\sigma = \theta, \quad \alpha + 2\nu k^2 = x\sigma\ \text{......(15)},$$

the biquadratic in question takes the form

$$(x^2 + 1)^2 = 16\theta^3(x - \theta)\ \text{.................. (16)}.$$

It is not difficult to shew that this has always two roots (both complex) which violate the restriction just stated, and two admissible roots which may be real or complex according to the magnitude of the ratio θ. If λ be the wave-length, and $c\,(=\sigma/k)$ the wave-velocity in the absence of friction, we have

$$\theta = \nu k/c = (2\pi\nu/c) \div \lambda\ \text{.................. (17)}.$$

Now, for water, if c_m denote the minimum wave-velocity of Art. 246, we find $2\pi\nu/c_m = \cdot 0048$ cm., so that except for very minute wave-lengths θ is a small number. Neglecting the square of θ, we have $x = \pm i$, and

$$\alpha = -2\nu k^2 \pm i\sigma\ \text{.........................(18)}.$$

The condition $p_{xy} = 0$ shews that

$$C/A = -2i\nu k^2/(\alpha + 2\nu k^2) = \mp 2\nu k^2/\sigma\ \text{............(19)},$$

which is, under the same circumstances, very small. Hence the motion is approximately irrotational, with a velocity-potential

$$\phi = Ae^{-2\nu k^2 t + ky + i(kx \pm \sigma t)}\ \text{.................. (20)}.$$

If we put $a = \mp kA/\sigma$, the equation (9) of the free surface becomes, approximately, on taking the real part,

$$\eta = ae^{-2\nu k^2 t} \sin (kx \pm \sigma t) \qquad (21).$$

The wave-velocity is σ/k, or $(g/k + T'k)^{\frac{1}{2}}$, as in Art. 246, and the law of decay is that investigated independently in the last Art.

To examine more closely the character of the motion, as affected by viscosity, we may calculate the angular velocity (ω) at any point of the fluid. This is given by

$$2\omega = \frac{dv}{dx} - \frac{du}{dy} = \nabla_1^2 \psi = \frac{a}{\nu} \psi$$

$$= \frac{a}{\nu} Ce^{my+ikx+at} \qquad (i).$$

Now, from (7) and (18), we have, approximately,

$$m = (1 \pm i) \beta, \text{ where } \beta = (\sigma/2\nu)^{\frac{1}{2}}.$$

With the same notation as before, we find

$$\omega = \mp \sigma k a e^{-2\nu k^2 t + \beta y} \sin \{kx \pm (\sigma t + \beta y)\} \qquad (ii).$$

This diminishes rapidly from the surface downwards, in accordance with the analogy pointed out in Art. 286. Owing to the oscillatory character of the motion, the sign of the vortex-motion which is being diffused inwards from the surface is continually being reversed, so that beyond a stratum of thickness comparable with $2\pi/\beta$ the effect is insensible, just as the fluctuations of temperature at the earth's surface cease to have any influence at a depth of a few yards.

In the case of a very viscous fluid, such as treacle or pitch, θ may be large even when the wave-length is considerable. The admissible roots of (16) are then both real. One of them is evidently nearly equal to 2θ, and continuing the approximation we find

$$x = 2\theta - \frac{1}{2\theta} + \ldots,$$

whence, neglecting capillarity, we have, by (15),

$$\alpha = -g/2k\nu \qquad (22).$$

The remaining real root is $1{\cdot}09\theta$, nearly, which gives

$$\alpha = -{\cdot}91\nu k^2 \qquad (23).$$

The former root is the more important. It represents a slow creeping of the fluid towards a state of equilibrium with a horizontal surface; the rate of recovery depending on the relation between the gravity of the fluid (which is proportional to $g\rho$) and the viscosity (μ), the influence of inertia being insensible. It appears from (7) and (15) that $m=k$, nearly, so that the motion is approximately irrotational.

The type of motion corresponding to (23), on the other hand, depends, as to its persistence, on the relation between the inertia (ρ) and the viscosity (μ), the effect of gravity being unimportant. It dies out very rapidly.

The above investigation gives the most important of the normal modes, of the prescribed wave-length, of which the system is capable. We know *à priori* that there must be an infinity of others. These correspond to pure-imaginary values of m, and are of a less persistent character. If in place of (6) we assume

$$\left.\begin{aligned}\phi&=Ae^{ky}\,.\,e^{ikx+at},\\ \psi&=(C\cos m'y+D\sin m'y)e^{ikx+at}\end{aligned}\right\}\text{ ......(iii)},$$

with

$$m'^2=-k^2-a/\nu\text{ ......(iv)},$$

and carry out the investigation as before, we find

$$\left.\begin{aligned}(a^2+2\nu k^2a+gk+T'k^3)A-i(gk+T'k^3)C-2i\nu km'aD&=0\\ 2ik^2A+(k^2-m'^2)C&=0\end{aligned}\right\}\text{ ......(v)}.$$

Any real value of m' is admissible, these equations determining the ratios $A:C:D$; and the corresponding value of a is

$$a=-\nu(k^2+m'^2)\text{ ......(vi)}.$$

In any one of these modes the plane xy is divided horizontally and vertically into a series of quasi-rectangular compartments, within each of which the fluid circulates, gradually coming to rest as the original momentum is spent against viscosity.

By a proper synthesis of the various normal modes it must be possible to represent the decay of any arbitrary initial disturbance.

303. The equations (12) and (13) of the preceding Art. enable us to examine a related question of some interest, viz. the generation and maintenance of waves against viscosity, by suitable forces applied to the surface.

If the external forces p'_{yy}, p'_{xy} be given multiples of e^{ikx+at}, where k and a are prescribed, the equations in question determine A and C, and thence, by (9), the value of η. Thus we find

$$\frac{p'_{yy}}{g\rho\eta}=\frac{(\alpha^2+2\nu k^2\alpha+\sigma^2)A-i(\sigma^2+2\nu km\alpha)C}{gk(A-iC)}\text{ ......(1)},$$

$$\frac{p'_{xy}}{g\rho\eta}=\frac{\alpha}{gk}\cdot\frac{2i\nu k^2A+(\alpha+2\nu k^2)C}{A-iC}\text{ ......(2)}.$$

Let us first examine the effect of a purely tangential force. Assuming $p'_{yy} = 0$, we find

$$\frac{p'_{xy}}{g\rho\eta} = \frac{i\alpha}{gk} \cdot \frac{(\alpha + 2\nu k^2)^2 + \sigma^2 - 4\nu^2 k^3 m}{\alpha + 2\nu k^2 - 2\nu k m} \qquad (3).$$

For a given wave-length, the elevation will be greatest when $\alpha = \pm i\sigma$, nearly. To find the force necessary to maintain a train of waves of given amplitude, travelling in the direction of x-positive, we put $\alpha = -i\sigma$. Assuming, for a reason already indicated, that $\nu k^2/\sigma$ and $\nu k m/\sigma$ are small, we find

$$p'_{xy}/g\rho\eta = 4\nu k\sigma/g, \text{ or } p'_{xy} = 4\mu k\sigma\eta \qquad (4).$$

Hence the force acts forwards on the crests of the waves, and backwards at the troughs, changing sign at the nodes. A force having the same distribution, but less intensity in proportion to the height of the waves than that given by (4), would only retard, without preventing, the decay of the waves by viscosity. A force having the opposite sign would accelerate this decay.

The case of purely normal force can be investigated in a similar manner. If $p'_{xy} = 0$, we have

$$\frac{p'_{yy}}{g\rho\eta} = \frac{(\alpha + 2\nu k^2)^2 + \sigma^2 - 4\nu^2 k^3 m}{gk} \qquad (5).$$

The reader may easily satisfy himself that when there is no viscosity this coincides with the result of Art. 226. If we put $\alpha = -i\sigma$, we obtain, with the same approximations as before,

$$p'_{yy} = -4i\mu k\sigma\eta \qquad (6).$$

Hence the wave-system

$$\eta = a \sin(kx - \sigma t) \qquad (7)$$

will be maintained without increase or decrease by the pressure-distribution

$$p' = \text{const.} + 4\mu k a\sigma \cos(kx - \sigma t) \qquad (8),$$

applied to the surface. It appears that the pressure is greatest on the rear and least on the front slopes of the waves*.

If we call to mind the phases of the particles, revolving in their circular orbits, at different parts of a wave-profile, it is evident

* This agrees with the result given at the end of Art. 226, where, however, the dissipative forces were of a different kind.

that the forces above investigated, whether normal or tangential, are on the whole urging the surface-particles in the directions in which they are already moving.

Owing to the irregular, eddying, character of a wind blowing over a roughened surface, it is not easy to give more than a general explanation of the manner in which it generates and maintains waves. It is not difficult to see, however, that the action of the wind will tend to produce surface forces of the kinds above investigated. When the air is moving in the direction in which the wave-form is travelling, but with a greater velocity, there will evidently be an excess of pressure on the rear-slopes, as well as a tangential drag on the exposed crests. The aggregate effect of these forces will be a surface drift, and the residual tractions, whether normal or tangential, will have on the whole the distribution above postulated. Hence the tendency will be to increase the amplitude of the waves to such a point that the dissipation balances the work done by the surface forces. In like manner waves travelling faster than the wind, or against the wind, will have their amplitude continually reduced*.

It has been shewn (Art. 246) that, under the joint influence of gravity and capillarity, there is a minimum wave-velocity of 23·2 cm. per sec., or ·45 miles per hour. Hence a wind of smaller velocity than this is incapable of reinforcing waves accidentally started, which, if of short wave-length, must be rapidly extinguished by viscosity†. This is in accordance with the observations of Scott Russell‡, from whose paper we make the following interesting extract:

"Let [a spectator] begin his observations in a perfect calm, when the surface of the water is smooth and reflects like a mirror the images of surrounding objects. This appearance will not be affected by even a slight motion of the air, and a velocity of less than half a mile an hour (8½ in. per sec.) does not sensibly disturb the smoothness of the reflecting surface. A gentle zephyr flitting along the surface from point to point, may be observed to destroy the perfection of the mirror for a moment, and on departing, the surface remains polished as before; if the air have a velocity of about a mile an hour, the surface of the water becomes less capable of distinct reflexion, and

* Cf. Airy, "Tides and Waves," Arts. 265—272; Stokes, *Camb. Trans.*, t. ix., p. [62]; Lord Rayleigh, *l. c. ante* p. 526.

† Sir W. Thomson, *l. c. ante* p. 446.

‡ *l. c. ante* p. 455.

on observing it in such a condition, it is to be noticed that the diminution of this reflecting power is owing to the presence of those minute corrugations of the superficial film which form waves of the *third order* [capillary waves].... This first stage of disturbance has this distinguishing circumstance, that the phenomena on the surface cease almost simultaneously with the intermission of the disturbing cause so that a spot which is sheltered from the direct action of the wind remains smooth, the waves of the third order being incapable of travelling spontaneously to any considerable distance, except when under the continued action of the original disturbing force. This condition is the indication of present force, not of that which is past. While it remains it gives that deep blackness to the water which the sailor is accustomed to regard as the index of the presence of wind, and often as the forerunner of more.

"The second condition of wave motion is to be observed when the velocity of the wind acting on the smooth water has increased to two miles an hour. Small waves then begin to rise uniformly over the whole surface of the water; these are waves of the second order, and cover the water with considerable regularity. Capillary waves disappear from the ridges of these waves, but are to be found sheltered in the hollows between them, and on the anterior slopes of these waves. The regularity of the distribution of these secondary waves over the surface is remarkable; they begin with about an inch of amplitude, and a couple of inches long; they enlarge as the velocity or duration of the wave increases; by and by the coterminal waves unite; the ridges increase, and if the wind increase the waves become cusped, and are regular waves of the *second order* [gravity waves]*. They continue enlarging their dimensions, and the depth to which they produce the agitation increasing simultaneously with their magnitude, the surface becomes extensively covered with waves of nearly uniform magnitude."

It will be seen that our theoretical investigations give considerable insight into the incipient stages of wave-formation. No sufficient explanation appears however to have been as yet given of the origin of the regular processions of waves of greater length which are so conspicuous a result of the continued action of wind on a large expanse of water.

304. The calming effect of oil on water waves appears to be due to the variations of tension caused by the extensions and contractions of the contaminated surface†. The surface-tension of pure water is less than the sum of the tensions of the surfaces of separation of oil and air, and oil and water, respectively, so that a

* Scott Russell's wave of the *first order* is the 'solitary wave' (Art. 234).

† Reynolds, "On the Effect of Oil in destroying Waves on the Surface of Water," *Brit. Ass. Rep.*, 1880; Aitken, "On the Effect of Oil on a Stormy Sea, *Proc. Roy. Soc. Edin.*, t. xii., p. 56 (1883).

drop of oil thrown on water is gradually drawn out into a thin film. If the film be sufficiently thin, say not more than two millionths of a millimetre in thickness, the tension is increased when the thickness is reduced by stretching, and conversely. It is evident at once from the figure on p. 374 that in oscillatory waves any portion of the surface is alternately contracted and extended, according as it is above or below the mean level. The consequent variations in tension produce an alternating tangential drag on the water, with a consequent increase in the rate of dissipation of energy.

The preceding formulæ enable us to submit this explanation, to a certain extent, to the test of calculation.

Assuming that the surface tension varies by an amount proportional to the extension, we may denote it by

$$T_1\left(1+f\frac{d\xi}{dx}\right) \qquad \text{(i)},$$

where T_1 is the tension in the undisturbed state, ξ is the horizontal displacement of a surface particle, and f is a numerical coefficient.

The internal motion of the water is given by the same formulæ as in Art. 302. The surface-conditions are obtained by resolving normally and tangentially the forces acting on an element of the superficial film. We thus find, in the case of free waves,

$$\left.\begin{aligned}\frac{p_{yy}}{\rho} &= T'\frac{d^2\eta}{dx^2},\\ \frac{p_{xy}}{\rho} &= \frac{dT'}{dx} = fT'\frac{d^2\xi}{dx^2}\end{aligned}\right\} \qquad \text{(ii)},$$

where $T'=T_1/\rho$. In the derivation of the first of these equations a term of the second order has been neglected.

Since the time-factor is $e^{\alpha t}$, we have $\xi = u/\alpha$, whence, substituting from Art. 302 (8), (9), (11), we find, as the expression of the surface-conditions (ii),

$$\left.\begin{aligned}(\alpha^2+2\nu k^2\alpha+gk+T'k^3)\,A - i\,(gk+T'k^3+2\nu km\alpha)\,C&=0,\\ i\,(2\nu k^2\alpha+fT'k^3)\,A+(\alpha^2+2\nu k^2\alpha+fT'k^2m)\,C&=0\end{aligned}\right\} \qquad \text{(iii)}.$$

If we write

$$\left.\begin{aligned}\sigma^2&=gk+T'k^3,\\ \sigma_0^2&=T'k^3\end{aligned}\right\} \qquad \text{(iv)},$$

the elimination of the ratio $A : C$ between the above equations gives

$$\alpha^2\{(\alpha+2\nu k^2)^2+\sigma^2-4\nu^2k^3m\}+f\frac{m}{k}\sigma_0^2\left\{\alpha^2+\left(1-\frac{k}{m}\right)\sigma^2\right\}=0 \qquad \text{(v)}.$$

This equation, with

$$m^2 = k^2 + a/\nu \qquad\qquad (vi),$$

determines the values of a and m. Eliminating m, we find

$$(a+\nu k^2)\{f\sigma_0^2(a^2+\sigma^2) - 4\nu^2k^4a^2\}^2 = \nu k^2[a^2\{(a+2\nu k^2)^2+\sigma^2\} - f\sigma^2\sigma_0^2]^2 \ldots (vii),$$

or, if we write

$$a/\sigma = y, \quad \nu k^2/\sigma = \theta \qquad\qquad (viii),$$

$$(y+\theta)\left\{\frac{f\sigma_0^2}{\sigma^2}(y^2+1) - 4\theta^2y^2\right\}^2 = \theta\left[y^2\{(y+2\theta)^2+1\} - \frac{f\sigma_0^2}{\sigma^2}\right]^2 \ldots (ix).$$

This equation has an extraneous root $y=0$, and other roots are inadmissible as giving, when substituted in (v), negative values to the real part of m. For all but very minute wave-lengths, θ is a small number; and, if we neglect the square of θ, we obtain

$$(y+\theta)(y^2+1)^2\frac{f^2\sigma_0^4}{\sigma^4} = \theta\left\{y^2(y^2+1) - \frac{f\sigma_0^2}{\sigma^2}\right\}^2 \qquad\qquad (x).$$

This is satisfied by $y = \pm i$, approximately; and a closer approximation is given by

$$y(y^2+1)^2 = \theta \qquad\qquad (xi),$$

leading to

$$y = \pm\left(1 - \frac{\theta^{\frac{1}{2}}}{2\sqrt{2}}\right)i - \frac{\theta^{\frac{1}{2}}}{2\sqrt{2}} \qquad\qquad (xii).$$

Hence, neglecting the small change in the 'speed' of the oscillations,

$$a = \pm i\sigma - \frac{\nu^{\frac{1}{2}}k\sigma^{\frac{1}{2}}}{2\sqrt{2}} \qquad\qquad (xiii).$$

The modulus of decay is therefore

$$\tau = \frac{2\sqrt{2}}{\nu^{\frac{1}{2}}k\sigma^{\frac{1}{2}}} = \frac{\lambda^{\frac{3}{2}}}{\pi^{\frac{3}{2}}\nu^{\frac{1}{2}}c_m^{\frac{1}{2}}}\cdot\left(\frac{c_m}{c}\right)^{\frac{1}{2}} \qquad\qquad (xiv),$$

in the notation of Art. 246.

Under the circumstances to which this formula applies the elasticity of the oil-film has the effect of practically annulling the horizontal motion at the surface. The dissipation is therefore (within limits) independent of the precise value of f.

The substitution of (x) for (ix) is permissible when θ is small compared with $f\sigma_0^2/\sigma^2$, or c small compared with fT'/ν. Assuming $\nu = \cdot018$, $T'=40$, we have $T'/\nu = 2200$. Hence the investigation applies to waves whose velocity is small compared with 2200 centimetres per second. It appears on examination that this condition is fulfilled for wave-lengths ranging from a fraction of a millimetre to several metres.

The ratio of the modulus (xiv) to the value $(1/2\nu k^2)$, obtained on the hypothesis of *constant* surface-tension, is $4\sqrt{2}\,(\nu k^2/\sigma)^{\frac{1}{2}}$, which is assumed to be small. The above numerical data make $\lambda_m = 1\cdot27$, $c_m = 20$. Substituting in (xiv) we find

$$\tau = \cdot30\lambda^{\frac{3}{2}} \times (c_m/c)^{\frac{1}{2}}.$$

For $\lambda = \lambda_m$ this gives $\tau = \cdot43$ sec. instead of $1\cdot41$ sec. as on the hypothesis of constant tension. For larger values of λ the change is greater.

When the wave-velocity c is great compared with 2200 c.s., we may neglect σ_0^2/σ^2 in comparison with θ. The result is the same as if we were to put $f=0$, so that the modulus of decay has, for sufficiently long waves, the value $1/2\nu k^2$ found in Art. 301. The same statement would apply to sufficiently minute crispations; but θ then ceases to be small, and the approximations break down *ab initio.* The motion, in fact, tends to become aperiodic.

305. Problems of periodic motion in two dimensions, with a *circular* boundary, can be treated with the help of Bessel's Functions*. The theory of the Bessel's Function, whether of the first or second kind, with a complex argument, involves however some points of great delicacy, which have been discussed in several papers by Stokes†. To avoid entering on these, we pass on to the case of a *spherical* boundary; this includes various problems of greater interest which can be investigated with much less difficulty, since the functions involved (the ψ_n and Ψ_n of Art. 267) admit of being expressed in finite forms.

It is convenient, with a view to treating all such questions on a uniform plan, to give, first, the general solution of the system of equations:

$$(\nabla^2+h^2)u'=0,\quad (\nabla^2+h^2)v'=0,\quad (\nabla^2+h^2)w'=0\ldots\ldots(1),$$

$$\frac{du'}{dx}+\frac{dv'}{dy}+\frac{dw'}{dz}=0\ldots\ldots\ldots\ldots\ldots\ldots\ldots(2),$$

in terms of spherical harmonics. This is an extension of the problem considered in Art. 293. We will consider only, in the first instance, cases where u', v', w' are finite at the origin.

The solutions fall naturally into two distinct classes. If r denote the radius vector, the typical solution of the First Class is

$$\left.\begin{aligned} u'&=\psi_n(hr)\left(y\frac{d}{dz}-z\frac{d}{dy}\right)\chi_n,\\ v'&=\psi_n(hr)\left(z\frac{d}{dx}-x\frac{d}{dz}\right)\chi_n,\\ w'&=\psi_n(hr)\left(x\frac{d}{dy}-y\frac{d}{dx}\right)\chi_n\end{aligned}\right\}\ldots\ldots\ldots\ldots\ldots(3),$$

* Cf. Stokes, *l. c. ante* p. 518; Stearn, *Quart. Journ. Math.*, t. xvii. (1881); and the last paper cited on p. 558.

† "On the Discontinuity of Arbitrary Constants which appear in Divergent Developments," *Camb. Trans.*, t. x. (1857), and t. xi. (1868).

where χ_n is a solid harmonic of positive degree n, and ψ_n is defined by

$$\psi_n(\zeta) = (-)^n \left(\frac{d}{\zeta d\zeta}\right)^n \frac{\sin \zeta}{\zeta}$$
$$= \frac{1}{1.3\ldots(2n+1)}\left(1 - \frac{\zeta^2}{2(2n+3)} + \frac{\zeta^4}{2.4(2n+3)(2n+5)} - \ldots\right) \qquad \ldots\ldots(4).$$

It is immediately verified, on reference to Arts. 266, 267, that the above expressions do in fact satisfy (1) and (2). It is to be noticed that this solution makes

$$xu' + yv' + zw' = 0 \qquad \ldots\ldots(5).$$

The typical solution of the Second Class is

$$\left.\begin{aligned} u' &= (n+1)\,\psi_{n-1}(hr)\frac{d\phi_n}{dx} - n\psi_{n+1}(hr)\,h^2 r^{2n+3}\frac{d}{dx}\frac{\phi_n}{r^{2n+1}}, \\ v' &= (n+1)\,\psi_{n-1}(hr)\frac{d\phi_n}{dy} - n\psi_{n+1}(hr)\,h^2 r^{2n+3}\frac{d}{dy}\frac{\phi_n}{r^{2n+1}}, \\ w' &= (n+1)\,\psi_{n-1}(hr)\frac{d\phi_n}{dz} - n\psi_{n+1}(hr)\,h^2 r^{2n+3}\frac{d}{dz}\frac{\phi_n}{r^{2n+1}} \end{aligned}\right\} \ldots(6),$$

where ϕ_n is a solid harmonic of positive degree n. The coefficients of $\psi_{n-1}(hr)$ and $\psi_{n+1}(hr)$ in these expressions are solid harmonics of degrees $n-1$ and $n+1$ respectively, so that the equations (1) are satisfied.

To verify that (2) is also satisfied we need the relations

$$\psi_n'(\zeta) = -\zeta\psi_{n+1}(\zeta) \qquad \ldots\ldots(7),$$

$$\zeta\psi_n'(\zeta) + (2n+1)\,\psi_n(\zeta) = \psi_{n-1}(\zeta) \qquad \ldots\ldots(8),$$

which follow easily from (4). The formulæ (6) make

$$xu' + yv' + zw' = n(n+1)(2n+1)\,\psi_n(hr)\,\phi_n \qquad \ldots\ldots(9),$$

the reduction being effected by means of (7) and (8).

If we write

$$2\xi' = \frac{dw'}{dy} - \frac{dv'}{dz}, \quad 2\eta' = \frac{du'}{dz} - \frac{dw'}{dx}, \quad 2\zeta' = \frac{dv'}{dx} - \frac{du'}{dy} \ldots(10),$$

we find, in the solutions of the First Class,

$$\left.\begin{aligned} 2\xi' &= -\frac{1}{2n+1}\left\{(n+1)\psi_{n-1}(hr)\frac{d\chi_n}{dx} - n\psi_{n+1}(hr)h^2r^{2n+3}\frac{d}{dx}\frac{\chi_n}{r^{2n+1}},\right. \\ 2\eta' &= -\frac{1}{2n+1}\left\{(n+1)\psi_{n-1}(hr)\frac{d\chi_n}{dy} - n\psi_{n+1}(hr)h^2r^{2n+3}\frac{d}{dy}\frac{\chi_n}{r^{2n+1}},\right. \\ 2\zeta' &= -\frac{1}{2n+1}\left\{(n+1)\psi_{n-1}(hr)\frac{d\chi_n}{dz} - n\psi_{n+1}(hr)h^2r^{2n+3}\frac{d}{dz}\frac{\chi_n}{r^{2n+1}}\right. \end{aligned}\right\} \quad \ldots\ldots(11);$$

these make

$$2(x\xi' + y\eta' + z\zeta') = -n(n+1)\psi_n(hr)\chi_n \quad \ldots\ldots\ldots(12).$$

In the solutions of the Second Class, we have

$$\left.\begin{aligned} 2\xi' &= -(2n+1)h^2\psi_n(hr)\left(y\frac{d}{dz} - z\frac{d}{dy}\right)\phi_n, \\ 2\eta' &= -(2n+1)h^2\psi_n(hr)\left(z\frac{d}{dx} - x\frac{d}{dz}\right)\phi_n, \\ 2\zeta' &= -(2n+1)h^2\psi_n(hr)\left(x\frac{d}{dy} - y\frac{d}{dx}\right)\phi_n \end{aligned}\right\} \quad \ldots\ldots(13),$$

and therefore

$$x\xi' + y\eta' + z\zeta' = 0 \quad \ldots\ldots\ldots\ldots\ldots\ldots\ldots(14).$$

In the derivation of these results use has been made of (7), and of the easily verified formula

$$x\chi_n = \frac{r^2}{2n+1}\left(\frac{d\chi_n}{dx} - r^{2n+1}\frac{d}{dx}\frac{\chi_n}{r^{2n+1}}\right) \quad \ldots\ldots\ldots\ldots(15).$$

To shew that the aggregate of the solutions of the types (3) and (6), with all integral values of n, and all possible forms of the harmonics ϕ_n, χ_n, constitutes the *complete* solution of the proposed system of equations (1) and (2), we remark in the first place that the equations in question imply

$$(\nabla^2 + h^2)(xu' + yv' + zw') = 0 \quad \ldots\ldots\ldots\ldots\ldots(16),$$

and

$$(\nabla^2 + h^2)(x\xi' + y\eta' + z\zeta') = 0 \quad \ldots\ldots\ldots\ldots\ldots(17).$$

It is evident from Arts. 266, 267 that the complete solution of these, subject to the condition of finiteness at the origin, is contained in the equations (9) and (12), above, if these be generalized by prefixing the sign Σ of summation with respect to n. Now when $xu' + yv' + zw'$ and $x\xi' + y\eta' + z\zeta'$ are given throughout any space, the values of u', v', w' are rendered by (2) completely determinate. For if there were two sets of values, say u', v', w' and u'', v'', w'', both satisfying the prescribed conditions, then, writing

$$u_1 = u' - u'', \quad v_1 = v' - v'', \quad w_1 = w' - w'',$$

we should have

$$\left.\begin{aligned} xu_1 + yv_1 + zw_1 = 0, \\ x\xi_1 + y\eta_1 + z\zeta_1 = 0, \\ \frac{du_1}{dx} + \frac{dv_1}{dy} + \frac{dw_1}{dz} = 0 \end{aligned}\right\} \quad \text{.....................(18).}$$

Regarding u_1, v_1, w_1 as the component velocities of a liquid, the first of these shews that the lines of flow are closed curves lying on a system of concentric spherical surfaces. Hence the 'circulation' (Art. 32) in any such line has a finite value. On the other hand, the second equation shews, by Art. 33, that the circulation in any circuit drawn on one of the above spherical surfaces is zero. These conclusions are irreconcileable unless u_1, v_1, w_1 are all zero.

Hence, in the present problem, whenever the functions ϕ_n and χ_n have been determined by (9) and (12), the values of u', v', w' follow uniquely as in (3) and (6).

When the region contemplated is bounded *internally* by a spherical surface, the condition of finiteness when $r = 0$ is no longer imposed, and we have an additional system of solutions in which the functions $\psi_n(\zeta)$ are replaced by $\Psi_n(\zeta)$, in accordance with Art. 267 *.

* Advantage is here taken of an improvement introduced by Love, "The Free and Forced Vibrations of an Elastic Spherical Shell containing a given Mass of Liquid," *Proc. Lond. Math. Soc.*, t. xix., p. 170 (1888).

The foregoing investigation is taken, with slight changes of notation, from the following papers:

"On the Oscillations of a Viscous Spheroid," *Proc. Lond. Math. Soc.*, t. xiii., p. 51 (1881);

"On the Vibrations of an Elastic Sphere," *Proc. Lond. Math. Soc.*, t. xiii., p. 189 (1882);

"On the Motion of a Viscous Fluid contained in a Spherical Vessel," *Proc. Lond. Math. Soc.*, t. xvi., p. 27 (1884).

306. The equations of small motion of an incompressible fluid are, in the absence of extraneous forces,

$$\left.\begin{aligned}\frac{du}{dt}&=-\frac{1}{\rho}\frac{dp}{dx}+\nu\nabla^2u,\\ \frac{dv}{dt}&=-\frac{1}{\rho}\frac{dp}{dy}+\nu\nabla^2v,\\ \frac{dw}{dt}&=-\frac{1}{\rho}\frac{dp}{dz}+\nu\nabla^2w\end{aligned}\right\}\quad\text{.....................(1)},$$

with

$$\frac{du}{dx}+\frac{dv}{dy}+\frac{dw}{dz}=0\quad\text{.....................(2)}.$$

If we assume that u, v, w all vary as $e^{\lambda t}$, the equations (1) may be written

$$\left.\begin{aligned}(\nabla^2+h^2)\,u&=\frac{1}{\mu}\frac{dp}{dx},\\ (\nabla^2+h^2)\,v&=\frac{1}{\mu}\frac{dp}{dy},\\ (\nabla^2+h^2)\,w&=\frac{1}{\mu}\frac{dp}{dz}\end{aligned}\right\}\quad\text{.....................(3)},$$

where

$$h^2=-\lambda/\nu\quad\text{..........................(4)}.$$

From (2) and (3) we deduce

$$\nabla^2p=0\quad\text{..............................(5)}.$$

Hence a particular solution of (3) and (2) is

$$u=\frac{1}{h^2\mu}\frac{dp}{dx},\quad v=\frac{1}{h^2\mu}\frac{dp}{dy},\quad w=\frac{1}{h^2\mu}\frac{dp}{dz}\quad\text{...........(6)},$$

and therefore the general solution is

$$u=\frac{1}{h^2\mu}\frac{dp}{dx}+u',\quad v=\frac{1}{h^2\mu}\frac{dp}{dy}+v',\quad w=\frac{1}{h^2\mu}\frac{dp}{dz}+w'\ \text{... (7)},$$

where u', v', w' are determined by the conditions of the preceding Art.

Hence the solutions in spherical harmonics, subject to the condition of finiteness at the origin, fall into two classes.

In the First Class we have

$$\left.\begin{aligned} p &= \text{const.}, \\ u &= \psi_n(hr)\left(y\frac{d}{dz} - z\frac{d}{dy}\right)\chi_n, \\ v &= \psi_n(hr)\left(z\frac{d}{dx} - x\frac{d}{dz}\right)\chi_n, \\ w &= \psi_n(hr)\left(x\frac{d}{dy} - y\frac{d}{dx}\right)\chi_n \end{aligned}\right\}\ldots\ldots\ldots\ldots\ldots(8);$$

and therefore $$xu + yv + zw = 0 \ldots\ldots\ldots\ldots\ldots\ldots\ldots(9).$$

In the Second Class we have

$$\left.\begin{aligned} p &= p_n, \\ u &= \frac{1}{h^2\mu}\frac{dp_n}{dx} + (n+1)\psi_{n-1}(hr)\frac{d\phi_n}{dx} - n\psi_{n+1}(hr)\,h^2r^{2n+3}\frac{d}{dx}\frac{\phi_n}{r^{2n+1}}, \\ v &= \frac{1}{h^2\mu}\frac{dp_n}{dy} + (n+1)\psi_{n-1}(hr)\frac{d\phi_n}{dy} - n\psi_{n+1}(hr)\,h^2r^{2n+3}\frac{d}{dy}\frac{\phi_n}{r^{2n+1}}, \\ w &= \frac{1}{h^2\mu}\frac{dp_n}{dz} + (n+1)\psi_{n-1}(hr)\frac{d\phi_n}{dz} - n\psi_{n+1}(hr)\,h^2r^{2n+3}\frac{d}{dz}\frac{\phi_n}{r^{2n+1}} \end{aligned}\right\}\ldots\ldots\ldots(10),$$

and $$x\xi + y\eta + z\zeta = 0 \ldots\ldots\ldots\ldots\ldots\ldots\ldots(11),$$

where ξ, η, ζ denote the component rotations of the fluid at the point (x, y, z). The symbols χ_n, ϕ_n, p_n stand for solid harmonics of the degrees indicated.

The component tractions on the surface of a sphere of radius r are given by

$$\left.\begin{aligned} rp_{rx} &= -xp + \mu\left(r\frac{d}{dr} - 1\right)u + \mu\frac{d}{dx}(xu + yv + zw), \\ rp_{ry} &= -yp + \mu\left(r\frac{d}{dr} - 1\right)v + \mu\frac{d}{dy}(xu + yv + zw), \\ rp_{rz} &= -zp + \mu\left(r\frac{d}{dr} - 1\right)w + \mu\frac{d}{dz}(xu + yv + zw) \end{aligned}\right\}\ldots(12).$$

In the solutions of the First Class we find without difficulty

$$\left.\begin{aligned} rp_{rx} &= -xp + P_n\left(y\frac{d\chi_n}{dz} - z\frac{d\chi_n}{dy}\right),\\ rp_{ry} &= -yp + P_n\left(z\frac{d\chi_n}{dx} - x\frac{d\chi_n}{dz}\right),\\ rp_{rz} &= -zp + P_n\left(x\frac{d\chi_n}{dy} - y\frac{d\chi_n}{dx}\right)\end{aligned}\right\}\quad\ldots\ldots\ldots(13),$$

where
$$P_n = \mu\,\{hr\psi_n'(hr) + (n-1)\,\psi_{n-1}(hr)\}\ \ldots\ldots\ldots(14).$$

To obtain the corresponding formulæ for the solutions of the Second Class, we remark first that the terms in p_n give

$$-xp_n + \frac{1}{h^2}\left(r\frac{d}{dr} - 1\right)\frac{dp_n}{dx} + \frac{n}{h^2}\frac{dp_n}{dx}$$
$$= \left(\frac{2(n-1)}{h^2} - \frac{r^2}{2n+1}\right)\frac{dp_n}{dx} + \frac{r^{2n+3}}{2n+1}\frac{d}{dx}\frac{p_n}{r^{2n+1}}\ldots\ldots(15).$$

The remaining terms give

$$\left(r\frac{d}{dr} - 1\right)u' = (n+1)\,\{hr\psi'_{n-1}(hr) + (n-2)\,\psi_{n-1}(hr)\}\,\frac{d\phi_n}{dx}$$
$$-\,n\,\{hr\psi'_{n+1}(hr) + n\psi_{n+1}(hr)\}\,h^2r^{2n+3}\frac{d}{dx}\frac{\phi_n}{r^{2n+1}}\ldots\ldots(16),$$

and

$$\frac{d}{dx}(xu' + yv' + zw') = n(n+1)(2n+1)\frac{d}{dx}\psi_n(hr)\,\phi_n$$
$$= n(n+1)\left\{\psi_{n-1}(hr)\frac{d\phi_n}{dx} + \psi_{n+1}(hr)\,h^2r^{2n+3}\frac{d}{dx}\frac{\phi_n}{r^{2n+1}}\right\}\ldots\ldots(17).$$

Various reductions have here been effected by means of Art. 305 (7), (8), (15). Hence, and by symmetry, we obtain

$$\left.\begin{aligned} rp_{rx} &= A_n\frac{dp_n}{dx} + B_nr^{2n+1}\frac{d}{dx}\frac{p_n}{r^{2n+1}} + C_n\frac{d\phi_n}{dx} + D_nr^{2n+1}\frac{d}{dx}\frac{\phi_n}{r^{2n+1}},\\ rp_{ry} &= A_n\frac{dp_n}{dy} + B_nr^{2n+1}\frac{d}{dy}\frac{p_n}{r^{2n+1}} + C_n\frac{d\phi_n}{dy} + D_nr^{2n+1}\frac{d}{dy}\frac{\phi_n}{r^{2n+1}},\\ rp_{rz} &= A_n\frac{dp_n}{dz} + B_nr^{2n+1}\frac{d}{dz}\frac{p_n}{r^{2n+1}} + C_n\frac{d\phi_n}{dz} + D_nr^{2n+1}\frac{d}{dz}\frac{\phi_n}{r^{2n+1}}\end{aligned}\right\}\ldots(18),$$

where

$$\left.\begin{aligned} &A_n = \frac{2(n-1)}{h^2} - \frac{r^2}{2n+1},\qquad B_n = \frac{r^2}{2n+1},\\ &C_n = \mu(n+1)\,\{hr\psi'_{n-1}(hr) + 2(n-1)\,\psi_{n-1}(hr)\},\\ &D_n = -\mu nh^2r^2\{hr\psi'_{n+1}(hr) - \psi_{n+1}(hr)\}\end{aligned}\right\}\ldots(19).$$

307. The general formulæ being once established, the application to special problems is easy.

1°. We may first investigate the decay of the motion of a viscous fluid contained in a spherical vessel which is at rest.

The boundary conditions are that

$$u=0, \quad v=0, \quad w=0 \qquad \text{(i)},$$

for $r=a$, the radius of the vessel. In the modes of the First Class, represented by (8) above, these conditions are satisfied by

$$\psi_n(ha)=0 \qquad \text{(ii)}.$$

The roots of this are all real, and the corresponding values of the modulus of decay (τ) are then given by

$$\tau=-\lambda^{-1}=\frac{a^2}{\nu}(ha)^{-2} \qquad \text{(iii)}.$$

The modes $n=1$ are of a rotatory character; the equation (ii) then becomes

$$\tan ha=ha \qquad \text{(iv)},$$

the lowest root of which is $ha=4{\cdot}493$. Hence

$$\tau={\cdot}0495\,\frac{a^2}{\nu}.$$

In the case of water, we have $\nu={\cdot}018$ C. S., and

$$\tau=2{\cdot}75\,a^2 \text{ seconds},$$

if a be expressed in centimetres.

The modes of the Second Class are given by (10). The surface conditions may be expressed by saying that the following three functions of x, y, z

$$\left.\begin{aligned}
\mathrm{u}&=\frac{1}{h^2\mu}\frac{dp_n}{dx}+(n+1)\psi_{n-1}(ha)\frac{d\phi_n}{dx}-n\psi_{n+1}(ha)\,h^2r^{2n+3}\frac{d}{dx}\frac{\phi_n}{r^{2n+1}},\\
\mathrm{v}&=\frac{1}{h^2\mu}\frac{dp_n}{dy}+(n+1)\psi_{n-1}(ha)\frac{d\phi_n}{dy}-n\psi_{n+1}(ha)\,h^2r^{2n+3}\frac{d}{dy}\frac{\phi_n}{r^{2n+1}},\\
\mathrm{w}&=\frac{1}{h^2\mu}\frac{dp_n}{dz}+(n+1)\psi_{n-1}(ha)\frac{d\phi_n}{dz}-n\psi_{n+1}(ha)\,h^2r^{2n+3}\frac{d}{dz}\frac{\phi_n}{r^{2n+1}}
\end{aligned}\right\}\qquad \text{(v)},$$

must severally vanish when $r=a$. Now these functions as they stand satisfy the equations

$$\nabla^2\mathrm{u}=0, \quad \nabla^2\mathrm{v}=0, \quad \nabla^2\mathrm{w}=0 \qquad \text{(vi)},$$

and since they are finite throughout the sphere, and vanish at the boundary, they must everywhere vanish, by Art. 40. Hence, forming the equation

$$\frac{d\mathrm{u}}{dx}+\frac{d\mathrm{v}}{dy}+\frac{d\mathrm{w}}{dz}=0 \qquad \text{(vii)},$$

we find

$$\psi_{n+1}(ha)=0 \qquad \text{(viii)}.$$

Again, since $$xu+yv+zw=0 \qquad \text{(ix)},$$
for $r=a$, we must have

$$\frac{1}{h^2\mu}p_n+n(n+1)(2n+1)\psi_n(ha)\phi_n=0 \qquad \text{(x)},$$

where use has been made of Art. 305 (7). This determines the ratio $p_n : \phi_n$.

In the case $n=1$, the equation (viii) becomes

$$\tan ha=\frac{3ha}{3-h^2a^2} \qquad \text{(xi)},$$

the lowest root of which is $ha=5{\cdot}764$, leading to

$$\tau=\cdot 0301\,\frac{a^2}{\nu}.$$

For the method of combining the various solutions so as to represent the decay of any arbitrary initial motion we must refer to the paper cited last on p. 558.

2°. We take next the case of a hollow spherical shell containing liquid, and oscillating by the torsion of a suspending wire*.

The forced oscillations of the liquid will evidently be of the First Class, with $n=1$. If the axis of z coincide with the vertical diameter of the shell, we find, putting $\chi_1=Cz$,

$$u=C\psi_1(hr)y,\quad v=-C\psi_1(hr)x,\quad w=0 \qquad \text{(xii)}.$$

If ω denote the angular velocity of the shell, the surface-condition gives

$$C\psi_1(ha)=-\omega \qquad \text{(xiii)}.$$

It appears that at any instant the particles situate on a spherical surface of radius r concentric with the boundary are rotating together with an angular velocity

$$\frac{\psi_1(hr)}{\psi_1(ha)}\omega \qquad \text{(xiv)}.$$

If we assume that $$\omega=ae^{i(\sigma t+\epsilon)} \qquad \text{(xv)},$$

and put $$h^2=-i\sigma/\nu=(1-i)^2\beta^2 \qquad \text{(xvi)},$$

where, as in Art. 297, $$\beta^2=\sigma/2\nu \qquad \text{(xvii)},$$

the expression (xiv) for the angular velocity may be separated into its real and imaginary parts with the help of the formula

$$\psi_1(\zeta)=\frac{\sin\zeta}{\zeta^3}-\frac{\cos\zeta}{\zeta^2} \qquad \text{(xviii)}.$$

If the viscosity be so small that βa is considerable, then, keeping only the most important term, we have, for points near the surface,

$$\psi_1(hr)=-\frac{1}{2h^2r^2}e^{(1-i)\beta r} \qquad \text{(xix)},$$

* This was first treated, in a different manner, by Helmholtz, *l. c. ante* p. 513.

and therefore, for the angular velocity (xiv),

$$a\frac{a^2}{r^2}e^{-\beta(a-r)} \,.\, e^{i\{\sigma t-\beta(r-a)+\epsilon\}} \qquad\text{(xx)},$$

the real part of which is

$$a\frac{a^2}{r^2}e^{-\beta(a-r)} \,.\, \cos\{\sigma t-\beta(r-a)+\epsilon\} \qquad\text{(xxi)}.$$

As in the case of laminar motion (Art. 298), this represents a system of waves travelling inwards from the surface with rapidly diminishing amplitude.

When, on the other hand, the viscosity is very great, βa is small, and the formula (xiv) reduces to

$$\omega\cos(\sigma t+\epsilon) \qquad\text{(xxii)},$$

nearly, when the imaginary part is rejected. This shews that the fluid now moves almost bodily with the sphere.

The stress-components at the surface of the sphere are given by (13). In the present case the formulæ reduce to

$$\left.\begin{aligned} p_{rx} &= -\frac{x}{a}p+\mu Ch\psi_1'(ha)\,y,\\ p_{ry} &= -\frac{y}{a}p-\mu Ch\psi_1'(ha)\,x,\\ p_{rz} &= -\frac{z}{a}p \end{aligned}\right\} \qquad\text{(xxiii)}.$$

If δS denote an element of the surface, these give a couple

$$N = -\iint(xp_{ry}-yp_{rx})\,dS = C\mu h\psi_1'(ha)\iint(x^2+y^2)\,dS$$

$$= \tfrac{8}{3}\pi\mu a^3\frac{h^2a^2\psi_2(ha)}{\psi_1(ha)}\,\omega \qquad\text{(xxiv)},$$

by (xiii) and Art. 305 (7).

In the case of small viscosity, where βa is large, we find, on reference to Art. 267, putting $ha=(1-i)\beta a$, that

$$2i\psi_n(ha) = (-)^n\left(\frac{d}{\zeta d\zeta}\right)^n\frac{e^{i\zeta}}{\zeta} \qquad\text{(xxv)},$$

approximately, where $\zeta=(1-i)\beta a$. This leads to

$$N = -\tfrac{8}{3}\pi\mu a^3(1+i)\beta a\omega \qquad\text{(xxvi)}.$$

If we restore the time-factor, this is equivalent to

$$N = -\tfrac{4}{3}\pi\rho a^5(\beta a)^{-1}\frac{d\omega}{dt}-\tfrac{8}{3}\pi\mu a^3(\beta a)\,\omega \qquad\text{(xxvii)}.$$

The first term has the effect of a slight addition to the inertia of the sphere; the second gives a frictional force varying as the velocity.

308. The general formulæ of Arts. 305, 306 may be further applied to discuss the effect of viscosity on the oscillations of a mass of liquid about the spherical form. The principal result of the investigation can, however, be obtained more simply by the method of Art. 301.

It was shewn in Arts. 241, 242, that when viscosity is neglected, the velocity-potential in any fundamental mode is of the form

$$\phi = A\frac{r^n}{a^n}S_n \cdot \cos(\sigma t + \epsilon) \quad\text{.........................}\quad \text{(i)},$$

where S_n is a surface harmonic. This gives for twice the kinetic energy included within a sphere of radius r, the expression

$$\rho\iint \phi\frac{d\phi}{dr}r^2 d\varpi = \rho n a\left(\frac{r}{a}\right)^{2n+1}\iint S_n^2 d\varpi \cdot A^2\cos^2(\sigma t + \epsilon) \quad\text{......}\quad \text{(ii)},$$

if $\delta\varpi$ denote an elementary solid angle, and therefore for the total kinetic energy

$$T = \tfrac{1}{2}\rho n a \iint S_n^2 d\varpi \cdot A^2\cos^2(\sigma t + \epsilon) \quad\text{.....................}\quad \text{(iii)}.$$

The potential energy must therefore be given by the formula

$$V = \tfrac{1}{2}\rho n a \iint S_n^2 d\varpi \cdot A^2\sin^2(\sigma t + \epsilon) \quad\text{....................}\quad \text{(iv)}.$$

Hence the total energy is

$$T + V = \tfrac{1}{2}\rho n a \iint S_n^2 d\varpi \cdot A^2 \quad\text{...........................}\quad \text{(v)}.$$

Again, the dissipation in a sphere of radius r, calculated on the assumption that the motion is irrotational, is, by Art. 287 (vi),

$$\mu\iint\frac{d \cdot q^2}{dr}r^2 d\varpi = \mu r^2\frac{d}{dr}\iint q^2 d\varpi \quad\text{......................}\quad \text{(vi)}.$$

Now
$$r^2\iint q^2 d\varpi = \frac{d}{dr}\iint \phi\frac{d\phi}{dr}r^2 d\varpi \quad\text{.....................}\quad \text{(vii)},$$

each side, when multiplied by $\rho\delta r$ being double the kinetic energy of the fluid contained between two spheres of radii r and $r+\delta r$. Hence, from (ii),

$$\iint q^2 d\varpi = \frac{n(2n+1)}{a^2}\left(\frac{r}{a}\right)^{2n-2}\iint S_n^2 d\varpi \cdot A^2\cos^2(\sigma t + \epsilon).$$

Substituting in (vi), and putting $r=a$, we have, for the total dissipation,

$$2F = 2n(n-1)(2n+1)\frac{\mu}{a}\iint S_n^2 d\varpi \cdot A^2\cos^2(\sigma t + \epsilon) \quad\text{......}\quad \text{(viii)}.$$

The mean dissipation, per unit time, is therefore

$$2\bar{F} = n(n-1)(2n+1)\frac{\mu}{a}\iint S_n^2 d\varpi \cdot A^2 \quad\text{..................}\quad \text{(ix)}.$$

If the effect of viscosity be represented by a gradual variation of the coefficient A, we must have

$$\frac{d}{dt}(T+V) = -2\bar{F} \quad\text{..............................}\quad \text{(x)},$$

whence, substituting from (v) and (ix),

$$\frac{dA}{dt} = -(n-1)(2n+1)\frac{\nu}{a^2}A \quad \text{(xi)}.$$

This shews that $A \propto e^{-t/\tau}$, where

$$\tau = \frac{1}{(n-1)(2n+1)}\frac{a^2}{\nu} \quad \text{(xii)*}.$$

The most remarkable feature of this result is the excessively minute extent to which the oscillations of a globe of moderate dimensions are affected by such a degree of viscosity as is ordinarily met with in nature. For a globe of the size of the earth, and of the same kinematic viscosity as water, we have, on the C.G.S. system, $a = 6{\cdot}37 \times 10^8$, $\nu = {\cdot}0178$, and the value of τ for the gravitational oscillation of longest period ($n=2$) is

$$\tau = 1{\cdot}44 \times 10^{11} \text{ years.}$$

Even with the value found by Darwin† for the viscosity of pitch near the freezing temperature, viz. $\mu = 1{\cdot}3 \times 10^8 \times g$, we find, taking $g = 980$, the value

$$\tau = 180 \text{ hours}$$

for the modulus of decay of the slowest oscillation of a globe of the size of the earth, having the density of water and the viscosity of pitch. Since this is still large compared with the period of 1 h. 34 m. found in Art. 241, it appears that such a globe would oscillate almost like a perfect fluid.

The investigation by which (xii) was obtained does not involve any special assumption as to the nature of the forces which produce the tendency to the spherical form. The result applies, therefore, equally well to the vibrations of a liquid globule under the surface-tension of the bounding film. The modulus of decay of the slowest oscillation of a globule of water is, in seconds,

$$\tau = 11{\cdot}2\, a^2,$$

where the unit of a is the centimetre.

The formula (xii) includes of course the case of waves on a plane surface. When n is very great we find, putting $\lambda = 2\pi a/n$,

$$\tau = \lambda^2/8\pi^2\nu \quad \text{(xiii)},$$

in agreement with Art. 301.

The same method, applied to the case of a spherical bubble, gives

$$\tau = \frac{1}{(n+2)(2n+1)}\frac{a^2}{\nu} \quad \text{(xiv)},$$

where ν is the viscosity of the surrounding liquid. If this be water we have, for $n=2$, $\tau = 2{\cdot}8a^2$.

The above results all postulate that $2\pi\tau$ is a considerable multiple of the period. The opposite extreme, where the viscosity is so great that the motion

* *Proc. Lond. Math. Soc.*, t. xiii., pp. 61, 65 (1881).

† "On the Bodily Tides of Viscous and Semi-Elastic Spheroids,...," *Phil. Trans.*, 1879.

is aperiodic, can be investigated by the method of Arts. 293, 294, the effects of inertia being disregarded. In the case of a globe returning to the spherical form under the influence of gravitation, it appears that

$$\tau = \frac{2(n+1)^2+1}{n}\frac{\nu}{ga} \quad \text{(xv)},$$

a result first given by Darwin (*l. c.*). Cf. Art. 302 (22).

309. Problems of periodic motion of a liquid in the space between two concentric spheres require for their treatment additional solutions of the equations of Art. 306, in which p is of the form p_{-n-1}, and the functions $\psi_n(hr)$ which occur in the complementary functions u', v', w' are to be replaced by $\Psi_n(hr)$.

The question is simplified, when the radius of the second sphere is infinite, by the condition that the fluid is at rest at infinity. It was shewn in Art. 267 that the functions $\psi_n(\zeta)$, $\Psi_n(\zeta)$ are both included in the form

$$\left(\frac{d}{\zeta d\zeta}\right)^n \frac{Ae^{i\zeta}+Be^{-i\zeta}}{\zeta} \quad \text{(1)}.$$

In the present applications, we have $\zeta = hr$, where h is defined by Art. 306 (4), and we will suppose, for definiteness, that that value of h is adopted which makes the real part of ih positive. The condition of zero motion at infinity then requires that $A = 0$, and we have to deal only with the function

$$f_n(\zeta) = (-)^n \left(\frac{d}{\zeta d\zeta}\right)^n \frac{e^{-i\zeta}}{\zeta} \quad \text{(2)}.$$

As particular cases:

$$\left.\begin{aligned} f_0(\zeta) &= \zeta^{-1}e^{-i\zeta},\\ f_1(\zeta) &= (i\zeta^{-2}+\zeta^{-3})e^{-i\zeta},\\ f_2(\zeta) &= (-\zeta^{-3}+3i\zeta^{-4}+3\zeta^{-5})e^{-i\zeta} \end{aligned}\right\} \quad \text{(3)}.$$

The formulæ of reduction for $f_n(\zeta)$ are exactly the same as for $\psi_n(\zeta)$ and $\Psi_n(\zeta)$, and the general solution of the equations of small periodic motion of a viscous liquid, for the space external to a sphere, are therefore given at once by Art. 306 (8), (10), with p_{-n-1} written for p_n, and $f_n(hr)$ for $\psi_n(hr)$.

1°. The case of the rotatory oscillations of a sphere surrounded by an infinite mass of liquid is included in the solutions of the First Class, with $n=1$. As in Art. 307, 2°, we put $\chi_1 = Cz$, and find

$$u = Cf_1(hr)\,y, \quad v = -Cf_1(hr)\,z, \quad w = 0 \quad \text{(i)},$$

with the condition $$Cf_1(ha) = -\omega \quad\text{.................................... (ii)},$$
a being the radius, and ω the angular velocity of the sphere, which we suppose given by the formula

$$\omega = \alpha e^{i(\sigma t+\epsilon)} \quad\text{.................................... (iii)}.$$

Putting $h=(1-i)\beta$, where $\beta=(\sigma/2\nu)^{\frac{1}{2}}$, we find that the particles on a concentric sphere of radius r are rotating together with the angular velocity

$$\frac{f_1(hr)}{f_1(ha)}\omega = \frac{\alpha a^3}{r^3}\frac{1+ihr}{1+iha}e^{-\beta(r-a)}\cdot e^{i\{\sigma t-\beta(r-a)+\epsilon\}} \quad\text{..............(iv)},$$

where the values of $f_1(hr)$, $f_1(ha)$ have been substituted from (3). The real part of (iv) is

$$\frac{\alpha}{1+2\beta a+2\beta^2a^2}\frac{a^3}{r^3}e^{-\beta(r-a)}\left[\{1+\beta(a+r)+2\beta^2ar\}\cos\{\sigma t-\beta(r-a)+\epsilon\}\right.$$
$$\left.-\beta(r-a)\sin\{\sigma t-\beta(r-a)+\epsilon\}\right] \quad\text{......(v)},$$

corresponding to an angular velocity

$$\omega = \alpha\cos(\sigma t+\epsilon) \quad\text{....................................(vi)}$$

of the sphere.

The couple on the sphere is found in the same way as in Art. 307 to be

$$N = -\tfrac{8}{3}\pi\mu a^3\omega\,\frac{h^2a^2f_2(ha)}{f_1(ha)}$$
$$= -\tfrac{8}{3}\pi\mu a^3\omega\,\frac{3+3iha-h^2a^2}{1+iha} \quad\text{........................(vii)}.$$

Putting $ha=(1-i)\beta a$, and separating the real and imaginary parts we find

$$N = -\tfrac{8}{3}\pi\mu a^3\omega\,\frac{(3+6\beta a+6\beta^2a^2+2\beta^3a^3)+2i\beta^2a^2(1+\beta a)}{1+2\beta a+2\beta^2a^2} \quad\text{......(viii)}.$$

This is equivalent to

$$N = -\tfrac{8}{3}\pi\rho a^5\,\frac{1+\beta a}{1+2\beta a+2\beta^2a^2}\frac{d\omega}{dt} - \tfrac{8}{3}\pi\mu a^3\,\frac{3+6\beta a+6\beta^2a^2+2\beta^3a^3}{1+2\beta a+2\beta^2a^2}\,\omega \quad\text{...(ix)}.$$

The interpretation is similar to that of Art. 307 (xxvii) *.

2°. In the case of a ball pendulum oscillating in an infinite mass of fluid, which we treat as incompressible, we take the origin at the mean position of the centre, and the axis of x in the direction of the oscillation.

The conditions to be satisfied at the surface are then

$$u=\mathrm{u},\quad v=0,\quad w=0 \quad\text{.............................. (x)},$$

for $r=a$ (the radius), where u denotes the velocity of the sphere. It is evident that we are concerned only with a solution of the Second Class. Again, the formulæ (10) of Art. 306, when modified as aforesaid, make

$$xu+yv+zw = -\frac{n+1}{h^2\mu}p_{-n-1} + n(n+1)(2n+1)f_n(hr)\,\phi_n \quad\text{......(xi)};$$

* Another solution of this problem is given by Kirchhoff, *Mechanik*, c. XXVI.

and by comparison with (x), it appears that this must involve surface harmonics of the *first order* only. We therefore put $n=1$, and assume

$$p_{-2}=Ax/r^3, \quad \phi_1=Bx \qquad \text{(xii)}.$$

Hence

$$\left.\begin{aligned} u&=\frac{A}{h^2\mu}\frac{d}{dx}\frac{x}{r^3}+B\left\{2f_0(hr)-f_2(hr)\,h^2r^5\frac{d}{dx}\frac{x}{r^3}\right\},\\ v&=\frac{A}{h^2\mu}\frac{d}{dy}\frac{x}{r^3}\qquad\qquad -Bf_2(hr)\,h^2r^5\frac{d}{dy}\frac{x}{r^3},\\ w&=\frac{A}{h^2\mu}\frac{d}{dz}\frac{x}{r^3}\qquad\qquad -Bf_2(hr)\,h^2r^5\frac{d}{dz}\frac{x}{r^3}\end{aligned}\right\} \qquad \text{(xiii)}.$$

The conditions (x) are therefore satisfied if

$$A=\mu h^4a^5f_2(ha)\,B, \quad 2f_0(ha)\,B=\mathrm{u} \qquad \text{(xiv)}.$$

The character of the motion, which is evidently symmetrical about the axis of x, can be most concisely expressed by means of the stream-function (Art. 93). From (xi) or (xiii) we find

$$xu+yv+zw=-\frac{2A}{h^2\mu}\frac{x}{r^3}+6Bf_1(hr)x=-\frac{\mathrm{u}x}{f_0(ha)}\left\{\frac{h^2a^5}{r^3}f_2(ha)-3f_1(hr)\right\} \ldots \text{(xv)},$$

or, substituting from (3),

$$xu+yv+zw=\left\{\left(1-\frac{3i}{ha}-\frac{3}{h^2a^2}\right)\frac{a^3}{r^3}+3\left(\frac{i}{hr}+\frac{1}{h^2r^2}\right)\frac{a}{r}e^{-ih(r-a)}\right\}\mathrm{u}x \ldots \text{(xvi)}.$$

If we put $x=r\cos\theta$, this leads, in the notation, and on the convention as to sign, of Art. 93 to

$$\psi=-\tfrac{1}{2}\mathrm{u}a^2\sin^2\theta\left\{\left(1-\frac{3i}{ha}-\frac{3}{h^2a^2}\right)\frac{a}{r}+\frac{3}{ha}\left(i+\frac{1}{hr}\right)e^{-ih(r-a)}\right\} \ldots \text{(xvii)}.$$

Writing

$$\mathrm{u}=ae^{i(\sigma t+\epsilon)} \qquad \text{(xviii)},$$

and therefore $h=(1-i)\beta$, where $\beta=(\sigma/2\nu)^{\frac{1}{2}}$, we find, on rejecting the imaginary part of (xvii),

$$\psi=-\tfrac{1}{2}aa^2\sin^2\theta\left[\left\{\left(1+\frac{3}{2\beta a}\right)\cos(\sigma t+\epsilon)+\frac{3}{2\beta a}\left(1+\frac{1}{\beta a}\right)\sin(\sigma t+\epsilon)\right\}\frac{a}{r}\right.$$

$$\left.-\frac{3}{2\beta a}\left\{\cos\{\sigma t-\beta(r-a)+\epsilon\}+\left(1+\frac{1}{\beta r}\right)\sin\{\sigma t-\beta(r-a)+\epsilon\}\right\}e^{-\beta(r-a)}\right] \ldots \text{(xix)}.$$

At a sufficient distance from the sphere, the part of the disturbance which is expressed by the terms in the first line of this expression is predominant. This part is irrotational, and differs only in amplitude and phase from the motion produced by a sphere oscillating in a frictionless liquid (Arts. 91, 95). The terms in the second line are of the type we have already met with in the case of laminar motion (Art. 298).

To calculate the resultant force (X) on the sphere, we have recourse to Art. 306 (18). Substituting from (xii), and rejecting all but the constant terms in p_{rx}, since the surface-harmonics of other than zero order will disappear when integrated over the sphere, we find

$$X=\iint p_{rx}\,dS=4\pi\left(B_{-2}\frac{A}{a}+C_1 Ba^2\right)\text{.................(xx)},$$

where $$B_{-2}=-\tfrac{1}{3}a^2,\quad C_1=2\mu haf_0'(ha)\text{.....................(xxi)},$$

by Art. 306 (19). Hence, by (xii) and (3),

$$X=\frac{2\pi\mu \mathrm{u}ha^2}{f_0(ha)}\{2f_0'(ha)-\tfrac{1}{3}h^3a^3f_2(ha)\}$$

$$=2\pi\mu \mathrm{u}h^2a^3\left(\tfrac{1}{3}-\frac{3i}{ha}-\frac{3}{h^2a^2}\right)$$

$$=-2\pi\rho a^3\sigma\mathrm{u}\left\{\left(\tfrac{1}{3}+\frac{3}{2\beta a}\right)i+\frac{3}{2\beta a}\left(1+\frac{1}{\beta a}\right)\right\}\text{........... (xxii)}.$$

This is equivalent to

$$X=-\tfrac{4}{3}\pi\rho a^3\left(\tfrac{1}{2}+\frac{9}{4\beta a}\right)\frac{d\mathrm{u}}{dt}-3\pi\rho a^3\sigma\left(\frac{1}{\beta a}+\frac{1}{\beta^2a^2}\right)\mathrm{u}\text{......(xxiii)}.$$

The first term gives the correction to the inertia of the sphere. This amounts to the fraction

$$\tfrac{1}{2}+\frac{9}{4\beta a}$$

of the mass of fluid displaced, instead of $\tfrac{1}{2}$ as in the case of a frictionless liquid (Art. 91). The second term gives a frictional force varying as the velocity*.

310. We may next briefly notice the effect of viscosity on waves of expansion in gases, although, for a reason to be given, the results cannot be regarded as more than illustrative.

In the case of plane waves† in a laterally unlimited medium, we have, if we take the axis of x in the direction of propagation, and neglect terms of the second order in the velocity,

$$\frac{du}{dt}=-\frac{1}{\rho_0}\frac{dp}{dx}+\tfrac{4}{3}\nu\frac{d^2u}{dx^2}\text{.....................(1)},$$

by Art. 286 (2), (3). If s denote the condensation, the equation of continuity is, as in Art. 255,

$$\frac{ds}{dt}=-\frac{du}{dx}\text{..........................(2)};$$

* This problem was first solved, in a different manner, by Stokes, *l. c. ante* p. 518. For other methods of treatment see O. E. Meyer, "Ueber die pendelnde Bewegung einer Kugel unter dem Einflusse der inneren Reibung des umgebenden mediums," *Crelle*, t. lxxiii. (1871); Kirchhoff, *Mechanik*, c. xxvi. The variable motion of a sphere in a liquid has been discussed by Basset, *Phil. Trans.*, 1888; *Hydrodynamics*, c. xxii.

† Discussed by Stokes, *l. c. ante* p. 518.

and the physical equation is, if the transfer of heat be neglected,

$$p = p_0 + c^2 \rho_0 s \quad \text{.......................(3)},$$

where c is the velocity of sound in the absence of viscosity. Eliminating p and s, we have

$$\frac{d^2u}{dt^2} = c^2 \frac{d^2u}{dx^2} + \tfrac{4}{3}\nu \frac{d^3u}{dx^2\,dt} \quad \text{.....................(4)}.$$

To apply this to the case of forced waves, we may suppose that at the plane $x = 0$ a given vibration

$$u = ae^{i\sigma t} \quad \text{.............................(5)}$$

is kept up. Assuming as the solution of (4)

$$u = ae^{i\sigma t + \beta x} \quad \text{.........................(6)},$$

we find

$$\beta^2 (c^2 + \tfrac{4}{3} i\nu\sigma) = -\sigma^2 \quad \text{.....................(7)},$$

whence

$$\beta = \pm \frac{i\sigma}{c}\left(1 - \tfrac{4}{3} i \frac{\nu\sigma}{c^2}\right)^{-\frac{1}{2}} \quad \text{..................(8)}.$$

If we neglect the square of $\nu\sigma/c^2$, and take the lower sign, this gives

$$\beta = -\frac{i\sigma}{c} - \tfrac{2}{3}\frac{\nu\sigma^2}{c^3} \quad \text{........................(9)}.$$

Substituting in (6), and taking the real part, we get, for the waves propagated in the direction of x-positive

$$u = ae^{-x/l} \cos \sigma \left(t - \frac{x}{c}\right) \quad \text{..................(10)},$$

where

$$l = \tfrac{3}{2} c^3/\nu\sigma^2 \quad \text{........................(11)}.$$

The amplitude of the waves diminishes exponentially as they proceed, the diminution being more rapid the greater the value of σ. The wave-velocity is, to the first order of $\nu\sigma/c^2$, unaffected by the friction.

The linear magnitude l measures the distance in which the amplitude falls to $1/e$ of its original value. If λ denote the wave-length $(2\pi c/\sigma)$, we have

$$\tfrac{2}{3}\nu\sigma/c^2 = \lambda/2\pi l \quad \text{.........................(12)};$$

it is assumed in the above calculation that this is a small ratio.

In the case of air-waves we have $c=3{\cdot}32\times10^4$, $\nu={\cdot}132$, C.G.S., whence

$$\nu\sigma/c^2=2\pi\nu/\lambda c=2{\cdot}50\,\lambda^{-1}\times10^{-5},\quad l=9{\cdot}56\lambda^2\times10^3,$$

if λ be expressed in centimetres.

To find the decay of *free* waves of any prescribed wave-length $(2\pi/k)$, we assume

$$u=ae^{ikx+\alpha t} \quad\text{.......................... (13);}$$

and, substituting in (4), we obtain

$$\alpha^2+\tfrac{4}{3}\nu k^2\alpha=-k^2c^2 \quad\text{.......................(14).}$$

If we neglect the square of $\nu k/c$, this gives

$$\alpha=-\tfrac{2}{3}\nu k^2\pm ikc \quad\text{..................... (15).}$$

Hence, in real form,

$$u=ae^{-t/\tau}\cos k(x\pm ct) \quad\text{.................. (16),}$$

where

$$\tau=3/2\nu k^2 \quad\text{........................ (17)*.}$$

The estimates of the rate of damping of aerial vibrations, which are given by calculations such as the preceding, though doubtless of the right order of magnitude, must be actually under the mark, since the thermal processes of conduction and radiation will produce effects of the same kind, of comparable amount, and ought therefore, for consistency, to be included in our calculations. This was first pointed out distinctly by Kirchhoff, who has investigated, in particular, the theoretical velocity of sound-waves in a narrow tube†. This problem is important for its bearing on the well-known experimental method of Kundt. Lord Rayleigh has applied the same principles to explain the action of porous bodies in absorption of sound‡.

311. It remains to call attention to the chief outstanding difficulty of our subject.

It has already been pointed out that the neglect of the terms of the second order (udu/dx, &c.) seriously limits the application of many of the preceding results to fluids possessed of ordinary

* For a calculation, on the same assumptions, of the effect of viscosity in damping the vibrations of air contained within spherical and cylindrical envelopes reference may be made to the paper "On the Motion of a Viscous Fluid contained in a Spherical Vessel," cited on p. 558.

† "Ueber den Einfluss der Wärmeleitung in einem Gase auf die Schallbewegung," *Pogg. Ann.*, t. cxxxiv. (1868); *Ges. Abh.*, p. 540.

‡ "On Porous Bodies in relation to Sound," *Phil. Mag.*, Sept. 1883.

degrees of mobility. Unless the velocities be very small, the actual motion, in such cases, so far as it admits of being observed, is found to be very different from that represented by our formulæ. For example, when a solid of 'easy' shape moves through a liquid, an irregular, eddying, motion is produced in a layer of the fluid next to the solid, and a widening trail of eddies is left behind, whilst the motion at a distance laterally is comparatively smooth and uniform.

The mathematical disability above pointed out does not apply to cases of *rectilinear* flow, such as have been discussed in Arts. 288, 289; but even here observation shews that the types of motion there investigated, though always theoretically possible, become under certain conditions unstable. The case of flow through a pipe of circular section has been made the subject of a very careful experimental study by Reynolds*, by means of filaments of coloured fluid introduced into the stream. So long as the mean velocity (w_0) over the cross-section falls below a certain limit depending on the radius of the pipe and the nature of the fluid, the flow is smooth, and in accordance with Poiseuille's laws; but when this limit is exceeded the motion becomes wildly irregular, and the tube appears to be filled with interlacing and constantly varying streams, crossing and recrossing the pipe. It was inferred by Reynolds, from considerations of dimensions, that the aforesaid limit must be determined by the ratio of w_0a to ν, where a is the radius, and ν the (kinematic) viscosity. This was verified by experiment, the critical ratio being found to be, roughly,

$$w_0a/\nu = 1000 \qquad\qquad (1)\dagger.$$

Thus for a pipe one centimetre in radius the critical velocity for water ($\nu = \cdot 018$) would be 18 cm. per sec.

Simultaneously with the change in the character of the motion, when the critical ratio is passed, there is a change in the relation between the pressure-gradient (dp/dz) and the mean velocity w_0. So long as w_0a/ν falls below the above limit, dp/dz varies as w_0, as

* "An Experimental Investigation of the Circumstances which determine whether the Motion of Water shall be Direct or Sinuous, and of the Law of Resistance in Parallel Channels," *Phil. Trans.*, 1883.

† The dependence on ν was tested by varying the temperature.

in Poiseuille's experiments, but when the irregular mode of flow has set in, dp/dz varies more nearly as w_0^2.

The practical formula adopted by writers on Hydraulics, for pipes whose diameter exceeds a certain limit, is

$$R = \tfrac{1}{2} f \rho w_0^2 \qquad (2),$$

where R is the tangential resistance per unit area, w_0 is the mean velocity relative to the wetted surface, and f is a numerical constant depending on the nature of the surface. As a rough average value for the case of water moving over a clean iron surface, we may take $f = \cdot 005$*. A more complete expression for R, taking into account the influence of the diameter, has been given by Darcy, as the result of his very extensive observations on the flow of water through conduits†.

The resistance, in the case of turbulent flow, is found to be sensibly independent of the temperature, and therefore of the viscosity of the fluid. This is what we should anticipate from considerations of 'dimensions,' if it be assumed that $R \propto w_0^2$‡.

If we accept the formula (2) as the expression of observed facts, a conclusion of some interest may be at once drawn. Taking the axis of z in the general direction of the flow, if $\bar{w}$ denote the *mean* velocity (with respect to the *time*) at any point of space, we have, at the surface,

$$\mu \frac{d\bar{w}}{dn} = \tfrac{1}{2} f \rho w_0^2,$$

if w_0 denote the general velocity of the stream, and δn an element of the normal. If we take a linear magnitude l such

$$w_0 / l = d\bar{w}/dn,$$

then l measures the distance between two planes moving with a relative velocity w_0 in the regular 'laminar' flow which would give the same tangential stress. We find

$$w_0 l = 2\nu / f \qquad (3).$$

* See Rankine, *Applied Mechanics*, Art. 638; Unwin, *Encyc. Britann.*, Art. "Hydromechanics."

† *Recherches expérimentales rélatives au mouvement de l'eau dans les tuyaux*, Paris, 1855. The formula is quoted by Rankine and Unwin.

‡ Lord Rayleigh, "On the Question of the Stability of the Flow of Fluids," *Phil. Mag.*, July 1892.

For example, putting $\nu = \cdot 018$, $w_0 = 300$ [C. S.], $f = \cdot 005$, we obtain $l = \cdot 024$ cm.* The smallness of this result suggests that in the turbulent flow of a fluid through a pipe of not too small diameter the value of $\overline{w}$ is nearly uniform over the section, falling rapidly to zero within a very minute distance of the walls†.

Applied to pipes of sufficient width, the formula (2) gives

$$-\pi a^2 \frac{dp}{dz} = 2\pi a R = \pi f \rho a w_0^2,$$

or

$$-\frac{1}{\rho}\frac{dp}{dz} = f\frac{w_0^2}{a} \quad \text{.......................} \quad (4).$$

The form of the relation which was found to hold by Reynolds, in his experiments, was

$$\frac{1}{\rho}\frac{dp}{dz} \propto \frac{\nu^{2-m} w_0^{\,m}}{a^{3-m}},$$

where $m = 1\cdot 723$.

The increased resistance, for velocities above a certain limit, represented by the formula (2) or (4), is no doubt due to the action of the eddies in continually bringing fresh fluid, moving with a considerable relative velocity, close up to the boundary, and so increasing the distortion-rate (dw/dn) greatly beyond that which would obtain in regular 'laminar' motion‡.

The frictional or 'skin-resistance'§ experienced by a solid of 'easy' shape moving through a liquid is to be accounted for on the same principles. The circumstances are however more complicated than in the case of a pipe. The friction appears to vary roughly as the square of the velocity; but it is different in different parts of the wetted area, for a reason given by W. Froude, to whom the most exact observations‖ on the subject are due.

* Cf. Sir W. Thomson, *Phil. Mag.*, Sept. 1887.

† This was in fact found experimentally by Darcy, *l. c.* The author is indebted for this reference to Prof. Reynolds.

‡ Stokes, *Math. and Phys. Papers*, t. i., p. 99.

§ So called by writers on naval architecture, to distinguish it from the 'wave-resistance' referred to in Arts. 221, 228.

‖ "Experiments on the Surface-friction experienced by a Plane moving through Water," *Brit. Ass. Rep.*, 1872, p. 118.

"The portion of the surface that goes first in the line of motion, in experiencing resistance from the water, must in turn communicate to the water motion, in the direction in which it is itself travelling. Consequently the portion of the water which succeeds the first will be rubbing, not against stationary water, but against water partially moving in its own direction, and cannot therefore experience as much resistance from it."

312. The theoretical explanation of the instability of linear flow, under the conditions stated, and of the manner in which eddies are maintained against viscosity, is at present obscure. We may refer, however, to one or two attempts which have been made to elucidate the question.

Lord Rayleigh, in several papers*, has set himself to examine the stability of various arrangements of vortices, such as might be produced by viscosity. The fact that, in the *disturbed* motion, viscosity is ignored does not seriously affect the physical value of the results except perhaps in cases where these would imply slipping at a rigid boundary.

As the method is simple, we may briefly notice the two-dimensional form of the problem.

Let us suppose that in a slight disturbance of the steady laminar motion

$$u=U, \quad v=0, \quad w=0,$$

where U is a function of y only, we have

$$u=U+u', \quad v=v', \quad w=0 \qquad \text{(i)}.$$

The equation of continuity is

$$\frac{du'}{dx}+\frac{dv'}{dy}=0 \qquad \text{(ii)}.$$

The dynamical equations reduce, by Art. 143, to the condition of constant angular velocity $D\zeta/Dt=0$, or

$$\frac{d\zeta}{dt}+(U+u')\frac{d\zeta}{dx}+v'\frac{d\zeta}{dy}=0 \qquad \text{(iii)},$$

where

$$\zeta=\tfrac{1}{2}\left(\frac{dv'}{dx}-\frac{du'}{dy}\right)-\tfrac{1}{2}\frac{dU}{dy} \qquad \text{(iv)}.$$

Hence, neglecting terms of the second order in u', v',

$$\left(\frac{d}{dt}+U\frac{d}{dx}\right)\left(\frac{dv'}{dx}-\frac{du'}{dy}\right)-\frac{d^2U}{dy^2}v'=0 \qquad \text{(v)}.$$

Contemplating now a disturbance which is periodic in respect to x, we assume that u', v' vary as $e^{ikx+i\sigma t}$. Hence, from (ii) and (v),

$$iku'+\frac{dv'}{dy}=0 \qquad \text{(vi)},$$

and

$$i(\sigma+kU)\left(ikv'-\frac{du'}{dy}\right)-\frac{d^2U}{dy^2}v'=0 \qquad \text{(vii)}.$$

* "On the Stability or Instability of certain Fluid Motions," *Proc. Lond. Math. Soc.*, t. xi., p. 57 (1880), and t. xix., p. 67 (1887); "On the Question of the Stability of the Flow of Fluids," *Phil. Mag.*, July 1892.

Eliminating u', we find

$$(\sigma+kU)\left(\frac{d^2v'}{dy^2}-k^2v'\right)-\frac{d^2U}{dy^2}kv'=0 \qquad \text{(viii)},$$

which is the fundamental equation.

If, for any value of y, dU/dy is discontinuous, the equation (viii) must be replaced by

$$(\sigma+kU)\,\Delta\left(\frac{dv'}{dy}\right)-\Delta\left(\frac{dU}{dy}\right)kv'=0 \qquad \text{(ix)},$$

where Δ denotes the difference of the values of the respective quantities on the two sides of the plane of discontinuity. This is obtained from (viii) by integration with respect to y, the discontinuity being regarded as the limit of an infinitely rapid variation. The formula (ix) may also be obtained as the condition of continuity of pressure, or as the condition that there should be no tangential slipping at the (displaced) boundary.

At a fixed boundary, we must have $v'=0$.

1°. Suppose that a layer of fluid of uniform vorticity bounded by the planes $y=\pm h$, is interposed between two masses of fluid moving irrotationally, the velocity being everywhere continuous. This is a variation of a problem discussed in Art. 225.

Assuming, then, $U=\mathrm{u}$ for $y>h$, $U=\mathrm{u}y/h$ for $h>y>-h$, and $U=-\mathrm{u}$ for $y<-h$, we notice that $d^2U/dy^2=0$, everywhere, so that (viii) reduces to

$$\frac{d^2v'}{dy^2}-k^2v'=0 \qquad \text{(x)}.$$

The appropriate solutions of this are:

$$\left.\begin{aligned} &v'=Ae^{-ky}, \text{ for } y>h;\\ &v'=Be^{-ky}+Ce^{ky}, \text{ for } h>y>-h;\\ &v'=De^{ky}, \text{ for } y<-h \end{aligned}\right\} \qquad \text{(xi)}.$$

The continuity of v' requires

$$\left.\begin{aligned} Ae^{-kh}&=Be^{-kh}+Ce^{kh},\\ De^{-kh}&=Be^{kh}+Ce^{-kh} \end{aligned}\right\} \qquad \text{(xii)}.$$

With the help of these relations, the condition (ix) gives

$$\left.\begin{aligned} &2(\sigma+k\mathrm{u})\,Ce^{kh}-\frac{\mathrm{u}}{h}(Be^{-kh}+Ce^{kh})=0,\\ &2(\sigma-k\mathrm{u})\,Be^{kh}+\frac{\mathrm{u}}{h}(Be^{kh}+Ce^{-kh})=0 \end{aligned}\right\} \qquad \text{(xiii)}.$$

Eliminating the ratio $B:C$, we obtain

$$\sigma^2=\frac{\mathrm{u}^2}{4h^2}\{(2kh-1)^2-e^{-4kh}\} \qquad \text{(xiv)}.$$

For small values of kh this makes $\sigma^2 = -k^2\mathrm{u}^2$, as in the case of absolute discontinuity (Art. 225). For large values of kh, on the other hand, $\sigma = \pm k\mathrm{u}$, indicating stability. Hence the question as to the stability for disturbances of wave-length λ depends on the ratio $\lambda/2h$. The values of the function in { } on the right-hand of (xiv) have been tabulated by Lord Rayleigh. It appears that there is instability if $\lambda/2h > 5$, about; and that the instability is a maximum for $\lambda/2h = 8$.

2°. In the papers referred to, Lord Rayleigh has further investigated various cases of flow between parallel walls, with the view of throwing light on the conditions of stability of linear motion in a pipe. The main result is that if d^2U/dy^2 does not change sign, in other words, if the curve with y as abscissa and U as ordinate is of one curvature throughout, the motion is stable. Since, however, the disturbed motion involves slipping at the walls, it remains doubtful how far the conclusions apply to the question at present under consideration, in which the condition of no slipping appears to be fundamental.

3°. The substitution of (x) for (viii), when $d^2U/dy^2=0$, is equivalent to assuming that the rotation ζ is the same as in the undisturbed motion; since on this hypothesis we have

$$\frac{du'}{dy} = \frac{dv'}{dx} = ikv' \qquad \text{(xv)},$$

which, with (vi), leads to the equation in question.

It is to be observed, however, that when $d^2U/dy^2=0$, the equation (viii) may be satisfied, for a particular value of y, by $\sigma + kU = 0$. For example, we may suppose that at the plane $y=0$ a thin layer of (infinitely small) additional vorticity is introduced. We then have, on the hypothesis that the fluid is unlimited,

$$v' = Ae^{\mp ky} \qquad \text{(xvi)},$$

the upper or the lower sign being taken according as y is positive or negative. The condition (ix) is then satisfied by

$$\sigma + kU_0 = 0 \qquad \text{(xvii)},$$

if

$$\Delta\left(\frac{dU}{dy}\right) = 0 \qquad \text{(xviii)},$$

where U_0 denotes the value of U for $y=0$. Since the superposition of a uniform velocity in the direction of x does not alter the problem, we may suppose $U_0=0$, and therefore $\sigma=0$. The disturbed motion is steady; in other words, the original state of flow is (to the first order of small quantities) *neutral* for a disturbance of this kind*.

Lord Kelvin has attacked directly the very difficult problem of determining the stability of laminar motion when viscosity is taken

* Cf. Sir W. Thomson, "On a Disturbing Infinity in Lord Rayleigh's solution for Waves in a plane Vortex Stratum," *Brit. Ass. Rep.*, 1880.

into account*. He concludes that the linear flow of a fluid through a pipe, or of a stream over a plane bed, is stable for infinitely small disturbances, but that for disturbances of more than a certain amplitude the motion becomes unstable, the limits of stability being narrower the smaller the viscosity. A portion of the investigation has been criticised by Lord Rayleigh†; and there can be no question that the whole matter calls for further elucidation‡.

* "Rectilinear Motion of Viscous Fluid between two Parallel Planes," *Phil. Mag.*, Aug. 1887; "Broad River flowing down an Inclined Plane Bed," *Phil. Mag.*, Sept. 1887.

† *l. c. ante* p. 574.

‡ The most recent contribution to the subject is a paper by Reynolds, "On the Dynamical Theory of Incompressible Viscous Fluids and the Determination of the Criterion," the full text of which has not yet been published. *Proc. Roy. Soc.*, May 24, 1894.

CHAPTER XII.

EQUILIBRIUM OF ROTATING MASSES OF LIQUID.

313. THIS subject had its origin in the investigations on the theory of the Earth's Figure which so powerfully engaged the attention of mathematicians near the end of the last and the beginning of the present century.

Considerations of space forbid our attempting more than a rapid sketch, with references to the original memoirs, of the case where the fluid is of uniform density, and the external boundary is ellipsoidal. With this is incorporated a slight account of some cognate investigations by Dirichlet and others, which claim notice not only on grounds of physical interest, but also by reason of the elegance of the analytical methods employed.

We write down, in the first place, some formulæ relating to the attraction of ellipsoids.

If the density ρ be expressed in 'astronomical' measure, the gravitation-potential (at internal points) of a uniform mass enclosed by the surface

$$\frac{x^2}{a^2}+\frac{y^2}{b^2}+\frac{z^2}{c^2}=1 \quad\text{..........................}\quad (1)$$

is

$$\Omega = \pi\rho abc\int_0^\infty \left(\frac{x^2}{a^2+\lambda}+\frac{y^2}{b^2+\lambda}+\frac{z^2}{c^2+\lambda}-1\right)\frac{d\lambda}{\Delta} \text{....}(2)^*,$$

where

$$\Delta = \{(a^2+\lambda)(b^2+\lambda)(c^2+\lambda)\}^{\frac{1}{2}} \quad\text{...............}\quad (3).$$

This may be written

$$\Omega = \pi\rho\,(\alpha_0 x^2+\beta_0 y^2+\gamma_0 z^2-\chi_0) \text{..............} (4),$$

where

$$\alpha_0 = abc\int_0^\infty \frac{d\lambda}{(a^2+\lambda)\Delta},\quad \beta_0 = abc\int_0^\infty \frac{d\lambda}{(b^2+\lambda)\Delta},\quad \gamma_0 = abc\int_0^\infty \frac{d\lambda}{(c^2+\lambda)\Delta}$$

............(5),

* For references see p. 534. The sign of Ω has been changed from the usual reckoning.

and
$$\chi_0 = abc\int_0^\infty \frac{d\lambda}{\Delta} \quad\text{.......................... (6).}$$

The potential energy of the mass is given by
$$V = \tfrac{1}{2}\iiint \Omega\rho\, dx\, dy\, dz \quad\text{...................... (7),}$$
where the integrations extend over the volume. Substituting from (4) we find
$$V = \tfrac{2}{3}\pi^2\rho^2 abc\,\{\tfrac{1}{5}(\alpha_0 a^2 + \beta_0 b^2 + \gamma_0 c^2) - \chi_0\}$$
$$= \tfrac{2}{3}\pi^2\rho^2 a^2b^2c^2 \int_0^\infty \left\{\tfrac{1}{5}\left(\frac{a^2}{a^2+\lambda} + \frac{b^2}{b^2+\lambda} + \frac{c^2}{c^2+\lambda}\right) - 1\right\}\frac{d\lambda}{\Delta}$$
$$= \tfrac{2}{3}\pi^2\rho^2 a^2b^2c^2 \int_0^\infty \left\{\tfrac{2}{5}\lambda\, d\left(\frac{1}{\Delta}\right) - \tfrac{2}{5}\frac{d\lambda}{\Delta}\right\}$$
$$= -\tfrac{8}{15}\pi^2\rho^2 a^2b^2c^2 \int_0^\infty \frac{d\lambda}{\Delta} \quad\text{.......................................(8).}$$

This expression is negative because the zero of reckoning corresponds to a state of infinite diffusion of the mass. If we adopt as zero of potential energy that of the mass when collected into a sphere of radius $\mathbf{a}$, $= (abc)^{\frac{1}{3}}$, we must prefix to the right-hand of (8) the term
$$\tfrac{16}{15}\pi^2\rho^2\mathbf{a}^5 \quad\text{.......................... (9).}$$

If the ellipsoid be of revolution, the integrals reduce. If it be of the *planetary* form we may put
$$a = b = \frac{(\zeta^2+1)^{\frac{1}{2}}}{\zeta}c \quad\text{...................... (10),}$$
and obtain*
$$\left.\begin{aligned}\alpha_0 = \beta_0 &= (\zeta^2+1)\,\zeta\cot^{-1}\zeta - \zeta^2,\\ \gamma_0 &= 2(\zeta^2+1)(1-\zeta\cot^{-1}\zeta)\end{aligned}\right\}\text{............(11),}$$
$$V = \tfrac{16}{15}\pi^2\rho^2\mathbf{a}^5\left\{1 - \left(\frac{\zeta^2+1}{\zeta^2}\right)^{\frac{1}{3}}\zeta\cot^{-1}\zeta\right\}\text{.........(12),}$$
provided the zero of V correspond to the spherical form.

For an *ovary* ellipsoid we put
$$a = b = \frac{(\zeta^2-1)^{\frac{1}{2}}}{\zeta}c \quad\text{...................... (13),}$$

* Most simply by writing $c^2+\lambda = (a^2-c^2)\,u^2$.

which leads to

$$\left.\begin{aligned}\alpha_0 = \beta_0 = \zeta^2 - \tfrac{1}{2}(\zeta^2-1)\zeta\log\frac{\zeta+1}{\zeta-1},\\ \gamma_0 = 2(\zeta^2-1)\left(\tfrac{1}{2}\zeta\log\frac{\zeta+1}{\zeta-1}-1\right)\end{aligned}\right\}\quad\text{.........(14)},$$

$$V = \tfrac{16}{15}\pi^2\rho^2\mathbf{a}^5\left\{1-\tfrac{1}{2}\left(\frac{\zeta^2-1}{\zeta^2}\right)^{\frac{1}{3}}\zeta\log\frac{\zeta+1}{\zeta-1}\right\}\quad\text{...... (15)}.$$

The case of an infinitely long elliptic cylinder may also be noticed. Putting $c = \infty$ in (5), we find

$$\alpha_0 = \frac{2b}{a+b},\quad \beta_0 = \frac{2a}{a+b},\quad \gamma_0 = 0\quad\text{...........(16)}.$$

The energy per unit length of the cylinder is

$$V_1 = \tfrac{4}{15}\pi^2\rho^2\mathbf{a}^4\log\frac{(a+b)^2}{4ab}\quad\text{.............. (17)},$$

if $\mathbf{a}^2 = ab$.

314. If the ellipsoid rotate in relative equilibrium about the axis of z, with angular velocity n, the component accelerations of the particle (x, y, z) are $-n^2x$, $-n^2y$, 0, so that the dynamical equations reduce to

$$-n^2x = -\frac{1}{\rho}\frac{dp}{dx} - \frac{d\Omega}{dx},\quad -n^2y = -\frac{1}{\rho}\frac{dp}{dy} - \frac{d\Omega}{dy},\quad 0 = -\frac{1}{\rho}\frac{dp}{dz} - \frac{d\Omega}{dz}$$
$$\text{..............(1)}.$$

Hence $$\frac{p}{\rho} = \tfrac{1}{2}n^2(x^2+y^2) - \Omega + \text{const.}\quad\text{..............(2)}.$$

The surfaces of equal pressure are therefore given by

$$\left(\alpha_0 - \frac{n^2}{2\pi\rho}\right)x^2 + \left(\beta_0 - \frac{n^2}{2\pi\rho}\right)y^2 + \gamma_0 z^2 = \text{const.}\quad\text{....... (3)}.$$

In order that one of these may coincide with the external surface

$$\frac{x^2}{a^2} + \frac{y^2}{b^2} + \frac{z^2}{c^2} = 1\quad\text{...................... (4)},$$

we must have

$$\left(\alpha_0 - \frac{n^2}{2\pi\rho}\right)a^2 = \left(\beta_0 - \frac{n^2}{2\pi\rho}\right)b^2 = \gamma_0 c^2\quad\text{........... (5)}.$$

In the case of an ellipsoid of revolution $(a = b)$, these conditions reduce to one:

$$\left(\alpha_0 - \frac{n^2}{2\pi\rho}\right) a^2 = \gamma_0 c^2 \qquad (6).$$

Since $a^2/(a^2+\lambda)$ is greater or less than $c^2/(c^2+\lambda)$, according as a is greater or less than c, it follows from the forms of α_0, γ_0 given in Art. 313 (5) that the above condition can be fulfilled by a suitable value of n for any assigned planetary ellipsoid, but not for the ovary form. This important result is due to Maclaurin*.

If we substitute from Art. 313 (11), the condition (6) takes the form

$$\frac{n^2}{2\pi\rho} = (3\zeta^2+1)\,\zeta\cot^{-1}\zeta - 3\zeta^2 \qquad (7).$$

The quantity ζ is connected with the excentricity e of the meridian section by the relations

$$e^2 = 1/(\zeta^2+1), \quad \zeta^2 = (1-e^2)/e^2.$$

The equation (7) was discussed, under slightly different forms, by Simpson, d'Alembert†, and (more fully) by Laplace‡. As ζ decreases from ∞ to 0, and e therefore increases from 0 to 1, the right-hand side increases continually from zero to a certain maximum (·2247), corresponding to $e = {\cdot}9299$, $a/c = 2{\cdot}7198$, and then decreases asymptotically to zero. Hence for any assigned value of n, such that $n^2/2\pi\rho < {\cdot}2247$, there are *two* ellipsoids of revolution satisfying the conditions of relative equilibrium, the excentricity being in one case less and in the other greater than ·9299. If $n^2/2\pi\rho > {\cdot}2247$, no ellipsoidal form is possible.

When ζ is great, the right-hand side of (7) reduces to $\frac{4}{15}\zeta^{-2}$ approximately. Hence in the case of a planetary ellipsoid differing infinitely little from a sphere we have, for the *ellipticity*,

$$\epsilon = (a-c)/a = \tfrac{1}{2}\zeta^{-2} = \tfrac{15}{16}\frac{n^2}{\pi\rho} \qquad (i).$$

If g denote the value of gravity at the surface of a sphere of radius a, of the same density, we have $g = \frac{4}{3}\pi\rho a$, whence

$$\epsilon = \tfrac{5}{4}\frac{n^2 a}{g} \qquad (ii).$$

Putting $n^2a/g = \frac{1}{289}$, we find that a homogeneous liquid globe of the same size and mass as the earth, rotating in the same period, would have an ellipticity of $\frac{1}{231}$.

* *l. c. ante* pp. 322, 367.

† See Todhunter, *Hist. of the Theories of Attraction, etc.*, cc. x., xvi.

‡ *Mécanique Céleste*, Livre 3me, chap. iii.

The fastest rotation which admits of an ellipsoidal form of revolution, for such a mass, has a period of 2 h. 25 m.

If $\mathbf{m}$ be the total mass, $\mathbf{h}$ its angular momentum, we have

$$\mathbf{m} = \tfrac{4}{3}\pi\rho a^2 c, \quad \mathbf{h} = \tfrac{2}{5}\mathbf{m}a^2 n \qquad (8),$$

whence we find

$$\frac{\mathbf{h}^2}{\mathbf{m}^3\mathbf{a}} = \frac{6}{25}\left(\frac{1+\zeta^2}{\zeta^2}\right)^{\frac{2}{3}} \{(3\zeta^2+1)\,\zeta\cot^{-1}\zeta - 3\zeta^2\} \quad \ldots (9).$$

This gives the angular momentum of a given volume of given fluid in terms of ζ, and thence in terms of the excentricity e. It appears from the discussion of an equivalent formula by Laplace, or from the table given below, that the right-hand side increases continually as ζ decreases from ∞ to 0. Hence for a given volume of given fluid there is one, and only one, form of Maclaurin's ellipsoid having any prescribed angular momentum.

The following table, giving numerical details of a series of Maclaurin's ellipsoids, is derived from Thomson and Tait*, with some modifications introduced for the purpose of a more ready comparison with the corresponding results for Jacobi's ellipsoids, obtained by Darwin (see Art. 315). The unit of angular momentum is $\mathbf{m}^{\frac{3}{2}}\mathbf{a}^{\frac{1}{2}}$.

e	$a/\mathbf{a}$	$c/\mathbf{a}$	$n^2/2\pi\rho$	Angular momentum
0	1·0000	1·0000	0	0
·1	1·0016	·9967	·0027	·0255
·2	1·0068	·9865	·0107	·0514
·3	1·0159	·9691	·0243	·0787
·4	1·0295	·9435	·0436	·1085
·5	1·0491	·9086	·0690	·1417
·6	1·0772	·8618	·1007	·1804
·7	1·1188	·7990	·1387	·2283
·8	1·1856	·7114	·1816	·2934
·9	1·3189	·5749	·2203	·4000
·91	1·341	·5560	·2225	·4156
·92	1·367	·5355	·2241	·4330
·93	1·396	·5131	·2247	·4525
·94	1·431	·4883	·2239	·4748
·95	1·474	·4603	·2213	·5008
·96	1·529	·4280	·2160	·5319
·97	1·602	·3895	·2063	·5692
·98	1·713	·3409	·1890	·6249
·99	1·921	·2710	·1551	·7121
1·00	∞	0	0	∞

* *Natural Philosophy*, Art. 772.

315. To ascertain whether an ellipsoid with three *unequal* axes is a possible form of relative equilibrium, we return to the conditions (5). These are equivalent to

$$(\alpha_0 - \beta_0)\, a^2 b^2 + \gamma_0 c^2 (a^2 - b^2) = 0 \quad \text{.........(10)},$$

and

$$\frac{n^2}{2\pi\rho} = \frac{\alpha_0 a^2 - \beta_0 b^2}{a^2 - b^2} \quad \text{...................(11)}.$$

If we substitute from Art. 313, the condition (10) may be written

$$(a^2 - b^2)\int_0^\infty \left\{\frac{a^2 b^2}{(a^2+\lambda)(b^2+\lambda)} - \frac{c^2}{c^2+\lambda}\right\}\frac{d\lambda}{\Delta} = 0 \text{.....(12)}.$$

The first factor, equated to zero, gives Maclaurin's ellipsoids, discussed in the preceding Art. The second factor gives

$$\int_0^\infty \{a^2 b^2 - (a^2 + b^2 + \lambda)\, c^2\}\, \frac{\lambda\, d\lambda}{\Delta^3} = 0 \text{...........(13)},$$

which may be regarded as an equation determining c in terms of a, b. When $c^2 = 0$, every element of the integral is positive, and when $c^2 = a^2b^2/(a^2 + b^2)$ every element is negative. Hence there is some value of c, less than the smaller of the two semiaxes a, b, for which the integral vanishes.

The corresponding value of n is given by (11), which takes the form

$$\frac{n^2}{2\pi\rho} = abc\int_0^\infty \frac{\lambda\, d\lambda}{(a^2+\lambda)(b^2+\lambda)\,\Delta} \quad \text{............(14)},$$

so that n is real. It will be observed that as before the ratio $n^2/2\pi\rho$ depends only on the *shape* of the ellipsoid, and not on its absolute size.

The possibility of an ellipsoidal form with three unequal axes was first asserted by Jacobi in 1834*. The equations (13) and (14) were carefully discussed by C. O. Meyer†, who shewed that when a, b are given there is only one value of c satisfying (13), and that, further, $n^2/2\pi\rho$ has its greatest value (·1871), when $a = b = 1{\cdot}7161c$. The Jacobian ellipsoid then coincides with one of Maclaurin's forms.

* "Ueber die Figur des Gleichgewichts," *Pogg. Ann.*, t. xxxiii. (1834); see also Liouville, "Sur la figure d'une masse fluide homogène, en équilibre, et douée d'un mouvement de rotation," *Journ. de l'École Polytechn.*, t. xiv., p. 290 (1834).

† "De aequilibrii formis ellipsoidicis," *Crelle*, t. xxiv. (1842).

If in the second factor of (12) we put $a=b$, and write

$$c^2+\lambda=(a^2-c^2)u^2,\quad c^2=(a^2-c^2)\zeta^2, \qquad \text{(iii)},$$

we find

$$\int_\zeta^\infty \left\{\left(\frac{1+\zeta^2}{1+u^2}\right)^2-\frac{\zeta^2}{u^2}\right\}\frac{du}{1+u^2}=0, \qquad \text{(iv)},$$

whence

$$\cot^{-1}\zeta=\frac{13\zeta+3\zeta^3}{3+14\zeta^2+3\zeta^4} \qquad \text{(v)*}.$$

It may readily be verified that this has only one finite root, viz. $\zeta=\cdot7171$, which makes $e=\cdot8127$.

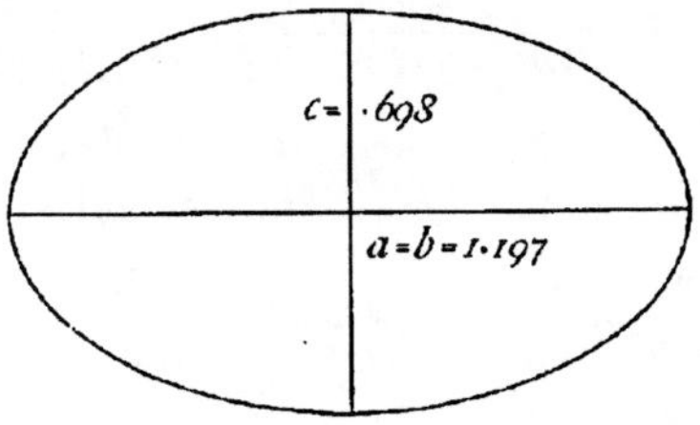

As $n^2/2\pi\rho$ diminishes from the above limit, the ratio of one equatorial axis of Jacobi's ellipsoid to the polar axis increases, whilst that of the other diminishes, the asymptotic form being an infinitely long circular cylinder ($a=\infty$, $b=c$).

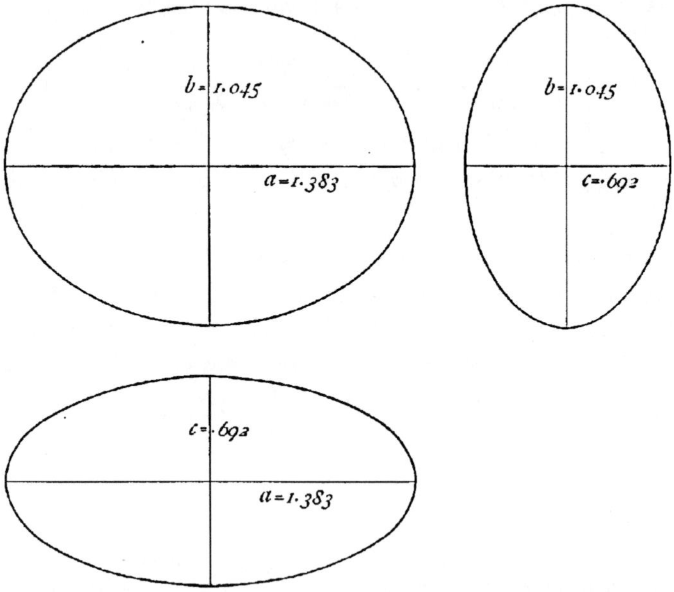

* Thomson and Tait, Art. 778′. The f of these writers is equal to our ζ^{-1}.

The following table of numerical data for a series of Jacobi's ellipsoids has been computed by Darwin. The subject is further illustrated by the annexed figures. The first of these gives the meridian section of the ellipsoid of revolution which is the starting point of the series. The remainder, adopted from Darwin's paper*, give the principal sections of two other forms.

Axes			$\dfrac{n^2}{2\pi\rho}$	Angular momentum
a/a	b/a	c/a		
1·197	1·197	·698	·1871	·304
1·216	1·179	·698	·187	·304
1·279	1·123	·696	·186	·306
1·383	1·045	·692	·181	·313
1·601	·924	·677	·166	·341
1·899	·811	·649	·141	·392
2·346	·702	·607	·107	·481
3·136	·586	·545	·067	·644
5·04	·45	·44	·026	1·016
∞	0	0	0	∞

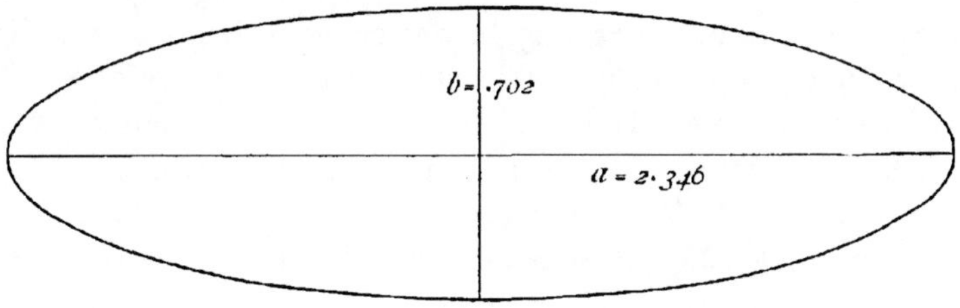

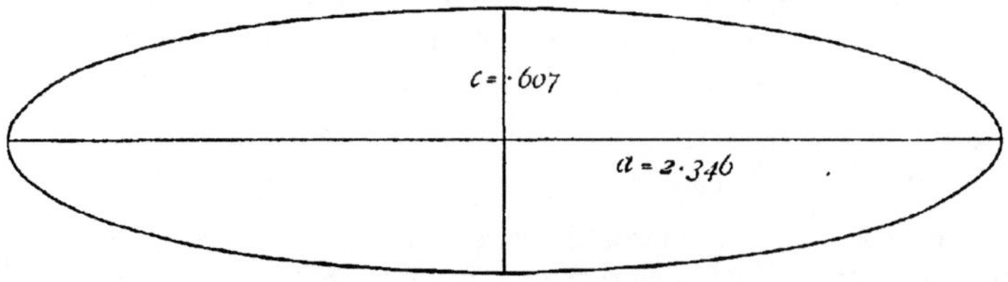

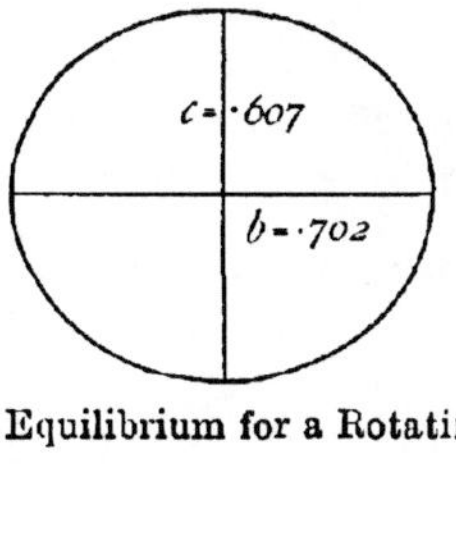

* "On Jacobi's Figure of Equilibrium for a Rotating Mass of Fluid," *Proc. Roy. Soc.*, Nov. 25, 1886.

There is a similar solution for the case of an elliptic cylinder rotating about its axis*. The result, which may be easily verified, is

$$\frac{n^2}{2\pi\rho} = \frac{2ab}{(a+b)^2} \qquad \text{(i).}$$

316. The problem of relative equilibrium, of which Maclaurin's and Jacobi's ellipsoids are particular cases, has in recent times engaged the attention of many able writers, to whose investigations we can here only refer. These are devoted either to the determination, in detail, of special forms, such as the annulus†, and that of two detached masses at a greater or less distance apart‡, or, as in the case of Poincaré's celebrated paper§, to the more general study of the problem, and in particular to the inquiry, what forms of relative equilibrium, if any, can be obtained by infinitesimal modification of known forms such as those of Maclaurin and Jacobi.

The leading idea of Poincaré's research may be stated as follows. With a given mass of liquid, and a given angular velocity n of rotation, there may be one or more forms of relative equilibrium, determined by the property that the value of $V-T_0$ is stationary, the symbols V, T_0 having the same meanings as in Art. 195. By varying n we get one or more 'linear series' of equilibrium forms. Now consider the coefficients of stability of the system (Art. 196). These may, for the present purpose, be chosen in an infinite number of ways, the only essential being that $V-T_0$ should reduce to a sum of squares; but, whatever mode of reduction be adopted, the number of positive as well as of negative coefficients is, by a theorem due to Sylvester, invariable. Poincaré proves that if, as we follow any linear series, one of the coefficients of stability changes sign, the form in question is as it

* Matthiessen, "Neue Untersuchungen über frei rotirende Flüssigkeiten," *Schriften der Univ. zu Kiel*, t. vi. (1859). This paper contains a very complete list of previous writings on the subject.

† First treated by Laplace, "Mémoire sur la théorie de l'anneau de Saturne," *Mém. de l'Acad. des Sciences*, 1787 [1789]; *Mécanique Céleste*, Livre 3me, c. vi. For later investigations, with or without a central attracting body, see Matthiessen, *l. c.*; Mme. Sophie Kowalewsky, *Astron. Nachrichten*, t. cxi., p. 37 (1885); Poincaré, *l. c. infra*; Basset, *Amer. Journ. Math.*, t. xi. (1888); Dyson, *l. c. ante* p. 166.

‡ Darwin, "On Figures of Equilibrium of Rotating Masses of Fluid," *Phil. Trans.*, 1887; a full account of this paper is given by Basset, *Hydrodynamics*, c. xvi.

§ "Sur l'équilibre d'une masse fluide animée d'un mouvement de rotation," *Acta Math.*, t. vii. (1885).

were the crossing-point with another linear series. For this reason it is called a 'form of bifurcation.' A great part of Poincaré's investigation consists in ascertaining what members of Maclaurin's and Jacobi's series are forms of bifurcation.

Poincaré also discusses very fully the question of stability, to which we shall briefly revert in conclusion.

317. The motion of a liquid mass under its own gravitation, with a *varying* ellipsoidal surface, was first studied by Dirichlet*. Adopting the Lagrangian method of Art. 13, he proposes as the subject of investigation the whole class of motions in which the displacements are linear functions of the velocities. This has been carried further, on the same lines, by Dedekind† and Riemann‡. More recently, it has been shewn by Greenhill§ and others that the problem can be treated with some advantage by the Eulerian method.

We will take first the case where the ellipsoid does not change the directions of its axes, and the internal motion is irrotational. This is interesting as an example of *finite* oscillation of a liquid mass about the spherical form.

The expression for the velocity-potential has been given in Art. 107; viz. we have

$$\phi = -\tfrac{1}{2}\left(\frac{\dot{a}}{a}x^2 + \frac{\dot{b}}{b}y^2 + \frac{\dot{c}}{c}z^2\right) \qquad\text{(1)},$$

with the condition of constant volume

$$\frac{\dot{a}}{a} + \frac{\dot{b}}{b} + \frac{\dot{c}}{c} = 0 \qquad\text{(2)}.$$

The pressure is then given by

$$\frac{p}{\rho} = \frac{d\phi}{dt} - \Omega - \tfrac{1}{2}q^2 + F(t) \qquad\text{(3)},$$

* "Untersuchungen über ein Problem der Hydrodynamik," *Gött. Abh.*, t. viii. (1860); *Crelle*, t. lviii. The paper was posthumous, and was edited and amplified by Dedekind.

† *Crelle*, t. lviii.

‡ "Beitrag zu den Untersuchungen über die Bewegung eines flüssigen gleichartigen Ellipsoides," *Gött. Abh.*, t. ix. (1861); *Math. Werke*, p. 168.

§ "On the Rotation of a liquid Ellipsoid about its Mean Axis," *Proc. Camb. Phil. Soc.*, t. iii. (1879); "On the general Motion of a liquid Ellipsoid under the Gravitation of its own parts," *Proc. Camb. Phil. Soc.*, t. iv. (1880).

by Art. 21 (4); and substituting the value of Ω from Art. 313 we find

$$\frac{p}{\rho} = -\tfrac{1}{2}\left(\frac{\ddot{a}}{a}x^2 + \frac{\ddot{b}}{b}y^2 + \frac{\ddot{c}}{c}z^2\right) - \pi\rho\left(\alpha_0 x^2 + \beta_0 y^2 + \gamma_0 z^2\right) + f(t) \qquad \text{.................(4).}$$

The conditions that the pressure may be uniform over the external surface

$$\frac{x^2}{a^2} + \frac{y^2}{b^2} + \frac{z^2}{c^2} = 1 \qquad \text{......................(5),}$$

are therefore

$$\left(\frac{\ddot{a}}{a} + 2\pi\rho\alpha_0\right)a^2 = \left(\frac{\ddot{b}}{b} + 2\pi\rho\beta_0\right)b^2 = \left(\frac{\ddot{c}}{c} + 2\pi\rho\gamma_0\right)c^2 \text{....(6).}$$

These equations, with (2), determine the variations of a, b, c. If we multiply the three terms of (2) by the three equal magnitudes in (6), we obtain

$$\dot{a}\ddot{a} + \dot{b}\ddot{b} + \dot{c}\ddot{c} + 2\pi\rho\left(\alpha_0 a\dot{a} + \beta_0 b\dot{b} + \gamma_0 c\dot{c}\right) = 0 \text{.........(7).}$$

If we substitute the values of α_0, β_0, γ_0 from Art. 313, this has the integral

$$\dot{a}^2 + \dot{b}^2 + \dot{c}^2 - 4\pi\rho abc\int_0^\infty \frac{d\lambda}{\Delta} = \text{const.} \text{............(8).}$$

It has been already proved that the potential energy is

$$V = \text{const.} - \tfrac{8}{15}\pi^2\rho^2a^2b^2c^2\int_0^\infty \frac{d\lambda}{\Delta} \text{..............(9),}$$

and it easily follows from (1) that the kinetic energy is

$$T = \tfrac{2}{15}\pi\rho abc\left(\dot{a}^2 + \dot{b}^2 + \dot{c}^2\right) \text{.................(10).}$$

Hence (8) is recognized as the equation of energy

$$T + V = \text{const.} \text{ .... (11).}$$

When the ellipsoid is of revolution ($a = b$), the equation (8), with $a^2c = \mathbf{a}^3$, is sufficient to determine the motion. We find

$$\tfrac{2}{15}\pi\rho\mathbf{a}^3\left(1 + \frac{\mathbf{a}^3}{2c^3}\right)\dot{c}^2 + V = \text{const.} \text{ ....(12).}$$

The character of the motion depends on the total energy. If this be less than the potential energy in the state of infinite diffusion, the ellipsoid will oscillate regularly between the prolate and oblate forms, with a period depending on the amplitude; whilst if the energy exceed this limit it will not oscillate, but will tend to one or other of two extreme forms, viz. an infinite line of matter coinciding with the axis of z, or an infinite film coincident with the plane xy*.

If, in the case of an ellipsoid of revolution, we superpose on the irrotational motion given by (1) a uniform rotation ω about the axis of z, the component angular velocities (relative to fixed axes) are

$$u=\frac{\dot{a}}{a}x-\omega y,\quad v=\frac{\dot{a}}{a}y+\omega x,\quad w=\frac{\dot{c}}{c}z \text{ .... (i).}$$

The Eulerian equations then reduce to

$$\left.\begin{aligned} \frac{\ddot{a}}{a}x-\dot{\omega}y-2\frac{\dot{a}}{a}\omega y-\omega^2x&=-\frac{1}{\rho}\frac{dp}{dx}-\frac{d\Omega}{dx},\\ \frac{\ddot{a}}{a}y+\dot{\omega}x+2\frac{\dot{a}}{a}\omega x-\omega^2y&=-\frac{1}{\rho}\frac{dp}{dy}-\frac{d\Omega}{dy},\\ \frac{\ddot{c}}{c}z\qquad\qquad\qquad&=-\frac{1}{\rho}\frac{dp}{dz}-\frac{d\Omega}{dz} \end{aligned}\right\}\text{ .... (ii).}$$

The first two equations give, by cross-differentiation,

$$\frac{\dot{\omega}}{\omega}+2\frac{\dot{a}}{a}=0 \text{ ....(iii),}$$

or

$$\omega a^2=\omega_0 a_0^2 \text{ ....(iv),}$$

which is simply the expression of von Helmholtz' theorem that the 'strength' of a vortex is constant (Art. 142). In virtue of (iii), the equations (ii) have the integral

$$\frac{p}{\rho}=-\tfrac{1}{2}\left(\frac{\ddot{a}}{a}-\omega^2\right)(x^2+y^2)-\tfrac{1}{2}\frac{\ddot{c}}{c}z^2-\Omega+\text{const.} \text{ ....(v).}$$

Introducing the value of Ω from Art. 313 (4), we find that the pressure will be constant over the surface

$$\frac{x^2+y^2}{a^2}+\frac{z^2}{c^2}=1 \text{ .... (vi),}$$

provided

$$\left(\frac{\ddot{a}}{a}+2\pi\rho\alpha_0-\omega^2\right)a^2=\left(\frac{\ddot{c}}{c}+2\pi\rho\gamma_0\right)c^2 \text{ .... (vii).}$$

In virtue of the relation (iii), and of the condition of constancy of volume

$$2\frac{\dot{a}}{a}+\frac{\dot{c}}{c}=0 \text{ ....(viii),}$$

* Dirichlet, *l. c.* When the amplitude of oscillation is small, the period must coincide with that obtained by putting $n=2$ in the formula (10) of Art. 241. This has been verified by Hicks, *Proc. Camb. Phil. Soc.*, t. iv., p. 309 (1883).

this may be put in the form

$$2\dot{a}\ddot{a}+\dot{c}\ddot{c}+2(\omega^2 a\dot{a}+\omega\dot{\omega}a^2)+4\pi\rho\alpha_0 a\dot{a}+2\pi\rho\gamma_0 c\dot{c}=0 \quad \text{............(ix)},$$

whence

$$2\dot{a}^2+\dot{c}^2+2\omega^2 a^2-4\pi\rho a^2 c\int_0^\infty \frac{d\lambda}{(a^2+\lambda)(c^2+\lambda)^{\frac{1}{2}}}=\text{const.} \quad \text{......... (x)}.$$

This, again, may be identified as the equation of energy.

In terms of c as dependent variable, (x) may be written

$$\tfrac{2}{15}\pi\rho\mathrm{a}^3\left\{\left(1+\frac{\mathrm{a}^3}{2c^3}\right)\dot{c}^2+\frac{2\omega_0{}^2a_0{}^4}{\mathrm{a}^3}c\right\}+V=\text{const.} \quad \text{............ (xi)}.$$

If the initial circumstances be favourable, the surface will oscillate regularly between two extreme forms. Since, for a prolate ellipsoid, V increases with c, it is evident that, whatever the initial conditions, there is a limit to the elongation in the direction of the axis which the rotating ellipsoid can attain. On the other hand, we may have an indefinite spreading out in the equatorial plane*.

318. For the further study of the motion of a fluid mass bounded by a varying ellipsoidal surface we must refer to the paper by Riemann already cited, and to the investigations of Brioschi†, Lipschitz‡, Greenhill§ and Basset‖. We shall here only pursue the case where the ellipsoidal boundary is invariable in form, but rotates about a principal axis (z)¶.

If u, v, w denote the velocities relative to axes x, y rotating in their own plane with constant angular velocity n, the equations of motion are, by Art. 199,

$$\left.\begin{aligned}\frac{Du}{Dt}-2nv-n^2x&=-\frac{1}{\rho}\frac{dp}{dx}-\frac{d\Omega}{dx},\\ \frac{Dv}{Dt}+2nu-n^2y&=-\frac{1}{\rho}\frac{dp}{dy}-\frac{d\Omega}{dy},\\ \frac{Dw}{Dt}&=-\frac{1}{\rho}\frac{dp}{dz}-\frac{d\Omega}{dz}\end{aligned}\right\} \quad \text{...................... (i)}.$$

If the fluid have an angular velocity ω about lines parallel to z, the actual velocities parallel to the instantaneous positions of the axes will be

$$\left.\begin{aligned}u-ny&=\frac{a^2-b^2}{a^2+b^2}(n-\omega)y-\omega y,\\ v+nx&=\frac{a^2-b^2}{a^2+b^2}(n-\omega)x+\omega x,\\ w&=0\end{aligned}\right\} \quad \text{........................(ii)},$$

* Dirichlet, *l. c.*.

† *Crelle*, t. lix. (1861).

‡ *Crelle*, t. lxxviii. (1874).

§ *l.c. ante* p. 589.

‖ "On the Motion of a Liquid Ellipsoid under the Influence of its own Attraction," *Proc. Lond. Math. Soc.*, t. xvii., p. 255 (1886); *Hydrodynamics*, c. xv.

¶ Greenhill, "On the Rotation of a Liquid Ellipsoid about its Mean Axis," *Proc. Camb. Phil. Soc.*, t. iii. (1879).

since the conditions are evidently satisfied by the superposition of the irrotational motion which would be produced by the revolution of a rigid ellipsoidal envelope with angular velocity $n-\omega$ on the uniform rotation ω (cf. Art. 107). Hence

$$u=\frac{2a^2}{a^2+b^2}(n-\omega)\,y,\quad v=-\frac{2b^2}{a^2+b^2}(n-\omega)\,x,\quad w=0\,\ldots\ldots\ldots\text{(iii)}.$$

Substituting in (i), and integrating, we find

$$\frac{p}{\rho}=\frac{2a^2b^2}{(a^2+b^2)^2}(n-\omega)^2(x^2+y^2)+\tfrac{1}{2}n^2(x^2+y^2)-\frac{2(b^2x^2+a^2y^2)}{a^2+b^2}n(n-\omega)$$
$$-\Omega+\text{const.}\ldots\ldots\ldots\ldots\ldots\ldots\text{(iv)}.$$

Hence the conditions for a free surface are

$$\left\{\frac{2a^2b^2}{(a^2+b^2)^2}(n-\omega)^2+\tfrac{1}{2}n^2-\frac{2b^2}{a^2+b^2}n(n-\omega)-\pi\rho\alpha_0\right\}a^2$$
$$=\left\{\frac{2a^2b^2}{(a^2+b^2)^2}(n-\omega)^2+\tfrac{1}{2}n^2-\frac{2a^2}{a^2+b^2}n(n-\omega)-\pi\rho\beta_0\right\}b^2$$
$$=-\pi\rho\gamma_0c^2\ldots\ldots\ldots\ldots\ldots\ldots\ldots\ldots\ldots\ldots\ldots\ldots\ldots\ldots\text{(v)}.$$

This includes a number of interesting cases.

1°. If we put $n=\omega$, we get the conditions of Jacobi's ellipsoid (Art. 315).

2°. If we put $n=0$, so that the external boundary is stationary in space, we get

$$\left\{\pi\rho\alpha_0-\frac{2a^2b^2}{(a^2+b^2)^2}\omega^2\right\}a^2=\left\{\pi\rho\beta_0-\frac{2a^2b^2}{(a^2+b^2)^2}\omega^2\right\}b^2=\pi\rho\gamma_0c^2\,\ldots\ldots\text{(vi)}.$$

These are equivalent to

$$(\alpha_0-\beta_0)\,a^2b^2+\gamma_0c^2(a^2-b^2)=0\,\ldots\ldots\ldots\ldots\ldots\ldots\text{(vii)},$$

and

$$\frac{\omega^2}{2\pi\rho}=\frac{(a^2+b^2)^2}{4a^2b^2}\cdot\frac{a^2\alpha_0-b^2\beta_0}{a^2-b^2}\,\ldots\ldots\ldots\ldots\ldots\ldots\text{(viii)}.$$

It is evident, on comparison with Art. 315, that c must be the least axis of the ellipsoid, and that the value (viii) of $\omega^2/2\pi\rho$ is positive.

The paths of the particles are determined by

$$\dot{x}=-\frac{2a^2}{a^2+b^2}\omega y,\quad \dot{y}=\frac{2b^2}{a^2+b^2}\omega x,\quad \dot{z}=0\ldots\ldots\ldots\ldots\ldots\ldots\text{(ix)},$$

whence

$$x=ka\cos(\sigma t+\epsilon),\quad y=kb\sin(\sigma t+\epsilon),\quad z=0\,\ldots\ldots\ldots\ldots\text{(x)},$$

if

$$\sigma=\frac{2ab}{a^2+b^2}\omega\,\ldots\ldots\ldots\ldots\ldots\ldots\ldots\ldots\ldots\ldots\text{(xi)},$$

and k, ϵ are arbitrary constants.

These results are due to Dedekind*.

* *l. c. ante* p. 589. See also Love, "On Dedekind's Theorem,...," *Phil. Mag.*, Jan. 1888.

3°. Let $\omega=0$, so that the motion is irrotational. The conditions (v) reduce to

$$\left\{\alpha_0-\frac{(a^2-b^2)(a^2+3b^2)}{(a^2+b^2)^2}\frac{n^2}{2\pi\rho}\right\}a^2=\left\{\beta_0-\frac{(b^2-a^2)(3a^2+b^2)}{(a^2+b^2)^2}\frac{n^2}{2\pi\rho}\right\}b^2=\gamma_0 c^2 \text{...(xii).}$$

These may be replaced by

$$\{\alpha_0(3a^2+b^2)+\beta_0(3b^2+a^2)\}a^2b^2-\gamma_0(a^4+6a^2b^2+b^4)c^2=0 \text{......(xiii),}$$

and

$$\frac{n^2}{2\pi\rho}=\frac{(a^2+b^2)^2}{a^4+6a^2b^2+b^4}\cdot\frac{\alpha_0 a^2-\beta_0 b^2}{a^2-b^2} \text{....................(xiv).}$$

The equation (xiii) determines c in terms of a, b. Let us suppose that $a>b$. Then the left-hand side is easily seen to be positive for $c=a$, and negative for $c=b$. Hence there is some real value of c, *between* a and b, for which the condition is satisfied; and the value of n, given by (xiv) is then real, for the same reason as in Art. 315.

4°. In the case of an elliptic cylinder rotating about its axis, the condition (v) takes the form

$$n^2+\frac{4a^2b^2}{(a^2+b^2)^2}(n-\omega)^2=\frac{4\pi\rho ab}{(a+b)^2} \text{....................(xv)*.}$$

If we put $n=\omega$, we get the case of Art. 315 (i).

If $n=0$, so that the external boundary is stationary, we have

$$\omega^2=\pi\rho\frac{(a^2+b^2)^2}{ab(a+b)^2} \text{............................(xvi).}$$

If $\omega=0$, *i.e.* the motion is irrotational, we have

$$n^2=4\pi\rho\frac{ab(a^2+b^2)^2}{(a+b)^2(a^4+6a^2b^2+b^4)} \text{....................(xvii).}$$

319. The small disturbances of a rotating ellipsoidal mass have been discussed by various writers.

The simplest types of disturbance which we can consider are those in which the surface remains ellipsoidal, with the axis of revolution as a principal axis. In the case of Maclaurin's ellipsoid, there are two distinct types of this character; in one of these the surface remains an ellipsoid of revolution, whilst in the other the equatorial axes become unequal, one increasing and the other decreasing, whilst the polar axis is unchanged. It was shewn by Riemann† that the latter type is unstable when the eccentricity (e) of the meridian section is greater than ·9529. The periods of

* Greenhill, *l. c. ante* p. 589.

† *l. c. ante* p. 589. See also Basset, *Hydrodynamics*, Art. 367. Riemann has further shewn that Jacobi's ellipsoid is always stable for ellipsoidal disturbances.

oscillation in the two types (when $e < \cdot 9529$) have been calculated by Love*.

The theory of the stability and the small oscillations of Maclaurin's ellipsoid, when the disturbance is unrestricted, has been very fully worked out by Bryan†, by a method due to Poincaré. It appears that when $e < \cdot 9529$ the equilibrium is thoroughly stable. For sufficiently great values of e there is of course instability for other types, in addition to the one above referred to.

320. In the investigations here cited dissipative forces are ignored, and the results leave undetermined the more important question of 'secular' stability. This is discussed, with great command of mathematical resources, by Poincaré.

If we consider, for a moment, the case of a fluid covering a rigid nucleus, and subject to dissipative forces affecting all relative motions, there are two forms of the problem. It was shewn in Art. 197 that if the nucleus be constrained to rotate with constant angular velocity (n) about a fixed axis, or (what comes to the same thing) if it be of preponderant inertia, the condition of secular stability is that the equilibrium value of $V - T_0$ should be stationary, V denoting the potential energy, and T_0 the kinetic energy of the system when rotating as a whole, with the prescribed angular velocity, in any given configuration. If, on the other hand, the nucleus be free, the case comes under the general theory of 'gyrostatic' systems, the ignored coordinates being the six coordinates which determine the position of the nucleus in space. The condition then is (Art. 235) that the equilibrium value of $V + K$ should be a minimum, where K is the kinetic energy of the system moving, as rigid, in any given configuration, with the

* "On the Oscillations of a Rotating Liquid Spheroid, and the Genesis of the Moon," *Phil. Mag.*, March, 1889.

† "The Waves on a Rotating Liquid Spheroid of Finite Ellipticity," *Phil. Trans.*, 1889; "On the Stability of a Rotating Spheroid of Perfect Liquid," *Proc. Roy. Soc.*, March 27, 1890. The case of a rotating elliptic cylinder has been discussed by Love, *Quart. Journ. Math.*, t. xxiii. (1888).

The stability of a rotating liquid annulus, of relatively small cross-section, has been examined by Dyson, *l.c. ante* p. 166. The equilibrium is shewn to be unstable for disturbances of a "beaded" character (in which there is a periodic variation of the cross-section as we travel along the ring) whose wave-length exceeds a certain limit.

component momenta corresponding to the ignored coordinates unaltered. The two criteria become equivalent when the disturbance considered does not alter the moment of inertia of the system with respect to the axis of rotation.

The second form of the problem is from the present point of view the more important. It includes such cases as Maclaurin's and Jacobi's ellipsoids, provided we suppose the nucleus to be infinitely small. As a simple application of the criterion we may examine the secular stability of Maclaurin's ellipsoid for the types of ellipsoidal disturbance described in Art. 319*.

Let n be the angular velocity in the state of equilibrium, and $\mathbf{h}$ the angular momentum. If I denote the moment of inertia of the disturbed system, the angular velocity, if this were to rotate, as rigid, would be $\mathbf{h}/I$. Hence

$$V+K=V+\tfrac{1}{2}I\left(\frac{\mathbf{h}}{I}\right)^2=V+\tfrac{1}{2}\frac{\mathbf{h}^2}{I} \qquad \text{(i)},$$

and the condition of secular stability is that this expression should be a minimum. We will suppose for definiteness that the zero of reckoning of V corresponds to the state of infinite diffusion. Then in any other configuration V will be negative.

In our previous notation we have

$$I=\tfrac{1}{5}\mathbf{m}\,(a^2+b^2) \qquad \text{(ii)},$$

c being the axis of rotation. Since $abc=\mathbf{a}^3$, we may write

$$V+\tfrac{5}{2}\,\frac{\mathbf{h}^2}{\mathbf{m}\,(a^2+b^2)}=f(a,\,b) \qquad \text{(iii)},$$

where $f(a, b)$ is a symmetric function of the two independent variables a, b. If we consider the surface whose ordinate is $f(a, b)$, where a, b are regarded as rectangular coordinates of a point in a horizontal plane, the configurations of relative equilibrium will correspond to points whose altitude is a maximum, or a minimum, or a 'minimax,' whilst for secular stability the altitude must be a minimum.

For $a=\infty$, or $b=\infty$, we have $f(a, b)=0$. For $a=0$, we have $V=0$, and $f(a, b) \propto 1/b^2$, and similarly for $b=0$. For $a=0$, $b=0$, simultaneously, we have $f(a, b)=\infty$. It is known that, whatever the value of $\mathbf{h}$, there is always one and only one possible form of Maclaurin's ellipsoid. Hence as we follow the section of the above-mentioned surface by the plane of symmetry ($a=b$), the ordinate varies from ∞ to 0, having one and only one stationary value in the

* Poincaré, *l. c.* For a more analytical investigation see Basset, "On the Stability of Maclaurin's Liquid Spheroid," *Proc. Camb. Phil. Soc.*, t. viii., p. 23 (1892).

interval. It is easily seen from considerations of continuity that this value must be always negative, and a minimum*. Hence the altitude at this point of the surface is either a minimum, or a minimax. Moreover, since there is a limit to the negative value of V, viz. when the ellipsoid becomes a sphere, there is always at least one finite point of minimum (and negative) altitude on the surface.

Now it appears, on reference to the tables on pp. 584, 586, that when $\mathbf{h} < \cdot 304\, \mathbf{m}^{\frac{3}{2}} \mathbf{a}^{\frac{1}{2}}$, there is one and only one ellipsoidal form of equilibrium, viz. one of revolution. The preceding considerations shew that this corresponds to a point of minimum altitude, and is therefore secularly stable (for symmetrical ellipsoidal disturbances).

When $\mathbf{h} > \cdot 304\, \mathbf{m}^{\frac{3}{2}} \mathbf{a}^{\frac{1}{2}}$, there are three points of stationary altitude, viz. one in the plane of symmetry, corresponding to a Maclaurin's ellipsoid, and two others symmetrically situated on opposite sides of this plane, corresponding to the Jacobian form. It is evident from topographical considerations that the altitude must be a minimum at the two last-named points, and a minimax at the former. Any other arrangement would involve the existence of additional points of stationary altitude.

The result of the investigation is that Maclaurin's ellipsoid is secularly stable or unstable, for ellipsoidal disturbances, according as e is less or greater than ·8127, the eccentricity of the ellipsoid of revolution which is the starting point of Jacobi's series†.

The further discussion of the stability of Maclaurin's ellipsoid, though full of interest, would carry us too far. It appears that the equilibrium is secularly stable for deformations of any type so long as e falls below the above-mentioned limit. This is established by shewing that there is no form of bifurcation (Art. 316) for any Maclaurin's ellipsoid of smaller eccentricity.

Poincaré has also examined the stability of Jacobi's ellipsoids. He finds that these are secularly stable provided the ratio $a : b$ (where a is the greater of the two equatorial axes) does not exceed a certain limit.

The secular stability of a rotating elliptic cylinder has been investigated directly from the equations of motion of a viscous fluid by Bryan‡.

* It follows that Maclaurin's ellipsoid is always stable for a deformation such that the surface remains an ellipsoid of revolution. Thomson and Tait, *Natural Philosophy* (2nd ed.), Art. 778″.

† This result was stated, without proof, by Thomson and Tait, *l. c.*

‡ *Proc. Camb. Phil. Soc.*, t. vi. (1888).

LIST OF AUTHORS CITED.

The numbers refer to the pages.

INDEX.

The numbers refer to the pages.

CAMBRIDGE: PRINTED BY J. & C. F. CLAY, AT THE UNIVERSITY PRESS.

11

CPSIA information can be obtained at www.ICGtesting.com
Printed in the USA
LVOW031953280812
296366LV00022B/13/P

9 781140 225812